The Year Book 1970

Cover Pictures. *Front:* Apollo 11 Moon man; Prince of Wales; Princess Anne; President Pompidou; Willy Brandt; Bernadette Devlin; Mrs Golda Meir; Al Aqsa mosque on fire; *Back:* Eisenhower; Tom Mboya; Ho Chi Minh; Concorde; President Nixon in Rumania; British troops in N. Ireland; Ann Jones.

Endpapers. Footprints of the first men on the Moon, Neil Armstrong and Edmund Aldrin, who on July 21, 1969, made "one small step for a man, one giant leap for mankind."

ISBN 0 7172 7801 8

© **THE HOUSE OF GROLIER, 1970**
Head Offices: Star House, Potters Bar, Herts, England.

Made and Printed in Great Britain by The Whitefriars Press Limited, London and Tonbridge, Kent.

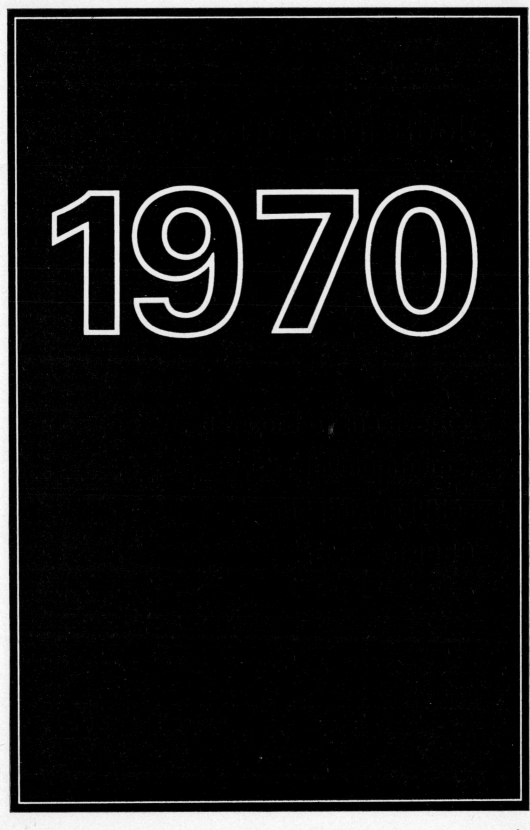

1970

Contents

Pictorial Features

Editor-in-Chief **ROBERT H. HILL**

Assistant David Tinkler

Art Editor **KENNETH POWELL**

Picture Research Derek Gilby

Fact Digest **ELIZABETH HOGARTH**

The Year 1969 in Headlines

January

Capricorn (The Goat), sign of the Zodiac for Dec. 21–Jan. 19

1 On first leg of four-day, 72-mile march from Belfast to Londonderry, Northern Ireland, civil rights marchers' attempt to enter Antrim is beaten back by Protestants.

Oldrich Cernik appointed Prime Minister of Czechoslovakia's federal government.

2 1,000 Protestant extremists converge on Maghera, 33 miles from Londonderry, and brawl with civil rights marchers.

Queen Elizabeth 2 arrives back at Southampton after trial cruise to the Canary Islands has shown up serious faults in her turbines.

3 In violence in Londonderry between civil rights supporters and militant Protestants, 35 people, including 5 policemen, are injured.

Senator Edward Kennedy is elected assistant leader and whip of Democratic majority in Senate by 31–26 votes.

4 Civil rights marchers on way to Londonderry are ambushed by Protestant extremists and others at Burntollet Bridge, but eventually reach the city. 50 people are taken to hospital.

Four people are killed and 11 injured when 8 p.m. Charing Cross to Folkestone and Dover express crashes in thick fog into back of parcels train near Marden, Kent.

Death of Montague Phillips, British composer, aged 83.

5 Sunday   In foggy conditions a Boeing 707 of Ariana Airlines of Afghanistan ploughs through house, killing parents of an 18-month-old girl (who survives), and crashes in field near Gatwick airport: 50 people are killed, 15 survive.

President-elect Richard Nixon appoints ambassador Henry Cabot Lodge as his chief negotiator at Vietnam talks in Paris.

7 At opening of Commonwealth Prime Ministers' Conference at Marlborough House, London, 1,000 demonstrators shout slogans and wave banners.

Trial of Sirhan Bishara Sirhan, charged with murder of Senator Robert Kennedy in June 1968, begins in Los Angeles.

8 14 people known to have died, and many missing, in bush fires near Melbourne, Victoria, Australia.

9 At Commonwealth Prime Ministers' Conference Britain refuses to reaffirm her pledge of no independence for Rhodesia before majority rule.

Freezing fog and black ice bring chaos to roads in southern England, causing dozens of crashes in which at least 8 people are killed. Accidents on M1 are worst since it was opened.

10 Apollo 8 astronauts (Borman, Lovell, and Anders) are given ticker-tape welcome in New York.

11 Civil rights marchers attack police road block in Newry, co. Down, N. Ireland, setting six

police trucks on fire, and during subsequent fighting 10 policemen and 18 civilians are injured and 23 demonstrators arrested.

Death of Richmal Crompton, author of "William" books, aged 78.

12 Sunday   1,300 police fight pitched battle in the Strand, London, against 4,000 demonstrators attempting to take over Rhodesia House and South Africa House; 17 policemen and 14 demonstrators injured, 31 people arrested.

Birth of son to Princess Benedikte of Denmark.

14 Russian spaceship, Soyuz 4, piloted by Lt.-Col. Vladimir Shatalov, is launched.

Explosions and fire in U.S. nuclear-powered aircraft carrier *Enterprise*: 13 men killed, 100 injured, and many missing.

Bruce Reynolds, last of the Great Train Robbery gang to be captured (Nov. 8, 1968), sentenced to 25 years in prison.

General strike throughout twelve towns in Sicily to call attention to plight of the thousands still homeless after earthquake of January 1968.

15 Russian Soyuz 5 spaceship is launched with three men on board—Col. Boris Volynov, Lt.-Col. Yevgeny Khrunov, and Alexei Yeliseyev.

Death of Dr. Frederic Arthur Cockin, former Bishop of Bristol, aged 80; and Dr. J. Dover Wilson, C.H., Shakespearean scholar, aged 87.

16 Soyuz 4 and Soyuz 5 link 150 miles above the earth, and Khrunov and Yeliseyev transfer from one to the other after an hour's "walk" outside the capsules. Volynov remains in Soyuz 5. The capsules then separate.

21-year-old Czech student Jan Palach sets himself on fire in

4th . . . Londonderry police barrier between mob and marchers

7th . . . London greeting to Commonwealth Prime Ministers

Wenceslas Square, Prague, in protest against Soviet occupation.

77-day deadlock in Vietnam peace talks in Paris is resolved by agreement to use a round table.

17 Soyuz 4 makes soft landing in Kazakhstan.

18 Over 4,500 armed police enter Tokyo University and use tear gas in an attempt to force out 300 extreme left-wing students.

Soyuz 5 lands in Kazakhstan.

19 Sunday Jan Palach (Jan. 16) dies of his burns; hundreds publicly mourn him as a martyr, and students demonstrate in Prague against Soviet occupation.

Cardinal Heenan, R.C. Archbishop of Westminster, preaches at Hinde Street Methodist Church, London.

20 Richard Milhous Nixon is inaugurated as the 37th President of the U.S.A.

Two more Czechs set themselves on fire during day of mourning for Jan Palach, when 50,000 people gather in Wencelas Square, Prague.

About 2,000 G.P.O. overseas telegraphists go on strike—first strike in the 98-year history of their trade union—over pay dispute.

21 Black mourning flags appear on public buildings in Prague, and hunger strikers camp in Wenceslas Square in demonstration against Soviet occupation.

2,000 student demonstrators in Tokyo dispersed by 7,000 policemen, but student violence spreads to Kyoto, where 120 are injured in fight between left-wingers and Maoists.

Johnny Famechon, Australia, beats Jose Legra, Spain, on points to win the world featherweight championship, at Royal Albert Hall, London.

22 Extreme Protestants, including the Rev. Ian Paisley and other clergy, demonstrate at St. Paul's

Cathedral, as Cardinal Heenan, Roman Catholic Archbishop of Westminster, preaches on Christian unity.

As cosmonauts of Soyuz 4 and 5 make triumphal drive through Moscow, shots are fired; cosmonauts are not hit, but chauffeur and police motor-cyclists are injured.

23 1,000 students clash with police in Paris streets, and 200 arrests are made. Rectorate building at the Sorbonne is occupied and sacked by students.

Tornado sweeps through Mississippi and Alabama.

24 London School of Economics closed after students smash newly installed iron gates and riot inside building.

Brian Faulkner, Northern Ireland deputy prime minister and Minister of Commerce, resigns from Captain O'Neill's government.

Modified martial law for 3 months is imposed in Spain, and press censorship re-introduced.

Björn Waldegaard (Sweden) wins Monte Carlo rally; Pat Moss-Carlsson takes ladies' prize for 7th time.

25 Hundreds of thousands of Czechs come to Prague for Jan Palach's funeral, and queue to pass the coffin.

Vietnam peace talks re-open in Paris.

Death of Irene Castle, U.S. dancer, aged 75.

26 Sunday In Wenceslas Square, Prague, police try to prevent the placing of tributes to Jan Palach, and use truncheons and tear gas to disperse student march.

State of California is declared a major disaster area after record rainfall and consequent mudslides, which are later shown to have killed at least 89 people and made more than 10,000 homeless.

William Morgan, Minister of Health and Social Services, resigns from Northern Ireland government.

27 11 men hanged on charges of spying and sabotage and their bodies publicly exposed in Liberation Square, Baghdad; 3 others hanged in Basra. They include 9 Jews.

Riot police and para-military servicemen clear Nairobi University of 1,200 students, on orders of President Kenyatta.

Ban on all overtime and Sunday working by U.K. Union of Post Office Workers; the parcels service has to be suspended.

28 Anti-government disorders in Peshawar, Pakistan; in last four days at least 24 people have died and 1,000 been arrested during demonstrations by opponents of President Ayub Khan.

The Australian Wheat Board announces sale of 2,200,000 tons of wheat worth $A125 million to Communist China. It is described as Board's biggest sale.

29 Death of Allen Dulles, former head of U.S. Central Intelligence Agency, aged 75.

30 U.K. postal strike in 19 cities causes massive backlog of mail, and 4d. post is suspended. More than 10,000 postal workers march through London.

Torchlight procession of 2,000 students through London, demanding re-opening of L.S.E. High Court makes orders banning 13 people from entering the School without consent, damaging the building, or interfering with its management.

Death of Father Dominique Pire, Dominican priest and Nobel peace prize-winner, aged 58.

31 Capt. Terence O'Neill, Northern Ireland prime minister, wins full support of all 12 members of his Cabinet.

U.K. Post Office pay dispute settled.

Pres. de Gaulle arrives in Rennes, Brittany, on 3-day visit.

19th . . . Cardinal Heenan

8th . . . Disastrous bush fires in Victoria, Australia

21st . . . Vigil for Palach

February

Aquarius (The Water-Carrier)
Jan. 20–Feb. 18

1 Rev. Ian Paisley leads hundreds of his supporters in march through Belfast.

2 Sunday In Quimper, Brittany, President de Gaulle announces spring referendum on reform of senate.
End of 4-day strike by 40,000 Italian petrol pump attendants over demand for bigger share of profits on sales.
Col. Frank Borman, commander of Apollo 8, arrives in London at start of good-will tour of eight European countries.
Death of Tom Arnold, British impresario, aged 73.

3 Capt. O'Neill announces that Northern Ireland Parliament will be dissolved on Feb. 4 and general election held on Feb. 24.
Dr. Eduardo Mondlane, president of the Mozambique Liberation Front, is assassinated by bomb on the outskirts of Dar-es-Salaam.
Death of Boris Karloff, British film actor, aged 81.

4 Col. Frank Borman and his family received by the Queen at Buckingham Palace.

5 Governor Reagan of California declares state of "extreme emergency" at University of California's Berkeley campus.
Dr. Antonio Salazar, former Portuguese Prime Minister, returns home from hospital where he has been since September 1968 after brain operation.

6 Population of break-away W. Indian island of Anguilla vote by 1,739 to 4 to adopt republican-type constitution, severing all links with the associated state of St. Kitts-Nevis-Anguilla and with British Crown.
Inquest jury find that 22 deaths in fire in Glasgow upholstery firm (Nov.

18, 1968) were due to "fault and negligence" of the firm.

7 Southern Aurora Sydney-Melbourne express crashes into goods train at Violet Town, Victoria, 104 miles from Melbourne, and 8 people are killed. Crash due to death from heart-failure of driver of Southern Aurora before the accident.
Biafran village of Umuohiagu, 25 miles N.E. of Owerri, bombed and strafed in second worst bombing incident of Nigerian civil war: between 200 and 300 people killed, and hundreds wounded.
Blizzards sweeping south across England bring towns and cities to a standstill and chaos to road, rail, and air traffic.

9 Sunday 7 people are killed and 35 injured when police open fire on mobs rampaging through central and north Bombay, in third day of violence by Marathi-speaking people protesting against immigration from Mysore.
Boeing 747 "jumbo jet" makes maiden flight over Puget Sound, near Seattle, U.S.A.
Worst snowstorm for 20 years paralyses much of U.S. east coast, including New York.
Death of George ("Gabby") Hayes, U.S. "western" film actor, aged 83.

10 Sir Paul Hasluck appointed Governor-General of Australia.

11 Harold Wilson arrives in Bonn for four-day visit to West Germany; Col. Frank Borman also arrives in Bonn on his good-will tour of Europe.
Leaders of the 15 trade unions at Ford Motor Co. agree to settlement which provides for equal pay for 1,600 women workers, rises for hourly paid workers, and financial penalties for unofficial strikers.
Half-day strike of Teesside teachers in support of five members of the National Association of Schoolmasters suspended for working to rule in protest against salary scales.

12 In Bonn students demonstrate against British policy in Nigeria, shouting "murderer" and hurling plastic bags containing blood from slaughterhouses at Harold Wilson's car.
Ford workers reject agreement made by their union leaders yesterday.
More teachers throughout Great Britain strike in sympathy with the N.A.S. members who have been suspended.
Rev. Ndabaningi Sithole, African nationalist leader, sentenced in Salisbury, Rhodesia, to 6 years' hard labour; he has already spent 4 years in prison after conviction for incitement to murder.

13 Final result of mid-term elections in West Bengal gives large majority to pro-Communist Front.
Death of Lew Stone, British dance band leader, aged 70.

14 Harold Wilson visits West Berlin and speaks on television.
25,000 London children affected by National Association of Schoolmasters' half-day strike. 2,000 schoolteachers demonstrate outside London's County Hall.
Death of Vito Genovese, Mafia leader in U.S.A., aged 71; and of Kenneth Horne, British comedian and businessman, aged 61.

15 Death of Charles (Pee Wee) Russell, U.S. jazz clarinetist, aged 62.

16 Sunday Four killed and 100 injured in demonstrations in Istanbul, Turkey, in protest against visit of ships of U.S. Sixth Fleet.
Pakistan's former Foreign Minister Zulficar Ali Bhutto is released after 3 months' imprisonment.
British Ford Motor Co. faces nation-wide strike from Feb. 24 over its plan (see Feb. 11) for financial penalties on unofficial strikers.
Col. Frank Borman is received by the Pope.
Death of Kingsley Martin, former editor of *New Statesman*, aged 71.

17 13 Africans die and more than 180 are injured when passenger train runs into blazing petrol fire over 800 yards of track on outskirts of Johannesburg.
Emergency regulations in Pakistan lifted after three years.

18 Four Arab terrorists machine-gun an Israeli airliner at Zürich airport: pilot, co-pilot, and 4 passengers injured, and one gunman killed by plane's guard.
Wedding of pop singer Lulu and Maurice Gibb of the Bee-Gees.

19 Gales and blizzards sweep southern England, and at Coire Cas, Aviemore, in the Cairngorms, Scotland, avalanche of snow and rocks buries seven climbers, four being seriously injured.
Wedding in Melbourne of Dame Zara Holt, widow of former Prime Minister of Australia, and Jeff Bate, Liberal member of Australian House of Representatives.
Death of Baroness Asquith of Yarnbury, formerly Lady Violet Bonham Carter, aged 81.

20 Seven more spies executed in Baghdad, the bodies being publicly hung in Liberation Square.
Death of Ernest Ansermet, orchestral conductor, aged 85.

21 President Ayub Khan of Pakistan promises to introduce a parliament elected by direct adult franchise, and announces he will not contest the 1970 presidential elections.

Terrorist explosive planted in Jerusalem supermarket kills two and wounds nine.

22 President Ayub Khan releases East Bengali leader Shaikh Mujibur Rahman, charged with conspiring to overthrow government of East Pakistan.

23 Sunday President Nixon arrives in Brussels on start of European tour.

Anti-Zionist demonstration by about 1,000 people, mostly Arabs, near Israel embassy, London.

Earthquake in Celebes islands, believed to be strongest recorded in the area: towns and villages destroyed and at least 600 killed.

Death of ex-king Saud of Saudi Arabia, aged 66.

24 Northern Ireland general election. Unionist Party retains absolute majority of seats, but in the Prime Minister's constituency of Bannside Capt. O'Neill's supporters (7,745) are outnumbered by those voting for Ian Paisley (6,331) and Michael Farrell (People's Democracy, 2,310).

10,000 out of possible 27,000 day-shift workers do not report for work at Ford's works throughout Britain (see Feb. 11, 12, and 16).

President Nixon arrives at London airport, and has talks with Harold Wilson at Chequers.

Israel planes bomb and strafe two Al Fatah training bases in Syria.

25 President Nixon lunches with Queen at Buckingham Palace, visits House of Commons, meets the three party leaders, and lays wreath at tomb of Unknown Soldier.

Split between the leaders of Ford's 15 unions in 9–6 vote against a motion to reject agreement of Feb. 11.

Opening of *Daily Mail* Ideal Home Exhibition is postponed because of unofficial disputes and strikes by men working on stands (see March 12).

26 Transport and General Workers Union makes Ford's strike official for its 32,000 members, and other unions follow suit.

Week of heavy rains causes mudslides and floods which drive 12,500 people from their homes in southern California, U.S.A.

Death of Levi Eshkol, Prime Minister of Israel, aged 73.

27 U.K. Bank rate is raised to 8 per cent.

In anti-American demonstration in Rome after arrival of President Nixon, one student is killed, 50 people are injured including 35 police, and 300 are arrested.

Ford's apply for court writs to ensure observance by trade unions of agreement of Feb. 11, and are granted temporary injunctions preventing the unions from taking further strike action.

Death of John Boles, former U.S. film actor, aged 73.

28 In Unionist parliamentary party meeting Capt. O'Neill receives vote of confidence (23–1, with one abstention), but only after 10 M.P.s have walked out.

President Nixon flies from Rome to Paris and has talks with President de Gaulle.

One of the biggest earthquakes ever recorded rocks Spain, Portugal, and N. Africa, but only 5 people are killed and 60 injured.

Death of Randolph Sutton, British music-hall artist, aged 80.

1st . . . Paisley leads Belfast march

2nd . . . Pres. de Gaulle speaks at Quimper

7th . . . Crash of Southern Aurora express in Victoria, Australia

4th . . . Astronaut Frank Borman at the Palace

25th . . . President Nixon lunches with the Queen

18th . . . Lulu marries Bee-Gee Maurice Gibb

March

Pisces (The Fishes) Feb. 19–March 20

1 Princess Anne carries out her first solo public engagement when she presents St. David's day leeks to Welsh Guards at Pirbright, Surrey.

2 Sunday Maiden flight for 28 minutes from Toulouse airport of Concorde 001, French-built prototype.
Chinese troops invade Soviet territory near the Nizhemikhailovka border post on the River Ussuri, part of the frontier between Soviet Far East and Manchuria. Shots are exchanged and men are killed and wounded.
President Nixon flies from France back to Rome, lands by helicopter in St. Peter's Square, has audience with Pope, and returns to Washington.

3 Apollo 9, carrying Col. James McDivitt, Col. David Scott, and Mr. Russell Schweickart, is launched from Cape Kennedy, and goes into Earth orbit, for rehearsal of separating and re-docking lunar module.
It is confirmed that Biafran troops have cut off Federal-held town of Owerri and severed its supply road from Port Harcourt.
High Court judge renews temporary injunctions granted to Ford's on Feb. 27.

4 Second day of demonstrations by thousands of Chinese outside Soviet embassy in Peking.

5 Dr. Gustav Heinemann, 69-year-old Minister of Justice, is elected West Germany's first Social Democratic President by Federal Assembly meeting in West Berlin, by majority of only six votes after three ballots.

6 Astronaut Russell Schweickart steps out of Apollo 9's lunar module and walks for 37½ mins. in space.
High Court judge ends writs of injunction granted to Ford's on Feb. 27, saying that such industrial agreements are "not enforceable at law."
Terrorist bomb explodes in cafeteria of Hebrew University, Jerusalem, injuring 29 students.
Death of Alexander Werth, author and journalist, aged 68.

7 Thousands of Russians demonstrate outside Chinese embassy in Moscow in protest against Chinese "brutality and mutilation" in border clash of March 2.
Apollo 9 spacecraft and lunar module re-dock after 6-hour separation.
Queen opens third stage of London Underground Victoria Line.

8 Artillery battle between Egypt and Israel along length of Suez Canal.
Chairman of trade union negotiating committee in Ford dispute, Mark Young of Electrical Trades Union, resigns.
Pakistan–England Test series abandoned after riot during third Test at Karachi.
Lionel Rose successfully defends his world bantamweight title in Melbourne against Alan Rudkin.

9 Sunday Lt. Gen. Abdel Riad, Egyptian chief of staff, killed by Israeli shell during Suez Canal artillery duel.
Three villages near Umuahia, Biafra, bombed by Federal Nigerian planes: at least 98 killed and 68 seriously injured.

10 James Earl Ray sentenced to 99 years' imprisonment in Memphis, Tennessee, U.S.A, for murder of Dr. Martin Luther King (April 4, 1968).
About 200 L.S.E. students stage all-night sit-in.
Death of Jimmy Wilde, British boxer, former world flyweight champion, aged 76.

11 Following 24-hour national strike in France in support of higher wages, President de Gaulle broadcasts his intention of defending the franc, the economy, and the republic.

In artillery duel across Suez Canal Israeli gunners hit three Egyptian ships in port of Suez.
About 80 L.S.E. students continue sit-in.

12 In Anguilla, William Whitlock, British parliamentary under-sec. in Foreign and Commonwealth office, reads out British government's proposals, then flees to Antigua at appearance of Ronald Webster, self-styled president, with armed followers.
Complete closure of all 23 Ford plants in Great Britain.
Gen. Lemnitzer's retirement as Supreme Commander of Allied Forces in Europe announced; successor is Gen. Andrew Goodpaster, now deputy commander of U.S. forces in Vietnam.
Mass anti-Russian rallies in Peking, Canton, and Hangchow.
Opening of *Daily Mail* Ideal Home Exhibition at Olympia, seven days late because of unofficial strikes.
Wedding at Marylebone, London, register office of Beatle Paul McCartney and Linda Eastman, U.S. photographer.

13 Apollo 9 successfully splashes down 180 miles east of Bahamas.

14 Day of violence in Belgian university towns of Ghent and Louvain ends after arrest of 100 students by police using tear gas, water cannon, batons, and rifle butts.

15 Shots fired in Manchurian-Siberian border incident between Russians and Chinese on Damansky (Chen Pao) island in Ussuri river.
Death of Miles Malleson, British actor aged 80.

16 Sunday Venezuelan airliner crashes and explodes on housing estate in Maracaibo, Venezuela, killing 76 on board and 30 on the ground.
Trade union chiefs and Ford management seen by Mrs. Barbara Castle, Minister of Employment and Productivity. Ford's make a new pay and holiday offer.
Mrs. Coretta King, widow of Dr. Martin Luther King, preaches in St. Paul's Cathedral, the first woman to do so.

17 Warsaw Pact powers conference in Budapest ends after 2-hour meeting—the shortest summit meeting of the powers ever held.

4th ... Anti-Russian march in Peking

7th ... Anti-Chinese march in Moscow

1st . . . Princess Anne hands out leeks

12th . . . Wedding of Beatle Paul

16th . . . Coretta King in St. Paul's

23rd . . . Anguillans "bury" Anthony Lee

30th . . . Eisenhower journeys to the Capitol

Mrs. Golda Meir is chosen prime minister of Israel.

Floods kill 300 people and make two thirds of population homeless in Sao Jose da Laje, Brazil.

Death of Winston Field, first Rhodesian Front party prime minister of Southern Rhodesia, aged 64.

18 Seven of crew of eight of Long-hope lifeboat found dead inside their inverted boat, 4 miles south of Orkney island of Hoy, whence they had set out during night to aid distressed cargo vessel.

Ford's dispute settled on basis of management's offer of March 16.

19 President Ayub Khan and Pakistan government, conceding that mob rule has taken over and that police and civilian forces are not strong enough to deal with situation, instruct administrations of East and West Pakistan to take urgent measures to quell disorders.

200 British paratroops and marines land on Anguilla at dawn.

1,260-ft.-high TV mast at Emley Moor, near Huddersfield, Yorks., crashes under strong winds and weight of ice.

20 Ronald Webster, "president" of Anguilla, demands withdrawal of British troops and proposes to hold referendum on the island's future.

John Lennon marries Yoko Ono in Gibraltar register office.

21 Ford's workers return to work.

22 Anguillans besiege island's administration building, denouncing the British commissioner Anthony Lee.

23 Sunday Mock funeral march for Anthony Lee staged by protesting Anguillans.

24 In attempt to check wave of murder, arson, and looting in East Pakistan—where in past month over 170 people have been killed by mob violence—police have arrested 250 people in Tangail and Jamalpur, and 172 in Dacca.

On a trial trip *Queen Elizabeth 2* sails from Southampton for first time since returning to port on Jan. 2 with faulty turbine rotors.

Death of Joseph Kasavubu, first president of Congolese Republic.

25 Ayub Khan resigns from presidency of Pakistan, and hands over administration to armed forces under Gen. A. M. Yahya Khan; martial law proclaimed.

At least 16 people killed and about 100 injured in head-on collision between two passenger trains at La Louvière, southern Belgium.

Death of Billy Cotton, British band-leader, aged 69; and of Alan Mowbray, film actor, aged 72.

26 Armed gang attack and tie up 16 members of staff of merchant bank in Hatton Garden, London, and escape with diamonds worth at least £350,000 and £8,000 in cash.

Death of Paul Panhard, French car manufacturer, aged 87.

27 Harold Wilson flies to Lagos for talks with Nigerian leaders in attempt to help find ways of ending war.

In by-elections, Conservatives win Walthamstow East from Labour, and hold Brighton (Pavilion) and Weston-super-Mare.

28 In wild Czech celebrations of second victory of their ice-hockey team over Russia in world championships in Stockholm, offices of Soviet airline Aeroflot in Wenceslas Square, Prague, are set on fire.

Lord Caradon, permanent British representative at the U.N., arrives in Anguilla to mediate.

Severe earthquake hits Izmir, Turkey: 1,300 houses are destroyed, 53 people killed, and 300 injured, the town of Alasehir being worst hit.

Death of ex-President of U.S.A. Dwight David Eisenhower, aged 78.

29 Earthquake in north-east Ethiopia kills 24, injures 168, makes several hundred homeless.

Grand National won by Highland Wedding, ridden by Eddie Harty.

30 Explosives cause £500,000 worth of damage to two electricity transformers at Castlereagh substation, near Belfast.

Gen. Eisenhower's coffin is taken to the Capitol in Washington for lying-in-state.

Lucien Bianchi, Belgian racing driver, killed during trial run at Le Mans.

31 B.O.A.C. pilots start strike at 1 a.m. over pay and productivity dispute; all B.O.A.C. flights grounded.

A joint agreement on early return to normality in Anguilla is announced by Lord Caradon and Ronald Webster.

Still seeking a means of ending the the war in Nigeria, Harold Wilson arrives in Addis Ababa for talks with Emperor Haile Selassie. Col. Ojukwu of Biafra refuses invitation to meet Mr. Wilson.

After funeral service in Washington National Cathedral, Gen. Eisenhower's body is taken by train for burial at Abilene, Kansas.

April

Aries (The Ram) March 21–April 20

1 Explosion in coalmine at Barro-teran, Mexico, kills at least 168 miners.

2 Harold Wilson returns to Great Britain from Africa.
Czechoslovak government and Communist party announce renewed press censorship and reinforcement of police, and publicly condemn popular liberal leader, Josef Smrkovsky.
Ghana's head of state, Lt.-Gen. Ankrah, resigns after admitting receipt of money for political purposes from a foreign company, and Brig. A. A. Afrifa takes his place.
Burial of Gen. Eisenhower at Abilene, Kansas.

3 On first anniversary of murder of Dr. Martin Luther King violence breaks out in many U.S. cities.

4 **Good Friday** U.S. bank rate is raised to 6 per cent.
More than 80 people injured and 275 arrested after second day of wild disorders in Chicago, in predominantly negro districts.

5 B.O.A.C. pilots strike (March 31) ends after 22 hours' negotiations.
Cambridge win the University Boat Race by 4½ lengths.

6 **Easter Day** Biafrans begin evacuation of their capital, Umuahia.

2,000 C.N.D. marchers in Trafalgar Square are addressed by Madame Nguyen Thi Binh, deputy leader of National Liberation Front delegation at Vietnam peace talks in Paris.
As Great Britain enjoys finest Easter for 45 years, rowdyism on beaches terrorises holidaymakers at Brighton, Margate, Skegness, and Southend.
Death of Monte Crick, British actor ("Dan Archer"), aged 63.

8 Arab guerrillas carry out pre-dawn rocket attack on Israel port of Eilat on Gulf of Aqaba; Israeli jets retaliate by bombing Arab rocket-firing positions at Aqaba.
Head-on collision of passenger and freight trains at Parkfields, Wolver-hampton, kills both drivers and injures 31 passengers.

9 At Battipaglia, near Salerno, Italy, in riots following closure of local tobacco factory, two are killed and about 150 injured, in fighting between 1,500 police and thousands of demonstrators.
Students at Harvard University, U.S.A., seize administration building during riots in protest against reserve officers' training corps programme.
Concorde 002, the British-built prototype, makes 22-minute maiden flight from Filton, Bristol.

10 Further rioting in Battipaglia; workers in other Italian towns rally in support; Communist Party call for nation-wide protest; and trade unions announce 3-hour general strike tomorrow.
400 police use clubs to move demonstrators at Harvard University, and 200 arrests are made.

11 In Battipaglia the entire popula-tion turns out for funeral of the two people shot dead on April 9; 24-hour general strike in Salerno, and violence in other Italian cities.

12 By defeating England 30–9 at Cardiff Arms Park, Wales secures international Rugby championship for first time since 1965, and triple crown for 11th time.
At Wembley, North Shields win the F.A. Amateur Cup by defeating Sutton United 2–1.

13 **Sunday** Lord Caradon leaves Anguilla, where the situation remains at an impasse.

14 Troop reinforcements are flown into Anguilla, and Ronald Webster calls off proposed referendum.
Biafran government completes evacuation of Umuahia.
Lin Piao, China's Defence Minister, is named at Communist party congress in Peking as eventual successor to Chairman Mao Tse-tung.
Prisoners riot in jails in Milan, Turin, and Genoa.
90 m.p.h. tornado hits region of Dacca, East Pakistan, totally destroying two villages, killing 1,000 people, and injuring several thousand.
Death of Jay Laurier, British comedian, aged 89.

15 U.K. Chancellor of Exchequer Roy Jenkins presents his Budget, which will increase revenue by an estimated £340 million in a full year.
North Korea claims to have shot down U.S. spy aircraft with 31 service-men on board.
Death of Victoria Eugénie, ex-Queen of Spain, aged 81.

17 Alexander Dubcek resigns as first secretary of Czechoslovakian Communist Party and is replaced by Dr. Gustav Husak (first secretary of the Slovakian Communist Party).
West German bank rate is raised from 3 to 4 per cent.
At Los Angeles, Sirhan Sirhan found guilty of murder of Senator Robert Kennedy (see April 23).
World record round-the-world flight completed by Dr. Alvin Marks (U.S.A.), president of Skymark Airlines, who touches down at Sacramento, California, 14 days after taking off in his single-engined Cessna.

18 Bernadette Devlin, a 21-year-old civil rights worker, becomes the youngest Westminster M.P. when she wins the Mid-Ulster by-election with a 4,211 majority.

19 In riot in Londonderry, petrol bombs are thrown; 69 people are injured (43 of them policemen) and 15 arrested.

9th . . . Battle in the streets of Battipaglia

10th . . . Milan workers protest about Battipaglia deaths

Whole system of state services in Italy brought to a halt by strike involving about 1,500,000 public employees.

Wedding of Federal Nigerian head of state Gen. Yakuba Gowon and Victoria Zakarir.

20 **Sunday**   As wave of violence spreads through Northern Ireland Capt. O'Neill requests help from British troops. Explosion damage to mains at Silent Water Reservoir, Mourne Mountains, co. Down, causes water shortage in Belfast.

Jail riot in Cagliari, Sardinia.

Anthony Lee leaves Anguilla on "holiday."

21 L.S.E. students vote overwhelmingly for boycott of all lectures, classes, and tutorials until two dismissed lecturers are reinstated, and demand immediate resignation of standing committee of governors and "democratic control" over all future appointments and dismissals.

Bruce Tulloh starts on 2,876-mile run from Los Angeles to New York.

22 *Queen Elizabeth 2* sails on her first passenger-carrying voyage from Southampton to the Canary Islands.

Robin Knox-Johnston sails his ketch *Suhaili* into Falmouth at the end of his trophy-winning non-stop round-the world solo voyage.

Israeli jets make heavy bombing attack on Egyptian radar installations in Jordan, and tension between the two countries is described as at its highest peak since 6-day war in June 1967.

Bernadette Devlin delivers her maiden speech in the House of Commons.

Italy's 12th prison revolt in 10 days, at Bologna.

President Saragat of Italy, beginning State visit to Great Britain, is welcomed by the Queen at Windsor Castle.

More than 100 British nurses stage sit-down at Department of Health and Social Security in London in protest against their conditions of work.

23 Capt. O'Neill persuades Northern Ireland Unionist parliamentary party to accept the principle of one-man-one-vote in local elections.

Biafra's capital, Umuahia, captured by Federal Nigerian forces after five days of almost constant shelling.

State of emergency declared throughout Lebanon after anti-government riots in which at least seven people have been killed and dozens injured.

Los Angeles jury decides on death penalty for Sirhan Sirhan, assassin of Senator Robert Kennedy.

24 Loch Neagh pipeline at Clady, co. Antrim, which carries one-fifth of Belfast's water supply, is damaged by explosion. At Annalong, co. Down, 54-inch water main supplying Belfast is blown up.

Lebanese Prime Minister, Rashid Karami, announces his government's resignation.

26 At Wembley, Manchester City win F.A. Cup, defeating Leicester City 1–0.

27 **Sunday**   Referendum in France on reforms of senate and regional administration.

Egyptian and Israeli forces exchange fire for nine hours along 75 miles of Suez Canal.

Death of President Rene Barrientos Ortuno, President of Bolivia, in helicopter crash; his successor is Vice-President Louis Adolfo Siles Salinas.

28 Gen. de Gaulle resigns as president of France after defeat in yesterday's referendum. Alain Poher, speaker of senate, takes over as interim president, pending election.

Capt. Terence O'Neill resigns from leadership of Ulster Unionist Party and premiership of Northern Ireland.

Bomb explodes in Central Electricity Generating Board Offices at Gabalta, Cardiff.

About 30,000 Italians, leaders of 1,300,000 civil servants, teachers, and railwaymen, begin 72-hour strike in protest against pay and conditions.

Avalanche overwhelms and kills five Americans and two Sherpas at 17,000 ft. on Dhaulagiri (26,810 ft.) in the Himalayas, and expedition is abandoned.

29 Anthony Lee is relieved of his post as commissioner in Anguilla, and replaced by John Cumber, acting commissioner since April 20.

Death of Julius Katchen, U.S. pianist, aged 42.

30 Australia's new Governor-General, Sir Paul Hasluck, is sworn in at Parliament House, Canberra.

19th . . . Wedding of Nigeria's Gen. Gowon   22nd . . . Bernadette at Westminster   10th . . . Police eject Harvard students

27th . . . France says *Non* to de Gaulle   24th . . . Belfast water supply pipe blown up at Annalong, co. Down

May

Taurus (The Bull) April 21–May 20

1 May Day strikes called in protest against U.K. Government's union reform legislation are supported by only 1 per cent of Britain's workers, but publication of all national newspapers is halted.

Major James Chichester-Clark is chosen leader of Unionist Party in Northern Ireland, and so becomes Prime Minister in succession to Capt. O'Neill.

Three L.S.E. lecturers accused of causing malicious damage to school gates and walls (Jan. 24) are acquitted, but two students found guilty.

2 Princess Anne launches Britain's biggest ship, *Esso Northumbria*, 253,000-ton tanker, at Wallsend, Northumberland.

QE 2 sails on her maiden voyage to New York.

Death of Franz von Papen, former German chancellor, aged 89.

3 Death of Dr. Zakir Husain, President of India, aged 72; Vice-President Dr. Varahagiri Venkata Giri becomes acting President.

4 **Sunday** Start of *Daily Mail* Transatlantic Air Race.

Death of Sir Osbert Sitwell, English poet, essayist, and novelist, aged 76.

5 The Queen and Prince Philip arrive in Austria for State visit.

Riot police battle with 5,000 Czech demonstrators in Pilsen on anniversary of city's liberation by U.S. forces in 1945.

6 Amnesty is declared in Northern Ireland for everyone serving sentences or facing charges arising from street demonstrations; Rev. Ian Paisley and Maj. Ronald Bunting are freed from jail.

7 King's Cross–Aberdeen night express crashes near Morpeth, Northumberland, derailing coaches: 6 killed and 103 injured.

Princess Anne joins her parents in Austria for remainder of State visit.

QE 2 receives tremendous welcome on arrival at New York on maiden Atlantic crossing.

8 Conservatives make sweeping gains of 633 seats in 320 boroughs of England and Wales in local government elections, Labour losing 639 seats and control of several major cities.

9 West German cabinet's refusal to revalue the Deutschemark has adverse effect on £, dollar, and French franc.

Israeli commandos cross Jordan and attack Arab guerrilla post 20 miles S. of Sea of Galilee.

The Queen, Prince Philip, and Princess Anne leave Austria at end of State visit.

10 Gen. de Gaulle and wife arrive for holiday at Heron Cove Hotel, near Sneem, co. Kerry, Ireland, 26 miles from Killarney.

England win Home International Football Championship Tournament by defeating Scotland 4–1 at Wembley.

11 **Sunday** Governors of 11 central banks meeting in Basle announce immediate action to reverse flow of funds into West Germany.

General election in mainland states of Malaysia today and yesterday results in much reduced majority for Abdul Rahman's coalition.

End of *Daily Mail* Transatlantic Air Race.

12 Following yesterday's central bankers' statement all currencies recover ground against the Deutschemark, and speculators' funds begin to drain away from Germany.

After meeting of T.U.C. general council and Harold Wilson and Mrs. Barbara Castle at 10 Downing Street to discuss proposed Industrial Relations Bill, Government agree to postpone publication of Bill.

Communists in Vietnam begin biggest assault since the 1968 Tet offensive.

13 After night of interracial Malay-Chinese rioting and arson in Kuala Lumpur, capital of Malaysia (50 killed and hundreds injured), army is called out to control rioters. State of emergency declared in Selangor; curfew imposed in Perak, Penang, and Province Wellesley.

Disciplinary committee set up at L.S.E., composed of 7 members of staff, with no student representation.

14 Pres. Nixon, in TV address to nation, puts forward an 8-point peace plan for Vietnam, proposing the phased withdrawal under international supervision of all non-South Vietnam forces from S. Vietnam, followed by free elections.

Another night of rioting and arson in Kuala Lumpur results in 50 more deaths and about 90 injured.

Devastating fire in Tromsö, Norway, does £3 million damage.

15 State of emergency throughout Malaysia declared: National Operations Council formed to run the country; publication of all newspapers suspended.

Biggest series of strikes in Australia for 20 years break out after arrest and imprisonment for contempt of court of Clarence O'Shea, secretary of Victoria Tramway Men's Union.

Force of 500 police use shotguns and tear-gas during battle with 2,000 demonstrators at University of California, Berkeley, U.S.A.

16 On 20th anniversary of formation of NATO the Queen reviews 61 ships of NATO fleet at Spithead.

More than 120 people injured in 5-hour battle in Berkeley, California, when students and hippies clash with police over use of parkland.

Third British heart transplant operation: Charles Hendrick (59) receives heart of Margaret Sinsbury (29) at Guy's Hospital, London.

Death of Sir Lewis Casson, British actor, producer, and husband of Dame Sybil Thorndike, aged 93.

17 Arab commandos launch co-ordinated attack on Israeli position 4 miles south of Damiya Bridge over Jordan.

Castleford win Rugby League Cup at Wembley, beating Salford 11–6.

Death of Cardinal Joseph Beran, exiled archbishop of Czechoslovakia, aged 80.

18 **Sunday** Apollo 10, manned by Col. Thomas P. Stafford, Cmdr. Eugene A. Cernan, and Cmdr. John W. Young, is launched from Cape Kennedy on rehearsal flight to moon.

19 Two rival groups of 500 students clash at Waseda University, Tokyo, and 600 riot police are called to restore order.

James Rector, aged 25, dies from gunshot wound received on May 15 at Berkeley, California.

Death of Coleman Hawkins, jazz saxophonist, aged 64.

20 In continuing Australian strikes more than 33,000 transport workers walk out, leaving Sydney without trains, buses, or ferries, and 6,000 waterside workers also stop work, leaving 40 ships idle in port.

Ian Smith broadcasts Rhodesian Front government's proposals for a republic and announces new constitution.

National Guard helicopter drops "CS" gas on demonstrators at Berkeley, California.

The Queen opens Church of Scotland's General Assembly in Edinburgh.

55 U.S. soldiers killed and 300 wounded in attempt to capture Vietcong stronghold Hamburger Hill (Ap Bia Mountain in north-west corner of Nam A Shau Valley, S. Vietnam).

Soviet Union gives first public demonstration of TU-144 supersonic airliner, in Moscow.

21 Clarence O'Shea is released from jail, but 150,000 trade unionists in Sydney are to continue with 24-hour strike beginning at midnight, as are the the West Australian trades and labour council.

Apollo 10 enters lunar orbit.

Commander Nigel Tetley, non-stop round-the-world solo yachtsman, is rescued after his trimaran, *Victress*, sinks east of the Azores.

22 Apollo 10 lunar module separates from command module, and Cernan and Stafford descend in it to within 10 miles of Moon's surface.

Conservatives retain Chichester in by-election, Labour losing deposit.

Viscount Hall is appointed chairman of new Post Office Corporation.

23 Apollo 10 lunar module re-docks with command module, and spacecraft leaves lunar orbit for return journey to Earth.

Helicopter and light aircraft drop tear gas on demonstrators at agricultural and technology college in Greensboro, North Carolina, U.S.A.

At least 496 people arrested at Berkeley, California, during demonstrations about death of James Rector (May 19).

Biafrans attack airport at Port Harcourt.

24 Colin Milburn, U.K. test cricketer, has his left eye removed after road accident.

25 Sunday Regime of Muhammad Mahgoub in Sudan is overthrown in bloodless military coup, and left-wing Abu Bakr Awadullah is appointed Prime Minister.

Five-mile-long oil slick causes holiday chaos on beaches from Southend to Shoeburyness.

26 Bank Holiday Apollo 10 splashes down in Pacific, only 25 seconds late after 600,000-mile journey.

Death of Allan Haines Lockheed, pioneer aircraft builder, aged 80; and of Alan Clark, B.B.C. radio sports commentator, aged 49.

28 Henry Cooper relinquishes the British heavyweight title he has held for a record 10 years and 4 months, because of dispute with the British Boxing Board of Control.

A.C. Milan win European Champions' Cup in Madrid, beating Ajax, Amsterdam, 4–1.

29 Violence breaks out in Cordoba, Argentina, between security forces and workers and students: at least 6 killed, and more than 100 wounded.

Wally Herbert, Dr. Roy Koerner, Alan Gill, and Ken Hughes reach land after their 3,620-route-mile walk across the Arctic ice.

30 General strike in Argentina in protest against policies of Minister of Interior.

Dutch marines and militia quell riot involving about 4,000 negroes on strike from Royal Dutch Shell Refinery, on Caribbean island of Curaçao.

20,000 demonstrators march through Berkeley, California.

1st . . . Chichester-Clark   7th . . . Aberdeen express crashes   16th . . . Royal review of NATO fleet

20th . . . Gas sprayed on students at Berkeley, California   30th . . . Willemstad, Curaçao, after strikers' riot

June

Gemini (The Twins) May 21–June 20

1 Sunday In first ballot in French Presidential election, M. Pompidou has commanding lead, but M. Poher refuses to concede victory; second ballot will therefore take place on June 15.

Announcement that Biafra has tried and sentenced to death 18 foreign oilmen captured with Nigerian troops in Okapi area between May 6 and May 10.

Death of Lord Hailey, O.M., aged 87.

2 Australian aircraft carrier *Melbourne* slices U.S. destroyer *Frank E. Evans* in two in manoeuvres in South China Sea: 73 U.S. seamen missing.

British Petroleum announces agreement in principle on £833 million merger of its U.S. oil interests with Standard Oil of Ohio.

4 Strike at British Leyland works in Lancashire, which started on May 19, has cost the company about £5 million in lost production, including £2½ million in exports; deadlock continues.

Prototype two-seat version of Harrier vertical-take-off fighter crashes on Salisbury Plain.

Reprieve of 18 oilmen sentenced to death in Biafra (June 1).

Derby won by Blakeney, ridden by Eric Johnson.

Death of Rafael Osuna, Mexican tennis star, in crash of Boeing 727 airliner near Monterrey, Mexico.

5 Emergency T.U.C. meeting called in Croydon to discuss proposed Industrial Relations Bill votes in favour of giving General Council of T.U.C. power to intervene in unofficial strikes and disputes between unions, and against Bill's penal clauses on unofficial strikers.

World Communist Congress opens in Moscow; 75 Communist parties are represented, but China, Albania, and Yugoslavia boycott the conference.

British, American, and Canadian veterans return to Normandy for ceremonies to commemorate D-Day landings in 1944.

6 Death of Gen. Sir Miles Dempsey, c.-in-c. British Second Army in 1944 invasion of Normandy, aged 72.

7 150,000 people attend free open-air "pop" concert in Hyde Park, London.

About 2,000 people demonstrate in Rome for changes in law to make divorce legal in Italy.

The Aldeburgh Festival concert hall and opera house–the Maltings, Snape, Suffolk–is gutted by fire.

8 Sunday At start of talks with President Thieu of S. Vietnam on Midway Island, President Nixon announces that 25,000 U.S. troops are to be withdrawn from Vietnam between July and end of August.

Spain closes customs post at La Linea, so sealing last land entry to Gibraltar; 4,500 Spanish workers return to Spain.

Death of Robert Taylor, U.S. film actor, aged 57.

9 At Wolverhampton, Enoch Powell speaks again on Great Britain's race problem, suggesting an immigrants' repatriation scheme.

U.S. bank rate is raised to record 8½ per cent.

10 Pope Paul visits Geneva, where he addresses the 50th anniversary conference of the I.L.O. and calls at the h.q. of the World Council of Churches.

Amalgamated Union of Engineering and Foundry Workers executive decide to make British Leyland strike (June 4) official.

Government announces that it has accepted findings by Board of Trade inquiry clearing the pilot, Capt. James Thain, of blame for Munich (Manchester United) air disaster of 1958.

11 Chinese and Soviet troops fight in mountainous border zone separating Soviet Republic of Kazakhstan from Sinkiang.

Mrs. Golda Meir, Israeli Prime Minister, arrives in London on 6-day visit for government talks and to attend Socialist International at Eastbourne.

Newcastle win Inter-Cities Fairs' Cup Final by defeating Ujpest Dozsa, Hungary, in Budapest, 3–2 in second leg, scoring 6–2 on aggregate.

Death of John L. Lewis, U.S. labour leader, aged 89; and of Frank Lawton, British actor, aged 64.

13 65 passengers injured when Paignton–Paddington holiday express leaves rails at Somerton, Somerset.

Death of Martita Hunt, British actress, aged 69.

14 Mike Bonallack (G.B.) wins British Amateur Golf Championship at Hoylake, Lancs.

15 Sunday In second ballot of French presidential election M. Pompidou defeats M. Poher by 15 per cent, and becomes new President of France.

More than 40,000 Japanese take part in nation-wide rallies against Vietnam war and U.S.A.–Japan security treaty.

Fifteen reported killed and 200 injured when roof of restaurant at San Rafael, Spain, collapses, bringing hundreds of tons of steel and concrete on 500 people having inaugural lunch.

16 Death of Field Marshal Earl Alexander of Tunis, aged 77.

18 Harold Wilson and Barbara Castle agree with T.U.C. leaders that there will be no legislation with penal sanctions against unions or unofficial strikers in life-time of present government in return for "solemn and binding undertaking" by T.U.C. to end 40 years of non-intervention in unofficial strikes.

General election in Republic of Ireland, won by Fianna Fail party.

Formula for ending British Leyland Lancashire factories strike reached after 10 hours of talks between unions and employers in York.

Robert Maxwell, M.P., announces plans for take-over of his publishing company Pergamon Press by U.S. company Leasco.

19 Gen. and Mme. de Gaulle return to France from Ireland.

Sir William Carr resigns as chairman of *News of the World* organisation; his successor will be Australian newspaper magnate Rupert Murdoch.

20 Georges Pompidou officially installed as 19th president of the French Republic; he appoints Jacques Chaban-Delmas to succeed Couve de Murville as prime minister.

In Rhodesian referendum Ian Smith's government obtains 81 per cent of votes in favour of severance of all ties with British Crown, and 73 per cent in favour of constitutional proposals.

New schools at Aberfan, replacing one destroyed in disaster of Oct. 21, 1966, opened by Harold Wilson.

Severe earth tremors felt in Melbourne.

21 Death of Maureen Connolly-Brinker ("Little Mo"), U.S. tennis player, aged 34.

22 Sunday Israeli jet planes raid Jordanian village, following night of commando skirmishes by Israeli and Egyptian forces.

Thousands of young people fight police at Rock music festival in Northridge, California, U.S.A.

In Hanover, West Germany, explosion of shells in truck of ammunition train, devastates goods yard, kills 12, and injures 11.

More than 100 Portuguese soldiers presumed drowned after barge in which they were attempting to cross Zambesi river in Mozambique founders in midstream.

Death of Judy Garland, U.S. actress, aged 47.

23 Dominican Airlines DC-4 cargo plane crashes into Miami, Florida, street, killing four-man crew and 10 people on the ground, and injuring 12.

Israeli forces blow up irrigation system in Jordan as troops on Suez Canal throw back Egyptian raiders.

24 Sir Humphrey Gibbs resigns Governorship of Rhodesia.

After saboteurs blow up oil pipeline at Haifa Israeli police detain 114 suspects, both Arabs and Jews.

Opening of All-England Open Tennis Championships at Wimbledon.

25 Bruce Tulloh ends his 2,876-mile run from Los Angeles to New York. His time of 64 days 21 hours 50 minutes beats 1964 record by Don Shepherd (S. Africa) of 73 days 8 hours and 20 mins.

In longest singles match ever played at Wimbledon (112 games, 5 hr. 20 mins), Pancho Gonzales, aged 41, beats Charlie Paserell, U.S.A., 22–24, 1–6, 16–14, 6–3, 11–9.

26 Liberals win Ladywood, Birmingham, by-election.

In bomb attacks in Buenos Aires on 21 supermarkets financed by family of Nelson Rockefeller, six are destroyed and 13 damaged.

27 Blast furnace men at Port Talbot start unofficial strike over pay dispute.

Gibraltar isolated from Spain by suspension of ferry service from Algeçiras.

29 **Sunday** Bombs explode in Argentina's main cities in continuing protest at visit of Governor Rockefeller.

Further race riots in Kuala Lumpur, Malaysia.

30 Federal Nigerian government announces that it is taking charge of all relief operations, so barring the International Committee of the Red Cross.

Power lines from Aswan dam to Cairo and Nile delta region damaged by Israeli commando action.

Time bomb explodes at post office in Cardiff, in the fourth bomb incident in the city in three months.

Divorce Reform Bill is passed by House of Lords.

Death of Moise Tshombe, former Congo president, aged 49, is reported.

2nd . . . U.S. destroyer *Frank E. Evans* is cut in two

15th . . . Restaurant roof falls in, at San Rafael, near Madrid

13th . . . Buckled lines derail British holiday express

15th . . . M. Pompidou elected President of France

25th . . . Gonzales wins Wimbledon's longest match

25th . . . Tulloh in New York

July

Cancer (The Crab) June 21–July 20

1 Investiture of Prince Charles as Prince of Wales at Caernarvon Castle.

State of siege is imposed in Argentina following murder of a trade union organiser.

56-day siege of Special Forces camp at Ben Het is relieved by S. Vietnamese force.

Dr. Gustav Heinemann takes oath as president of West Germany.

2 Prince Charles starts four-day tour of Wales.

Brian Jones, former member of Rolling Stones pop group, is found dead in swimming pool at his Sussex home.

3 In Turin 4,000 rioters, protesting against high rents and evictions, clash with police, 50 of whom are injured.

More than 250 London Transport Underground signalmen stage 24-hour unofficial strike over pay.

4 Harold Wilson starts his first official visit to Sweden.

Ann Jones wins Wimbledon ladies' singles—the first British girl to do so for 8 years—by defeating Billie-Jean King.

5 Tom Mboya, Kenya's Minister of Economic Planning, is assassinated in Nairobi street, and riots break out throughout the country.

Prince Charles ends his tour of Wales, receiving the freedom of city of Cardiff.

Rod Laver wins Wimbledon men's singles by defeating John Newcombe.

Death of Wilhelm Backhaus, pianist, aged 85; and of Dr. Walter Gropius, architect, aged 86.

6 Sunday Agreement reached in London between Nigerian, British, and Red Cross representatives on relief measures for Biafra.

Thousands of mourning Africans file past the body of Tom Mboya at Nairobi home, while fights between Luo and Kikuyu tribes take place.

7 Start of three-day unofficial strike by 350 Eastern Region railway signalmen.

Death of Gladys Swarthout, U.S. opera singer, aged 64.

8 Biggest air battle since six-day war between Israeli and Syrian planes.

Russian-Chinese shooting incident on Goldinsky Island on Amur River border.

In Nairobi 800 police fight with more than 30,000 demonstrators during memorial service for Tom Mboya.

First plane-load of the 25,000 U.S. troops being withdrawn from S. Vietnam arrives home.

Eastern Region signalmen's strike (July 7) spreads to London and northern sections of the region.

9 7,000 London teachers strike in support of pay claim; 5,000 march to county hall and Westminster.

Tom Mboya's funeral procession forced to leave planned route when 100,000 rioting Luo tribesmen block Kisumu centre; crowd throw stones at Pres. Kenyatta's car.

Railway signalmen's strike spreads to Southern region.

10 Railway signalmen announce another three-day strike for July 22–24.

Non-stop round-the-world solo yachtsman Donald Crowhurst's trimaran *Teignmouth Electron* is found abandoned 700 miles west of the Azores.

11 After trial lasting 8 months Laurence Gandar, editor-in-chief of *Rand Daily Mail*, Johannesburg, and senior reporter Benjamin Pogrund, are found guilty of publishing articles on S. African prison life without taking reasonable steps to verify them, and Gandar is fined £117 and Pogrund given suspended 6 months' prison sentence.

Tom Mboya buried according to tribal rites in his home village on the island of Rusinga, Kenya.

Air search for Donald Crowhurst (July 10) is called off.

12 In Northern Ireland Orangemen's marches lead to violent Protestant-Roman Catholic clashes in Belfast and Londonderry.

Tony Jacklin (G.B.) wins the British Open Golf championship at Royal Lytham, Lancs.

13 Sunday Renewed rioting in Londonderry, where 40 people are arrested and 20 policemen injured; and in Dungiven, where police besieged in Orange Hall are subjected to barrage of petrol bombs.

Of 50,000 Oxfam marchers starting from 11 points around London, about 40,000 reach Wembley Stadium.

Russian unmanned spacecraft, Luna 15, is launched towards the moon.

14 Rioting in Belfast and London-derry; police reinforced by about 150 soldiers in Londonderry.

One-day strike by U.K. Post Office engineers disrupts trunk lines and ITV programmes.

More than 100 people feared killed when goods train rams back of passenger train 25 miles north of Cuttack, India.

Les McAteer wins British middle-weight title by defeating Wally Swift in 11 rounds.

15 El Salvador army reported to have intruded 40 miles into Honduras, and Honduran troops said to have crossed into El Salvador.

President Kekkonen of Finland and his wife arrive in London on four-day State visit.

16 As El Salvador army is advancing on Tegucigalpa, Honduras, and Nueva Ocotepeque is captured by Salvadoran forces, Organisation of American States calls for cease-fire.

U.S. spacecraft Apollo 11, carrying Col. Edwin Aldrin, Col. Michael Collins, and Mr. Neil Armstrong, is launched from Cape Kennedy at 2.32 BST, on flight for the first moon-landing.

17 Luna 15 goes into orbit round the moon. Apollo 11 passes half-way stage to moon.

18 Senator Edward Kennedy crashes his car off bridge on Chappa-quiddick Island, Massachusetts, and his passenger, Mary Jo Kopechne, is drowned.

Governments of Honduras and El Salvador agree to cease-fire.

Frank Cousins takes his leave of Transport and General Workers Union, of which he has been general secretary for 13 years, at closing session of union's biennial conference at Douglas, I.O.M.

Armed men dressed as security guards steal £129,000 from bank in Crickle-wood, N.W. London.

19 Apollo 11 goes into lunar orbit. John Fairfax, British oarsman, becomes first man to row the Atlantic single-handed when he steps ashore near Fort Lauderdale, Florida, after 178 days at sea.

20 Sunday Apollo 11's lunar module, "Eagle," touches down on moon's surface at 9.18 p.m. BST, with Armstrong and Aldrin aboard.

Luna 15 goes into orbit which brings it to within 10 miles of moon's surface.

21 At 3.56 a.m. BST Armstrong opens "Eagle's" hatch, and steps on to moon's surface, where he is joined 19 minutes later by Aldrin; 2 hours and 40 mins. later they return to "Eagle," and at 6.54 p.m. BST blast off moon, joining up with command module "Columbia" at 10.33 p.m. BST.

Senator Edward Kennedy charged with misdemeanour of leaving scene of car accident in which Mary Jo Kopechne was killed (July 18).

22 General Franco names Prince Juan Carlos as his successor; Prince is sworn in on July 23.

23 President Nixon leaves for Pacific Ocean rendezvous with Apollo astronauts, to be followed by Far East tour.

30 passengers injured when Pullman express is derailed at Sandy, Beds.

24 Apollo 11 astronauts splash down safely in Pacific, enter quarantine quarters, and are greeted by Pres. Nixon.

Gerald Brooke, British lecturer imprisoned in Russia since 1965, is freed.

20 killed and 4 injured when Norwegian super-tanker *Silja*, 102,000 tons, explodes after collision with French cargo ship 20 miles off Toulon.

Civil rights marches are banned in Northern Ireland.

25 Speaking on U.S. TV and radio, Senator Edward Kennedy gives his account of what happened on night of July 18.

Death of William Dubilier, U.S. wireless and telegraph pioneer, aged 81.

27 **Sunday** Tom McClean, commando in Special Air Service, becomes first man to row Atlantic from west to east single-handed when he lands at Blacksod Bay, co. Mayo, having taken 72 days to row the 2,500 miles from Newfoundland.

President Nixon arrives at Djakarta, Indonesia, and is greeted by President Suharto.

28 Senator Edward Kennedy is notified that his driving licence has been suspended for a year.

The Queen and members of the Royal Family visit Western Fleet at Torbay.

1,000 people involved in racial demonstrations in Leeds, following death by stabbing of youth near a

Pakistani-owned cafe. Pakistani labourer charged with murder.

President Nixon arrives in Bangkok, where he is met by King of Thailand.

Johnny Famechon (Australia) becomes world featherweight champion, defeating Masahiko (Fighting) Harada (Japan) after referee has declared fight a draw and police decide winner after checking score card.

29 The Queen presents new colour to the Fleet, in the hangar of the 43,000-ton aircraft-carrier *Eagle*.

30 President Nixon visits S. Vietnam, sees U.S. troops at Di An base, and has talks with President Nguyen Van Thieu.

Russian author Anatoli Kuznetsov is granted asylum in U.K.

31 President Nixon arrives in Delhi and has talks with Mrs. Gandhi, Indian Prime Minister.

Pope Paul arrives in Kampala, Uganda, where he is welcomed by President Obote.

1st . . . Charles, Prince of Wales

21st . . . TV picture of Armstrong and Aldrin, the first men on the moon

1st . . . Pres. Heinemann

24th . . . Gerald Brooke released

11th . . . Funeral procession of Tom Mboya

August

Leo (The Lion) July 21–Aug. 21

1 Pope Paul addresses Uganda parliament and has unavailing talks with Nigerian and Biafran representatives.

In West Berlin mounted police disperse 500 student demonstrators demanding the release of seven West German military deserters.

2 President Nixon arrives in Bucharest, Rumania, for 27-hour visit, and receives tremendous welcome.

Violence breaks out again in Belfast when 2,000 Protestants stone block of flats.

3 Sunday In fighting in Belfast between Roman Catholics and Protestants petrol bombs are thrown and armoured cars charge burning vehicles used as barricades; during this week-end's riots more than 80 civilians and 17 police are injured, and 19 arrests made.

President Nixon leaves Rumania, flies to Mildenhall U.S. air force base, Suffolk, where he has 4-hour talk with Harold Wilson, and returns to U.S.A.

Almost 30 million people affected by widespread flooding in many parts of India, including states of Gujarat, Madhya Pradesh, and Orissa.

4 Owing to failure to settle unofficial blast furnace men's strike at Port Talbot the steelworks closes down and 12,000 steel-workers are laid off.

6 Mrs. Barbara Castle, U.K. Minister of Employment and Productivity, orders court of inquiry into steel strike at Port Talbot (see Aug. 20).

Devastating tornado in north central Minnesota.

7 The Queen, Duke of Edinburgh, Prince Charles, Princess Anne, Prince Andrew, and Prince Edward arrive in Bergen, Norway, at start of unofficial 6-day visit to western Norway.

Timo Makinen, Finland, and co-driver Pascoe Watson, win the first

Daily Telegraph and B.P. Round Britain Powerboat Race.

8 France announces devaluation of the franc by 12½ per cent from Aug. 11.

Princess Alexandra represents the Queen at State banquet in Singapore Conference Hall during week-long 150th anniversary celebrations of the founding of modern Singapore.

"Ritual" murder at Beverly Hills, Hollywood, of actress Sharon Tate and four others.

10 Sunday Apollo 11 astronauts leave quarantine chamber with a clean bill of health.

Duke and Duchess of Kent begin 3-week official visit to Australia and New Guinea.

11 President Kaunda of Zambia announces that the state will take over all mineral rights in the country.

Police and civil rights supporters clash at Dungannon, co. Tyrone.

Jon Erikson of Chicago, aged 14, becomes youngest male to swim English Channel.

12 March of 15,000 Protestants in traditional Apprentice Boys' Parade provokes Londonderry's worst night of rioting, during which 82 police are injured.

The Queen leaves Norway at end of her visit.

13 In further violence in Londonderry petrol bombs and paving stones are thrown, cars set alight, and buildings burnt: 33 police injured. Fighting also breaks out in Belfast.

Jack Lynch, Prime Minister of Irish Republic, in TV broadcast, demands that a U.N. Force should replace Royal Ulster Constabulary and British troops in the North, and that Mr. Wilson should open talks about partition.

Report from Russia of battle between frontier guards and hundreds of Chinese troops who have crossed the Sino-Soviet border in central Asia.

14 During "open warfare" between Protestants and Roman Catholics in Armagh and Belfast five men are shot dead, machine-guns and petrol-bombs are used, and buildings are set on fire. British troops occupy Bogside area of Londonderry.

Death of Leonard Woolf, British author and publisher, husband of Virginia Woolf, aged 88.

15 600 more British troops and two British police chiefs go to Northern Ireland. Troops use CS gas to disperse rioters in Belfast.

16 Death of George Western, surviving member of Western Brothers variety act, aged 74.

17 Sunday British troops bring uneasy calm to Northern Ireland cities. In London demonstrations by Irish Republican supporters, 65 are injured.

Fires started by Arab guerrillas in three Jewish-owned stores in West End of London.

Death of Dr. Philip Blaiberg, longest surviving heart transplant patient, in Groote Schuur hospital, Cape Town, aged 60; and of Professor Mies van der Rohe, architect, aged 83.

18 In Belfast Maj. Chichester-Clark calls conference of leaders of responsible opinion in attempt to find solution to religious disputes.

Hurricane Camille strikes Mississippi and Louisiana; winds gusting up to 200 m.p.h. cause 200,000 people to flee to safety; at least 400 killed.

Death of Leslie Hutchinson ("Hutch"), British West Indian singer and pianist, aged 69.

19 Seven-point declaration on Northern Ireland issued from 10 Downing Street, after meeting between Harold Wilson and Maj. Chichester-Clark.

On eve of anniversary of invasion of Czechoslovakia by Warsaw Pact countries' troops in 1968, thousands of Czechs demonstrate in Prague.

20 Czech troops and police use fixed bayonets, machine guns, and armoured vehicles to disperse crowd of 20,000 assembled for demonstration in Wenceslas Square, Prague.

Varahagiri Venkata Giri, independent Communist candidate supported by Mrs. Gandhi, is elected new President of India.

Government's court of inquiry recommends that Port Talbot strikers should receive the demanded pay rises.

21 Mosque of Al Aqsa in Old City of Jerusalem is damaged by fire. Arabs blame Jews and threaten "holy war."

Czech army sends tanks into Prague to subdue crowd of 50,000. Czechs boycott public transport, and wear mourning. In Brno 5,000 people stage demonstration.

Hurricane Camille sweeps across Virginia and West Virginia, and out into the Atlantic.

Bernadette Devlin M.P. arrives in New York on fund-raising visit.

Leasco withdraws offer for Robert Maxwell's Pergamon Press.

22 Riots break out again in Brno, Czechoslovakia. In four days of demonstrations 1,377, including 66 foreigners, have been arrested.

British army in Northern Ireland announces that it will take control of arms issued to "B" Specials.

An Australian, Michael Rohan, member of Church of God, is charged with setting fire to Al Aqsa mosque.

23 Czech government takes emergency powers to "maintain public order," including abolition of guarantees of freedom of the individual passed in 1966 and 1986, and the right of appeal.

President Nguyen Van Thieu appoints Gen. Tran Thien Khiem new premier of S. Vietnam.

24 Sunday Port Talbot steel workers return to work.

Forest fires on French Riviera rage over 29-mile-long area from Menton to Cannes.

V. V. Giri sworn in as India's fourth president in the Central Hall of Parliament, New Delhi.

25 15 men—2 Jews, 4 Christians, and the rest Moslems—convicted of spying for Israel and the U.S. Central Intelligence Agency, are executed in Baghdad.

Arab terrorist time-bomb explodes in Regent Street, London, office of Israeli shipping firm.

At Sydney court martial commanding officer of aircraft-carrier *Melbourne* is cleared of blame for sinking of U.S. destroyer *Frank E. Evans* (June 2).

1,673-ton Australian National Line frigate *Noongah* founders in heavy weather off the N. coast of N.S.W., with loss of 21 lives.

City panel on take-overs and mergers begin investigation into Leasco's withdrawal of offer for Pergamon Press.

In Los Angeles Ruben Olivares (Mexico) wins world bantamweight title by knocking out Lionel Rose (Australia).

26 Bernadette Devlin has talks with U.N. Secretary-General U Thant in New York.

27 James Callaghan, Home Secretary, beginning visit to Northern Ireland, tours riot-torn areas of Belfast.

Start of unofficial strike at Standard-Triumph's Liverpool factory which is to continue for 11 weeks, lead to 11,000 workers being laid off, and cost the company £11 million in exports.

Israeli raiding force stages attack on Egyptian h.q. at Macuba, in the Nile valley.

28 Leasco and Pergamon Press agree terms for a merger, which is approved by City panel on take-overs and mergers.

James Callaghan visits Bogside area of Londonderry, and meets Rev. Ian Paisley.

29 U.S. airliner with 113 passengers and crew, hijacked by Arab terrorists, lands safely at Damascus, minutes before time-bomb in cockpit explodes.

In first free elections in Ghana since 1956, Dr. Kofi Busia is elected prime minister.

Death of Philip Slessor, BBC announcer and compere, aged 59.

30 Six Israelis from hijacked plane are held in Syria; remainder of passengers and crew are released.

31 Sunday Bob Dylan gives 1 hour performance before 200,000 fans at Isle of Wight pop music festival.

Death of Charles Hendrick, Great Britain's third and only surviving heart transplant patient (May 16); and of Sir Cyril Osborne, Conservative M.P aged 71.

2nd . . . President Nixon dances in Rumania

21st . . . Jerusalem's Al Aqsa mosque is set on fire

12th . . . Londonderry barricade in flames

15th . . . British troops quell Belfast riots

20th . . . Armoured cars roll through Wenceslas Square

September

Virgo (The Maiden) Aug. 22–Sept. 22

1 King Idris of Libya is deposed in his absence abroad by a military junta who proclaim a socialist republic.

Brazilian president Arturo Costa e Silva having suffered a stroke, military leaders assume power.

Death of Drew Pearson, U.S. journalist, aged 71.

3 Death of Ho Chi Minh, North Vietnamese leader, aged 79.

4 U.S. ambassador in Brazil, Charles Burke Elbrick is kidnapped by terrorists who promise to spare his life if 15 named political prisoners are released into a "neutral" country.

5 Brazilian government agrees to free 15 political prisoners in exchange for release of kidnapped U.S. ambassador.

Chinese delegation led by Chou En-lai leave Hanoi a few hours after their arrival for Ho Chi Minh's funeral, to avoid meeting Russian delegation.

Frank Cousins makes farewell retirement speech to T.U.C. and, with George Woodcock, is awarded gold medal of Congress.

Lt. William Calley, U.S. Army, is charged with murder of at least 109 non-combatants during a "search-and-destroy" mission by his platoon on March 16, 1968, at My Lai (village known to soldiers as "Pinkville"), 6 miles N.E. of Quang Ngai, South Vietnam. (This news is not released until Nov. 12.)

By defeating Worcestershire, Glamorgan make certain of county cricket championship for first time since 1948.

Death of Josh White, U.S. negro singer of folk songs, aged 60.

6 Brazilian air force plane flies 15 political prisoners to Mexico City.

Sheila Scott lands in Nairobi after record solo flight from London of just under 48 hours.

Death of Gavin Maxwell, British author and naturalist, aged 55.

7 Sunday In Brazil, kidnappers release U.S. ambassador Elbrick unharmed.

Mr. Kosygin, leading Russian delegation to Hanoi for Ho Chi Minh's funeral, meets North Vietnamese leaders.

British troops use CS gas to stop crowd of Protestants advancing into Catholic district of Belfast.

8 After death by shooting of a Protestant vigilante, violence increases in Belfast, and 500 British troops are transferred from Londonderry to reinforce the 2,900 already in the capital.

Teenage Arab guerrillas throw bombs at Israeli embassies in Bonn and The Hague and at the Brussels office of El Al, the Israeli airline.

Israeli ship-borne raiders destroy two torpedo boats at Egyptian base on Red Sea coast 15 miles S. of Suez.

In Vietnam, 3-day truce of mourning for Ho Chi Minh begins.

Libyan military junta name an 8-man cabinet under a civilian prime minister and including only two army officers.

In Norwegian general election held yesterday and today, the 4-party non-Socialist coalition government retains power with reduced majority.

By defeating Tony Roche in the men's singles of the U.S. tennis championships Rod Laver becomes the first man to win twice the "grand slam" (championships of Australia, France, U.S.A., and Wimbledon).

9 Major Chichester-Clark announces that a 1½-mile-long barbed wire "peace line" will be erected by army between the Catholic Falls Road and Protestant Shankill Road areas of Belfast, and orders that all other barricades must be removed.

Israeli forces invade Egypt in a 10-hour combined land, sea, and air operation across the Gulf of Suez.

Approaching Indianapolis airport, a DC-9 jet airliner of Allegheny Airlines collides with a private light aeroplane and crashes, killing all 82 on board.

Wild rioting in Caserta, near Naples, after relegation of the town's football club.

Funeral of Ho Chi Minh.

Wedding of Marion Coakes, British show-jumping champion, and National Hunt jockey David Mould.

10 Traffic curfew between 9 p.m. and 6 a.m. instituted in Belfast.

Start of 24-hour strike of French train drivers, and of a million Italian metal and car workers.

11 Mr. Kosygin interrupts his return flight from Hanoi for surprise visit to Chou En-lai in Peking.

End of 3-day truce in Vietnam.

West German bank rate raised from 5 to 6 per cent.

New Libyan government (Sept. 8) is sworn in.

Wedding of Gary Sobers, West Indies cricketer, and Australian Prudence Kirby, at Basford, Notts.

12 Cameron commission's report on Northern Ireland disturbances of Aug. 1968–April 1969 denounces religious extremists on both sides, and finds complaints of discrimination and gerrymandering justified.

French railway strike is extended; 660,000 Italian construction workers begin 48-hour strike; unofficial strikes take place in Kiel, West Germany, shipyards; and immediate pay negotiations are demanded by W. German railway, paper and printing, and leather workers.

W. German miners (having won a 14 per cent wage rise) and iron and steel workers (having been given an 11 per cent increase) return to work after unofficial strikes.

13 Leasco withdraws its take-over bid for Pergamon Press.

14 Sunday Constitutional amendment permitting Pres. Park of South Korea to stand for a third term is passed.

In south coast floods following heavy rainstorms in South Korea, 107,000 are homeless, 268 dead, 150 injured, and 104 missing.

British combat troops withdrawn from Anguilla.

Death of Tom Burke, British operatic tenor, aged 79; and of Helen Sobel (U.S.A.), the world's best bridge-player in the 1940s and 1950s, aged 59.

15 In Italy, strike of dairy farmers stops Milan's milk supply; transport workers in Palermo start 24-hour strike; and metal workers start series of guerrilla strikes. Altogether strikes by 2½ million workers are planned for this week.

Melbourne-Sydney express, Spirit of Progress, derailed 80 miles S. of Sydney, injuring 30 passengers.

Death of "Monsewer" Eddie Gray, British comedian and juggler, aged 71.

16 President Nixon announces the withdrawal from Vietnam of a further 35,000 troops by Dec. 15.

18 French railway service returns to normal after strike, except for Paris Metro. Bus workers strike in Paris, Marseilles, and Montpellier.

President Nixon addresses U.N. General Assembly for first time.

Board of London Weekend TV company terminate contract of its managing director Michael Peacock.

Death of J. R. Campbell, a founder of the British Communist party and one-time editor of *The Daily Worker*, aged 74.

19 Wave of "wildcat" strikes in West German tram and bus services: Italian metal workers in Milan and Turin go on strike; 24-hour general strike paralyses Florence.

President Nixon cancels draft of 50,000 men due for call-up in November and December.

Six senior executives resign from London Weekend TV company after dismissal of Michael Peacock.

21 Sunday A thousand soldiers move into Ahmedabad, Gujarat, India, to quell Hindu-Muslim riots which have raged for the past three days.

Large force of London police evict 500 hippy squatters from Piccadilly mansion which they have occupied for a week.

22 First Chinese underground nuclear test explosion at Lop Nor, Sinkiang.

Violent storms strike Scandinavian coasts and cities, killing 15 and causing many injuries.

23 President Nixon approves construction of a U.S. supersonic transport aircraft to rival Anglo-French Concorde and Russian Tu-144.

Unofficial strike of London dustmen starts in Hackney.

24 A further 3,000 troops move into Ahmedabad (Sept. 21).

A man dies in Protestant-Catholic street battle in Londonderry.

25 Foreign exchange market in West Germany is closed until after general election on Sept. 28.

Level-crossing collision at Hal, Belgium, between Paris-Amsterdam express and a tanker lorry kills 3 and injures 25

26 In view of threatened demonstration by 10,000 opponents, final pre-election rally of Adolf von Thadden's National Democratic Party at Nuremberg is banned by police.

Pres. Siles Salinas of Bolivia ousted in bloodless coup by military led by Gen. Alfredo Ovando.

28 Sunday General election in West Germany: Christian Democrat and Christian Social Union candidates returned in 242 seats; Social Democrats in 224; and Free Democrats in 30

In renewed Protestant-Catholic violence in Belfast, petrol bombs are thrown at troops and 15 fires are started; barricades are re-erected; and c.-in-c. requests more troops.

Alexander Dubcek is removed from speakership of Czechoslovakian federal parliament.

Death of Sir Bruce Seton, British actor ("Fabian of the Yard"), aged 60.

29 West German government decides to allow Deutschemark to "float."

Labour Party Conference opens at Brighton.

Dustmen in three more London boroughs go on unofficial strike.

South Africa's most violent earthquake kills 6 and causes widespread damage.

30 Further earth tremors in South Africa kill 11 and render 1,000 homeless at Tulbagh, 90 miles from Cape Town.

Dustmen's unofficial strike spreads to four more London boroughs.

9th . . . British troops erect barbed wire "peace line" in Belfast

9th . . . "Football" battles and street riots in Caserta, Italy

9th . . . Funeral of Ho Chi Minh

11th . . . Kosygin meets Chou En-lai

11th . . . Wedding of Gary Sobers

October

Libra (The Scales) Sept. 23–Oct. 22

1 Mao Tse-tung makes first public appearance since May 19, at 20th anniversary celebrations of Chinese People's Republic in Peking.

Earthquakes in northern California injure 15 people and cause much damage; and in Junin, Peru, 54 are killed, 50 injured, and about 300 houses destroyed.

2 Willy Brandt, leader of West German Social Democrats, announces that his party and the Free Democrats have reached agreement on forming a coalition.

3 $4\frac{1}{2}$ million people now affected by London dustmen's strike.

4 British journalist Anthony Grey released after 26 months' house arrest in Peking.

Death of Doris Arnold, pianist and first woman BBC variety show producer.

5 **Sunday** Harold Wilson announces government changes including: reduction of cabinet from 23 to 21 ministers; enlargment of Ministry of Technology, which takes over the Ministry of Power and some industrial responsibilities of the Board of Trade; creation of a new secretaryship of state for local government and regional planning, with responsibility for housing and transport.

In Belfast, troops use CS gas against illegal procession of about 500 Orangemen to Rev. Ian Paisley's new church; later a soldier on patrol is wounded by sniper's bullet.

6 Opening of trial of Michael Rohan, charged with setting fire to the Al Aqsa mosque in Jerusalem on Aug. 21.

Dustmen, now on strike in 30 of London's 32 boroughs, are joined by other local authority workers.

Death of Walter Hagen, U.S. golfer, aged 76.

7 While 150,000 Young Communists celebrate 20th anniversary of founding of German Democratic Republic (East Germany), between 1,000 and 2,000 youths clash with Communist police near Berlin wall, and 50 are arrested.

In Montreal, Canada, when police and fire-fighting forces go on 16-hour strike over pay dispute, a civilian and a policeman are killed, ten banks robbed, windows smashed, shops looted, fires started, and petrol bombs thrown.

Gen. Emilio Gerrastazo Medici is named president of Brazil by armed forces command, in succession to Marshal Arturo Costa e Silva (Sept. 1).

8 French bank rate is raised to 8 per cent, its highest ever.

U.K. Home Secretary James Callaghan begins four-day visit to Northern Ireland.

On 14th day of "the worst rains for a thousand years" the Tunisian government launches international appeal for aid for devastation caused by floods.

9 Cook National Day in New Zealand to commemorate the 200th anniversary of the landing of Capt. Cook at Poverty Bay.

Pay settlement for London and other dustmen agreed in Edinburgh by National Joint Council for local authority workers.

10 Leaders of London dustmen reject yesterday's pay agreement, and unofficial strike continues.

6 people reported killed at Selaigneaux, Belgium, when Paris–Hanover express crashes into rear of freight train in dense fog.

Robert Maxwell voted off board of Pergamon Press by shareholders.

11 In overnight 8-hour battle in Belfast between troops, police, and 2,000 Protestants trying to advance into Catholic area, automatic rifles, sub-machine guns, shot-guns, petrol bombs, and tear gas are used, three are killed, and many are wounded.

In Chicago battle between militant students and police 50 people are injured and more than 250 arrested.

U.S.S.R. spacecraft Soyuz 6 launched, with Lt.-Col. Georgy Shonin and Valery Kubasov aboard.

12 **Sunday** Nearly 500 British paratroops are flown to Belfast in response to call for reinforcements. Violence again breaks out when 400 Protestants fight British troops. Police and troops seize arms, ammunition, and a pirate radio transmitter, and arrest 69 people.

Soviet Union launches Soyuz 7 spacecraft, carrying Lt.-Col. Anatoly Filipchenko, Lt.-Col. Viktor Gorbasko, and Vladislav Volkov.

Anthony Grey (Oct. 4) arrives in London from Karachi, where he has been since leaving China on Oct. 9.

Death of Sonja Henie, Norwegian skating film star, aged 59.

13 In fifth week of strikes and unrest in Italy bus and taxi drivers jam Naples streets; cement workers start 3-day national strike; lightning strikes hit Pirelli plant in Milan; and Taranto farmers block roads in protest over milk prices.

More than 70,000 miners go on strike in Yorkshire coalfields, in support of trade union demands for 40-hour working week.

Soyuz 8, carrying Shatalov and Yeliseyev, is launched and carries out manoeuvres with Soyuz 6 and 7.

Jack Bodell beats Carl Gizzi on points to win vacant British heavyweight boxing championship; and Vic Andreetti retains his British junior welterweight title by knocking out Des Rea in 4th round.

14 Apollo 11 astronauts (Armstrong, Aldrin, and Collins) and their wives arrive in London, where they are received by the Queen at Buckingham Palace, and dine with the Prime Minister.

15 First Vietnam Moratorium Day in U.S.A., when millions of people march, hold rallies, and read aloud the roll of the 40,000 war dead. Apart from clash between police and about 100 black militants outside the White House, the protest is peaceful.

Announcement that Alexander Dubcek and Joseph Smrkovsky have resigned as speakers of Czechoslovak parliament.

President Abdel Shermarke of Somalia shot dead by members of his own police force in Las Anod, N. Somalia.

U.K. dustmen's strike spreads to more provincial towns, and in London 500 dustmen stage protest march.

16 Northern Ireland government issues orders prohibiting sale of alcohol in Belfast after 7 p.m. on Fridays and Saturdays, and all day on Sundays.

Soyuz 6 lands safely.

17 Police raid Melbourne, Australia, home of Ronald Biggs, last of Great Train Robbers still free, but find he has left. His wife is arrested on charge of illegally entering Australia.

National Coal Board agrees to pay increase for 154,000 mineworkers, but does not improve its offer on working week.

Soyuz 7 lands safely.

Death of Father Charles Boulogne, world's longest living heart transplant patient, aged 56.

18 Bomb blasts in Athens injure 6 passers-by, damage Greek National Bank offices and other buildings, and blow up an electricity distribution unit.

Soyuz 8 lands safely.

19 Sunday Polish airliner carrying over 60 passengers hijacked by two young East Germans and forced to land at West Berlin, where they are given political asylum.

20 More than 120,000 miners at 132 of Britain's 306 colleries go on unofficial strike in support of shorter hours for surface workers.

21 Bundestag elects Willy Brandt West Germany's first Social Democrat Chancellor for 40 years.

Anti-Vietnam war riots and demonstrations by Japanese students, of whom about 1,400 are arrested, 1,000 of them in Tokyo.

Bloodless coup in Somalia by army and police.

22 Lebanese Prime Minister Rashid Karami resigns after disclaiming responsibility for clashes between Lebanese troops and Palestinian commandos in south Lebanon.

Explosions in Haifa destroy four blocks of flats, killing one man and injuring 11 others.

24 German government revalues Deutschemark upwards by $8\frac{1}{2}$ per cent (3.66 DM to U.S. dollar.)

In riot in Parkhurst, Isle of Wight, top security prison, 12 prison officers and 40 prisoners are injured.

Peter and Helen Kroger, American-born spies for Russia, fly to Poland after their release from U.K. prisons.

25 In Australian Federal general election, of the 125 seats in the House of Representatives Liberal-Country Party coalition win 66 seats, and Labour Party 59 seats.

26 Sunday In further clashes between army and guerrillas in Lebanon, 3 people are killed, bringing total casualties to 12 dead and many wounded in Tripoli alone.

27 Earthquake devastates Yugoslav town of Banja Luka and four near-by villages, killing 20 and injuring 400.

28 In general election in Israel Mrs. Golda Meir is returned to power, but with reduced majority.

Death of Eric Maschwitz, composer and former head of BBC light entertainment, aged 68.

30 Armoured units of Lebanese army fight Palestinian guerrillas in 12-hour artillery, rocket, and machine-gun battle for village of Rachaya, 50 miles south-east of Beirut.

In by-elections at Paddington North, Islington North, Gorbels, Glasgow, and Newcastle-under-Lyme, Labour retain seats with reduced majorities; and at Swindon lose seat to Conservatives after two recounts.

Death of Lord Douglas of Kirtleside, aged 75.

31 Mrs. Charmaine Biggs, wife of train robber Ronald Biggs, released from custody on Oct. 20, is given temporary permit to stay in Australia.

3rd . . . Dustmen's strike affects 4½ million Londoners

7th . . . Montreal's night of crime during police strike

12th . . . More British troops in position in Belfast

15th . . . First Vietnam Moratorium Day in Washington, D.C.

November

Scorpio (The Scorpion) Oct. 23–Nov. 22

1 U.S. Marine Cpl. Raphael Minichiello is captured outside Rome after having hijacked Boeing 707 on night flight from Kansas City to San Francisco, forcing pilot at gunpoint to fly 6,868 miles to Rome with refuelling stops at Denver, New York, Bangor (Maine), and Shannon, Eire.

2 **Sunday** Indian Congress Party finally splits into two warring groups—one headed by Prime Minister Mrs. Gandhi, and the other by the Congress Working Committee.

3 President Nixon, in Washington speech, discloses secret long-term plan for withdrawal of U.S. forces from Vietnam and the handing over of the defence of S. Vietnam to her people.
Announcement that Northern Ireland ban on alcohol sales (Oct. 16) is to end.
Leasco files suit in U.S.A. against Robert Maxwell and others in connection with take-over of Pergamon Press.
Violent hurricane strikes Stockholm.

5 John Lindsay, standing as a Liberal, wins New York mayoral election, receiving 42 per cent of the vote.
U.K. farmworkers receive pay rise, with reduction of one hour in working week.

7 John Gorton is re-elected leader of Australian Liberal Party and thus remains Federal Prime Minister.
65 men die in dynamite explosion at Buffelsfontein gold mine in West Transvaal, S. Africa.
Full return to work at Standard-Triumph's Liverpool factory (Aug. 27).

8 Nine people arrested and 12 hurt at Leicester during anti-apartheid demonstrations at Springboks v. Midland (East) rugby match.

9 **Sunday** Egyptian destroyers shell northern coastal strip of Israel-occupied Sinai.
Further disturbances in Montreal where fire bombs are thrown and windows smashed; and in Quebec, French Canadian separatists demonstrate against the judiciary.

10 Sir David Rose, Governor-General of Guyana, killed by scaffolding falling from ninth storey of building in Whitehall Place, London.
In Memphis, Tennessee, protest march by 2,000 negroes is broken up by police using tear gas.

11 Time-bombs explode in three New York skyscrapers; an anti-Vietnam war organisation claims responsibility.

12 Meeting of Congress Party expels Mrs. Gandhi (see Nov. 23).
First of teachers' half-day strikes being organised throughout U.K. takes place in Lancashire.

13 Second Vietnam Moratorium in U.S.A. starts at 6 p.m., with march from Arlington National Cemetery, Washington.
Quintuplets, all girls, born in Queen Charlotte's Hospital, London, to Mrs. Irene Hanson, aged 33, who has been given a fertility drug.

14 In Vietnam Moratorium about 1,000 marchers an hour pass through Washington to the Capitol, each wearing a card bearing the name of an American soldier killed or a S. Vietnamese village destroyed.
21st birthday of Prince of Wales.
Apollo 12 blasts off from Cape Kennedy shortly after 8 p.m. B.S.T., manned by Cmdrs. Charles ("Pete") Conrad, Richard Gordon, and Alan Bean. Although main electrical systems fail momentarily, separation from 3rd stage rocket occurs successfully 25 minutes later.

15 In last day of Vietnam Moratorium, coffins containing names of war dead are carried from the Capitol to the Washington Monument.
Fighting at Springboks v. Swansea rugby match between anti-apartheid demonstrators and police and stewards.

16 **Sunday** During violent 6-hour demonstration in Tokyo by thousands of left-wing students protesting against possible extension of Japan's security treaty with U.S.A., 50 are injured and 1,690 arrested.
Explosive charges placed by Arab frogmen damage Israel cargo ship and excursion boat in Eilat.

17 First meeting between Russian and U.S. delegations at strategic arms limitations talks (SALT), in Helsinki, Finland.
Anti-Vietnam war protest demonstrations and ceremonies in Australia, at Canberra, Sydney, Melbourne, and Adelaide.
Israeli planes bomb and strafe artillery units in Jordan for 2hrs. 20 mins.

18 Half-day strikes by London teachers affect 30,000 children.
Death of Joseph Kennedy, aged 81; and of Ted Heath, British band leader, aged 67.

19 Apollo 12 astronauts Conrad and Bean land on Moon in lunar module "Intrepid" at 7.54 a.m. B.S.T., and work on surface from 12.44 p.m. to 4.30 p.m. B.S.T.

20 After second work period (6.35 a.m. to 9.46 a.m.) Apollo 12 astronauts blast off the Moon, and link up with command module "Yankee Clipper" at 18.45 B.S.T. "Intrepid" is then fired to hit Moon at 3,700 m.p.h.
White House announcement that Henry Cabot Lodge, chief U.S. negotiator at Vietnam peace talks in Paris, and his deputy Laurence Walsh have both resigned.
87 passengers and crew die when Nigerian Airways VC 10 airliner crashes in jungle near Lagos.
Strike of 10,000 teachers in Inner London affects children at 1,000 schools.

21 Apollo 12 leaves lunar orbit and begins return journey to the Earth.
Death of D. B. Wyndham Lewis, British author, aged 78; and of Norman Lindsay, Australian artist and writer, aged 90.

22 Fire destroys part of Anne Hathaway's cottage, Stratford-on-Avon: man is charged with arson on Nov. 26.
Springboks v. London Counties rugby match at Twickenham is halted several times by demonstrators, and later an attempt is made to rescue arrested people held at Twickenham police station.
Death of Sir Frederick Mutesa ("King Freddie"), the exiled Kabaka of Buganda, aged 45.

23 **Sunday** At Congress Party conference in Delhi Mrs. Gandhi is reinstated to the party (see Nov. 12), and Mr. Nijalingappa, party president, is dismissed.
British Skynet (military communications) satellite is launched by U.S. rocket at Cape Kennedy.

24 Crew of Apollo 12 splash down safely in Pacific 400 miles south-east of Pago Pago, at 9.58 p.m. B.S.T.

U.S. Army announces that Lt. William Calley (see Sept. 5) is to be tried by general court martial on charges of killing Vietnamese civilians in "Pinkville" massacre.

Helicopter search for five Austrian climbers last seen 12 days ago on Himalayan peak of Dhaulagiri is abandoned.

Death of Howard Marion-Crawford, British actor, aged 55.

25 President Nixon renounces use of all methods of biological warfare, promising destruction of existing stockpiles.

Half-day strike by 26,000 teachers in 55 areas of Great Britain.

Strike of British Road Services lorry drivers brings 47 of 90 parcel depots to a standstill.

Oil rig capsizes and sinks in 60 m.p.h. gale, 95 miles off Flamborough Head, Yorks.

26 Following 9-month ban by London dockers on opening of its new container ship terminal at Tilbury, Overseas Containers Ltd. decides to transfer its operations to Antwerp.

At end of Al Aqsa mosque arson trial in Jerusalem, court adjourns to consider judgement.

Over 2,000 police prevent 7,000 anti-apartheid demonstrators from interrupting Springboks v. Northern Counties rugby match at Stratford, Manchester.

27 VC 10 airliner with 69 people on board safely makes emergency landing at London airport (Heathrow) after explosion and fire put both its starboard engines out of action.

Two Jordanians throw hand-grenade into Athens office of Israel airline El Al, injuring 14 people, one of whom —a 2-year-old child— subsequently dies.

28 Italian parliament passes controversial Divorce Bill by 325 votes to 282.

100,000 Italian metal workers on strike for more pay march through Rome, joined by university students.

29 General election in New Zealand: National Party is returned for fourth consecutive time but with majority of only four seats. Mr. Holyoake remains prime minister.

Lt. William Calley (see Nov. 24) is additionally charged with murdering a man in Quang Ngai province about 6 weeks before "Pinkville" massacre.

1st . . . Minichiello, longest hijacker

7th . . . Gorton re-elected leader

15th . . . Coffins carried past Washington Capitol in 2nd Vietnam Moratorium

15th . . . Anti-apartheid demonstrators on Swansea pitch at Springboks game

24th . . . Apollo 12 crew (Conrad, Gordon, and Bean) return and enter quarantine

December

Sagittarius (The Archer) Nov. 23–Dec. 20

1 At opening of 2-day summit meeting of Common Market leaders at The Hague, Willy Brandt, West Germany, presses for Britain's entry, and President Pompidou, France, admits application should be discussed. Outside, over 1,000 demonstrators protest against delays in uniting Europe.

British teachers at more than 320 schools in 81 local authority areas start 2-week strike.

2 At The Hague, Common Market leaders agree to open talks with Britain and other applicants by the end of June 1970.

98 anti-apartheid demonstrators arrested in Aberdeen after mass invasion of pitch during Springboks' first Scottish match.

Death of Stephen Potter, British author and humorist, aged 69.

3 An Air France Boeing 707 crashes into sea and explodes 5 miles from Maiquetia airport, Venezuela, killing all 70 on board.

Death of Marshal Voroshilov, ex-President of U.S.S.R., aged 88.

4 In by-elections, Conservatives win Wellingborough from Labour and retain Louth.

Death of Lord Carron, former President of Amalgamated Engineering Union, aged 67; of John Byrne, former general secretary of Electrical Trades Union, aged 66; and of Jack Payne, British band leader and impresario, aged 70.

5 About 30,000 Italian senior civil servants strike; it is also third day of strike by half a million Italian municipal employees, and first day of 2-day strike by bank employees.

Two Israelis who have been detained in Syria for 98 days after the hijacking of a Trans World airliner (Aug. 29) are returned to Israel in exchange for 13 Syrians.

Death of Princess Andrew of Greece, mother of Prince Philip, aged 84; of aviation pioneers Hugh Oswald Short (British), aged 86, and Prof. Claudius Dornier (German), aged 85.

6 In primary elections in Kenya five members of President Kenyatta's cabinet and two out of every three existing M.P.s are voted out.

Death of Baroness Horsbrugh, first woman Conservative Cabinet Minister, aged 80.

7 **Sunday** Crowd of between 200,000 and 500,000 attend open-air pop concert (including The Rolling Stones), at Tracey, California, during which one man is stabbed to death; one is drowned; 2 people are killed when car runs over them; hundreds suffer from drug hallucinations; and four babies are born.

8 Olympic Airways four-engined domestic aircraft on flight from Crete crashes on Mount Paneion, 23 miles south-west of Athens, killing all 90 on board.

12 members of militant negro group, the Black Panthers, barricaded in their h.q. in Los Angeles, fight 4-hour battle with 300 armed police before surrendering. Fred Hampton, Black Panther leader, aged 21, is shot dead.

9 In House of Commons motion for change in government policy over Nigerian civil war, 254 vote for government but 86 vote against, the largest number yet.

Los Angeles grand jury brings in indictments against Charles Manson, leader of a "Satanic" cult, and five of his followers for murder of Sharon Tate and others (Aug. 8).

10 President Emile Zinsou of Dahomey, W. Africa, assassinated in army coup led by chief-of-staff Lt.-Col. Maurice Kouandete.

John Roger Nicholson, financial editor of *Rhodesian Herald,* sentenced to 18 months' hard labour for passing economic information about Rhodesia to agents of unspecified foreign power.

Funeral of Fred Hampton (Dec. 8) in Chicago ends two days of mourning.

11 Test and County Cricket Board at Lord's decide unanimously that South Africa's 1970 cricket tour of England shall take place.

12 Greece withdraws from Council of Europe, after majority of 18 member nations, meeting in Paris, decide to vote for her suspension.

14 killed in bomb explosion at National Agricultural Bank, Milan; other explosions in Rome.

104,400-ton Dutch Shell tanker *Marpessa*, built in Japan, catches fire following explosion while on her

maiden voyage: she sinks on Dec. 15, the largest ship ever to sink at sea.

Chairman of U.S. House of Representatives Armed Services Committee orders a new investigation into alleged Pinkville massacre, following a week of secret hearings by his sub-committee.

13 Two Arab commandos attempting to hijack Ethiopian Boeing 707 between Rome and Addis Ababa are disarmed and killed; plane makes forced landing at Athens.

Farmers' demonstration at Newton Abbot, Devon, in protest against agricultural prices, halts traffic for an hour while farm machinery slowly circles town centre.

14 **Sunday** At University College Hospital, London, sextuplets (one stillborn) are born to Mrs. Rosemary Letts, who has received fertility drug; survivors are 4 girls and a boy.

Death of Lord Hill of Wivenhoe (formerly Ted Hill, secretary of the Boilermakers' Union), aged 70.

15 100,000 follow funeral in Milan of 14 victims of bomb explosion (Dec. 12).

British teachers' trade unions reject pay-rise offer worth £24 million.

16 U.K. House of Commons vote by 343 to 185 to abolish permanently the death penalty for murder.

500 protesting Devon dairy farmers march down Whitehall and attempt to take cow into House of Commons.

17 Nation-wide strikes leave Italy without transport, phones, or mail, and schoolchildren without teachers.

Death of Marshal Arturo da Costa e Silva, former president of Brazil, aged 67.

18 House of Lords vote by 220 votes to 174 for permanent abolition of death penalty for murder.

19 Dr. Milton Obote, President of Uganda, is shot and slightly wounded by unknown gunman in Kampala.

U.S. State Department announces partial lifting of its 19-year-old embargo on trade with Communist China.

20 Church bells all over Great Britain toll from 11 a.m. to noon to mark "hour of giving" in aid of afflicted in Biafra and Nigeria.

21 Opening of Arab summit conference at Rabat, Morocco.

22 Strike of all public transport in Italy.

Swiss court sentences to 12 years' hard labour each of three Palestinian Arab terrorists who attacked the El Al airliner at Zürich on Feb. 18.

End of SALT talks in Helsinki (Nov. 17).

In Londonderry court, Bernadette Devlin, M.P. for Mid-Ulster, is found guilty on four of 13 summonses concerning offences in the city during the August troubles; she receives six months' prison sentence, but is granted bail pending an appeal.

Death of Josef von Sternberg, U.S. film director, aged 75.

23 Arab conference at Rabat breaks up in disarray.

24 Five new gun-boats built for Israel in France slip out of Cherbourg, where they have been blocked under France's total embargo on arms for Israel.

25 Israeli jet aircraft shower rockets, napalm, and heavy explosives on targets along Suez Canal front to a depth of 10 miles.

26 Israeli commandos steal complete secret Russian-built low-level radar station at Ras Ghareb, on the Gulf of Suez, taking it apart

and flying it to Israel strapped under helicopters.

Deaths in U.K. from influenza and its consequences reported to be over 700 since Dec. 20.

11 people die and two are seriously injured when fire guts hotel in Saffron Walden, Essex.

27 In Japanese general election Prime Minister Eisaku Satu and his Liberal Democratic Party retain power with increased majority.

In Ceylon, floods caused by incessant rains over recent weeks have killed 25 and left a million homeless.

Death of Sir William Russell Flint, British artist, aged 89.

28 **Sunday** Ex-President Lyndon B. Johnson in U.S. TV interview says, among other revelations, that he never wanted to be president of the U.S.A.

Nearly 300 firemen and 50 fire engines fight blaze at Great Britain's largest oil refinery at Fawley, near Southampton.

Death of Henry Oscar, British actor, aged 78.

29 Fire breaks out aboard Shell super-tanker *Mactra*, 205,000 tons d.w., after explosion.

Mrs. Muriel McKay, wife of deputy chairman of *News of the World*, is reported missing from her Wimbledon home.

30 Denis Rohan found by Jerusalem District Court not be punishable under law, because when he set fire to Al Aqsa mosque (Aug. 21) he acted under uncontrollable pathological impulse. He is committed to a mental hospital.

Edward Heath wins Sydney–Hobart ocean sailing race on handicap, in his 32-ft. sloop *Morningcloud*. Another British yacht *Prospect of Whitby* is second on handicap, and Sir Max Aitken's *Crusade* is first to cross finishing line.

Detective shot dead and three other policemen wounded—one of whom dies later—in Glasgow when police, investigating bank raid, call at houses in the city. Three men later charged with murder and attempted murder.

31 Following arrival of the 5 Israeli gun-boats at Haifa, two French generals are suspended after 4½-hour cabinet meeting inquiring into the boats' "escape" from Cherbourg (Dec. 24).

At midnight the half-crown ceases to be legal tender in the U.K.

5th... Rome strikers demand "Arms for the workers"

14th... Sextuplets born in London, five alive

23rd... Rabat conference breaks up in disarray

31st..."Escaped" Israeli gunboats arrive at Haifa

God Bless the Prince of Wales!

ELIZABETH HOGARTH

On JULY 1, 1969, on a day of pomp and pageantry, and enormous security precautions, H.R.H. Prince Charles was invested by the Queen as the 21st Prince of Wales. From early in the morning the streets of the small town of Caernarvon, gay with heraldic banners and decorations, were lined by some 200,000 people, many of whom had waited all night to be sure of a good view of the procession. Television sets all over the world were switched on by an estimated 500 million people, waiting for the beginning of a ceremony last held when Prince Charles's great-uncle, the Duke of Windsor, was invested by King George V.

Prince Charles, who was created Prince of Wales by the Queen in 1958 at the end of the Empire and Commonwealth Games in Cardiff, had thoroughly prepared himself for what must have been the most significant and nerve-racking day of his life, and for his subsequent role of Prince of Wales. Ignoring the threats of the Welsh Nationalists, and the disquieting bomb incidents which had occurred in previous months, he spent the summer term of 1969 at the University College of Wales, Aberystwyth, where he took a nine weeks' "crash course" in the Welsh language and Welsh culture and history. Meeting as many Welsh people as he could, he disarmed and won over many of the critics.

On the grey morning of the Investiture about 4,000 guests gathered inside the walls of Caernarvon Castle. Under a canopy of transparent plastic, resting on four huge spear-shaped supports and decorated with a version of the Prince of Wales's feathers taken from a medieval design, the circular grey slate dais with its three simple thrones made of slate, each with a scarlet cushion, formed the focal

point at one end of the lawn. Outside, in the fitful sunshine which was to continue, interspersed with a little drizzle, throughout the day, the first of the processions was on its way through the town's streets to the Castle. First came the Queen's Heralds and Pursuivants of Arms, in their splendidly embroidered and colourful uniforms; then representatives of Welsh youth, Welsh M.P.s, the Prime Minister and Mrs. Wilson, mayors, and bards robed in the costume of a bygone age. Then followed the procession of peers, the Queen's Bodyguard of the Yeomen of the Guard, and the Honourable Corps of Gentlemen-at-Arms.

Shortly after 2 p.m. guns boomed out their salute over the town as the first members of the royal family began to alight from the royal train. The carriage procession of the Prince of Wales, wearing the uniform of Colonel-in-Chief of the new Royal Regiment of Wales, decorated with the Order of the Garter, was the first to leave. Riding in an open landau, with George Thomas, Secretary of State for Wales, and accompanied by an escort of the Household Cavalry, he drove, waving and smiling, through the cheering crowds to the Water Gate of the Castle where his uncle, the Earl of Snowdon, Constable of the Castle, was waiting with the mayor of Caernarvon to greet him. A fanfare of trumpets rang out from the battlements, the investiture choir sang "God Bless the Prince of Wales," the crowd roared its applause, and the Prince was led by Lord Harlech, the Archdruid of Wales, and other Welsh dignitaries to the Chamberlain Tower, within the Castle walls.

The Queen's procession was by this time on its way. Wearing a yellow coat and matching hat, she rode in an open carriage with the Duke of Edinburgh, in naval uniform, accompanied by Princess Anne, in turquoise

---

Top of page: **first official portrait of the Prince of Wales, a coroneted head by David Wynne.**

blue. Behind, in another open carriage, were the Queen Mother, in apple green, and Princess Margaret, wearing a peach-coloured outfit. When the Queen's carriage, escorted by the Household Cavalry, drew up at the Water Gate, an equerry hammered on the heavy door and demanded entrance in her name. The Earl of Snowdon came out carrying the key of the Castle on a wooden tray, and made her the traditional presentation before the Castle was opened to her. Again the fanfares rang out, and preceded by the Marquess of Anglesey bearing the sword of state, by the Duke of Norfolk, and the Kings and Heralds of Arms, the Queen and the Duke were led to their thrones on the dais. As the Queen stood before taking her place on the throne the emotional Welsh national anthem was played, followed by the more sober "God Save the Queen."

Next the Queen ordered the Earl Marshal to convey her summons to the Prince. He gave this order to the Garter King of Arms, Sir Anthony Wagner, who walked slowly across the lawn to the Chamberlain Tower. After a pause, in which it seemed that those waiting held their breath, a fanfare sounded as the Prince, bareheaded, walked at a level pace towards her. He was accompanied by the Secretary of State for Wales, and by Earl Lloyd-George of Dwyfor carrying the sword, Lord Ogmore the coronet, Lord Heycock the sceptre, Lord Maelor the gold ring, and Lord Harlech the purple velvet mantle with its ermine cape. All the insignia, with the exception of the coronet, had been made for the 1911 investiture.

The Prince, with the Welsh peers around him, bowed three times before kneeling on a cushion in front of the Queen. James Callaghan, Home Secretary, read, in English, the letters patent creating him Prince of Wales, and then, as the Secretary of State for Wales repeated them in Welsh, the Queen invested her son with the insignia. She placed the sword about his waist, the gold ring on his finger, the mantle about his shoulders, and the golden rod in his hand. After she had placed the coronet, designed by Louis Osman, on his head the Prince put up his hands to adjust it and a slight smile passed between them. The Prince then placed his hands between those of the Queen and in a clear, confident voice spoke the words of the traditional promise of homage:

"I, Charles, Prince of Wales, do become your liege man of life and limb and of earthly worship, and faith and truth I will bear unto you to live and die against all manner of folks."

The kiss of fealty was then exchanged, the Queen raised him up, and he went to take his seat at her right hand. After the loyal address, delivered by Sir Ben Bowen Thomas, President of the University of Wales, Aberystwyth, in Welsh and English, Prince Charles rose to reply. He delighted the Welsh people by giving his speech first in Welsh—he is the first Prince of Wales ever to have had any knowledge of the Welsh language—and then in English. In his address he expressed his intention to associate himself with as much of the life of Wales as possible, and his desire to contribute to its heritage. He referred to the fact that Wales had produced not only singers and scholars, but also, and here he allowed himself to smile, a distinguished "Goon," Harry Secombe.

A religious service in both languages brought the ceremony to an end, but it remained for the Queen to present the Prince to his people, first at Queen Eleanor's Gate, then at the King's Gate, and finally at the Lower Ward of the Castle, lifting his right hand to the crowds standing below.

The undergraduate Prince, with his equerry, during his course in Welsh language, culture and history at the University College of Wales, Aberystwyth.

The Queen presenting the Prince of Wales to the Welsh people at Queen Eleanor's Gate, Caernarvon Castle, after his investiture—an important part of the traditional ceremony.

As the Prince and his parents emerged from the Castle before driving away, R.A.F. Phantoms and Lightnings of Strike and Air Support Commands, with precision timing, flew overhead in close formation. The royal banner was struck and the carriages returned

along the processional route to the applause of the enthusiastic crowd.

Having spent a night on the royal yacht off Llandudno, the Prince began a 400-mile tour of Wales, during which he took part in some 40 official functions, and, what was perhaps more important, spoke to many of the Welsh people, sometimes delaying his official time-table in order to do so. The success of this tour cannot be doubted, for everywhere he went, in town and country district alike, he was cheered and welcomed by large demonstrative crowds. He travelled through Snowdonia, Montgomeryshire, and Cardigan to Swansea, where he announced the Queen's decision to confer city status on the borough, and where the dockers gave him a rousing welcome. As he continued his journey through South Wales the miners and steelworkers took up the welcome, and through the rural areas on his way to Newport thousands of waving people lined the route to cheer him on his way. On the last day of his tour he was given a civic welcome in Cardiff, received the freedom of the city, and in the evening attended a concert given by the Welsh National Youth Orchestra.

The investiture and the tour were a triumph for Prince Charles. Any fears about the reception he might receive from the majority of the people of Wales were ill-founded, for the Welsh showed in no uncertain manner that they had taken their new Prince to their hearts.

Immediately after the investiture the Prince of Wales made a 400-mile "meet the people" tour of Wales. On the second day he was driven round Carmarthen Park (*below*) to receive the enthusiastic greetings of a huge crowd.

HERE MEN FROM THE PLANET EARTH
FIRST SET FOOT UPON THE MOON
JULY 1969, A. D
WE CAME IN PEACE FOR ALL MANKIND

NEIL A. ARMSTRONG
ASTRONAUT

MICHAEL COLLINS
ASTRONAUT

EDWIN E. ALDRIN JR
ASTRONAUT

RICHARD NIXON
PRESIDENT UNITED STATES OF AMERICA

"One Giant Leap for Mankind"

Six hundred million people, glued to their television sets
the world over, held their breath as Neil Armstrong carefully placed his left foot on the Moon's surface on July
21, 1969—the climax of Man's greatest scientific and
technical achievement and the opening of a new era in
human history. *Top:* the plaque left behind on the Moon
by the first men to walk on its surface; and the three Apollo
11 astronauts—(*left to right*) Edwin Aldrin, Michael
Collins, and Neil Armstrong. *Above:* Aldrin descending
from the lunar module (*left*), photographed with a "still"
camera by Armstrong; and (*right*) walking on the surface,
his companion and the module reflected in the visor of
his space helmet. *Left:* as the world saw the men at work
—television picture of Aldrin setting up apparatus while
Armstrong (*foreground*) photographs the scene.

Facing page 33

First Men on the Moon

L. J. CARTER

Secretary of the British Interplanetary Society

On JULY 21, 1969, with the words "That's one small step for a man, one giant leap for mankind," the American astronaut Neil Armstrong became the first man to step on the surface of the Moon—man's first direct physical contact with a major celestial body. The epic flight of the crew of Apollo 11, Armstrong, Col. Edwin Aldrin, and Col. Michael Collins, began on July 16 with the launch of a giant Saturn 5 rocket from Pad 39A at Cape Kennedy, after a 28-hour countdown, watched by a million eye-witnesses and a world TV audience of around 600 million—the greatest ever audience for any single event.

The purpose of Apollo 11 was simple and basic—to demonstrate that men can travel to the Moon, land, and return safely to Earth again. It was eight years before, in May 1961, that President Kennedy first propounded the goal that the U.S.A. should land men on the Moon "in this decade." From then on, more than 400,000 people participated in the designing, building, testing, and operation of the machinery required for the assignment. Rockets and spacecraft, tracking antennae, computers, launch facilities, and recovery systems were needed, and astronauts had to be selected and trained for the task no one had ever attempted before. Almost everything connected with the project seemed to be either the first, the only, the largest, the heaviest, the most powerful, or the most expensive of its kind.

'Columbia' & 'Eagle'

The launch proceeded smoothly. Within 12 minutes the first two stages of the Saturn 5 rocket had fired and been jettisoned, and the third stage was placing Apollo 11 in Earth-orbit. Less than 3 hours later, the third stage engine was fired again to boost Apollo 11 to a speed of 24,200 m.p.h. and send it into a path which would lead it towards the Moon over 230,000 miles away. As the spacecraft moved farther from the Earth, the lunar landing craft (code-named "Eagle") was separated from the main command ship (code-named "Columbia") to turn round and re-dock into its landing position.

On the 19th the astronauts reported that the view of the Moon already filled about three-quarters of the hatch window. The next day Armstrong and Aldrin crawled into the lunar module, leaving Collins behind in the command module. The two craft were then separated, Collins firing the command ship's rockets, while Armstrong and Aldrin fired the landing craft to reduce speed and drop down on to the Moon's surface. As they approached, they saw below a crater about the size of a football field, covered with large rocks, so Armstrong took over manual control to steer the craft to another spot and settle down gently. Immediately he had done so, he radioed to Earth: "This is Tranquillity Base—'Eagle' has landed." It was 21.18 B.S.T., on July 20.

'One small step . . .'

No one who saw the historic moment $6\frac{1}{2}$ hours later when Neil Armstrong's foot touched the Moon will forget the indescribable feeling of excitement and pride that it created in the mind. Calmest of all perhaps was Armstrong himself, as he coolly reported that the lunar surface was fine and powdery and stuck to the layers of his boots like powdered charcoal. The impression of his footprints in the soil was only a small fraction of an inch deep, so that there was no difficulty in moving about. Shortly afterwards he was joined by "Buzz" Aldrin and, from a leg of the spacecraft, the astronauts took an American flag, its top edge braced by a wire spring to keep it extended on the windless Moon, and placed it on a staff pressed into the surface. Their first graphic impression of the Moon (reported at a press conference afterwards) was as follows: "It seemed as though it was like swimming in the ocean with 6–8 feet swells and waves. In that condition, you never can see very far away from where you are and this was exaggerated by the fact that the lunar curvature is so much more pronounced."

The next task was the collection of lunar rocks and soil samples and setting up three lunar experiments. Later in the day, after a 22-hour stay, the lunar module was restarted, using the descent stage as a launch pad, and re-docked with the command module 4 hours later, while circling on the far side of the Moon. Two hours later the landing craft was jettisoned and the command module's engine was fired for the return trip.

Photo taken by Schweickart on "Spider" of Scott standing in the open hatch of Apollo 9's "Gumdrop."

A variety of objects were left behind on the Moon, besides the scientific experiments. These included the lunar module descent stage (which bore a small plaque bearing the signatures of the three astronauts and that of President Nixon), the U.S. flag, miniature messages from the heads of foreign countries, TV camera and tripod, many tools, and various pieces of equipment not needed for the return flight.

The plaque bore the images of the two hemispheres of the Earth and the inscription: *Here men from the planet Earth first set foot upon the Moon, July 1969, A.D.—We came in peace for all mankind.* An opportunity for stamp collectors to share in the voyage arose from the fact that the astronauts carried a master die which made the round trip to the Moon. This, on return, was used to print a special commemorative 10c. U.S. postage stamp, showing a spaceman stepping on the Moon's surface and inscribed "First Man on the Moon." The astronauts also carried a "Moon letter," the postmark on which was printed by them while they were there.

The TV programmes direct from the spacecraft, watched by hundreds of millions, were all in colour, except for the period when the astronauts stepped on to the Moon's surface; only black and white could be transmitted then because of the reduced power available from the lunar module. The show on July 18 lasted for 1 hour 36 minutes as Armstrong and Aldrin prepared to enter "Eagle" for checkout. The next day there was a telecast of the lunar surface beamed to the Earth for 34 minutes. On the 21st the TV carried scenes from the moment Armstrong stepped on to the Moon's surface. On the 23rd, a colour programme

showed the astronauts eating a meal, and the next day a final programme from Apollo 11 showed the approaching Earth.

The spacecraft splashed down in the Pacific Ocean, south west of Honolulu on July 24, and the crew were greeted by President Nixon on board the aircraft carrier *Hornet*. As they entered a long period of quarantine while scientists examined the possibility that they might be contaminated by lunar "germs," he told them: "This has been the greatest week since the Creation."

Apollo 9—'Gumdrop' & 'Spider'

Before Apollo 11 could set its crew down safely on the surface of the Moon, two important test flights had to be carried out. The first of these was the 10-day flight of Apollo 9, with the astronauts Col. James McDivitt, Col. David Scott, and Mr. Russell Schweickart. This was the critical launch of a Saturn 5 rocket from Cape Kennedy, to undertake the first manned orbital test of the lunar module.

Blast-off was on March 3. It was a flawless flight. After entering a near-circular orbit about 120 miles high, the crew carried out docking manoeuvres which were so precise that they were hardly more than "a pencil's width" from the planned trajectories. The programme included evaluating rendezvous and docking techniques, flight-testing the new lunar module descent and ascent engines, checking the propulsion system for flight manoeuvres, and providing the first chance to use the Apollo suit and its portable life-support equipment. Schweickart performed a "space walk" that lasted over half an hour.

The flight also demonstrated the remarkably clear communications system, including a number of TV programmes to Earth, showing views of the docked spacecraft and the Earth below. Schweickart and McDivitt entered the lunar module ("Spider") several times and on the third occasion moved it to a different orbit, the separation distance exceeding 100 miles. Six hours later, there was a brief re-docking for crew transfer, and the lunar module then separated again and moved to a different orbit under ground command. The Apollo 9 astronauts continued with a leisurely programme of experiments lasting for a further five days, including landmark sightings, simulation of a return flight from the Moon, and multi-spectral photography for Earth-resources study, particularly in connection with agriculture.

The Apollo 9 command module ("Gumdrop") splashed down in the Atlantic Ocean on March 13, 3 miles from the aircraft carrier *Guadalcanal*. The recovery was televised to a

Apollo 10's lunar module descended to within 10 miles of the Moon's surface, in rehearsal for the Apollo 11 landing. As it returned (*left*) to rejoin the command module (*right*), "Snoopy" and "Charlie Brown" photographed each other.

world audience through the Intelsat communications satellite network.

Apollo 10—'Charlie Brown' & 'Snoopy'

Apollo 10's mission was a final rehearsal for the Moon landing. It was designed to simulate a manned lunar landing in every respect except the actual touchdown, and to check every spacecraft system. The three astronauts, Col. Thomas P. Stafford, Cmdr. Eugene A. Cernan, and Cmdr. John W. Young, left Cape Kennedy on May 18, splashing down in the Pacific eight days later, 3 miles from the predetermined spot.

After launch, the third stage engine inserted the spacecraft into a nearly circular orbit round the Earth and was then shut down while the astronauts spent two Earth orbits undertaking a thorough checking of the system. As everything was working well, over Australia and in their second orbit the crew was given the "go" for injection into the lunar flight path. During the flight the freeze-dried diet, now standard for manned flights, was supplemented by individually wrapped sandwiches. The only sour note struck by the astronauts was their distaste for the chlorinated drinking water.

On May 21, Apollo 10 entered a high elliptical orbit round the Moon, subsequently circularised at about 60 miles. The crew provided vivid descriptions of the lunar features over which they were passing; they found the "dark" side of the Moon surprisingly well-lit by Earth-shine, and had no trouble in picking out landmarks. Cernan commented that the side away from the Earth was "lit up like a Christmas tree." The closest descent was to within 10 miles of the lunar surface for a close-up inspection of the planned Apollo 11

landing site in the Sea of Tranquillity. In two circuits of the Moon, the landing radar was checked, and the crew undertook extensive surface photography and landmark tracking.

Once their low-altitude tasks were done— after about 8 hours of independent flight— Stafford and Cernan jettisoned the descent stage of the lunar module (code-named "Snoopy"), fired the ascent engine and flew up to join Young in the command module (code-named "Charlie Brown"). There were a few chilling moments when the lunar module gyrated wildly as the descent stage was cast off 15 miles above the surface of the Moon, and again at the moment of re-docking when, Young said, "all hell broke loose." But all was well and on May 23, when on the far side of the Moon, the crew fired the main engine to escape from lunar orbit and entered the narrow corridor to take them back to Earth again. So exact was the burn that the speed achieved was only 4 m.p.h. less than planned, and midcourse corrections written into the programme were eliminated as unnecessary.

For millions of viewers all over the world, the high points in this exciting flight were the live TV programmes. A 15-lb. colour TV camera, specially developed for this flight, recorded the initial docking manoeuvre after Apollo 10 and the Saturn third-stage had entered the lunar flight-path, and showed the Earth from space, crew activity inside the cabin, and the Moon from various angles and distances.

Apollo 12—'Yankee Clipper' & 'Intrepid'

The second manned lunar landing began on Nov. 14, 1969, when the Apollo 12 astronauts, Cmdr. Charles Conrad, Cmdr. Richard Gordon, and Cmdr. Alan Bean, were launched

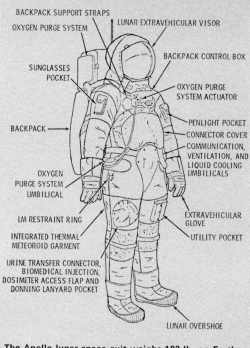

BACKPACK SUPPORT STRAPS
OXYGEN PURGE SYSTEM
LUNAR EXTRAVEHICULAR VISOR
BACKPACK CONTROL BOX
SUNGLASSES POCKET
OXYGEN PURGE SYSTEM ACTUATOR
BACKPACK
PENLIGHT POCKET
CONNECTOR COVER
COMMUNICATION, VENTILATION, AND LIQUID COOLING UMBILICALS
OXYGEN PURGE SYSTEM UMBILICAL
LM RESTRAINT RING
EXTRAVEHICULAR GLOVE
INTEGRATED THERMAL METEOROID GARMENT
UTILITY POCKET
URINE TRANSFER CONNECTOR, BIOMEDICAL INJECTION, DOSIMETER ACCESS FLAP AND DONNING LANYARD POCKET
LUNAR OVERSHOE

The Apollo lunar space-suit weighs 183 lb. on Earth, but only 13 lb. under the Moon's low gravity.

The Apollo 12 astronauts: Charles Conrad (*left*) **and Alan Bean** (*right*)**, who landed, and Richard Gordon** (*centre*)**, who piloted the command module.**

from Cape Kennedy by a Saturn V rocket during a thunderstorm. A lightning discharge cut out the electrical system immediately after launch, and the craft went over to batteries, but the power supply was righted after a few minutes and within 11 minutes the astronauts were in orbit round the earth. After 1½ orbits to check that all systems were working normally, Apollo 12 entered its trajectory towards the Moon. The first of several live TV transmissions which followed, less than 4 hours after

launch, showed the receding Earth and the interior of the spacecraft.

On November 19, after detaching from the command module ("Yankee Clipper"), the lunar module "Intrepid" approached the Moon at a shallow angle. Dust proved troublesome on landing; so much was stirred up that the last 20 ft. of the descent was "blind." "Intrepid" landed in the Ocean of Storms, only 600 ft. from the robot craft Surveyor 3, which had lain in a 650-ft. crater for 2½ years. The Ocean of Storms is similar to the Sea of Tranquillity—where the Apollo 11 astronauts landed—but on the Western side of the Moon and about 955 miles from the Apollo 11 landing site.

"Intrepid" landed early in the Moon's morning. The sun was only 5° above the horizon and cast very long shadows. (On the Moon these long shadows help astronauts to distinguish rocks, craters, and other surface features more easily.) Conrad and Bean stayed on the Moon's surface for 31½ hours. During this time, they made two excursions over the lunar surface. They gathered over 100 lb. of material and set up an elaborate set of scientific instruments—including a seismometer, laser beam reflector, instruments to record the Moon's temperature, a gauge to detect possible lunar magnetism, and a more sophisticated instrument to measure the "solar wind." They also visited Surveyor 3 which, they discovered, had changed from a dazzling white colour to brown. Several parts of it were collected for return to Earth, including the TV camera, sections of tubing, and the scoop that had given man his first idea of the load-bearing characteristics of the lunar surface. Unfortunately the TV camera which should have shown the world all these activities by Conrad and Bean was set up by them facing the sun, so that its sensitive light-cells were burnt out. After a few seconds there were no TV pictures,

One of the Apollo 12 crew setting up experiments on the Moon's surface, November 19, 1969.

but still photos were taken. Gordon, alone in the command module, occupied many of his solitary hours in making a comprehensive survey of the Moon. He used a stereo camera and also infra-red and spectrographic processes.

Listeners on Earth were impressed with the high spirits of the astronauts as they explored the Moon's surface. These were not hesitant or cautious steps, but those of men moving with self-confidence. They whistled and sang while they worked, and discovered that, in the Moon's lesser gravity—only one sixth that of the Earth—they could move with ease and with less effort and fatigue than similar activities would generate on Earth.

On November 20, Conrad and Bean blasted off from the Moon and began to chase "Yankee Clipper" for a rendezvous. Earth viewers saw live and in colour, intensely thrilling TV pictures as "Intrepid," at first a mere speck on the screen, grew to fill it as it

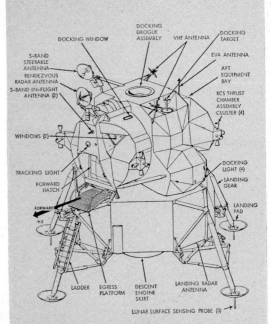

The Apollo lunar module, although weighing 32,000 lb., is too fragile to function under Earth's atmospheric pressure and high gravity.

closed at 25 m.p.h. for a perfect space docking. Subsequently, "Intrepid" was crashed on to the Moon's surface at about 3,600 m.p.h., to prevent danger to later astronauts using the same orbital track and to allow the seismometer to be calibrated.

"The year of Apollo" ended with the splash-down of "Yankee Clipper" on November 24, in a far from peaceful Pacific Ocean, 10 days 4 hours and 42 minutes after launch.

FUTURE APOLLO FLIGHTS

Eight further flights—at the rate of two or three each year—are scheduled to follow Apollo 12, designed to explore a wide variety of lunar formations. Those currently planned are as follows:

Apollo 13—the *Fra Mauro formation* along the western equator, a flattened highland mantled by massive ejecta from the Imbrium basin to the north. The Apollo 13 crew may be asked to drill a core sample through the mantle, because the area is presumed to be a stratigraphic blanket over original crust material.

Apollo 14—the crater *Censorinus,* a small, relatively new impact structure in uplands along the southern edge of the Sea of Tranquillity. Censorinus, a noted landmark, was used as a tracking aid by the crews of Apollos 8, 10, and 11.

Apollo 15—the *Littrow Rim,* one of a series of rille networks on the eastern border of the Sea of Serenity.

Apollo 16—*Tycho,* the most prominent of all Earth-side lunar craters at full Moon. Its rim also was the soft-landing site of Surveyor 7 in January 1968. The Apollo 16 crew will be asked to examine that long-quiescent spacecraft in detail.

Apollo 17—the *Marius Hills,* a cluster of cones and domes near the centre of the Ocean of Storms and to the west-northwest of the crater Marius.

Apollo 18—*Schroter's Valley,* which lies in the Aristarchus plateau and displays a sinuous depression to a depth of about 4,300 ft. from the floor to the rim. It includes the spectacular *Cobra Head* feature, although that rugged area is not suitable for landing.

Apollo 19—the crater *Hyginus* and its rille, a low-rimmed, 6·2-mile feature notable for numerous small domed masses on the floor. Its most prominent landmark is a great cleft—the linear rille pock-marked by many chain craters.

Apollo 20—the crater *Copernicus,* probably the most conspicuous feature of the Moon's Earth side, and potentially the most geologically rewarding in that its walls expose about 2½ miles of the original lunar stratifications.

Apollo 12 Moon-man setting up the umbrella-like communications antenna for transmitting data.

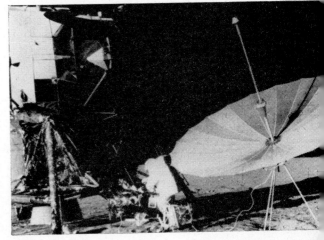

Centenary Occasions of 1969

ELIZABETH HOGARTH

In 1969 MANKIND as usual showed its regard for famous people and events by holding many and varied commemorations of their hundredth anniversaries. Notable were those held in honour of the Indian leader, Mahatma Gandhi, who was born on October 2, 1869. On that day, a hundred years later, temple bells rang out throughout India, and thousands of people attended a ceremony at the Rajghat memorial on the holy Yamuna river banks where he was cremated in 1948. The British, who in his lifetime had at first seemed unaware of his existence, then feared and imprisoned him, and eventually revered and even loved him, held three celebrations in London on January 30, the 21st anniversary of his assassination. A memorial ceremony took place at India House; a memorial service was held at the Quaker Meeting House, St. Martin's Lane; and, in the evening, Lord Mountbatten of Burma and the Archbishop of Canterbury paid tribute to him at a service in St. Paul's Cathedral, which was attended by people of all denominations and creeds. On August 13, the Post Office issued a special 1s. 6d. stamp bearing his portrait, the first U.K. postage stamp to commemorate an overseas leader. The Prince of Wales, the Prime Minister, and a host of other prominent persons attended a special concert in the Royal Albert Hall on October 21.

It was on October 7, 1769, that Capt. James Cook first sighted New Zealand, and in Gisborne, where he landed, celebrations of the bicentenary of the event started in July. These included events as varied as art exhibitions, badminton championships, theatrical productions, and a yacht race. The chief celebrations took place in "Cook week," October 4–11, when ten warships from five countries cruised into Gisborne harbour, and a naval ceremony, attended by the Prime Minister, Mr. Holyoake, and other dignitaries, took place at the Cook memorial. It was decided that a Captain Cook Memorial Park, including a statue to the great navigator at the top of Kaiti Hill, should be created in Gisborne. Regional celebrations were also held in other parts of the country known to have been visited by Captain Cook. It was in 1869 that the clipper *Cutty Sark* was launched, and a hundred years later a special exhibition, centred upon the original figurehead, was held on board the ship, which is docked at Greenwich.

In Australia the city of Darwin celebrated the centenary of its selection in 1869 as the site for the chief town on the north coast. In Egypt another city remembered its much older creation: Cairo, the largest city in Africa, celebrated its thousandth year, for its history began in A.D. 969 when Gawhai the Sicilian, after conquering Egypt for the Caliph, chose the desert site on which to build a new capital. Egypt celebrated, too, the opening of the Suez Canal in November 1869, and to mark the occasion the Cairo Opera House staged a production of *Rigoletto*, the first work to be performed at its opening a hundred years before. *Aïda* had been composed by Verdi for the occasion, but its production was held up until 1870.

In 1769 two of the most famous soldiers of their time were born: Arthur Wellesley, 1st Duke of Wellington, on April 29; and on August 15, Napoleon Bonaparte, Emperor of the French, whose bicentenary was celebrated in France by exhibitions, special stamp issues, a son-et-lumière show at Les Invalides, the striking of two medals, and ceremonies at Ajaccio, Corsica, his birthplace. In Great

Mahatma Gandhi's centenary inspired the first British stamp to commemorate a foreigner—designed by fellow-Indian, Binam Mullick.

May 10, 1869, saw the completion of the first coast-to-coast railway in the U.S.A., when the Central Pacific tracks met those of the Union Pacific at Promontory, Utah. Pioneer photographer Andrew J. Russel recorded the conjunction.

Britain less attention was paid to the Iron Duke; even Edmond Hoyle, writer on card and other games, who died on August 29, 1769, and whose rules for whist gave rise to the expression "according to Hoyle," received almost as much notice.

Music and the Arts

Of the musical anniversaries which fell in 1969 few can have noted that Alexander Dargomizhsky, the Russian composer, died on January 7, 1869; that the German composer Hans Pfitzner was born on May 5, 1869; or that the British composer and conductor Sir Henry Walford Davies was born on September 6, 1869. But the hundredth anniversary of the death of the French composer, Hector Berlioz, which fell on March 8, was widely commemorated. In France, concerts of his music were given, and an exhibition devoted to his life and work was held in Paris, while in Britain a bigger programme of events included a performance of *The Trojans* in full at the Royal Opera House, London, an exhibition at the Victoria and Albert Museum, and performances in many towns and cities. Special performances of Berlioz's music were also given in Antwerp, Lisbon, Milan, Rome, Rotterdam, Tokyo, and Boston, U.S.A.

A musician remembered with deep affection in Great Britain was the founder-conductor of the Promenade Concerts, Sir Henry Wood, and on the hundredth anniversary of his birth on March 3, 1869, a performance of Verdi's *Requiem* was given at the Royal Albert Hall, London. The capacity audience included the Queen and Princess Anne. On May 25, 1969, the Vienna State Opera House was packed for a special concert to celebrate the inauguration of a centenary festival at this famous theatre. In addition to the musical events—28 different operas were performed in 28 days—a set of nine stamps showing operatic scenes was issued, and a huge exhibition of items in the history of the State Opera was held. London, too, celebrated this centenary with an exhibition at the Royal Festival Hall.

Literary centenaries were world-wide, and included the births of Booth Tarkington, American novelist (July 29); Laurence Binyon, British poet (August 10); Charlotte Mew, the tragic poetess who, unrecognised and poverty-stricken in her life-time, took her own life in 1928 (November 15); André Gide, French poet and critic (November 22); Algernon Blackwood, supreme author of ghost stories (December 10); and Stephen Leacock, English-born Canadian professor of economics and humorous writer (December 30). May 3 was the 500th anniversary of the birth of the Florentine political writer, Niccolo Machiavelli, and to mark the occasion celebrations took place in San Casciano where, in retirement, he wrote his most famous work *The Prince*. An international congress was held in Florence, where he worked as a civil servant and died in 1527; performances of his play were given; and a special postage stamp bearing his portrait was issued. In Moscow at an exhibition held to celebrate the publication of Tolstoy's *War and Peace* in 1869, editions from many countries were on view, as well as MS. pages.

39

In 1869 R. D. Blackmore published his evergreen story *Lorna Doone*, and the heroine's hundredth birthday was exuberantly celebrated on Exmoor. Local people played the parts of the chief characters in the novel, and from April, when the Dunkery beacon was fired, until September, when the Dance of the Doones took place, there were many pageants, fêtes, and other commemorative events. It was in 1869, too, that Louisa M. Alcott published *Good Wives*, the sequel to *Little Women*, and W. S. Gilbert his *Bab Ballads*.

The tercentenary of the death of Rembrandt on October 4, 1669, was widely commemorated. In the National Gallery in London there was an exhibition of his prints, drawings, and paintings, as well as of some by his associates, pupils, and followers. Other exhibitions of his work were held in Amsterdam, the city of his birth, in Canada, and in the U.S.A. His self-portrait also appeared on an Austrian stamp issued to commemorate another event, the bicentenary of the beginning of the Albertina collection of graphic works, the

largest of its kind in the world. Other artists commemorated during 1969 were Fra Filippo Lippi (died October 8, 1469); Pieter Brueghel the elder (died September 5, 1569); and Henri Matisse (born December 31, 1869).

This Austrian stamp—bearing a graphic reproduction of a Rembrandt self-portrait—was issued during 1969 to celebrate the 200th anniversary of the foundation of the Albertina Collection of Graphic Art, Vienna.

Two famous architects were born in 1869—the British Sir Edwin Lutyens, whose works include the Cenotaph in Whitehall, London, on March 29; and the American, Frank Lloyd Wright, born on June 8. A Lutyens centenary exhibition, held at the Royal Institute of British Architects, included the famous 5 ft.-high, 14-room Queen's Dolls' House, designed by Sir Edwin in 1921 as a gift for Queen Mary.

An exhibition in the Science Museum, London, celebrated the 200th anniversary of the birth of Sir Marc Isambard Brunel, the civil engineer who constructed the first Thames tunnel, between Rotherhithe and Wapping, 1825–43, and the father of a better known son. The Dutch and Flemings celebrated the birth of Erasmus on October 27, 1469, a date only recently authoritatively established by historians. In Rotterdam a village was recreated in the style of his day as an open-air museum, and special exhibitions of the works of this great humanist were held throughout the Low Countries.

Two items in our diet began their life a hundred years ago. In response to an offer by Napoleon III of an award to any scientist who could help to feed the vastly increasing French population by producing a substitute for butter, the chemist Hippolyte Mège-Mouriès invented in 1869 an emulsion of beef fat and milk, and claimed the prize: margarine, so called because under a microscope it resembled a pearl (Greek *margarites*), had come to stay. And in August 1869 at Ryde, near Sydney, Australia, Mrs. Maria Ann Smith found some rotting apples in a barrel of gin and threw them into her orchard. For some still unknown reason, from the pips grew a new type of apple in the name of which Granny Smith is immortalised,

Other Centenaries of 1969

Births

Neville Chamberlain, British Prime Minister (March 18); John Robert Clynes, British trade union leader (March 27); Albert Roussel, French composer (April 5); Harvey Cushing, American surgeon (April 8); Sir Herbert Barker, manipulative surgeon (April 21); George Morrow, humorous artist (September 5); Sir George Robey, "Prime Minister of Mirth" (September 20); Baron Duveen, art patron (October 14).

Deaths

Alphonse de Lamartine, French poet (February 28); Charles Augustin Sainte-Beuve, French critic (October 13); Edmond George Stanley, 14th Earl of Derby, British Prime Minister (October 23); George Peabody, American philanthropist of "Peabody Buildings" fame (November 4); Friedrich Overbeck, German artist (November 12); Thomas Creswick, British landscape painter (November 28); Giulia Grisi, Italian soprano (November 29).

Events

Mendeleev's announcement of his periodic law of chemical elements (March); Foundation of University of Otago, Dunedin, New Zealand (June 3); Foundation of Girton College, initially College for Women, Hitchin (October 16); Opening of Blackfriars Bridge by Queen Victoria (November 6).

Transport

*Ice-breaking tanker
"Manhattan" making the
North-West Passage*

Monza saw one of the closest ever G.P. finishes: Stewart won by feet from Rindt, with Beltoise third.

Cars on Circuit and on Show

PETER GARNIER, Editor of *Autocar*

I N THE SPHERE of car racing the year 1969 was remarkable chiefly for three occurrences: Jackie Stewart's victories in five of the first six G.P. races, which gave him the championship halfway through the season; the runaway victory of the Porsches in sports car racing; and the debut of formula 5000 racing in Great Britain. The racing year started as usual with the Tasman Championship series in Australia and New Zealand. This developed into a battle between Chris Amon (Ferrari) and Piers Courage (Brabham), with Graham Hill and Jochen Rindt (both Lotus) intervening. Amon won the N. Z. Grand Prix at Pukekohe, with Rindt second and Courage third; the front hub of Hill's Lotus broke on his 13th lap. Amon was again the victor at Levin, and Courage was second; both the

Lotuses suffered mechanical faults, Rindt's crashing after brake failure. At Christchurch the Lady Wigram Trophy was won by Rindt in a new Lotus; Hill and Amon were second and third.

At Teretonga it was Courage's turn to win in Frank Williams's Brabham-Ford, with a commanding lead from the third lap onwards; Hill was second and Amon third. The Australian Grand Prix at Lakeside saw Ferraris take first (Amon) and second (Derek Bell) places; third was a Lotus-Repco driven by a local boy, Leo Geoghegan. Hill "closed the gate" on Courage who had tried to outbrake him, and both retired with resultant damage. Amon and Courage were now rivals for the title, but at Warwick Farm Courage crashed on the opening lap and Rindt ran away with the victory; Bell's Ferrari was second, and Frank Gardner's Mildren-Alfa third. Amon thus became Tasman Champion after an exciting series.

The World Championship

Jackie Stewart in a Matra-Ford started the season as he meant to go on with a runaway victory in the South African Grand Prix; he broke Jim Clark's record on his third lap, and finished 20 seconds ahead of Hill (Lotus), followed by Denny Hulme (McLaren) and Jo Siffert (Lotus). Only nine of the 18 starters finished. Only five of 14 starters finished in the Spanish Grand Prix at Barcelona, which Stewart won, his Matra-Ford finishing two laps ahead of Bruce McLaren, with Jean-Pierre Beltoise (in another Matra) third. This race was notable for the first accident directly attributable to an aerofoil wing: Rindt crashed

1969 World Champion by the wide margin of 26 points—Jackie Stewart, with his wife Helen.

The all-conquering Matra-Ford, with Jackie Stewart in the cockpit, winning the British G.P. at Silverstone.
Autocar

and totally destroyed his Lotus, but escaped serious injury. After this incident, the Automobile Club de Monaco issued a ban on aerofoil wings, supported by the F.I.A. and the *Commission Sportive Internationale*, who also banned them for the Dutch Grand Prix. At the end of June, after the Dutch Grand Prix, at a meeting between the C. S. I., the racing car constructors, and the race organisers it was resolved in effect to ban aerofoils permanently, the only kind of spoilers permitted being those attached to the sprung mass of the body and contained within the width between the wheels (except ahead of the front ones) within a maximum depth of 80 cm.

Graham Hill won the Monaco Grand Prix for the fifth time, after playing a waiting game in third place until Stewart (in the lead) broke a drive shaft and Amon (second) broke his gear-box. In the Dutch Grand Prix it was a close battle between Stewart, Hill, and Rindt, the last named taking the lead on lap 3 and holding it until his car failed on lap 17. Behind this struggle was an even more exciting one between Hulme, Amon, McLaren, Brabham, and Ickx, who fought wheel to wheel until the finish. Stewart won the race, and in the French

Grand Prix at Clermont Ferrand he pulled it off yet again, completely dominating the race from the start. After a tremendous battle with Jacky Ickx in a Brabham-Ford, Beltoise in the other works Matra went ahead in the very last lap to take second place by only 0·2 second, nearly a minute behind Stewart.

Stewart won his fifth Grand Prix of the season at Silverstone at the end of July. Rindt harried him hard until the 62nd lap, when he had to make a pit stop while in the lead, but at the flag Stewart led Ickx by 41 seconds, with McLaren third 6 seconds behind Ickx. Jacky Ickx took his revenge in the German Grand Prix, which he won in a Brabham-Ford. Stewart came second, 18 seconds behind. But this made his total of points for the world championship 51, which was 29 more than any other driver in the season, and in the breathtaking Italian Grand Prix at Monza he clinched the title with an untouchable 60 points, against McLaren's 24 and Ickx's 22. This final European round of the series was the most exciting, the first four cars (Stewart, Rindt, Beltoise, and McLaren) crossing the line with no more than 50 yards between them all. The lead changed hands continuously, and

Other winning drivers of the year's great races included (*left to right*): Mario Andretti, who won the Indianapolis 500 with a record average speed of 156·87 m.p.h.; Jochen Rindt of Austria (Lotus), who set a new lap record of 128·69 m.p.h. in his victory at Watkins Glen; Oliver (*left*) and Ickx, whose Ford won the fiercely fought Sebring 12-hour endurance race; and Chris Amon (New Zealand), who carried off the Tasman Championship in his Ferrari.

Graham Hill, in a wheelchair after his accident, presented Jackie Stewart with a trophy marking his succession to the presidency of the World Champion Drivers' Club.

even in the last few laps it was anybody's race. Graham Hill contested the lead during the last 20 laps, but mechanical trouble put him out of the race.

Once across the Atlantic, Stewart's formula 1 fortunes changed, and in the Canadian Grand Prix at Mosport Park Jacky Ickx won after taking the lead from Stewart about a third of the way through the race in a controversial accident. Brabham cars came in first and second. Both the Lotus team cars went out with mechanical troubles, both works BRMs blew up, and altogether 13 cars failed to finish. Jochen Rindt's turn finally came at Watkins Glen, where he won from Piers Courage by nearly a minute, having set a new lap record of 128·69 m.p.h. Stewart retired on the

Porsche winning the 1,000 km. at the Nurburgring.

35th lap. Graham Hill crashed when a tyre on his Lotus went flat, and he overturned several times at very high speed; on the second roll he was thrown out (he had not refastened his seat belt after pushing the car to start it after a spin), and broke both legs.

In the last race, in Mexico, Hulme took the flag first, Ickx came in second, with Jack Brabham third. Stewart was no better than fourth, but in the final placings he came out with 63 points, ahead of Ickx's 37 and McLaren's 26.

In the classic Indianapolis 500, Mario Andretti, driving a Hawk-Ford, fought off an early challenge by A. J. Foyt and Roger McClusky, and a later one by Lloyd Ruby, to win at an average speed of 156·867 m.p.h. This race speed was a new record, despite the running of 14 laps with the yellow caution lights on. Second man was Dan Gurney in his own Eagle-Ford, while Bobby Unser was third in a four-wheel drive Lola-Offenhauser.

Motor racing suffered the loss of several prominent drivers during 1969. Chris Williams was killed testing at Silverstone just before Easter, Lucien Bianchi practising at Le Mans, and Gerhart Mitter in practice at the Nurburgring. And the band-leader Billy Cotton, a former Brooklands driver and grand old man of racing, died of a heart attack while watching a boxing match.

Formula 5000 Racing

Formula 5000 racing made its debut at Oulton Park at Easter when the first of a series of events for the Guards Trophy was run. The race was won by Peter Gethin in a McLaren-Chevrolet from David Hobbs in a Surtees-Chevrolet. On the following Monday, at Brands Hatch, Gethin made it a double, while Hobbs went out with suspension trouble. In the fourth round, at Mallory Park, Gethin won again, Hobbs again finished second, and Mike Walker drove a Lola into third place. The first-ever Dublin Grand Prix was won by Hobbs; the race was run as two 42-lap heats and, despite engine trouble in the second, Hobbs won on aggregate from Mike Hailwood in a Lola.

Interest began to hot up when Gethin could not start at Snetterton, and blew his engine up at Oulton Park. Trevor Taylor came to the fore after winning at Coxyde in Belgium and Zandvoort in Holland. But in September, at Oulton Park again, he broke a cam follower, and the championship was open between Gethin, Taylor, Holland, Walker, and Hailwood. In the final round at Brands Hatch Mike Hailwood won in a Lola, but Gethin set a new lap record and took the championship on points, after crashing along with Trevor

Taylor when they tangled with a back-marker on the 9th lap.

A new regulation to restrict power and cut the escalating cost was introduced for formula 5000 at the end of August to take effect from December 1. It states that no fuel injection may be fitted, and that only Weber 48 IDA carburettors, with no interconnection between ports, may be used.

Sports Car Racing

Although the season developed into a Porsche benefit, it started with victories by other makes—Lola-Chevrolets (first and second) in the Daytona 24-hour race; Fords (first, second, and third) in the Riverside 500, a top U. S. stock car race; and a British Ford (driven by Jacky Ickx and Jackie Oliver) in the hotly contested Sebring 12-hour. Porsche started their walk-away in the B.O.A.C. 500 run at Brands Hatch, the third round of the championship, when they came home 1-2-3, the drivers being respectively Siffert and Redman, Attwood and Elford, and Mitter and Schutz

Siffert and Redman came first again in another 1-2-3 Porsche victory in the 1,000-km. race at Monza; this time Hermann and Ahrens were second in another works 908, and Koch and Dechent third in a private 907. In the lamentable Targa Florio in Sicily, Porsches went one better by taking the first four places. The start was chaotic—after a 25-minute delay the drivers set off on their own. There were pit stops galore throughout the six hours, and three cars were destoyed by fire. This time Mitter and Schutz were first, Elford and Maglioli second, Hermann and Stommelen third, and von Wendt and Kauhsen fourth. The Siffert-Redman Porsche won the 1,000-km. race at Spa, Belgium, and when this invincible make took the first five places in the 1,000 km. at the Nurburgring the German factory was assured of the sports car manufacturer's championship. Meanwhile Trevor Taylor in a Lola had won the Oulton Park Tourist Trophy after 74 laps, when the race was stopped after Paul Hawkins's fatal accident in another Lola had blocked the track.

The Le Mans 24-hour race saw Porsche (Hermann and Larousse) ousted from first place by a JWA Ford GT 40, but only by 0·07 of a mile after 3,000 miles of hard racing. Another Ford GT 40 came third. The two Fords were driven by Ickx and Oliver, and Hobbs and Hailwood. Of the remaining six races in the season, four were won by Porsches: they took the first three places at Watkins Glen, the first four in the Spa 24-hour endurance race, the first and third in the Austrian Grand

The JWA Ford GT 40, driven by Jacky Ickx and Jackie Oliver, winning the Le Mans 24-hour race—one of the few big sports car events not won by Porsche.

Prix, and the first, third, fourth, and fifth in the *Tour de France*, revived after a lapse of five years and decided on eleven hill climbs and road races and nine circuit races. In the CanAm race at Watkins Glen, McLaren and Hulme finished nose to tail at an average of 126·06 m.p.h., and the rain-soaked 84-hour blast round the Nurburgring (which has replaced the old Liége-Rome-Liége rally) was won by a Lancia, only 19 out of 66 starters managing to finish.

Rallies of the Year

As 183 starters set out on the 1969 Monte Carlo Rally in January it was anybody's guess who would win the most glamorous of all rallies. First to reach Monaco were Aaltonen

Porsche took the first four places in the Spa 24-hours.

and Liddon in a Lancia Fulvia HF, but the real testing time starts later—up in the mountains behind the Principality: 158 cars were left in for the special stages, 111 of them with clean sheets. By the final stage only 44 cars remained in the running, and only 27 of those finished the gruelling 12-hour dash through snow and ice. The winner was Waldegaard in a Porsche 911S, closely followed by team-mate Larousse; third was Jean Vinatier in an Alpine-Renault. Ford's new French driver, Piot, managed to bring an Escort Twin-Cam into fourth place. Pat Moss-Carlsson took the *Coupe des Dames* in a Lancia Fulvia.

In the Swedish Rally, run on the traditional ice-covered roads and tracks ploughed through the snow on frozen lakes, Waldegaard in a Porsche won, ahead of Lampinen and Hertz in a Saab and Eriksson and Johansson in an Opel Rallye Kadett. The 1969 East African Safari, which was claimed to be the roughest and fastest event ever held, was won by Robin Hillyar and Jock Aird in a German Ford 20M, with a Volvo second and a Datsun third. Dust was the main problem, and many cars left the road or crashed into banks; only 32 of the 91 starters finished. Nevertheless, the winner averaged 60 m.p.h. for the entire distance.

Roger Clark won the Circuit of Ireland in a very special 1·8-litre Twin-Cam Ford Escort, built to conquer the works BMC Mini-Coopers, which, however, took second, third, and fourth places. On its second outing, the Escort won the Welsh International Rally, and in the Tulip Rally in Holland a British works-built Ford Twin-Cam won from a starting field of 86 cars. Just to show their versatility, Porsche won the Acropolis Rally in Greece, but Roger Clark and Jim Porter drove a works Twin-Cam Ford Escort into second place. Only 15 cars finished in this event. In the Scottish Rally through the forests it was a win for Simo Lampinen navigated by A. Hertz in a Saab 96, with a Hillman Imp second, and a Ford Escort third. Rosemary Smith in another Escort took the *Coupe des Dames* with sixth place overall. Vinatier won the Alpine Rally for the second time in an Alpine-Renault, second and third places being taken by the same make. The 2,400-mile R.A.C. Round Britain rally in the snow and ice of November was won by the Swedes Kallstrom and Haggbom in a Lancia Fulvia. Scandinavian drivers took eight of the first ten places.

New Models at the Shows

The year started with the announcement of major styling changes to the big Triumph sports car which became the TR6. Mechanically there was little difference; the 2½-litre fuel injection engine and all-independent rear suspension were retained, but the outside took on the most integrated sleek shape that the TR has ever boasted. Alfa Romeo announced detail changes to their 1300 and 1600 models, with improved braking and roadholding and

Ford Capri 2000 GT

Peugeot 504 coupé

Opel Diplomat

Citroen Ami 8

some improvements to trim and comfort. Reliant took over Bond Cars, both firms having complementary models of three and four wheelers with glass-fibre bodies.

Ford broke entirely new ground when they put their new Capri on the market in the last week of January. This fastback four-seater was a stylish attempt to break into the "sporty" car market. Mechanically the new model was based on existing components, with Cortina-like suspension, Escort-type rack-and-pinion steering, and a choice of engines spanning the whole Ford range from 1300 c.c. to 3-litre vee-6. As well as being built in the U.K. the Capri was Cologne-built for Common Market consumption, the later cars being fitted with the German range of engines. Early in March Opel announced a very sophisticated new range of large saloons, the models being called Kapitan, Admiral, and Diplomat. Bosch electronic fuel injection was introduced as a new option, and a complex but very effective independent rear suspension made the ride and handling outstanding.

In France Peugeot introduced convertible and coupé bodies for their very successful 504 model, with styling by Pininfarina. Fiat announced first details of their new prestige car, the 130, powered by a new 2·9-litre o.h.c. vee-6 engine; automatic transmission is standard in this car, and suspension is independent all round, with coil-spring struts at each corner. In readiness for the Geneva Motor Show in

March, Lancia introduced a new 2-litre coupé version of their Flavia, with front-wheel drive and a sleek new body by Pininfarina, and Citroen brought out a new small derivative of their famous 2CV, called the Ami 8. In the U.S.A., Ford's new small car, designed to combat the invasion by European and Japanese cars, was called the Maverick. Reckoned to be the American idea of what a third family car should be like, it was entirely conventional in styling and mechanical specification, with an in-line six-cylinder engine and live rear axle.

The long-awaited new BMC 1500 was unveiled on April 24 by British Leyland. Called the Austin Maxi, it is a five-door dual-purpose vehicle, with transverse engine and front-wheel drive. The engine is a new overhead camshaft unit, with an output of 74 b.h.p. net at 5,500 r.p.m. Hydrolastic suspension is used all round, and the car features many advanced items such as five-speed gear-box, servo-assisted disc brakes, two-speed wipers, and reclining seats fore and aft. Almost at the same time, Fiat announced a new front-drive 1100 model called the 128. This, too, featured a single-overhead camshaft engine mounted transversely and driving the front wheels. In engineering it followed established Autobianchi practice, with the gear-box at one side of the engine driving through unequal length shafts. Soon after, Autobianchi showed their new A111, based on the same bodyshell but

Austin Maxi 1500

Hillman GT

Fiat 128 (1100 c.c.)

Mini 1275 GT

powered by the Primula 1,438 c.c. pushrod engine. It utilised the same engine installation as the 128, but with different front and rear suspension systems.

Mercedes startled the motoring world in the middle of August by suddenly announcing details of an experimental Wankel-engined GT coupé. It had a bold wedge profile and a triple-rotor engine developing 280 b.h.p. There were no plans for production at that time, but several seem to have been built. After many rumours and "sneak" pictures, the long-awaited Volks-Porsche was produced in time for the Frankfort show in September. It was a mid-engined sports two-seater, with either a four-cylinder Volkswagen or a six-cylinder Porsche engine. Mercedes came out with a new 3·5-litre vee-8 engine for their prestige cars, and Opel showed two experimental coupés, one based on the Rekord, the other on their new Diplomat. Peugeot brought out a new model called the 304, which was based on the little 204, with larger (1,288 c.c.) engine and longer overhangs at front and rear. Shortly after came the new Renault 12, another small 1300 saloon with front-drive like the Peugeot; in the Renault the engine is placed ahead of the front wheels for the first time.

As a start to the British motor show season, Rootes announced a new version of their Hunter, with more powerful engine and less luxurious trim. Called the Hillman GT, it is based on the 1968 London-Sydney Marathon-winning car. More exciting was the introduction of a new vee-8 engine for the Aston Martin BBS, with overhead cams and Bosch fuel injection. It is claimed to give the car a of top speed of 171 m.p.h., making this the world's fastest four-seater.

British Leyland updated their 1100/1300 models with a new GT version, and Vauxhall re-introduced the VX 4/90 based on the Victor 2000. Daimler announced a new version of the Sovereign, which was little more than an XJ6 with distinguishing touches; and the 3-litre vee-6 version of the Ford Capri finally reached production. British Leyland continued their face-lift programme with a new front and revised interior for the Mini, and new front and rear ends on the Triumph 2000. The Austin and Morris prefixes for the Minis were dropped, the models becoming the Mini Clubman and Mini 1275 GT. The Triumph also received a new interior, plus wider rear track and a much bigger boot. All the BLMC sports cars were updated to comply with the latest U.S. Federal safety regulations, with more interior padding and distinctive exterior changes. Just before the Turin show, Autobianchi introduced a new front-drive minicar, with Fiat 850 engine mounted transversely. Fiat themselves put bigger engines in their Dino and 124 Sport models, and announced the terms on which they had taken over control of Lancia.

Renault 12 (1289 c.c.)

New Sunbeam Alpine

Volks-Porsche sports

Triumph 2000 Mark II

The Anglo-French supersonic airliner Concorde 001 touching down at Toulouse after its maiden flight in March.

New Shapes in the Sky

G. R. WRIXON, A.R.Ae.S.

MAN'S FIRST FOOTSTEPS on the moon fired the world's imagination almost to the exclusion of his more mundane achievements in aviation here on Earth. But 1969 will go down as a milestone in aeronautical history primarily because supersonic transports proved they will fly, and fly at the speeds for which they have been designed; jumbo jets, too, not only flew but also began to come off the mass-production lines; and perhaps the year's final claim to fame is that, sadly, the oldest aircraft manufacturer in the world was only saved at the eleventh hour from going into liquidation.

Keeping their promise made some years ago, the Russians just managed to fly the world's first supersonic transport on the last day of 1968. The Tupolev Tu-144 swept into the air for the first time at an unnamed airport near Moscow two months ahead of its Western rival, the Anglo-French Concorde, which first flew at Toulouse on March 2. Indecision still dogged the American SST, which suffered a major setback in 1968 when Boeing was forced by increasing design weight to abandon its swing-wing design in favour of a fixed double-delta configuration. It was not until September 23, 1969, that President Nixon made up his mind and gave the aircraft the go-ahead.

Concorde 002, the second prototype, assembled by the British Aircraft Corporation at Bristol, took to the air on April 9, so that by the time of the Paris Aero Show in June it was possible for both Concordes to be seen

together in the air over Le Bourget. Hotly denied rumours that the Russian Tu-144 had crashed were largely dispelled when the official Soviet news agency claimed the aircraft had exceeded the speed of sound for the first time on June 5. Concorde 001 had to wait until October 1 before she achieved this distinction. It was during the 45th flight of the French prototype that chief test pilot André Turcat and Jean Pinet held the aircraft at a speed of Mach 1·05 for about 10 minutes during a 110-minute flight. At a height of 36,000 ft. supersonic flight was possible overland close to Toulouse because at that speed no shock wave would be heard on the ground below. At present fitted with Rolls-Royce Olympus 593 Phase 2A engines, 001 is capable of Mach 1·3, but with Olympus 593-3B engines both 001 and 002 should be able to exceed Mach 2. The British prototype is expected to be the first to reach the double sonic speed.

Rising costs, however, still proved embarrassing to both the French and British governments, who, during the year, admitted officially that the development cost of the Concorde had risen to some £730 million. Other estimates made earlier in the year (taking into account the effects of inflation and devaluation) suggested that some £485 million of British public money is at risk, and a total of nearly £1,000 million between both countries. Assuming that sales of the Concorde amount to

D

The American Boeing 747—known as the "jumbo jet"—left the ground in February, ran into engine trouble later in the year, but made her first passenger-carrying flight with a cargo of journalists successfully in December.
The Boeing Company

some 200 aircraft, rather less than half of the cost is likely to be recoverable. The cost of the one-year delay in the first flight, originally scheduled for February 28, 1968, is alone estimated to be of the order of £100 million.

General Ziegler, chief of Sud-Aviation, said, during 1969 that the Concorde might not be in operational service before 1974. Although, admittedly, the pressure has been reduced by the delays to the Boeing SST, this new date is a reflection of the cumulative result of the first flight delay and many other factors. Design refinements proposed by the manufacturers during the year, applicable to production line aircraft, were put forward in order to ensure that the Concorde has a healthy margin of payload over and above the 25,000 lb. Sud-Aviation and B.A.C. have always guaranteed. Slight modifications are to be made to the wing leading edges and air intakes, and the fineness ratio (streamlining) of the rear fuselage and fin is to be improved. But the results of the flight tests proved very encouraging. The two companies are no longer worried about the fuel consumption at subsonic speeds. If supersonic transports are not allowed to fly at their normal Mach 2-plus speeds over land, the Concorde will still be a viable commercial proposition for airlines when flying subsonically during part of its journey.

It should be possible to have two prototypes of the Boeing SST flying by the end of 1972.

An artist's impression of Concorde's projected rival, the Boeing SST, prototypes of which should fly in 1972. President Nixon approved this aircraft in September 1969.

Nearly £320 million has been allocated for the next five years, which is claimed to be sufficent to achieve this aim. Total cost of the overall programme is likely to approach £2,000 million, nearly three times the original estimate. Boeing had expected that after selling 300 SSTs it would start making a profit, but with this colossal escalation of costs the break-even point is no longer clear. The decision to go ahead with the Boeing will, strangely enough, help Concorde sales; indecision about the American plane made prospective purchasers rather dubious about all SSTs, but with the U.S.A. in the league supersonic transports have become "internationally respectable."

The Boeing 2707-300 (as the new version of the SST is designated) is to be built primarily of titanium alloy, which will permit cruising flight at Mach 2·7 at altitudes of 60,000 ft. to 70,000 ft. It will be powered by four General Electric GE4/J5P afterburning turbojets, each of 67,000-lb. take-off thrust. The passenger cabin, 176 ft. long, will seat, in the all-tourist configuration, 298 passengers seated six abreast.

Another Boeing product was the first of the new large-capacity jets to fly. This was the Boeing 747, which has earned the popular description of "jumbo jet." Chief test pilot Jack Waddell eased the 747 off the runway at Paine Field near the Everett factory north of Seattle for the first time on February 9, only seven weeks after the original target date. During an 80-minute flight it reached 300 m.p.h. and 15,000 ft. The 231-ft.-long Boeing 747, which weighed 300 tons, took about 4,500 ft. to get airborne. Observers commented on the quietness of its four giant Pratt & Whitney JT9D engines. After this good start and its impressive appearance at the Paris Aero Show, it was disappointing that by September apparently all was not well, for completed 747s without their engines were standing idly at Everett. Towards the end of the year Pan American announced that it would have to postpone the first 747 service from New York to London, from December 15 to January 22, 1970, after Boeing had admitted that delivery of the aircraft would be up to two months late. The hold-up in delivery of the engines was due to an increase of 5 per cent on estimated fuel consumption, and the failure of the engine to maintain its guaranteed 43,500-lb. thrust. The engine casings were suffering from distortion under load.

The Boeing 747, which can carry 490 one-class passengers, and 362 in its first-and-tourist-class version, will be the long-haul airliner of the 1970s. Two other large-capacity jets under development in the U.S.A. are the Lockheed L-1011 TriStar and the McDonnell Douglas DC-10, although these are intended for somewhat shorter stages than the Boeing. They are in direct competition, and the year saw a growing rivalry between the two manufacturers as each announced new, bigger, and longer-range derivatives. Lockheed's TriStar is powered by the British Rolls-Royce RB.211 fan engine, while the DC-10 will have the American General Electric CF6. Both companies, however, are having to consider the use of versions of the Pratt & Whitney JT9D favoured by certain customers because of its use in the 747. The L-1011-8·4, as the long range version of the TriStar is called, will be powered by 52,500-lb.-thrust RB.211-56 engines, and should weigh 575,000 lb. for take-off. Normal load is 280 passengers, and certification should be obtained by the autumn of 1973. Assembly of the first TriStar began at the end of August, and deliveries of the early version will begin in 1971. Short Brothers at Belfast, Northern Ireland, will build the TriStar's ailerons, spoilers, wing tips, and engine pods.

Assembly of the first DC-10 began on June 23, 1969, 14 months after the go-ahead was given. The DC-10 Series 10 (the standard American domestic version) weighs 410,000 lb. and is powered by three GE CF6-6 engines each of 40,000-lb. thrust. A version with 45,000-lb.-thrust JT9D-15s is known as the DC-10 Series 20, while the Series 30 will have 49,000-lb.-thrust CF6-50A engines and a gross weight of 530,000 lb. This last version will carry a mixed class load of 253 passengers, but the aircraft should be capable of carrying up to 345 if necessary; it has been ordered by KLM, Swissair, Sabena, and UTA (called from their initials the KSSU group).

Towards the end of 1968 the European Airbus consortium, made up of Sud-Aviation, Hawker Siddeley Aviation, and Deutsche Airbus, decided on a revised configuration for the A-300 aircraft, which was to be smaller and powered by Rolls-Royce RB.211 engines instead of the bigger RB.207 engines originally specified. The British government had long declined to commit itself to a decision to go ahead with its share of the project, and seized upon the new configuration as an excuse for "further reconsideration." Tired of waiting

Seating up to 345 passengers, Lockheed's TriStar was one of the competing long-haul jets under construction in 1969.
Lockheed Aircraft Corporation

A model of B.A.C.'s short-haul airbus, the Three-Eleven which may rival the European A-300 project.
B.A.C. photo

for a British decision, France and Germany decided to go ahead alone with the airbus, and after a meeting in London on April 10 the British government finally pulled out. It had always been a British condition that the Rolls-Royce engine should be chosen, but now the French and Germans felt free to consider the use of two American CF-6 or JT9D engines instead of the Rolls-Royce.

Hawker Siddeley Aviation, which had played a leading part in the design of the A-300 project, was left high and dry by the British government. But it was prepared to put up some of its own money for the project, with or without the British government's co-operation, and on July 24 the company reached an agreement in principle with the French and German partners that it would play the role of design consultant. Germany was believed to be putting up 75 per cent of the launching costs, and Hawker Siddeley was likely to contribute more than £10 million. By October Hawker Siddeley reported that it was buying materials and setting up jigs to produce six sets of wings for the airbus. The prototype of this product of European co-operation is due to fly in 1972.

Two other contenders for the short-haul airbus market are in the running—the B.A.C. Three-Eleven and the Dassault Mercure II.

Work started on a smaller Continental airbus, the Dassault Mercure II, during July.
Avions Marcel Dassault

The plan for the Three-Eleven is that the British government might meet half the costs, but only when 50 firm orders have been obtained. The Three-Eleven uses the same RB.211 engines as the Lockheed TriStar, and B.A.C. was discussing with Lockheed the possibility of the American company's building the nose and flight deck under sub-contract. In August, in response to the reactions of international airlines, B.A.C. increased the payload of the Three-Eleven, and it now stands at 62,500 lb. over a range of nearly 1,700 nautical miles. Eight-abreast seating will provide tourist class accommodation for 214 passengers, but up to 294 seats nine-abreast can be provided for inclusive tour passengers.

Dassault showed a full-scale mock-up of the 130–160-seat twin-jet Mercure at the Paris Aero Show. Two 15,000-lb.-thrust Pratt and Whitney JT8D-11 engines will provide the power. The French government has agreed to meet 56 per cent of the costs, and 30 per cent will be provided by Italy, Spain, Belgium, and Switzerland. Dassault itself will put up the remaining 14 per cent. With characteristic initiative Dassault was already building the plane by the end of July.

Handley Page Ltd., which became a public company on June 17, 1909, can rightly claim to be the oldest aircraft manufacturer in the world. It refused to join one of the great mergers of British aircraft companies set up in 1960. Three days after it celebrated its 60th anniversary, financial troubles were revealed which led to the appointment of a receiver on August 8. Handley Page built famous aircraft at Cricklewood and Radlett throughout its 60 years, notably the O/400 and V/1500 bombers of the First World War, the highly successful HP.42 civil airliners of the 1930s, and the Hampden and Halifax bombers of the 1939–45 War. In 1966 the company broke away from its traditionally large aircraft to embark on the twin turboprop Jetstream feeder-line and business aircraft, which was to be the first of a line of smaller types of up to 15,000 lb. gross weight. Delays due to attempts to solve the problem of excess weight set the programme back about nine months, but by early January 1969 the first production Jetstream had gone to the American agents for fitting out, and CSE Aircraft Services had received the first for a U.K. customer, also for fitting out and painting.

At the time that the Handley Page board suffered a complete change of directors on June 20, there were 91 firm orders for the Jetstream and negotiations were in progress on another 90. Despite this the company had to announce, on August 8, that it was without

The year saw the equipment of the R.A.F.'s first Phantom Mark 2 squadron. Similar fighters will eventually be phased out by the Royal Navy.

the financial resources to carry on, and creditors were forced to foreclose. Talks were opened with the K. R. Craven Group of St. Louis, Mo. (owners of the American distributors of the Jetstream), to see if the injection of American capital could save the company, and on October 20 terms were agreed, and Handley Page became the property of an American consortium headed by Craven's. The U.K. Ministry of Technology helped to make this possible by promising to give Handley Page a £20 million contract for converting Victor Mark 2 bombers into tankers for the R.A.F. By the beginning of 1970 the company was advertising for more workers.

The year saw other notable developments in the commercial aviation scene. Briefly, these include the publication of the Edwards Report on British air transport, which looks for a powerful civil aviation authority to encourage more competition between the state airline corporations and the independents; the cheering news that both B.O.A.C. and B.E.A. made substantial profits during 1969, despite the former's loss of £8 million due to a prolonged strike by the pilots; and developments at London's Heathrow Airport where the new Terminal One was opened by the Queen to cater for the capital's domestic services to points within the U.K.

Edwards proposed the creation of a National Air Holdings Board which would have financial and policy-making control over B.O.A.C. and B.E.A.—suggesting that the corporations should engage in inclusive tour and charter operations. The report said that private airlines should be encouraged to group together as a "second force" operator, and that some subsidies were justified on certain

domestic routes on the grounds of regional policy.

Military Aviation

Nothing made its mark more surely on the military scene than the public demonstrations of the Hawker Siddeley Harrier vertical take-off fighter in London and New York afforded by the *Daily Mail* Transatlantic Air Race (see pp. 213–216). In the U.S.A. the demonstrations must have had a profound influence on the confirmation of the order for twelve Harriers, placed by the American government for the U.S. Marine Corps to use possibly in South-East Asia. Meanwhile in Britain the first R.A.F. squadron of Harriers (No. 1 Squadron) was formed at Wittering in Northamptonshire; the Harrier T2, a two-seater trainer version, flew (and unfortunately the prototype was seriously damaged in a crash which injured test pilot Duncan Simpson); and another Harrier carried out shipborne trials at sea on H.M.S. *Blake*.

Hawker Siddeley's Harrier, a vertical take-off fighter which can operate from a clearing no bigger than a tennis court.
Hawker Siddeley

53

The Anglo-French Jaguar, a tactical support fighter and trainer, flew in time for the Paris Aero Show, in June.
B.A.C. photo

Phantoms continued working up with the Royal Navy at Yeovilton, and the first R.A.F. Phantom squadron (No. 6) was forming during January at Coningsby. These aircraft will have a limited life with the Royal Navy, which will be phasing out its aircraft carriers during the early 1970s. The R.A.F. will inherit the Navy's aircraft. It is already receiving new versions of the Hawker Siddeley Buccaneer naval strike aircraft, which went into R.A.F. service with an Operational Conversion Unit at the Royal Navy's airfield at Lossiemouth during the year. The Royal Navy's future role in aviation will be the operation of helicopter task forces, and the first of the American-designed, Westland-built Sea King anti-submarine helicopters were delivered to the naval station at Culdrose in Cornwall in 1969.

Among other new aircraft the R.A.F. took delivery of the first of its Hawker Siddeley Nimrod anti-submarine aircraft in October. The Nimrod, which is based on the design of the civil Comet 4C, carries sophisticated radar and sonar detection gear and allows its crews to carry out their long ocean patrols comfortably. France and Britain went steadily ahead with the Jaguar tactical support and trainer aircraft. By the time of the Paris Aero Show four French prototypes had flown, and the first British-assembled Jaguar made its first flight late in the year. The first four were two "E" two-seat trainers and two "A" single-seat tactical support versions.

Farther in the future, there is the European multi-role combat aircraft (M.R.C.A.), in which Britain, Germany, and Italy are interested. Holland, originally a partner, withdrew during the year. About 1,000 M.R.C.A.s are to be built for service with the R.A.F. and the German and Italian air forces from the mid-1970s. They will be powered by Rolls-Royce RB.199 engines. The 24 American-built F-111 fighters for the Royal Australian Air Force will be delivered after all. Training of R.A.A.F. crews in America was halted when cracks were found to have developed during tests in the aircraft's wing carry-through box—part of the swing-wing mechanism. For some time it seemed likely that the Australian government was trying to opt out of its contract to buy the aircraft but, with massive guarantees, deliveries will now go ahead.

In October the R.A.F. received the first of its Nimrods—Hawker Siddeley's anti-submarine aircraft based on the Comet 4C.
Hawker Siddeley Aviation

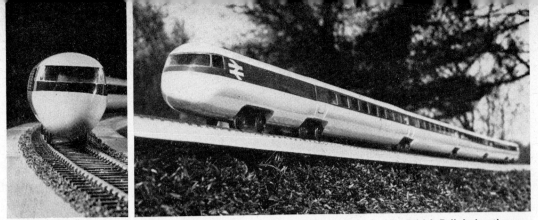

A sleek model of the APT (Advanced Passenger Train) which was being researched by British Rail during the year. The coaches will tilt inwards as they round curves (*left*) at up to 150 m.p.h. *British Rail*

Brighter Future for Railways

CECIL J. ALLEN, M.Inst.T., A.I.Loco.E.

GREAT INTEREST was shown during 1969 in the APT (Advanced Passenger Train) project which is being worked out by the British Railways Research Establishment at Derby. It is generally conceded that this is the largest and best-equipped research centre of its kind owned by any railway system in the world other than the Japanese, and it is not surprising that the five-year research programme is attracting world-wide attention. Indeed, the best-known U.S. firm building high-speed railway rolling stock is already in negotiation for a licence to build trains of the APT type as soon as the production stage is reached.

In the design a complete break-through in railway technology is being aimed at. The main features will be a revolutionary reduction in train weight compared with the present standard designs of rolling stock; a mechanism for tilting the coach-bodies on curves to make it possible to traverse these at speeds higher than any previously attempted, without risk or discomfort to passengers; and propulsion by gas turbine instead of diesel or electric power, although the latter may be used later for APTs that may come into service on electrified lines.

Lightness will be achieved in two ways. Using well-tried aeroplane techniques, each coach-body will be of stressed-skin aluminium construction; and each coach will be carried on two axles only, instead of on the normal four-wheel bogies. Precisely what form the suspension will take is at present a secret, as patent applications are pending. The sides of each train will be completely streamlined, with rubber fairings joining coach to coach, so as to present an uninterruptedly smooth surface from end to end, with skirts reaching down almost to rail level. Bullet-nosed motor-coaches will cut down head-end air-resistance to a minimum.

The first line selected for APT operation is to be from King's Cross to Newcastle. Needless to say, higher speeds round curves will involve the smoothing out of existing curves to the utmost extent that finance will permit, and the present stretches of automatic signalling north of York will need to be extended to cover the whole route from King's Cross. Part of the research is being devoted to a new system of train control, known as the "wiggly wire" method because it involves laying down between the running rails two continuous wires which change places from time to time. In conjunction with coded currents passing through the running rails the wires will indicate to drivers precisely what is the state of the line ahead of them, and also will permit conversations between drivers and control centres, showing in the latter the exact position and speed of every train in the controlled area.

Some 14 miles of the disused London Midland main line between Melton Mowbray and Leicester are being prepared for thorough testing of the new trains before they go into service. The tests should begin in 1970 or 1971, but it will probably be 1974 before Advanced Passenger Trains are in regular service. The aim is for speeds up to 150 m.p.h. (the trains will actually be capable of speeds up to 200 m.p.h.). With 150 m.p.h. over suitably aligned sections it will be possible to bring the present fastest time of 3 hours 35 minutes between London and Newcastle

The "wiggly wire" system of train control which, in conjunction with coded currents passing along the rails, shows on the driver's indicator panel (*left*) the exact state of the line ahead.   *British Rail*

down to 2 hours 40 minutes. But for the preliminary stage 125 m.p.h. may be the limit.

Setbacks and Successes

In North America the electric "Silverliners" of the Penn Central railroad, introduced at the end of 1968, were beset by teething troubles, and by the autumn of 1969 no more than six six-coach trains had come into operation. Five of these, renamed "Metroliners," were covering the 226½ miles between New York and Washington in 2 hours 59 minutes, including five intermediate stops; while the sixth, for the first time in U.S. history, was making the run non-stop in 2¼ hours, at an average of 90 m.p.h., despite the slow running needed round the curves in Philadelphia and Baltimore and the slow entrances to and exits from the New York and Washington terminals. The revolutionary "turbo-trains" of Canadian National Railways, between Montreal and Toronto, were even less fortunate; their early troubles were so serious that they had to be taken out of service altogether.

On the Continent trains are getting faster and faster, especially in France and Germany. Although the first short lengths of line in each country over which 125 m.p.h. speeds are authorised have not been extended—doubtless because of the costly speed control equipment required—speeds of up to 100 m.p.h. are now being run freely over many main lines in both countries. The famous French "Mistral," re-equipped with a magnificent set of new coaches (including such amenities as a hairdressing salon and a small shop), runs the 535½ miles from Paris to Marseilles in 6 hours 40 minutes, at an overall average of 80·3 m.p.h., including four intermediate stops. On the other side of the country the new Paris–Madrid "Puerta del Sol," introduced in 1969, takes just under 4¼ hours for the 359¾ miles from Paris to Bordeaux, running this distance non-stop at an average of 85·3 m.p.h.

As yet no European run approaches the speeds of the famous New Tokaido Line in Japan, over which the daily runs scheduled at over 100 m.p.h. from start to stop have now

The French "Mistral's" new coaches include a hairdressing salon (*left*) and a boutique.   *S N.C.F*

reached a total of 114, including 54 booked at 106·5 m.p.h., with many others nearly as fast. These speeds are over a brand new main line, laid out regardless of cost expressly for speed, with no restrictions whatever other than a general limitation to 130 m.p.h. In the densely populated industrial countries of Western Europe similar new lines engineered for high speed would be a godsend, but the deterrent, of course, is finance. Yet this prospect has been, and is being, faced in both Italy and France.

The Italian State Railways in 1927 and 1934 opened two new main lines laid out at great expense for high-speed travel, the first from Rome to Naples, and the second (including the 11½-mile Apennine tunnel) from Bologna to Florence; both these *direttissima* routes avoided the severe gradients and curvature of previous routes, and this made possible substantial accelerations. Now a still more ambitious line is planned from Florence to Rome, reducing the 196¼-mile route to 160 miles, and making possible a time of 90–100 minutes in place of the present fastest of just under 3 hours. Some 38 miles of tunnelling will be needed, and the layout will permit speeds of up to 150 m.p.h.

The French National Railways are similarly thinking of a possible new direct line between Paris and Lyons, using the existing main line for 15 miles out of Paris and 10 miles into Lyons, but the remainder being entirely new. With the help of much tunnelling the proposed line, with no curves of less than 2 miles radius and no gradients steeper than 1 in 333, would cut the present distance of 317½ miles to between 265 and 270 miles. There would be no lineside signals, but, as on the Japanese New Tokaido Line, the entire working would be controlled electrically from a panel in Paris.

Electrification would be unnecessary; a high-speed half-hourly service would be maintained by four-coach streamlined sets driven by gas turbines. If a speed as high as 300 km.p.h. (186 m.p.h.) proved practicable, the duration of the Paris–Lyons journey could be brought down from its present fastest of 3¾ hours to less than 2 hours. French engineers calculate that such a line could be built at a cost of £350,000 per mile, compared with £910,000 per mile of the Japanese New Tokaido Line, but engineers of other countries are sceptical. French National Railways are already introducing gas-turbine-driven trains over routes which do not carry sufficient traffic to justify electrification; the first of these is between Paris (the St. Lazare terminus) and Cherbourg.

The Talgo building (*below left*) stands astride the point at which differing gauges meet at Port Bou on the Franco-Spanish frontier. As coaches pass through it (*bottom*) their bogies are changed for the track ahead; giant jacks (*below right*) lift the locomotives for bogie-changing.
S.N.C.F. and R.E.N.F.E.

Bogie-changing at Frontiers

The new "Puerta del Sol" express has brought about a new method of working between the French and Spanish capitals. The French track gauge, like that of Great Britain and most European countries, is 4 ft. 8½ in., but that of Spain and Portugal is 5 ft. 6 in.; yet the "Puerta del Sol" sleeping cars run through across the frontier. It is done by lifting the coaches bodily with special equipment at the frontier station of Hendaye, and changing the 4 ft. 8½ in. gauge bogies for those of the 5 ft. 6 in. gauge. The frontier stop for this purpose lasts 45 minutes.

On the other side of the two countries a similar operation is carried out at Port Bou with a train called the "Catalan," which runs between Barcelona and Geneva by way of Narbonne, Avignon, and Grenoble. The "Catalan" is a "Talgo" train, of a unique type which has been running in Spain for some years. Each "Talgo" train is like a snake, with very short coach units of which the ends of adjacent coaches are carried on a single pair of wheels. The Port Bou installation can deal with three coaches at a time, and is so expeditious that the frontier stop lasts no more than 20 minutes.

The idea of bogie-changing is not new. The Russian track gauge of 5 ft. also differs from that of the rest of Europe, and some time ago the Russians installed bogie-changing facilities at Brest-Litovsk, on the Russo-Polish frontier. The idea at first was to make possible through running between the U.S.S.R. and other Iron Curtain countries, but today massive Russian sleeping cars are also run through between Moscow and points all over Europe, including the Hook of Holland, Ostend, Paris, Vienna, Copenhagen, Stockholm, Oslo, and Rome. The Russian bogie-changing equipment, which also involves the bodily lifting of each coach or wagon, is considerably slower in action than that at Hendaye or Port Bou; normally some 2 hours are allowed for the frontier stop, including passport and customs formalities. Bogie-changing was—and still is—carried out in Australia, where different gauge tracks have severely impeded railway development for a hundred years. In 1970 the first trans-continental standard gauge passenger train from Sydney to Perth has become possible through the relaying of stretches of both narrow and wide gauge. The story of this achievement is told elsewhere (see "Australia Moves—Faster, Faster," pp. 280–284).

Continuous Welded Rails

The trend towards higher speeds demands simultaneous developments in track design. Until now the only changes from past practice have been the welding of rails into long continuous units and the substitution of pre-stressed concrete for timber sleepers.

During 1969 the continuous welding of rails was much in the public eye, mainly because the derailment of two express trains in unusually hot weather was thought to have been due to the buckling of continuously welded track. It was little short of miraculous that when the Tees–Tyne Pullman left the rails at Sandy, Beds, at between 90 and 100 m.p.h., presumably from this cause, no more than a few minor injuries were suffered by passengers —a tribute to the effectiveness of the British (and American) buckeye couplers between coaches, which like a series of firm steel handclasps often succeed in keeping the coach-ends in line even in serious accidents. Less fortunate were the 65 injured when a Paignton–Paddington holiday express left the rails at Somerton, Somerset, at an estimated speed of between 60 and 70 m.p.h.

It is a good many years since rail-welding first began, and in some countries, such as Germany, it has gone considerably farther than in Great Britain. The rail-joint is the weakest point in the track, and because of the battering that it receives as the wheels pass over the gaps, small though they are, the rails tend to get depressed at the joint, which needs frequent packing up on the ballast in order to keep the running surface of the rails perfectly level. Vibration from this cause also increases the wear-and-tear of rolling stock. The main reason for welding the rails together is to close these gaps, and so reduce the cost of maintaining both track and rolling stock; that the

Russian sleeping car in a Paris terminus.   *S.N.C.F.*

This gigantic German "train" picks up old rails and sleepers and lays new, as it moves continuously forward at a speed of 750 ft. per hour.

passenger gets a smoother and quieter ride is an incidental benefit.

The question invariably asked is how the rails manage to expand in hot weather if no gap is left between them. The answer, proved by experience, is that if they are held sufficiently tightly, the tendency to expand or contract with extremes of temperature is confined within the steel as a stress which is relieved only when they return to the temperature at which they were laid. A vital part in the secure holding is played by the ballast. It is essential that this shall be ample in quantity, and tightly packed round the sleeper ends, as in very hot weather any weakness in the holding of the sleepers may allow the rails to buckle. That this is so rare an occurrence shows that continuous welding

British experimental paved concrete track.

is reasonably safe, and it is now regarded as standard procedure.

In central depots the 60-ft. rails are electrically welded into lengths of 300 ft. or more, which are then run in specially equipped rail trains to the site; here the long lengths are welded again into continuous lengths often broken only by switch and crossing work. In earlier continuous welding practice, "breather" joints, in form like splices, were laid between one long length and the next, to give a little more scope for expansion than ordinary joints, but in general such special provision is no longer thought to be necessary.

Experiments are now being made in both Great Britain and Germany in the continuous support of rails on concrete. One system consists of a framework made up of longitudinal as well as transverse concrete slabs; another is a paved track of concrete 1 ft. thick and 8 ft. 6 in. wide, on which the rails are mounted with no ballast. New methods are also being developed to expedite the replacement of worn track. One Continental firm is now producing equipment with which a gang of 51 men can relay a stretch of track completely at a speed of 750 ft. per hour (over a mile in a single 8-hour shift), no preparatory or follow-up work being needed. The new track, completely assembled, is brought to the site on a rail train which also carries away bodily the track which is being replaced. In this and other ways the former lengthy operation of relaying, with its "C" and "T" ("Commences" and "Terminates") lineside boards compelling all trains to reduce speed severely over a matter of weeks, is being replaced by quicker methods. Altogether, as we enter the 1970s, the railways of the world can be said to be facing a brighter future.

The Shape of Things at Sea

PETER R. FISHER
of *Lloyd's List and Shipping Gazette*

Tanker of about 214,000 tons d.w. discharging crude oil at Milford Haven. This is the most profitable size for tankers at present. *BP photo*

OVER THE LAST FIVE YEARS the shipping industry has made tremendous technological advances: tanker sizes have rocketed beyond the 300,000-ton deadweight mark, combination carriers have passed 150,000 tons, and the container ship has arrived. 1969 saw no comparable gigantic strides forward, but was rather a year when the industry took stock. This was particularly so in the tanker field.

The total world tanker tonnage continued to grow. During the year over 18 million tons was added to the world fleet—some 68 per cent more than was delivered in 1968, which was itself a record. The size of individual tankers also continued to grow. As the Gulf Oil giants of 325,000 tons d.w. began to scurry to and fro between the Persian Gulf and Bantry Bay the question shipping men all over the world were asking was which country would be the first to break the 400,000-ton barrier. Leading shipbuilders and the classification societies—the associations which work out the "rules" about strength of materials and the construction of ships—were already preparing to design these mammoth tankers. Indeed, one Japanese oil company ordered a 370,000-tonner, and was negotiating for one between 420,000 and 450,000 tons. British shipbuilders were actively studying the design problems involved in building two tankers, one of 400,000 tons and one of 1,000,000 tons.

Logically, the bigger the tanker the cheaper it is to build; and the more cargo it can carry the lower is the cost of transport. However, there are other factors to be taken into account. One is the enormous insurance rates to be paid, particularly in respect of third-party liability. For example, when a really big tanker is involved in a collision or runs aground she may disgorge some 300,000 tons of crude oil; the *Torrey Canyon* disaster of 1967 showed what damage (the compensation was £3 million) this can cause to beaches (and consequently tourism) and to marine and bird life. British

Petroleum, Gulf Oil, Mobil Oil, Shell International Petroleum, Standard Oil of California, Esso Transport Company, and Texaco agreed in September that from October 6, 1969, should any of their tankers cause pollution, they would pay in compensation up to £45 per gross registered ton of the offending ship or £4,200,000, whichever is the less, to governments for expenses incurred in clearing fouled beaches. The agreement, known as the Tanker Owners Voluntary Agreement on Liability for Oil Pollution (TOVALOP), was reached in 1968, but only came into operation after owners of half the world's tanker tonnage had subscribed to it. (Japanese owners, with one of the world's largest tanker fleets, have not signed.) Owners pay increased insurance premiums to cover possible claims; the rates vary, those owners whose tankers carry dirty crude oil paying the most.

It is not surprising that the big oil companies are tending to move away from the really mammoth tanker and to concentrate on the economical 210,000-ton class. Cautious owners are waiting for the market to digest the full impact of the new tanker generation, and also to see whether there is any possibility of the reopening of the Suez Canal. At the other end of the scale, the oil companies will certainly no longer require vessels under 45,000 tons except to carry clean cargoes such as refined petroleum products.

Transport of oil "over the top of the world" became a matter of importance with the discovery in 1968 of gigantic deposits on the Northern Slope of Alaska, and opened up again the historic question of the possibility of the North West Passage—a challenge to adventurous seamen since John Cabot's first attempt in 1498. Amundsen made the passage in 1906, and six ships had completed it since then, but 1969 saw the first all-out attack on it in recent times. It was made by the most powerful U.S. merchant vessel, the 115,000-ton tanker *Manhattan*, 1,005 ft. long, strengthened and almost rebuilt for the voyage. She had been split into four sections and re-assembled, and given a 9-ft. wide steel belt round her hull, a new special bow, and underwater rudder-guards. On her historic voyage she was escorted by helicopters and smaller icebreakers, and carried a mixed party of 95 sailors, journalists, and scientists.

Leased by the Humble Oil company, she set out from Chester, Pennsylvania, called at Halifax, Nova Scotia, and entered the ice-bound waterway in the early part of September. She easily crushed the thinner ice of the first leg, but became stuck in Melville Sound on September 9 and again in McClure Strait on the 12th. She crashed her way through the first barrier, but in face of the second retraced her path and took the easier route through the Prince of Wales Strait into the Beaufort Sea. Finally, on September 20 she reached Prudhoe Bay, site of the biggest oil strikes, and took aboard a symbolic gold-painted barrel of oil in token of her epoch-making success in making the North West Passage.

Tramps and Liners

It is not only the tanker that has increased in size in recent years. Dry cargo ships have also made rapid strides both in size and speed. But the profitability of this type of vessel depends not only on the size of the ship but also on the size of the cargo openings to get the cargo in and

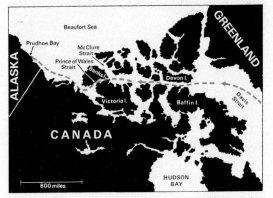

Route taken by the American ice-breaking tanker *Manhattan* on its historic sailing of the North West Passage in September.

out faster, as well as the fitting of sophisticated cargo-handling equipment to reduce the time spent in port. Twenty years ago the hatches into a ship's cargo holds were sealed by wooden slabs and tarpaulins, and to close or open them was a long and laborious process. Today hatches are usually made of steel and operated either hydraulically or electrically for rapid opening and closing. Modern cargo liners' speeds approach 30 knots—a far cry from the days of the old "tramp" which ploughed the seas at a steady seven knots or less. But up-to-date tramp ships are still produced in large numbers. The SD14, for example, designed and built on the River Wear, is one, and the *Conqueror*, designed by a London naval architect, is another. Others are the *Freedom* (built in Japan and Spain and designed by a Canadian), the Japanese standard, the joint German yard standard, and the Blöhm & Voss 4-alternative standard. All these are worthy replacements for the wartime Liberty ships which were designed to last 10 years and are still carrying cargoes 25 years later.

The biggest shipping event in 1969 was the eventual departure of Britain's newest liner,

Typical of the new generation of "tramp" steamers, the SD14 cargo vessel *Carina* (9,072 gross tons) was built by Austin and Pickersgill of Sunderland.

Skyphotos

The *Queen Elizabeth 2,* showing her great expanse of sheltered decks which include two swimming pools.

Queen Elizabeth 2, which finally sailed four months late from Southampton's Ocean Terminal on Friday, May 2, 1969, on her maiden North Atlantic voyage. A huge crowd gave her a big send-off with streamers and balloons, fireboats saluted her with high jets of water, and Buccaneers of the Fleet Air Arm wheeled overhead. New York gave her a similar welcome, televised live by satellite to her home country. The celebrations happily clouded public memory of her disastrous debut in December 1968, when her first sea trips had revealed serious engine defects which led to an open squabble between her owners and her builders and the appointment of a neutral expert to examine her troublesome turbine rotors. Instead of sailing on her first cruise in January 1969 she lay at Southampton while the rotors were taken out and flown back to Clydebank to be realigned. Further trials held in late March and early April proved successful, and she was handed over to Cunard on April 22. But the sad story was a bitter blow to the Upper Clyde Shipbuilding Group.

The *QE2* has passenger accommodation of the highest standard ever offered by a shipping line. While engaged on the North Atlantic she carries 2,025 passengers in two classes, and a crew of about 900. When cruising, accommodation is limited to 1,400 one-class passengers. Many luxury suites are available, and

the majority of passengers have cabins overlooking the sea. Glazed promenades cover the whole ship, and aft is a great expanse of terraced sheltered deck. There are two outdoor and two indoor swimming pools. The liner is fully air-conditioned. Space is available for 80 cars, which can be driven on board by means of special ramps, lifts being provided to take them to their deck positions. Conveyors, lifts, and escalators ensure swift handling of stores and baggage. There is space for 156,400 cubic ft. of cargo, lifted by two 5-ton cranes forward. The ship's vital statistics are:

Gross tonnage	..	..	65,863 tons
Overall length	..	..	963 ft.
Breadth	..	..	105 ft.
Height (keel to funnel base)			134½ ft.
Height of funnel structure	..		69½ ft.
Height (keel to masthead)	..		203 ft. 9¼ in.
Draught maximum	..	..	32 ft. 6 in.
Service speed..	..	..	28½ knots
Horsepower	..	..	110,000
Propellers	..	..	Two, six-bladed
Main boilers	..	..	Three
Steam pressure	..	..	850 lb.
Steam temperature	..	..	950°F.
Evaporation (sea water to fresh water)	..	..	1,200 tons daily
Number of decks	..	..	13
Deck space	..	..	6,000 sq. yd.
Theatre seats	..	..	530
Restaurant capacities:			
"The Columbia"	..	..	500
"The Grill Room"	..	..	100
"The Britannia"	..	..	815
Lifts	.. .. ..	..	22

One of the most talked-about features of the liner's silhouette is her single tall funnel. It appears to be something of an anachronism, but twenty designs were produced and tested in the wind tunnel at the National Physical Laboratory, Teddington, before it was approved. In spite of her inauspicious birth-pangs the *QE2* is far from the white elephant that some predicted. On North Atlantic service she had a load factor of 84 per cent, carrying over 40,000 passengers during the season; and her success helped to convert Cunard's 1968 passenger-ship loss of £1,100,000 into a profit of about £1 million.

Cruising Holidays

Another big passenger liner making her maiden voyage in 1969 was the German Atlantic Line's 25,000-ton gross, 23-knot liner *Hamburg,* which sailed on a first cruise to West Africa and South America on March 31. She has accommodation for 800 passengers and a crew of 400. Built by Deutsche Werft A.G., Hamburg, she was delivered on time, 12

The 25,000-ton liner *Hamburg*, largest passenger ship built in Germany since 1945, made her maiden voyage on March 31.

months after launching. Her public and social rooms are situated on the lido deck and promenade deck, while the cabin accommodation is arranged on three cabin decks. The passenger area has been provided with main stairways, fore and aft, each with two automatic lifts. All rooms are fully air-conditioned. The cabins are sound-proofed, and complete with bath, TV, radio, and telephone; each can be converted to either a lounge or a bedroom. There are numerous bars, a swimming pool, a theatre with 290 seats, and a banqueting hall for 272. A large dining saloon on "B" deck seats 294 passengers, another on "C" deck takes 198 passengers, and there is a grill room for 128 passengers.

There is no doubt that cruise holidays are a growing form of relaxation. International demand for this type of holiday—particularly on large liners—is growing year by year. In the U.S.A. alone, there has been a rise of 112 per cent in cruises over the past 10 years. The outlook augurs well for passenger lines running regular services in the season and cruising out of season.

Exceptional was the decision of the P. & O. Line to stop their passenger ships calling at Indian ports from February 1970—after 140 years. The closure of the Suez Canal has rendered it uneconomic for ships sailing from Europe to S.E. Asia and Australia to make a diversion to India. British Royal Mail Lines also decided to close a century of passenger service to the River Plate. It ceased with the sailing from Buenos Aires of the 18,575-ton gross liner *Aragon*. But she is not to be lost sight of for, renamed *Arawa*, she is now on the U.K.–Australia–New Zealand run, with her sisters *Amazon* and *Arlanza*, which have also been withdrawn from the River Plate run. The reason for the liners' withdrawal was a drop in refrigerated meat cargoes for Britain from Argentina, coinciding with a decrease in passenger bookings. At the end of 1967 Britain suspended imports of Argentine beef following the disastrous outbreak of foot-and-mouth disease in England. Exports were later resumed, but, instead of shipping bulky beef quarters, Argentina is now allowed to send only mostly choice cuts which require smaller holds.

One of the most interesting repair, or rather rebuilding, jobs was completed in August by a Dutch yard. Two 500-ton coasters—*Hada II* and *Hermes*—were joined together side by side to make one ship, *Gloria-Siderum*. The object was to provide a vessel for heavy single loads of up to 300 tons. The *Gloria-Siderum* is propelled by two 800-h.p. engines, one in each component vessel, but there is central engine control. She is 184 ft. in length, 67 ft. in breadth, and only 13 ft. in depth. Her carrying capacity is 1,905 tons.

Barge-carrying Ships

Barge-carrying ships are a recent innovation, like car-carrying trains. The first LASH (lighters aboard ships) vessel to be seen in Europe was the Japanese-built, Norwegian-owned, American-chartered *Acadia Forest*, a 43,500-ton ship carrying 73 lighters, which arrived on December 1 at Rotterdam after her maiden Transatlantic voyage from New Orleans. She left 46 of the lighters (each of which holds 370 tons of cargo) to be towed along Europe's inland waterways to their individual destinations, and sailed on to Sheerness, Isle of Sheppey, Kent, where she unloaded the remaining 27 lighters to be towed to Thamesside wharves. The lighters are carried on her deck or in her hold, and are lowered into, or raised from, the water by her own stern gantry crane, at the rate of one every 15 minutes.

A novel "Siamese twin" heavy-load-carrying vessel, the *Gloria-Siderum*, made in Holland by joining two 500-ton coasters side to side. She has two engines—one in each half.
N.V. Scheepsbouwwer v/h De Groot en Van Vliet

The world's first "lighters aboard ship" vessel, the *Acadia Forest*. Above: lighter being lowered by the huge crane at the stern. Left: a train of lighters, lowered from the ship, being manoeuvred by a tug (*at rear*) and a leader barge (*foreground*) to a riverside wharf.

A development of LASH is the British BOB (barges on board) system, in which barges of 400–500 tons' capacity will be similarly carried on ships of 30,000–40,000 tons. The barges, floating in and out through hinged openings in the side of the ship, will be transferred by crane to watertight holds fore and aft.

Beyond these holds are stowage spaces for containers.

A most unusual completion in 1969 was an unmanned ocean-going barge for the shipment of sawn timber, pulpwood, limestone, and other bulk cargoes. The first of its type to be built in Europe, it is a 10,000-ton vessel. The hull consists of a pontoon provided with stabilisers. On the top of the pontoon there is a deck for heavy concentrated loads, while fences protect the cargo from the sea. Inside the pontoon there are oil-carrying tanks with a capacity of 424,000 cubic ft. The barge is towed by a 4,500–5,000 h.p. tug, at about 10 knots fully loaded. It operates between Sweden and ports in northern Europe.

This artist's impression of BOB (barges on board), shows how a fleet of 400–500-ton barges would float in and out of the sides of a large container-carrying mother ship, delivering and picking up cargo at ports with no deep-water facilities.

Turnbull Marine Design Co. Ltd., Sale, Cheshire

Science and Power

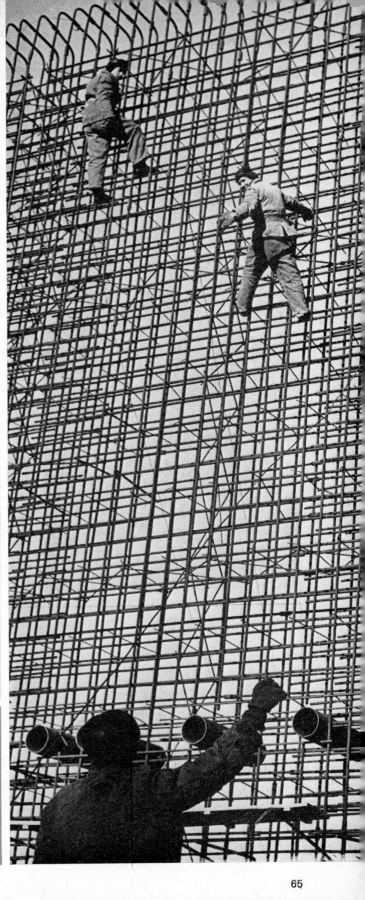

*Russian spider-men
at work on an extension to a
nuclear power station*

E

Striking Structures of 1969

WILLIAM MORSE, B.Sc., A.M.I.Mech.E., P.Eng.

Building mounted on rubber. Because three railway lines (one on the surface and two underground) pass so near, the £250,000 six-storey extension to the St. Mary's Hospital Medical School, Paddington, London, opened on July 8, 1969, by the Queen Mother, is mounted on rubber. Otherwise, vibration from the trains would seriously interfere with the hospital's research work and, indeed, would make it impossible to use its two electron microscopes.

The resilient foundations, designed by the consulting engineers for the project, Oscar Faber & Partners, have a natural frequency of 6 cycles per second vertically and 4 cycles per second horizontally. The main foundation consists of a reinforced concrete platform carrying four columns, each with its own vibration-resistant bearing, supporting one-quarter of the total load, *viz*. 650 tons. The foundation bearings are simple in concept: each has a shallow V with its trough on the centre line of the column. A 4-in.-thick pad of natural rubber is fitted between the convex-V at the base of the column and the corresponding concave-V in the foundation, as shown in the diagrams below.

In this way, both the vertical and horizontal components of ground vibration are taken care of. The thickness of the pads and the V-angle were determined by the mass of the completed building and the required resonant frequencies.

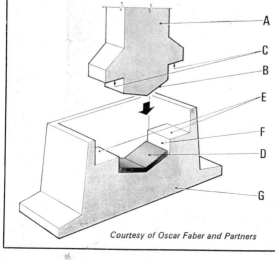

Courtesy of Oscar Faber and Partners

A. Column of building.
B. V-shape at base of column.
C and E. Jacks can be inserted between these faces.
D. 4-inch-thick rubber pad.
E and F. These faces are not touched by the column when it rests on the rubber.
G. Foundation of reinforced concrete.
H. Metal studs measuring deflection of rubber bearing pad.

Water Towers

The rather modern-looking reinforced concrete construction water tower shown at left is located at Lahti, about 50 miles north of Helsinki in Finland. There are two reservoirs in the cone, the total capacity being 225,000 gallons. The exterior of the tower is clad with asbestos cement panels, and the whole of the structure is insulated with a mineral wool lining.

The novel and attractive structure shown at right is a steel water tower at Herouville Saint Clair, near Caen, Normandy, France. It was designed by Société Industrielle Delattre-Levivier (SIDL) whose aim was to create an eye-catching structure that would harmonise well with the surroundings. It has a total capacity of 330,000 gallons. The design consists of three independent cylindrical tanks, each carried on a tubular foot, so arranged that any one of the three tanks can be isolated, leaving two thirds of the total capacity available during maintenance periods.

The Polar Sea Cathedral (*below*) at Tromsö, Norway, 250 miles inside the Arctic Circle, is the farthest-north cathedral ever built. The entire structure is cast in light-weight concrete, to reduce the weight, because of the difficulties of carrying out construction work under Arctic conditions. The elements were precast by A/S Norsk Leca, and transported to the building site. Other advantages of using concrete of this kind are that it provides efficient thermal and acoustic insulation and gives a pleasant interior surface by painting alone. The roof slabs, which are 12 in. thick and 16 ft. wide, vary in height up to 80 ft. The roof is covered with stove-lacquered aluminium sheets chosen for their durability and decorative finish. Enormous windows fill the great triangles at front and rear and long narrow windows are inserted between the roof sections.

Photo, Teigens, Oslo

The Gazebo Hotel, Elizabeth Bay, Sydney, N.S.W. *(above left)*, designed by the Fischer Group of Companies, is owned by the Master Hosts Hotel Group. The circular tower of 18 storeys contains 201 suites in which it can accommodate 500 residents, a restaurant, convention room, and roof-top swimming pool. Through the extensive use of precast concrete it was erected at the rate of one floor per week. It is built on the flat plate principle, with 13 load-bearing external precast concrete columns. The columns are continued up into a conical roof superstructure crowned by a belvedere tower.

Australian News and Information Bureau

An inflatable and mobile dam or weir, which can be installed in a quarter of an hour, has been invented by Dutch engineers for the closing of a canal or other watercourse in an emergency. It consists of a long steel box, with a lid divided into two flaps inside which a "balloon" is fitted. The box lies permanently on the canal bed. When required its lid opens and the "balloon" fills with water, expanding until it emerges above the surface to form a shallow dam. In the lower cross-section diagram at right, A is the steel box, to which the flaps (C) are fixed by watertight hinges (B). The rubber-coated nylon "balloon" (E) is inserted between the edges (D) of the flaps. G are pipes through which water is pumped to inflate the dam. The photos below show (*upper*) a floating crane lowering the steel box into the water, the first stage of installation; and (*lower*) that the inflated dam is strong enough to carry pedestrians and light vehicles. When not in use the "balloon" is deflated into its box, the lid is closed, and boats can then pass freely over it.

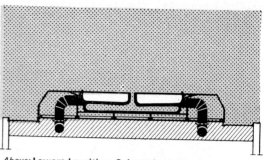

Above: Lowered position. Coloured area represents water.

Below: Inflated position.

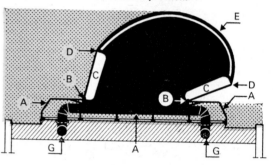

Airport Developments. As aircraft get larger and larger, so too do the hangars that house them for service, as witness BOAC's Boeing 747 hangar at London Airport (Heathrow), completed in December 1969, for the twelve jumbo jet aircraft on order. The hangar, which has a clear span of 453 ft. and measures 273 ft. from front to rear, provides an open workshop area of more than 100,000 sq. ft., so that two of the 350-seater aircraft can be housed side-by-side. Constructed by Holland & Hannen & Cubitts (Southern) Ltd., the hangar has a 2,140-ton roof, built of tubular steel on two levels and supported by the biggest diagonal steel grid in the world. The front girder (fascia beam) is 27 ft. deep by 5 ft. wide, and the spine beam 48 ft. deep by 11 ft. wide. Each girder is more than 550 ft. long and consists of four 18-in. diameter circular steel tubes as main boom members, connected together to form a boxed lattice structure. There are six doors each 75 ft. square and weighing about 45 tons. The 14-in. thick floor contains about 9,000 cubic yd. of concrete, while there are 36,000 cubic yd. of concrete in the aprons outside.

In order to give access to the engines, wing, and front fuselage, the aircraft is manoeuvred on to a specially contoured steel mezzanine. floor, 16 ft. up from ground-level; thus movable steps and gantries are not required. Likewise, while the aircraft is supported in a cradle at its normal level the floor below the wheels can be lowered mechanically to provide a spacious inspection pit 60 ft. long, 32 ft. wide and 17 ft. deep.

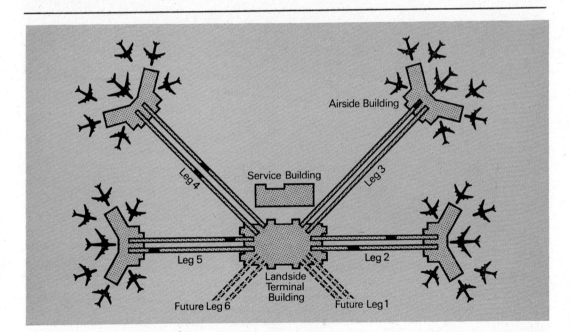

Airports are getting bigger too, and the larger they become the more inconvenient it is for passengers to get to and from their planes For this reason, the Hillsborough County (Florida) Aviation Authority are introducing their "Landside-Airside" passenger transfer system, to be opened in 1970 at the Tampa international airport, Florida. This is how it works. Landside functions, such as parking, baggage-handling, and the issue of tickets, are carried out in a central building and kept quite separate from Airside functions such as apron operations, gate checks, and passenger holding, which are performed in (or near) buildings located radially outwards at some distance from the central Landside building.

The important feature of the system is that each Airside building is connected to the central Landside building by two elevated road-ways 30 ft. apart, on each of which a single automatic vehicle shuttles back and forth. (There is a walkway between, for use in an emergency.) Thus a passenger has to walk at most only 230 yards from his parked car to the plane. The automatic vehicle has four doors; passengers enter on one side and leave on the other. Each car is designed to carry 100 passengers per trip. The vehicles have rubber tyres that run on concrete surfaces, locked to the roadway by guide wheels that follow a centre-beam. They are powered by 3-phase alternating current electric motors and controlled automatically by equipment carried in the car or on the roadway, control signals and voice communications being transmitted to and from the vehicles by antennae.

Mersey Road Tunnel. An interesting feature of the second Mersey Tunnel, between Liverpool and Wallasey, under construction during 1969 was the use of resin-bonded rock bolts of the Selfix type, made by E.C.P. Resins Ltd., Alfreton, Derbyshire. These have been far more successful than normal rock-bolting techniques; mechanical bolts were, in fact, not too effective in the soft sandstone. The photograph above shows a hole being drilled for one of the new bolts in the embankment of the Wallasey approach road.

The Selfix rock bolt unit consists of a high-tensile steel bolt and a capsule containing a synthetic resin with a catalyst resting on the surface of the resin (after the fashion of the toothpaste with a mouthwash in the stripes). The capsule is inserted in the borehole, followed by the bolt; the bolt is then rotated so that the bolt-end ruptures the capsule. This causes resin and catalyst to mix and form an extremely hard synthetic cement. The resin compounds harden in two stages: the initial gel stage, when the resin forms a plastic mass; and the cure stage, when it becomes a solid, resilient mass. Complete hardening, over a temperature range from 40°F. to 120°F, takes place in only four minutes.

With the Selfix system, the rock around the anchorage is effectively sealed from the air by the strong and durable synthetic cement. Tests show a load-bearing strength in excess of requirement in all strata that have been tried. Loads as great as 500 tons have been applied without failure. The holes for the bolts are driven with an air-powered rock drill mounted on an air-leg; and a rotary drill is used for rotating the bolt in order to rupture the resin capsule.

Nuttall, Atkinson, & Co., who were responsible for driving the tunnel, used a 48-ft.-long, self-propelled giant mechanical mole for the purpose. This rock-cutting machine is claimed to be the largest of its kind in the world. It had the job of enlarging a 12 ft. by 12 ft. pilot tunnel, driven in 1966 by a previous contractor. The new Mersey Tunnel has an internal diameter of 31 ft. 7 in., giving a roadway width of 24 ft. for two lanes of traffic. It will be about $1\frac{1}{4}$ miles long. The first Mersey Tunnel, between Liverpool and Birkenhead, is $2\frac{1}{4}$ miles long, and took $8\frac{1}{2}$ years to build; the second is expected to be completed in about $2\frac{1}{2}$ years from the start of the work in April 1968. Sir Alfred McAlpine & Sons Ltd. were responsible for the approach roads.

1 **2** **3** **4**

Walking Excavator. An extremely clever British design of excavator, the model 360/15 made by Richard Smalley (Engineering) Ltd., Sleaford, Lincolnshire, moves itself about on site by means of its own digging mechanism. The great advantage is that there is no need for a heavy engine or transmission, and there are, in consequence, great savings in weight, cost, and maintenance. The machine, which has 360-degree slew, is most manoeuvrable. The sequence illustrations above show how the machine propels itself (in this instance, from left to right) by manipulating the jib and dipper arm. 1. *The jib and dipper reach forward.* 2. *The bucket is placed on the ground.* 3. *The main body of the machine is pulled forward on its two wheels by the "scissors action" of the jib and dipper. At the same time the stabilisers are raised so that the wheels can carry the excavator.* 4. *When the movement of the jib is complete, the cycle of operations can be repeated.* With this method of propulsion, the machine can move forwards, backwards, and sideways, and can walk into apparently inaccessible parts of a site. Because of its 360-degree slew, the excavator can move in any direction and dig or unload at any angle. The hydraulically operated stabiliser legs make it possible for the machine to work even on a 25-degree gradient.

"Giraffe" Platform. During cut and-fill mining in the high-production slopes of the Thompson mine of the International Nickel Company of Canada, Limited, a safe and steady platform for sealing, roof-bolting, and other work is provided by a specially designed "Giraffe" platform mounted on a boom (*right*). It does away with the need for building stages. The carrier is powered by a 17-h.p. air motor, while a 7.5-h.p. hydraulic motor operates the stabiliser and boom. It is said that labour-saving machinery of this kind will help INCO to increase its Canadian nickel production to more than 600 million lb. a year by the end of 1971.

Courtesy of International Nickel

A 15,000-ton steel storage tank, shaped like an inverted funnel, with a capacity of half-a-million barrels of crude oil, has been built by Dubai Petroleum Company (a subsidiary of Continental Oil Company of America), as part of the Fateh off-shore oilfield production scheme in the Persian Gulf. The 270-ft.-diameter tank was built on land and floated in only 8 ft. of water, before being towed by tugs (*above*) to the site, some 58 miles off Dubai, where its bottom rests on the sea bed 160 ft. below the surface. Well-secured by pilings it acts as a storage tank for crude oil from the surrounding wells, easily accessible to giant tankers. The system operates on the principle that oil floats on water. As oil flows into the top stem, which projects about 40 ft. above the sea, the water in the underlying shell is forced out through escape holes around the perimeter of the base. Automatic devices sense when the tank has reached capacity and stop the flow. When oil is withdrawn into tankers, sea water flows back again into the tank. Production from the oilfield, which began in the autumn of 1969, is expected to reach 100,000 barrels a day by the end of 1970.

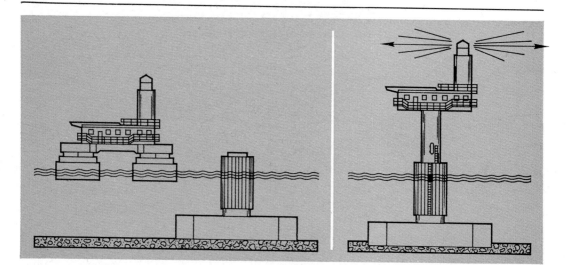

The New Royal Sovereign light. An interesting procedure was used by Christiani & Nielsen in constructing for the Corporation of Trinity House a light tower which has replaced the Royal Sovereign lightship in the English Channel eight miles off Beachy Head, Eastbourne. Both the substructure (caisson and tower) and the cabin superstructure were built in dry dock at Newhaven. The substructure was towed to the site and sunk in position. The superstructure was then floated out on pontoons, and the two parts joined. Finally, the cabin tower was raised into position by jacks. The diagrams above show (*left*) moving the cabin to sea, with the substructure already in position; and (*right*) the parts joined, and the cabin raised and in operation.

One of the precious samples of Moon rock brought back by the Apollo 11 astronauts.

Mysteries of the Moon

A. G. BROWNE
who is science correspondent of the Press Association

THE YEAR OF man's first steps on the Moon was for astronomers, as well as for the hundreds of millions who watched the historic excursion on television, a year of intense interest in lunar matters. Old problems were revived and new ones came to light, but none was completely solved by the Apollo flights. Indeed, in view of the conflicting explanations of some of the flights' findings the Moon was even more of a mystery at the end of the year than it had been at the beginning. One definite and important early conclusion from an examination of the 60 lb. of dust and rocks brought back by Apollo 11 was a dating of that material to something over 3,000 million years, which seems to place a lower limit on the age of the Earth-Moon system.

One new problem of the Moon is that of the "mascons"—concentrations of mass which cause gravitational anomalies in the "seas." Before the flight of Apollo 11, twelve mascons had been discovered through distortions in the orbits of space probes round the Moon, of the Lunar Orbiter series of unmanned craft, and of the Apollo 8 and 10 flights. As an orbiting spacecraft approaches a mascon it is accelerated and its path changed. This could have profound consequences for a landing. An attempted landing at the time of Apollo 8 might have brought disaster. Even Apollo 10

was four miles off course at its point of closest approach, despite increased knowledge of the mascons. Apollo 11 was on course, although it had to change its landing place at the last moment. Apollo 12 was "spot on". By then much was known of the effects of mascons, but it was still unclear what they are.

One explanation is that they are the remains of vast meteorites which, early in the Moon's history, collided with it to form the "seas" and now lie buried beneath the surface. But mathematical studies show that mascons are too big for that theory. At the lowest speed at which it is likely to have approached, a meteorite big enough to form a "sea" by explosive impact would be just one-tenth the size of the mascon in that "sea." At higher speeds a smaller meteorite would provide a large enough explosion, but would probably be vaporised. Another theory is that the "seas" were formed by volcanic action instead of meteoritic impact, but it is very unlikely that mascons are accumulations of lava. Russian and American space probes have indicated that the Moon rocks are akin to basalt on Earth, which was formed in high temperature, and many astronomers have been ready to accept that the smoothness of the surface of a "sea" is due to the fact that it is composed of lava flows. But lava is unlikely to produce positive gravitational anomalies. To do so, it would have to be denser than the rocks it displaced on the surface, and of either an unreasonable thickness or a quite unexpected density.

Lunar "Seas" of Water?

One interesting explanation has been put forward by an American astronomer, J. J. Gilvarry, who has argued for some years that the Moon once had an atmosphere and enough water to form a layer two kilometres deep. He has pointed out that the "seas" are far shallower than meteoritic craters should be, and suggests that they were formed when the Moon was elastic enough to allow some compensation in its surface features, when projections above the surface would sink and depressions would rise. But this would be insufficient to explain the shallowness of the "seas," and Gilvarry goes on to argue that they must have been partly filled up by material carried in from elsewhere.

This material, he says, was transported by water from the highlands to the "seas" (which were actual seas of water), and he claims that the mascons are formed of sedimentary rocks. Space probe studies, he says, fit shales better than basalts. Sedimentation took place, he suggests, when the Moon was no longer elastic enough to provide compensation for its surface features. So much material was carried into the "seas" that even when the water evaporated there was still enough extra mass supported by the underlying rocks to provide the mascons. His theory can also account for the "negative mascons" which appear in some "seas." These appear to be at a higher level and would result from smaller sedimentary deposits—too small to make up for loss of mass through evaporation of water.

The Moon today seems to be a solid body, supporting its surface features by the sheer strength of its underlying structure, and not a body with a liquid core like the Earth. But some of the Moon's surface features do seem to have been formed by long trails of liquid, and there are astronomers besides Gilvarry who believe that that liquid may well have been water, carried out from the interior of the Moon during its early life. Lava is hardly likely to have continued as a molten stream for 250 miles, which is the distance required to explain some features.

Volcanoes on the Moon?

In its early life the Moon may have been heated by internal radioactivity to the point where it was capable of some volcanic activity. Recent detailed photographs of its surface

The Moon's craters remain something of a mystery. Photo taken from Apollo 10's lunar module.

support those who believe in a volcanic origin for some of its surface features. Those who believe it is now a cold world enthusiastically welcomed results from Apollo 11 and 12 as supporting them. The ascent stage of Apollo 12's lunar module was hurled back to the Moon's surface to produce a 20-foot crater. From this impact the seismometer, 40 miles away, amazingly recorded seismic waves for over 30 minutes, an unthinkable effect on Earth. If the whole Moon is a highly resonant object, then it would seem to be a cold solid world. But the result could be accounted for in other ways—perhaps a less dense layer beneath the surface acted as a sounding chamber, or perhaps the impact triggered off a succession of landslides. It could be a purely local effect. Earlier, Apollo 11's seismometer, after initially appearing to report "moonquakes" similar to earthquakes, settled down to record happenings which were interpreted as showing that the Moon beneath its crust is, in the words of NASA geologists, "a great brittle ball, fractured into huge rock blocks, probably from the impact of great ancient meteors," and was never thoroughly molten.

This last suggestion is only tentative, not yet subjected to rigorous mathematical examination. It could be contrasted with the interpretation of another finding—namely, that half the dust brought back by the Apollo 11 astronauts was made up of tiny glass spheres and rods. This was interpreted by some as evidence of wide-scale volcanic activity on the Moon at a time when there was some sort of atmosphere. It was argued that tiny glass spheres could be formed only if there was an

The prominent rille that extends from the crater Hyginus. Could it once have carried water?

atmosphere present; otherwise they would "seize" and stick together in irregular shapes. Volcanic eruptions, it was suggested, could have released enough gas to form a sufficient temporary atmosphere.

Origin of the Moon

Rigorous studies are being made of the various theories of the formation of the Moon. One Apollo 11 finding, mentioned earlier, gives a lower limit to the age of the surface of over 3,000 million years. If the Moon is, as generally believed, about 4,500 million years old, then it could have had an active early history of 1,500 million years before lapsing into its present condition. Thus theories of the origin of the Earth–Moon system cannot rely on some catastrophic action 1,000 million years ago, for that would be sure to have left some evidence on Earth (which geologists have so far not found) and, even more certainly, on the Moon.

Perhaps the most popular present theories are that the Moon was once an independent small planet captured in some way by the Earth. But many such theories can take the history of the system back only halfway or less to that figure of 3,000 million years. In capture, too, the Moon would arrive with hyperbolic energy, or "escape" speed; and although it might remain caught for 10 or even 100 years, that hyperbolic energy would eventually take it far away again. If it was to stay captured, there must have been some outside intervention to reduce its energy, such as collision with a giant meteorite or involvement with an Earth atmosphere much greater than its present extent.

Dr. R. A. Lyttleton, the Cambridge astronomer, in the course of an exhaustive mathematical analysis of theories about the origin of the Moon, has shown that such an intervention need not be so large as to be impossible. In fact, the only theory about the Moon ruled out by his examinations is the simple fission theory, that the Moon was just ejected from the Earth. The Moon, only $\frac{1}{81}$ the size of the Earth, is too small. For the fission theory the smaller body must be about one-eighth the size of the larger. But, Lyttleton points out, the planet Mars, which is about one-ninth the mass of the Earth, fits the theory neatly. The Moon could have been a smaller droplet left between the two separating masses; mathematics shows that it would have been retained by the larger body while the second body became another planet.

Carrying on this argument, Prof. W. H. McCrea of the University of Sussex has suggested that the original super-Earth (now Earth, Mars, and Moon) could have had a counterpart in another planet which divided into Venus and Mercury. One problem about the inner planets is the wide variation in their density. If formed independently in much the same conditions, they should have the same density. Support for the idea that Mars was thrown out from the Earth, perhaps leaving

The seismometers set up on the Moon by the Apollo 11 and 12 crews sent some puzzling messages.

behind the great gash of the Pacific Ocean, is that Mars and the Moon have a density similar to that of the outer layers of the Earth. Prof. McCrea pointed out—what was apparently unnoticed before—that a Venus–Mercury planet would have the same density as the Earth–Mars–Moon planet to within two parts in a thousand. The two large planets, according to the theory, collapsed, perhaps as they lost light gases, and so rotated more rapidly. (The increase in rate of spin would follow in exactly the same way as an ice-skater's spin speeds up as she brings her arms in, concentrating her mass nearer the centre of her body.) The giant planets speeded up to the point when they became unstable and split up, but in the case of the planet nearer the Sun (Venus-Mercury) it was the core that divided. The smaller part, carrying off less of the lighter exterior matter, became Mercury, which is slightly denser than Venus.

More about Pulsars

The sensation of 1968 was the discovery of pulsars—sources of regular pulses of radio waves. New light was thrown on them during 1969—literally so, for one pulsar, in the Crab nebula, was found to give flashes of light at the same rate as radio pulses. The output of energy is so prodigious that probably all the radiation from the Crab nebula depends on this one object. The Crab nebula is a supernova remnant—900 years old as we see it, for the Chinese observed its explosion in the 11th century—but 12,500 light years away. It may be that all pulsars are remnants of supernova explosions. When they were first reported it was clear that the flashing radio pulses must come from oscillating or rotating stars far denser than ordinary stars. At first it seemed that white dwarfs, stars in which matter is highly compressed, were the source; they provided the right order of oscillating time, and their size accounted for the length of the individual pulse. But the Crab nebula pulsar put that idea out of court when it was found to oscillate with a period of less than one-thirtieth of a second. No white dwarf could oscillate so rapidly, nor could it rotate at that speed. The alternative idea of a neutron star is now generally accepted.

A neutron star, with its protons and electrons forced together into neutrons, is compressed even more than a white dwarf, with a density a thousand million times as great—a teacupful would weigh more than 1,000 million tons. Such an object would oscillate far too rapidly to account for the Crab nebula pulsar, but it could easily *rotate* at that speed. An original theory of Professor

T. Gold is that pulsars are rotating neutron stars with a "hot spot" on the surface which sends out a beam of energy, like a celestial lighthouse.

The rotational theory received support when it was found that the Crab nebula pulsar was slowing down; that is to be expected in a rotating object losing energy. But then came a shock when V. Radhakrishnan and R. N. Manchester at the Radiophysics Laboratory in Sydney, Australia, and P. Reichley and C. S. Downs of "Cal Tech," U.S.A., observed that the pulsar in the constellation Vega in the Southern Hemisphere had suddenly speeded up. Between February 24 and March 3 the pulse rate increased by two parts in a million. The Australians suggested that, if the object was a neutron star ten kilometres in radius, the speeding-up could be caused by a shrinkage of only one centimetre.

The mechanism by which intense radio waves are produced in a very strong gravitational field are imperfectly understood. To explain the "hot spot," Freeman Dyson, of the Institute for Advanced Study, Princeton, U.S.A., suggested that it is a volcano on the surface. The material expands as it rises, and a jet is likely to reach escape velocity. Somehow the energy of the escaping neutrons is converted into electromagnetic radiations. To account for the tremendous energy of the Crab nebula pulsar at least a million grams of matter per square centimetre per second must reach the surface. Dyson suggested that the quantity of volcanic material may well be large enough to produce the collapse of the mantle by about a centimetre at intervals of a few years. Thus the change observed in the Vega pulsar should not be a rare occurrence.

Whatever their nature and origin, pulsars are providing an important astronomical instrument for mapping interstellar space. They are the first real means of determining the strength of magnetic fields in space, and they also constitute a tool for determining the density of ionised hydrogen. From this, temperature can be deduced, and from fluctuations in density more can be learnt of the dynamics of the motions of interstellar gas and, possibly, of the formation of stars. One other claimed achievement was a further confirmation of Einstein's theory of relativity. At Arecibo, Puerto Rico, the delay in the arrival of pulses from the Crab nebula pulsar, caused by the Sun's gravitational field, was measured. The signals, it was found, were slowed by just the amount expected by the relativity theory—about one ten-thousandth of a second after their journey of about 12,500 years.

Putting Science to Work

RONALD SHARP

ALTHOUGH OVERSHADOWED by the supreme achievement of applied science—the first landings of men on the moon—human inventiveness in other fields was as active and productive as ever in 1969. This was particularly true of research and exploration of the other extreme from the moon—the sea-bed. Of recent years there has been a growing interest in the sea and the sea-bed as a source of minerals and a centre of industrial activity. Indeed, marine technology has become a very active field for scientists and engineers who have been busy devising means of exploring the sea-bed—and the strata beneath it—and extracting the oil, gas, and other minerals to be found there. Underwater vessels of all shapes and sizes for exploring the depths of the ocean have been designed in large numbers, and the first international congress and exhibition on the subject of "oceanology" was held in England during the year.

British shipbuilders, together with the government-sponsored National Research and Development Corporation (NRDC), designed and built a manned vehicle capable of travel-ling along the sea-bed as deep as 600 ft. The vehicle, which is towed to its working location where it is submerged, moves about on the sea-bed on large vaned wheels. Power comes through a cable fed from generating and control modules mounted on the deck of a support ship. The hull of the underwater vehicle is divided by bulkheads into three compartments, one housing the crew and all their instruments in normal atmospheric pressure, one accommodating the divers in a high-pressure atmosphere, and one a transfer department through which the divers emerge to work on the sea-bed. Both the normal and high-pressure compartments have sleeping and toilet accommodation, and the former is also equipped with cooking facilities. It is not necessary to raise the vehicle to transfer personnel to and from the surface. This is done by means of a submersible diving chamber which is locked on to the transfer compartment, allowing easy passage in and out of the crew compartment.

This sea-bed vehicle can be fitted with a wide range of power tools and mechanical equipment to carry out such functions as trench-

Artist's impression of a new underwater vehicle for work 600 ft. down, designed by British shipbuilders in conjunction with the NRDC. It moves about on the sea-bed on large vaned wheels. *Cammel Laird & Co. Ltd.*

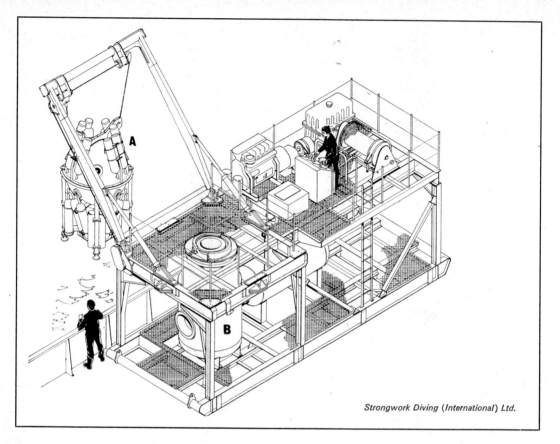

Strongwork Diving (International) Ltd.

digging for pipelines and telephone cables, core-drilling for geological samples, and the operation of cranes and excavators for salvaging and undersea mining.

The NRDC had a hand in the design of another new deep-diving system which is also capable of operating at a depth of 600 ft. (illustrated in this page). Designed as a package unit, the system comprises two compression chambers, a winch, an hydraulic control system, and a diving access platform. When the system is in position on the surface, two divers enter the submersible compression chamber which is quickly lowered to the required depth. The divers breathe a gas mixture supplied from the cylinders around the chamber. On reaching the sea-bed, the divers can leave the chamber and walk for a distance of up to 65 ft. They receive their air supply through flexible pipes connected to the chamber. When their work is finished, the divers re-enter the chamber which is brought to the surface, where it is mated with the transfer

In this new British deep-diving system, divers descend in a diving bell (A in diagram). On return to the surface (photo, left) the bell is locked on to a transfer chamber (B), which the men enter for partial decompression. The diving bell is then separated for immediate use by other divers.

chamber. The divers spend some time in this under pressure before later entering a master compression chamber in which they are gradually brought back to normal atmospheric pressure. Meanwhile, the submersible chamber can be taken over by another pair of divers to continue the work on the sea-bed.

Not all undersea work necessitates a visit to the ocean bed. There are such tasks as inspecting ships' hulls and harbour installations and investigating marine life which call for mobility during fairly long periods beneath the surface. The ability of swimmers to perform underwater tasks depends on their equipment and their stamina. Although a man can swim casually for a considerable time with the aid of his air cylinders, as soon as he starts exerting himself he begins to use up his air at a faster rate. Limitations of this kind have been removed by a series of vehicles designed and constructed by the British Ministry of Defence Admiralty Materials Laboratory. The most successful is a two-man vehicle operated by

Sea-Lab III, in which it was planned that American aquanauts should live for 60 days at the bottom of the sea. *Left:* artist's impression of a transfer capsule approaching the submerged Sea-Lab, which is linked by cables and pipes with its support vessel on the surface. *Below:* the main working area of the underwater "house." On the day (February 17th, 1969) when the experiment was to begin, a diver died while swimming from the transfer capsule to the Sea-Lab, and the project was postponed indefinitely.

In this British underwater vehicle two swimmers lie side by side on top of the hull, one operating the controls by hand and foot.

Admiralty Materials Laboratory, U.K. Ministry of Defence

two swimmers lying side by side on top of the hull. One man controls the vehicle with a foot-operated rudder bar and hand-controlled fore and aft hydroplanes. The vehicle carries a complete range of navigation instruments and can be fitted with a homing device to locate an underwater beacon.

It is powered by a silver-zinc battery operating through a D.C. motor and a reduction gear providing a speed of more than 3 knots, which is about the maximum a swimmer can withstand. Later developments are likely to be streamlined vehicles with the swimmers enclosed and protected against the effects of water flow, thereby making it possible to achieve greater speeds and a wider range.

Although the death of a diver caused the postponement of the American Sea-Lab III project 600 ft. down off the Californian coast, four U.S. aquanauts did break the underwater endurance record in 1969 by remaining for 60 days under the sea. They lived 50 ft. under the Caribbean in Tektite I, two steel cylinders mounted on a rectangular base, moored off St.

John in the Virgin Islands, and were able to leave their underwater home to explore marine life and return to it at will.

A problem constantly associated with the sea came a step nearer solution when scientists in Israel devised a method of removing crude oil from the surface of water. Part of Lake Tiberias was contaminated by crude oil flowing down from the Golan Heights when a pipeline was damaged. A recognised method of absorbing oil on water is to cover the affected area with polyurethane flakes, which not only soak up the oil but also can be "squeezed" so that much of it can be recovered. The problem so far has been the collecting of the oil-soaked flakes from the sea. The Israeli scientists developed a new construction of polyurethane, with increased oil-absorbing and water-repellent properties. Then they bound the flakes into "carpets" which were floated on top of the oil patches. The carpets soaked up the oil and were removed from the lake in one piece without harming any of the fish in the lake. The idea was so successful that it is being patented all over the world and could well be used in the future wherever oil contaminates water.

Land and Air Transport

Concentration on space and underwater vehicles does not mean that land travel has been neglected by inventors. Two futuristic trains made their appearance in France in 1969. One is a "hovertrain" which runs on a special track at 270 m.p.h., stabilised by cushions of air produced by a special engine. It is powered by a petrol engine, assisted by rockets which come into use when higher speeds are required. The other train, called the "RailJet," runs on a conventional track and is propelled by motors on each bogie which enable the train to reach speeds of up to 200 m.p.h. The electric field between the motors and the rails prevents slewing and pro-

The French "hovertrain" which in experimental runs has reached a speed of 270 m.p.h.

Another experimental French train, the "RailJet," with motors on each bogie, has attained 200 m.p.h.

vides remarkable stabilisation at the highest speeds, and the brakes are applied immediately the current is reversed. The "Rail-Jet" is the first example of the application of aircraft-building techniques to rail vehicles.

The "hovertrain" is similar in principle to a new vehicle developed in the U.S.A. with a view to providing a direct link between the John F. Kennedy Airport and New York City, 20 miles away. The journey by road can take up to two hours, but the "tracked air cushion vehicle," as it is called, can do it in only four minutes. It operates on the hovercraft principle, riding on a cushion of air an inch and a half above a single central track. To ensure that it does not "jump the track," two cushions of air between the sides of the vehicle and a pair of guide rails hold it steady.

A perennial problem facing airports is fog.

In the Second World War, the Royal Air Force kept airfields open by burning fuel oil alongside the runways and dispersing the fog with the heat of the flames. The system was christened FIDO (from the initials of Fog Intensive Dispersal Operation). Such a method would not be practical on civil airports, and less dramatic means are being tried. One device, which has become known as "the long-snouted fog eater," consists of a powerful blower with a collapsible hose. It is towed on to the runway, extended to its full height of 100 ft., and rotated through a vertical arc while spraying fog-dispersing chemicals.

An odd application of the hovercraft principle was a hovering scarecrow which made its debut in England during the year. A dummy of a man holding a rifle was mounted on a platform which was powered by a fan to

Drawing of the locomotive of an American "hovertrain," planned for speeds of up to 300 m.p.h.

The "long-snouted fog eater," which sprays fog-dispersing chemicals, is here seen retracted and (right) extended to its full height of 100 ft. and in operation at an airport.

hover about an inch above the ground. The scarecrow proved successful in keeping birds away from seeded fields, and could find a use in keeping them away from airports.

Another agricultural device which made its appearance in 1969 was a driverless tractor called the "Autotrack." An ordinary tractor fitted with an electronic sensing device is guided by a grid of wires buried in the ground deep enough not to be fouled by implements. The sensor picks up from the wires and relays to the power steering unit instructions that keep the tractor on course and tell it when to raise or lower the plough or other implement when one run is ended and another starts. Once the tractor has been set on course, it will cultivate a whole field without manual supervision. The underground wires can be laid quite quickly and cheaply, and will last almost indefinitely.

Electrical Devices

One of the most difficult tasks for electrical engineers is checking generators which consist of wire coils. It is easy enough to trace a fault once it has occurred; the problem is to spot a

American electrical engineers using the new "radio stethoscope" for detecting and locating faults in the coils of a generator by picking up radio "noise" caused by incomplete insulation.   *Westinghouse Corporation, Pittsburgh, U.S.A.*

weakness before the fault causes a power breakdown. American engineers have devised an instrument to do this. It is a kind of radio stethoscope that pinpoints the source of trouble by detecting radio noise in coil insulation. The device is an electromagnetic probe consisting of a horseshoe electromagnet about the size of a hand. With it routine tests are carried out regularly, particularly in generators made up of hundreds of coils which are expected to last more than 30 years.

New from the U.S.A. is a heart pacemaker powered by a nuclear battery, developed by the U.S. Atomic Energy Commission. The device had been under test for three years; success finally came in 1969 when the nuclear-powered pacemaker was implanted in a dog, which can look forward to a trouble-free heart for the next ten years.

Battery-operated pacemakers are not new in heart surgery, but the usual mercury cell and other conventional batteries need frequent checking since battery failure could be fatal to the patient. The active material in the nuclear pacemaker is half a gram of plutonium-238. This isotope emits alpha particles which have high energy but such low penetration that they can be stopped by an ordinary sheet of paper. Danger from stray radiation is thus no greater than that from a luminous wrist watch.

The atomic battery produces a current by turning the energy of the alpha particles into heat and then, through a thermocouple, into electricity. The thermocouple is made from a copper-nickel and a nickel-chromium alloy drawn into strands and woven into a glass tape. The resultant current passes to an ordinary

This man is holding a new power source under development by G.E.C. of America—the magnesium-salt battery, one of which provides as much current as the pyramid of conventional batteries at right. It is refuelled by adding fresh thin magnesium plates, a handful of salt, and water.

pulse generator which supplies the pacing pulses to the electrodes that stimulate the heart muscles. The nuclear pacemaker is also thought to have an important future in other bio-medical fields, such as blood pressure control and diaphragm stimulation to help breathing action.

Power from the Sun

The production of heat and power from non-mineral fuels is important not only in anticipation of the time when coal and oil supplies will be exhausted, but also for countries which have no native deposits of those fuels and cannot afford to import them in sufficient quantity. The two leading fuels of the future are nuclear energy and solar energy. It is a paradox that nuclear power has become a successful reality, despite all the theoretical and technical problems of producing it, whereas solar energy, which has existed for all to see since the universe began still eludes man as a practical, or at least an economic, proposition. Solar cells, such as convert the sun's radiation into electrical energy in spacecraft, are too expensive to be considered for everyday use. Indeed, the silicon monocrystal cells used in the American space programme cost a hundred dollars for every watt of electricity they produce.

However, new hope arose in 1969 for those who look to the sun for a cheap source of power. A team of scientists at the Israel National Council for Research and Development designed a cadmium sulphide solar cell costing a fraction of the silicon monocrystal cells. And the new cells were successfully used to illuminate traffic lights and a lighthouse in

A tiny atomic battery that produces 100 times the power of a chemical cell of the same size.

"Fear no more the heat o' the sun"

This experimental solar furnace at Odeillo, near Font-Romeu in the Pyrenees, cost France £8 million. Eight tiers of mirror-lined screens (the backs of four are seen at right) reflect the sun's heat upon the huge curved surface of the main structure (above). The latter is also lined with mirrors (shown closer below), which concentrate the heat on to the furnace, the small raised building in front of the main structure. Temperatures of up to 6,000 °F. can be produced within a few minutes.

The furnace and the 20,000 mirrors in the whole array are controlled electronically from the control room (bottom right). Furnaces of this type could revolutionise power-production in tropical regions, and might even one day be set up on the moon.

the Straits of Tiran. Each cell is made from layers of polycrystalline cadmium sulphide, deposited on glass. The principle is that the cell absorbs the sun's radiation and stores it for use as and when required.

Other scientists have been working on another revolutionary but simple form of fuel—body heat. Everyone knows how quickly a cold room warms up when it is full of people, and it occurred to an American engineer, William Custer, that this heat could be put to work. He designed a system at Pittsburgh University in which the body heat from students and staff helps to warm ten buildings. The system also utilises heat from electric lights, kitchens, and sunlight coming through windows. It is so successful that no conventional heating is required even in the coldest winter. Called "Heat-Reclaim," the system works on the principle that cool water absorbs heat. Heat, extracted through ceiling louvres from areas where it is surplus or not needed, warms chilled water passing through a series of pipes to a central unit where it is raised to a higher temperature by compression in a condenser. It is then piped to hot-water radiators in the areas which need heating. When all heating requirements are met, any surplus heat is stored in insulated tanks to be fed into the system automatically at weekends or holidays or at night when there is no heat available to be reclaimed. The heart of the system is a centrifugal water chilling machine (basically a refrigeration unit) installed in the basement of the university.

Helping the Handicapped

Great is the satisfaction of scientists, engineers, and inventors who are able to help handicapped people. A recent invention of particular merit is a page-turning device which allows anyone to enjoy reading without using the hands. Page-turners are not a new idea, but they are generally expensive. The one produced by staff at the Waltham Forest Technical College, London, cost less than £3 in materials. Based on an idea from the Royal National Orthopaedic Hospital, the device consists of an adjustable support for the book, to the top of which is fitted a small board carrying the mechanism. Two micro-switches control a small battery-driven motor. The user operates one switch by moving a lever in one direction with his mouth. This starts the motor, which moves a rubber roller across the book and up towards the top corner of the page. Before it reaches the corner, the sideways movement of the roller is stopped, but it continues to rotate and draws the corner of the page back. As soon as the corner is free of the roller, the user moves the lever in the opposite direction to operate the other switch, which brings the roller back across the book with the page in front of it, thus turning the page. If allowed to continue, it will roll up to the opposite corner and turn the page back again.

1969 brought the introduction of several devices to enable blind people to read ordinary print. One was a converter which changes printed letters into a form that can be sensed by the fingertips. Reflected light from a printed

A portion of a gigantic array of solar cells for creating electric power in space, made by Lockheed in the U.S.A. It will be launched folded, and opened out at the required height.

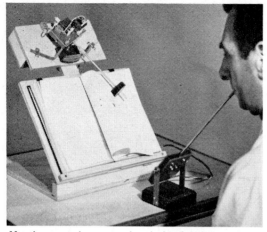

Mouth-operated page-turning device for the paralysed reader, described in the preceding page.

letter goes to an optical sensor which is linked by cable to 144 photo-electric cells, arranged in six rows of 24. Each cell is connected to a separate crystal to which blunt pins are attached. When the sensor picks up the shape of a letter its signal vibrates the pins in a pattern which can be identified by the user's fingertips. Reading speed is only 20 to 35 words a minute, compared with 100 words a minute with Braille, but the advantage of the new device is that it can be used by people who cannot read Braille or for short extracts of ordinary printed matter which it is not worth copying into Braille.

The Argonne National Laboratory in America also produced an invention to make reading easier for the blind. It is a machine somewhat smaller than a portable typewriter that can take symbols recorded on ordinary magnetic tape and play them back in the form of the raised dots of Braille on an endless plastic belt. The user reads by running his fingertips along the belt, the speed of which can be adjusted to suit his reading speed. At the end of each complete pass the dots are erased and a new pattern is made of the next group of words.

Another invention will make a blind typist as skilled as a sighted person by giving her the power to check her own work. This is a typewriter developed at the Israel Physics Laboratory in Jerusalem, which simultaneously produces both a normal typescript and a Braille tape. Each typewriter key automatically produces two symbols, one in Braille which is embossed on the tape and the other a normal character on ordinary paper. After typing a piece, the blind typist by checking the Braille tape can discover if she has made any errors in the normal typescript.

Contact lenses have in the last decade been a boon to many people with eyesight problems. Now a new type of contact lens has even restored sight to blind people. This near miracle was achieved at the University of Florida, where a number of people blinded by diseased or damaged corneas have regained their sight by the glueing of tiny plastic lenses to the corneal surface of one or both eyes, after removal of the diseased area where necessary.

The cornea is the transparent membrane which forms the outer coat of the exposed part of the eyeball. It is vulnerable to various kinds of disease and injury which can cause it to become temporarily or permanently opaque, blinding the victim. Fitting the lens is a simple process taking about ten minutes, and if necessary it can easily be removed. Although it is emphasised that the technique is still experimental, it does offer considerable hope to people with corneal trouble.

New Uses for Lasers

The laser is a familiar feature among modern scientific achievements, and in 1969 a number of interesting applications were introduced. For example, dental cavities may soon be prevented before they start by a process known as "laser glazing." The technique uses the pinpoint accuracy and instantaneous heat of a laser beam to seal the enamel coating of the teeth. Moreover, it can be done without pain or damage to the mouth. The American scientist who invented the technique used a ruby laser to control a light beam with enough heat energy to glaze a tooth in less than a fiftieth of a second. The laser unit, which

A new British dental X-ray machine that can X-ray the whole jaw in one sweep.

"Panorex": photo, Harold King

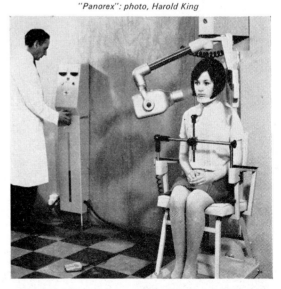

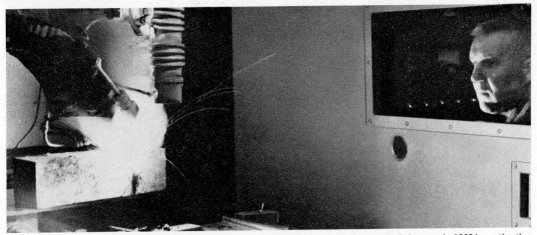

A 9,000-watt electron beam cutting through a block of granite. Westinghouse in the U.S.A. were in 1969 investigating this use for electron beam rock cutters in mining and tunnelling.

should cost no more than conventional dental X-ray equipment, could well become a standard tool in the dental surgery within two years.

Another invention that could become standard equipment in dental surgeries is a new British machine which can X-ray the entire jawbone in one sweep, as compared with the conventional dental X-ray method which needs 14–18 separate film exposures. With the new machine the patient rests the chin in a half-collar support, and the X-ray camera swivels round in an arc, photographing as it goes. The first of these machines were installed in two British hospitals.

Lasers have also been used successfully to penetrate thick fog and snow with the aid of a newly devised portable hand-held instrument. Light from a 20-watt gallium arsenide laser is sent out in short bursts and reflected back to an infra-red receiver. The receiver is normally "off," but it can be switched on by a strong reflection striking a photocathode tube. While back-scattered light from fog particles is not strong enough to activate the receiver, the reflection from solid obstacles switches it on long enough for the image to be identified. In this way, only solid objects are "seen" through the fog.

Lasers have for some time been used to drill holes in diamonds, and it came as no surprise to learn of their use in Switzerland to make watch bearings from rubies and other jewels. The significance of the development is that the lasers are not used on an individual basis but in mass production. An automatically controlled feed system conveys the jewels into position, shoots rapid bursts from an yttrium aluminium garnet laser, and passes them on to a collection point. The process, which allows several bearings to be drilled every second, is very much faster than the conventional method of using steel needles coated with diamond dust.

Drilling and Grinding

This, however, was one of the very few instances in which industrial diamond has been replaced by something more efficient. Indeed, diamond, being the hardest material known to man, is finding more and more uses in industry, as a precision cutting tool, a grinding abrasive, and a drilling material. In 1969, engineers perfected a plating process that locks diamond particles into a metallic compound. Metal bonding of diamond to saws and cutting tools is not a new idea, but the new process, which took nearly two years to perfect, succeeds in distributing diamond more uniformly than by conventional methods. The process itself is a trade secret, but the results are quite remarkable. For example, it is possible to apply a diamond coating to wafer-thin metallic discs which are used as circular saws to cut the hardest and most brittle ceramics without damaging them.

Diamond is also used in ultrasonic machining. This is the system which uses extremely high frequency sound waves to apply the impact pressure. Usually, the type of diamond employed ultrasonically is in the form of either a loose abrasive slurry or a metal probe impregnated with diamond grit. Now an entirely new method has been devised using a tool tipped with a single diamond—and it was designed specially to drill *square* holes! Moreover, the holes are only 0·038 in. across, and they were drilled in a ceramic wafer 0·01 in. thick. Ceramics, as well as being as hard as rock, are extremely brittle, and it seemed quite impossible to drill any kind of hole, let alone square ones, into this minute thickness without shattering the material. However, by applying ultrasonic impacts 20,000 times a second it was possible to cut a square hole in 10 seconds to an accuracy of one thousandth of an inch. The idea was successful because each individual impact was of such short duration that the ceramic did not have time to absorb it; it was the sum total of impacts that made the actual penetration.

The year also brought the solution of a problem which has been facing diamond technologists for many years—namely, the grinding of steel. The difficulty has arisen not because steel is so hard but because it is too *soft* to be successfully ground with diamond; metal particles have tended to clog the grinding wheels between the diamond particles, producing a smooth surface on the wheel and robbing it of its abrasiveness. The innovation is to coat the diamond particles with nickel before bonding them to the wheel; this has made it possible to take advantage of diamond's hardness, which is many times greater than that of the abrasives hitherto used for steel grinding.

The next hardest material to diamond has always been silicon carbide. Now, scientists and engineers have succeeded in coming closer to the hardness of diamond by producing a material twice as hard as silicon carbide. It is a cubic form of boron nitride known as "Borazon," a crystalline substance made by subjecting ordinary boron nitride to a pressure of 1,000,000 lb. per sq. in., and temperatures in the region of 3,000°F. Like diamond, "Borazon" is metal-coated for bonding to grinding wheels. One of its big advantages over ordinary abrasives is that "Borazon" grinding wheels do not need frequent dressing to restore their worn shape. It also has one notable advantage over diamond—namely, a remarkable resistance to heat. The carbon from which diamond is formed will "burn" at 1,600°F., whereas "Borazon" will go to 2,500°F. without any change in structure. It looks as if diamond is at long last faced with a serious competitor in industry.

Not all cutting relies on the hardness of the cutting medium. Indeed, a machine has been devised which depends as much on mode of action as on the abrasive used. It can cut through a 6-in.-diameter piece of titanium in only two minutes—and titanium is one of the hardest of alloys. It makes easy work of such materials as high-carbon alloys, tungsten, and high-speed steels. The main feature of the machine is its pecking action. This prevents excessive build-up of frictional heat which can cause physical changes in materials; in

A linesman can safely work on a 400,000-volt power system while wearing this new "conductor suit". Composed of steel wire and cotton, it forms a protective cage round him.

materials like titanium, which is used extensively in aircraft construction, such dangerous changes must be prevented.

New Methods of Cutting

Another novel cutting machine, devised in the U.S.A., clamps itself to a large pipe and crawls round it, cutting as it goes. It is particularly useful for field work in laying water or gas mains or other large conduits that have to be adjusted or cut to shape and size on the spot because they are too big to be moved. The spinning cutter head is driven by compressed air, to reduce the danger of explosion when working on gas or sewer installations. The crawling cutter is clamped to the pipe by a belt which it also uses to pull itself around the circumference of the pipe. It needs only 10 in. clearance when cutting a pipe in a trench. It takes about 10 minutes to fit, and the cutting speed is an inch a minute. The device will cut steel, cast iron, asbestos-cement, or concrete pipe from 6 in. to 6 ft. in diameter.

A British company has developed a method of cutting and shaping metal without tools. The process is called chemical milling. The basic idea is to transfer a drawing photographically to the sensitised coating of a workpiece and etch away the unmasked areas, leaving behind the desired shape. The resulting shaped piece is free from burrs and rough edges, and has none of the internal stresses which are often left by conventional cutting methods. The method allows very complex shapes to be cut in extremely thin metals.

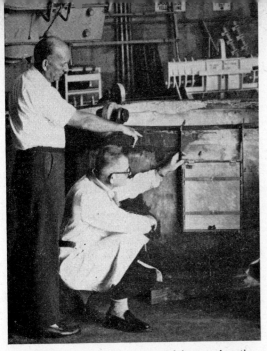

Placing a film cassette on a large stainless steel casting, preparatory to X-raying it. The X-raying of metals is a valuable new technique for testing their behaviour.

Another jet device uses the conical pressure wave caused by a jackhammer piston in water. The wave shoots out a portion of the water at a speed of 25,000 ft. per second, which represents the incredibly high pressure of 50 million lb. per sq. in.

X-rays are playing an important part in the world of metals. One of the latest devices allows the internal atomic structure of metals revealed by X-rays to be displayed on a television screen. Previously, studies of this kind have had to be made on film. The new device, combining X-ray apparatus with a light magnifier of the kind used by astronomers, can produce a continuous picture of a metal's structure. It is possible to watch exactly how the metal behaves when it is deliberately deformed with, for example, heat. Metallurgists need to know precisely how the atomic structure of a metal will react to various physical treatments and environments; with this knowledge it will be possible to improve all manufactured products which rely on the specific properties of metals.

Practical Uses for TV

Television may be revolutionised in years to come by a completely new kind of screen developed in 1969. It is made up of thread-like crystals sandwiched between two layers of glass which become translucent under the influence of electricity. Under voltages of 3–30 volts D.C., the phenomenon occurs at any temperature between 0° and 175°F. The degree of translucence depends on the voltage; the amperage is quite small. Another type of picture can be produced by a newly invented ciné camera that translates output figures from a computer into easily understood animated films of professional standard. One interesting application is to record the movement of satellites and heavenly bodies and measure them from the film at leisure. This avoids the hit-and-miss problem of trying to measure fast movements as they occur.

Japanese engineers in 1969 invented the world's smallest colour-TV camera, one-twentieth of the weight of conventional models. But a British company produced a black-and-white one which is certainly the smallest TV camera of any kind. It measures $4\frac{3}{4}$ in. by 1 in. It is, of course, a special-purpose camera devised for closed-circuit use in inaccessible places, such as the inside of pipes or boiler tubes. It can be pushed along considerable lengths of tube, avoiding the time and expense of dismantling machinery or digging up buried pipes. The camera consists of two units: the cylindrical camera head, complete with integral lens and lighting unit; and a

The process is in six steps. First, an accurate drawing of the part to be produced is made; it is drawn several times life-size and is photographed and reduced to actual size, so that two masks can be made, one representing the part and the other its mirror-image. These are registered facing each other so that the metal part can be etched from both sides. The metal, coated with a photo-resistant material, is placed between the two masks and exposed to ultra-violet light, which produces a photo-image on both sides. An etching medium is then applied and this eats away the unmasked areas, leaving the desired shape. All that is necessary then is to remove the etching chemical and photographic coating. Chemical milling is expected to have many applications, particularly in the electronics industry where many components of complicated shapes are made in thin materials.

Another new method of cutting metal—or stone—is to use "slugs" of water. For metalworking the advantage is that no heat is developed, while for rock cutting in mines the method eliminates the need for explosives. The principle is that energy sent into a body of water is concentrated on speeding a small slug of the water into the metal or rock. The idea was developed by the U.S. army, who produced a "water cannon" that delivered blasts of water ten times a second with an impact pressure of 40,000–80,000 lb. per sq. in., which is more than enough to break granite. The cannon derives its power from a compressed air generator.

The tiny cylinder at left is the smallest ever TV camera, used for inspecting pipes and tubes.
E.M.I. Electronics Ltd.

control unit. The two are connected by 50 yards of cable, and together are light enough to be carried comfortably by one man. There is a built-in air pump to cool the head and allow the camera to operate in temperatures of up to 125°F.

Another kind of underground inspection device was invented by scientists at Oxford University. This is a supersensitive metal detector. One of its first uses was to help archaeologists in the hunt for King Arthur's Camelot at South Cadbury Hill, Somerset. It can be used to locate underground pipe-lines, buried treasure, sea-bed wrecks, or skiers buried in snow. The device is a pulse induction detector; it works by beaming a magnetic field which, when contact is made with metal, induces into the metal an electric eddy current that can be picked up and indicated by a moving needle. The detector can locate the presence of gold, silver, copper, iron—in fact, any metal. At South Cadbury Hill, it was used to pinpoint postholes of ancient buildings by locating the remains of nails and other metal fragments. It was also used to search the wreck of the Spanish galleon, *Santa Maria de la Rosa*, off the west coast of Ireland, and in the hands of a diver located cannon and other metal remains, including gold and silver coins.

Detection of another kind will be facilitated by a machine that can identify a person by measuring his hand as positively, it is claimed, as by his fingerprints. The machine is likely to be used by police in crime detection and prevention, and by banks to identify the holders of credit cards. People whose identity must, for any reason, be kept on file have their hand measured, the data being magnetically recorded on a card. When it becomes necessary to prove the person's identity he puts his hand into a slot of the machine while the record card is fed into another slot. The machine measures the width and thickness of the hand, fingers, and knuckles, and compares the measurements with the data on the card.

In Great Britain, the unusually fine summer of 1969 prompted many men to buy light-weight suits for the first time. But knowing the unpredictability of the climate they were anxious about the effect of being caught in a sudden downpour. Fortunately, the growing sophistication of man-made fibres has made lightweight clothing materials less susceptible to damage by rain. This certainly applies to a new material developed in the U.K. in 1969. Known as Northylon 106, it is as light as the lightest summer suiting fabrics, yet ten times as strong. It is a plastic-coated nylon material which does not succumb to twisting; although it weighs only 8 ounces to the square yard, its tear strength is ten times that of conventional plastic-coated rayon or cotton fabrics.

Automation Extended

Automation knows many forms. One of the last fields in which one would expect to find it is in the administration of anaesthetics. In 1964 Dr. Harry J. Lowe, of the Pritzker School of Medicine at the University of Chicago, started researching into a method of administering anaesthetics automatically. Five years later he was able to claim success with a programming machine which he describes as an "automatic anaesthetist." His research involved measuring the solubility of several anaesthetics in human tissues, and calculating the anaesthetic requirement for the average man or woman. This requirement is modified according to individual factors, such as the patient's weight, and the information is transferred to the programmer. The latter then injects anaesthetic into a closed-circuit breathing system minute by minute to meet the patient's requirements, at the same time recording the amount given. Exhaled oxygen, carbon dioxide, and anaesthetic are returned to the breathing circuit.

Factory automation was extended to an operation that hitherto has always required some degree of manual supervision—painting by spray-gun. Formerly even machine-operated spray-guns had to be confined to those production lines where all the products were identical in shape, size, and colour. In a French motor-car factory, however, there has appeared a new machine which not only paints mass-produced cars at high speed but also can be programmed to apply any one of 20 different colours on six different models intermixed on the same production line. The machine consists of two opposite-profile paint-

An unmanned amphibious bulldozer, radio-controlled by the man standing on dry land, at work dredging in shallow sea water. This Japanese development is said to be the first of its kind in the world. Its chief uses are in river improvement and land reclamation.

ing units—a master and a slave—facing each other across the production line. They are fitted to cam-driven arms which hold the spray-guns in the correct plane throughout the stroke and apply an even coat of paint over the surface.

The painting units are controlled by a photo-electric cell which reads the programme from a reflective tape wound round a rotating drum syncronised with the conveyor belt. Light reflected from the tape is detected by a photo-electric cell which controls the spray-gun triggers. By blacking out portions of the tape a spraying pattern can be built up to match the contours of any shape of vehicle. It is not necessary to mask the car bodies because the machine follows the silhouette and applies the paint only where it is needed.

One of the most useful features of the machine is the colour-change valve. Ordinarily, colour changes involve considerable wastage of paint when solvent has to be used to clean off the previous colour from the hoses. With the new system this wastage is minimised because the hose between the spray-gun and colour-change valve is only 8 in. long and $\frac{1}{8}$ in. in diameter, instead of the usual 6 ft. and $\frac{1}{2}$ in.

In complete contrast, another automatic device invented in 1969 was an automatic pig-feeding system that can feed 500 pigs in ten minutes. It consists of a bulk bin holding up to 20 tons of meal, a 600-gallon water tank, a mixing unit, pump, and control board. Wet feed is pumped to the pig pens through 2-in.-diameter plastic piping and delivered through pneumatically operated outlet valves. The system operates on a continuous cycle. As the feed level drops in the mixer, water and feed meal are metered out and automatically fed into the mixing chamber. One pen is fed at a time; when the pre-set amount of feed has

passed through the first outlet valve the control valve closes it down and opens the outlet valve in the next pen. For automatic operation the system is fitted with time switches, but it can also be used manually. This is a new British invention, which could become a boon to farmers, especially those who find themselves short of staff.

Another new device which is very close to the land is a portable water purifier which "squeezes" the impurities from water by the reverse osmosis process used to turn sea water into fresh water. The purifier, which is powered by a tiny petrol or electric motor, is capable of turning brackish water into pure drinking water at the rate of 100 gallons a day.

A portable water purifier that works on the principle of reverse osmosis.

Inside the Atom

R. E. H. STRACHAN, M.A.

RESEARCH DURING THE last quarter of a century has shown that the atom, far from being the smallest particle of matter, is itself composed of a large number of "building bricks" called subatomic particles. The familiar protons, electrons, and neutrons of which all atoms are composed have been joined by some 200 other particles of various masses, some charged, some neutral, and most having a life to be measured in a small number of microseconds. These short-lived particles usually turn up during atomic transformations produced by particle accelerators. Their number is so great that efforts are continuously being made to arrange them in some ordered fashion, much as the elements have been arranged in the periodic table. A further goal is to find what might be termed the ultimate subatomic brick—some fantastically minute particle of matter from which all other particles are derived. The name "quark" was proposed for these ultimate subatomic particles by the American physicist Dr. M. Gell-Mann, from a word made up by the writer James Joyce. Scientists had looked for quarks for many years, but only in 1969 did anyone claim to have found some.

Irish-born Australian physicist Professor Charles B. McCusker, who announced in September to a conference on cosmic ray studies in Budapest that he had discovered "quarks," the ultimate sub-atomic particles of which all matter may be composed.

If his work is confirmed the name of Professor C. B. McCusker of the University of Sydney may rank with those of Thomson, Rutherford, Bohr, Wilson, and Cockcroft as a major contributor to man's knowledge of the structure of the atom. What McCusker claimed to have discovered was evidence of quarks produced by the action of very intense cosmic rays. In five photographs out of about 60,000 examined he detected the presence of particles which seem to have a charge equal to about $\frac{2}{3}e$ (e is the charge on the electron). This is exactly what had been predicted for one type of quark. The hunt is now on, and work to produce quarks in the laboratory, as well as to detect the other predicted type (which has a charge of $-\frac{1}{3}e$), has been intensified. The possibility that McCusker misinterpreted his photographs was estimated by him as less than 1 per cent, but some physicists were more sceptical. If he is right he will have triumphed where others, using more elaborate and expensive equipment, have so far failed.

Quarks versus Dyons

Gell-Mann's concept of the quark is only one theory to account for the complexities which result from the proliferation of the so-called fundamental particles. Other simplifications have also been suggested. A proposal put forward in 1969 by Dr. Schwinger of Harvard postulated the existence of what he termed "dyons." These, like quarks, would have a charge of $\frac{2}{3}e$ or $-\frac{1}{3}e$, but would also possess a magnetic charge. Schwinger claims that his dyons, if they are ever identified, will dispose of a number of the anomalies which are recognised in existing atomic theory. It may even be that what McCusker found are dyons—but this is a possibility that must be reckoned as very remote.

In the meantime four new subatomic particles have recently been discovered, of which at least two fit into one of the more hopeful patterns of symmetry which have been proposed for the previously known particles. The four particles were detected in hydrogen bubble chambers, both at the European Nuclear Research Centre (CERN) in Geneva and at Brookhaven in the U.S.A. Designated by the Greek letter Xi, they are among the heaviest of the 200 or so subatomic particles known. The experiments at Brookhaven involved the photography of some 700,000 events in the bubble chamber, and after detailed examination of all these photographs only about 150 were found to contain crucial

Great Britain's first SGHWR (steam generating heavy water reactor), at Winfrith Heath, Dorset. Heat generated by uranium dioxide pellets boils light water, the steam passing to a turbo-alternator which is capable of producing an output of 100 megawatts of electricity.

evidence for the existence of the Xi particles. When accelerators of even higher energy are available (such as the proposed 300GeV machine at CERN) even more discoveries about the fundamental particles may well be made.

A New Bubble Chamber

Bubble chambers, which are direct derivatives of the cloud chambers which C. T. R. Wilson developed at Cambridge, are probably the most effective weapons in current use for detecting the existence of rare and very short-lived subatomic particles. The principle is to maintain a tank of liquid gas, such as hydrogen or helium, under pressure and at a temperature a little above its normal boiling point. When fast moving subatomic particles enter this mass of liquid gas, their paths can be seen, when the pressure is suddenly released, as a line of minute bubbles. The bubbles are produced by the vaporising of the liquid by the heat developed as the particle passes through it. The motion of the particles in the magnetic and electric fields which can be established in the bubble chamber, and the effects of collisions, can give evidence of the charge and mass possessed by the particles.

A new technique under development at CERN promises to allow researchers to dispense with the bulky pressure equipment, and at the same time take photographs at a much faster rate. This is a matter of major importance, since it is common for hundreds of thousands of photographs to be taken before

physicists find a record of the rare chance event for which they are looking. The new device replaces the pressure equipment by a beam of ultrasonic waves. These are pressure waves of very short wavelength, and when they pass through a liquid they produce a progressively moving pattern of high and low pressure points. Since the wavelength is short the high pressure points are close together. The speed of sound in the liquid gas is low compared with the speed of the particles. The intensity of the waves is adjusted to be just too low to start boiling the helium except where additional energy is supplied by the passage of a moving particle; then bubbles form at the peaks of the pressure points. The tracks of protons and pions have already been observed in this new chamber, but the quality of the photographs is not yet equal to that obtainable with conventional equipment.

Approach to Absolute Zero

Temperature is a measure of the average energy of motion possessed by the molecules of a material. Thus, while there should be no theoretical upper limit to temperature, a lower limit should occur when molecular motion becomes zero. It is well known that a study of the behaviour of gases reveals that this absolute zero occurs at a temperature very close to $-273°C$.

The size of the effort being made by physicists all over the world to devise methods of getting ever closer to absolute zero is not due alone to its intrinsic interest; all materials undergo remarkable changes of property as their temperature approaches absolute zero—super-fluidity and super-conductivity are well-known examples. A research team of the University of California at San Diego announced in 1969 a new technique for reaching temperatures very close to $-273°C$. The scheme, which uses an isotope of helium, He3, involves mechanical operations only. When in the liquid state the nuclei of this isotope spin at random in all directions, but at temperatures very close to absolute zero the direction of spin becomes regular. The new technique is to compress the liquid He3 at a very low temperature until the spins line up. When this happens the temperature drops. This sounds simple, but the difficulties of working at these very low temperatures are enormous; it is particularly hard to maintain the temperature and once it has been reached, there are fundamental difficulties in its measurement.

All electrical conductors possess some resistance, which causes the development of heat when currents flow in them and thus wastes a percentage of the electrical energy. But at very low temperatures metals become superconducting—that is, lose all their electrical resistance. Although the temperature at which superconductivity occurs differs in different metals, in all cases the temperature is so low that liquid helium must be used as a coolant. At present the highest temperature at which superconductivity occurs is 18°C. above absolute zero, the conductor in this case being an alloy of niobium and tin. If scientists could produce superconductivity at tempera-

tures of the order of 28°C. above absolute zero, then liquid hydrogen could be used as a coolant and the transmission of power along superconducting transmission lines could become an economic possibility.

Scientists at the Brookhaven National Laboratory at Rochester and in New York have suggested on theoretical grounds that a material made up of thin films of silicon and vanadium should become superconducting at 40°C. above absolute zero. The reasons are not understood, but it has been found that if films of materials some few atoms thick are built up into a sandwich, the sandwich becomes superconducting at higher temperatures than a simple mixture of the materials. Similar work is being carried out with other materials at the solid state laboratory at Orsay in France.

Discovery of "Polywater"

Water, the most common of all compounds on our planet, owes much of its usefulness to a number of important and unusual properties. These include its high specific heat (which, among other things, has a profound effect upon climate), its high latent heat, and its so-called anomalous behaviour, which is responsible for the convenient fact that water masses do not freeze solid throughout their bulk but freeze from on top, so that the rate at which the remaining water can lose further heat is diminished. All three properties are dependent on the variety of ways in which simple water molecules, represented by the formula H_2O, can associate into more complex polymers of

High-voltage generator capable of producing 5 million million watts to simulate the flash of gamma radiation, built for the U.S. Atomic Energy Commission at Albuquerque, New Mexico.

Construction in 1969 at Cadarache in the Rhône valley of a new French nuclear reactor, *Phoenix*, which will have an output of 250 megawatts.

the general formula $(H_2O)_n$ where n can have a variety of integral values.

Some evidence is now appearing of the existence of a type of water which consists predominantly of one of the possible polymers. The names "anomalous water," "super-water," and "polywater" have been proposed for this. Investigations have been carried out in Great Britain at the Unilever Research Laboratories at Port Sunlight, in the U.S.A. at the University of Maryland, and in Russia. The researchers at Port Sunlight exposed very fine capillary tubes to saturated water vapour for several days, and found that the water which condensed in some of them differed in density, viscosity, and volatility from ordinary water. It is thought that the effect was due to some surface effect of the glass which imposed an ordered structure on the water molecules. The fascinating possibility has been envisaged that much the same sort of events may occur in living cells, and work in this connection is proceeding at the Aerospace Medical Centre in Pennsylvania.

Infra-red from Space

All bodies at temperatures above absolute zero emit thermal radiations, the quality and quantity of which depend in general on the temperature and on the nature of the radiating surface. Physicists employ the concept of a perfectly black body as one which, at any temperature, is an ideal absorber or radiator of all thermal radiations: that is, the quality and quantity of radiation from a "black body" depend only on its temperature. It is found, however, that if the quantity of radiant heat radiated per second by a "black body" at various wavelengths is plotted against those

wavelengths, the graph always has a maximum value. The sharpness of the maximum, and the wavelength at which it occurs, depend only on the temperature of the radiator. This has been used as a method for determining the temperature of the sun: it is only necessary to determine the wavelength of the radiation at which maximum energy of the sun is radiated and assume that the sun is an ideal radiator (i.e. a "black body"). The technique reveals that the outer layers of the sun are at a temperature of about 5,700°C.

Recent work at Cornell University, U.S.A., has concentrated on thermal radiations from outer space. Any material in space, away from stars and similar hot bodies, must be extremely cold, so that the thermal radiation emitted will have very long wavelengths. If the wavelength for which the energy is a maximum can be determined, this should give an estimate of the temperature at its place of origin. Rockets fired above the blanket of the atmosphere have been used to carry infra-red detectors cooled by liquid helium. Results have suggested that the background radiation originated at temperatures around 8° above absolute zero. More elaborate work is now being prepared, and it is hoped that a clearer picture of the distribution of energy between different wavelengths will reveal a more accurate and perhaps lower estimate of the background temperature. This detailed knowledge might have some significance in deciding what were the events which led to the development of the universe.

Measuring Liquid Density

The determination of the densities of liquids is an operation which can be carried out to a very high degree of accuracy, provided that the quantity of liquid available has a volume of at least 50 c.c. An ingenious technique developed by the Commonwealth Scientific and Industrial Research Organisation in Australia allows the density of samples having a volume of only about 1 c.c. to be determined with a probable error of only two parts in 100,000. The method involves the use of a small glass float which contains a magnet. The mass of the float and magnet must be such that when they are placed in the liquid the float just sinks. A magnetic field is then applied in a vertical direction, and its size is adjusted until the float is just held in suspension. The strength of the field needed will vary with the density of the liquid, and thus can be used to calculate the density. The technique is of particular use when the density of rare biological samples is required, since the volume of liquid needed is very small, and very little of it is lost during the measurements.

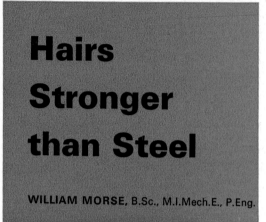

Polyacrylonitrile fibres, three ten-thousandths of an inch thick, before the heat treatment that turns them into carbon fibres.

Rolls-Royce Ltd.

Hairs Stronger than Steel

WILLIAM MORSE, B.Sc., M.I.Mech.E., P.Eng.

THE NEW SCIENCE of "fibre technology" came firmly to the fore in 1969, when the experimental stages of creating new composite materials strengthened with fibres finer than a human hair were emerging into practical industrial uses. For many years, glass-fibre-reinforced plastics (GRP) have been used for car bodies, boats, fishing rods, roofing, vaulting poles, and hundreds of other things, because of their good strength-to-weight ratio, ease of fabrication, corrosion resistance, and cheapness. Their strength-to-weight ratio is better than that of metals like aluminium, titanium, and steel, but their stiffness-to-weight ratio is about the same.

The new carbon, boron, and other fibres, often referred to as "advanced materials," go one better than glass fibres and give really remarkable high-strength low-density composites. Carbon-fibre-reinforced plastics (CFRP), for example, have a strength-to-weight ratio about 50 per cent higher than that of GRP composites, and a stiffness-to-weight ratio about six or seven times higher. In all these composites, the fibres are the load-bearing elements, and the matrix the load-sharing element. The strength in the direction parallel to the fibres is far greater than that in the transverse (or any other) direction. The composite is, in fact, said to have unidirectional strength properties.

In Great Britain, production has been concentrated on carbon fibres, made by a wholly British process resulting from work done at the Royal Aircraft Establishment (RAE), Farnborough, Hants, using an organic textile fibre (polyacrylonitrile) as the precursor. This is a chemical relative of the dress fabric Courtelle. The National Research Development Corporation (NRDC) holds the patents on the process and has licensed Rolls-Royce, Courtaulds, and Morganite Research & Development Ltd. to manufacture it, but none of these companies yet manufactures carbon fibres on a large scale.

The carbon fibres consist of small graphite crystallites aligned so that most of their basal planes are along the fibre axis. There are two basic types: the first is intended for applications calling for a very high stiffness; and in the second the stiffness is somewhat reduced, but the tensile strength is greater. Courtaulds also market another type (Grafil A) having a lower modulus than these two.

For some years it was known that polyacrylonitrile fibres behave differently from other polymers. When heated to about 200°C.

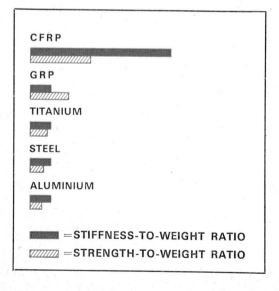

CFRP

GRP

TITANIUM

STEEL

ALUMINIUM

■ =STIFFNESS-TO-WEIGHT RATIO

▨ =STRENGTH-TO-WEIGHT RATIO

they become intensely black through partial decomposition, but do not melt and retain their original fibre form. Very little interest was shown in the end product until scientists at the RAE found that, by restricting shrinkage of the fibres in the oxidation stage, vastly superior properties could be obtained.

The polyacrylonitrile used in the RAE process, specially developed for the purpose by Courtaulds, is in the form of a continuous multi-filament tow of 10,000 fibres, each with a diameter of about 0·0003 in. When heat-treated in air at 200°C., it loses weight and tends to shrink, but this is prevented by a frame and the fibres are thereby put in tension. A second heat treatment at 1,000°C. carbonises them, and during subsequent heat treatment in an inert atmosphere, the material loses its nitrogen and hydrogen (and some of its carbon), leaving a residue of exceedingly high-strength pure carbon fibres. Tows of these are placed side by side to form a sheet and laid in a solution of epoxy or other resin in a volatile solvent, which is then evaporated, to give an even, predetermined thickness of "pre-preg" sheet (as it is called, from the word "pre-impregnated"), containing known proportions of carbon and resin.

Rolls-Royce call their preimpregnated carbon fibre material Hyfil; Morganite Research & Development Ltd. use the name Modmor; and Courtaulds call their range of products Grafil. Le Carbone Lorraine Co. in France use the name Rigilor.

Industrial Applications

One of the most publicised uses of carbon fibres is for the low-pressure compressor (fan) blades of the Rolls-Royce advanced technology aero-engine the RB 211. The fan blades are nearly 3 ft. long and have a tip chord of 1 ft. If made of titanium, a possible alternative, the blades would weigh almost three times as much as in Hyfil, and this would naturally greatly increase the overall weight of the engine, because the casing and shaft would have to be heavier to suit.

Rolls-Royce manufacture their high-duty composite components by a process of building up from thin laminations which are cut from unidirectional sheet in the manner known as cross-plying or cross-bracing (see diagrams in next page). Once the complicated preform

shapes have been established by extremely accurate lofting techniques, the shapes can easily be cut out by unskilled labour. The cut sheets of pre-preg are placed together in the correct sequence and have sufficient tackiness to remain in position until the whole assembly is placed in a matched die. The die is then closed and subjected to a controlled cycle of pressure and temperature.

In structural applications carbon-fibre composites are chiefly being employed in conjunction with existing materials to give increased strength and stiffness where they are most required. On the Ford GT 40 car, which won at Le Mans in 1968 and 1969, a combination of CFRP and glass-fibre cloth produced a stronger and stiffer body structure,

Comparison of beams of various materials 12 in. long and 1 in. thick, designed to support 10,000 lb. at the centre under a deflection of 0.1 in.

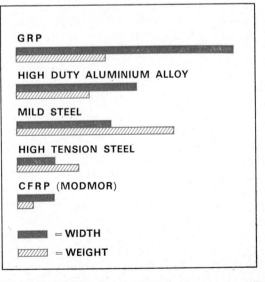

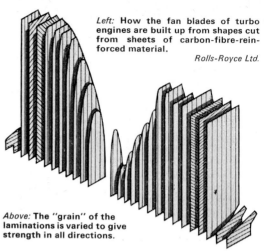

Above: The "grain" of the laminations is varied to give strength in all directions.

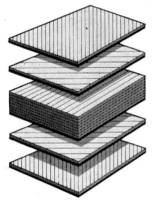

Left: Cross-plying or cross-bracing of layers of CFRP, so that its unidirectional strength can be utilised in a multidirectional manner.

and so cured the vibration drumming previously encountered at high speeds, as well as saving 60 lb. on body weight. In the Lola GT sports car the ultra-lightweight nose section, made by Specialised Mouldings Ltd. of Huntingdon, is of glass-fibre-reinforced polyester resin, with a network of Grafil HM carbon fibres, which give a 20 per cent weight-saving with increased stiffness. Grafil is used also in all the Maclaren Can-AM series of cars, as well as in the Maclaren Formula 1 bodies.

In aircraft design, where there is a constant search for materials that will give the same strength for less weight, CFRP is being tried out in the BAC-311 for reinforcing the flanges of conventional light-alloy metal floor beams, support members in the pressure bulkhead, and in other places where its unidirectional properties are particularly valuable. Students at the College of Aeronautics, Cranfield, have been investigating the use of CFRP in a plastic matrix of Araldite, which lends itself well to the design of wing spars. Sandwich flooring, developed by William Mallinson Ltd., and made up of carbon-fibre composite and balsa

wood, is 25 per cent lighter than conventional aluminium-faced flooring, so that on an aircraft like the BAC-111, with a floor area of 600 sq. ft., about 150 lb. can be saved.

Gears, Boats, Golf Clubs

Chopped carbon fibres have been used by British Rail in nylon gears produced by the injection moulding process. Experimental work is being carried out by Ian Proctor Metal Masts Ltd. on the use of carbon fibres in conjunction with metal for masts of the Flying Dutchman class of yacht; it is thought that the basic section of the mast will be reduced to three-quarters of that normally used. Grafil was successfully used in a boat manufactured by Parkers of Boston, which won the National 505 sailing championship at Plymouth in July 1969. In this instance the carbon fibres acted as reinforcement for glass fibres. A similar technique was employed in the canoes supplied by Streamlyte Mouldings to the British competitors in the World Canoe and Kayak Championships held in France in the summer of 1969.

Carbon-fibre paper webs and laminates have been designed and patented by W. & R. Balston Industrial Ltd. for use in bearings, containers, and vessels. At the Summerfield Research Station of Imperial Metal Industries Ltd., work on carbon fibres in an epoxy resin has been going on since late 1966. High-stiffness material has been used for a honeycomb sandwich and for a satellite structure, the resulting weight of which is 30 per cent less than that of a similar structure of aluminium alloy. Filament-wound tubes have also been made there. The National Engineering Laboratory at East Kilbride is investigating the possibilities of carbon fibres for sports goods (tennis rackets, golf clubs, and so forth), and have produced an experimental golf club that is claimed to lengthen the drive by 30 yds. The shaft is reinforced with carbon fibres to give greater stiffness and less weight. Chemical plant may be an important outlet for carbon fibres, too; combining the chemical resistance of the carbon with that of a suitable resin can provide corrosion-resistant pump impellers, casings, stirrer shafts, and pressure vessels. The Atomic Energy Establishment at Harwell has produced a carbon-fibre-reinforced glass twice as strong as ordinary glass and capable of withstanding a sudden temperature change from 550°C. to 4°C. without cracking.

Boron-Fibre Composites

Fibre-reinforced composites using a plastic matrix are suitable only for fairly low temperatures. For higher temperatures a metal matrix is required, but there is always a possibility that the fibres will react with the molten metal, and there can be difficulty in obtaining enough "wetting." A technique has been developed by the Fulmer Research Institute, U.S.A., to overcome this problem by coating the carbon fibres with tungsten, but for high temperature applications it would seem that boron fibres in a metal matrix are more practical.

Boron fibres have been developed mainly in the U.S.A. Details published by Goodyear Aerospace on a composite of boron in an epoxy resin matrix for a high-pressure moulding used for an engine-gear housing show that it weighs considerably less than the light-metal housing that was considered for the job, and has about twice the stiffness. The General Technologies Corporation, Virginia, has tried boron fibres in a magnesium matrix, since the two do not react. The boron-fibre bundles are passed through a molten bath of magnesium, and the composite put through suitable forming rolls, as it cools, to make rods; tubes, I-sections, and other shapes are also possible.

One of the most important applications to date for boron fibres is in the Pratt & Whitney JT8D turbofan engine, which has experimental first-stage fan blades made entirely of boron (Borsic)-aluminium composite. With a diameter of 40 in. the fan blade is the largest rotating engine component so far made of metal matrix composites. In the current JT8D engines in the Boeing 727 and 737, and the Sud Aviation Super Caravelle commercial transport aircraft, there are 30 blades, each of which weighs 15½ oz. compared with 26 oz. for titanium blades.

The main difference between the new fan and its conventional counterpart is the absence

Shrouds

In the Pratt and Whitney JT8D aero engine, fan blades made of titanium (*upper*) need the support of part-span shrouds, while those made from boron-fibre-aluminium composite (*lower*) require no such stiffening.

of the part-span shrouds which are needed in the titanium version to stiffen the blades against vibration. As a result blade efficiency is improved, because the drag of the shrouds is eliminated. Weight-savings throughout the engine result from the lighter blades, for centrifugal forces on the rotor are thereby reduced. In fact, overall engine weight reductions of about 12 per cent may be possible for supersonic turbofans, when the lighter materials are applied to other components, such as discs, stators, cases, etc.

The Borsic-aluminium tape used for the blades, which was developed by United Aircraft Research Laboratories, is available in many widths and lengths. It is composed of a monolayer of parallel Borsic fibres interspersed with plasma-sprayed aluminium and backed by aluminium foil. About 50 per cent of the tape's total weight is made up of Borsic filament, spaced at 175 fibres per inch of tape width. The method of manufacture is similar to that used in making carbon-fibre-reinforced blades. Tapes of appropriate shapes are cut to the right lengths, stacked in a jig duplicating the shape of the blade, and bonded together under pressure and heat.

Thanks are due to many companies that have supplied information for this article, particularly Morganite Research & Development Ltd., Rolls-Royce (Composite Materials) Ltd., Courtaulds Ltd., Fothergill & Harvey Ltd., Imperial Metal Industries Ltd., and Pratt & Whitney Aircraft.

The Telephone's Resounding Tinkle

PAT HAWKER

IN TELECOMMUNICATIONS, 1969 saw the industry's most spectacular success yet—the relaying of live speech and television pictures direct from the surface of the moon and their immediate distribution to hundreds of millions of homes. But it is in the development of everyday communications that the long-term significance of any year must be judged; in this respect we continued to witness the growing marriage of computers with communications techniques, the steady enlargement of global space communications and ocean cable networks, and improvements in the millions upon millions of local telephone subscriber connections.

Despite the growth of telecommunications over the past decade, there remain enormous variations in the extent to which the basic telephone services have developed in different countries. Whereas there are over 100 million telephones in service in the U.S.A. (representing almost 52 telephones per 100 population), the figures for other countries, even the highly industrialised ones, are notably smaller: Australia has some 3·1 million telephones (27 per 100); the U.K., 12 million (22 per 100); Japan, 18 million (18 per 100); France, 6·9 million (14 per 100); South Africa, 1·3 million (7 per 100); Brazil, 1·4 million (2 per 100). Only Sweden with 3·9 million (50 per 100), and Canada with 8·3 million (41 per 100), approach the U.S. telephone saturation level. There is an equally wide variation in the use made of the telephone, from some 670 calls per person per year in the U.S.A. and Canada to 200 in Australia and 60 in France. The telephone statistics of the emergent countries fall far below these figures. It is thus in the growth of what has been called the "plain ordinary telephone service," where the vast majority of conversations are between persons only a few miles apart, that the main development is still to come. And for the vast majority, it is the "plain ordinary telephone service" that is most in demand.

Yet one of the fastest growing services during the year was not the telephone but the Telex, by which messages are transmitted and received by automatic typewriter-teleprinter machines located within subscribers' premises. In the U.K. this service is growing at a rate of about 15 per cent a year. By the end of 1969, some 30,000 machines were in use—double the figure for 1965. Similarly, facsimile (picture telegraphy) and data-transmission services continued to grow in importance, although the volume of data traffic is still well below the volume of speech, even in the U.S.A. Data-transmission (Datel) services range in speed from roughly 48,000 bits per second downwards. (A "bit" is a single binary numeral— 0 or 1—by which most computers calculate.) The increasing adoption of push-button dialling telephones ("keyphones") will have far-reaching consequences for the remote control of many types of apparatus, and also for transmitting small amounts of data to remote computers

New Dials and Cables

Business users of telephone services are increasingly being offered various forms of "repertory diallers." These are phones that can be programmed with a repertoire of the telephone numbers most frequently needed by the user, so that a simple operation (pressing one of a number of buttons, or two digit-

The push-button telephone is handy for the ordinary subscriber but vital for manual data transmission.

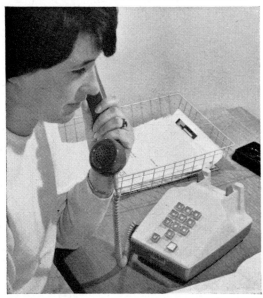

Model of the new British Post Office Research Station at Martlesham Heath near Ipswich, in which the famous old Dollis Hill centre will be rehoused. £11 million a year is spent by the Post Office on research.

dialling) can automatically put through a local, trunk, or even international call to any such number. With the long calling codes now in use, these facilities offer an important simplification for a busy switchboard operator. Many countries continue to experience difficulties in meeting the exploding demands for telecommunications facilities of all types: even New York City, one of the major telephone webs, faced problems in handling telephone and computer-data transmission during 1969, and there were several temporary breakdowns in some of the large switching centres. The British Post Office claimed a "world first" in its major use of aluminium instead of copper in cables linking subscribers' telephones with local exchanges. This use of aluminium follows recent solutions of difficulties previously experienced in the jointing of aluminium cables and in preventing corrosion. A new crimping tool compresses wire ends inside an insulated connector without stripping off the plastic insulation. Corrosion on underground cables is largely prevented by packing cables with petroleum jelly.

The G.P.O. itself experienced a major change in its administrative structure on October 1, 1969, when it ceased to be a department of state under the Postmaster General, and became a commercial Post Office Corporation run by a board of directors. The main effect of the change is to separate its commercial activities from its other functions, which have now passed to a new Ministry of Posts and Telecommunications. To continue the long tradition of Post Office research activities, some £11 million is being spent annually. For many years the centre of research has been at Dollis Hill in N.W. London, but the building of a new research station at Martlesham, near Ipswich, began during the year.

Computer-Controlled Phones

During 1969, the Australian Postmaster General invited tenders for the development of a nation-wide data transmission system, which is expected to begin operation in some areas of Australia during 1971. The existing telecommunications network will be augmented by the installation of computer-based switching centres in the capital cities. Progress in the extension of the high-capacity trunk system during 1969 included the bringing of Perth within the network, which now links all Australian State capitals. The contract for the Sydney electronic trunk exchange was awarded in November, to Standard Telephones and Cables Pty. Ltd. of Sydney. This is for a "Metaconta" system (originally developed by the Bell Telephone Manufacturing Company of Antwerp, Belgium), which incorporates stored programme control and built-in facilities for push-button dialling, call transfers, traffic measurement, and centralised supervision.

In the search for new electronic techniques to aid the rapid switching of telephone circuits, the future importance of the computer is widely accepted. Many of the various systems under development are based on the use of central computers as the heart of large telephone exchanges. However, a technique disclosed by Plessey during 1969, and likely to be the first British system to incorporate stored programme control, uses a multiplicity of small processors on an interchangeable function basis. Advantages claimed for this approach include reliability, flexibility, relatively low initial cost, and easy expansion of the system when required.

A new "voice with a smile" automatic telephone call intercept system is to be installed in a number of American cities. This equipment informs callers who have dialled an incorrect or unassigned number on the correct action to be taken. A 96-track magnetic drum contains recorded phrases, words, and digits that can be assembled under computer control to cope with a large number of circumstances. The recordings, although used for composite messages, have been arranged to sound as natural as possible. A central exchange has a disc memory on which will be stored unassigned numbers and whether these have previously been used, and this information enables the central processor to assemble the phrases in the main drum store. The disc stores can be readily updated by using a typewriter keyboard; this will allow, for example, a patient to be given information on how to reach a doctor who is absent from his surgery. The system can also be used for various answering services, including weather forecasts, sports information, time checks, and the like.

Help for the Handicapped

While the telephone is a useful aid for everyone, there is one section of the community to whom its value is incalculable: for the badly disabled or handicapped person it may be a line to life. For this reason, the major telecommunications administrations are constantly striving to develop techniques which would bring the benefits of the telephone service to the paralysed, to the deaf and hard of hearing, and to the dumb. During 1969, many prototype devices for this purpose were described and some were undergoing field trials. The British Post Office was initiating tests of a system whereby severely paralysed people who, as a result of spinal cord injuries or the after-effects of polio, have little controllable movement in their bodies below the neck, could dial their own telephone calls by puffing and sucking at a tube. This is based on the use of "patient-operated selector mechanisms" in conjunction with a loud-speaking telephone, and converts pneumatic signals from the mouth into electrical outputs by means of diaphragm-operated micro-switches controlling uniselectors.

Another device, called the Code-Com, has been developed by Bell Telephone Laboratories for people who are totally deaf, deaf and blind, or deaf and mute. This consists of a conventional telephone and a special signal unit containing light bulbs, a vibrating disc, and a telegraph sending key. In effect, the handicapped person uses the telephone line to communicate by Morse code, using a flashing light to attract a deaf person, who could then use the vibrating disc or lights to receive the code signals. A disadvantage is the need for training users in the operating code.

Limited trials were also in progress in the U.S.A. of a combination of a telephone with a teleprinter (teletypewriter) and flashing-light calling device. In practice, a deaf person would place his telephone instrument in a coupling box and then use the teletypewriter to communicate his messages. Western Electric were making a dual-frequency tone ringer which is more effective than conventional ringers in summoning persons with partial hearing. Another aid is the amplifying telephone, with adjustable volume control to serve users with either normal or impaired hearing.

Undersea Links

During 1969, work began on the laying of the new TAT5 ocean cable to link the U.S.A. with Spain and also with many other main telephone cable routes including those with the U.K., South Africa, and Mediterranean countries. When the 3,500-nautical-mile TAT5 comes into service during 1970 to carry up to 720 telephone circuits, it will be by far the highest capacity cable yet linking America with Europe. Much of the special lightweight cable for the system has been made at Southampton, England, by Standard Telephones and Cables. An interesting feature of the

Laying a new undersea telecommunications cable across the Western Mediterranean between Barcelona and Pisa.

The new generation of Intelsat satellites launched in 1969 required a new set of ground stations. *Left:* lifting a new 81 ft.-wide dish aerial into position at Pleumeur Bodou, France. *Right:* Goonhilly 2 ready for action.

shore end laying of TAT5 is the use of a "ploughing vehicle" to bury the cable some inches in the sea bed to provide added protection against breakage by trawlers.

The year also saw the first use of telephone cables linking the U.K. with Portugal, and Portugal with South Africa. While the coming of satellite communications has slowed down the extension of the world's telephone ocean cable networks, the importance of this form of international telecommunications has by no means been lost.

Satellite Communicaticns

The international civil satellite system continued to grow rapidly in scope and importance until, by the end of 1969, it could fairly be considered as rapidly approaching a global network. Many new satellite earth stations, with their enormous dish aerials, were either commissioned or under construction. The civil satellites are operating under the aegis of Intelsat (International Telecommunications Satellite Consortium). This is an international organisation set up under a 1964 agreement with the object of establishing a world system of satellite communications, and now including almost 70 nations. The management organisation for the international body is the American Communications Satellite Corpo-

ration (Comsat). The interim international agreement signed in 1964 is expected to be replaced by a more permanent agreement in 1970, and during 1969 negotiations were continuing on this question. Under the interim agreement, the U.S.A. has held a majority share in Intelsat. Main abstainers from the system are the U.S.S.R. and its associated countries, who have announced their intention of forming an Intersputnik civil communications system; but they may eventually participate in Intelsat. The U.S.S.R. operates her own Molniya satellites for communication between her European and Asiatic extremes; two replacement Molniya satellites were sent up in April and July 1969.

During the year, the British Post Office formally brought into use a new twin-aerial station at Goonhilly Downs, Cornwall, with a 90-ft.-diameter aerial for operation with Intelsat's Atlantic satellites; and the earlier 85-ft.-diameter aerial is now allocated for the Indian Ocean satellite. New earth stations were opened by Cable & Wireless at Hong Kong and Bahrein, with a second aerial soon to be erected in Hong Kong and a further station planned for Jamaica.

Intelsat III satellites were successfully launched during 1969 for both the Pacific and Indian Ocean stations, but an attempt to

R.A.F. operator's view at Oakhanger, Hants, headquarters of the British military satellite system called Skynet.

During the Apollo moon voyages, television pictures were successfully transmitted from the command modules by means of a specially developed colour camera. For the first moon-landing, the camera set up on the surface was limited to 320-lines, monochrome, 10 pictures per second. Special communications techniques were utilised to bring these pictures back to earth, where they were distributed over the Intelsat network to many countries. Interest was so high in Europe that even at 3 a.m. G.M.T. electric power consumption was reported as exceptionally high in many cities because of the number of viewers watching the historic transmissions. On the second landing the surface camera unfortunately failed after a few minutes.

Progress also continued on other communication applications of the new tool of space satellites. A new giant American military satellite makes it possible to extend the system down to relatively small tactical units equipped with their own little dish aerials. During 1969 the British military Skynet system was prepared in readiness for full operational use in 1970. From the main centre of this system at Oakhanger, Hants, both communications and control signals are transmitted to transportable earth stations in Cyprus, Gan, Bahrein, Singapore, and Hong Kong—and also to ships. This is a multiple access system allowing independent circuits to be set up between the different earth stations to a total of some 22 duplex speech circuits through the satellite.

In Europe, members of the European Broadcasting Union have been planning to use satellites to form a permanent television network linking together the national networks of most European countries, as a substitute for the more costly terrestrial networks at present in use. It was also announced that plans are being made for the trial use of an ATS3 satellite of the National Aeronautics and Space Administration (NASA) for television broadcasting directly to community receivers in Indian villages. Such a system could be the forerunner of the extensive use of synchronous space satellites for broadcasting to small local master aerials or even directly to individual viewers' homes.

launch a replacement for the Atlantic Ocean failed. These satellites have to be put up into the special synchronous orbit 22,300 miles above the earth's equator, in which position they orbit the earth at the same speed as the earth's rotation, so that they appear to stay in the same position. Unfortunately, the main Atlantic Intelsat III satellite developed a temporary fault on June 29, 1969, and was unavailable for the relays of the Apollo 11 moon-landing or for the investiture of the Prince of Wales, but coverage of these events was relayed between North America and Europe via Japan and, as a further step, the original Early Bird (now called Intelsat I) was brought back into use after having been "retired" early in 1969 after four years. Later, the fault in the Atlantic Intelsat III satellite—the rotating aerial joint was affected by differences in temperature between various parts of the satellite—was overcome, and the satellite was brought back into service. Twenty-four circuits on the Intelsat III satellite over the Pacific were leased for trans-Australian (Sydney to Perth) telephone calls from November 20—the first instance of the use of a "stationary" international satellite for internal communications over a mainland on a regular commercial basis. It will cease when the trans-Australia microwave radio system becomes operational in mid-1970.

At the beginning of 1969 there were about 23 earth stations, in 15 countries, capable of working with the Intelsat satellites. By the end of the year, the number had increased to 43 stations in 26 countries. During the year work continued also on the development of the next satellite generation (Intelsat IV), which will be able to handle an even greater number of telephone and television circuits than Intelsat III.

Man and his Environment

F. E. G. COX, B.Sc., Ph.D.
Reader in Zoology in the University of London

EVERY ANIMAL is a product of its genetic make-up moulded by the environment in which it finds itself. In most cases life is a compromise between the potentialities of the animal and the hazards of the environment. Man is no exception to this rule. In 1969 biological research turned away from molecular and cellular biology towards Man himself and his environment, and as a result of discoveries made during the year certain well established beliefs were changed and new horizons opened. Much is now known of how the genetic make-up of an individual determines his behaviour, how a human egg can be fertilised in a test tube, and how an animal might receive cells directly from its mother. It is now clear that certain body activities thought to be involuntary can be controlled, while the voluntary activities of Man have made the environment impossible for other animals. It also became clearer how Man and other animals overcome viral infections and how certain deficiencies result in disease.

Chromosomes and Crime

Chromosomes are elements in every cell of the body carrying the heredity factors called genes. A normal woman's cells possess two X chromosomes, and a normal man's one X and one Y. It seems from this that maleness is determined by the presence of a Y chromosome, but the Y chromosome itself is not enough to convey this trait, for a number of cases have been recorded of women with a Y chromosome as well as two X chromosomes. In fact, a considerable number of people possess an extra chromosome of one sort or the other. Dr. N. Maclean and his colleagues in Great Britain analysed over 12,000 patients in mental hospitals and found that the proportion of such people with an extra X chromosome is greater than the proportion in the normal population. Schizophrenics, for example, had more than twice the number of abnormalities. In general it was concluded that the presence of an extra X chromosome could be correlated with mental disturbance. Dr. Maclean was careful to point out that this does not mean

that the extra chromosome *causes* mental disturbance, but it can cause physical changes which in themselves could well lead to mental disturbance.

The presence of an extra Y chromosome is even more disturbing. Dr. D. J. Bartlett of the Medical Research Council's Population Genetics Unit at Oxford and his colleagues examined 204 male inmates of a maximum security prison hospital, and found that 47 of them possessed XYY chromosomes. In normal populations the proportion of these "super-males" is about 1 in 2,000. Most of the men were intelligent and tall, but nearly all had a long history of crime and had shown resistance to conventional training and treatment. It seems therefore that some criminal activities should be regarded as a disease. In late 1968 an Australian court accepted proof of an extra Y chromosome in an accused man as evidence in support of a plea of diminished responsibility.

The Permeable Placenta

It has long been one of the fundamental concepts of immunology that the placenta protects the foetus from the immunological responses of its mother by acting as a physical barrier. Experiments by a group of scientists at the Institute of Child Health in London have shown that this is not true. They found that eggs transplanted from one strain of mouse to another developed into animals containing the cells of the host mother. This can only mean that whole cells can cross the placenta. Of the various possibilities emerging from these experiments the most important is that the foetus can be regarded as a mosaic. This may explain why the foetus is not rejected by the mother, for the cells may be regarded as "self" and not recognised as "foreign." Another possibility is that the extra chromosomes mentioned above may be acquired in this way.

Test-tube Fertilisation

The first step towards the growth of human beings in test tubes is the fertilisation of the egg by the male sperm. This has now been done by

Dr. R. G. Edwards of Cambridge and his colleagues Drs. B. D. Bavister and P. C. Steptoe. Hitherto the incidence of fertilisation under laboratory conditions has been very low, but Dr. Edwards and his colleagues have succeeded by using a technique developed in experiments with hamsters. The significance of the discovery is that it opens the way for experiments on the growth of human multi-cellular blastocysts under controlled conditions. Once this has been done it will be possible to investigate the various defects which occur during the early stages of embryo growth—for example, the effects of physical damage or the activity of enzymes. The journal *Nature* pointed out that this work does not herald "1984," but reminded scientists that they must explain their purpose in performing experiments of this kind.

Experiments in Learning

Two types of animal behaviour have long been recognised. They are those based on voluntary and those based on involuntary actions. In performing a voluntary action—for example, moving an arm or leg—an animal "knows" what it is doing and can control the action. Involuntary actions, which cannot be controlled by the animal, include such activities as pulse rate and the secretion of digestive substances in mammals. Dr. Neal Miller, of the Rockefeller University, New York, reported in 1969 on experiments which show that the separation of actions into voluntary and involuntary is misleading, for he demonstrated that certain involuntary activities can be learned. Salivation in dogs is a classical involuntary action, yet Dr. Miller trained dogs to increase their salivation by rewarding them for increased output. Similarly he was able to teach them to decrease their production of saliva.

In other experiments animals were trained to alter their rate of heart beat and even to constrict or dilate certain blood vessels. All precautions were taken to avoid the possibility that voluntary muscles were involved, and it must be concluded that the two kinds of behaviour do grade into each other. In another series of experiments Drs. Shapiro, Tursky, Gershon, and Stern of Harvard demonstrated that human volunteers could be trained to alter their blood pressures by rewarding the desired effect. It is likely that some of the mysteries of human control over body activities—for instance, the practices of holy men in India—may be explained in terms of trained voluntary behaviour.

Human speech is one of the most sophisticated learnt techniques, and yet many humans are able to communicate by sign language without resorting to words. Chimpanzees kept in the company of children perform as well as the children for about three years, and then lag behind. It is possible that this is because chimpanzees cannot be trained to talk. Drs. R. A. Gardner and B. T. Gardner have studied communication in chimpanzees by teaching them to use simple sign language limited to the use of the hand or arm. The results are promising: one chimpanzee learned in just over a year to use nineteen signs and understand more. Such experiments make considerable contributions to our understanding of the processes of learning and speech.

Trends in Pollution

All biologists are fully aware of the dangers of pollution by substances ranging from insecticides to industrial wastes, and there are signs that the general public, too, is being made aware of the dangers. DDT, one of the most effective and widely used insecticides, is a chlorinated hydrocarbon and as such is so stable that it accumulates in water and soil. It can end up in the carnivores of the final stages of food chains, since these animals feed on others which have been in contact with the insecticide. An article in *Nature* by workers from several American universities put the blame for the declining populations of many birds on the use of DDT, and in particular cited the peregrine falcon, which is now nearly extinct in the eastern States of the U.S.A.

The sale of DDT compounds had already been prohibited in Sweden, and in 1969 Denmark placed a ban on their use and Canada introduced restrictions which allowed them on only a few crops. In the U.S.A., Michigan and California banned and Arizona restricted them. Australia also restricts their use. It appeared likely that Great Britain would soon follow these good examples.

Although DDT may disappear from the market, polychlorinated biphenyls (PCBs), used in some industrial processes, may replace it as a pollutant. These substances are being found in birds and eggs in Europe and the U.S.A., and they were considered one possible contributor among others to the death of thousands of sea birds along the west coast of Great Britain in August–October.

While substances that are actually responsible for pollution are receiving some attention, those which are bound to cause trouble in the future are not. Two kinds of pollution which are not yet serious problems are those caused by nitrogen and by hot water wastes. According to Dr. Barry Commoner, of Washington University, the nitrogen waste

ISOLATION OF A SET OF GENES

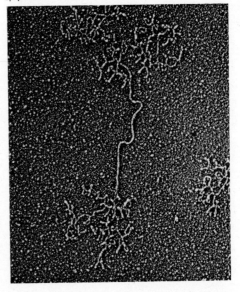

In November Drs. J. Beckwith, J. Shapiro, and L. Eron at Harvard Medical School for the first time isolated an operon (a specific group of genes like those shown above) from the DNA (deoxyribonucleic acid, life's basic genetic material) in the chromosome of a bacterium. The scientists caused the bacterium to be attacked by two viruses which, when they broke away, carried bacterial DNA, including the operon, with them. DNA is arranged in a double spiral (*below left*) ; each strand will combine only with its own mate. When separated strands of DNA from the two viruses were brought together (*right*), they combined at the operon, which they had in common, but nowhere else. By removing the uncombined portions (the ragged ends at top and bottom of the photo) the scientists were left with the pure group of genes (the smooth central portion). The scientists themselves warned of the potential danger of their achievement. By the introduction of genes for "desirable" characteristics, human beings of specialised types could be bred in "people factories"—a terrifying power in the wrong hands.

All these photographs were magnified scores of thousands of times by means of the electron microscope. The historic photo above shows for the first time genes (the carrot-shaped structures) actually producing RNA (ribonucleic acid), which instructs every cell how to build up protein to make its individual character.

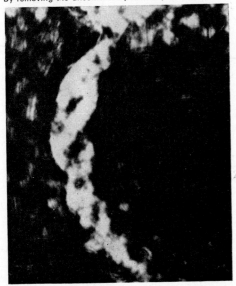

from sewage has increased in the U.S.A. by 70 per cent in 25 years, while nitrogen from fumes of various kinds has increased by 300 per cent and from fertilisers by 1,400 per cent. The important question is where this nitrogen ends up. Initially, waste nitrogen compounds, in the form of nitrates, entering water may cause excessive growth of algae, which in turn reduces the amount of oxygen present, causing the death of plants and animals both invertebrate and vertebrate.

But this is not the only danger. Nitrates are converted into nitrites, which are toxic, by certain bacteria living in the alimentary canal of Man and probably other animals: therefore the pollution of water supplies and foodstuffs must be prevented. In certain parts of the U.S.A. the nitrogen content of drinking water has already exceeded the maximum permitted level of 10 parts per million, and in Europe the nitrogen content of vegetables is approaching the danger level. The direct effects of nitrogen excess are greatest in young children, yet large amounts of nitrates have been found in baby foods.

Few people would regard hot water as a problem, yet thermal waste is becoming increasingly important in the pollution of water. Most hot water comes from the cooling systems of generating plant from which it is pumped into streams or the sea. In an article in *Scientific American* in March 1969, Dr. John Clark drew attention to the long-term effects of thermal pollution. The animals affected are cold-blooded ones whose metabolic activities are seriously altered by changes in the environmental temperature.

In general, metabolic activities double with every 10°C. increase in temperature. Thus the whole life of an animal is changed by an increase in temperature: it moves faster, breathes faster, and requires more oxygen. But such increases in activity cannot go on unchecked, and eventually thermal death occurs. An increase in temperature unleashes an unpredictable chain of consequences which are different in different areas. Dr. S. K. Eltringham, for instance, found increased activity among wood-boring crustaceans in Southampton Water, which reduces the life of piers and piles. Thermal pollution can be prevented by the sensible use of cooling towers, but in the U.S.A. the difference between the temperature in some rivers and the temperature at which no native fish can live is less than 3°C.

The Body's Defences

All higher animals are able to recognise substances injected into them as "foreign" and to react against them. At one time it was thought that the single term "antibody" embraced all such reactions, but it is now clear that several mechanisms are involved. The body produces antibodies against viruses, but some years ago it was realised that another antiviral substance is also produced which is not an antibody. This substance, called interferon, is produced as the result of damage to cells by viruses. Interferon limits the course of an infection, but in most animals the amount produced is insufficient to bring a viral infection under control. However, certain substances, called interferon inducers, have been found which elicit the production of interferon, and Dr. J. H. Park of the New York Medical College, and Dr. S. Baron of the National Institute of Allergy and Infectious Diseases, have used such a substance to *cure* a viral infection. The substance was artificial double-stranded RNA, and the infection cured was that caused by the herpes virus in rabbits. The protective effects of interferon are not limited to viruses, for two groups of U.S. biologists, one at the National Naval Medical Centre, Bethesda, and the other at the New York University School of Medicine, have produced evidence that interferon and interferon inducers give some protection against malaria.

Interferon apart, the normal response to invading organisms is the production of antibodies. Within the last decade the role of the thymus gland in the immune response has become clear. The thymus is a small endocrine gland situated in the chest. It appears that there are two distinct and separate immunological systems, one concerned with the cellular response, including the rejection of skin grafts and organ transplants, and the other concerned with the circulating antibodies. The cellular response is thymus-dependent, while the circulating antibody response is not. For many years cases have been recorded of people suffering from a deficiency of antibody. Such people cannot overcome infections by producing antibodies, but can reject "foreign" tissue and can exhibit a hypersensitive reaction (allergy). Such cases indicate the existence of two immunological systems. It was only in 1969 that confirmatory observations were made on children without an active thymus. Drs. R. Kretschmer, B. Say, D. Brown, and F. S. Rosen, at the Harvard Medical School, reported that such children are unable to reject foreign tissue or exhibit hypersensitivity, although quite able to produce normal antibodies. Thus the cause of another series of immunological diseases has been traced. The cure is probably a thymus transplantation.

The Human Sciences

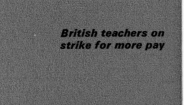

British teachers on strike for more pay

Filling in the Details of History

GEOFFREY RIDSDILL SMITH, M.A.

An Australian mining engineer, having an early morning wash in the Cleland Hills beside the Thomas Reservoir 200 miles west of Alice Springs in 1961, suddenly saw on the massive blocks of sandstone all round him a number of carvings pencilled in shadow by the rising sunlight. There was even one beside his wash-basin. Until that moment no one had noticed these drawings of concentric circles, human faces and bodies, footprints, animal tracks, and abstract forms, for weathering had rendered them invisible except in certain oblique lights. Originally they would have stood out, for the pre-aboriginal artists, with their flake-tools, cut through to the light rock beneath the surface. Analysis of rock samples may show the nature of the weathering and its rate of development, which will in turn help to date the carvings. Since archaeological experts began to survey the find in earnest no less than 387 of these petroglyphs have been recorded, but the origin of their design remains a mystery. The facial expressions range from happy to sad, though all have round eyes, large foreheads, and narrow chins. The bodies are in two parts, with the head and trunk separated from the pelvis to which arms and legs are attached. It is hoped that more such drawings will be found at two other waterholes in the area where men may once have settled.

It was a more sophisticated worker in stone who, in A.D. 200, carved the Jupiter column outside the villa of a Roman farmer near the German town of Heilbronn in the Neckar valley. The column stands 25 feet high and was erected to induce the god to send good weather for the harvest. Jupiter rides his horse on top of the column which is embossed with oak leaves and acorns. The capital is supported by the four seasons, round the pedestal are the seven days of the week, and on the base is an inscription bearing the name of the villa's owner, Caius Vettius Connougus.

A Roman villa recently excavated at Sparsholt, near Winchester, has produced what is described as "a text-book example of what a prosperous Roman farmstead looked like." Indeed it has been possible to reconstruct the villa in model form, with its open fields to the west, traced from aerial photographs, and what may have been vineyard terraces in the eastern valley. The farmstead consisted of three or four buildings round a walled farmyard in the entrance of which the ruts of farm wagons are still discernible. The roofs were of Purbeck stone slates or brick tiles, and the walls mostly of flint with string courses of shaped stone, rendered with mortar outside and gaudily painted plaster inside.

The oldest building, not yet completely excavated, was once a roomy aisled hall where the farm-workers probably lived. One end of this hall had been converted to a bath suite, with undressing room, cold bath, warm room, hot room, and hot bath. The main house had a verandah running all along its front with an entrance in the middle. Brightly coloured geometric panels decorated the walls of the reception room and on the floor there was a very fine geometric mosaic. This room appears to have been heated by a brazier, for one can still see the floor discoloured where it stood, as in a smaller room which may have been a study. The centrally heated living room, with hypocaust room beyond it, would have been more comfortable. Winchester was only a 20-minute carriage drive away, and it is

Above and in facing page: pre-aboriginal rock carvings discovered in Australia. *Right:* the Jupiter column that stood outside a Roman villa near Heilbronn, West Germany. *Below:* mosaic floor of the reception room of a Roman villa excavated at Sparsholt, near Winchester.

Top, South Australian Museum; photos by Robert Edwards. Right, "Current Archaeology"

The commanding officer of a Roman garrison dropped and lost his gold signet ring in his lavatory at a fort on Hadrian's Wall (*above*). It was found some 1,750 years later, and this impression (*left*) was taken of the seal.

Above, "Current Archaeology"; left, Ministry of Public Building and Works

intervals seems to have led to a demarcation dispute at Chester, where the wall-builders and fort-builders appear to have met simultaneously and the wall-builders carried on with their foundations through the middle of the fort which was already under construction. At Housesteads, the best known fort, the Commandant's house is now being excavated, and in the well-preserved lavatory a fine gold signet ring was found with a garnet seal with a theatrical mask carved on it. One can imagine the commotion when the C.O. discovered his loss!

More is being learnt in that Roman Wall country of upland sheep farms, undisturbed by modern ploughing, of how the native inhabitants lived. The earliest settlements were groups of timber houses within a wooden stockade. Then the stockade was succeeded by a stone or earth rampart, and the settlement became a small hill-fort. With the Roman occupation stone houses replaced the wooden ones and spread out beyond the obsolete ramparts. At one settlement, Huckhoe, a recent carbon-14 dating of charcoal has predated by 400 years the hitherto accepted Iron Age date of the 1st or 2nd century B.C. The average area of a stockade was one acre, though a few were up to 18 or 20 acres. These would have been tribal centres. One of them, at Burnswalk, was not taken over by the Romans, who built a new fort three miles off, but was possibly used as a field-firing range, for lead sling bullets and stone balls were found around a dummy paved gateway and, sited at catapult range, are three mounds which could have been catapult emplacements. What better target could an artilleryman have had than a real enemy stronghold, even though it was undefended?

Four seasons of excavation on South Cadbury Hill, Somerset, have revealed a continuous occupation of this natural stronghold through the Neolithic and Bronze Ages down to Saxon times. Among the most recent discoveries are the remains of an early 1st century A.D. wooden building which was probably a temple, possibly Druidical. Whole carcases of cattle and sheep were buried round it as sacrificial offerings. The first, and only, human skeleton to be found was that of a youth aged about 20. He may also have been sacrificed, for his skeleton, buried in the foetal position, was crammed into a grave in the pre-Roman rampart—as if to afford ghostly protection to the community against attack. Of the same date are the hearths and furnaces of an armourer's workshop, littered with iron swords, daggers, knives, and cauldrons. The houses of the settlement were round, about 30 ft. in

thought that the owner of this pleasant villa was probably a decurion, one of the town councillors.

Roman and Pre-Roman

Up on Hadrian's Wall, at the northern boundary of Roman Britain, each year's excavations shed more light on the life of the Roman soldier once stationed there—which Kipling so vividly recreated in *Puck of Pook's Hill*. The Wall, which took eight years to complete, was built in sections by detachments of two legions, the XX and II, who set up inscribed stones in the mile-castles. The VI legion, also employed on wall construction, may have laid the foundations, while the other two legions built the wall itself which, in places, is only 8 ft. wide on 10 ft. foundations. This was possibly done to speed up the work. Each legion had five miles of wall to build, the XX for instance, building from the 7th to the 12th mile-castle, the II from the 12th to the 17th, and so on.

A subsequent decision to strengthen the defences with forts on the Wall at four-mile

Relics of the faithful in medieval Ireland, dug up in Dublin in 1969, included a leaden seal of Pope Innocent III (*left*) and a pewter pilgrim's badge (*right*), both showing St. Peter and St. Paul.
National Museum of Ireland

diameter, with walls of thick wooden planks or wattle and daub, and cobbled floors in which storage pits have been found cut into the rock. This Celtic way of life ended savagely when the Romans stormed Cadbury in A.D. 45. A systematic destruction of the defences followed, during which time the soldiers lived in wooden huts and cooked their food in field ovens. But scrapped weapons and equipment tell their tale of the bitter fighting which preceded the fort's surrender.

After the Roman withdrawal from Britain, Cadbury, with its defences strengthened to four ramparts, became a centre of British resistance to the Saxon invaders. The south-west gateway appears to have had a high wooden fighting platform, protected by a parapet and stabilised by packed earth and stones round its base. Some of the stones came from a Roman building. The rock-cut post-holes of a great timber hall, 30 ft. by 60 ft., were found at the centre of this fortified area in 1969. The hall probably had a central nave with aisles, and a screen to divide the nobility from their retainers. Here, at last, is a find the archaeologists have been waiting for, something commensurate with the Arthurian legend!

Antiquities of Ireland

The latest of the great passage graves in the Boyne Valley, co. Meath, to be excavated is Knowth. These royal burials, of which the most famous is Newgrange, are more than 4,000 years old. The mound at Knowth covers 10 acres and excavation of it has so far revealed two tombs. The passage leading to the main tomb is 113 ft. long and 3 ft. high, rising to 8 ft. 6 in. It is lined with engraved orthostats (upright stones), and roofed with stone lintels, and it leads into a cruciform chamber which has three recesses. The largest of these, 11 yards wide, has been called "the mound's sanctum sanctorum" for here, under a 19-ft. dome built by the corbelling technique, had been placed a stone basin 4 ft. in diameter. Carved round the inside is a groove, and in the centre a circle with lines radiating from it. Outside, as the central motif, are three concentric circles, and running round the body seven deep horizontal grooves. It is thought that in this carved basin the ashes of the dead chieftain were deposited. Two other souterrains, leading to smaller chambers, have been opened up; and round the outside of the mound four more "satellites" were located, bringing the number of these smaller mounds up to fifteen.

Redevelopment in Dublin has unearthed, for the first time, the original Viking and Norman settlements. These dwellings were made of wood and wattle coated with clay, and the footpaths were also made of wood. More sophisticated houses of the 12th and 13th centuries were of squared timbers, mortised and tenoned, with weather-boards fastened with iron nails. Good examples of handiwork found included pairs of shoes, children's boots, and ornamental sheaths lying in 4 ft. of leather clippings. There were also animal bones with trial carvings on them for reproduction in metal decoration for domestic and ecclesiastical objects; and combs, knife handles, dice, and chessmen carved from antler horn. Among other relics of that age of faith found in Dublin during the year is a leaden seal, or bulla, which had been attached to an Apostolic Letter. The seal has Saints Peter and Paul on one side and on the reverse the name of the Pope who issued it, Innocent III (1198–1216). There is also a pewter pilgrim's badge which depicts St. Peter with a key and St. Paul with a sword; loops at its corners allowed the pilgrim to sew it to his clothing. It probably came from

Rome, where the badges were made by the Canons of St. Peter's (who had the monopoly), and it perhaps belonged to an Irish bishop or abbot who had attended the Fourth Lateran Council in 1215. Such finds are rare. Last of the religious relics is a bronze pilgrim's flask, or ampulla, with a dedicatory inscription to the Virgin Mary and St. Wulfstan who was canonised in 1203. The pre-canonisation investigation was held in Worcester and the Archbishop of Dublin attended it; this flask may well have belonged to him, or to one of his retinue.

Temples of Lebanon

In the Bekaa, a fertile Lebanese valley watered by the Litany river, there have been recent excavations of some of the *tells* which date from the Neolithic to the Iron Age. Finds include bronze arrowheads, iron daggers and sickles, much pottery, and a number of 12th and 11th century B.C. ovens in which meat was cooked and bread baked. When the debris got too high for an oven to be used, the inhabitants, who lived in tents or reed huts, would build another at a higher level. At Tell el Ghasill, four temples have been exposed, one on top of the other. The stones

Divers of the sub aqua club of Royal Naval Air Command with amphorae recovered in 1969 from a Roman ship that sank in Ognina Bay, Sicily, about 300 B.C.

from the latest temple, on top, had mostly been removed for other buildings; but the temple below still had its pebble foundations, taken from the river, topped with sun-dried brick. This temple was dedicated to two gods, probably Baal the god of storms, and Astarte the goddess of fertility. In the third temple was found the paved floor of the holy of holies, with sumps to hold wine jars which had pointed bases.

In the fourth, and earliest, temple there were two silos of sun-dried brick. Under the floor of one, three cylindrical seals were found. The first, of blue paste, depicts two horned animals with a bird flying overhead; the second, also of blue paste, shows a man in a tunic holding a staff with a star on top and three birds flying over him; the third, of white paste, has a horned animal rampant before an incense-burner, looking towards a man in a long tunic, again with a bird flying over him.

On a fourth seal, carved in haematite and found in another room, we see a goddess (perhaps Astarte) in a long robe, apparently juggling with apples. Beside her is a winged griffin, below which a man is swimming (perhaps a river god), and next to the griffin is a man wearing a pointed hat—who may be Baal. He holds a spear in one hand and a heifer by the horns with the other.

Muslim Art in India

A curious incident occurred in 1842 at the end of the first Afghan War (fought to create a buffer state between India and Russia) when General Pollock had the richly carved doors removed from the marble tomb of Sultan Mahmud in Ghazni, Afghanistan, and taken to Agra, where they were set up in the Red Fort. He did this because of a legend that Mahmud had looted them from the temple of Siva at Somnath, in Gujarat, when in A.D. 1024 he sacked this fabulously rich Indian shrine, which was so popular that 3,000 barbers were needed to shave the heads and beards of the pilgrims. There was no truth in the legend, however, for the doors—extremely rare examples of Islamic woodwork—could obviously never have stood in a Hindu temple.

Not until 1967 does anyone seem to have noticed the havoc wrought on them by ants, souvenir-hunters, and general decay. When told of this, Zakir Husain, the first Muslim president of India, immediately ordered a complete restoration, using wood of a different colour where necessary to distinguish it from the original. Thus India, the fortuitous heiress to these alien treasures, shows how conscious she is of their worth.

A Year of Ferment in the Schools

Compiled by
BARBARA LOWTHER

THROUGHOUT THE WORLD the year 1969 might well be seen as one of educational revolution. Policies have been questioned, concepts examined, ideas proposed, and changes wrought. In Great Britain an unfortunate adjunct to this ferment has been financial stringency.

The school population has increased as a result of the rising birth rate and the fact that more children are remaining at school after the permitted leaving age. At the same time the cost of upkeep and school equipment has soared; yet the government imposed a 3½ per cent limit on increases in expenditure for the year 1969–70. Progress was arrested in many directions: schemes for "Nuffield" science, introduced several years before, had to be curtailed; the adoption of new approaches to mathematics was postponed because there was insufficient money for textbooks and other equipment; children were prevented from taking the newer G.C.E. syllabuses since neither teachers nor facilities were available.

Specific problems of local authorities highlighted the national predicament. At the beginning of the year West Suffolk anticipated 1,400 extra pupils but no increase in the number of part-time teachers. Warwickshire had already overspent by March. Kent decided to appoint 40 fewer teachers, Lancashire to cut maintenance grants to universities. Nottinghamshire made a heavy reduction in maintenance work on educational premises, and employed a minimum of part-time teachers. Most authorities made cuts in "fringe" awards—school prizes, grants, and subsidies—and also reduced expenditure on school books and equipment. The nursery school situation exemplified the struggle between the central government and the local authorities. In order to implement its promise to carry out the provisions of the Plowden report the government offered local authorities a 75 per cent grant towards the cost of nursery schools and classes. Some authorities refused this first chance since 1945 to develop nursery education, insisting that the government should meet the whole cost.

Student Troubles

World-wide student unrest continued throughout the year, spreading in many areas to secondary schools. In Japan it led to clashes with the police and long-term closure of universities. Nerve gas was used and troops called in to quell riots in American colleges and universities. In Britain the London School of Economics was closed after militant demonstrations early in February. However, greater representation for students on university and college councils, with more control over their own discipline, seems to have satisfied all but the most belligerent. In Australia disturbances were settled by agreements along the following lines: (a) each faculty of a university to have an education committee composed of staff and students in equal numbers; (b) three students at each faculty meeting with the right to vote; (c) four students on the unversity council of 38 members; (d) increased student representation on the seven sub-committees of the council.

As if in response to the cry of the insurgent forces of the National Union of Students— "All academic courses must reflect the needs of society"—the idea of an Open University, or University of the Air, conceived some three years before, rapidly became a reality (see Open University in Fact Digest). The university should be able to offer four courses in 1971, and the normal degree course is expected to take four years. Colleges of education attracted considerable criticism regarding the quality of teachers produced. There were still differences of opinion whether students should be judged according to their practical teaching ability or by their academic attainments.

Question of "Comprehensives"

In Great Britain the biggest subject of controversy was still "comprehensive" education. The publication in March and October of two "Black Papers" on education fanned into a flame the dying embers of the fire of antipathy towards comprehensive schools. The first appeared on March 13 under the title of *Fight for Education*. Its editors were Professor C. B. Cox of Manchester University and Professor A. E. Dyson of East Anglia University, and contributors included Kingsley Amis, Angus Maud, M.P., John Sparrow (Warden of All Souls, Oxford), and Robert

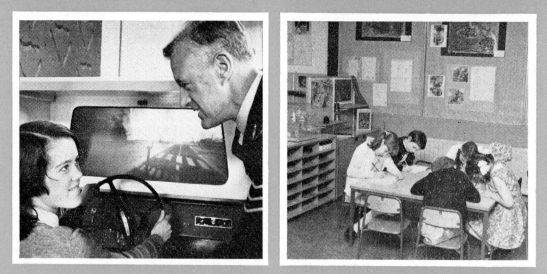

In spite of financial stringency new teaching methods and school buildings made some headway in Great Britain in 1969. *Left:* learning to drive by "auto-tutor." *Right:* open-plan classroom at a new primary school in the City of London.

Conquest. In chapters headed with such titles as *The Egalitarian Threat* and *In Praise of Examinations*, they advocated a return to more rigid syllabuses and examinations, the retention of selection at 11-plus, and concentration on the three Rs. In his article *Egalitarianism and an Academic Élite* John Sparrow condemned ". . . schools where intelligent and stupid children are included in the same large comprehensive classes (and) the teaching has to be geared to the capacity of the slowest and least intelligent of the pupils in order to meet the humanitarian demand that they should not be left behind in the race . . . Against this gain in social justice must be set the over-all loss involved in the slowing down of the educational machine and consequent slowing down of the academic standard achieved." More than 15,000 copies of this publication were sold. Edward Short, Secretary of State for Education, exclaimed "This is the blackest day for education in 100 years!" He explained that the Black Paper was more than just an attack on the comprehensive secondary school —it was an attack on liberal ideas in education generally.

The second Black Paper, published on October 7, did not swing the pendulum back quite so far. One article suggested that comprehensive schools were acceptable if they followed a certain pattern. This was written by Dr. Rhodes Bayson, headmaster of Highbury Grove School, Islington, a comprehensive school for 1,400 boys. He runs the school on a house system along public school lines. He warned against the use of comprehensive

principles as political propaganda. In all, 25 academicians, psychologists, headmasters, and teachers contributed to the second Black Paper. One of them, Tibor Szamuely, a former convinced communist, once rector and professor of history at Budapest University, attempted to explode the myth that comprehensive education can achieve a classless society and equal opportunity for all. He quoted the complaint of Mrs. Shirley Williams, U.K. Minister of State for Education and Science, that of all British university students only 26 per cent were of working-class origin, and pointed out that this is the highest proportion in Europe. In other countries, working-class undergraduates number 10 per cent in Denmark, 8·3 per cent in France, 5·3 per cent in West Germany, and 4 per cent in Switzerland.

While the grammar schools had formerly allowed gifted children the opportunity to break down class barriers, he went on, the comprehensive system tended to encourage class distinction by drawing school populations from a limited area, inhabited by a definite stratum of society. In this he was supported by the eminent but aged educational psychologist Sir Cyril Burt, who cited Chelsea, Hampstead, and Lewisham as having six times as many non-manual as manual workers. In certain neighbourhoods, therefore, comprehensive schools offer the working-class child less opportunity to escape to a better education than the grammar school system did.

The case against comprehensive schools was emphasised by facts culled from the Russian example. Mr. Szamuely quoted a complaint by the director of the Machine Tool Building Trust in Leningrad (Russia's leading city in education) about the increasing number of young workers joining his staff who had had only 5–7 years' education. He reported the opinions of three professors of Moscow University who suggested that an "unequal" system of education should be established, on the lines of the British!

Professor Pollard, who holds the chair of English at the University of Hull, attacked in the second Black Paper the trend towards so-called "free expression" or "creativity" in schools, and recommended a return to the basic teaching of spelling, grammar, and punctuation. He used "O" and "A" level results over past years to demonstrate the inferior marks gained by comprehensive school pupils in comparison with those in grammar schools. There were also constructive articles relating to education in primary schools and universities, and a general agreement that education in the future should select the best from both traditional and modern methods. The comment that the money at present allocated to education is well below the minimum requirements is probably the truest and most incontrovertible statement to be found in the two Black Papers.

Despite such voluble opposition, the Queen's speech on October 29 made it clear that the government was determined to further the cause of comprehensive education in practical terms: "A Bill will be introduced requiring local education authorities to prepare plans for reorganising secondary education on comprehensive lines." Hitherto local authorities had been only asked for their plans, and at least 17 of the biggest, including Birmingham, had failed to produce them. If the bill becomes law they will be forced to do so.

Age-Grouping Dilemmas

The decision to raise the school-leaving age in the U.K. to 16 in 1972–73 has exacerbated the difficulty of where to educate the 16–19 age-group. They could continue in the sixth form at school, they could go to a College of Further Education, or they could transfer to a Technical College. Many educationalists favour transferring them to a sector of education designed especially for them—Sixth Form Colleges. In February, W. H. G. Armytage, Professor of Education at Sheffield University, suggested that the fusing of sixth forms and Further Education Colleges is essential if we are to make economic use of specialist staff and allow students to make "skill-based, realistic choices for the future." It is also argued that Sixth Form Colleges can offer the widest choice of educational pursuits, from a scattering of G.C.E. "O" levels for those who failed the first time to academic subjects of an advanced standard, while at the same time offering music, drama, and other leisure pursuits, together with languages, commercial subjects, engineering, domestic science, and career guidance.

Antagonists to this tertiary scheme look to the Leicester High School system (14–19 age-group) as the best solution. They argue

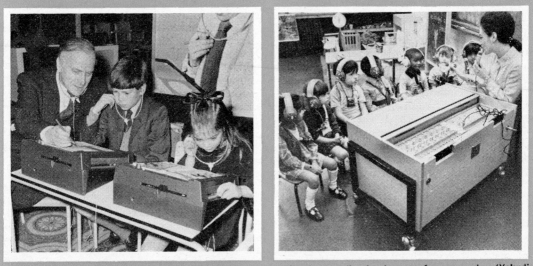

Mechanical aids to teaching introduced during the year included (*left*) an audio-visual system for non-readers (Yehudi Menuhin created its music course); and a sound transmitter with which deaf children can be taught singly or together.

that children who need to re-sit an examination or wish to take additional subjects would be at a disadvantage in moving to another school for a short period of study. Since teachers have an opportunity within this age-range of teaching to both "O" and "A" level, it makes a fairly economic use of specialist staff. Another favourable factor in schools of this age group is that those who stay on after the age of 16 do so because they want to, which enhances the tone and general discipline of the school.

Another successful experiment has been the pairing together of two comprehensive school sixth forms, each school specialising in certain subjects and the children moving from school to school as necessary.

Other countries have different views on the break between primary and secondary education. The U.S.S.R. decided in 1969 to amend its ten-year education scheme by moving the top year of the primary school into the secondary range because of the fact that children are maturing younger and therefore need to specialise at an earlier age. Norway approved a scheme to raise the school-leaving age to 16 on a 7–13, 13–16 pattern of primary and secondary education; schoolchildren are to have a 40-week year of 25 hours a week, with a maximum of 30 children to each class. Spain introduced free and compulsory education for the first time, for all children aged from 6 to 13 years.

"Q" Levels and "F" Levels?

On December 9 the U.K. Schools Council added a final ingredient to the fermenting pot of education by publishing a joint statement by two working committees which recommended a complete revision of the examination system. The aims seemed to be three-fold: to take account of the raising of the school-leaving age to 16, to set a higher standard for university entrance, and to arrest the tendency to early specialisation, by which most grammar-school children have to opt for arts or sciences as early as 13. If the proposals are accepted, all secondary school children will study eight subjects to the age of 16; these will be attested by the school and not externally examined, unless the pupil wishes it in which case he or she will be able to sit the G.C.E. "O" level or C.S.E. examinations as at present. G.C.E. "A" level will be abolished, and replaced by two examinations:

(1) "Q" (Qualifying) level, taken at 17 in five subjects grouped so that both arts and science are represented. The standard will be between the present G.C.E. "O" and "A" levels, and "Q" levels in five subjects will be

the minimum general entry requirement for all higher education, including technical colleges and teachers' training colleges. "Q" level examinations will start in 1975.

(2) "F" (Further) level, taken at 18 in two or three subjects, which will specifically qualify the student for entrance to a particular faculty or department of a university. "F" levels will approximate to the present "A" levels, but the "factual" or "memory" content of the courses will be reduced and greater emphasis laid on intelligent approach to the subjects. "F" level examinations will start in 1976.

Both "Q" and "F" levels will be single-subject examinations. The two committees who produced the proposals were the Schools Council's own working party on examinations and the Standing Conference on University Entrance.

Subjects and Methods

For better or for worse, comprehensive education is now a reality in Great Britain. An extra £4 million was spent in 1969 on school buildings to ease the transition to the system, and 15 authorities were given permission to start on new building programmes. Nevertheless, there are still many controversial issues relating to teaching methods to be settled, regardless of the type of educational establishment involved. In October, Edward Short announced his aim to remove the emphasis from examinations and to replace them with teachers' records, which would include details of progress, character, and aptitude. There were protests from people who preferred a more objective method of assessment.

Controversy over the question of religious education was also much in evidence. The National Secular Society made direct contact with "pupil power" in the attempt to encourage schoolchildren to boycott "Scripture" lessons. Several hundred pamphlets were distributed to sixth-formers, asking them to campaign against compulsory morning worship. It is apparent, however, that most parents are in favour of some form of religious instruction at school.

A report was published on a six-year study carried out by two professors from Manchester University into the value of the method of teaching reading known as the Initial Teaching Alphabet (i.t.a.). The system attempts to eliminate the confusion that arises during the early stages of learning to read by using an alphabet of 42 characters, with one letter representing one sound only. The report gives cautious approval to the method, and recom-

A series of planned guerrilla half-day teachers' strikes began in England in November, developing in December into full-scale two-week strikes at selected schools. Schoolchildren looked on with mixed feelings as teachers walked out.

mends the setting up of a large-scale experiment. The general impression is that i.t.a. helps children to make an early start in reading, but that gains are not noticeable by the time children leave the infants' school.

Another undoubted success was the introduction in 1969 of electronic video recording machines, which play films through an ordinary television set. It is possible to stop the film on a single frame for as long as required. The films have a long life, but cost about £10 each, while the machine costs about £150. Although films are at present manufactured only in black and white, it is anticipated that colour will soon be available.

The biology department of Sydney University successfully tried tape-recorded lectures linked with specially selected slides; 120 students carried out their practical microscope work in individual booths fitted with earphones and tape recorders. Unlike conditions in large lecture rooms and overcrowded laboratories, this system allows each student to work at his own pace, turning back the tape for a repeat when a matter is not fully understood the first time. Results were promising: from a random selection of 50 students at the end of the first year, 15 achieved marks of over 80 per cent and only 7 were under 50 per cent.

Teachers on Strike

Whatever the form of organisation, whatever the new methods and gadgets introduced, the standard of education depends ultimately on the quality of the teachers, and this, it is argued, depends in turn on the importance of teaching as a profession in terms of status, and therefore of money. In Western Australia new pay scales showed an 8–12 per cent increase;

newly qualified, two-year trained teachers begin at 2,960 Australian dollars (£1,369) and four-year trained teachers get 3,985 dollars (£1,843). Even that pay is small compared with 6,000 U.S. dollars (£2,500) for the young teacher in Philadelphia. But account must be taken of the high cost of living in both countries.

In British schools there was a gradual move towards strike action for more pay. On January 3 a teachers' panel met to work out a revised salary claim and agreed to demand a basic scale of £860–1,615. Later that month the proposal for continuous service increments by the National Association of Schoolmasters was rejected, precipitating a half-day walk out by N.A.S. members, their suspension by their employers, and short strikes in their support. Through the year unrest in the teaching profession grew. Teachers saw other essential workers gain considerable increases through strike action, and this, together with their frustration by lack of the tools with which to do a proper job, put the profession in general in a fighting mood—so marked that for the first time ever the rival teachers' unions (N.U.T. and N.A.S.) sank their differences to fight a joint battle for salary increases. The "employers" (the management side of the Burnham committee) offered an increase of, first, £50 a year and, later, £100 for the lower and £80 for the higher paid. But the teachers' unions were adamant in their demand for a general rise of £135. Half-day and whole-day guerrilla strikes took place in the spring and autumn, and on December 1 full-scale strikes by 4,000 teachers were ordered at selected schools throughout the country.

Medicine in the Space Age

OLIVER GRANT

UNDOUBTEDLY THE MOST publicised piece of medicine of 1969 was the examination of the American astronauts after the first visit to the Moon in July. The lengthy period of quarantine to which they were subjected— and in which they were joined by others thought possibly to have been contaminated by contact with lunar material—is a measure of the fears that new disease germs might have been brought back to Earth. The dreaded hostile invaders from outer space are not beings of superior intelligence which might treat us as we treat lesser species, but new viruses and microbes which might treat us as our present stock of viruses and microbes do, but in an unexpected and possibly more deadly way. In fact, the likelihood of any disease invasion from the Moon always was extremely small—so small, in the view of many, as to be completely discounted.

Even if there are bacteria on the Moon— and the existence cannot be completely ruled out in the absence of a full study of conditions there—it is still certain that those bacteria are not practised in coping with animal organisms like ourselves. Nobody believes that there are Selenites, as H. G. Wells described them— Moon versions of man or Moon versions of other animals—in that inhospitable environment. Therefore any bacteria or other organisms would not have developed the unfriendly activity against host animals which we call disease. That is not to say that they could not, given the chance—and that awakens the unpalatable thought that the quarantine of the astronauts was pointless not just because there was no disease to show up, but because, if there are going to be Moon-germ diseases, they will only come when the germs have kept quiet about their presence long enough to develop their weapons against us.

On earth there is no doubt that the most awkward disease invaders are the ones that cross national boundaries from one part of the world to another. Holidays abroad are a source of danger. One example of this came in the late summer with an outbreak of typhoid among a group of people who stayed at a hotel in Tunisia. At least 38 cases occurred, 8 in Britain, 16 in Germany, 13 in Switzerland, and one in Holland. One English and one German patient died. Apart from the occasional outbreak, such as the one in Aberdeen in 1964, most cases of typhoid in Great Britain nowadays originate abroad. Precautions can, of course, be taken to reduce the danger of contracting the disease abroad. One of the best (and most congenial) is to drink wine at meals, instead of local water— or stick to bottled mineral water. Packets of sterilising tablets can be carried to deal with local water and even to treat soft-skinned fruit. Inoculation well beforehand can give 70 per cent protection, unless one is unfortunate enough to be the victim of a mass onslaught from contaminated food.

Thromboses and the Pill

Such diseases as cancer and degenerative heart conditions occupy the attention of most medical research today. One of its most important weapons is still epidemiology, the techniques which were first developed to study infectious diseases such as diphtheria and scarlet fever, and which helped to reduce them to their present relatively innocuous position in our society. Epidemiology is the study of the frequency with which disease occurs in different populations. One modern use was in the survey by Sir Austin Bradford Hill and Professor Richard Doll which showed the association between cigarette-smoking and lung cancer. Epidemiological studies on coronary heart disease have implicated worry, sedentary living, and over-eating, as well as smoking. But one such study this year should bring relief to people with a sweet tooth. The proposition of Professor John Yudkin that a high sugar intake is the chief dietary factor in heart disease received a "not proven" verdict from a study of 1,328 men working for the Atomic Energy Authority.

One unexpected finding about the incidence of coronary disease in Great Britain, reported by Professor Melvyn Howe of the University of Strathclyde, was that it did not agree with the universally accepted theory that this disease is associated with prosperity. In Britain the reverse is the case. There are fewer cases in the economically favoured south. This, suggested Howe, could be due to other aspects of diet. Heart diseases are more common in the areas where "high tea" is a common meal, and he also pointed to the popularity of sweets, cakes, and buns (foodstuffs rich in carbohydrates but deficient in trace elements) in Scotland, and of butter in Wales. Geographical differences in the pattern of disease might also stem from trace elements in the soil. Although not absolutely proved, it does seem that pernicious anaemia can be associated with a local deficiency of iron and cobalt; heart disease with a lack of calcium in the water; and nervous diseases with the presence of lead. Lung cancer is certainly more common in areas of heavy industry, and this could be associated with atmospheric pollution, including lead in petrol engine fumes, as well as with smoking.

Being better-off provides a health bonus to British women. Cancer of the breast is now less troublesome among well-to-do women than it was once. This is presumably because it is now the "in" thing for women in the higher social classes to breast-feed their babies. Cancer of the breast is known to be most common in unmarried women, women without children, and women who have not breast-fed their babies. On the other hand, the disease is becoming more common in the lower social groups, probably because women going out to work cannot breast-feed.

Professor Doll, who had already established a link between blood-clotting in the veins and the Pill, reported during the summer of 1969 that the risk of cerebral thrombosis is increased sixfold among women who use oral contraceptives, although the risk from that and pulmonary embolism is still only one quarter of the risk of dying in a motor accident and about 2 per cent of the risk of dying from all causes. No link between the Pill and coronary thrombosis has been shown, but in 1969 reports began to appear of a connection between arterial and venous thrombosis and the taking of the compounds oestrogen and progestogen present in oral contraceptives. Later it was established that oestrogen is probably the guilty element in the Pill, and on December 11 a warning was published by the U.K. Committee on Safety of Drugs that the administration of high-dosage oestrogen pills should cease and that the 700,000 women taking them should as soon as possible change to low-oestrogen pills.

Cancer Progress

Considerable efforts are being made in laboratories all over the world to discover the mechanism by which cancers form and grow. This is closely linked with immunology, the study of the mechanism by which the body fights invading cells, either disease germs or foreign tissue. A tumour can be considered "foreign"; why, then, does the body not reject it as vigorously as it does, say, a heart transplant? The probability is that there *is* a rejection process against tumours. As long ago as 1953, Dr. N. A. Mitchison showed that transplanted tumours could be rejected by lymphocytes—the cells that take part in the organ rejection process—though not by the antibodies that play the major part in combating disease. Since then it has been shown that cancer cells do generally carry foreign antigens (the molecules that provoke the immune response). It is possible that the rejection process which causes so much trouble in transplant surgery was designed to fight cancer, but fails in some cases to do so.

A new technique of fusing cells to produce hybrids, by mixing them with an inactivated virus, has opened up new fields of research. A team led by Professor Henry Harris, of Oxford University, hybridised mouse tumour cells of extreme malignancy with non-malignant cells, named A9, and found malignancy enormously reduced. Something in the A9 cell appeared to suppress malignancy, though previously such hybrids had always been malignant and malignancy was thought to be a dominant characteristic. But malignancy returned in some daughter cells of these hybrids which lost certain chromosomes. At the least this work could provide a better understanding of the dependency of malignancy on the genetic make-up of the cell, and it could perhaps provide chemical methods of suppressing malignancy. The work had other results: A9 cells carry a strong complement of those antigens which invoke rejection, while the hybrids lost this characteristic, as if the antigens were being cloaked by some activity of the tumour cell. This could give a lead in the battle against organ rejection.

In September came a report of a step towards the objective of invoking the organ rejection process against cancer. Two workers in the same Oxford laboratory, Dr. J. F. Watkins and Dr. L. Chen, reported they had greatly increased the resistance of mice to one form of tumour by inoculating them with hybrid cells formed from the same tumour cells and normal hamster cells. The hybrid cells were rejected, and when the mice were later injected with the tumour cells alone these were also rejected, up to a certain maximum dose. Ten thousand times as many cells were needed for a lethal dose in the inoculated animals as in mice that had not been inoculated. Thus there is the possibility of invoking an immune response against a specific human cancer by

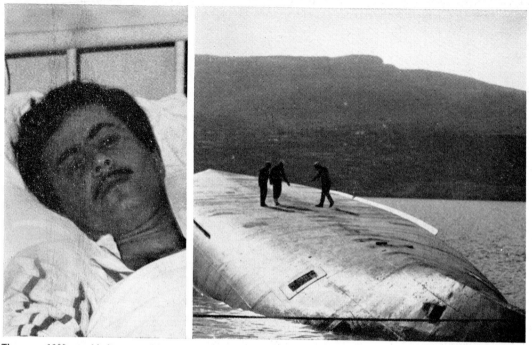

The year 1969 provided two striking examples of the miracle of human survival in what would normally be fatal circumstances. The first was Second Engineer Sabbahedine Ozen seen recovering in hospital (*left*) after being trapped for four days in an upturned tanker (*right*) in March. His ship, the small Turkish gas tanker *Aygaz*, capsized in mountainous seas off the southern coast of the Peloponnese in March. Royal Navy frogmen heard him tapping and cut a hole (*foreground*) in the hull to haul him to safety. The only member of the 15-man crew to survive, he had been breathing a small pocket of air fortunately trapped between the gas and the hull.

inoculations of hybrids of the cancer cells with easily rejected cells.

The desired result, sharpening the rejection process against cancer, in the clinical treatment of leukemia may have been achieved in Russia, according to a report in *Nature*, although no dramatic claims of a cure were made. Professor Skurkovitch of Moscow and his team reported a stimulated reaction of the immune system to destroy cancerous blood and marrow cells. They started from the assumption that the patient tolerates his own leukemic cells, and from that attempted to see if "foreign" leukemic cells could restore immunological activity. Twelve children were divided into six pairs, the children in each pair being given injections of each other's leukemic cells. This was followed by similar injections of plasma. In eight children there was remission of the disease and in three the remission was complete, all traces of leukemic cells disappearing. At the time of the report remission had continued for six months, and in one case of complete remission no further treatment of any kind had been given.

Transplant Surgery

Nowadays no survey of medicine would be complete without a reference to transplant surgery. In 1968 enthusiasm was high; in 1969 however, there were growing concern and declining enthusiasm by the public and some surgeons, particularly with regard to heart transplants, where the problem of rejection is as difficult as ever. There was some despond at the death of Philip Blaiberg in July, although he had survived 593 days with his new heart. In October the second longest living heart transplant patient, Father Charles Boulogne, of France, died 17 months and 5 days after his operation. By the time of these deaths, heart transplants had ceased at Houston, Texas, which had been the most active world centre, with the admission that considerable advances were needed in antirejection techniques before the mental anguish and the cost—about £10,000 per operation—were worth while. Out of 140 recipients of new hearts in the world, only 35 had by then survived.

Britain's third recipient of a heart graft, Charles Hendrick, survived from May 16 to August 31 before succumbing to cardiac arrest following a lung infection. There was considerable controversy about his operation, however, following the disclosure that the donor (a student nurse who had received severe head injuries in a road accident) had

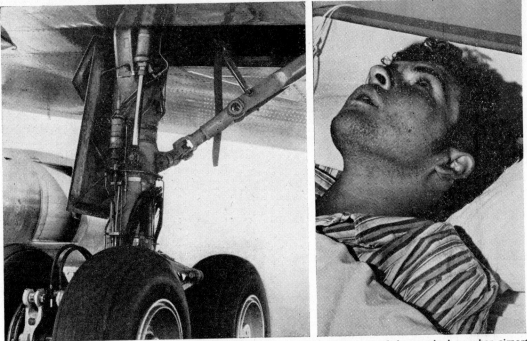

A 22-year-old Cuban, Armando Socarras Ramirez, became the medical guinea-pig of the year in June when airport workers in Madrid found him blue with cold, insensible, and "frozen stiff" in the wheelbay (*left*) of the DC-8 jet he had selected as an escape route from Havana. For nine hours and over 4,000 miles he had existed, frozen in suspended animation like a science fiction hero, as the plane crossed the Atlantic at 29,000 ft. Doctors were amazed to find that Armando survived and later recovered in a Spanish hospital (*right*). They also pointed out the paradox: had the temperature been a little higher he would have died from exposure.

been moved to Guy's Hospital, London, where the transplant was carried out, from Putney Hospital, and that the machine which kept her heart beating had been switched off before the operation. The hospital declared that she had been moved there in her own interests, for a fuller examination, and that she could have survived only a very short time if the machine had continued to support her heart action. The previous month the British Medical Association had declared that it was not ethical for a dying patient to be moved solely to be near a transplant recipient. This dictum formed part of the rules for the guidance of surgeons and doctors drawn up by the Association's ethics committee. It also said that, if consent for a transplant could not be obtained from the donor during his life-time, positive consent must be obtained from the next-of-kin; and also declared that pronouncement of death should be made by two fully registered practitioners one of whom must have been registered for a period of at least five years, both being independent of the transplant team. These rules had the backing of the General Medical Council.

Kidney transplants were becoming almost a routine matter, and a greater measure of success was reported in lung and liver transplants. The B.M.A. Planning Unit recommended an increased effort on kidney transplants, for both humane and economic reasons—they could prove cheaper than long-term use of kidney machines—but declared that heart and lung transplants should be carried out on only a small scale for research purposes.

On the anti-rejection front anti-lymphocytic-serum (ALS), a substance which could counter rejection while leaving the body resistant to infection, had been used in a successful series of kidney grafts in the U.S.A. Work reported by Professor Roy Calne, of Cambridge, gave hope that ultimately the body might be made to tolerate grafts from a specific person. This, known as specific immunological tolerance, has been achieved in pigs. Professor Calne had already shown that pigs could receive liver grafts from their own species without any bother, surviving without any anti-rejection treatment. His advance was to show that the temporary transplant of an extra liver into a pig, or an injection of extract of liver, would enable the animal to accept from the same donor grafts of kidney or skin which it would normally quickly reject. The pig may be unique, but the discovery opens up an avenue of hope.

A Time of Violence

GEORGE CHINN

VIOLENCE IS NOTHING NEW in the history of man. It is nothing new in the history of crime. Why then in Great Britain did the Lord Chancellor, the judges, and the magistrates express such concern about it in 1969? It was not only the amount of violence that worried them; it was the purposelessness of much of it, not only in criminal activities but also on occasions which used to be just times for leisure and pleasure. Of the criminal aspect a prosecuting counsel could say, at the most notorious murder trial of the year—that of the Kray brothers—"There was no patent reason, no provocation—just sheer anger and spite." The Krays and their like can be dealt with in the fashion prescribed by law. But what is to be done about the violence increasingly connected with the simple game of football, not so much on the field as among the spectators?

Sometimes it can be dealt with straightforwardly and intelligently, as when the police at one match early in the 1969–70 season made youths take off their steel-tipped boots, let them watch the game in stockinged feet, and returned the boots well after all opportunities for kicking fights had passed. At other times the police came in for criticism, as when, in September, they turned off a train in Bedfordshire five hundred Tottenham Hotspur supporters who had seen their team beaten 5–0 by Derby County. The "fans" had shown their displeasure by smashing train fittings and repeatedly pulling the communication cord. After being put off the train they went marauding through two villages, smashing windows and terrorising inhabitants. Some threw stones at cars and uprooted road signs. Eventually police from all over Bedfordshire were called on to quell the rioting, herd the fans together again, and put them on other trains back to London.

Special mobile police squads were set up in London to stamp out Soccer thuggery after a London "local Derby" between Tottenham Hotspur and Chelsea. In expressing their grief at Chelsea's defeat some supporters did thousands of pounds of damage to Underground stations, and put the new Victoria Line out of action for 20 minutes; others roamed the streets terrorising passers-by. On the same day a Birmingham public house was wrecked and coaches smashed by fans on the rampage after Oxford City had held Crystal Palace to a draw. Another London club, West Ham, had the "Mile End Mob" among its supporters; closed-circuit TV was installed to keep an eye on their steel-capped boots and Japanese flick knives. Wooden mallets and cudgels and five-inch wide belts were taken from youths at a match at Luton where more than 100 people were injured or treated for shock. At a Glasgow–Newcastle match in April, Glasgow supporters threw bottles from the terraces and invaded the pitch; nearly 100 people were injured during the match and in the rampaging afterwards. Hooligans are a small minority but it is the innocent bystander who often gets hurt. The sight of someone knocked unconscious by a misthrown half-brick being lifted over the heads of a crowd was not unknown, although less common than that of goalkeepers deliberately felled by missiles.

Fines Not Enough

Firmer treatment of the Soccer hooligans was called for by Dennis Howell, U.K. Minister of Sport, a football referee himself. Fines were completely useless, he said; a whip-round among a convicted man's friends soon raised the money. Those who terrorised innocent people should be sent to prison, or ordered to report to a police station every Saturday afternoon. The day after his statement magistrates at Greenwich ordered a youth to spend two hours at a detention centre on each of the next six Saturday afternoons, to keep him away from football matches. In November clubs were recommended to appoint stewards to patrol the "football special" trains. Other constructive suggestions were made in the Lang report published in December (see under Football in Fact Digest).

But British Soccer violence could not compare with what went on elsewhere. At Caserta, Italy, battles between police and fans went on for 24 hours after the local team had been relegated for attempting to bribe other players. And a full-scale war with bombing

Growing violence by law-breakers demanded improved protection for the police and others. *Left:* British postman's goggles to save his eyes from ammonia. *Right:* plastic visors and shields for Rome riot police.

raids and ground battles was triggered off by football enmity between El Salvador and neighbouring Honduras.

At one end of the scale much violent destruction is done "for kicks"—shots fired at cars on motorways, and widespread vandalism in railway carriages, telephone kiosks, and schools, the latter sort often ascribed to children. At the other end, in the first five months of 1969 there was 24 per cent more violent crime than in the same period of 1968, and the 1968 crime statistics had shown a disappointing return to the upward trend. Convictions for violence against the person increased by 7·4 per cent, and for robbery by 14 per cent. Offences involving firearms in England and Wales (only 731 in 1964) reached 2,500 in 1968; there were 875 offences in which firearms were used or presented, 352 cases of wounding by shooting, and 40 of killing by shooting. Nobody was safe, but shop assistants, post office employees, bank clerks, and policemen were most exposed to the bullet. As usual, television programmes were blamed for their example of violence. In the U.S.A. a gang of young people carried out shotgun raids on betting shops, post offices, and banks in emulation of the exploits seen in the "Bonnie and Clyde" film; four members were sentenced to a total of 22 years' imprisonment.

The business of crime continued to flourish in 1969. Perhaps the biggest haul was the £350,000 in gems and cash reported to have been seized by a masked gang, armed with a sawn-off shotgun, which broke into a Hatton Garden bank in March. Staff were tied and gagged as they arrived. The assistant manager, with the keys, was forced to open a safe in the strong-room. Newspapers called the gang the "Cockney gents" after the comment of a girl assistant: "They spoke with Cockney accents, but they were real gents." Art thefts were especially prevalent; paintings to a total value of £755,000 were taken in only five of the robberies in England during the year. Some proved too hot to handle, but many others disappeared into the mysterious market for easily identifiable masterpieces. Vast sums of cash were stolen: £129,000, in old and new notes, from a van in front of a bank in Cricklewood, London, in July; £33,000 from another van in Stoke-on-Trent in the same month; £94,000 in wage boxes from a security cash depot in Clerkenwell in September; and £158,000 from the vaults of a bank in Liverpool in August.

The End of the Krays

The Kray twins and their brother Charles were sentenced after the longest murder trial in British history. The twins, Ronald and Reginald, received life imprisonment, with the recommendation that they should not be released before 30 years—Ronald for the murder of George Cornell at the "Blind Beggar" public house in March 1966, and for the murder of Jack ("the Hat") McVitie in October 1967, and Reginald for the murder of McVitie. Their elder brother Charles was sent to prison for 10 years for being an accessory after the McVitie murder by assisting in the disposal of the body.

The conviction of Ronald Kray and his henchman John Barrie (sentenced to at least 20 years) for the "Blind Beggar" murder depended on the eye-witness story of a barmaid who told how after the murder she fled, terrified for her life, to hide in a cellar. Kray and Barrie had walked into the public house, carrying pistols. Cornell, commenting "Look who's here," was shot in the head by Kray, and he and Barrie turned on their heels and walked out. It was, said Mr. Kenneth Jones, prosecuting counsel, "horrifying and deadly effrontery that two men could walk into a public house and in cold blood slay another human being." The murder of Cornell, it was suggested after the trial, was the first step in an all-out war with the Richardson torture and extortion gang of south London. The Krays' "manor" was in east London.

After the murder of Cornell, said Mr. Jones at the trial, Ron used to taunt Reg during family arguments, saying "I have done one. It's about time you did yours." The reason for McVitie's murder was that "Reg Kray had decided to show he was an equal to his twin brother in violence, and that he could kill, too." Selected as the victim, McVitie was lured to a basement flat in Stoke Newington, under the pretence that he was being taken to a party. Soon he found it was no party for him. "Terrified and bathed in sweat, liked a caged animal, he tried to escape by throwing himself at a window and smashing it," said Mr. Jones. A gun failed to fire, and as Ron held McVitie from behind Reg plunged a knife repeatedly into him.

Members of the "Firm," as the Kray gang was called, told of extortion and violence. Club "protection" was one of the main activities; "customers" usually paid under the threat of force and weapons. If they did not, then "either they get hurt or people are sent into the club to have fights and things like that, but nine times out of ten they get hurt," one witness said. Once he had to shoot and wound a man in the man's own home, in front of his wife.

The Kray twins were also charged with the murder of Frank Mitchell, the "Mad Axeman"; the prosecution alleged that they plotted his escape from Dartmoor because they thought he would be useful to them, but found him a burden and paid £1,000 to have him murdered. During the hearing, stories were told of Mitchell's life at Dartmoor which, said the judge, sounded like "cloud cuckoo land." The licensee of the "Peter Tavey Inn," six miles

from Dartmoor, said Mitchell came in about eight times over a period of two months, dressed in what looked like a golfing jacket, wellington boots, and waterproof hat. He usually had a considerable amount of cash, changed £5 notes and on one occasion a £10 note, and took away bottles of whisky, vodka, brandy, and cider. There were references to Mitchell's "love nest," a hayloft littered with empty bottles on Bagga Tor. In this atmosphere, it was suggested, the Krays planned his escape, sending a minicab proprietor to make the arrangements. The latter was sentenced to 18 months' imprisonment and Reginald Kray to five years', concurrent with his other sentences, for plotting the escape. But Ronald and Reginald were found not guilty of Mitchell's murder.

With the Krays joining the Richardsons in prison the two main centres of organised crime in London were officially said to have been broken up. But there was talk later of the "McVicar gang," led by John McVicar, on the run from sentences of 23 years for armed robbery, using firearms, and shooting at the police. A fitness fanatic, McVicar escaped from Durham prison's "E" wing by picking his way through a bathroom wall and scaling a 35-foot wall.

Echoes of Past Crimes

Another famous prison escape—that of the spy George Blake from Wormwood Scrubs in 1966—was recalled when the man who engineered it, Sean Alphonsus Bourke, was assured of his freedom by the Irish courts. The U.K. government had applied for his extradition, but on Bourke's appeal the Irish judges took the view that his was a political rather than a criminal offence. Another pair of spies, American-born Peter and Helen Kroger, sentenced in 1961 to 20 years' imprisonment for obtaining and selling British naval secrets to the U.S.S.R., were released in October 1969, after serving only 8½ years, and flown to Poland. Their freedom was part of an agreement with the U.S.S.R.; the latter in return had three months earlier released the English lecturer Gerald Brooke, sentenced in 1965 for distributing anti-communist literature, and in October released two British men imprisoned for importing drugs into the Soviet Union, and also made some concessions concerning the marriages of British to Russian nationals.

Even in 1969, six years after its commission, the Great Train Robbery refused to lie down. In January, Bruce Reynolds, the last of the gang to be sentenced, who had been found in Torquay in November 1968, was given 25 years' imprisonment, having pleaded guilty.

New means of catching criminals included (*left*) a nylon net fired from a "pistol," for trapping wage-snatchers; and (*right*) the Sussex Constabulary diving unit for underwater searches in harbours and rivers.

In October, Ronald Arthur Biggs, the only member of the gang still at large, who escaped from Wandsworth prison in 1965, was discovered to be alive and well and living in Melbourne, Australia. Only hours before the police arrived to arrest him he vanished from the house he had shared with his wife and three children, while earning his living as a carpenter. Melbourne was combed in vain, but Eric Flower, who, though not a member of the train robbery gang, had escaped with Biggs from Wandsworth, was captured in Sydney, N.S.W., a week later. When a newspaper offered Mrs. Biggs a sum said to be £30,000 for her "story," the outraged public turned its sympathy towards the driver of the robbed train, Jack Mills, who was still an invalid as a result of injuries inflicted by the robbers. A fund for him and his wife was opened, and by the middle of December £34,000 had been received—enough to ensure them a comfortable home and income for life.

The Cannock Chase murder of 7-year-old Christine Darby in 1967 was resolved on February 18, 1969, when a 39-year-old engineer was sentenced to life imprisonment for it. The Court of Appeal on November 11 refused him leave to appeal. The appeal of George Marshall, sentenced to life imprisonment for the murder of "Baba" Elgar in February 1968, was allowed on May 16, 1969, and he was released.

Reform of the Courts System

Increased crime means increased work for the courts. At the Old Bailey (Central Criminal Court), in the words of the Royal Commission on Assizes and Quarter Sessions, the situation had become intolerable. Even with 14 or 15 courts sitting every day there were 391 cases awaiting trial at the end of June 1969. On average a case could not be tried in less than $4\frac{1}{2}$ months from committal. After sitting for three years under the chairmanship of Lord Beeching, the Royal Commission recommended a new system of criminal courts for England and Wales, with the separation of criminal and civil business in the higher courts.

The Supreme Court would be reconstituted to comprise the Court of Appeal, the High Court (with civil jurisdiction), and a new Crown Court (handling criminal work above the level of magistrate). The Central Criminal Court would cease to be a separate entity, but would remain the most important centre for sittings of the Crown Court. The Crown Court would be served by High Court judges and a new bench of circuit judges supported by part-time recorders. Judges would no longer visit 33 of the present 61 assize towns, but would sit at seven additional towns not visited at present. In the 69 towns where quarter sessions now sit, there would normally no longer be a court above magistrates' court level.

The High Court, dealing with cases throughout the country, would sit when and where needed. County courts would continue under circuit judges, with increased responsibilities. A new administrative court service would be responsible for the efficient running of all higher criminal and civil courts.

A Turbulent Year in the Churches

Rev. KENNETH SLACK

Minister of the City Temple, London

IF 1969 PRESENTED no religious event comparable in its public impact to the Pope's encyclical *Humanae Vitae* the previous year, and was not marked by great representative gatherings like the 1968 Lambeth Conference and Uppsala Assembly, it certainly cannot be described as a year of serene ecclesiastical calm after the "alarums and excursions" that had gone before. Turmoil and confusion reigned. Radicals saw this as possibly the prelude to the essential revolution if the Church is to be relevant in the closing years of the twentieth century; traditionalists often put it down to the irruption of godlessness within the very Church of God.

There was certainly confusion in regard to ecumenical progress—the march of the Churches towards closer relationships. The visit of the Pope to the headquarters of the World Council of Churches headquarters in Geneva on June 10 was not only unprecedented, but so remarkable that had it been predicted merely three or four years before it would have been dismissed as an ecumenist's pipe dream. It is true that the announced major purpose of his Genevan visit was to address the fiftieth anniversary celebrations of the International Labour Office. But one may question whether the I.L.O. would have seen the Pope if the World Council headquarters has been elsewhere.

Without a moment's doubt the visit marked the wholly new relationship between the Church of Rome and the major instrument for Christian co-operation of the non-Roman Churches of the world. But it did not do much more than that. The Pope's words were guarded. Positively he said that his visit was "truly a blessed encounter, a prophetic moment, the dawn of a day to come and yet awaited for centuries," but with caution he added: "In fraternal frankness, we do not consider that the question of the membership of the Catholic Church in the World Council is so mature that a positive answer could or should be given."

Within the United Kingdom the words "Protestant" and "Catholic" became the labels of the contending parties in Ulster in a situation in which public order could only be precariously maintained by large forces of troops. However much, rightly, it was argued that these labels more truly represent deep historic divisions of a sociological kind than divisions of Christian belief, the fact remained that the world watched an incredible breakdown of civic order apparently based on religious differences. Roman and Protestant leaders spoke out together, and together visited the torn community of Londonderry pleading for reconciliation, but this was offset by the identification of the hard-core Protestant resistance to any change with Ian Paisley, the self-appointed Moderator of the "Free Presbyterian Church of Ulster" (a small body having no links whatever with historic Presbyterianism). Earlier in the year, when Cardinal Heenan was received by the Archbishop of Canterbury at St. Paul's Cathedral during the Week of Prayer for Christian Unity, Paisley and one of his lieutenants figured in incidents leading to police action and summonses; and in June he was refused admission to Switzerland when he arrived to protest against the Pope's visit to the World Council of Churches headquarters.

A Scottish ally of Ian Paisley, Pastor Glass, and his followers forced the suspension of the sitting of the General Assembly of the Church of Scotland by creating an uproar when for the first time a fraternal delegate from the Roman Catholic Church was being received by the Assembly. There was greater public notice of this incident because the Queen was present, having decided to attend in person instead of appointing a Lord High Commissioner, as has been customary for centuries.

These flare-ups of ancient sectarian bitterness were not offset by dramatic advance in the one large decision on church relationships which fell to be made in 1969. Tuesday, July 8, was decision-day in regard to the first stage of the proposed new relationship between the Church of England and the Methodist Church. The Convocations of Canterbury and York, meeting jointly in London, and the Methodist Conference meeting in Birmingham, voted at the same time. It had already been agreed that no less than a 75 per cent vote in favour would be adequate. In the event this was easily achieved in the Methodist Conference—77·4 per cent were in favour. But the requisite votes were not secured in the Anglican convocations, the overall majority being only 69 per cent. In a television interview after the vote the Archbishop of Canterbury, Dr. Ramsey, did not disguise his deep disappointment. The bishops, all but six of whom voted for the new relationship, reacted by strongly encouraging every kind of closer co-operation, both centrally and locally, with the Methodists that can be achieved within the present set-up.

As well as those who were opposed to the scheme there was a growing number of Christians who regretted the expenditure of spiritual and other energy upon so "churchy" a concern. They divided into those who thought a decision in favour worth making if it were made swiftly enough for energies then to be turned to larger issues, and those on the other hand who thought the whole business of intercommunion irrelevant in times when men had walked on the moon. Both groups were united in thinking that the real concerns for Christian conscience today are ecumenical in no ecclesiastical sense but in the original meaning of the word, i.e. concerned with "the inhabited earth." The struggle against racism and world poverty, highlighted in the previous year at the Uppsala Assembly, loomed large in the Christian mind in 1969.

A world consultation on racism was held by the World Council of Churches in Notting Hill, an area of inner London which has been the scene of not a few racial riots and is the home of a substantial immigrant community. The consultation was marked by incursions of "Black Power" leaders which matched those of James Forman and others into the worship of many leading American churches during 1969 with demands for financial reparations by white Christians to the black people whom they had "oppressed." The report emerging from this consultation called on the Churches in the World Council to take massive action against racism, and demanded that this should be symbolised by the allocation of a sizeable part of the Council's narrow financial reserves towards the programme.

The report was also startlingly outspoken in Christian support of the use of violence to achieve racial justice. In this, however, it did not go anything like as far as Colin Morris, the Methodist missionary in Zambia (who has taken up appointment as minister to the historic Wesley's Chapel, City Road, London). He followed up his controversial *Include Me Out!* with an even more hard-hitting book, *Unyoung, Uncoloured, Unpoor*, which presented an original reading of the New Testament that made Jesus the apostle of violence. This book, published in September 1969, may be seen as the manifesto of the revolutionary left among Christians. The pacifism which marked the Christian left in the 1930s has been succeeded by a militancy in regard to the racial struggle and the demand of the Third World for a new deal which is a new feature of the Christian scene.

Many denominations made a swift response during 1969 to the call of the Uppsala Assembly for voluntary gifts to be made until the governments of affluent countries could be persuaded officially to allocate 1 per cent of their gross national product to world develop-

Left: Rev. Ian Paisley (*centre*), the virulent Belfast anti-papist, figured in the sectarian tumult that scarred Northern Ireland during 1969, and was heard elsewhere trumpeting discord to ecumenical harmonies. *Right:* His new £200,000 church opened in October in Belfast.

I

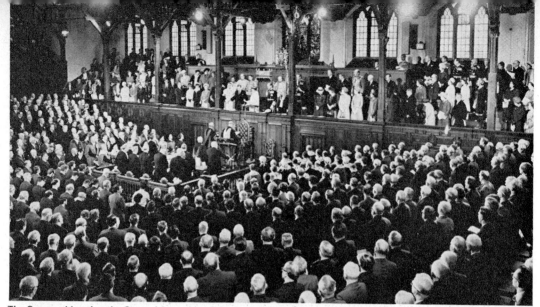

The Queen addressing the General Assembly of the Church of Scotland in Edinburgh on May 20. This was the first time since 1603 that a reigning monarch had attended a regular Assembly—which was disrupted by a Paisleyite faction.

ment. A number of churches appointed days on which the gifts of congregations, of either one day's pay or 1 per cent of "take-home pay," were gathered. In 1969 it appeared that this kind of giving, and the kind of education it requires, may well come to occupy the place in church life earlier held by missionary giving and education (although it is stressed that such new gifts should in no way impinge upon the Church's existing mission at home and abroad). Such reinforced giving towards world need has been accompanied by a new emphasis upon political action that will ensure that voluntary giving is only a stop-gap until essential governmental action is taken. The most striking illustration of this was the National Sign-In, jointly sponsored and organ-

The year saw the continued involvement of the Church in social welfare. *Below:* Focus on Famine demonstration at St. Martin in the Fields.

ised by the Roman Catholic Church and the British Council of Churches and held in December. This offered the opportunity for Christians to "stand up and be counted" as pleading with the British Government for positive action.

All this outward-going activity on the part of the Churches in Great Britain has certainly been made from a diminishing base of actual worshipping numbers. Dr. John Robinson celebrated his move from the suffragan see of Woolwich (to which he has given world-wide fame, and in which he is succeeded by David Sheppard, the cricketer and evangelical leader) to be dean of Trinity College, Cambridge by publishing an article packed with depressing statistics. He called it "The Dramatic Dip." He showed that in the London area the number of baptisms in the Church of England had dropped by 32·8 per cent in the ten years to 1966 (the last year for which figures are available). Confirmations in his own diocese of Southwark had dropped by 48·9 per cent in seven years. The number of those recommended for training for the priesthood throughout the country had fallen by the staggering figure of 58·9 per cent in only five years.

These figures reflect a questioning of the institutional life of the Church which certainly knew no lessening in 1969. Even the Roman Catholic Church, seemingly impervious at many points to the spirit of the age, is seeing a great change. The fall in the number of conversions in England and Wales of 47·6 per cent in eight years is striking. Nor is it limited to Britain. During 1969 it was revealed that the number of Roman seminarians in the

Thirty-three newly created Cardinals celebrating Mass with the Pope in St. Peter's Basilica on May 1. October saw a synod of Catholic Bishops held in Rome at which tentative steps were taken towards the devolution of papal power.

U.S.A. had dropped from 45,267 to 33,065 in the brief period of four years.

The Roman Catholic Church in fact continued to face the effects of the Second Vatican Council. The appointment in April of Monsignor Jan Willebrands, for long the secretary of the Secretariat for Christian Unity, both to be a Cardinal and to succeed the late Cardinal Bea as president of the Secretariat, was reassuring to those who feared some withdrawal from ecumenical engagement.

Some features of the Synod of Bishops held in Rome in October were disturbing before the bishops actually began their journeys. The designation of the gathering as "extraordinary," the secret agenda, and evidence of moves by the Curia to avoid too great content being given to the concept of collegiality (i.e. the Pope ruling within a college of bishops, which had been one of the keynotes of the second Vatican Council)—all this created some anxiety. In the event fears seem to have been unjustified. Advances made were modest, but they were real. From now on the Pope will be expected to consult the bishops before issuing statements about faith and discipline. This must, of course, be reciprocal: Rome must be consulted by any bishop before he makes any such declaration. Local conferences of bishops will be given much greater power, and the lines of communication between Rome and the bishops are to be improved.

Cardinal Suenens of Malines-Brussels emerged in 1969 as the recognised leader of the forces hoping for change within the Roman Catholic Church. A lengthy interview which he gave to the editor of *Informations Catholiques Internationale* was widely translated and reproduced. It reinforced what he had already said in his book, *Co-responsibility in the Church*. This title was significant, and the fact that a leader long regarded as an intimate of Pope Paul should choose to move by book and interview suggested that he despaired of the power of quiet diplomacy, for which he had up to then been more widely known. The fierce reaction of the Curia, and the pained reaction of the Pope himself, revealed the shock which the words of so widely respected and highly placed a churchman had given. However, at the Synod of Bishops the Cardinal seems to have adopted a more pacific role. Controversy continued to rage in the Roman communion on the issues of priestly celibacy and the prohibition of contraception otherwise than by the "natural" rhythm method. There was a marked new questioning among English Catholics of the method of appointment of bishops. Altogether it may be said that the main question that became more sharply focused in 1969 was the overarching one: "Who should make the rules, or decisions, in the Christian Church?"

Worship continues to be one of the areas most sharply affected by the spirit of change. The International Consultation on English Texts produced at the end of April suggested new versions of such basic items of common worship as the Lord's Prayer, the Nicene and Apostles' Creeds, and the Gloria and the Sanctus. Two of the changes proposed for the Lord's Prayer were bold—"glorify your name" instead of "hallowed be thy name," and "save us from the time of trial" instead of "lead us not into temptation." Since the Consultation represented the major Christian Churches

131

The first Papal visit to Africa: Paul VI greeted by President and Mrs. Obote on arriving in Uganda on July 31.

throughout the English-speaking world, the versions it has put out for experimental use and comment may prove a considerable contribution not only to the better understanding by the people of what they are saying in worship but also to ecumenical advance.

The Church of England proposed during the year considerable changes in its calendar and lectionary, i.e. the shape of the Christian Year and the lessons of scripture read during it. These proposals also derived from very wide consultation with other Churches. The main effect would be to rid the calendar of such quaintly named Sundays as Quinquagesima and Sexagesima (which are meaningless titles to virtually everybody), and to concentrate on the three great feasts of Christmas, Easter, and Pentecost, naming other Sundays in relation to them. Thus both Advent and Lent would go from the titles, and nine Sundays before Christmas and Easter would be named accordingly. The faithful churchgoer would certainly get ample warning of the number of shopping weeks to Christmas!

While this kind of work in 1969 tried to make the life of the Church more meaningful

Ecumenical exchange: Cardinal Suenens, primate of Belgium (left) and Dr. Ramsey, Archbishop of Canterbury, met and swopped books in January.

to a secularised generation, there was a lessening of confidence even within the ranks of the Church. In the U.S.A. Bishop James Pike, already deeply involved in controversy over many years, crowned it by leaving the Church as no longer a credible institution for conveying the Gospel; and set about founding an institute for the care of those who had been led to take the same step. (Later in the year he tragically died of heat exhaustion on a journey to the Holy Land when his car ran out of fuel in the Dead Sea area.) No equally prominent Christian leader in Great Britain left the Church in this fashion, and Bishop John Robinson sharply contradicted the suggestion that his move back to academic and pastoral life in Cambridge was to be interpreted in that way.

Nevertheless, the signs of a lessening of confidence were there. Most sharply it revealed itself in the reduction of the number of candidates for the ministry of all the Churches. The closing of theological colleges has become commonplace. Again, a Church grown more aware of world need and recognising the call to make a Christian response has felt guilty in asking for increasingly large sums for the maintenance of the expensive and ageing church fabrics that have been inherited from the past. The televised sight of starving Biafran children has made the appeal for the decaying bell-tower or the worm-eaten aisle roof look rather irrelevant. There has been awareness, too, of the strength of feeling in the younger generation that care of people must take total priority over maintenance of buildings. In the Church of England and in the World Council of Churches preparatory steps were taken in 1969 to draw the younger generation more fully into the areas of the Churches' life where decisions are made.

In Great Britain the plight of the homeless and the ill-housed was brought before church people, and the general public, with brilliant publicity by "Shelter," a charity enjoying strong Christian support. Collections for "Shelter," for Biafran orphans, and for the victims of the Vietnam war have become as commonplace in church life as those for direct propagation of the Gospel were a generation ago. Thus the period of turbulent change invites the contrasted responses referred to in the opening paragraph of this survey. The traditionalist sees much of this movement as taking refuge from lack of Christian conviction in mere humanitarianism; the radical sees it as the beginning of a new Christian concern to break out of the vestry mentality and into a world that needs more than anything else the witness of caring.

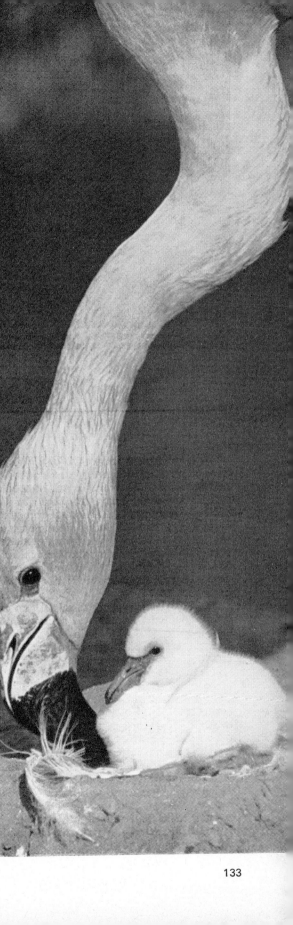

Nature

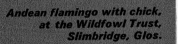

*Andean flamingo with chick,
at the Wildfowl Trust,
Slimbridge, Glos.*

Desolate olive groves near Tunis, photographed on October 24 after a month of torrential rainfall—described as "the worst for a thousand years." By this date the Tunisian death toll had exceeded 500 and 132,000 people were homeless.

The Violence of Nature

JOHN GROGAN

"Once in a thousand years" is a large claim too commonly made. Perhaps, over the whole surface of the earth something will happen each year, in a selected spot, which could be expected only once in a generation or even once in a century. But in 1969 some meteorologists were ready to volunteer that phrase "once in a thousand years" to describe the calamitous flooding of Tunisia. Certainly something very unusual happened over North West Africa and Western Europe in the autumn of 1969. The floods in Tunisia and Algeria were unprecedented. The dryness and sunniness of the month of October in Britain, which brought water restrictions to much of the country, were unprecedented. The high winds in Scandinavia, which killed more than a score of people, were unusual. Some scientists suggested a link between all these events, though what it was they were unable to say. "Unprecedented" in the British case meant that a century or two of records could not produce a counterpart. In North Africa it meant a demonstration of the violence of nature and man's helplessness before it which must have come as a shock to holiday-makers who had gone there in the expectation of clear skies and unbroken sunshine. For a month heavy rain fell almost continuously over countryside which, if not quite arid

desert, suffers more commonly from drought than from excessive rain. Villages were drowned in water or engulfed in chocolate-coloured liquid mud. Wadis (dried up water-courses) became torrents as wide as the Thames, carrying animal and human dead and the other grim debris of disaster. Small salt lagoons swelled to become lakes which swallowed up homes and crops.

A month after the rains had started on September 25, the toll in Tunisia was officially put at 501 dead, 132,000 homeless, 55,000 houses destroyed. In Algeria there were then 76 dead, 3 missing, 237 injured, 63,000 homeless, 14,000 homes destroyed. During early October reports to the British Disaster Emergency Committee (made up from the Ministry of Overseas Development and charitable organisations) told of one third of Tunisia being under water. The site of the town of Kairouan, a large holiday resort, was a lake without either electricity or drinking water, and helicopters were striving to maintain essential supplies. The phosphate mines of Gafsa were flooded, putting 25,000 miners out of work and depriving the government of £2 million a week in phosphate revenue alone. One fifth of the country's animals had been swept away. Other major towns, Sousse, Kasseine, and Sfax, were isolated, dependent on makeshift communications and supply routes. With widespread pollution of water supplies, scores of thousands of doses of typhoid vaccine were rushed to the country. Great stretches of roadway and railway were destroyed and many bridges washed away, thus hampering the work of rebuilding when the rains began to lighten in mid-October. Then, as salvaging got under way, torrential rains fell once again, and even parts of the capital, Tunis, itself, were cut off by the rushing tongues of water that swept into the town.

Floods in the Far East

Holidaymakers go to Tunis in the late summer expecting sunshine as a right: when it rains enough to drown hundreds it is headline news. But calamity through flood is as expected in some parts of the world as earthquakes are in Turkey. When a hundred people are swept away and perish in the monsoon rains of India the fatalism of the East and the unconcern of the West mean it is accepted as something inevitable. But the floods in the state of Andhra Pradesh, caused by a cyclone which swept in from the Bay of Bengal in May, went far beyond the normal Indian disaster. Perhaps a thousand people died (early official estimates were 800) in what were called the worst floods of the century. Among the dead were 21 fishermen who put out to sea just before the storm broke. Fifty-three people were overwhelmed when an irrigation tank gave way. Vijayavada, the second city of the state, recorded 25 inches of rain in five days, a year's supply for south-eastern England and over half a ton of water on every square yard! Three million acres of farmland were flooded, and over these floated the carcases of thousands of cattle.

In Korea similar tropical storms brought the worst floods since 1959; between 9 and 14 inches of rain fell in a torrential downpour in the southern coastal districts, leaving 257 people dead, 81 missing, 90 injured, and more than 60,000 homeless. In Formosa, 38 people were dead and 28 missing after a typhoon hit the northern part of the island; half a million people were said to have suffered in one way or another. Across the world, in Brazil, an incomplete casualty count gave 293 dead after floods swept through the town of São Jose da Laje. In Persia, flooding in January drowned about 100 people and sent thousands more in hill villages fleeing before an invasion of thousands of poisonous snakes, themselves flying from the floods. In Syria the same storms found helicopters helping to rescue 10,000 marooned villagers, and the 50,000 population of one town being supplied by air. Again in Persia, three months later, another 40 people were drowned in further flooding and almost 50,000 left homeless as houses were destroyed in nearly 400 villages. The death toll in Portugal when it was hit by heavy rain in the spring was small in comparison, with four people drowned. But disaster areas were declared as the rivers Tagus and Douro overflowed their banks, sweeping away property and crops worth millions of pounds.

America's Worst Hurricane

In the U.S.A. tornadoes, hurricanes, and storms brought death and destruction which even that rich and scientifically advanced nation cannot avoid. As usual the passage of the dreaded "twister" winds along "Tornado Alley," up through the central states, brought death to many. In the space of a few summer months 17 people were killed and 100 injured in northern Minnesota, 5 killed in Missouri, and 14 killed and 400 injured in Cleveland, Ohio, as tornadoes swept across Lake Erie. The bodies of two children and their mother were found in a wrecked and abandoned school after one tornado passed through Cincinnati

A Formosan village inundated by the heavy rains that followed in the wake of Typhoon Flossie in October.

in August, injuring another 231. Dozens of people were evacuated from a four-storey block of flats just before the two top floors were sucked off by the wind. The worst tornado, however, came to Mississippi in January. It killed 29 people and left a 50-mile-long swathe of destruction. Houses crumpled as if made of cardboard, and cars and lorries were sent flying in the air. In the town of Hazelhurst, probably the worst hit, it was said that timber and furniture "rained" from the sky.

But the state of Mississippi suffered most in the summer, from Hurricane Camille, the most ferocious storm in American history. It brought winds of 200 m.p.h. and tides 20 ft. above normal along the Gulf coast. The death toll in Mississippi was around 250, in Virginia around 100, with more casualties in Louisiana and Alabama. At one time it appeared that the death toll was much higher, but then it was realised that embalmed corpses, washed out of a cemetery, were being counted too! The towns of Biloxi and Gulfport suffered badly. In Biloxi, on America's Riviera, 5,000 families lost their homes and 40,000 buildings were damaged. Some parts were under 20 ft. of water and the damage was put at 10 million dollars in that one town alone. In Bay St. Louis 50 people died in one block of flats, and 10–20-foot breakers swept across the foreshore into hotels, uprooting smaller houses and depositing them in the hotel gardens. As Gulfport lay under water the horrified pilot of one plane reported sighting 40 bodies floating together. Virginia only got the tail end of the storm, but this was sufficient to bring its worst flooding in a century, with 130 bridges shattered, 5,238 homes destroyed, and another 11,667 suffering major damage. The material possessions of whole communities in the State's west central area were destroyed. Some victims were swept down mountainsides in landslides following in the wake of the hurricane, others were carried away in streams swollen to rivers, and in rivers that burst calamitously through their banks to flood whole countrysides. The James River rose to a record height of 28 ft. 6 in.—19 ft. 6 in. above ordinary flood level—and when it receded 60 bodies were left behind with a further 10 of the local population still missing. As the winds died down and the waters receded and people counted the cost of Camille, immediate insurance claims were lodged for 100 million dollars.

On the other side of the U.S.A., in California, the worst storm for 30 years killed at least 100 people in January, though over half the deaths were officially reported as occurring in road accidents connected with the deluge. As in the case of the autumn floods in S.E. England the previous year, part of the blame for the unwonted severity of the flooding was ascribed to the pace and density of housing construction. Interference with the natural drainage of the land leads to faster run-off and a quick rise in flood waters. Brush fires, too, had destroyed the trees and bushes which could have held in place the thin topsoil, and so mudslides moved in great masses into residential areas, thrusting aside houses in their path.

Forecasting Disaster

But while man's mistakes sometimes help to exacerbate the blows he takes from misfortune,

Remains of the small town of Hazelhurst, Mississippi, after a tornado had swept through it in January. The "twister" cut a 50-mile swathe of destruction through the state.

Like a litter of dolls' houses thrown on to a scrap-heap, the town of Buras, Louisiana, after Hurricane Camille had passed in August. Mississippi, Virginia, and Alabama were also hit by the hurricane—the worst in American history.

his attempts to use his intellect to soften the blows do have an effect. Thanks to modern forecasting techniques using the information provided by meteorological satellites and other advanced instruments, the blows do not come quite so unexpectedly. The grievous toll of Camille was probably only a fraction of what it might have been: warning of its coming was given in time for a quarter of a million people to flee from the main line of its advance. What happens when such warning is not available was shown when a tornado at Dacca in East Pakistan killed an estimated 1,000 people and injured several thousand.

Little can be done, however, when the birth of a hurricane has been discovered to weaken its development or change its course. Camille's successor Debbie was bombarded with silver iodide crystals to provide nuclei on which water droplets could grow. One hope was that treating one side of the hurricane in this way might cause it to veer off its path; but whether any good came of it is doubtful. The paths of hurricanes are erratic and little understood, and Debbie's movements did not seem to differ from what might normally be expected. Another technique proposed to counter hurricanes is to cover the sea in their path with a layer of chemicals to prevent the evaporation of moisture which fuels the storm's growth. How likely this is to have any effect is uncer-

tain—but hurricanes, like all the world's weather, *are* affected by the interaction between the sea and the atmosphere. The atmosphere is a vast engine in constant motion, powered by the sun, and a great part of the sun's energy working on the atmosphere is reflected back from the land and sea, and, in the case of the sea, partly locked in water vapour. American meteorologists are carrying out a project, off Barbados, to study the sea-air interaction in that birthplace of hurricanes.

Russian scientists have announced a grandiose project to study the weather-making process on a global scale, by means of land stations manned and unmanned, a greatly enlarged fleet of oceanographic and weather ships, automatic floating stations, rockets, and satellites. Some fears were expressed that the intention was not merely the understanding of the present world weather, but the study of the total effect of schemes for changing the geography and weather of the U.S.S.R. If, when all is known, a change of climate for the better in Central Asia or the U.S.A. means a change for the worse in Western Europe, who will decide what should be done?

One type of disaster for which forecasting techniques are urgently wanted is the earthquake. Work to this end started in a disused railway tunnel, 360 ft. beneath the moors between Bradford and Halifax in Yorkshire.

Geophysicists from Cambridge University, using a laser measuring tool, were studying the pattern of earth movements and relating them to known earthquakes to try to find an association. Similar work was going on round the world, and it was reported that in Russia studies were even being made of the apparent ability of some animals to sense the coming of a quake. At a conference in Madrid it was reported that a Russian, S. A. Fedotov, had accurately predicted the place in Japan where an earthquake occurred on May 16, 1968, from his study of weather phenomena, electric currents through the earth's crust, and previous earthquake patterns.

Earthquakes and Fire

According to the U.S. Geological Survey one major destructive earthquake is likely to occur somewhere in the world each year. Over the past thousand years earthquakes have probably claimed 3–5 million victims. 1969 did not bring any large-scale earthquakes, although about 50 people died in each of two earthquakes in Iran and West Turkey. One, in January, was in the Korassan province of Iran, where thousands had died in one of the worst of all calamities the previous summer. The other, in March, was around the town of Alasehir in West Turkey (the original Philadelphia of classical times, which was completely destroyed by an earthquake in 17 B.C.).

The best recorded earthquake of 1969 was one which did not take place. For much of the year there was foreboding that there was to be an even more calamitous repeat of the great 1906 earthquake that destroyed much of San Francisco. After speculation by some scientists that the stresses building up in the great fault running beneath California might,

A severed house in suburban Los Angeles, perched over an earthslide caused by heavy January rainstorms.

after 60 years, be on the point of relieving themselves again, some religious groups began predicting that the State would split in two and the heavily populated towns would slide into the sea on Good Friday. Professor Charles Richter, whose name is given to the scale used for recording the strength of earthquakes, had to issue a statement describing the rumours as ridiculous. There *was* an earthquake about the time predicted, but the most it achieved was to shake tinned foods off supermarket shelves. Later in the year came two quakes which were the worst in the State for 12 years but, although injuring 12 people, they took no lives.

In September the worst earthquake in South Africa for 37 years killed nine. But in October the town of Banja Luka, Yugoslavia, and the villages around were shaken by an earthquake as violent as that which devastated Skopje, although fortunately the toll in lives was far less. Only 20 were killed, but 80 per cent of the buildings were reported destroyed or badly damaged and the town's 80,000 inhabitants had to camp out following the second and worse of the two shocks. This earthquake was recorded as 9 on the destruction scale of 12 degrees, probably the most violent of the year. The other main earthquake zone, on the Pacific side of South America, had its shock in October, in Lima, Peru, where 10 died. In June the heaviest earthquake recorded this century in Melbourne rocked the southern part of the State of Victoria, sending thousands of people fleeing into the streets from their homes but causing no serious casualties.

Bush fires swept through Victoria in January, engulfing the small town of Lara (36 miles south-west of Melbourne). Some 50 homes were destroyed, including this one, which burst into flames as the holocaust passed by. Within minutes only ashes marked the spot.

The town of Banja Luka, Yugoslavia, was devastated by earthquake in October—yet only 20 were killed.

Victoria, in January, had its worst bush fires for many years. They ravaged thousands of acres only a month after the disastrous fires of the Blue Mountain area in New South Wales. In one series of fires between Melbourne and Geelong 16 lives were lost. Temperatures were near 90°F. on the coast and around 100°F. inland, and strong gusty winds added to the fire risk. A 30-mile-wide wall of flame engulfed the little town of Lara, 36 miles south-west of Melbourne, destroying 50 homes, two churches, and a school, and leaving 150 homeless. The fires were the worst in the State since 1943. Official estimates were that more than 300 square miles of farming land in Victoria were burned out in a week, and records showed that thousands of sheep and cattle were killed.

In France, in August, two people, one a mentally subnormal youth, admitted adding to the fires which devastated 25,000 acres of forest and brushwood in the Midi's worst blaze since 1956. But the main culprits were the long hot summer and the steady blowing of the mistral. A catastrophic drought in Poland resulted in many fires there. In August it was reported that there had been 16,000 outbreaks in two months, with 16,250 acres of forest destroyed.

The summer was so dry and sunny that Great Britain also had more than her quota of bush fires. Part of the ancient Caledonian Forest was involved in one of the most devastating fires in the Scottish Highlands for many years. In the one month of April, forest fires caused more damage to Forestry Commission property in three weeks than in the whole of 1967 and 1968 together.

Too Hot or Too Cold?

No matter how good a summer Great Britain has, it rarely results in widespread deaths from heat. In Mexico, thousands of people fled to the mountains in August to escape a heat wave which had killed 94, mostly children killed by exhaustion and dehydration. The temperature reached 125°F.

Deaths directly attributable to the weather during the year in Great Britain may have been few, but every year it kills in a more insidious way. According to a former professor of medicine, Dr. Geoffrey Taylor, in the U.K. 60,000–90,000 succumb to cold each year. Unheated homes take five years off our lives, compared with centrally heated ones, he stated. So reports sent from Greenland by Danish and American scientists should give us cause to think: according to them it will be colder in 1985. They base their conclusions on a study of a core of ice four fifths of a mile long, removed from the Greenland ice cap. Its layers were said to reveal 100,000 years of climatic history and to show cycles of warmth and cold which should bring a cold low in 20–30 years from now. Other scientists, pointing to the amount of carbon dioxide being liberated into the atmosphere, predict that the temperature might rise by a few degrees, because of a greenhouse effect. Such a rise might be enough to produce floods which would dwarf all those hitherto experienced. The icecaps and glaciers could start melting, and the seas might rise over such cities as New York, London, and Leningrad. Either a fur coat or a swimming costume, it seems, will be the correct weather wear at the end of the century.

Pyromaniacs played their part in starting forest and bush fires which, fanned by the steady mistral, ravaged 25,000 acres of the French Riviera in August. The long hot summer had rendered the region tinder dry, and the conflagration was the Midi's worst blaze since 1956.

Restoring the Balance of Nature

JOHN CLEGG

MUCH OF THE NEWS of animal life, and of the steps being taken to conserve it, during 1969 came from Australia. Mounting concern about the danger to the country's unique flora and fauna from widespread economic development and indiscriminate hunting led, in April, to an announcement by the Prime Minister, John Gorton, that a Federal-State conference would be called to discuss ways of tackling conservation on a national basis, and to draw up a national wildlife policy. Previously the Federal government had been reluctant to take active steps for fear of upsetting individual States, but the slowness of some State governments to set aside areas of land for nature reserves or to support private conservation organisations led inevitably to Federal action. The government's initiative in calling this conference should break through the deadlock and at last make possible sensible co-operation on game laws, the creation of nature reserves that cross State boundaries, and unified research—especially into a comprehensive survey of the state of Australia's wildlife in general. In March a delegation of scientists from the Australian Academy of Science urged the Australian government to set up a national institute to study native animals and plants. The delegation submitted a detailed report pointing out that "the Australian fauna is vanishing at a rate which is not understood, or appreciated, by the casual observer of the Australian scene. The introduction of grazing animals and their diffusion through the country has changed the whole ecological character of vast areas, and has led to the disappearance of many native species from much of their former range."

Meanwhile, one of the animals about which concern has been felt was the subject of an interesting experiment. In May a company was registered in Sydney to set up Australia's first kangaroo farm! Kangaroos are much more efficient than sheep at converting plant food into animal protein and they are better adapted to Australia's inland environment as they can withstand drought. The company proposed initially to stock between 1,200 and 1,500 kangaroos on 2,000 acres of land in order to prove that it is possible to farm kangaroos humanely and economically.

Australian nature reserves announced during 1969 include Pilliga, 160,000 acres in New South Wales, straddling the Newell Highway, between Coonabarabran and Narrabri. The N.S.W. government has dedicated the area as a reserve because it is one of the major plant and animal communities of the central north-west and has a wealth and variety of interesting creatures. Grey kangaroos and ring-tailed possums are plentiful, and emus, koalas, and spiny anteaters are all known to occur in the area. In Queensland 17,500 acres at Southwood, near Moonie, will probably be reserved as the Brigalow National Park. In Victoria the Little Desert National Park and the Wilson's Promontory National Park were extended, and the Lower Glenelg National Park, near Portland, and the Captain James Cook National Park, near Cape Everard, have been created. In Tasmania the South West Fauna District of 475,000 acres (only half the area originally recommended) has been gazetted.

Destruction by Starfish

Perhaps Australia's most spectacular nature reserve, although it is not dedicated as such, is the Great Barrier Reef stretching for 1,260 miles off the north-eastern coast. As a tourist attraction it is estimated to be worth £30 million per annum. Naturalists, therefore, have been shocked to learn that this wonderful natural feature is threatened on no less than four counts: the granting of licences to prospect for off-shore oil; an application to mine coral detritus on Ellison Reef; the destruction of large numbers of giant clams by the crews of foreign fishing vessels; and finally, and most insidiously, a plague of starfish called the crown-of-thorns (*Acanthaster planci*) which attacks the coral polyps.

In May a symposium of 500 conservationists met at Sydney University to discuss ways in which the uncontrolled exploitation of the reef for commercial purposes could be stopped, and they recommended the setting up of a commission with members from both the Commonwealth and Queensland governments. The Federal Minister for Education and Science summed up the situation when he told the symposium: "Uncontrolled commercial de-

During 1969 marine scientists waged war on the poisonous, hydra-limbed, crown-of-thorns starfish (*left*) which, thanks to its coral diet and spectacular rise in numbers, threatens the Great Barrier Reef and the Pacific islands. Living coral, the nursery for teeming marine life (*centre*), becomes after destruction by the starfish a sterile wilderness (*right*).

velopment of the reef could lead to the destruction of habitat and the extermination of most indigenous plant and animal species."

The damage done by the crown-of-thorns, however, will not be remedied merely by holding conferences; indeed it is one of the greatest puzzles biologists have ever had to solve. The starfish averages about 15 in. across but can grow to 2 ft., and has up to 17 arms covered with long, curved, and poisonous spines. It extrudes its stomach over the coral colony and absorbs the delicate coral polyps, leaving behind only the empty coral covering, which with no animals inside to make new coral, soon crumbles and breaks up. A single adult starfish can eat as much as 24 square inches of live coral every day; a thousand can consume a reef at the rate of an acre a month, and can destroy in a few years an atoll that may have taken centuries to form.

The reason why these starfish have recently multiplied in such a spectacular way is still a mystery. Ten years ago a single crown-of-thorns spotted near Green Island in the Great Barrier Reef was enough of a rarity to send naturalists diving with snorkels to study its graceful movements. One theory is that one of its natural predators, and perhaps its only one, the huge, foot-long triton shellfish, the shell of which is prized by collectors all over the world, has been overcollected in the reef area, but this is disputed by some biologists. The Great Barrier Reef is not the only place where countless thousands of the crown-of-thorns have been destroying coral reefs. There are reports of similar damage on a large scale to the coral reefs of the U.S. territory of Guam, to islands off the east coast of Malaysia, and to Borneo, New Guinea, the Fiji Islands, and elsewhere—right across the Indo-Pacific Ocean. Pacific islanders face the erasure of

their islands, but before this happened they would starve—for their reefs and atolls are vital to the spawning and feeding of fish.

During the summer of 1969 an international team of marine scientists, armed with hypodermic syringes and diving gear, mustered on Guam, under the leadership of Dr. Chesher, of the Institute of Marine Science in Miami, Florida. The operation did not call for brute force—for when a crown-of-thorns is cut into pieces each piece grows another set of tentacles. Instead Dr. Chesher had devised a hypodermic syringe with which a diver can inject the starfish with a fatal dose of formalin. This has proved so effective that on one occasion a team of four scientists killed 2,589 starfish at Guam in four hours. Tests were also made with a new type of electric gun which, it was claimed, would kill the starfish by electric shock.

Turtles and Tortoises

One of the larger animals of the Great Barrier Reef is the marine turtle, of which there are five kinds: the green turtle, loggerhead,

Newly hatched turtles heading for the sea. These increasingly rare creatures were given full protection—at least from Man—by the Queensland government during 1969.
Australian News and Information Bureau

Baboons inspecting visitors to the wildlife park at Longleat, Wilts. Wild animals' acceptance of the motor car as a "natural" facet of their environment is a feature of such parks, both in their native homes and in their exile.

hawksbill, flatback, and leathery turtle. The Queensland government has set a good example to the world by giving these five species full protection along the State's entire 3,200-mile-long coast and the whole of the Barrier Reef. The survival prospects of marine turtles in other waters, however, are not so rosy. It is believed that two or even three species may become extinct within the next five or six years. This is because they are being ruthlessly exploited for commercial purposes. Turtles provide oil for cosmetics, leather for bags and shoes, shell for many ornamental purposes, and, of course, meat, eggs, and soup made from the calipee—which is the yellow

Chung Nam Kim, the Korean sailor who fell overboard off Nicaragua and survived 17 hours before he was rescued—after clinging for two hours to the back of a giant turtle.

gelatinous substance found above the turtle's lower shell. In some undeveloped tropical countries turtle eggs are an essential source of protein, but in the prosperous West there is no excuse for indulging in luxuries which threaten the extinction of the species from which they are obtained. In 1969 the World Wildlife Fund urged the general public to stop buying

anything made from turtle products, and Peter Scott, the chairman of the British national appeal, said "I really believe that people (some Lord Mayors for example) ought to 'lay off' turtle soup—which anyway almost entirely depends upon the quality and quantity of sherry put into it!"

One man who had especial reasons for being grateful that turtles were not yet extinct was a Korean sailor who, in August, was picked up from the back of a giant turtle about 110 miles off Nicaragua in the Pacific. He said he had fallen overboard from a Liberian vessel and, after swimming for over 15 hours, clung to the creature's back for two hours, while the turtle, mercifully, refrained from diving!

The land-bound relatives of the turtle, the tortoises, have been giving rise to concern for some years. From Morocco alone some half a million tortoises are exported to Britain as pets each year, and similar numbers go to other countries. It seems unlikely that tortoise populations can stand this heavy annual drain, for they are slow-breeding animals. In the spring of 1969 the Fauna Preservation Society, with the help of a grant from the World Wildlife Fund, supported a study of the wild populations of tortoises in Morocco, with special reference to their size and age structure. The report on this study will be awaited with great interest by those societies who

Some 40 million fish were poisoned in the Rhine, during June, after a large quantity of the insecticide endosulfan had been dumped into the river.

deplore this trade. These unfortunate reptiles often die soon after their arrival in the United Kingdom, either from damage received in transit, or from ignorance of their requirements in captivity on the part of their owners.

Statistics showing the rate of other animals imported to the U.K. were given in a government report published during 1969. This gave figures for 1967, which were greeted with great concern. For instance, during that year licences had been issued for the importation of over 26,000 primates, mostly Old World monkeys wanted primarily for scientific research. Direct importation by zoos accounted for only 260 primates. Another publication issued during the year contained the remarkable information that in Britain alone "one new zoo or bird garden is said to open every six weeks." There are now over 120 zoos of various kinds in Britain, many of which belong to the Federation of Zoological Societies set up in 1966. This body tries to ensure that any member zoo is well maintained and its animals properly looked after. Before a zoo is admitted to membership it has to be inspected by an independent panel of experts.

Wildlife Parks and Zoos

Wildlife parks, smaller versions of the great game parks of Africa, are a new development among private zoos in recent years, and more

Claimed to be the world's largest nesting box, this 120-ft. tower, built at Lake Charles, Louisiana, as a war memorial to men who have died in the war in Vietnam, offers accommodation for 5,280 purple martin swallows.

have opened this year. Visitors can go "on safari" in their own cars through such parks, and see animals unenclosed and at close quarters, for they soon become accustomed to the traffic. Indeed they take little notice of visitors unless they stop their cars and get out—a dangerous and strictly forbidden operation at parks such as that belonging to the Marquess of Bath at Longleat, Somerset, where lions are present in large numbers. Lions in the Kruger National Park in South Africa have become so used to cars that they now use lines of parked tourists as cover while stalking such animals as impala returning from drinking places!

Among the more attractive wildlife parks are those that specialise in water birds, and of these in Britain the grounds of the Wildfowl Trust at Slimbridge are the most popular, attracting thousands of visitors every year. Here for the first time in 1969 no less than three species of flamingo bred. Up to June 1968 it was believed that no flamingoes of any kind could be reared in Britain. Then the Caribbean flamingoes, the most brightly coloured of all the breed, produced a single youngster which by the end of 1969 was in full adult plumage. In July 1969 the Trust announced the first breeding in captivity anywhere in the world of the Andean flamingo, and in August no less than nine pairs of the Chilean flamingoes produced their single eggs. Flamingoes are gregarious birds and need the social stimulation of the flock to achieve breeding condition. The success of the Wildfowl Trust in breeding these birds is no doubt

Chemicals called polychlorinated biphenyls may be implicated in the death of thousands of seabirds washed up on the Irish Sea coasts in September and October.

due, partly at least, to the large size of its flamingo stocks.

Pollution by Pesticides

The poisoning of our environment continues to worry responsible governments and their peoples. Not only the land but rivers, seas, and the air now carry a frighteningly high concentration of the highly toxic and persistent chemicals used as insecticides and weedkillers. The *Newsletter* of the Wildlife Preservation Society of Queensland reported that Australia uses proportionately more pesticides than any other country. By a unanimous vote the U.N. General Assembly passed a resolution sponsored by Sweden and more than fifty other members calling for an international conference in 1972 to consider ways of co-operating in the fight against environmental pollution.

A new danger to wild life is indicated in the news that some substances used in the manufacture of plastics, paint, and cosmetics, called the polychlorinated biphenyls, have found their way into the tissues of many species of wild animals in North America. There was no evidence of their presence in British wild life until the disastrous poisoning of more than 10,000 sea birds in the northern Irish Sea in late September and October. Bodies washed up on the coasts of Northern Ireland, south west Scotland, and Anglesey, many in a very emaciated condition, were found to contain 400 parts per million of residues of the PCBs. It appeared that they were probably not taken in with the birds' food or directly from the water.

Everyone knows that organo-chlorine pesticides such as DDT are responsible for a catastrophic decline in peregrine falcons, ospreys, bald eagles, and other birds of prey. Research by a scientist of the Nature Conservancy, the results of which were published on April in the Zoological Society's *Journal of Zoology*, indicates that badgers in Britain are being poisoned by organo-chlorine pesticides. It is believed that the animals eat wood-pigeons which have been feeding on spring-sown corn that has been treated with the pesticide in defiance of a voluntary ban imposed in 1961. Some of the badgers had residues of the poison dieldrin in their liver as high as 46 parts per million.

Pollution of rivers by pesticides used in agriculture is also suggested as one of the reasons for the serious decline in otters in Britain. A report by the Mammal Society, incorporating information from the Masters of Otter Hounds' Association and published in May, showed that there has been a severe decline over most of southern and eastern England, although in the north and west numbers are about normal. This will be sad news to naturalists and also to those who have gained an affection for otters by reading the best-selling book, *Ring of Bright Water*, the author of which, Gavin Maxwell, died in September. The otter he described was, of course, not the native British species; nevertheless the book conveys a very vivid picture of the beauty and playfulness of these delightful animals.

One of the worst cases of river pollution ever recorded occurred in June 1969, when the Rhine was poisoned by 200 lb. of an insecticide called endosulfan, chemically similar to DDT, which was released into the river from a factory in Germany. It was estimated that 40 million fish died as a result, a striking demonstration of the deadliness of the growing range of chemicals now used so widely by farmers. That the long-term effect of the use of these powerful chemicals can rarely be forecast, was illustrated in a remarkable case described in the American journal *Natural History*. A mosquito control programme in Borneo sponsored by the World Health Organisation involved spraying large quantities of DDT, which effectively killed off the mosquitoes. Soon after, however, the natives' houses began falling down, and it was found that they were being eaten by a caterpillar which had not been affected by the DDT; but the wasps which normally prey on the caterpillar and keep it under control had been killed off in large numbers. At the same time DDT was sprayed in the houses to kill houseflies. This time the little lizards called geckos, which live in the houses, ate the poisoned flies and died. The cats then ate the geckos and also died, and then rats invaded the houses. As they brought a risk of plague, fresh cats had to be parachuted into the area to try to restore the balance!

Theresa, a porpoise, was under training as a "diver's mate" during 1969. American experts predict that Theresa will prove invaluable during salvage operations—fetching and carrying tools between the surface and divers below.

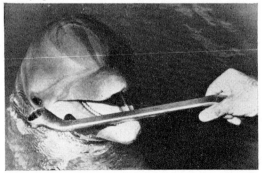

Mud choked saturated British acres as the year began—but by August (*right*) farmers were bringing home bumper harvests.
Photos, British Farmer

Nature Paid her Debt to Farmers

PETER BELL
Associate Editor of *British Farmer*

"ALL IS SAFELY gathered in." The words of the old harvest hymn rang out at thanksgiving services all over Great Britain as September gave way to October, and for once they could be sung with sincerity as well as fervour. The wet summer and autumn of 1968 and the long, cold winter that followed had as their sequel four of those kindly, compensating months that turn disaster into success in an industry where the weather is the ultimate arbiter. In these pre-packed, quick-frozen, oven-ready days it is easy to forget that Nature has the first word—and the last.

At the end of May 1969, some 120,000 acres in the North and East of England lay fallow, still saturated by the drenching rains that had seemed to have no end. Where there should have been green upthrusting wheat and barley, potato rows ready for earthing up, sugar beet marching in long straight lines, and peas and beans podding up, there were only vast stretches of mud and plastic, intractable and sullen. Even in many of the "better" fields there were great bare patches and places where the plants were yellow and sickly with water choking their roots. But by July the picture had changed dramatically. Now a lush, burgeoning verdancy met the farmer's approving eye. Once again it was a land of promise: a promise that was largely fulfilled. The southern half of Britain chalked up yields of

grain well above average, while the North, which the 1968 deluge had hit hardest, at least pulled up to achieve returns much above expectations. Root and potato yields were down, but the crops could be gathered in good conditions. Speaking at the time of the grain harvest, Dr. Clare Burgess, president of the National Association of Corn and Agricultural Merchants, said he was sure wheat production would show an increase over 1968's, despite a smaller acreage; and he forecast a total barley crop of between 8½ and 8¾ million tons, compared with 1968's 7·95 million tons.

Not many years ago Lord Boyd Orr was forecasting world starvation in a matter of a few decades, when population growth, he said, would outstrip the world's ability to feed itself. In 1969, after a tour of Australia and New Zealand, farmer-writer John Cherrington began a report in the *Financial Times* with the cheerful predictions that the world can feed itself; it could feed double its present population of 3,000 million (which should become necessary about A.D. 2000), and it could almost certainly support even double that population (12,000 million) if it ever became necessary. Cherrington was quoting Dr. C. P. McMeekan, the leading New Zealand agriculturist, who told the World Bank that there was more land unused than used in the world, and more land under-farmed than well farmed, and that the

K

resources of modern technology in cultivation and animal husbandry were being applied in only a handful of countries. John Cherrington even questioned the assumption that two thirds of the world's population are under-nourished.

The report of the Food and Agriculture Organisation of the United Nations, which came out in late September, stated that "combined world agricultural, fishery, and forestry production increased in 1968 by about 3 per cent—roughly in line with the average rate of increase over the past ten years and ahead of a world population growth rate of 2 per cent." In the developing countries combined, the increase in agricultural production was some 2 per cent, and in food production alone 3 per cent, while population growth was 2·6 per cent a year. Dr. Boerma, F.A.O. Director-General, described 1968 as an average year, and it is certain that when the next report is published the year 1969 will be described as above average.

In short, the swinging pendulum of production is providing enough food for all—so long as the politicians have the sense to see that it gets to the people. Indeed, the bogey word of 1969 was not *shortage*, but *surplus*. The wheat-exporting countries clocked up a 60-million-ton stock—double the current level of export needs. The figure in 1968 was 37 million tons. The reasons for this accumulation were increased yields on the one hand, and decreased demand from importers, including some developing countries, on the other. Grain is not the only product in surplus. The Common Market alone, besides stocks of 7 million tons of wheat and 1 million of barley, has 350,000 tons too much butter and 400,000 tons of dried milk.

The F.A.O. report pointed out that the agricultural surpluses problem is not new. It said: "Aside from North America and Western Europe, significant surplus stocks appeared in 1967 and 1968 in other high-income countries, such as Australia (wheat), Japan, where larger rice stocks now constitute a major problem, and the U.S.S.R., where vast stocks of butter have accumulated for the first time." The estimate for the 1968–69 Australian wheat harvest was a record 530 million bushels—almost double the drought-affected crop of 1967–68, and 63 million bushels above the record set in 1966–67. Barley, too, at 75 million bushels, was at an all-time high, and meat production is put at 1,725,000 tons—more even than the record output of 1964–65. Total production of all commodities was expected to reach its highest ever level—21 per cent above 1968, and 7 per cent above the previous record year 1966–67. The picture in New Zealand was comparable, with new peaks being attained in

both dairy products and meat. All the pointers indicated a continued rise: her dairy herd started 1969 3·2 per cent bigger than the year before—2,304,000 cows in milk against 2,232,482. Beef cattle went up from 4,549,143 to 4,786,000.

With Great Britain her primary market, it is not surprising that New Zealand is taking a painfully close interest in developments in Europe and in the increased likelihood of Britain's joining the Common Market following the resignation of President de Gaulle. No sooner had the great man left the scene than the British reached for their E.E.C. files, dusted them, and re-read their contents. Much had happened in the Community since Britain was last turned down. Its farm policy, in particular, had borne some bitter fruit, proving itself to be impossibly expensive and in need of a complete revision. For this reason the top agriculturist on the E.E.C. Commission (the Community's civil service), Dr. Sicco Mansholt, had produced a plan for reducing the number of farmers, slashing the dairy herds, and putting producer prices at more realistic levels. This suggestion was not received eagerly by the Community, and most of 1969 was spent in discussing it, together with farm problems generally—without ever coming to firm conclusions.

But, as opinion polls held during 1969 showed, feelings in the U.K. had changed, and the Common Market no longer held the attractions that it once did. Ranks of the anti-Marketeers in all parties made themselves heard at the autumnal political conferences. Even Edward Heath, who had long urged the virtues of entry, said that it would be folly to rush in while affairs in the E.E.C. were in a state of flux. The National Farmers' Union of England and Wales, which had always been highly dubious about membership, at least had the satisfaction of feeling that its lack of enthusiasm had been justified.

This attitude was endorsed by comments from influential sources in Holland, France, and elsewhere that the U.K. system of farm support was much better than the European one, and that, far from Britain adapting her system, the E.E.C. should change to the British model. This view was further tacitly endorsed when France, on devaluing the franc, was promptly excommunicated from the common agricultural policy—thus breaking a rule which Britain had been told was immutable. It ceased to be immutable over-night.

Whatever the overall advantages of the British deficiency payment system, there are few occasions more likely to cause violent anti-government reaction among farmers than the

Agrotechnology 1969

Left: This hand-held high-pressure crop-sprayer, developed in 1969, uses "ultra-low" amounts of an oil-based pesticide. *Right:* Plastic "raincoats" for sheep: Australian graziers find these reduce losses after shearing.

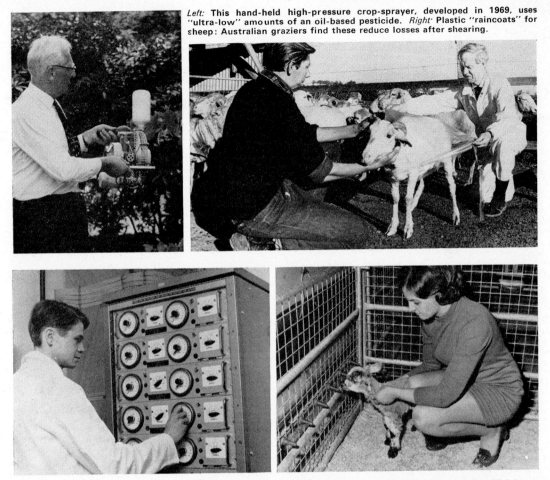

Left: the control panel of "Autoween" an electronic wet-nurse, which regulates milk substitutes to 400 artificial teats that collectively feed lambs or calves at pre-determined times. *Right:* lamb at the receiving end.

Above: A French farmer-inventor (*left*) demonstrating his fruit-picking aid— adaptable platforms mounted on a mobile base. *Right:* another anti-backache boon, the electric "Horticar," for such tasks as weeding or strawberry picking.

annual price review. These reviews have taken place every spring since the Second World War. Government and farming representatives get round a table and, over many weeks, attempt to thrash out commodity producer prices for the year ahead. Occasionally the N.F.U. men have endorsed the rates proposed, which are, of course, the basis of the country's cheap food policy—a policy which benefits the consumer. (The so-called "feather-bedding" subsidies are really consumer subsidies to keep down the price of food, rather than farm subsidies. Take them away and the poorer section of the community would soon appreciate that fact—as they will if Britain goes into Europe.)

In 1969 the government, having announced with great firmness that it endorsed an agricultural expansion programme, was expected to give effect to it at the review. The Treasury-bound Minister of Agriculture, however, was unable to get much of a deal for his industry. He got some joy in cereals and meat, but that did not satisfy his flock, who gave him a rough time at the meetings he addressed in the spring. If the Government had not spoken such encouraging words beforehand, the review would have been regarded as reasonable. But when you are invited to a banquet and then offered cold mutton and a stale crust you are not inclined to be enthusiastic, even if you are hungry! The outlook for expansion was not made any brighter later in the year by the continuous rise in prices of basic necessities and the restriction of credit. By the end of the year there was growing militancy among farmers.

The Government's land use policy is not regarded as adequate either. Unlike Australia's and New Zealand's, Britain's green acres are at a premium. The huge and growing population sees to that. Some 50,000 acres are taken annually for urban developments of all kinds. In 1969 the new city of Milton Keynes in North Bucks was designated; with its construction will go the destruction of some 23,000 acres of good farm land. Then there is the land swallowed up by reservoirs. The N.F.U. fights a perpetual rearguard action against water interests anxious to drown large areas of productive land. If it holds out long enough, a study of the practicability of putting a barrage across the Wash may be completed, and the Government of the day may decide that the plan to get fresh water by this means is a practical proposition. Use of underground waterbearing strata, already under test in the Thames basin and in Norfolk, is another promising prospect. Or desalination of sea water may become cheaper. The longer the N.F.U. can delay the approval of surface reservoirs the better the chance of finding other ways of supplying people's taps.

Factory Farmers' Code

In October the British animal welfare codes of practice, which were the sequel to the report on intensive husbandry practice made by a committee set up in 1964 under the chairmanship of Professor Rogers Brambell, received parliamentary approval. But it was a near thing. The codes gave rather more latitude to the farmer than Brambell envisaged. Another zoologist, Professor Hewer of Imperial College, had been charged with the task of drafting the codes for cattle, pigs, chickens, and turkeys. He and a nine-man committee were asked to build with the Brambell bricks and the results of the latest research and their own investigations. Their handiwork—which took them about two years—was approved by veterinary surgeons and welcomed by farmers, but accepted only in part by animal welfare bodies.

The code for tethered or penned calves said that they should have sufficient room and freedom of sideways movement to be able to groom themselves, lie down on their sides, and extend their legs. Brambell had stipulated, in addition, enough room for them to turn round—a much larger space. On calves' diet, the code required the inclusion of roughage *unless* the milk substitute is complete in all known essential nutrients. That "unless" allows the omission of roughage; this, said some objectors, could be cruel to calves which, in their craving for roughage, sometimes eat the wood of the partitions in their pens. Hewer replied that a calf that had never received roughage would not develop a rumen (first stomach) and therefore would not have the craving! The pig code allows the small space of 5 sq. ft. each for fatteners and maiden gilts of about 125 lb.; and the poultry codes allow birds to be compressed into 1 sq. ft. per 7 lb. live weight for broilers, and into spaces varying from 1 sq. ft. per 4 lb. to 1 sq. ft. per 8 lb. for caged birds and turkeys.

The Minister of Agriculture accepted the Hewer codes more or less *in toto*, and had his own experts graft on sections covering extensive, as well as intensive, practice. When the final drafts were placed before parliament they passed fairly swiftly through the Lords, but endured an intense chewing-over in the Commons. A division was only averted by an undertaking by the Minister that he would consider members' sources of worry (primarily battery hens and penned calves) and would have the state vets make a report on how things were going during 1970.

See also Antibiotics, Pesticides, in Fact Digest.

The Arts

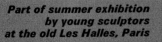

*Part of summer exhibition
by young sculptors
at the old Les Halles, Paris*

Fashion Followed the Natural Line

BETTY HALE Editor of *Fabulous*

Trousers were vital for feminine followers of fashion—especially with tunics, waistcoats, or long jackets.

THE FASHION STORY of 1969 was a gentle, rather romantic one. For both girls and men the emphasis was on the slimmer figure, with everything pared down. For girls there were mini busts, mini waists (usually belted), and mini hips. There was a big fabric saga with plenty of new man-made jerseys in glorious colours. There was also "unisex" (clothes for male and female alike), which was more important than ever in the fashion world.

For girls the most vital item was trousers. They had had long pants before, but 1969 saw the full blossoming of the fashion. Admittedly it was not universally accepted as office wear for secretaries or receptionists, or proper for school teachers, except in the most open-minded circles, and it still did not appear as an item in girls' school uniforms. But it did gain a far greater hold than in previous years. Previously the big problem with trousers was what to wear with them. In 1969 the answer was a mini dress, or a tunic, or a blouse and waistcoat, or a long jacket. This made a more

complete outfit than the shirt or sweater and trousers which had been the combination hitherto. Trouser suits early in the year, for indoor wear, consisted of a high-necked tunic, fingertip length, and matching wide trousers, often with turnups.

Sleeveless waistcoats, often with exaggeratedly large armholes and with varied fastening (four buttons in a line, or a single top button or hook, or just held together by a belt at the waist), were extremely popular. They came in various lengths, but commonly, like tunics, as far as the fingertips. They matched either trousers or a skirt in the same fabric, or they were in a contrasting colour or in a contrasting material like leather, suede, or hand-worked wide-mesh woollen crochet. As "trousers and sweater" were out, so were "skirt and blouse" and "skirt and sweater." Always there was the plus of either a waistcoat or a sleeved or sleeveless jerkin. Skirts, as short as possible, were A line, flared, or pleated.

When the weather became a little warmer and the sweater look did reappear it was markedly modified, being very brief. Many of the most advanced jumpers were sawn off before they reached the top of the skirt, leaving an inch or two of bare midriff. The waistcoat gradually developed into the sleeveless coat worn over a co-ordinating dress: for instance, plain over stripes, or a striped coat over a plain dress. Colours were gentle, like pink stripes with navy, grey with white, beige with white, or pale green with navy or white. White cropped up all the time for accessories, shoes, everything. In the winter the "in" colour was black, but as spring came white took over.

Pinafores and See-Throughs

As big a fashion feature as the waistcoat was the pinafore dress: in jersey, tweed, suede, or leather, with very narrow, even laced, shoulders, with round or V neck, and invariably flared in skirt or with an inverted pleat or two. Pinafores came in all colours and in horizontal multi-stripes such as white, black, brown, yellow, or yellow, white, blue, black.

Summer dresses had a see-through look, but did not, in fact, reveal anything. Especially popular were easy-care voile prints, paisley pattern being a favourite, made into lean, button-through shirt-style dresses, frequently with long sleeves and pointed white collars and cuffs. Mostly they were worn over mini slips or, by the more adventurous, a body stocking. Twiggy Dresses (sponsored by the well-known

model) produced a very popular white cotton lace see-through shirt-style dress. Also seen a great deal were lacy crochet dresses, hand-made with scalloped hem and sometimes with ribbon slotted at the waist or under the bust. Crochet trousers and tops were worn at the discotheque and parties. The tops were brief, like shortie sweaters, and the midriff bare.

For beach or after-six wear there was a range of bare-midriff pants-and-top suits, some with not much more than a bra top and others with long-sleeved tops which finished just below the bosom. Also for evenings were charming Victorian-type long dresses, with high granny necks, frills, long sleeves, and bows. They were very "girlie" in nylon organza, sprigged cotton lawn, and Tricelon crepe. For day time there were plenty of dress-and-trouser suits in one of the new man-made jerseys like Tricel Tricol (soft and shimmery), Dicel Satin, Celon Jersey, Lancola Jersey, or Tricelon Ninon (soft and romantic). These silky easy-falling fabrics were trouble-free and made in glorious plain colours: geranium, pewter, butterscotch, lolli-pop pink, mimosa, aubergine, tangerine, navy, and of course white. Some pants outfits were styled with slightly flared trousers and match-ing slim tunic with open neckline and collar. Others had white trousers teamed with a flowered tunic. More elaborate were very full, pleated trousers. There were also catsuits in lightweight jerseys, plain, patterned, or in "wet-look" ciré. Usually the trouser legs were fully flared, coming in to a slim hip. For the beach, catsuits were made in stretch towelling.

As well as man-made fibres, cotton was seen a good deal in summer, as were crepe and bonded crepe (which had a satinised finish inside, making it hang softly against the body). There was also a small boom in patchwork; it was revived by St. Laurent and Dior in Paris early in the year, and appeared in London as fabric by the yard and in skirts, dresses, and pants. Knitted dresses were popular, very simply styled with or without sleeves, round-necked, and with slightly flared skirts. Gold and silver lurex yarns were highly favoured.

Two small items made big fashion news during the year. One was chains. Metal chains of all kinds, sizes, and shapes were used both for necklaces (the more the better, up to about a dozen) and for belts. Many chains doubled as necklaces one day and belts the next. Early in the year golden chains were the things to wear; later on, silver became more fashionable. Chain belts with round, square, or triangular links were worn singly and in twos and threes on shirt dresses, tunics, pinafore dresses, with knitted dresses, even with swim-suits and on bare midriffs. The other notable small item was the scarf. An outfit was not complete without a contrasting, matching, blending, anything-you-like scarf. It could be tied kerchief style at the neck, used as a belt, tied like a man's tie, knotted to a chain belt, or tied round the head in bandeau, pirate, mill-girl, or turban style. It might even be tied round the thigh of a trousered leg.

Swimwear was brief. Bikinis were in, either in the genuine two-piece style or with a link between the two halves in the form of a small strap or a couple of brass rings. One-piece swimsuits had plunging necks, low backs, and cheeky chunks cut out of the sides.

Minimum Underwear

Tights were mostly classic in style, although some were tinted to team with the rest of the outfit. But colours were gentle see-through black, white, pink, green, yellow, or silver—not the hard strident shades of a year or two before. Underclothes were reduced to the minimum for the overall slim look; some girls wore only tights beneath their top clothes, some a brassiere and a pantie girdle, and a few the new throw-away paper knickers. Some micro-skirted summer dresses had matching knickers, often with decorative back pockets.

Shoes were still quite clumpy, but not as heavy in the summer months as in the winter. Almond or square toes were everywhere, and not a point to be seen. Heels were medium low and fairly thick. Nearly all shoes were styled

Fringes swished.

Long waistcoats and scarves draped.

Catsuits slunk.

Maxi coat trailed.

in a combination of two or three colours. Black gradually went out as beige/white, beige/scarlet, blue/white, all white, and other muted colour combinations came in. Vamps were mostly high, and buckles and tabs were the usual decoration. In the early part of the year boots were all the rage, the taller the better. They were forecast for summer, too, but in fact were rarely seen. Autumn boots were designed in "Mary Poppins style" to go beneath ankle-length skirts or trousers.

In the late autumn, as the weather began to get colder and girls went out to buy their new winter coats, there were more and more full-length ones to be seen. It was the one fashion that they all wanted to follow. Manufacturers could hardly keep pace with the demand. The drab colours (grey, R.A.F. blue, dull green, brown) were in, as well as clear scarlet, yellow, and black. After half-hearted efforts in the past to introduce longer coats, at last the full length had arrived. Styles were usually belted and cut on slim lines, buttoning to the waist or just below. It was the fashion innovation of the year, and it was not confined to London, as is sometimes the case with the more exaggerated styles. Heads were often made small in close-fitting rib-knit or crochet caps pulled on to hide every scrap of hair.

Unisex clothes, styled similarly for girls and men, invaded the fashion scene. With so many girls taking to trousers, it had to happen. In July, Mick Jagger of The Rolling Stones met the girls half-way by appearing before an audience of 250,000 at a free concert in London's Hyde Park wearing what looked exactly like a girl's dress in white voile with a gathered skirt and laced front, over flared-from-the-knee white trousers. It was quicky copied in white Tricel and sold—to girls. There were "his-and-hers" slacks, shirts, pyjamas, swimming trunks ("hers" had a bra top, of course), catsuits (not so popular with the men), and trouser suits. Both girls and men wore the same scarves, belts, and even boots and shoes. One boutique attached to a London store sold unisex under-pants of cotton voile in white spotted with red or navy.

The Male Silhouette

Generally men's fashion did not set the world on fire. The jackets that were flared from the waist in late 1968 became a little longer and leaner by early 1969. The whole male silhouette was narrowing down, and the waist was less accentuated. There was a sobering-up of style and colour. The flare in trousers was tailing off into the tubular pipeline look. Lapels continued to get wider all the year; shoulders were concave. In cloth there was a slight 1930s influence and a return to Harris and herringbone tweed. Coats and jackets were very much double-breasted, with the buttons in either straight lines or graduated (starting wide apart at the top and coming closer together at the waist). As in girls' fashion, men's jackets and coats became pro-

152

Jagger in unisex.

Cut-away swimwear.

The safari suit.

Shirts in floral prints
and broderie anglaise.

gressively longer, ending up in the autumn with a pipeline top-coat that ended at mid-calf or even went down to the ankle.

While formal suits remained fairly conservative, leisure suits were varied and exciting. The safari-style suit was well to the fore, with four flapped pockets on a full-belted jacket; it came in linen/Terylene mixtures, crushed velvet, and even suede and leather. There were co-ordinated shirts and trousers for informal wear: for instance, printed damask shirts with identically printed trousers. Ties were often made by the shirt makers to link up with or exactly match the shirts. Lace shirts in a variety of pale plain colours were popular from April onwards (there were also lace trousers). Satin and nylon ciré were other fabrics used for shirts. Also widely seen were (like the girls') semi-see-through voiles, broderie anglaise, and fine floral prints in pastel colours.

The Fitted Shirt

Apart from a few odd exceptions like the lace-up shirt (reflected in the Mick Jagger "dress" and also in laced-up trousers first seen at St. Laurent), the shirt story was mainly one of fabric, not of style. The style change was the new slim, body-hugging line and deeper collar. In very informal wear, fringing was a favourite addition, on sleeves and trouser legs and shirt yokes. It came into girls' wear too.

In an unexpected boom, what used to be Dad's three-buttoned round-necked short-sleeved undervest emerged as a fashion

garment in many different colours both plain and knot-and-dip dyed. These vests were worn by men and girls. The "skinheads"—teenage boys with close-cropped hair—wore them with their jeans, braces, and boots which were slightly reminiscent of the Nazi look. On the leisure scene the "wet look" in jerkins and shirts persisted, as did the waistcoat suit (suit with sleeveless jacket worn with fancy shirt or sweater). The wide-brimmed hat made an impact, probably because Mick Jagger was seen in one. It went with the safari suit.

There was no very positive change in footwear. Shoes still had buckles and straps, and were slightly square-toed. Prince Regent and page-boy styles were well to the fore, with big front flaps. Dark leathers and patent were popular, as well as uppers in corduroy velvet or canvas in casual summer shoes.

Men's underwear was brief with cut-away legs, and was usually very gay. There were pants in scarlet, sky-blue, and black paisley printed on gold, red, or blue. There were striped pants in boxer style, and even lacy mesh ones, too. The most popular men's version of the girls' shortie sweater was the 1930s-style multi-coloured, sleeveless, V-necked, skimpy, Fair Isle pullover worn by Paul McCartney; it looked the right size for a 13-year-old boy. All the men's trendy sweaters were brief and close-fitting—a far cry from the old "sloppy Joe," and in harmony with the natural slim silhouette that was the keynote of all 1969 fashions.

Angled balconies sprout like exotic nests from this 21-storey block of flats built in Hamburg, Germany, in only ten months.

New Building Private and Public

BARBARA AULD, B.A.(Arch.), A.R.I.B.A.

In THE LAST FEW YEARS a paradoxical situation has arisen in and around most big cities. As more people enjoy cheap car and air transport for travel and tourism, so more are being affected by congestion and aircraft noise. Many want to live somewhere beyond the suburbs in small village communities, or in entirely new cities such as those planned in England at Milton Keynes in Buckingham-shire and Telford in Shropshire. Some people are ready to face hours of travelling to their work each day so long as their families can grow up away from the noise and strain of big cities. Further, in giving evidence to the Roskill Commission on the siting of London's third airport, architects and town planners in the Royal Institute of British Architects' working group suggested that, unless the supporting city is built at a considerable distance from the airport, noise protection would raise building costs by 20–30 per cent.

These considerations emphasise the serious problem of siting new housing so that people can enjoy peaceful and even rural surround-ings. A 20th-century village in such sur-roundings is New Ash Green in Kent, planned to house eventually about 6,000 people, many of them "commuting" to London. The house groups of 100–150 are tightly packed and set in common land linked by "short cut" foot-paths to the village centre. In Eric Lyons's design for Span Developments costs are kept relatively low by using a standard house *width*, and varying the *depth* to give different amounts of accommodation.

Killingworth township in Northumberland is being developed round an old hamlet north of Newcastle as a place primarily to live and work in. Some industry is already established there, and a town centre is growing up dominated by a twin-towered office block. This was designed by Ryder and Yates and Partners, a young local firm of architects who were responsible for the Northern Gas Board's headquarters and for the Gas Research Station (winner of a Royal Institute of British Architects award in 1969). There will be a preponderance of family houses, but some ten-storey flats are being built, approached from street decks which link the blocks and the town centre. A competition for a large number of houses as well as flats and maisonettes was won by Ralph Erskine, a British architect who practises in Sweden.

The Greater London Council's Thamesmead housing development on flat land beside the Thames estuary at Woolwich–Erith won an international award for the best architecture and town planning project submitted to the *Union Internationale des Architectes*. Some of the housing already built runs in a nearly unbroken sweep for about half a mile. It follows an irregular line varying from two to five storeys, with flats and maisonettes facing in either direction from a zigzag central spine. Garages and stores are on the ground floor. Most of the thirteen-storey tower blocks of flats are being built in the Balency system of concrete construction.

Matching Houses to Sites

At La Luz, a few miles to the north-west of Albuquerque in New Mexico, about two dozen houses for a small new community have been built by three young men, two developers and their architect, Antoine Predock. They aim to improve the beautiful site overlooking the Rio Grande rather than destroy it, as happens so often when building takes place in open country. The houses, built of unburnt sundried bricks, are tightly packed, with curved garden walls. The whole development looks like a small Spanish fortress town.

Three houses for individual families which in imagination match the beauty of their site have been built recently, two in Britain and one in the U.S.A. At Feock in Cornwall, Richard Rogers, Norman Foster, and Wendy Foster have designed a house (called Creek

Work was in progress during the year on the G.L.C.'s Thamesmead housing development by the river at Woolwich. Here the first of the twelve 13-storey blocks that comprise Stage 1 stands completed in October. Each block will contain 48 apartments.

Vean) to take full advantage of lovely views over a small creek and the countryside beyond. The ground slopes steeply, and the upper level living room is approached from the car park by a bridge. The owner wanted wall space to hang his collection of modern

Linear housing on the Greater London Council's Thamesmead development. The project won an international award for the best architectural and town planning scheme submitted to the *Union Internationale des Architectes* during the year.
Photo, Greater London Council

"Creek Vean," a private house overlooking Pill Creek, near Feock, Cornwall. Designed by Richard Rogers, and Norman and Wendy Foster, it won the 1969 Royal Institute of British Architects award for the South-Western region. The interior walls (*right*)—like the exterior—are of honey-coloured concrete blocks. *Photo, Brecht-Einzig Ltd.*

paintings: so the corridor of the lower floor is planned as a gallery with one long blank wall. Doors on the other long side of the gallery, opening into a study, bedroom, and self-contained flatlet, slide into recesses in the walls so that the whole space can be opened up. The walls, inside and out, are of honey-coloured concrete

This sculptural home of an American architect tops an 8,000-ft. mountain near Denver, Colorado. The $100,000, three-bedroomed, three-level house has a lift instead of stairs and a view over 80 miles of mountain scenery.

blocks, and the floors of Cornish slate. The house won a 1969 Royal Institute of British Architects award. Richard and Su Rogers designed a highly insulated, zipped-together, component house on stilts, adjustable to fit any ground, that won second prize in Du Pont's competition for a house for today.

Elegant Dwellings

On the site of an old stable yard, a house for the first principal of the new University of Stirling overlooks a gently wooded hillside. Designed by Morris and Steedman, the house uses two of the stone walls of the original courtyard. It has a wide-angled L-shaped plan, with the main rooms for entertaining looking out over the valley. The family bedrooms and guest bedrooms are grouped on either side of the living area. At Manchester, Connecticut, the architects of Mr. and Mrs. Jack Goldberg's house have made use of a sloping, densely wooded site to design a house on split levels, with rooms for the children a half level below the living area. The main living and dining room opens on to a wide terrace which has a fine view of the city of Hartford nearby. The charm of the house lies in its combination of curved and rectangular shapes, and in the natural cedar boarding, finished with bleaching oil, with which all walls inside and out are lined. In contrast, a small Japanese-looking house for a bachelor was designed by Timothy Rendle in a pastoral setting near the Thames at Barnes, London. Here the natural colours of the roof timbers forming the ceiling (the main beams are stained black), brown quarry tile floors, and wooden venetian blinds create a gentle interior.

Brave New Buildings of 1969

Left: an arresting model of a 20-storey hotel being built by the East Germans during 1969 at the skiing resort of Oberwissenthal.

Below: this Catholic church in Bettlach, Switzerland, with its massive, carved appearance, testifies to the strengthening link between contemporary architecture and sculpture.

Above: each floor of this new office building at Stade, West Germany, is separately suspended from two reinforced concrete arches—a novel method of construction.

Below: the Sheikh of Bahrein's cool new British-designed administration block in scorching Manama. Triangular concrete screens flank the structure, shielding windows from the blinding sun, while, within, air-conditioning prevails.

Below: model of an elegant addition to the Chicago skyline, the First National Bank of Chicago. The sweeping lines of this new structure, completed in 1969, contain 60 storeys, and are faced with marble.

157

A ramp for passengers' cars rises to the first floor of London Airport's new £11 million Terminal One. The largest of the three airport terminal buildings, it was opened by the Queen on April 17, 1969.

As passenger traffic increases, at all large international airports additional buildings are constantly needed. At London Airport, Heathrow, the third and largest passenger terminal building, designed by Frederick Gibberd and Partners, was opened during 1969. The lower level of this long rectangular building deals with arriving passengers, and the upper level with departing passengers. The building is approached by an elevated ramped road. In Sydney, N.S.W., the second stage of the Kingsford Smith international airport was rapidly going ahead. The Y-shaped passenger concourse will project out from the terminal building on to the apron area, so that arriving and departing aircraft can taxi close up to one of twelve bays for unloading and loading. The scheme is due to be finished during 1970.

Model of the hall and common-room for St. Antony's College, Oxford, which was being built during 1969. *By courtesy of the architects, Howell, Killick, Partridge, and Amis.*

As cruising and holidays in the sun attract more and more people, new tourist hotels are in much demand. Some built recently on the island of Malta were designed by Richard England. Their boldly designed shapes fit in admirably with the vernacular architecture and dominate the rocky landscape like Crusader castles. A conference centre designed by Trevor Dannatt, now being built at Riyadh in Saudi Arabia to house 1,500 people, has its own hotel attached. Two open-sided triangular courts form a big W on plan, and the bedrooms, which are approached by balcony access, open into shaded patios.

New University Buildings

Massive university building programmes are steadily being realised. The Pathfoot building is the first completed phase of the new Stirling University, designed by Robert Matthew, Johnson-Marshall, and Partners. On one of the most beautiful university sites in Britain, it is planned in a series of long, low buildings along the hillside, and is easily adaptable to future needs. This building also won a Royal Institute of British Architects award for 1969. In Glasgow, William Whitfield's complex of towers form the first stage of a new university library. It is planned so that the whole floor area can be used as reading space, with open access bookstacks rather than the more usual arrangement of separate reading room and bookstacks.

A hall and common-room building is under construction for St. Antony's College, Oxford, designed by Howell, Killick, Partridge, and

Amis. It is the first of a group of communal residential and teaching buildings which will form an open-sided quadrangle with an existing convent building. Both the dining hall on the first floor and the common room on the second floor have protruding splayed concrete window surrounds. These rooms are top lit through openings in the web-like concrete roof. The Oxford Centre for Management Studies on the outskirts of the city has teaching, communal, and residential blocks all designed by the architects Ahrends, Burton, and Koralek so that they can be extended. The 24 study-bedrooms are split-level, part for study and part for sleeping. The whole of the south-west face, including the double-glazed studio-like windows, is sloped back, and much of the building is clad in zinc.

The new agronomy building by Ulrich Franzen on the campus at Cornell University, U.S.A., is a large fort-like structure, faced in rust-coloured brick. The laboratories in this thirteen-storey windowless tower run in two lines off a central corridor. The outside walls of the labs are blanked off by galleries for reaching the service ducts which run in the floors.

In the German medieval town of Neviges, North Rhine-Westphalia, a spectacular new pilgrimage church now replaces the old parish

The new pilgrimage church at Neviges, West Germany, was built to Gottfried Böhm's prize-winning design. *Above:* the vaulted and irregularly roofed interior, showing the pulpit and central altar. *Below:* the huge, polygonal, jagged, concrete exterior, in something approaching the style of a medieval fortress. *Photos, Werner Ellerbrock, Duisburg*

church, where the Virgin Mary was traditionally honoured. Professor Gottfried Böhm's design for a huge polygonal concrete structure was chosen after two architectural competitions. Irregularly shaped chapels and choir galleries on different levels cluster round the central floor space, and the jagged shapes of the concrete roof form the ceiling inside.

The office and research centre for the steel firm of Dorman Long at Middlesbrough promises to be another brilliant design in James Stirling's characteristic glass and metal style. This one, unlike his engineering building at Leicester University and history faculty library at Cambridge, will stand in a gaunt industrial landscape. In this long slab of building the lower floors, housing the larger offices, diminish in size as they go up, giving a sloped wall surface on one face. Above this the smaller offices rise vertically, and the whole structure is enclosed in glass inside the steel frame.

Qantas Airways have started to build a new headquarters in Sydney overlooking the southern approaches to the Harbour bridge. The site lies to the south of the downtown Rocks area of the city for which large-scale redevelopment has been planned. The 48-storey tower of offices designed by the Sydney firm of Joseland and Gilling will be surrounded by pedestrian spaces and a new public square. A second and sightly lower tower adjoining the first is envisaged for about 1983. A computer centre, sited below ground level for temperature control, will be in the base of the tower. Four huge concrete corner piers, 60 ft. wide and 5 ft. thick, have been designed to take the very heavy wind loading encountered in buildings of this height, and also to support the floors.

Ship's Architecture

It may seem strange to include a ship in a survey of architecture, but British architects played a large part in the design of the *Queen Elizabeth 2*. Her size and shape were determined not only by the depth of water in the harbours and canals to and through which she has to travel, but also by the vital ratio of size to power and speed. Stability and strength to meet the huge Atlantic rollers were also essential design factors. The *QE2* emerged as a rather narrow, high ship, the only open sides being on the top deck. The public rooms, two open-air swimming pools, and even the restaurants are on the top five decks, some stretching the full width of the ship. The five decks below are for passenger cabins and luxury suites, with as many as possible having portholes.

Visual design was shared between Cunard's naval architect Dan Wallace; the architect James Gardner, co-ordinator for the overall appearance and external details; and the architect Dennis Lennon, co-ordinator for the interior, all working in close collaboration with Upper Clyde Shipbuilders. Many other architects and interior decorators were employed in designing the public rooms and cabins, but Dennis Lennon and Partners managed to unify the whole ship by designing some of the sequences of rooms themselves, as well as the entrance lobbies and staircases, and by keeping some control over the other rooms.

The Queen's Room, a huge lounge running the full width of the ship, was subtly divided by its designer Michael Inchbald. He created two delightful promenades with chairs and green climbing plants running fore and aft, separated from the slightly lower central lounge and dance floor by rows of mushroom-shaped white fibreglass columns. The room is lit through glazed slots in the fibreglass ceiling, and mirrors behind perforated screens at the ends of the room give an illusion of greater space. Michael Inchbald also designed the white shell chairs on mushroom-shaped bases which echo the columns.

Beyond the Queen's Room the promenades converge and lead down a few steps into a series of restaurants and bars designed by Lennon. Colour plays an important part in setting the mood all over the ship: in the Columbia Restaurant tones of brown have been used for the carpet, leather chairs, and leather wall panels, and pale apricot for the curtains, with varying colours for the table linen according to the time of day. The exclusive Grill Room beyond has dark red velvet wall panels, built-in red seating, and ivory silk curtains; four charming figures made entirely of things from the sea, such as shells and coral, seem to have stepped from the ballet *Ondine*. Lennon also designed the cheerful Britannia Restaurant in red, white, and blue, the predominantly red Theatre Bar, and the green Midships Bar lit by brass lamps.

David Hicks, in association with Garnett, Cloughley, Blakemore Associates, designed the sophisticated Q4 room in black, white, grey, and red, to act as a bar for the first-class outdoor pool by day and as a night club. A double-height lounge on the upper and boat decks designed by Jon Bannenberg can be used for informal or formal occasions such as dances. The Coffee Shop in "pop art" style on the sports deck was designed by Elizabeth Beloe and Tony Heaton, who were then students at the Royal College of Art, London.

QE 2's Elegant Interior

Landlubbers played a part in the design of the new Cunarder, *Queen Elizabeth 2*, and especially left their mark on the liner's opulent cabins and assembly rooms. *Top left:* the Queen's Room, designed by Michael Inchbald, stretches along the aft end of the quarter deck, separated by sliding glass doors from the promenades to port and starboard. Inchbald has subtly given the illusion that the room is longer and wider than its 105 ft. by 100 ft., and also (by using an open perforated screen for a ceiling, lit from behind) higher than its scant 9 ft. *Top right:* Beige and blue predominate in Dennis Lennon's Upper Deck Library. *Above:* the Double Room, by Jan Bannenberg, is the largest public room in any passenger ship and occupies the aft end of the upper and boat decks. As its name implies, the Double Room is divided into two levels which are connected by a sweeping 24ft.-wide staircase. Opposite these stairs is the bandstand, behind which rears a curving wall of sepia-tinted glass. *Left:* the Britannia restaurant, another design by Dennis Lennon, seats 800 in an appropriate red, white, and blue setting. The imposing Britannia figure-head was a gift from Lloyd's of London.
Photos, Council of Industrial Design

This cool example of Minimal Art, by the American sculptor, Jules Olitski, testifies to the school's concern with pure form rather than matters human or metaphysical. *Whip Out*, with its rippling and sweeping sheets of lacquered aluminium, was in a show of Olitski's work held in New York during April.   *Metropolitan Museum of Art, New York*

Two Faces of Today's Art

KENNETH COUTTS-SMITH

Mᴏʀᴇ ᴛʜᴀɴ ᴀɴʏᴛʜɪɴɢ ᴇʟsᴇ the exhibitions during 1969 emphasised the division of the preoccupations of the contemporary artist into two distinct areas. These areas have been in existence for some time, and have been continually interacting; one can see, though, that they are the contemporary expression of defined and established traditions. The two traditions are, on the one hand, that of today's formal painting and sculpture, expressed largely in the area of Minimal Art (developed from Cubism, Constructivism, and the Bauhaus), and, on the other, one that is descended from Dadaism, through Surrealism to Pop. Two exhibitions mounted in London illustrated the division very clearly. The *Art of the Real* at the Tate Gallery presented and explored the whole area of Minimal and "reductionist" art, while an exhibition called

An essay in studied caprice by Graham Boyd, a subtle heir to the Conceptual tradition which extends beyond form to image—in this case an elaborate metaphor explained by the work's title, *Seed Box*. This oeuvre exploits a surrealist juxtaposition of organic subject and inanimate materials—perspex, nylon line, and lead shot.

When Attitudes Become Form at the Institute of Contemporary Art brought forward remarkable new developments in what has been called "the other tradition." The dichotomy between the post-Cubist concept of significant form, and the post-Dada emphasis on the *conceptual* in art was made extremely evident.

The catalogue of the Tate Gallery exhibition explicitly defined the position held by the exponents of reductionist form. "Today's 'art of the real'," it stated, "makes no direct appeal to the emotions, nor is it involved in uplift, but instead offers itself in the form of the simple irreducible, irrefutable object." The essential idea is that the art-object is presented as a self-contained entity, eschewing symbolism and referring to nothing outside itself. There is no "content" in the traditional sense of the term; the subject matter is rather the confrontation between the spectator and the work. The idea of "environment" in art is not new, but the Minimal artists have taken it to an extreme sophistication. Colour plays a new role; in the work of many artists it has achieved an extraordinary subtlety, and one sometimes has the feeling that the sculpture or painting is "about" colour. The retinal experiences of Op and Kinetic art have been incorporated into "significant form."

Work of individual artists in this school includes the contemplative mandalas of Ad Reinhardt and Barnett Newman, the diffused space of Mark Rothko, the austere boxes of Donald Judd and Robert Morris, the environmental structures of Tony Smith, the delicate colour vibrations of Kenneth Noland and Morris Louis. But at the Tate exhibition it was possible to realise how far back in time this movement stretches. A "typical" Barnett Newman austere vertical stripe picture was painted in 1949, and the almost abstract Ellsworth Kelly *Window* in the same year, and the Alexander Liberman purist statement *Minimum*, a single white circle on a dark background, dates from 1950. But the early reductionist work of Georgia O'Keefe goes back to 1929, and this astonishing artist, little known in Europe, in *Blue Lines* of 1916, achieved proximity to the minimal two years before the Russian constructivist Malevitch's famous canvas *White on White*.

The Art of Ideas

The *Art of the Real* was a completely American exhibition, organised by the Museum of Modern Art, New York; but *When Attitudes Become Form*, although the majority of exhibitors were American, was sponsored by Phillip Morris, Europe (a fine example of industrial patronage), and was first mounted at the Kunsthalle, Berne. After being seen in London, it travelled to the Avignon Festival, the National Gallery of Modern Art, Rome, the Louisiana Museum, Copenhagen, and the Modern Museum, Stockholm. The contributors to this exhibition were concerned with "conceptual," not "perceptual" art. So far no one has managed to give this form a satisfactory name or category; various labels, such as *Anti-form, Micro-Emotive Art, Possible Art, Concept Art, Arte Povera, Earth Art,* each describe only one aspect of the style. There is an obvious opposition to form—an emotional involvement that accepts the accidental configuration of the *objet trouvé*, the use of mundane materials even more unstable and unaesthetic than those used by the "junk" sculptors of some years ago, Earth itself, the place where we live, as both a medium and a work-place.

Some of the works concerned with the so-called Earth Art are projects executed in isolated places, such as mile-long trenches dug in the desert. This art work is, of course, not exhibited, indeed is hardly ever seen; the object presented is a dossier of plans and blueprints, photographs and geological samples. Frequently the "project" is never executed. The blueprint is enough. The essence of the aesthetic experience lies in the concept.

Felt Pieces, by Robert Morris, was part of the first major exhibition of recent, post-Dada conceptual forms, *When Attitudes Become Form,* which arrived in London during August.

Emanating the primitive malevolence of a voodoo fetish, *Little Magician*, by Wim de Haan, is an example of "junk art," constructed from scraps.
Louise Van Der Veen

Where the Minimal is stripped of ideas, *Concept Art* is almost nothing *but* ideas. For instance, space has been one of the major preoccupations of the artist since the Renaissance. The Conceptual artist takes a new look at space; for him it is not only that volume bounded by the dimensions of the art-object, it can also be the space it inhabits or traverses. Douglas Huebler, with his *Duration Piece No. 9*, in his own words ". . . used an aspect of the United States Postal Service for six weeks to describe over 10,000 miles of space." He posted a clear plastic box measuring 1 in. by 1 in. by $\frac{3}{4}$ in. by registered mail to an address in Berkeley, California; on being returned "undeliverable," it was left intact and enclosed in a larger container and posted to Riverton, Utah, and once more returned to the sender as undeliverable. The process was repeated to four further addresses which accomplished the marking of a line joining the two coasts of the U.S.A. during a period of six weeks. The final container, all the registered mail receipts, a map, and a statement of the work process, completes the work, and constitutes the object to be exhibited.

The I.C.A. exhibition was full of constructions made from all sorts of mundane materials—earth, cloth, plaster, rope. The young English artist Victor Burgin presented a disturbing image by laying a series of full-sized photographs across some 12 ft. of the floor. The photographs were of the floor itself, revealing all the graining, marks, and scratches of the planking, and, accurately overlaying the depicted object itself, they raised disturbing questions about the nature of reality, posing the question which was object and which was image.

Sculpture in Steel

In the Minimal mainstream, Anthony Caro's large exhibition at the Hayward Gallery, London, was an important occasion. Without doubt the leading British exponent of this idiom, Caro, who received in 1968 a major presentation at Venice Biennale, was able to present for the first time his whole development in a large retrospective exhibition. The purity, elegance, and refinement of his vision, achieved with materials deliberately chosen for their non-aesthetic associations—such as girders and industrial sheet steel—were subtly demonstrated, and brought out Caro's peculiar ability for "drawing in space." Caro was much influenced by the pioneer American Minimalist, David Smith. Another American artist of that pioneer generation is Barnett Newman, who mounted his first show for ten years at the Knoedler Gallery, New York. The breaking of a decade's silence showed that the old master had lost nothing of his touch. Pure fields of colour bisected by scrupulously and exactly placed vertical bands are the idiom that has obsessed this artist from the beginning.

Of the younger English reductionists, Mark Lancaster in his exhibition at the Rowan Gallery demonstrated a greater concern with colour; his new canvases seem to have loosened up a little, with floating fields of bright modulated colour laid upon a grid reminiscent of graph paper. Michael Michaeledes consolidated his growing reputation with an impressive exhibition at the Il Giorno Gallery, Milan. This Greek-born but London-resident artist stretches plain untreated canvas across shaped formers, relying on a delicate play of light and shadow to carry the image. William Pye in his second exhibition at the Redfern Gallery mounted an impressive sculptural statement using highly polished tubular chrome steel. Pye's sculptures, which seem to make a point of confrontation between the technological world and the archetypal world of archaic symbols, reminiscent as they were of temples and shrines, marked one of the most stimulating exhibitions by a young artist in 1969.

Magritte and Apollinaire

The "other tradition" is nowhere more obvious than in certain Surrealists, most notably Magritte. A major exhibition mounted by the Arts Council at the Tate

After Summer 1968, in sheet steel, by the leading British Minimal sculptor Anthony Caro, was displayed at his January exhibition at the Hayward Gallery, London.

Gallery provided an opportunity to see and reassess many previously unfamiliar paintings by this Belgian artist, who died in 1967. The paradoxes that René Magritte raised, his technique of presenting enigmatic images in a manner that raises a sort of mental flicker analogous to the retinal and optical flicker of Op art, seem to remain entirely fresh and pertinent, while the work of most Surrealist painters seems to have dated.

A fresh look at Magritte could not have been better timed, for 1969 saw a profound reassessment of the "irrational" in art—that is to say, the whole Dada–Surrealist line. The Institute of Contemporary Art mounted for their major winter show an exhibition dedi-cated to Apollinaire, the great French poet, friend and champion of the Cubists, precursor of the Dada movement and inventor of the abstract poetry-cum-painting which he called *calligrammes.* Marking the 50th anniversary of his death, the exhibition showed first many paintings and documents of the period, and secondly invited works by 35 British and foreign artists done in the spirit of and in homage to this important figure, who stood at the fountain head of the modern movement. Artists from abroad who participated included Jim Dine, Pol Bury, Liliane Lijn, Enrico Baj, and François Dufrêne. Among the English participants were Richard Hamilton, Joe Tilson, Derek Boshier, Richard Smith, Clive

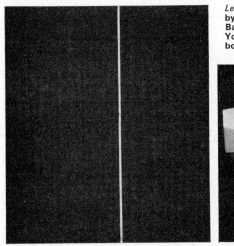

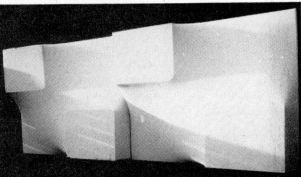

Left: *The Three,* a pure field of black cut by a vertical band of raw canvas, by the pioneer American Minimalist, and mentor of the school, Barnett Newman—who mounted his first show for ten years in New York during 1969. Below: *White Relief* by Michael Michaeledes, a Greek-born London-based exponent of reductionism.
Left, M. Knoedler & Co. Inc. New York

Les Promenades d'Euclide, a typical paradox from the enigmatic brush of the great Belgian surrealist, the late René Magritte. An important Magritte exhibition graced the Tate in 1969.   *Alexander Iolas Gallery. New York*

Barker, Gerald Scarfe, John Latham, Laurence Burt, John Furnival, Christopher Logue, and Edward Lucie Smith. Running concurrently was a one-man exhibition of paintings by the Liverpool painter-poet Adrian Henri, for whom Apollinaire is a major inspiration.

Pop art seems now to be a spent force. Nevertheless, the Hayward Gallery put on a large exhibition called *Pop Art Redefined,* organised by John Russell and Suzi Gablik. This was a major art-historical event since the

show, and an accompanying book, "defined" the idiom properly for the first time. With the benefit of some nine years' hindsight it was made clear that Pop proper is concerned purely with images from the various "admass" media, and that it is, if not a specifically American movement, at least one whose basic imagery is American pop-vulgarism as evident in images culled from the cinema, pulp fiction, and advertising. It appears now to have quite run its course, and to have given way to Neo-Dada preoccupations of the as yet unnamed idiom represented in the *When Attitudes Become Form* exhibition.

"Earth Art" on Site

A distinct category already noticed in the *When Attitudes Become Form* show is the so-called Earth Art or "site art." Here certain artists, mostly Americans, have executed enormous "structures" in isolated places like the Mojave Desert. Walter de Maria, for instance, had the poetic concept of *Mile Long Drawing,* two parallel chalk lines twelve inches apart running along the floor of the desert for exactly one mile. Dennis Oppenheimer has made large works covering an enormous acreage of ground by delineating patterns in grass with a motor mower and filling the swathes with a sprinkling of iron filings. Another artist, Michael Heitzer, has executed the enormous number of 22 separate "works" in dry lake areas of depressions cut into the earth and lined—with all evidence of the process such as footprints, tyre-marks, etc., carefully erased from the surroundings.

In England, Mark Boyle chooses points at random in a city, usually by throwing a dart at a map, and subsequently takes a large mould from an area of street or pavement and

The "secret" Tantric art of India—the visual equivalent of Yoga, through which initiates "penetrate. . . the mystery of the universe"—caused a stir in the Western world during 1969. *Below:* a 17th-century painting of this mystical school, showing Hindu symbolism and the wheel of life. *Right:* A typical Tantra sculpture—a meteorite rounded and honed.

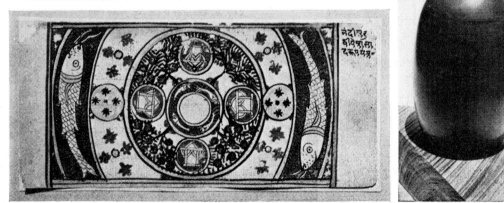

Mark Boyle (*right*), the English master of "Earth Art," with one of his works—an exact reconstruction of a cobbled street selected at random by hurling a dart at a map.

from India, exhibitions of which were mounted by Cianciamino and Axiom Gallery. Tantra can be regarded as the visual branch, as it were, of the philosophy of Yoga, and its purpose has been described as "to penetrate the enigmatic silence, the mystery of the universe." In painting, the typical image is a mandala-like circular form, the wheel of life, or a curious image of the ups and downs of spiritual progress involving snakes and ladders. (Indeed, it was from this image that the idea for the well-known board game was taken.) In sculpture the forms are simple—the stones of meteorites rounded and highly polished into mystical egg-like shapes. The sudden rediscovery of Tantra is part of the wide interest in Oriental mysticism evident in the "hippy" world, and is related to the recently emerged school of "psychedelic" painting. It is not surprising that Tantric painting has long remained hidden, for it was intended only for the initiated and has been a "secret" art form for many centuries.

Mass-Produced Art

The opposite of "secret" art is the concept of mass-production and the use of industrial methods in art. For example, the market for prints has enjoyed a boom—possibly due to the sharp rise in price of original works which has taken them out of the reach of the majority of would-be collectors. 1969 saw the inauguration of the first International Print

reproduces it exactly in resins or other plastics. The technique reproduces exactly not only the form of the ground, but also all the random elements of earth, litter, organic matter, and so on. Several are of beach sites; one final panel shows the markings and form of the sand dictated by the movement of the sea and tide.

Back to the Masters

Preoccupation with the latest thing in art did not prevent the mounting of several major historical exhibitions during the year. Some of Leonardo da Vinci's drawings were seen by the public for the first time in a big show of his work from the royal collection at the Queen's Gallery, Buckingham Palace; the British Museum put on a didactic show of "Picaresi, his predecessors, and his heritage," which demonstrated the great influence of this 18th-century artist on stage design and on the generation that immediately followed him; Amsterdam honoured the tercentenary of the death of Rembrandt with a careful selection of his very best; London showed 100 paintings and 100 drawings by Van Gogh, destined for a new museum in Amsterdam; and even the pre-Raphaelite William Holman Hunt was dusted off for a large exhibition.

Even more historical but much more "new" is the art world of Tantric painting, a school of religious and meditative painting

David Hockney's poster for the first International Print Biennale was called *Trees and Grass.*

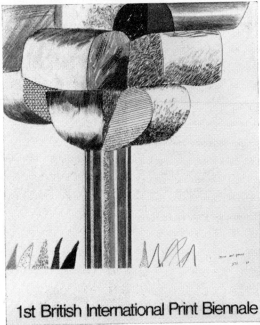

1st British International Print Biennale

Environmental art by Timothy Drever was part of the 1969 Camden Festival at Kenwood, Hampstead. Spectators were encouraged to rearrange the shapes, thus becoming part of a continuous creative process.

Biennale at Bradford city art gallery. Over 2,000 entries were submitted, from which the jury selected 300 prints in the open section. Perhaps more than anything else, this exhibition marked the final acceptance of silk-screen and photo-litho printing as valid forms for contemporary fine art.

Multiples, another form of mass-produced art, as a form of luxury toy have spread, and many more galleries have given over space and investment to them. But in general the original idea of cheap mass-produced art within the pocket of anyone interested has not been allowed to develop, for most galleries have restricted reproductions to very small editions, highly priced for an élitist minority. Consequently many artists have begun to feel an antipathy for the commercial gallery system, and they are beginning to try to find direct co-operative ways of by-passing the middle-man.

S.P.A.C.E. (Space Provision: Artistic, Cultural, Educational), largely the inspiration of the painter Peter Sedgley, has set up a community studio and workshop in an old warehouse in St. Katharine's Dock, East London, and others are by-passing the commercial galleries by mounting private and studio exhibitions. The most enterprising are eight young sculptors, mostly from the St. Martin's School of Art, who have taken over as studio and exhibition space a disused brewery in South London, the Stockwell Depot. On a different level, F.A.C.O.P. (Friends of the Arts Council Operative) have been pointing out the need for an *Artists'* Council and for direct participation in organisations run by art "bureaucrats." This sort of direct participation and direct action may be a pointer towards important future developments in the arts.

An engaging "primitive" oil painting by Margaret Baird, which was included in an exhibition of sporting pictures staged during the year by the Grosvenor Gallery, London.

New Books of 1969

HUMPHREY BROCKHOLST

FOLLOWING THE "year of student revolt," 1969 was a year of slim revolutionary volumes and thick revolutionary bank-balances. Among well-known exponents of this suddenly fashionable genre were the veteran poet and polemicist Stephen Spender, with *The Year of the Young Rebels*; the dreaded "Danny the Red," Daniel Cohn-Bendit, (and brother Gabriel) with *Obsolete Communism: the Left-Wing Alternative*; and the notorious Tariq Ali, who stole the thunder from his rival comrades by launching his oeuvre *New Revolutionaries* with a minor public outcry accounted for by the appearance on the book's fly-leaf of a diagram demonstrating how to construct a Molotov cocktail. His book was an uneven yet interesting anthology containing essays by some 18 "new revolutionaries" and bearing the imprint of their diverse ideologies, while, in his summing up, the editor performed syntactical acrobatics, slipping in the odd qualifying dependent clause, no doubt hoping thereby to satisfy both the rabid fanatic and the hesitant fellow-traveller.

If none of these little red books set the Thames on fire, one tome published in England during 1969 did win the curious distinction of causing its author to be burnt in effigy. This latter-day Guy Fawkes was the axed press tycoon, Cecil Harmsworth King, whose vitriolic autobiography, *Strictly Personal*, not only lacerated his own family but turned sourly upon some famous names, including that of

Mohammed Ali Jinnah, founder of the state of Pakistan. King's casual assumption that the Father of the Nation was a homosexual was not well received in Rawalpindi, or indeed by Pakistanis in London, some of whom occupied the offices of the *Sunday Times*, which had serialised the book.

Other autobiographies of 1969 included offerings by Sir Gerald Nabarro, *NAB 1: Portrait of a Politician*; Bernadette Devlin, *The Price of My Soul*; Jack Dash, *Good Morning, Brothers!*; Christopher Mayhew, *Party Games*; and Mary Rand, the "golden girl" of British athletics, *Mary*. Prominent among those works that radiated class enough to slip into the year's autobiographical élite was the eighth octave of *My Life and Times*, Sir Compton Mackenzie's mammoth retrospective opus, which appeared promptly in January to receive its annual critical garlands. The third volume of Harold Macmillan's memoirs, *Tides of Fortune*, took the reader, with characteristic aplomb, through the decade 1945-55, during which the unflappable author climbed deftly up the rungs of power as far as the Exchequer. Bertrand Russell celebrated his 97th birthday by presenting the third and final volume of his life, logically nomenclatured *The Autobiography of Bertrand Russell, 1944-1967*, which proved compulsively readable—in parts. From its cover the noble author glared imperiously out at the bewildering folly of humanity while within he steered a dry, self-righteous, homiletic,

The prolific Pakenham family, six of whom published books in 1969, at a literary luncheon in their honour in June. *Left to right:* **Lady Catherine Pakenham** (killed in a car crash in August), **Rachel Billington** (*All Things Nice*), **Antonia Fraser** (*Mary Queen of Scots*), **father Lord Longford** (*Humility*), **mother Lady Longford** (*Wellington—The Years of the Sword*), **Thomas Pakenham** (*The Year of Liberty*), **Judith Kazantsis** (*Women in Revolt*), and **Kevin Pakenham.**

Seven of the world's poets who congregated in London in July for the four-day Poetry International '69, at which they read from their own works. *Left to right:* Anthony Hecht (U.S.A.), Edward Brathwaite (West Indies), Ogden Nash (U.S.A.), W. H. Auden (Great Britain), Robert Bly (U.S.A.), Vasko Popa (Yugoslavia), and Janos Pilinsky (Hungary). The photograph was taken on the roof of the Arts Council's Piccadilly offices.

and somewhat bizarre course, charting the lethal absurdities of the Cold War with the inadequate instruments of reason; dismissing the failure of a marriage in a line; surviving an air-crash off the Norwegian coast by swimming calmly shorewards; walking into a conference here, a rose garden there—in short, sorting through the accumulated jumble of a rich retrospective attic.

The most anticipated autobiographical work of the year was Laurie Lee's sequel to *Cider with Rosie* entitled *As I Walked Out One Summer Morning*, which proved to be an account of a youthful trek through Spain in which the author's potent powers of evocation haunted and hovered about an alien landscape. Something of the nostalgia of *Cider with Rosie* was discernable in *The Vanished World*, a lyrical account of his childhood by H. E. Bates, while another sequel, Gerald Durrell's *Birds, Beasts, and Relatives*, was reminiscent of Laurie Lee's second book in that it, too, records an English response to an exotic environment—in this case, of course, Corfu.

Lives of the Great

The biography of the year was without question Antonia Fraser's *Mary Queen of Scots*, which rode high among the best-sellers throughout 1969. The subject was well suited to popular appeal, and the dramatic themes of love, murder, intrigue, rape, incarceration, and decapitation were the weft to a woof of detailed minutiae that revealed, for example, that when the executioner raised Mary's severed

head on high, her auburn wig fell from it to unveil a grizzled pate! Antonia Fraser is the daughter of the erstwhile Lord Privy Seal, Lord Longford, whose highly literate family was well represented on the bookstalls during the year. Not only did the paternal earl himself release an edifying treatise, modestly titled *Humility*, but his wife, Lady Longford, the distinguished biographer, published an excellent life of Wellington. Two other daughters, besides Antonia, also burst into print: Rachel Billington with a novel based on her experiences as an innocent in America, *All Things Nice*; and Judith Kazantzis with *Women in Revolt*. Their brother, Thomas Pakenham, brought out a major historical work concerning the Irish rebellion of 1798, *The Year of Liberty*.

J. B. Priestley, the unflagging Grand Old Man of English letters, who celebrated his 75th birthday during 1969, produced an opulent biography, *The Prince of Pleasure*, a life of the Prince Regent, published in good time to catch the Christmas market. A storm of controversy heralded the publication of another biography, *The Secret Lives of Lawrence of Arabia* by Phillip Knightley and Colin Simpson, which demolished the fashionable view of T. E. Lawrence as a mystical and gullible idealist who conquered large stretches of desert for the Arabs and was duped by the crafty Foreign Office. Lawrence emerged from the new investigation as an active agent of imperial policy, fully aware of British ambitions in the Middle East. This interpretation raised a furore—indeed it was even alleged that a distinguished and powerful cabal had waged a protracted campaign to prevent the book's publication. Other distinctive books on famous lives included *A Talent to Amuse*, Sheridan Morley's story of Noël Coward; *Visionary and Dreamer* by Lord David Cecil, an evocative account of Samuel Palmer and Edward Burne-Jones; *Churchill: Four Faces of the Man* by A. J. P. Taylor (and others); *Disraeli* by Robert Blake; *The Empress Brown* (Queen Victoria) by Tom Cullen; and, in Gandhi's centenary year, *Gandhi's Truth: On the Origins of Militant Non-violence* by Erik H. Erikson, a Freudian scrutiny of the Mahatma's youth, and *The Life and Death of Mahatma Gandhi* by Robert Payne.

Tracts for the Times

In that field of literary endeavour conveniently described by librarians as "non-fiction," 1969 saw the publication of an originally presented opuscule that should find a place on many a shelf. This was *Akenfield: Portrait of an English Village* by Ronald Blythe, a sound yet far from definitive analysis of the shifting fabric of village life in the 1960s. Shifting fabric was the theme of the most curious work of the year to excite massive interest, Christopher Booker's *The Neophiliacs*, a "study of the revolution in English life in the Fifties and Sixties." What Western Civilisation was to Spengler, so stands the King's Road to the brooding Booker. As an angry analysis of trend-hysteria the book excelled, yet its mystical mini-historicism proved too idiosyncratic to be convincing. A more ephemeral note still was struck in *Scratch an Actor* by Scott Fitzgerald's protégé of many summers since, the famed and feared Hollywood gossip columnist, Sheilah Graham. There were four notable additions to the *Bluffer's Guide* series during the year, with treatises on the art of bluffing on Cinema, Folk and Jazz, Antiques, and Management, from the same house that had the incalculable nerve to unleash the *International Joke Dictionary*—a multilingual anthology of hoary chestnuts. There also appeared a fascinating compendium of facts pertaining to that agile irritant *The Complete Flea*, based on the personal investigations and tribulations of a Mr. Lehane, who became unwittingly infested while inhabiting inexpensive rented accommodation in Dublin.

Another expert on the animal kingdom (long a stranger to inexpensive accommodation) is Dr. Desmond Morris, who in 1969 capped his run-away success *The Naked Ape* with *The Human Zoo*, which received open-eyed attention and some sharp critical thrusts accusing the author of peddling erotica in the

The Case of Kuznetsov

On the afternoon of Tuesday, July 29, 1969, two incongruous figures sat peering through the smoke-hazed gloom of a Soho striptease club. The earnest individual gazing abstractedly through thick glasses was Anatoli Kuznetsov—at 40 one of the leading members of the younger generation of Russian writers, and author of *Babyi Yar*. By his side sat his "interpreter"—watchdog of the Soviet secret police—whom the writer had to elude if his well-laid plans to "choose freedom" were to succeed. As the show crescendoed to a stop the pair filed out, blinking into the afternoon sunshine, and Kuznetsov announced his intention of seeking a girl. The watchdog—convinced of his charge's devotion to Soviet Communism (was he not in London to research a book on Lenin?)—agreed to meet him later at their Kensington hotel and left the writer to his own devices.

Immediately Kuznetsov made his way to Fleet Street and walked into the offices of *The Daily Telegraph*, clutching a scrap of paper bearing the name of a Russian-speaking journalist employed by that newspaper. After some time he reached, by telephone, the ear of David Floyd—the *Telegraph's* expert on communist affairs—who gave the novelist his address, to which he sped by taxi. Thus began the great literary "happening" of 1969—an affair which involved Soviet agents and Whitehall diplomats; the well-trimmed lawns of English country houses; the well-worn face of Mr. Malcolm Muggeridge; and the activities of a London publishing house.

On the evening of July 30, Anatoli Kuznetsov was granted asylum in Britain, a decision that infuriated Russian embassy officials. They demanded an interview with the author, but he refused to meet any of them. While Soviet agents allegedly scoured the metropolis for him, Kuznetsov was spirited down to the West Country where, as the guest of old world gentry, he composed an account of his reasons for defecting. Interviewed for B.B.C. television by the ubiquitous Muggeridge, he declared that he had been impelled to escape from Russia because his novels were consistently mutilated by censors acting as agents of "Socialist realism" and his footsteps were dogged by informers. He had made his dangerous flight to freedom, abandoning country, friends, and family, in order that his works should appear *as he wrote them*, unscathed by officious censorship. Ironically, in October the harassed émigré was driven to complain, in a letter to *The Daily Telegraph*, that a London publishing house was, "despite my emphatic prohibition," planning to reprint one of his "emasculated" novels (*Babyi Yar*) and to issue another one (*Fire*) in its Soviet-censored form.

Two of the British women novelists of distinction who brought out new books during 1969: Margaret Drabble (*left*), who published *The Waterfall*, and Brigid Brophy, who wrote *In Transit*.

name of science. The eminent zoologist, however, brushed such crude assaults aside. Mrs. Joy Adamson emerged from the African bush to publish *The Spotted Sphinx* (a leopardian equivalent of her best-selling account of Elsa the lioness), and, having done so, returned whence she came.

V. S. Naipaul, a novelist of such rare distinction that he can hardly poke his nose out of doors without having a prize hung on it, abandoned fiction during the year and turned to history. His book, *The Loss of Eldorado*, concerned the early colonial days of polyglot Trinidad; the conquistador Antonio de Berrio; and Sir Walter Raleigh. Hammond Innes turned to the same basic theme with his sterling work, *The Conquistadors*. Russell Braddon's *The Siege* was an outstanding account of the siege of Kut—a primitive settlement on the Tigris where, after Gallipoli, 13,000 British and Indian troops held out against the Turks for 147 days. An original

Graham Greene (*left*) produced another of his "entertainments," *Travels with my Aunt*, in 1969. Henry Miller (*right*), 78-year-old "father of the four-letter word," belied his respectable appearance with a new book *Sexus*

slant on the history of the Second World War was given by *The People's War*, a tribute to British civilians on the home front by Angus Calder. Another was provided by *Dowding and the Battle of Britain* by Robert Wright, opportunely released to coincide with the fuss engendered by the *Battle of Britain* film.

Women at Work

There can be no street of reasonable social standing and average length in the western world in which there is not at least one housewife crouching behind her typewriter, surrounded by screaming infants, distracted husband, broken crockery, shopping lists and rejection slips, with blue stockings kicking on the washing-line. Two international stars of the "woman's lot" school of novelists, Edna O'Brien of Ireland, and Mary McCarthy of the U.S.A., remained mute during 1969, but Brigid Brophy—who had subsisted for five years without publishing—brought forth *In Transit*. This cannot be recommended as a model for the sisterhood, as Miss Brophy appears to have had an aberrant stab in the general direction of James Joyce. A translation of Simone de Beauvoir's *La Femme Rompue* (The Woman Destroyed) that appeared during the year was more typical: delicate and penetrating, or friable and boring, according to the reader's taste. Margaret Drabble, an engaging dominie of the school, published another testament to female misery, *The Waterfall*, a tiresome tale told by a neurotic wife relentlessly pursuing the reader with incredibly long sentences.

Among established female novelists concerned with more universal thematic content were Iris Murdoch with *Bruno's Dream*; Doris Lessing with *The Four Gated City*, the fifth portentous volume of her interminable undertaking, *Children of Violence*; and Muriel Spark with "a tale for all ages," *A Very Fine Clock*.

A Few Notable Novels

Tip to the spear side of the year's quality book list was the English publication of Kasunari Kawabata's Nobel-prize-winning *House of the Sleeping Beauties*—a dream evocation featuring an eccentric in a brothel—which earned its oriental author flattering attention as the "Japanese Proust." Other notable fiction included Graham Greene's *Travels with My Aunt*; Henry Miller's aptly titled *Sexus*; Norman Mailer's *Why Are We in Vietnam?*; and John O'Hara's anthology *And Other Stories*. Kingsley Amis turned to the occult for *The Green Man*, and Henry Williamson turned the last leaf of his 15-volume chronicle of English life over two generations in *The Gale of the World*. John Fowles assumed the quill of a 19th-century novelist to write *The French Lieutenant's Woman*, a superb re-creation of Victorian England that earned him comparison with Hardy.

The humorous novels of 1969 included, as ever, in their midst an offering dashed from the indefatigable pen of the 88-year-old P. G. Wodehouse. This one was *A Pelican at Blandings*, in which Emsworth plays reluctant host to Alaric, Duke of Dunstable—of whom it is said that "if an opportunity presents itself of running a mile in tight shoes to chisel someone out of twopence, he springs to the task." That fastidious recluse, J. P. Donleavy, resumed his haunted quest for personal dignity amidst a world of sharks and picaresque buffoons, under the fictive cloak of one Balthazar B, whose *Beastly Beatitudes of Balthazar B* echo the lamentations of *The Ginger Man* from the tenements of Dublin to those of Maida Vale. *Portnoy's Complaint* by Philip Roth contained a patient's comically obscene confession to his psychiatrist, while *And To My Nephew Albert I Leave The Island What I Won Off Fatty Hagan in a Poker Game*, by David Forrest, proudly boasted the longest title of the year.

Helen MacInnes presented the thriller of 1969, *The Salzburg Connection*, in which a British agent dredges up a chest full of Nazi documents—and thus shakes the various governments of Europe. Another riveting political thriller was *The Smile on the Face of the Tiger*, by Messrs. Osmund and Hurd, which chillingly charts the crisis that erupts when a future British Government is faced with a Chinese ultimatum to withdraw from Hong Kong. *The English Agent* by the late F. L. Lucas is involved in derring-do during the Peninsular War, while another 19th-century gentleman abroad in 1969 was *Flashman*. This book, professing to represent the edited memoirs of the famous bully licked by Tom Brown during the latter's well-documented schooldays, was presented to the world by G. M. Fraser. It traced the bounder's caddish progress as an officer in the Indian Army and, unbelievably, was received by a brace of American professors of literature as a genuine autobiographical discovery.

The best genuine literary fraud of 1969, however, was perpetuated by 25 American journalists masquerading under the name Penelope Ash, whose book, *Naked Came the Stranger*—a torrid tale of sex in the suburbs—was written, tongues firmly in cheeks, in three weeks flat under their leader's rigid ordinance: "True excellence in writing will be pencilled into oblivion . . . there will be an unremitting emphasis on sex." Needless to say the book became a best-seller, and its authors plan a sequel—*Stranger than Naked!*

New Books for Younger Readers

GRAHAM ACKROYD

OF THE MANY STRIKING HISTORICAL BOOKS published during 1969, perhaps Erik Haugaard's *The Rider and His Horse* was the best. This exciting story takes place in Palestine after the destruction of Jerusalem by the Romans, and relates the adventures of a boy called David who joins the people of the Masada—led by the warrior Eleazar Ben Ya'ir—in a last desperate stand against the enemy. How the Masada survived the onslaught of the Roman legions and how David reached manhood in an age of bloodshed and cruelty is told with compassion by a writer who understands the powerful desire of young people to be free to make their own decisions. The background to *Charlie Is My Darling* by Jane Oliver is the story of the 1745 Jacobite rising. Those savage fighters, the Highlanders, capture Edinburgh Castle thanks to the hero of this authentic novel, young Sandy MacDonald. Later, when Sandy follows the army to England, he learns that life is not always a sucession of victories but that defeat must be taken with fortitude and courage. Also outstanding was Iona McGregor's *The Popinjay*, the name given to a tough, quick-thinking boy who, in Scotland's war-swept 16th century, learned to stand on his own feet in a world of savage cruelty and gross indifference to human suffering. This again was an authentic and vivid account of a part of our history

notable for gore. Tales of events in Roman Britain are told (with outstanding skill) by Molly Wheeler in *The Farthermost Fort*, in which some young people are involved in the adventurous affairs of their Uncle Flavius, known as Constantine III, elected by the Britons to be their Emperor—much to the anger of the Romans. Tara, one of the young heroines of these stories, enjoys a life of continuous adventure, experiencing fights against the Gauls and Saxons and the defence of the hill-forts. The violence is never overdone, and humour is always in evidence. Another fine historical adventure was *The Voice of the Great Elephant* by Jenny Seed, which told the tale of an African boy living during a time when the Zulus were the most feared warriors on the Dark Continent.

Modern Excitements

Madeleine L'Engle, one of the most successful authors of children's books writing today, is best known for *A Wrinkle in Time* which won the Newberry Award. Her latest novel of suspense, *The Young Unicorns*, is notable for its realistic dialogue and adult attitude to young people. The main character, Dave, driven to despair because of a broken home, joins a vicious gang of thuggish teenagers involved in kidnapping and drug-taking.

When Dave deserts the gang its members make repeated efforts to draw him back into their orbit. How he, his family, and friends avoid total destruction provides the climax of a book the main theme of which is the conflict between good and evil. Sylvia Sherry, famous for *Street of the Small Market*, hit the jack-pot again in 1969 with another sparkling story of life in the raw, *A Pair of Jesus Boots*. Rockey, who lives in a slum district of Liverpool, cannot decide whether he wants to be a footballer or a big-time crook. In an atmosphere of dirty streets, down-and-outs, and petty thieves, he comes into contact with real crime and learns that it is far more dangerous and terrible than he ever imagined: indeed had it not been for his sandals (the "Jesus boots") he might never have survived!

Boris, by Jaap ter Haar, a Dutch writer, has for its background the siege of Leningrad in the Second World War. It tells how after five hundred days of attacks by the German army, the youthful Boris, accompanied by his friend Nadia, has to make a perilous journey across no-man's-land in search of food. A meeting with a German patrol changes his life, sets him on the road to manhood, and provides an unforgettable story of courage overcoming man's inhumanity to man. In *A Herd of Deer* by that well-established writer Eilis Dillon, a young man who owns some poor land decides to increase his meagre income by keeping a herd of deer, much to the local people's anger. How he overcomes their prejudices with the help of a young friend is told with charm and humour.

Crime and Adventure

Those readers who enjoy crime, science-fiction, and fantasy will relish all these elements in Joan Clark's outstanding story *Foxon's Hole*. Three children take part in an enthralling adventure which involves a secret establishment high on the moors, the skeleton of a Stone Age boy, and a strange lad found half-dead—all spicily flavouring 300 pages of suspense by a writer who knows how to keep action on the boil! For sheer excitement Paul Capon's mystery story *Strangers on Forlorn* takes a lot of beating. The ingredients include an island, a crashed aircraft and its teenage passengers, frightened islanders suspicious of uninvited guests, a hint of civil war, a shot in the dark, mystery, and fear. From Australia came *Untamed* by H. M. Peel, a first-rate yarn with many dramatic illustrations, telling the story of Jago, a man-hating, untamed stallion and the jealous leader of a herd of wild horses. Anne Henderson and her husband set out to capture one of the herd's fillies and even before they come face to face with Jago they encounter a perilous journey across the desert with dust storms, snakes, and the threat of death by thirst.

Readers who enjoy humour should not miss Nils-Olof Franzen's hilarious story *Agaton Sax and the Scotland Yard Mystery*, bearing in mind the author's solemn warning: "When speaking of Inspector Lispington try if possible never to mention the Goat Beard!" And watch out for Hairy Herbert, Cauliflower Charlie, Four-eyes Harris, and many other weird villains. One of the most unusual stories of 1969 was Reiner Zimnik's fantastic and enchanting tale of a young man's love for his crane—the tallest in the world. The way he made it work when the world was covered with water is only part of this dream-like book, *The Crane*, illustrated with many witty drawings.

Moa Valley by Anne de Roo is the story of a hiking holiday in New Zealand undertaken by a girl called Marion and her young friends in a search for the moa bird. The children find themselves lost in unexplored territory with no prospect of being found by a scouting party for a week. In *Lotta Leaves Home* Astrid Lindgren tells the charming story of a little girl who decides to live alone in the loft of a shed because nobody understands her. *Salt Boy* by Mary Perrine is an unusual tale of a Red Indian boy's many adventures. The way he learns to lasso a black horse makes wonderful reading. Also from New Zealand, and for the youngest readers, came one of the most beautiful picture-story books of the year, *A Lion in the Meadow* by Margaret Mahy, with illustrations by Jenny Williams: a story as short as a beautiful dream.

Information Books

The outstanding work of non-fiction published in 1969 was *The Story of Britain* by R. J. Unstead, the famous "young readers'" historian. Illustrated in colour and black and white, it tells the story of Great Britain and of her people. In *Roman London* Alan Sorrell brings to life, with the aid of illustrations, the London and the Londoners of Roman times. *Man and his Music*, a superbly illustrated series of books with magnificent colour plates, traces the part this art has played in the service of man throughout European history. Those who wish to know everything there is to know about keeping small pets from ants to tree-frogs should consult *A Zoo On Your Window-Ledge* by Joy Spoczynska. Budding young engineers will find all the information they require about bridges in P. S. A. Berridge's *The Girder Bridge*. Those readers interested in diminishing and lost tribes, their legends and customs, will find a fascinating world in *What Became of the Australian Aborigines?* by R. Gamack, one of a series which includes books on the Mayas, the Maoris, and the Mamelukes—the slave-kings of Egypt.

For sheer excitement and interest young climbers could not do better than Walter Unsworth's *The North Face*, about mountaineering in the Alps, while Michael Brown's *Shackleton's Epic Voyage* tells the thrilling and true story of 27 brave men who endured the perils of the Antarctic. The real story of football from the very beginning to its present world-wide popularity is told by J. Edmundson in *All About Football*, with superb action photographs. If you enjoy poetry you will find a lively selection, old and new, in *Poet's Corner*.

Cockatoo Talk

In April a hoot of national laughter greeted the Australian Postmaster General's N.S.W. Department's curious refusal to "transmit by post" the last novel of the late D'Arcy Niland, *Dead Men Running*, because of "objectionable language" in it. So withering was the press reaction to this bureaucratic edict that the luckless P.M.G. himself had to wade into the fray and—with a barrage of face-saving phrases—back down. The laughter came from Australians who had acquired a copy of the book without recourse to the mails, and eagerly scoured its pages to discover the offending obscenity. They found a work of manifold merits but little to bring the blood rushing to a maiden's cheek. At last the search was narrowed down to a solitary use on page 163 of the famed four-letter word of Anglo-Saxon origin that occurs in *Lady Chatterley's Lover*—not even spoken directly by a character in D'Arcy Niland's novel, but quoted as the utterance of . . . a white cockatoo.

The

Performing

Arts

A Mixed Bag in the Theatre

ROY STACEY

Managing Editor of *Amateur Stage*

AFTER A YEAR free of stage censorship in Great Britain it is possible to make a reasonable assessment of the way theatre managements have exercised their new-found freedom. The Theatres Act, which came into force in September 1968, abolished the Lord Chamberlain's powers, but, despite some public protests in the press, on TV, and on the radio, no prosecutions were brought under the Act. Until the first test case is brought there exists no established precedent on the legal interpretation of the new Act—so, for the time being, almost anything goes.

As might have been expected, the greatest change has been in the use of freer language, sometimes liberally spattered with four-letter words and obscenities which the Lord Chamberlain would undoubtedly have deleted. To be fair, playwrights and managements have rarely exploited "bad language" solely for sensational and commercial purposes. But they have "cashed in" on the other censor-free development—nudity on the stage. Most examples on the British stage have emanated from the U.S.A. *Hair* got in first, the day after the new Act came into force, but others speedily followed. Paul Raymond, king of strip - clubland, took over the Whitehall Theatre, and chose as his first presentation a feeble American comedy, *Pyjama Tops*, for which £10,000 was spent on the installation of a swimming bath on stage, to allow for some nude female bathing. Various other examples of nudity hit the headlines, mostly originating in experimental fringe theatres. A vicious play set in a Canadian reformatory, *Fortune and Men's Eyes*, transferred to the West End from Charles Marowitz's Open Space, where we also had a Lady Macbeth sleepwalking without a stitch; the Living Theatre Co. from America even managed to obtain some audience participation in throwing off their inhibitions, and their clothes; and the Arts Lab. and the Roundhouse, two other fringe establishments, achieved much press publicity for similar exploits.

Kenneth Tynan more than repaid the U.S.A. with his *Oh, Calcutta!* in New York, in which he had promised "elegant erotica." This was almost universally damned by the critics, but the black-marketeers in seats are making such a fortune that productions of this piece are planned for London, Melbourne, and other capitals. Perhaps the best summing-up of the situation came in an article in the *Daily Telegraph* which concluded: "It is a bleak prospect if the Anglo-Saxon theatre in the seventies is to be swamped with *Calcutta* imitators, each one seeking to be a shade more brazen than the last . . . Our ultimate deterrent is, perhaps, public ennui."

Life in the Regions

A less sensational, but, for the future of the British theatre, infinitely more important development has been the astonishing revival of regional theatre during the past decade. The past was often overshadowed by the dismal news of theatre closures, and it is true there are now many fewer theatres than before. The weekly "rep"—typical of provincial theatre up to the 1950s—has virtually vanished. The public, fed cosily at home on a varied diet of TV drama, will not venture out and pay to see tatty, second-rate live theatre. The theatres that survive now present plays once every two or three weeks, with consequently improved standards. An encouraging factor is the acceptance by an increasing number of local councils that in a civilised, cultured community a theatre is as much a necessity for a self-respecting town as a library or swimming bath. Some have saved existing commercial theatres by making them civic, others give a subsidy, and others have built, or assisted in building, new theatres.

This change of attitude in the provinces is evident not only in the standard of performance but also in the calibre of programmes presented: many provide a far higher proportion of quality plays than London has to offer at any one time. Though London is still their Mecca, more actors, following John Neville's example, are willing to play in the provinces. New professional companies are doing really interesting work. Manchester, for example, has two new theatres—the Stables (under the aegis of Granada TV), and the flexible university theatre housing the '69 Theatre Company, which has included among its coups Vanessa Redgrave in *Daniel Deronda*.

Nor is it merely a coincidence that some of

the most exciting theatrical experiences in London's West End have originated in regional theatres, and often from young British playwrights. From Nottingham came Peter Barnes's *The Ruling Class*, a bizarre farcical fantasy without logical plot or shape, but crackling with vivid theatrical images and invention, about the self-preservation instinct of the ruling classes. In contrast, Barry England's *Conduct Unbecoming*, from Bristol, was old-fashioned in the best sense of the term, with the completely absorbing story of two young subalterns in a famous British cavalry regiment towards the end of last century.

Arturo Ui, originating in Glasgow, was hailed as the best production of a Brecht play by a British company, with a magnificent performance by Leonard Rossiter in the title role. The "limited season" in London of Goldsmith's *The School for Scandal* from Manchester had to be extended, giving London a too rare opportunity of observing the development of Tom Courtenay as a major actor. When Cambridge's Prospect Theatre Company, one of the very few touring companies, took *Richard II* and *Edward II* to the Edinburgh Festival and to London for a short season at the Mermaid, some critics gave Ian McKellen's Richard the accolade of the best Shakespearean performance of the year.

Local Documentaries

London is now too vast for its theatre to have any real roots in the local community: it caters for the comparatively small nucleus of theatre devotees who live within easy reach of the West End, that much larger floating population of people who just want "a night out" (often with a coach-load of neighbours), and the ever-increasing number of visitors. But the most successful post-war regional theatres have tilled the local soil diligently, knowing that their future depends on becoming an integral part of the community.

One manifestation of this is the success of what may be called documentaries, often with music. The Victoria Theatre, Stoke-on-Trent, under director Peter Cheeseman, has especially rich local soil which produced *The Knotty*, about the old North Staffs railway. This it was invited to show at the Florence international theatre festival—a tribute indeed to such a small theatre company. Other Stoke successes include *Potters and Rebels* and *Anna of the Five Towns*, adapted from Arnold Bennett's novel. Another example of the musical documentary came from Newcastle— *Close the Coalhouse Door*, by Alan Plater. This was transferred to London (and to the BBC),

Ginger Rogers on top of the moon in *Mame*, one of the box-office pulls of the year in London.

but it did not flourish in the south as successfully as it merited.

Like Stoke (with Peter Terson), the Northcott, Exeter, has a resident playwright, Jack Emery, whose research, allied to company co-operation, produced *The Bastard King* (based on the Monmouth rebellion) and *Wesley: a Man against his Age*. Two documentaries

Another American musical transplanted to London, *Dames at Sea*, with (*left to right*) Sheila White, Joyce Blair, and Rita Burton, satirised the naive back-stage plots and characters of the Hollywood extravaganzas of the 1930s.

Woody Allen's *Play it Again, Sam* was a vehicle for Dudley Moore. Also involved Patricia Brake and Bill Kerr.

concerning famous criminals were Alan Cullen's *The Life and Times of Charlie Peace* (Sheffield) and *Anything You Say will be Twisted* (Bolton), on the life of Jack Sheppard, which was transferred to the Mermaid, London.

Regional festivals suffered mixed fortunes. Chichester had its most successful season ever in 1969, with *Antony and Cleopatra*, *The Caucasian Chalk Circle*, *The Country Wife*, and *The Magistrate*; all were offered transfers to London, but it was found practicable only for the last-named, with Alastair Sim reaching the heights of farcical fooling. But two Scottish Festivals, Edinburgh and Pitlochry, though

Left to right: Dame Flora Robson, Joan Miller, and Joyce Carey starring in the West End revival of the Rodney Ackland-Hugh Walpole thriller, *The Old Ladies.*

continuing to achieve high artistic successes, found rising costs a heavy burden.

Old Wave Renewed

A surprising phenomenon of 1969 was the continuing success of *The Secretary Bird*, a "french-window" sophisticated comedy of the style so popular in the 1930s, which everyone thought had been killed in 1956 by *Look Back in Anger* and the new wave of playwrights. But this wave has petered out into a thin trickle, leaving behind much flotsam and jetsam and a mere handful of playwrights with staying power, such as Harold Pinter and John Osborne. *The Secretary Bird* could be a portent of the swing of the pendulum back to "straight" entertainment, but its success was more probably sparked off by Kenneth More's (and later John Gregson's) superb performance. Several more "vehicle" plays, exploiting the talents and pulling power of a star name, appeared in the West End during the year. The most blatant example was *Highly Confidential*, a ridiculous farce about an international spy, but a peg for Hermione Gingold's famous revue act. In *So What about Love?* by Leonard Webb, Sheila Hancock demonstrated her versatility as a sex-mad, introspective "bed-sit. girl." One critic, Harold Hobson of the *Sunday Times*, bitterly condemned its amorality; and the same criticism could be made of *The Crunch*, by Felicity Dawson and Basil Douglas, in which Andrew Cruickshank (television's "Dr. Cameron") played a headmaster tempted by a football pools swindle. Rex Harrison, in his first London stage part for eight years, in another comedy of rather dubious moral standards, *The Lionel Touch*, by George Hulme, proved his impeccable expertise in getting laughs out of feeble material.

Among the more off-beat pieces were *Spitting Image*, by Colin Spencer, about homosexuals who conceive a baby; and Joe Orton's last play, *What the Butler Saw*, a zany farce set in a private madhouse, on which the talents of players of the calibre of Sir Ralph Richardson and Coral Browne were wasted. Imports from America were in general more successful than home-bred products. *The Price*, a powerful study of the enmity between two brothers whose father had been ruined by the Wall Street crash of 1929, gave Arthur Miller his longest London run. It is doubtful if *The Boys in the Band*, by Mart Crowley, could have been produced in the Lord Chamberlain's era, however lenient he might have become to plays about homosexuality. *Out of the Question* took an amusingly satirical look at Britain's brain drain, by an American writer, Ira

Wallach. It did not rest too heavily on its stars, Michael Denison and Dulcie Gray, as did *Play it Again, Sam*, by Woody Allen, on Dudley Moore as a neurotic little man who has fantasies of sexual conquests. *Plaza Suite*, a triple bill by Neil Simon (currently America's most successful light comedy writer), linked by a common setting in a New York hotel bedroom, was mildly amusing. Another multi-bill, *Mixed Doubles*, comprised eight short duologues by contemporary British playwrights, the linking subject being marriage.

The soaring costs of production, exacerbated by Selective Employment Tax, are driving musicals in London nearer to the American pattern—with little between the smash hit and the crashing failure. Two American film stars made their first appearances in London—Ginger Rogers, in *Mame*, received the true star treatment; Betty Grable, in *Belle Starr*, was less fortunate. Two "Ann's," based on old novels, suffered opposite fates: an unsophisticated family musical, set in Edwardian Canada, *Anne of Green Gables*, was surprisingly successful; while an adaptation of H. G. Wells's *Ann Veronica* failed. An adaptation of Dickens's *Tale of Two Cities* deserved a better fate, but *Mr. & Mrs.* (adapted from Noël Coward) did not. *Promises, Promises*, a slick American musical, was a success.

The National Repertories

The National Theatre offered a varied bag—two classics, *Love's Labour's Lost* and *The Way of the World*; two new plays by British writers, *H* by Charles Wood, a savage anti-war piece set at the time of the Indian Mutiny, and *The National Health*, by Peter Nichols (author of *A Day in the Death of Joe Egg*); and a revival of the whole of Shaw's massive *Back to Methuselah*, which is precisely the kind of work, impossible to produce commercially, which the leading subsidised British theatre should be presenting.

The second theatre in this category, the Royal Shakespeare, continued to play to record audiences (over 1,000,000 a year) and record box-office receipts, but also ran up a record deficit (over £160,000). As ever, its strength lies in Shakespeare (still the biggest box-office draw). In London it mounted fine productions of *Troilus and Cressida* and *Much Ado about Nothing*; two poetic but undramatic pieces by Pinter, *Landscape* and *Silence*; an unsuccessful new play by David Mercer, *Dutch Uncle*: and formidable revivals of two neglected plays—O'Casey's controversial anti-war piece, *The Silver Tassie*, and Ben Jonson's comedy about London life, *Bartholomew Fair*.

The Royal Court repertoire was notable

Shogo (Jack Shepherd) menacing Georgina (Gillian Martell) in Edward Bond's *Narrow Road to the Deep North*.

chiefly for an Edward Bond season (*Saved*, *Narrow Road to the Deep North*, and *Early Morning*), and several modern realistic plays by young writers—*This Story of Yours* by John Hopkins, *In Celebration* and *The Contractor*, both by David Storey, and *Life Price* by Michael O'Neill and Jeremy Seabrook (widely publicised by the offer of free seats to all).

The Mermaid celebrated its tenth anniversary with a boisterous revival of its opening production, *Lock Up Your Daughters*. Other productions included the first performance of a 60-year-old play by Henry James, *The Other House*, which proved him a better novelist than

Left to right: **National Theatre players Robert Walker, Lionel Guyett, Robert Lang, and Bernard Gallagher in *H*, Charles Wood's play set at the time of the Indian Mutiny.**

playwright; and a breakaway from the perennial Christmas *Treasure Island* with an imaginative production of *Gulliver's Travels*, cleverly employing projected scenery. The year's *tour de force* was Roy Dotrice's remarkable performance in *Brief Lives*, adapted by Patrick Garland from the anecdotes of the 17th-century antiquary John Aubrey, which beat all box-office records for a single-handed performance.

One delightful new theatre opened during the year—the Thorndike at Leatherhead, on the boards of which Dame Sybil Thorndike celebrated her 87th birthday. And, at long last, a start was made on both the National Theatre on the South Bank of the Thames, and the Royal Shakespeare Company's new home at the Barbican in the City; both are scheduled for completion by 1973. An old music hall was transformed into the exciting new Greenwich Theatre, which is trying to emulate the best of the regional theatres in a London suburb; with three new plays as its opening productions, this venture promises well. The University of Sussex opened its Gardner Centre for the Arts, a £300,000 building the hub of which is a flexible new theatre designed by Sean Kenny.

In the amateur field, full-length entries in the National Student Drama Festival, held at Exeter University, for the first time consisted entirely of new plays. This proved so successful that in 1970 every entry, one-acters included, will have to be original. A number of productions from the 1969 Festival were taken up by professional theatres, and the winning play, *Zoo, Zoo, Widdershins Zoo*, by Kevin Laffan, had a professional production at the Edinburgh Festival.

Theatre in Australia

In 1968–69 the newly formed Australian Council for the Arts adopted the policy of channelling its meagre financial resources into one professional company each in Sydney, Melbourne, and, to a lesser extent, Adelaide. The Melbourne Theatre Company and the Sydney Old Tote Company were chosen to be the major grant-receiving theatres, to the extent of about $A80,000 a year each. This brought forth cries of outrage from the older-established theatres in Sydney—the Ensemble and the Independent—and the newer Community Theatre, all of which were "in the red." Their directors banded together in a sustained campaign against the Arts Council which, in its 1969–70 programme, changed its policy so far as to allocate $A20,000 to the three companies to encourage them to make more country and school tours.

The Arts Council's aim is to create one strong professional company of a high standard in each capital city, which, they argue, is a more effective policy than distributing limited funds over a number of small companies, who would at best be able to reach only a competent level. While this may sound reasonable in theory, in practice it has virtually snubbed the older-established theatres, and in particular the work of some of the real pioneers of live theatre in Australia, such as Irene Mitchele (St. Martin's, Melbourne), Hayes Gordon (Ensemble), and Doris Fitton (Independent), without whose work the Old Tote and the Melbourne Theatre Company would probably not exist today.

Censorship was a fiercely debated topic throughout the Commonwealth. The debate was sparked off by Sydney's New Theatre production of *America Hurrah!* A complaint was lodged with the chief secretary for New South Wales, who stopped further performances of *Motel*, one of the plays in this collection. "The Friends of *America Hurrah* Society" was formed and gave private performances. Some of these, and public demonstrations, were broken up by police, and there were numerous discussions on radio and TV, and opinion surveys. The result was that the theatre in Sydney became almost free from state interference: *The Boys in the Band* and *Hair* hardly caused a ripple, and a production of *Oh, Calcutta!* was planned.

Elsewhere in Australia the attitude was different. For example, actors in the Melbourne production of *The Boys in the Band* were fined for using obscene language, and members of the Vice Squad quizzed the leading actor and caused the deletion of a "four-letter word." And in Brisbane, Twelfth Night Theatre were engaged in legal proceedings for six months over a production of *Norm and Ahmed*, by rising young Australian writer Alexander Buzo, following the arrest of the actors on stage.

From the more conventional, commercial theatre there was the customary diet of imported musical and dramatic successes, but regrettably few worthwhile indigenous plays. St. Martin's, Melbourne, had the greatest success in this respect, with Hal Porter's *Eden House*, which might well have international appeal, although not particularly contemporary in style. A number of experimental fringe theatres continued, without making much impact on the general public. In particular the Jane Street Theatre, Sydney, staged try-out seasons of new plays, notably by Rodney Milgate, Tony Morphett, and Alexander Buzo.

Three Ladies of Quality circling a Gentleman of Parts: Royal Ballet dancers Alfreda Thorogood, Margaret Barbieri, Elizabeth Anderton, and Hendrik Daval, in Anthony Tudor's *Knight Errant*.

Royal Ballet, Covent Garden

Blueprint for Ballet

PETER WILLIAMS Editor of *Dance and Dancers*

INVOLVING AS IT DOES several arts on a high level, ballet can never support itself economically unless it is used in a purely commercial way in film or stage musicals or in that now almost extinct theatrical form the music hall. In the past, its survival depended on the enthusiasm and dedication of rich patrons or far-sighted private organisations. With the Second World War and the disappearance of private wealth on any large scale, it became obvious that if the creative arts were to survive in Great Britain the state must give assistance in the form of subsidies such as already existed in several European countries. A start was made by the setting-up of a council known as C.E.M.A. (Council for the Encouragement of Music and the Arts) which, throughout the war and into the postwar period, did splendid work. In 1946 C.E.M.A. developed into what is now known as the Arts Council of Great Britain, a body designed to take account of the expansion in artistic activities inevitably resulting from the increase in leisure time.

Ballet, although becoming the most popular art in the whole field of lyric theatre, did not receive as much attention as it deserved from the Arts Council until 1966 when the Council, realising the situation, set up a board of inquiry to consider what ballet was available in Great Britain and how it could be used to serve the whole country in the future. The result of the inquiry was a Report on Opera and Ballet in Great Britain, published in November 1969, which may well become the blueprint for the development of ballet not only in Great Britain but also in other countries.

From the evidence it is apparent that Britain now has ballet companies that can reach most geographical and intellectual areas. They form three tiers, according to size. In the first tier come the two sections of the Royal Ballet and London's Festival Ballet, which can play only in the large theatres. The two sections of the Royal Ballet act as a kind of National Gallery of dance in preserving the classics and the best works by the greatest choreographers of this century. The Festival Ballet follows a similar policy but aims at a wider audience.

In the next tier come the medium-sized companies—Ballet Rambert and Scottish Theatre Ballet (formerly Western Theatre Ballet)—which can not only play in smaller theatres but can also concentrate on works using modern scores and ideas more in tune with the mood of our time and with a greater bias towards the schools of contemporary dance. Not only do these companies appeal to the younger middle section of the audience (aged from about 18 to 30); they are also ideal for festivals, university towns, and areas where there are enlightened arts associations.

In the third tier come the small companies and groups which can play in towns and villages where it is impossible for larger companies to operate. Examples are the Royal Ballet's Ballet for All company and a similar group formed by the London School of Contemporary Dance. Both are developing a form of presentation which includes lecture demonstration in a theatrical way.

The report stressed the importance of each company's having a permanent base, whether in London or the regions, and stated that greater attention in the future should be paid to developing creative talent by giving opportunities to promising choreographers. It is interesting to consider what each company

London's Festival Ballet offered exotic fare. *Left:* André Prokovsky clutching the Queen of the Morphides, Galina Samtsova, in John Taras's *Piège de Lumière.* *Right:* The Unknown Island, Jack Carter's homage to Berlioz.
Festival Ballet, London Coliseum

did in this present respect in the 1968–69 ballet season.

"First Tier" Companies

The larger Royal Ballet, based on Covent Garden, showed a new work by Frederick Ashton in October 1968. This ballet, *Enigma Variations*, instead of treating Elgar's music as an abstract work delved into the nature of the various friends to whom he dedicated his music in the words "to my friends pictured within." Ashton has linked the variations with a narrative which shows the loneliness of Elgar (beautifully played by Derek Rencher) and his sorrow at not having yet achieved international recognition (the Variations were composed in 1898). The ballet ends with a telegram from the great conductor Richter, saying that he will conduct Elgar's music at his concerts. Ashton's beautiful and poetic work is also one of the most typically English ballets in the Royal Ballet's repertory. The mood of the period has been lovingly underlined by the designing of Julia Trevelyan Oman.

Rather less satisfactory was the Royal Ballet's new production of the Tchaikovsky-Petipa *Sleeping Beauty*, which went on at Covent Garden on December 20, 1968. Britain owes its eminence in world ballet to the *Sleeping Beauty* more than to any other work because it established the Royal Ballet at Covent Garden in 1946 and in America in 1949. After 23 years the old production, designed by Oliver Messel, was looking tired. The new one, however, involved too many people and

emerged as a piecemeal affair. The most satisfactory element was Frederick Ashton's contributions, including a beautiful new *pas de deux* for Princess Aurora and Prince Florimund after the Princess has awakened from her hundred-year sleep. The new production gave more scope to the Prince's role, which in the past has been shadowy, to say the least; and it proved ideal for Anthony Dowell, who is rapidly becoming one of the world's most important male dancers. Oddly enough the production came off better on BBC 2 colour TV than it did in the theatre.

A year of great activity for the larger section of the Royal Ballet included a revival of Antony Tudor's *Lilac Garden*, but this curiously did not suit the company any more than its revival of Kenneth MacMillan's *Olympiad*, originally created for West Berlin. The disaster of the year—and every company is entitled to occasional disasters—was a creation by Roland Petit, *Pelléas et Mélisande*, specially for Margot Fonteyn and Rudolf Nureyev.

Continual touring prevents the Royal Ballet's smaller company from putting on many new works, but in 1969 it managed to mount several. One was *Knight Errant* by Antony Tudor to some Richard Strauss music. Based on an 18th-century French novel, *Les Liaisons Dangereuses*, this comedy of manners about an amorous gentleman's involvement with three married ladies had moments of wit, especially when the gentleman was danced by David Wall. But the subtleties of comedy are hard to realise in dance form, and the work can

Contemporary attitudes at the Ballet Rambert. *Left:* Glen Tetley's *Embrace Tiger and Return to Mountain,* Chinese exercises danced to an electronic score. *Right:* John Chesworth's *Pawn to King 5,* to music by the Pink Floyd.

Ballet Rambert, Jeannetta Cochrane Theatre

be considered only a partial success. Following the policy of giving new choreographers a chance, this section of the Royal Ballet also included in one programme a new work by Geoffrey Cauley, *In the Beginning*, and a revival of a work which David Drew originally created for Royal Ballet students, *Intrusion*. Both were excellently danced, but neither seemed worthy of a permanent place in the repertory of a major company. The most important aspect of this company's year was that their Covent Garden season, while the larger company made another tour of the U.S.A., was a sell-out—evidence that at last both sections of the Royal Ballet have achieved equal status in the minds of the public.

Sir Frederick Ashton will retire from the artistic directorship of the Royal Ballet in 1970, when he will be replaced by John Field, who has been largely responsible for bringing the smaller section up to its present standard, and by Kenneth MacMillan, who until recently was artistic director of the West Berlin Opera Ballet. The effect of the new blood is unpredictable, but it will be hard for anybody to follow in the footsteps of Sir Frederick, who with his perfect taste and sensitivity as a choreographer has probably contributed more to the quality of British ballet than any other single person.

London's Festival Ballet has also been going through direction changes, Beryl Grey becoming artistic director and Wilfred Stiff administrator, replacing Donald Albery. But policy remained unchanged during their first year. The company gave a new full-length version

of *Coppélia* by Jack Carter, who also created a work to mark the Berlioz centenary, *The Unknown Island*. Also new to the repertory was a revival of John Taras's *Piège de Lumière* (Light Trap), originally created for the company of the late Marquis de Cuevas. This work about convicts catching butterflies in a jungle was distinguished by the dancing of Galina Samtsova as a Morphide, and of André Prokovsky as the convict who catches her. Apart from the success of its foreign tours the most important feature of the Festival Ballet's year was that its London season took place at the Coliseum instead of on the converted concert platform of the Royal Festival Hall. Possibly the highlight of the season was the return of Lynn Seymour as guest ballerina to dance Princess Aurora in *Sleeping Beauty* partnered by Danish Peter Martins.

The "Second Tier"

Ballet Rambert, continuing its policy of producing contemporary works, brought another creation by Glen Tetley into its repertory, *Embrace Tiger and Return to Mountain*. Based on Chinese exercises of T'ai-chi to an electronic score by American composer Morton Subotnick, it proved to be one of the most original and beautiful ballets of recent years and brought success to the re-shaped company both in Britain and on its first European tours. Norman Morrice created a *Pastorale Variée* which used the interesting idea of repeating the same music (by Paul Ben-Haim) twice— in the first section for the general ensemble, then in an extended *pas de deux* for the second

Marilyn Rowe and Kelvin Coe, of the Australian Ballet, dancing *The Last Vision*, a pas de deux specially created for them by the Russian choreographer, Igor Moiseyev.

part. Differing from Morrice's previous works in that it was extremely lyrical, it could well serve the same purpose in the repertory as *Les Sylphides* with more classical companies.

Ballet Rambert also has been developing the choreographic talents of the company. John Chesworth created a work to music by the Pink Floyd, *Pawn to King 5*; and Christopher Bruce used Handel music for his first work, *George Frideric*. Both works have been useful in the regular repertory. Bruce's is a straightforward piece of classical dancing, but with decided contemporary overtones; Chesworth's, in its attitude towards violence within the context of a discotheque, reflects certain less agreeable aspects of today and proved very successful on the company's tour of Germany.

Western Theatre Ballet, moving north of the border and becoming the Scottish Theatre Ballet based on Glasgow, had little time for new creations; the process of establishing the first regional company, working in conjunction with Scottish Opera, naturally led to much readjustment and re-thinking. The company is not to be confined to Scotland: Scottish Theatre Ballet made tours of Britain in 1969 and gave a London season (probably to become an annual event) at Sadler's Wells, when a new three-act ballet by Peter Darrell, *Beauty and the Beast*, with a specially commissioned score from Thea Musgrave, had its world première. The genesis of another regional company took place in the spring in Manchester where Laverne Meyer showed an embryonic version of what by September had become Northern Dance Theatre. Twelve dancers appear in a repertory of short works which, although classically based, are contemporary in outlook and use mainly contemporary music; two new dancers will be added to the group each year.

The "Third Tier"

An interesting development in 1969 was the use of dance in mixed-media events—performances in which dancers, actors, light, and sound are used in a natural relationship. Possibly the most exciting was a performance by Geoff Moore's Moving Being at the Institute of Contemporary Art which produced a stimulating, disturbing, and beautiful series of events. Moore and several other creators in mixed-media also took part in *Explorations* at The Place. This building on the northern edge of Bloomsbury, London, formerly the headquarters of the Artists Rifles regiment, was acquired, and entirely reconstructed inside, by Robin Howard as a home for the London School of Contemporary Dance. It can also provide space for all kinds of events, of which *Explorations* was the first; and if *Explorations* is any indication it seems possible that The Place, as a much needed platform for the experiments of creative artists, may become one of Europe's most valuable sources of ideas for art forms.

The London School of Contemporary Dance itself has started to blossom fruitfully with a company directed by one of Martha Graham's principal male dancers, Robert Cohan, and including several dancers from the Graham company. There are also a splinter group for taking contemporary dance to smaller towns, and a lecture-demonstration group for even smaller towns, schools, and universities. In 1969 performances were given abroad and in the regions, and the first London season opened at The Place on September 2.

Ballet Scene Abroad

In Australia Peggy van Praagh and Sir Robert Helpmann have based Australian Ballet, which they jointly direct artistically, on the Royal Ballet in that they mix well-known classics with triple bills of more modern works. The company is building up an interesting and well-balanced repertory. In 1969 it gave a new production of the full-length *Coppélia*, a revival of Ashton's *The Dream*, and Tudor's *Pillar of Fire*. Tudor also created a new work, *The Divine Horseman*, to Werner Egk music and based on a Caribbean theme; other world premières included *Arena* by Jack Manuel, and *The Last Vision* by the famous Soviet choreographer Igor Moiseyev. Australia also has a group, Athletes and Dancers, which performs the same kind of function as Ballet for All in Britain. Directed by former Western Theatre

Ballet dancer Suzanne Musitz, this group tours small towns and villages, with a demonstration group relating classical dance training with athletic training in a form of theatre.

The Canadian National Ballet has also been shaped on the lines of the Royal Ballet by its director Celia Franca, who was once a distinguished member of the English company. For more modern works the smaller Royal Winnipeg Ballet performs the same kind of function for Canada as Ballet Rambert for England; during the year it made a successful tour of Eastern Europe and Russia. The third major Canadian company, Les Grands Ballets Canadiens, is still too young to have formed a very definite policy. To date its major contribution has been ballets based on the trilogy of the German composer Carl Orff—*Carmina Burana, Catulli Carmina,* and *Trionfo di Afrodite.* These were shown in London when the company gave its first London season at Sadler's Wells in the spring. But apart from some excellent dancers, the company created a rather disappointing impression.

Most notable among other visits to London was the return of Netherlands Dance Theatre with a large repertory, including very distinguished works by Glen Tetley and Hans van Manen. This company showed how it is possible to mix the classical and contemporary dance schools in a form of dance language that is totally valid and is a pointer to the way that dance may well move in the future. Also at Sadler's Wells was the Alwin Nikolais Dance Theatre, which seemed to be the very essence of what we believe about dance in mixed-media at its very highest. Nikolais creates every part of these works himself—choreography, design, lighting, and sound—and his dancers form an integral part of some of the most beautiful images ever seen on the stage. That this form of dance theatre is what the

The disappointing London debut of Les Grands Ballets Canadiens was redeemed by excellent individual performances. Here Sanson Candelaria plays a pinioned swan to Carl Orff's music in *Carmina Burana.*

younger audiences want was proved when they packed the theatre at every performance.

The most distinguished visitors from the classical side of ballet were the Bolshoi. If the main part of their Covent Garden season was disappointing, owing to inferior productions of the great classics, everything was saved by *Spartacus.* This spectacular, on the Slave's Revolt in ancient Rome, was excellently constructed by the choreographer Grigorovich. He contrived to make the narrative understandable while creating one of the most "all-dancing" ballets ever seen. It was superbly danced by the four principals—Liepa as Crassus, Timofeyeva as his mistress Aegina, Lavrovsky as Spartacus, and Bessmertnova as his wife Phrygia—and by a male *corps de ballet* such as only the Bolshoi can produce.

The visiting Bolshoi's superb *Spartacus,* by Grigorovich, was the highlight of the year at Covent Garden.

An ecstatic Barbra Streisand outlines her matrimonial designs to a bemused Walter Matthau—a scene from *Hello, Dolly!* 20th Century-Fox

Richard Chamberlain—noted for his bedside manner as young Dr. Kildare—clasps a recumbent Katherine Hepburn in *The Madwoman of Chaillot.* Warne-Pathé

Dearth of the Family Film

ANNE WILSON

IN THE CINEMA, 1969 was a year of challenge, controversy, and change, which began gratifyingly with record-breaking successes by films such as *Pendulum*, a tautly written, well directed thriller starring George Peppard, and *Bullitt* with Steve McQueen in the title role. Another early box-office bonanza was *The Lion in Winter*, set in the 12th century at the time of Henry II, the success of which was due mainly to the magnificent performance of Katharine Hepburn as the intelligent, ambitious, cunning, and devious Eleanor of Aquitaine, but also to that of Peter O'Toole as the blustering, wily Henry.

But films designed for a mass audience gave way to a great extent to those with more limited appeal during the year. Thus, films in the *Sound of Music* class survived only marginally with *Hello, Dolly!* starring Barbra Streisand and Michael Crawford; *Goodbye Mr. Chips*, a romantic story with music; *The Madwoman of Chaillot*; and, perhaps most successfully, with *Funny Girl*. This true rags-to-riches tale of Fanny Brice and her determination to become one of America's show business "greats" was Barbra Streisand's first film and Omar Sharif's first musical. Produced by Ray Stark (Fanny Brice's son-in-law), it was an amusing, effervescent, sentimental, and colourful spectacle which unleashed a superb talent in Miss Streisand. Her self-mocking humour, sensitivity, and radiance made Fanny Brice a real character, completely over-shadowing Omar Sharif.

U-certificate films in the all-round entertainment field were fewer than ever before. Of the few, most notable were *Run Wild, Run Free* and *Ring of Bright Water*. The former provided a second starring role for Mark Lester (who had played the title role in *Oliver!*); the latter was a popular follow-up by husband and wife Bill Travers and Virginia McKenna to their successful *Born Free*.

Crazy comedy was represented, somewhat inadequately, by such films as *Monte Carlo or Bust* and *The Love Bug*, a simple all-round entertainer from the Disney stable about a magical Volkswagen called Herbie. Also in this category were *Where's Jack?* starring Tommy Steele as the notorious highwayman Jack Sheppard; *Sinful Davy*, in a similar vein; and another in the *Carry On* series, *Carry On Camping*, with the usual outrageous fun.

Apart from the wide-screen re-release of *The Jolson Story* and also *The Longest Day*, re-released to mark the 25th anniversary of D-Day, big screen entertainment produced only three memorable films: *Sweet Charity*, starring Shirley MacLaine as Charity Hope Valentine, a guileless girl searching for love,

184

Inca King Atahualpa (Christopher Plummer) kneels before Spanish conquistador Pizarro (Robert Shaw) in the film of Peter Shaffer's play *The Royal Hunt of the Sun*. *Rank*

Sammy Davis Jr., *Sweet Charity's* high priest of the Rhythm of Life, with his acolytes John Martin and Shirley MacLaine. *Rank*

which offered brilliant and colourful choreography by Bob Fosse; Cinerama's *Krakatoa East of Java*, which was effective because of its volcanic shots, even though the story was not particularly strong; and *The Royal Hunt of the Sun*, based on Peter Shaffer's play and starring Robert Shaw and Christopher Plummer, an absorbing, powerful epic about the Spanish conquest of Peru.

The introduction of a new and interesting concept of the multiple-star film proved to be highly successful in money-making terms. *Oh! What A Lovely War*, for example, succeeded through the engaging performances of a whole group of talented and well-known actors including Vanessa, Corin, and Michael Redgrave, John Gielgud, Laurence Olivier, Ralph

Richardson, and Maggie Smith. The film, exceptionally well directed by Richard Attenborough, was derived from Joan Littlewood's stage production. *The Battle of Britain*, a meticulously researched account of one of Britain's greatest historical episodes, also had a large and impressive cast which included Michael Caine, Trevor Howard, and Michael Redgrave. Yet Laurence Olivier was the only real character to emerge in a rather disappointing film which fell between documentary and fiction. But super-stars could not always guarantee a box-office success, a fact emphasised by the comparative disinterest in *Boom*, a Tennessee Williams drama starring Elizabeth Taylor, Richard Burton, and Noël Coward.

John Mills clutches feathered friend in one of the few family films of the year, *Run Wild, Run Free*. Onlookers are Mark Lester, youthful star of *Oliver!*, and Fiona Fullerton.

Columbia

Brighton pier, bizarre location for *Oh! What a Lovely War,*
looms behind this Edwardian "snap," from the film.
Paramount

With the emphasis on content rather than stars, the year saw a number of films concerned with subjects hitherto ignored or forbidden. Among the most successful was *Midnight Cowboy.* A disturbing, depressing, and sentimental film with an unsavoury and at times perverted theme, it yet showed an extraordinary understanding of the bitterness and humour of human relationships. It was well made and contained good acting by newcomer Jon Voight as an innocent Texan dishwasher who went to New York to make his fortune by seducing rich women, and also by Dustin Hoffman, who played a crippled con-man with intuitive sympathy. *Rosemary's Baby,* written and directed by Polish director Roman Polanski, which broke box-office records at the beginning of the year, also succeeded by reason of its satanic dramatic content.

The generation gap, a subject which aroused great interest during the student uprisings of 1968, was the theme of one of the most important and interesting films of the year, *If . . .* Directed by Lindsay Anderson, and starring unknowns Malcolm McDowell, David Wood, and Richard Warwick, the film dealt with a group of public-school boys staging an armed rebellion. As one of the invited entries to the Cannes Film Festival, *If . . .* was the first British film to win the Grand Prix since *The Knack* five years before.

The other invited British entry, *The Prime of Miss Jean Brodie,* was, however, unsuccessful. This film, adapted from Muriel Spark's novel and chosen for the Royal Film Performance earlier in the year, was concerned with the rise and fall of an eccentric Scottish schoolteacher (Maggie Smith) and her idiosyncratic theory of education. Another film at the Festival, *Easy Rider,* starring and produced by Peter Fonda, caused a major row and was accused of showing a distorted view of America; surprisingly, however, the film—about a bearded hippy nicknamed Captain America—was passed for release by the British film censor.

An equally well-made and self-critical, but completely different, piece of American social comment was *Goodbye Columbus,* a comic look at middle-class American surburbia, starring Ali MacGraw and Richard Benjamin. The tricks and entanglements of human relationships was also the theme of such films as *Secret Ceremony* with Mia Farrow and Elizabeth Taylor; John Osborne's *Inadmissible Evidence,* starring Nicol Williamson; and *Justine,* the four books of Lawrence Durrell's *Alexandrian Quartet* combined into one film.

Sex, Violence, and Censorship

The year was indeed to prove a difficult one for film censorship. It soon became obvious that some film directors felt that commercial pull in this permissive era lay in the more unusual sexual themes. Foreign companies undoubtedly acted with less discretion than British, which produced one or two tasteful and perceptive films of the kind. *The Killing of Sister George,* Beryl Reid's stage success in London and New York, was the bitter tragedy of a jealous, neurotic, hard-drinking Lesbian, the star of a marathon-running television series, whose problems began when she realised her part was to be written out. *The Sergeant,* emotionally acted by Rod Steiger, was a psychological drama of army life, the story of a latent homosexual army sergeant, ruthless and inhuman on the surface but vulnerable underneath. In similar vein, *Staircase,* released later in the year, was a vivid tale of male homosexuality starring Rex Harrison and Richard Burton.

During the first four months of the year the number of X-certificate films released in Great Britain was higher than the number of A and U certificates combined. They included two extreme and somewhat superfluous films, *Candy* and *Baby Love.* The former starred young Swedish actress, Ewa Aulin, opposite a number of well-known actors such as Richard Burton, Marlon Brando, and Charles Aznavour in short sexual fantasy sequences. *Baby Love,* starring 15-year-old Linda Hayden, was a sensational drama about an illegitimate girl who came home from school to find that her mother, a prostitute, had committed suicide.

Malcolm Arnold conducting the orchestra as they recorded Sir William Walton's music for *The Battle of Britain*.

Another controversial film which surprisingly passed the censor was *Can Hieronymus Merkin Ever Forget Mercy Humppe and Find True Happiness?* directed, produced by, and starring Anthony Newley. Like its title, this was an extravagant, even pretentious, but never boring piece of work.

The decline of mass-audience films disturbed the Director of the British Board of Censorship, Mr. John Trevelyan, as well as the main cinema chains ABC and Rank, and the police committee in Belfast even considered a total ban on X-certificate films when in mid-May they were showing at twelve of the city's nineteen cinemas! In spite of the publicity given to X films on sexual subjects, however, it was agreed that screen violence was a still greater cause for concern, as seen in such films as *The Wild Bunch* and *Twisted Nerve*, an immensely moving and horrific drama about a young psychopath played with impeccable sympathy by Hywel Bennett.

Early in the year Mr. Trevelyan announced that the Board was considering a plan to change censorship grading. "If the plan is adopted," he said, "the letters will be discarded for numbers (1 to 4) indicating the suitability of films for children and adults. This change will reflect the growing maturity of young people and the urgent need for more flexibility in rating films. We are considering widening the scale slightly in one respect and tightening it in another, relaxing the requirement that children need a responsible adult with them for some films, but raising the age by two years at which the present X film is viewable. This should please exhibitors who feel that the way the X has been associated with sex and violence has got their business a lot of bad publicity. The grading would be as follows: 1—equivalent of the present U certificate; 2—similar to the present A, but will require children under 14 to be accompanied by an adult; 3—anyone over the age of 14 will be able to see the film unaccompanied by an adult; 4—banned to anyone under 18."

One man determined to support John Trevelyan in his plans to prevent the market from being flooded by sensational X-certificate films was Bryan Forbes, the British actor and director who was chosen during the year to be the new £35,000-a-year production chief of Associated British Pictures. He made it plain

Captain America (Peter Fonda) savours bouquet as beaded hippie (Dennis Hopper) looks on: scene from the controversial picture *Easy Rider*.   Columbia

Judy Geeson played a nubile hitch-hiker, and Rod Steiger an erring husband, in *Three Into Two Won't Go.*   *Rank*

that he appreciated the value of such X-certificate comedies as *Three Into Two Won't Go* and *The Graduate*, but banished X films completely from his first £7 million production programme of thrillers, comedies, classics, and a musical. For these he signed up an impressive list of talent including Roger Moore, Peter Sellers, and John Mills.

While Britain tentatively questioned its rules of censorship, Australia was going through its own cultural purge, including some harsh treatment of films. The censors forbade the screening of films depicting violence, such as *Pretty Poison*, starring Anthony Perkins, which mingled black humour with sex and realistic murder, and *100 Rifles*, a violent and lethal Mexican and Indian adventure starring Jim Brown and Raquel Welch. There was also much local heart-burning over the choice of Mick Jagger to play the hero-outlaw Ned Kelly.

The year showed an increased interest in the major international film festivals. The British entry at San Sebastian in June was *The Italian Job*, a light-hearted crime comedy exactly suited to the cockney humour of Michael Caine, although in fact the best comedy acting in it came from Noël Coward. Chosen for the Berlin festival was *A Touch of Love*, adapted from Margaret Drabble's novel *The Millstone*, an emotional, well-acted film starring Sandy Dennis. Invited also was *Three Into Two Won't Go*, the story of a young hippy hitch-hiker (Judy Geeson) who was casually used by a married man (Rod Steiger) for his own sexual pleasure, until he realised she was more than a match for him in every way. This

was one of the best acted films of the year. Two films invited to the Locarno festival were *Otley*, an amusing, light-hearted secret service comedy starring Tom Courtenay and Romy Schneider, and *The Virgin Soldiers* with Hywel Bennett and Lynne Redgrave, which concerned the sexual obsessions of young British soldiers in the Far East.

Also noticeable in Britain was a greater awareness of foreign-language films, although even the most important found only a limited audience. *In The Town of S*, a Russian adaptation of a Chekhov story, was an intelligently amusing film of bitter romance. From Hungary came *Silence and Cry*, directed by Miklos Jancso, a grim village drama of a young Red Army soldier hiding after the defeat of the first Hungarian communist government in 1919. *Stolen Kisses* from France, directed by François Truffaut, was a charming, light-hearted study of adolescence. Finally, the most eagerly awaited film of the year was Russia's adaptation of Tolstoy's *War and Peace*, a 70-mm. feature film in colour, in which the creative force lay in its battle scenes. Said to be the most expensive film ever made, it was shown in two three-hour parts.

Tastes may change, but Westerns and adventure films will remain close to the British filmgoer's heart. This was shown in 1969 by the popularity of films such as *The Wild Bunch*, *The Stalking Moon*, *Where Eagles Dare*, and *The Boston Strangler*. *Che*, starring Omar Sharif, was less successful; the story, relevant for people interested in the revolutionary guerrilla leader Che Guevara, was not exciting enough for general appeal. Similarly, *The Fixer*, a horrific drama of anti-semitism set in period but with an up-to-date message, was brutal and powerful but rather too serious for general success. *The Thomas Crown Affair* and *Ice Station Zebra*, however, had much to recommend them in style, suspense, exciting action, and good casts.

Moves to find an alternative to American monopoly investment in British films were made by Commonwealth United Entertainment, who signed a contract with the U.S.S.R. for a joint venture to produce a film of Tchaikovsky's *Nutcracker Suite*. Shooting will begin in the spring of 1970 at Mosfilm Studios, Moscow. Commonwealth United will have distribution rights in the Western Hemisphere and various other countries. This company, originally Hollywood-based, moved to London at the beginning of 1969, and in the first six months of the year made history by the speed at which it took its position beside the major film companies, its first releases being *You Are What You Eat* and *Cold Day in the Park*.

The Piper and the Tune

BARRIE HALL

H E WHO PAYS the piper calls the tune. If that was ever true, it is true no longer in the world of music. It is doubtful if the Prince Esterhazy who paid Haydn to conduct and to write for his household orchestra would have dictated how Haydn should compose. Had he done so, Haydn could not have been the towering influence and the great innovator that he was. But it is as relevant now as at any time to consider who "pays the piper." The financial situation is basically the same anywhere in the world. Music-making costs more money than audiences can be expected to provide. The cash goes to composers, performers, and designers, in the rent of concert halls and the salaries of stage and managerial staffs, and in printing and advertising. The total sums can be enormous.

Patronage of one kind or another is nearly always necessary to bridge the gap. America supports most of its orchestras and other forms of music-making almost entirely by a form of private patronage (which may also be business patronage, as with the Glyndebourne Opera in Great Britain). Committees of interested individuals raise truly colossal sums. A city as wealthy as Houston, Texas, for instance, can find the money to fly in the Metropolitan Opera from New York for one performance, with a great party afterwards for the cast, and then fly it back again. As a result many American orchestras are extremely rich. So is the Berlin Philharmonic, with players well paid, plenty of rehearsal time, and tours abroad subsidised. But in that case it all comes from the state. The state supports music in Germany, and in Italy (with a long tradition of opera and concerts in all large towns), and carries on where the princely patron had to leave off. Russian and Eastern European music is similarly state-financed. Music-making in Australia follows the pattern of Geneva: the broadcasting organisation runs the principal symphony orchestras, which also give public concerts in addition to their radio work.

Threat to BBC Orchestras

Great Britain has evolved a compromise. Music is partly state-supported by Arts Council grants, and the BBC owns several symphony orchestras in various regions of the country. But the function of the latter is principally to broadcast. With some exceptions (for example, BBC symphony concerts at the Royal Festival Hall, London) these orchestras do not play outside the studios except to invited audiences; in other words, they only use outside halls as extra studios. Consequently proposals made by the BBC in 1969 concerning its own orchestras aroused intense interest—and dismay. The crisis, for such it was, arose through money, or the lack of it. The BBC is financed through licence fees paid by listeners and viewers; it is left to individual honesty, mildly harried by threats of detector vans owned by the Post Office, to pay these fees. Not surprisingly, there are some who do not pay up; the gap in 1969 was put at £7 million.

British television is on the advance, so it was to radio that the BBC turned in order to balance its ledgers. After much heart-searching, it proposed to do away with some of its orchestras as a means of saving itself from financial catastrophe in the years to come. The reaction was predictable up to a point. The Musicians' Union clearly would have gone on strike had the plans been implemented. But the proposals provoked surprising support from all quarters for the BBC's music-making potential. They brought out into the open a strong underlying pride of possession in the regions where the BBC has orchestras outside London. It is not enough that concerts could be broadcast from anywhere in the country (music has even been beamed in from commercial "pop" pirate ships offshore, after all); and gramophone records are not enough, either (although the collapse, in 1969, of Florida's only serious music programme, all on records, brought such a public outcry in America that another sponsor had to be found). Live music-making by live orchestras is a real need. The BBC's orchestras were seen to be far more than the BBC's private concern, and the proposals entered a more public stage, involving the whole fabric of music in Great Britain, with discussions at national level with the Arts Council about the best use to which the orchestras can be put in the general public interest beyond that of the radio audience. What may emerge could be something on the Australian pattern, with the BBC retaining its orchestras, which would also receive public finance in order to give more concerts to paying audiences.

The BBC had approached the crisis on the basis that alone and unaided its own funds were unequal to maintaining the orchestras. But the prospect of losing them struck far more deeply at the nation's cultural life than the provision of broadcast music. No man is an island—nor any orchestra, either. Reduce orchestras in a country, and you reduce the jobs available to musicians—which eventually reduces the music academies and schools, who cannot go on producing players for whom there will never be any work.

Maker of Audiences

In Great Britain there is a man, just turned 90 but as active and brisk as ever, who has spent a life-time being an audience-maker. Sir Robert Mayer spent part of his own fortune in providing concerts for schoolchildren, now a part of Jeunesses Musicales and a huge national organisation in Britain. The late Sir Malcolm Sargent conducted and explained the music, at the beginning of Sir Robert's great experiment. Hundreds of thousands of young people had their first taste of symphonies and concertos through Sargent's efforts and Sir Robert Mayer's enthusiasm for giving children the best. No one knows how many of today's fathers and mothers take *their* children to concerts because Sir Robert gave them a taste for music when they themselves were children.

Sir Robert Mayer, who has introduced three generations of children to music, was 90 on June 5, 1969—an occasion celebrated by a concert in his honour at the Royal Festival Hall, London, which the Queen attended.

Probably many of "Mayer's children" were among those who protested against the BBC's proposals. There is no long tradition of supporting orchestras and opera-houses in Britain. One cannot imagine Germany or Italy proposing to do away with an orchestra or an opera-house; pride of possession and public support are too firmly rooted. Nevertheless, it is in Great Britain, with a comparatively shallow tradition, that the music-lover has the most to choose from. Certainly this is true of London, where there are fifteen or more full concerts every week, plus chamber concerts and recitals, and two opera-houses.

Music in Australia

In Australia, modern music progresses; fourteen composers discussed their work at the Perth Festival, and at Sydney thirteen works were introduced in the season, with three Australian composers talking about theirs. At the other end of the time-scale, where would you expect to find a concert of Iberian and French music of the 13th to 16th centuries, played on vielle, citole, lute, and Moorish guitar? It was at the ninth Easter Music Festival in Mittagong, 80 miles south-west of Sydney. An Australian operatic event in London was a performance of Malcolm Williamson's *The Growing Castle*, given in Australia House by the Australian Music Association of London, backed by four business firms in Australia. Naturally, there were Australian singers, Ronald Dowd, Geoffrey Chard, Margreta Elkins, all working in London's opera-houses. It is said at Sadler's Wells Opera that if the Australians were taken away there would be no principals (and if the Welsh were taken away there would be no chorus).

Sydney's opera-house is still a-building; but it is doing better than Edinburgh, where the city only just saved one theatre from becoming a bingo hall, while it is no nearer starting a proper opera-house for one of the world's great international festivals. Benjamin Britten's new opera-house, the Maltings at Snape (created for his Aldeburgh Festival), was gutted by fire in the middle of the 1969 Festival. On the point of cancelling, Britten had a feeling of "wild, hysterical courage," and housed the events elsewhere. He is determined to resurrect the Maltings by 1970.

A ghost was finally laid in London's famous Royal Albert Hall, when the long-standing echo disappeared after 109 fibreglass "saucers," from 6 to 12 ft. in diameter, were hung from the dome; an inexpensive exercise in exorcism, the acoustic work cost only £8,000. The backs of the saucers are covered with plastic-topped sheets of glass wool, which absorbs the unwanted middle frequencies and reflects the top and bottom frequencies. The Henry Wood Promenade Concerts sounded all the better for this work. World-wide concern was aroused by the BBC's proposal to omit *Land of Hope and Glory* from the Last Night of the

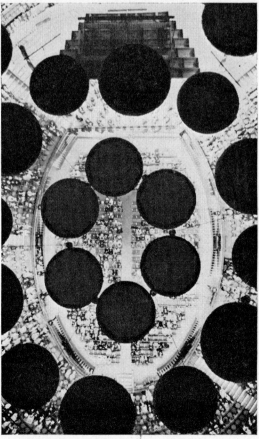

Above: The world-wide celebrations of the centenary of Berlioz's death included this production at Covent Garden of *Les Troyens* complete.

Left: The Royal Albert Hall's notorious echo was finally stilled by the installation in January of more than a hundred fibreglass "saucers" suspended from the dome, from which this striking photo was taken.

Below: Walter Susskind conducting young players from the U.S.A. at the first International Festival of Youth Orchestras at St. Moritz, Switzerland.

Proms. In the event, it was played by popular demand, though its future is uncertain. One faction would like to make the final concert less of a carnival. The other maintains that, having listened attentively to music from Dunstable to Boulez for 51½ nights, letting one's hair down for the last half-evening is not too much. The Proms did well by Berlioz in his centenary year. Georg Solti at Covent Garden (where Colin Davis conducted the complete version of *The Trojans*) pointed out that Berlioz might really have been an English composer, for France did little to celebrate the event, whereas 160 performances were given in England during the first half of 1969 alone.

Conductors in Double Harness

Colin Davis will take over from Solti at the Royal Opera House in 1971, where he will direct jointly with Peter Hall. Sydney's Charles Mackerras takes over at Sadler's Wells, retaining his connection with Hamburg opera. Double harness is becoming quite customary for conductors. Georg Solti takes over Chicago's orchestra, and also joins Bernard Haitink at the London Philharmonic. Haitink already has the Amsterdam Concertgebouw, in the Mengelberg-Van Beinum tradition of being conductor of both. Pierre Boulez, appointed to succeed Colin Davis at the BBC Symphony, tops everyone by accepting also the prestigious New York Philharmonic and the Cleveland Symphony as well. But André Previn, conducting the London Symphony, lost his connection with the Houston Symphony. Leonard Bernstein made his last tour with the New York Philharmonic during 1969, and became their conductor laureate for life. Things are not so happily arranged at the New York Metropolitan Opera. Always about to cancel a season because of strikes and pay demands (it always comes back to money, as general manager Rudolf Bing said of the latest disputes, involving eleven unions), in 1969 for the first time in Bing's eventful twenty years the season did not start—and it showed little sign of ever starting again.

It was a good year for anniversaries. The New York Philharmonic and the *Musical Times* reached their 125th birthday. David Oistrakh celebrated his sixtieth with five long-playing records, an honorary professorship in Budapest, and an honorary D.Mus. at Cambridge, England. For the centenary of Rachmaninov, the Russians began work on a museum in Ivanovka to be opened in 1973. Rimsky-Korsakov's flat in Leningrad is to be restored, too, with the help of his son and daughter, both in their eighties. Schubert's house in Vienna was renovated and re-opened; and as we approached the 1970 bicentenary of Beethoven, his complete works were being issued in a new Henle-Novello edition.

Death . . . and Life

On the other hand, it was also a year for musical mourning. Conductors Ernest Ansermet, Karl Rankl, Fritz Stiedry, Constantin Silvestri, Tauno Hannikainen, and Charles Munch all died; so did the French organist Jeanne Demessieux, pianists Wilhelm Backhaus and Julius Katchen, composer Franz Reizenstein, tenor Giovanni Martinelli, and the Australian baritone John Brownlee, a Melba discovery, who became president of the Manhattan Music School in New York.

In the midst of death, however, we are in life. Young life, vigorous and forward-looking, asserted itself in an International Festival of Youth Orchestras at St. Moritz. Started in Britain by Blyth Major, who conducts minors in his Midlands Youth Orchestra, the Festival involved ten countries, with Switzerland as host. The money came from business; it was all backed by Investors Overseas Services, investing also in the future of music the world over. Thirteen orchestras arrived with their own conductors, and played under them and under Walter Susskind; and in the last concert the leading players from each formed one orchestra playing under Leopold Stokowski, an octogenarian who has always encouraged youth.

Mrs. Rosemary Brown, the London housewife who claimed to have taken down musical compositions dictated by the spirits of long dead composers.

Death's sting was also somewhat drawn during the year by a London housewife, Rosemary Brown, who claimed to have been for some years in regular communication with Liszt, Schubert, Haydn, Beethoven, and scores of other composers on the "other side," and to have taken down music at their dictation. The results were sufficiently impressive for some of the pieces to be published and recorded, including an Impromptu which Schubert not only did not leave unfinished but did not even start.

The television picture of the year: President Nixon, seated in the White House, spoke on July 21 to astronauts Armstrong and Aldrin on the moon, watched live by a vast TV audience of chairbound earthlings.

Broadcasting in Britain

M. J. BRYDEN

IT WAS, ABOVE ALL, a political year for broadcasting. Even the "greatest outside broadcast of all time," the first moon landing—which was watched "live" by hundreds of millions of television viewers throughout the world—was variously pronounced a propaganda triumph for the West; a fillip for American morale, sagging under the relentless pressures of the Vietnam war; or the first glorious step towards inevitable global unity. Television played an integral part in the adventure; a TV camera was attached to the lunar module itself and another actually set up on the moon's surface by the astronauts—who were acutely aware of (and played to) their vast earthbound audience. Indeed, the tremendous impact of the landing stemmed not so much from its heroic, exploratory, or technological elements, but from the fact that the people of the world had *seen* it! It was as if the whole population of earthlings, gazing through their communal electronic eye, had been actually present at this historic moment in the life-time of man.

On the British wavelengths it was more specifically politics—the internal wrangles of broadcasting itself and the way the wider political world shaped, or was shaped by, the medium—that was the dominant theme of 1969. Only the long-awaited advent of colour on BBC 1 and ITV momentarily distracted serious observers of the medium from the high-pitched buzz of battle emanating from behind the screen.

In April an episode in Granada's crime serial *Big Breadwinner Hog* emphasised the increasing public concern with the question of violence on the television screen. An example of gratuitous sadism sparked off one of the biggest single TV rumpuses ever: thousands of viewers telephoned the ITA to complain—indeed a spokesman estimated that "it was probably the greatest number of complaints ever received." The public outcry, including a Commons debate, led inevitably to a tightening of ITA screening procedure. BBC television came in for its perennial share of criticism. In February it was censured for "flippancy" following David Dimbleby's TV commentary on President Nixon's visit to London; it was later attacked savagely (by John Braine, Bernard Levin, and others) for its alleged Left-wing bias; and it was condemned for the sort of shallow, trend-conscious insensitivity that led, in September, to the image of Christ being used as a "plug" for a comedy show on the front cover of *Radio Times*.

Violence on the Screen

From a wider perspective the whole of British broadcasting came in for some searching questioning as to how much it actually *shaped* the world it professed merely to *reflect*.

Upper: **Farewell to the BBC from Simon Dee** (*left*) **who in October signed a £100,000 two-year contract with London Weekend; the Dales, axed in April, with** (*left to right*) **Dorothy Lane (Mrs. Freeman), Charles Simon (Dr. Dale), and Jesse Matthews (Mrs.'Dale); announcer Alvar Lidell, who retired after 37 years.** *Lower:* **Six London Weekend executives resigned after Michael Peacock's September sacking—Frank Muir** (*second from left*), **Joy Whitby** (*next*), **Derek Granger** (*next*), **Terry Hughes** (*sixth from left*), **Doreen Stephens** (*next*), **and Humphrey Burton** (*third from right*). **Others left later.**

Among the incidents that gave concern to many people was the case of the BBC film producer who, while making a *cinéma verité* documentary about a gang of hooligans, calmly filmed the thugs as they rampaged through a small town. It was the fact that the BBC had apparently received information that trouble was in the offing and, instead of informing the authorities, had merely set up their cameras in strategic positions, that infuriated the town's inhabitants. Moreover, who could say whether the raid would have taken place at all had the protagonists not known that their deeds would shine upon the screens in countless homes. Another example came in September when a judge of the Court of Appeal blamed Granada Television for the month-long detention of an Indian immigrant farmer. The detention followed the Indian's fourth attempt to enter the country—an attempt allegedly sponsored by Granada with the object of making a documentary and, in the words of the judge, "causing trouble for the authorities."

During the troubles in Northern Ireland illegal radio stations, broadcasting encouragement and strategic advice to both factions, had to be jammed by army engineers. More significantly, "live" news coverage on television served to alert all partisans in the neighbourhood of any incident. A situation that was difficult to begin with became more so once the TV cameras began to whirr and viewers left their sets for the streets. Moreover, the presence of cameras tends to aggravate a crowd's behaviour. For these reasons the Americans, with their painful experience of street fighting, have abandoned "live" coverage of riots. It seemed, in 1969, that the British authorities might soon have to face the same prickly dilemma: for although "live" coverage tends to exacerbate disorder, at least the viewer knows that he is seeing the truth and cannot complain about biased editing. There remains the question how far the fast-growing wave of politically motivated street violence is actually spawned by television. Mass demonstrations with deliberate manifestations of violence are believed by many to result from a thirst to catch the eye of the camera, and as the public becomes increasingly inured to shock, so each new demonstration has to step up the pace to secure attention.

Unfulfilled Promises

The internal politics of broadcasting itself —in most years merely trivial—assumed a larger significance in 1969. It was the first full year of the new ITV companies (Harlech,

Yorkshire, and London Weekend) following the reshuffle of contracts in 1968. Throughout the year controversy and criticism howled and snapped at the heels of the new companies, chiefly because of their conspicuous failure, in the face of commercial pressure, to fulfil their lofty pre-contract pledges, and the bland manner in which they sought to excuse themselves. This failure was symbolised neatly in May when London Weekend, which had won its contract on a prospectus that specifically emphasised current affairs, actually closed down its Public Affairs Department.

All the new contractors had won their franchises by reflecting in their proposals the modish enthusiasms of the intelligentsia. Great play had been made of "current affairs," "in-depth documentaries," "regionalism," and, inevitably, "the arts," regardless of the fact that most viewers have a far from avid interest in such matters. This specious concern with "raising standards" may have won the new companies their contracts, but doomed them to financial loss. Not only were their ideas uncommercial, but they revealed a shallow conception of quality. Clearly "raising standards" should mean improving the basic TV fare—making poor drama good, good comedy excellent, and so forth—rather than screening low-grade high-brow at peak hours.

Whatever the inherent weakness of the new companies' proposals, the fact that they received their contracts on the strength of them means that they have a moral duty to fulfil them. Moreover, the ITA (the authority which, representing the public interest, presides over the various independent companies, dispenses the franchises, and has the power to withdraw them) has an obvious duty to the public to see that promises are kept. It was therefore a shock to that section of the public

ingenuous enough to believe that statements of intent are made to be honoured, when in August the ITA dismissed criticism of the new companies' shortcomings by announcing that it had not expected them to carry out their pledges anyway! The climax of the controversy arrived on September 18, with the dismissal, following a protracted boardroom battle, of London Weekend's Managing Director, Michael Peacock, the ex-BBC "whiz-kid" who above all others had been identified with expectations of an increased "cultural content" in programmes. Following Peacock's departure six of L.W.T.'s top executives resigned, and a massive political argument erupted over the future of independent television.

BBC's Abortive Plans

The biggest behind-the-screen rumpus of 1969, however, came from the BBC. The year had opened with rumour and speculation concerning the future policy of the Corporation, which was under review by a policy study group. It was known that this committee was concentrating particularly on sound radio, and in May provisional plans were mooted for the scrapping of the existing six regions (Scotland, Wales, Northern Ireland, Midlands, North, South and West) and the introduction of more local radio stations. The tentative proposals were finally crystallised in a report called *Broadcasting in the Seventies*, published on July 10. In this document the BBC announced proposals to alter the whole structure of radio, axing three orchestras, the BBC Chorus, the training orchestra, the Third Programme title, and replacing the three English regions by eight smaller regions. The new scheme outlined plans for a new educational radio channel; declared that Radio Two was to become a light music programme;

Chairman Lord Hill, with Director General Curran (*right*) and Managing Director (Radio) Gillard, facing the critics at a press conference on the BBC's plan for *Broadcasting in the Seventies*.

ordained that Radio Three should broadcast its classical music and serious talks only on the VHF waveband; and set out a blueprint for 40 local stations similar to the eight experimental—and somewhat unsuccessful—local radio stations already operating. These plans were seen as a sacrificial gambit on the part of the BBC to (*a*) save money, and (*b*) spike the guns of the Conservative party, which favours local *commercial* radio stations. The Corporation was suffering from a desperate lack of money and estimated to be losing between £4 million and £5 million per annum, thanks to an unrealistic licence fee (which, for political reasons, the Government was loath to raise) and to the scale of licence evasion, together with the extra demands of the Open University, or University of the Air, starting in 1970, and the tremendous cost of colour television.

Broadcasting in the Seventies was particularly attacked by music lovers enraged over the proposed liquidation of orchestras (see "The Piper and the Tune," page 189), but the lobby mustered against the plans was much wider. Indeed, the document was criticised sharply in the House of Commons by the Postmaster General himself. Machiavellian observers saw behind the BBC's proposals a subtle attempt to force the Government to raise the licence fee, and, sure enough, following talks between the Prime Minister and Charles Curran—the new Director General of the BBC—the Postmaster General announced, on August 14, an increase of 10s. (to £6 10s.) for the combined black-and-white TV and radio licence, to take effect on April 1, 1971, when the separate home and car radio fees of £1 5s. will be abolished. It was further decreed that the orchestras were to be kept "broadly at their present level"; the cultural Radio 3 would not be restricted to VHF (which can be received by only about 33 per cent of the nation's radio sets) but continue on the medium band; and the nation-wide local radio plan would come into effect, 12 stations being added to the 8 already existing before September 1970, and another 20 by 1974.

Programmes of the Year

On the other side of the screen the public observed a decline in programmes, linked perhaps to the enormous costs involved in colour television. Behind the rainbow hues there was a high degree of rubbish revolving round a stupefying staple of old films and "chat shows." Some high peaks, however, stood out from the generally low level, the most prominent being Sir Kenneth Clark's mammoth BBC 2 series *Civilisation*. This cultural epic cost a suitably heroic sum, most

of which must have been expended in transporting the noble savant and his camera crew about the continent of Europe in order to find apposite backcloths. The programmes consisted of lectures on Western civilisations, illustrated by manifold changes of scene, countless works of art, and the cultivated ambience of the ubiquitous lecturer—all of which was excellent television.

Montreux Silver Rose for Marty Feldman.

Civilisation from Sir Kenneth Clark.

One of the most surprising and welcome television successes of 1969 was ITN's extended *News at Ten*. This uncluttered and mature presentation earned such high ratings that the BBC were ruffled enough to give a "new look" to the rival *Twenty-Four Hours* and invent an early evening regional news round-up, called *Nationwide*. In the field of comedy—always a fertile one for quality—Marty Feldman raised the biggest laugh at the Montreux Festival in April but missed the Golden Rose award, taking the Silver. The play of the year was undoubtedly Dennis Potter's *The Son of Man* (BBC 1), a powerful and inevitably controversial portrait of Christ. The most important documentary was the joint BBC–ITV film *Royal Family*, shown in June, an opulent piece of television that caught the subtle mystique of monarchy far more surely than the lengthy "live" coverage of the Investiture of the Prince of Wales on July 1.

A number of "informal" television programmes featuring both Harold Wilson and Edward Heath marked the year, and the public was in some confusion whether these were party political broadcasts or merely programmes of general interest concerning the lives of public figures (which was the case). The most important of these shows was ITV's *The Prime Minister and Mrs. Wilson at Home* (to David Frost). The performance of neither leader could have advanced him far in public favour, but it is significant that they both tried. One day, no doubt, a politician will arise who can play the medium like a stringed instrument. Meanwhile the amateurism of current political leaders is salutary.

The Isle of Wight became a Mecca for Bob Dylan fans on the summer bank holiday weekend. Some 200,000 of them—from all over the world—made the pilgrimage to hear the folk-singer's first public performance since his motor-cycle accident in 1967. He sang 13 songs (for a reputed £35,000) at the three-day Festival, Aug. 30–Sept. 1. Dylan (*inset*) was more lyrical than of old, his voice had softened, and his philosophy appeared to have mellowed.

Pop Grows Up

BOB DAWBARN

Features Editor of *Melody Maker*

POPULAR MUSIC HAS ALWAYS been subject to swift change—yesterday's idols are today's forgotten men. But in 1969 the changes were so rapid and revolutionary that it will take at least another year to assimilate them. At the basis of the revolution was the fact that yesterday's groups had grown up. After a year or two on the scene musicians found that their techniques and musical knowledge had grown to the point where they were no longer satisfied with providing instantly hummable, and equally instantly forgettable, tunes to be sold on innumerable single discs and then forgotten. The signs had been there for some time. The Cream probably laid the foundations although they had split up the previous year. The music they played, at first based on the blues, became more and more complex towards the end,

and surprisingly they had taken their audience with them.

Others followed their example, many rising from the minor boom in blues which encouraged so many pop musicians to try their hands at solos in the jazz style. The new heroes were no longer the prettiest looking aimed at the youngest section of the community. They were groups with names like Fleetwood Mac, Jethro Tull, Nice, Deep Purple. Or long-established groups who had begun to prove their point, like The Who, Moody Blues, Pink Floyd, or Soft Machine.

Unexpectedly the movement paid off. A group like Colosseum, led by a proven jazz drummer, Jon Hiseman, and including one of Britain's best saxophone players, Dick Heckstall-Smith, could not only find an audience for its complicated and exciting music, but could find itself working virtually every night for around £350 a date. The reason was largely the increasing age and affluence of the average pop fan. At the beginning of the year, it was revealed that, for the first time, LPs were outselling single discs; in other words audiences were accepting longer (and more expensive) works than before. With the comparative eclipse of the single, the Hit Parade lost the vice-like grip it had exerted for the last decade.

A major section of the audience was the college and university circuit. Here was a ready-made audience with the intelligence to be able to select the best in the music and, more important perhaps, the funds to pay for it. As the year progressed the colleges became

as Amen Corner, Marmalade, and Love Affair. Equally surprising was the fact that the first of the concerts to sell out starred the esoteric folky Incredible String Band and The Family.

Arrival of Jazz-Rock

One trend, mainly influenced by the recorded success of American groups like Blood, Sweat, and Tears and the Chicago Transit Authority, was a pop-jazz entente—Jazz-Rock as it was called—with groups using brass, reeds and other non-rock instruments and including more and more improvisation in their arrangements. Colosseum were early protagonists in this field; King Crimson and Circus were others. Curiously, Eric Clapton, whose work with the Cream had done so much to

New stars of 1969: (*left to right*) Peter Sarstedt—younger brother of Eden Kane and erstwhile wandering folk-singer—came in from the cold to figure in the hit parade and star in his own TV series; Clodagh Rodgers shot to fame with *Bend Me, Shape Me*; Desmond Dekker—exponent of Reggae and chart-topper with *Israelites*; Bobbie Gentry established herself in London, starring on television and producing a hit—*I'll Never Fall in Love Again.* Photos, *"Melody Maker"*

more and more important, as the power of the smaller beat clubs and ballrooms—so long the basis of the pop business—declined. It was the students who built up groups like Ten Years After, Jethro Tull, Fleetwood Mac, and Chicken Shack into major draws.

Of course, the Beatles, too, had a lot to do with the striving for better music. Their "Sergeant Pepper" album was the lever that had opened the floodgates for more ambitious music. Oddly enough, the Beatles themselves seemed content to mark time in 1969. They had their usual quota of hits and publicity, but their work on LP seemed largely a confirmation of past statements. The broadening of horizons they left largely to others—and there were plenty of willing inheritors.

The way things were changing was highlighted at the end of June when the first Pop Proms were held for a week at London's Royal Albert Hall. The one night that caused the promoters some financial concern was the very night that would have paid for the whole thing a year before—the show aimed at the younger fans with such "teeny-bopper" idols on the bill

launch progressive pop, was to disappoint many of his fans with his new group, Blind Faith, formed with his ex-Cream colleague Ginger Baker. The group made its debut before 150,000 fans drawn from all over the world—a plane-load even travelled from Australia—at a free concert in London's Hyde Park. Whatever the truth of the criticism that Clapton was deliberately underplaying his blues associations, Blind Faith recorded an album, but then retired from view.

Not all the old names went down. The Rolling Stones made a much-publicised comeback with another Hyde Park concert and had a rave tour of America on their first visit there for two years. Mick Taylor, from the group led by the high priest of British blues John Mayall, had earlier replaced Brian Jones with the Stones. Jones died tragically a few weeks later. Mick Jagger, who remained the dominating member, was involved in the biggest pop sensation of the year when he was controversially cast as Ned Kelly in a film about the famous Australian outlaw.

The biggest event in Great Britain was the second Isle of Wight Festival. The first had been something of a débâcle, organised too hurriedly and with few facilities. This time the organisers had a real ace up their sleeves—the first public appearance by Bob Dylan since his motor-cycle accident in 1967. The profits were enormous, the gigantic crowds were well-behaved, but Dylan sounded little like his old self: he was gentler, the hard edge having left his voice and the social comment in his songs having been reduced.

The year brought endless problems for another major group, the Bee Gees, who had ridden high since arriving from Australia a couple of years before. First Vince Melouney left. Then, after months of fraternal strife, Robin Gibb went solo, leaving brothers Barry and Maurice—the latter newly wed to Lulu—to carry on with drummer Colin Peterson. Finally, Peterson went, in a cloud of legal actions which left Barry and Maurice as the sole rightful Bee Gees. There were other splits. Dave Dee, despite continuing success, left his team-mates Dozy, Beaky, Mick, and Tich to carry on without him. Julie Driscoll parted company with organist Brian Auger and the Trinity, and went into seclusion to re-think her career. Noel Redding left the Jimi Hendrix Experience to form a new group, Fat Mattress. The Mothers of Invention, arch-satirists of pop, broke up. Steve Marriott left The Small Faces and formed Humble Pie. Manfred Mann gave up his hugely successful group, and with his drummer Mike Hugg formed Chapter Three, jazz-based, complete with brass and saxes.

Newcomers to the Scene

A couple of interesting newcomers were Clodagh Rodgers and Peter Sarstedt, both of whom sold a lot of records. Clodagh had been trying for some time to establish herself as a country and western singer when she was given a straight pop song, *Bend Me, Shape Me*, to record. It made her a star overnight. Sarstedt was a little more unusual. The brother of Eden Kane, who had been a regular maker of hits in Britain in the early 1960s before leaving for Australia, he wrote all his own songs. They were sophisticated and often both humorous and witty. BBC series on both TV and radio assured him of a large following.

Undoubtedly the most curious phenomenon of the year was Reggae. This was the old West Indian blue beat and ska of former years dressed up with a new name. Its heroes were largely Jamaicans like Desmond Dekker and Max Romeo; it was Dekker who made the breakthrough with a chart-topping single disc called *Israelites*. The music relied on a

Rolling Stone Mick Jagger singing to some 150,000 fans at a free concert in London's Hyde Park in June. A similar Rolling Stone concert held near Tracy, California, in December, attracted about 300,000.

heavy beat and the utmost simplicity; the lyrics were frequently highly suggestive. That Reggae should catch on was odd enough. Odder still was the fact that its devotees were largely the white teenagers who came to be known as "skinheads," the crop-headed gangs who wore boots and braces and allegedly caused trouble at football matches in their general search for violence and mayhem. No doubt they were reacting against the intellectualisation of pop which their elders and "betters" preferred. By the end of the year, Reggae had become so big that the mere name guaranteed full houses.

Revival of Big Bands

British groups continued to dominate the American scene, notably the long-running Who who hit a peak with their pop opera *Tommy*, Led Zeppelin, a tough, rocking group led by Jimmy Page and formed after the demise of The Yardbirds, and the aforesaid Rolling Stones. But, in reverse, an odd off-shoot of this odd year was the success of old-fashioned dance bands imitating the style of Glenn Miller. In the year of the 25th anniversary of Miller's death they mushroomed in Great Britain—and drew the crowds. Big bands, too, returned to make an impact on the British jazz scene. There were the usual tours by Duke Ellington and Buddy Rich, but the biggest impact was made by two bands visiting the country for the first time, both playing at Ronnie Scott's London club. The first, the Kenny Clarke-Francy Boland Big Band, was remarkable not least for the fact that its members were drawn from some seven countries, including the U.S.A., the U.K., Belgium, and Yugoslavia. Between them they made the band swing as bands have not swung since the 1930s. The second band, America's Thad Jones-Mel Lewis Orchestra, also had two leaders and a personnel that read like a *Who's Who* of jazz. It concentrated more on its soloists and arrangements than on the uninhibited ensembles favoured by the Clarke-Boland outfit.

There were celebrations to mark the birthday of Duke Ellington, unbelievably 70, and joy over the recovery of Louis Armstrong who bounced back with the famous grin after almost a year's lay-off including a long spell in hospital. As is unhappily so often the case, it was the jazz deaths that caught the imagination. Three giants were all silenced in 1969. First was George Lewis who, with Bunk Johnson, did so much to popularise New Orleans jazz in the earliest days of the Revival in the 1940s. Then there was Pee Wee Russell, most individual of all jazz clarinettists. Finally, there was the death of Coleman Hawkins, the man who almost single-handed had dragged the tenor saxophone to respectability as a solo instrument in the early 1930s. Others were the veteran drummer Paul Barbarin, and two British musicians, guitarist Dave Goldberg and trumpeter Bert Courtley.

A brighter note was struck by the tenth anniversary celebrations of Ronnie Scott's club. Many had thought Scott demented

John and Yoko Lennon staged a week-long "lie-in for peace" at the Amsterdam Hilton, during March

when he started to run a full-time London jazz night club in 1958. It has had its ups and downs since, but it still remains the most important club in Great Britain and still feeds its regulars with a diet of the best American, as well as British and Continental, musicians.

In general, economics still made full-time jazz playing a virtual impossibility for most musicians. Musically, things were highly encouraging. The younger musicians, like Keith Tippett, Alan Skidmore (tenor saxist son of a tenor saxist father), and Mike Westbrook were erasing the cool, unconcerned image of many older jazzmen; they brought to jazz club stands enthusiasm and excitement that had been missing for 20 years. Alan Skidmore —and guitarist Louis Stewart from the Tubby Hayes Quartet—received recognition by winning the annual Montreux Jazz Festival and being offered scholarships at America's famous Berklee music school. Stewart decided to accept the offer, but Skidmore declined.

The difficulties of the new breed of *avant garde* jazzmen were highlighted when John Surman left Great Britain to live and work on the Continent only months after being the first local musician to be voted "Musician of the Year" in the annual poll of jazz critics conducted by *Melody Maker*. For many British jazzmen—the brilliant young Australian alto-saxist and flautist Ray Warleigh was a good example—the new Jazz-Rock groups provided the answer to financial problems, and many of them worked regularly on the same stands as pop musicians. 1969 was, in fact, musically one of the most exciting years in British jazz and pop for a long time.

RECORDS THAT TOPPED THE HIT PARADE IN 1969

Compiled from "Melody Maker's" weekly chart

Lily the Pink	The Scaffold	1 week
Ob-la-di Ob-la-da	Marmalade	3 weeks
Albatross	Fleetwood Mac	2 weeks
Blackberry Way	The Move	1 week
Half as Nice	Amen Corner	2 weeks
Where do You Go to?	Peter Sarstedt	4 weeks
I Heard it through the Grapevine	Marvin Gaye	3 weeks
Israelites	Desmond Dekker	1 week
Get Back	The Beatles	5 weeks
Dizzy	Tommy Roe	2 weeks
Ballad of John and Yoko	The Beatles	3 weeks
Something in the Air	Thunderclap Newman	1 week
In the Ghetto	Elvis Presley	1 week
Honky-Tonk Woman	Rolling Stones	5 weeks
In the Year 2525	Zager and Evans	3 weeks
Bad Moon Rising	Creedence Clearwater Revival	2 weeks
I'll Never Fall in Love Again	Bobbie Gentry	2 weeks
Sugar Sugar	The Archies	6 weeks
Yester-me Yester-you Yesterday	Stevie Wonder	1 week
Two Little Boys	Rolf Harris	4 weeks

Exploration and Adventure

*Statue in a suburb of
Malaga, Spain, to the
crew of Apollo 11,
commemorating the first
Moon landing*

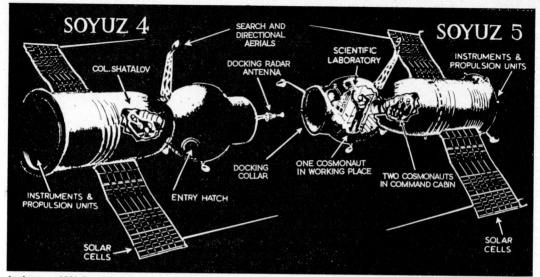

SOYUZ 4 — COL. SHATALOV — SEARCH AND DIRECTIONAL AERIALS — DOCKING RADAR ANTENNA — SCIENTIFIC LABORATORY — SOYUZ 5 — INSTRUMENTS & PROPULSION UNITS — INSTRUMENTS & PROPULSION UNITS — ENTRY HATCH — DOCKING COLLAR — ONE COSMONAUT IN WORKING PLACE — TWO COSMONAUTS IN COMMAND CABIN — SOLAR CELLS — SOLAR CELLS

In January 1969 Russia's Soyuz 4 (carrying one man) and Soyuz 5 (carrying three) docked some 130 miles above the Earth. After two cosmonauts had transferred from 5 to 4, the spacecraft separated and landed safely 500 miles apart.

Soyuz, Space Probes, and Satellites

L. J. CARTER
Secretary of the British Interplanetary Society

WHILE THE MOON-LANDINGS by the crews of Apollo 11 and 12 overshadowed all other space news during 1969 it was by no means an inactive year for space exploration by other men and other spacecraft. Most interesting was the resumption by the U.S.S.R. of manned orbital flight. This began with Soyuz 4 and 5. First, Soyuz 4, carrying Col. Vladimir Shatalov, was launched from Baikonur on January 14 into a 108–140 mile orbit, subsequently increased to 129–148 miles. Soyuz 5 followed the next day, placing its crew of Col. Boris Volynov, Lt.-Col. Yevgeny Khrunov, and Alexei Yeliseyev into an initial 125–144 mile orbit several hundred miles N.E. of Soyuz 4, but travelling at the same speed. Soyuz 5 increased its speed for the next 24 hours to close the distance: on January 16, when the craft were less than 20 miles apart, an automatic approach system was switched on in both command modules, Soyuz 4 being the active spacecraft and Soyuz 5 the passive. The two spacecraft were then joined together for about 4½ hours before separating again.

A "space walk" by Yeliseyev and Khrunov took place on the 35th orbit of Soyuz 4 and the 18th of Soyuz 5, after which they transferred to Soyuz 4. Although the men spent an hour in the space environment, their actual time outside the spacecraft was only a few minutes. Soyuz 4 landed on the 17th, 25 miles N.W. of Karaganda. The actual re-entry was performed automatically, using the lifting-body characteristics of the descent module. Soyuz 5, now carrying Volynov alone, continued in orbit to perform some additional manoeuvres, landing the following day 125 miles S.W. of Kustani and about 500 miles W. of the Soyuz 4 landing point.

The Russians moved closer to their goal of constructing a permanent manned station in

Crews of Soyuz 4 and 5. *Left to right:* Lt.-Col. Yevgeny Khrunov, Col. Vladimir Shatalov, Col. Boris Volynov, and civilian Alexei Yeliseyev.

Crews of Soyuz 6, 7, and 8. *Left to right:* **Col. Shatalov** (also in Soyuz 4), **Lt.-Col. Viktor Gorbasko, Valery Kubasov, Lt.-Col. Anatoly Filipchenko, Alexei Yeliseyev** (also in Soyuz 5), **Vladislav Volkov,** and **Lt.-Col. Georgy Shonin.**

space with the flights of Soyuz 6, 7, and 8, launched from Tyuratam on successive days beginning on October 11. Soyuz 7 (with Lt.-Col. Anatoly Filipchenko, Vladislav Volkov, and Lt.-Col. Viktor Gorbasko) was launched on the 12th, about 10 minutes before Soyuz 6 (carrying Lt.-Col. Georgy Shonin and Valery Kubasov) was due to pass almost directly overhead, with the result that the two spacecraft were placed in nearly identical orbits only a few miles apart. At one point Soyuz 7 and Soyuz 8 (carrying Shatalov and Yeliseyev) were within 1,500 ft. of each other and flew in formation for several hours. Over 50 orbital changes were made by the three spacecraft during their mission. During the flight experiments were carried out with three different welding techniques—electron beam welding, consumable electrode welding, and compressed-arc-plasma welding—all vitally necessary before large antennae can be built in space, or manned space platforms assembled.

The three craft landed safely at one-day intervals beginning on October 16. They were manually orientated for retro-fire, with final recovery by parachute and rocket braking.

Space Probes to Venus and Mars

Modified Vostok rockets were used by the Russians to launch two probes towards the planet Venus—Venus 5 on January 5 and Venus 6 on the 10th. Both were designed to make "soft" descents into the atmosphere of the planet on the side away from the Sun, in mid-May. Two identical craft were used in order to cross-check results from various points as they moved along their Earth–Venus trajectory, to provide data from different parts of the planet on arrival, and to cover the failure of either of them during flight.

A capsule from Venus 5 was ejected on May 16 and one from Venus 6 the following day. The two capsules, about 185 miles apart, showed that the pressure of the atmosphere on Venus was probably 70–90 times that of the Earth, instead of 15–20 times as had previously been thought. As a result, the capsules were probably crushed as they descended by parachute. Before ceasing to transmit, they showed a temperature rising from 13° to 28°C. and an atmosphere consisting of 93–97 per cent carbon dioxide, 2–5 per cent nitrogen and other gases, and only about 0·4 per cent oxygen.

The Americans launched two probes to Mars, both by Atlas-Centaur rockets, from Cape Kennedy. Mariner 6 set out on its fly-by mission on February 24, carrying two TV cameras, an infra-red spectrometer, and ultra-violet spectrometers to probe the atmosphere of the planet. Mariner 7, an identical "back-up" spacecraft, followed on March 28. The total distance covered by Mariner 7 to reach Mars was 197,137,830 miles: it was 61,869,120 miles from Earth at the point of nearest encounter. Mariner 6 travelled 241,838,160 miles to reach the planet, and was 59,525,861 miles from Earth at its nearest encounter with Mars.

On July 30 Mariner 6 passed by the planet at a distance of 2,120 miles, and obtained spectacular photographs of its equatorial belt, revealing thousands of Moon-like craters. Mariner 7 passed by at the same distance on August 5, and obtained detailed photographs of the southern polar cap. Mariner 6 took 74 pictures, 24 of them during the near-encounter; Mariner 7 took 91 pictures, 33 of them during the near-encounter. In the pictures the craters did not appear as high or as sharply marked as those on the Moon. "Snow" deposits were seen near the South Pole, lining crater walls, on the floors of maria, and in valleys and low areas; they are unlikely to be frozen water, and are more likely carbon dioxide.

Although it seems to resemble a cratered, arid Moon, Mars has some quite distinctive features, including a particularly chaotic area

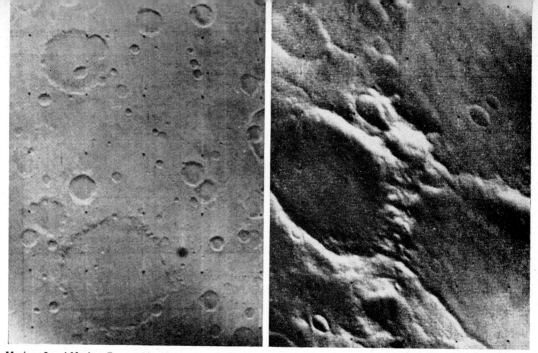

Mariner 6 and Mariner 7 passed by Mars at 2,120 miles. *Left:* Mariner 6's view of a few of the craters in the equatorial belt. *Right:* Enlargement of the "Giant's Footprint," two craters in the South polar cap, recorded by Mariner 7.

of nearly 500,000 sq. miles and a "featureless" region, a plain of unrelieved flatness. No evidence of clouds was found in the pictures, but Mars has an atmospheric haze. This was deduced from looking at pictures of the edge of the planet taken with blue, green, and yellow filters. The haze appears to be between 5 and 10 miles thick, and starts at a height of 10 miles above the planet. It is, of course, extremely thin. The air on Mars is at least 98 per cent carbon dioxide—perhaps even 100 per cent—and has no trace of any of the life-sustaining elements, such as nitrogen and oxygen. Mars is an exceptionally cold place; temperatures during the day range from $-63°$ to $62°F.$, and at night-time they range from $-63°$ to $-163°F.$ Life as we know it on Earth seems very improbable on Mars. If there are any life-forms, they are most likely to be only microscopic.

On August 27 the 147-lb. Pioneer 10, containing seven scientific experiments, was launched into a highly unusual solar orbit which will keep the spacecraft relatively close to the Earth, yet outside its magnetosphere, for 3–4 years, at distances ranging from 2 million to 10 million miles. This orbital arrangement will allow the greatest amount of information about solar environment to be received, since the satellite will remain close enough to the Earth to make maximum use of its data return system. Pioneer 10 was the last of the initial series, but design studies, using the same technology, have extended the value of the craft to undertake deep-space missions as far out as the planet Jupiter in 1972–73.

Scientific Satellites

The half-ton Orbiting Geophysical Observatories (OGO) continued to provide a new concept of near space—an invisible but furiously active world of hypersonic, highly energised particles which occasionally penetrate the Earth's protective magnetic envelope. OGO-5, in a highly elliptical orbit that takes it 70,000 miles from the Earth, mapped for the first time a large part of the sky in the intensity of Lyman Alpha radiation from hydrogen gases in the Milky Way. It was followed by the 1,400-lb. box-like OGO-6, on June 5, which carried a further 25 experiments into a 248–683 mile polar orbit, to add to the 1·2 million hours of scientific data already returned by earlier OGOs and completing a programme which first began in 1964.

Interesting results were received from the 414-lb. radio-astronomy satellite Explorer 38, orbiting 3,640 miles above the Earth. This satellite has four 750-ft.-long tubular antennae, which, extended in orbit, give it an overall length of 1,500 ft. The satellite showed that the Earth, like the planet Jupiter, sporadically emits low-frequency radio signals, provided the first low-frequency radio map of radio emissions in our galaxy, and also revealed that the Sun is a much more active source of radio outbursts in the lower frequencies than had been expected. This is quite important because it can provide the only means apart from space probes of studying the Sun's atmosphere out to the 36-million-mile distance of the orbit of Mercury.

On June 21, 1969, Explorer 41 (the seventh in the Interplanetary Monitoring Platform series) entered a very elongated orbit extending 135,000 miles into space, carrying twelve experiments to study the solar plasma, magnetic fields, and cosmic rays. It was designed to continue the study of Earth–Moon radiation environment, which began with the launch of Explorer 18 in 1963.

Two more spacecraft were launched to examine the Sun—the 641-lb. Orbiting Solar Observatory OSO-5 into a 335–349 mile orbit on January 22, and the 640-lb. OSO-6 into a 300–340 mile orbit on August 9. Both entered near-circular orbits and contained comparable experiments, but OSO-6 included a new feature which allowed its two Sun-pointing telescopes to study in detail the ultra-violet and X-ray spectra at any point on the Sun's disc, and so provide further information about the Sun's atmosphere as well as its corona. These Sun-monitoring satellites also provide a valuable early warning of solar flares, for radiation from major Sun-storms could be a potential threat to astronauts on the Moon, besides affecting the weather on Earth and disrupting long-distance radio communications. The four previous OSO craft have returned more than 10,000 hours of scientific information about the Sun.

Interesting results were received from the 4,400-lb. Orbiting Astronomical Observatory OAO-2, launched on December 7, 1968, and circling in a 480-mile almost-circular orbit. The largest and most complex of the American scientific satellites, it has a pointing stability comparable to that of a marksman holding his rifle sight for many minutes on a bullseye less than 2 inches across at a distance of 1 mile. The 11 telescopes in OAO-2 are studying the extremely hot young stars, which emit most of their energy or light in the ultra-violet—the blue portion of the spectrum invisible to the human eye or ground observatories because of the Earth's atmosphere. One package of four telescopes scans about 700 stars daily; the other, a group of seven telescopes, is focused on single stars.

The 2-ton OAO-2 mapped about a quarter of the sky in 6 months, taking over 1,000 pictures of individual stars, constellations, and galaxies, a quarter of which were "unique"— that is they showed either new stars previously undetected or known stars seen in a new light. Some of the stars appear to be "ageing" about twice as fast as was previously thought, by burning their hydrogen at a very rapid rate. But a mystery is the discovery of intense light from several old galaxies, e.g. the Andromeda Galaxy (M31), and very little from others.

On January 30 the 532-lb. Canadian-built ISIS-1 satellite entered a 356–2,184 mile orbit. This was the third ionospheric satellite to be launched in a U.S.A.–Canada project to continue the study of the ionosphere from above. On October 1 the 176-lb. ESRO 1B satellite (christened *Boreas* on launch) successfully entered a near-circular orbit with eight experiments, to study the polar ionosphere, the Northern Lights, and related phenomena. This was a back-up version of ESRO 1 (*Aurora*) which was successfully placed in a highly

Examples of the varied unmanned probes and satellites that explored space in 1969. *Left:* a Russian Venus probe, topped by a capsule such as was launched to land on Venus in May. *Centre:* American OGO-6 (Orbiting Geophysical Observatory), launched in June. *Right:* American ATS-5 (Applications Technology Satellite), launched in August into sychronous orbit 22,300 miles above the Earth; this is an experimental communications and navigation satellite.

elliptical near-polar orbit on October 3, 1968, and was still operating, but *Boreas* had only a short life-time, re-entering the Earth's atmosphere on November 23. *Boreas* was a co-operative project between the U.S.A. and the 10-nation ESRO organisation.

Shortly afterwards, on November 8, the first satellite in a co-operative space programme between Germany and the U.S.A. was launched in a near-polar orbit. This was *Azur*, a 157-lb. satellite which carried seven scientific experiments to study the Earth's radiation belt, the aurorae, and solar particles.

The 1,900-lb. ATS-5 was launched from Cape Kennedy on August 12, to carry 13 experiments into space, and joined its two companions in synchronous orbit 22,300 miles above the Earth. It carried an L-band repeater which uses an as yet uncrowded set of frequencies in the upper reaches of the radio spectrum, to help develop an improved system of using satellites for aircraft communications and navigation.

Of weather satellites, ESSA-9 on February 26 entered an almost circular 900-mile near-polar orbit to join its companions in providing Earth-weather reports which have now been transmitted continually for almost a decade. On April 14 the 1,200-lb. *Nimbus*-3 successfully entered a 675–703 mile orbit. This 10-ft.-tall

craft, the most advanced weather satellite yet built, was designed to measure for the first time the atmospheric temperature from ground to space, and to interrogate weather-data instruments such as balloons, ocean buoys, aeroplanes, and ships for relay to a ground station for analysis. Besides two new infra-red electronic sensors to measure temperature—a key ingredient in weather forecasting—*Nimbus*-3 carried advanced TV cameras for day and night-time pictures of cloud systems. Some 400 stations in 43 countries can pick up local overhead cloud pictures directly from this satellite.

Preliminary results average 5,000 readings each day from the Earth's surface to an altitude 15 miles high, covering the entire globe once every 12 hours. Later *Nimbus* satellites will monitor the vast uncovered oceans and poles as well as the land areas, immediately, cheaply, and repeatedly. Tens of thousands of radio-sondes (weather-data-gathering balloons) now in use will gradually be eliminated.

Two Soviet weather-gathering satellites also appeared during the year. Meteor 1 entered a 400–430 mile orbit on March 26, followed by Meteor 2 in a similar orbit on April 6. Both were designed to measure cloud cover, to detect the presence of snow, and to record the Earth's heat-energy balance.

Example of the photographs taken by satellites that meteorologists use as a basis for weather forecasts. It shows cloud cover over the Pacific Ocean, from Australia and New Zealand *(bottom left)* to the U.S.A. *(top right)*.

Three lone yachtsmen high and dry in June: Robin Knox-Johnston, the first non-stop single-handed circumnavigator (*left*), chatting to thwarted rival Nigel Tetley (*centre*) and Sir Francis Chichester.

Feats of Courage and Endurance

JACK MAXWELL

IN A YEAR THAT bristled with daring exploits—fabulous feats and desperate failures—there can be no doubt which proved the epic of them all: the incredible climax, and anti-climax, of the round-the-world non-stop single-handed yacht race sponsored by the *Sunday Times*, London. The summer of 1968 had seen the start of this ambitious event with competitors sailing from British ports between June 1 and October 31. By 1969 wind, wave, and ill-health had already taken their toll, and of the nine competitors five had been forced to withdraw. Of the four that remained only one was to reach his destination, yet all were to loom dramatically in the headlines of the year.

The leading contestant, Robin Knox-Johnston, in his slow-but-sure 32-ft. ketch *Suhaili*, had set out on June 14, 1968, and had not been heard from since he was seen off New Zealand on November 21. As the months went by there were many who thought that the gigantic seas off Cape Horn had battered his already damaged craft to pulp and swallowed her gallant helmsman. Meanwhile Bernard Moitessier in his fast 42-ft. all-steel ketch *Joshua*, who had left Plymouth on August 28, 1968, was hot favourite for both the Golden Globe trophy for the first man home and the £5,000 prize for the fastest circumnavigation. On February 10, 1969, he was sighted off the Falklands, and experienced yachtsmen

confidently estimated that he would arrive in Plymouth on or about April 24. In fact the most gifted of nautical pundits could not have foreseen the incredible course events—and *Joshua*—were to take. For on March 18 Moitessier and his yacht were seen scudding past Cape Town, thousands of miles off course, and heading round the world for the second time!

He had succumbed to a mystical brand of sea fever and sailed on, still observing the rules of the race he had abandoned, for another three months until he dropped anchor at Papeete in Tahiti, where he emerged bearded, bronzed, and fit having completed the longest non-stop solo voyage ever made. He had sailed 35,000 miles at an average speed of 117·2 miles a day, but explained to reporters: "Talking of records is stupid, an insult to the sea. . . . You have to understand that when a man is months and months alone, he evolves; some say people go nuts. I went crazy in my own fashion. For four months all I saw were the stars. I didn't hear an unnatural sound. A purity grows out of this kind of solitude."

On April 5, some weeks after Moitessier had abandoned the race, the "missing" Robin Knox-Johnston was sighted by a tanker 500 miles west of the Azores. He had not been heard from for 134 days. His self-steering gear was broken, his fresh-water tanks had been flooded, but he was now on the last leg of his incredible voyage, with his head set firmly towards his port of embarkation, Falmouth. Here he arrived just after 5 p.m. on April 22, amidst an armada of small craft and two escorting mine-sweepers. The first man home had spent 312 days at sea (nine more than Moitessier, although he covered less distance), so that although he had secured the Golden Globe trophy, the race for the £5,000 was still in dispute, and one of the two trimarans sailed by Nigel Tetley and Donald Crowhurst seemed destined to win it.

Bernard Moitessier, the French competitor in the non-stop single-handed round-the-world race who started a second circumnavigation, ending by having sailed 35,000 miles.

Tetley, in his swift trimaran *Victress*, had already rounded the Horn and on the day of Knox-Johnston's triumph he had crossed his own outward track—thus becoming the first man to round the world in a multi-hulled craft. But three weeks later he radioed England with news of a battering from the north-east trade winds that had nearly sunk the *Victress*. Several of her bow deck timbers had shifted, and she was "leaking like a colander."

Tetley approached the Azores with reports that his rival for the big prize, Donald Crowhurst, had rounded the Horn and that there was likely to be a close race for the money. On May 22, however, came the news that, tantalisingly close to home, the *Victress* had sunk in high winds 100 miles north of the Azores. Nigel Tetley had been woken from sleep at midnight, May 21, alerted by an ominous scraping sound which proved to be the port bow adrift and rubbing against the centre hull. Water was gushing in so fast that the lone sailor had barely time to rush to his radio to send out a "mayday" signal before abandoning the vessel. By mid-morning the following day, one of the searching aircraft from the U.S.A.F. base in the Azores spotted him waving from his rubber dinghy, and he was eventually picked up by a Liberian tanker bound for the West Indies, where he landed on May 29.

Attention now turned to the only remaining contestant still at sea, Donald Crowhurst, who was then expected at his home port of Teign-

mouth about July 1—a certain winner of the £5,000 prize. As the weeks went by *Teignmouth Electron* was reported heading steadily homewards. On June 22 the *Sunday Times* reported that Crowhurst's estimated position was 600 miles south-west of the Azores—only two weeks' sailing from Teignmouth where the citizens were busily preparing a gigantic welcome. Thus it was a tremendous shock when the communications centre at Plymouth received the following message from the British Royal Mail ship *Picardy* on Thursday, July 10: "Trimaran *Teignmouth Electron*, Bridgwater, regret found abandoned, position 33° 11' N. 40° 28' W. Hoisted on board. The owner lone sailor Donald Crowhurst. Personal papers, logs, BBC films and tapes, etc., found on board. Vessel unharmed. Yachtsman is missing."

Not only was the yacht's log book undisturbed, so were her dinghy and emergency life-raft. The mainsail was furled, but the fact that the two foresails were lying on the deck gave rise to the theory that Donald Crowhurst had slipped and fallen overboard while hoisting canvas. For two days a fruitless air search scanned the area. There the matter would have rested had not a close examination of Crowhurst's papers revealed the startling fact that, during her entire voyage of 243 days, *Teignmouth Electron* had never left the Atlantic Ocean but had followed an erratic course while her skipper had radioed misleading signals about his position. He had moreover put into Brazil for repairs, thus breaking the cardinal rule of the non-stop race. Whether Crowhurst had set out deliberately to defraud or whether the stress of his lone battle with the sea had undermined his judgment and integrity is not known. All that can be said is that the films and tapes he recorded for the BBC (which were shown to the viewing public on July 26) revealed him as relaxed, cheerful, and as well-balanced as a man alone on the ocean could reasonably be expected to be. Only his private log testified that he was under mental stress.

Walking across the Arctic

Another adventure of epic scale that was well under way as the year began was the British Transarctic Expedition that had set out in February 1968 to walk the 3,800 miles of treacherous ice that spans the Arctic Ocean. During January 1969 the four-man team and their 35 huskies were still in winter camp, perched on a tiny ice floe and drifting slowly in the wrong direction. Their position lay some 250 miles from the North Pole, and their original plan—which had been to build

Adventurers Afloat

Above: Robin Knox-Johnston—the only competitor to complete the round-the-world single-handed yacht race—greets a passing ship with a raucous rendering from *The Pirates of Penzance*. The lone circumnavigator is standing in the cockpit of his 32-ft. Indian-built ketch *Suhaili*, and this picture clearly shows the craft's canoe stern which he found an invaluable asset while sailing in heavy seas. Knox-Johnston arrived in Falmouth on April 22, 1969, where he was able to reply to the customs officer's obligatory question "Where from?" with the satisfying answer "Falmouth!" He had been 312 days at sea.

Left: The papyrus craft *Ra* built by the Norwegian anthropologist and adventurer of *Kon-Tiki* fame, Thor Heyerdahl, in which he and a brave six-man crew attempted to sail the Atlantic to lend weight to his theory that the ancient Egyptians crossed to Central America in similar primitive boats to found early ci ilisations there. The strange vessel's square sail (furled here) carried an emblem reminiscent of a Van Gogh sun—the symbol of the boat's namesake, Ra, the ancient Egyptian sun-god. Heyerdahl confidently predicted that the papyrus craft would stand up to a journey of three or four months from the Moroccan port of Safi to the Caribbean islands. Experts on papyrus were less sanguine, forecasting a wet shark-delighting end to the voyage in less than three weeks. In the event Fate worked out a compromise and, almost two months after leaving Safi, it was announced on July 20 that the "ancient mariners" had been forced to abandon a sodden sinking *Ra* and take to an escorting vessel 625 miles from Barbados.

The Round Britain Powerboat Race 1969

The year saw the first *Daily Telegraph* and B.P. £10,000 Round Britain Powerboat Race. At 9 a.m. on July 26, Prince Philip pressed a button (*top right*) and the crack of a maroon rang over Portsmouth, followed by a thunderous roar as the 43 competing craft accelerated away on the first of the ten punishing legs and 11 days of the 1,700 nautical mile race. The overall winner was **Avenger Too** (*above*) piloted by Timo Makinen—the "Flying Finn"—(festooned *left*), co-piloted by Pascoe Watson (wielding the champagne), and crewed by Brian Hendicott. The early stages of the race featured a duel between **Avenger Too, Maltese Magnum Twin, U.F.O.,** and **Gee**. The Inverness to Dundee leg, however, raced in thick fog, saw **Magnum Twin** wrecked on a sand bank and **U.F.O.** stuck beside her—losing five hours—while **Gee** retired with mechanical trouble. Meanwhile the foxy Finn trailed a vessel equipped with radar through the fog and built up an unassailable lead. Tim Powell in **U.F.O.**, however, did his best to catch him, finishing in second place only 19 minutes behind the winner. Of the 43 competing craft (worth some £500,000) only 24 finished. Nevertheless, the event proved so popular that it may well become an annual fixture on the sporting calendar.

The four-man British Transarctic Expedition (*above*) were the first men to walk the 3,800 miles of shifting ice that spans the Arctic Ocean. Map (*below*) shows their incredible route from Point Barrow to Spitsbergen via the Pole.

their winter camp where the drift of sea-ice would carry them steadily on their way, beyond the Pole, towards Spitsbergen—had misfired when they had lost vital time through injury.

While this was frustrating, other more palpable causes for anxiety arose to disturb the explorers' equanimity as they went about their 13-hour-day, seven-days-a-week winter work programme, gathering scientific data and preparing for the grind ahead. Colliding floes, fractures in the ice, and temperatures as low as 77° below zero all served to harass, but the most pressing worry was the condition of Alan Gill who had injured his back in a fall the previous autumn. An attempt to rescue Gill by aircraft soon after the accident had failed owing to adverse weather conditions, and, strapped to a sled, he had been hauled to the winter camp where he was gradually nursed back to fitness. By the time the team were preparing to break camp, Gill was up and about, but there remained serious doubts whether his back could stand up to the rigours ahead. Indeed by mid-February it had been decided to evacuate him, and a substitute was standing by in Canada ready to take his place as soon as the Polar night had rolled away and conditions favoured a landing. In the event, however, Alan Gill proved fit enough to remain on the ice. Sledging began on February 24, following a dramatic crack in the floe which split the winter camp in twain.

As the team headed their dogs over the first of the 1,500 miles that lay between them and Spitsbergen, they knew that they were engaged in a race against the as yet unseen sun. For with the coming of full daylight, the ice—treacherous enough in the cast-iron cold of winter—would begin to melt. With this constantly in mind, Wally Herbert and his comrades inched their battered sleds and spurred their huskies over the shifting sheaf of broken sea-ice throughout March, sometimes spending whole days hacking their way through

jagged ribs of ice rearing high into the air. On March 27, when the Royal Canadian Air Force dropped them supplies, they were still 90 miles from the Pole and the sun was shining overhead. The dogs, however, reinvigorated by fresh meat dropped by the Canadians, picked up speed and on April 5 the explorers reached the North Pole, the first Britons ever to do so on foot.

Herbert sent the following message to the Queen: "I have the honour to inform your Majesty that today, April 5, at 0700 hours G.M.T., the British Transarctic Expedition, by dead reckoning, reached the North Pole, 407 days after setting out from Point Barrow, Alaska. My companions of the crossing party, Alan Gill, Major Kenneth Hedges, R.A.M.C, and Dr. Roy Koerner, together with Squadron-Leader Church, R.A.F., our radio relay officer at Point Barrow, are in good health and spirits, and hopeful that by forced marches and a measure of good fortune the expedition will reach Spitsbergen by Mid-

o

summer's Day of this year, thus concluding, in the name of our country, the first surface crossing of the Arctic Ocean."

Only two days later the team's soaring morale was drastically lowered when a fire engulfed and completely consumed one of their two tents, ruining Alan Gill's sleeping bag. A month later, when they were 360 miles from Spitsbergen and averaging 11 miles a day, another hair-raising episode underlined the dangers of the trek when the luckless Gill, his sled, and its dog team narrowly missed being swallowed by ice "boiling like stew." Another hazard came on four legs—polar bears constantly menaced the party. Roy Koerner hurled a boot at one lumbering bear that came too close: the beast caught the missile and, with two massive crunches, ate it. Visiting bears proved completely fearless; indeed the only emotions they displayed were curiosity and an eager desire to eat the members of the expedition, who were forced, on occasions, to shoot for their lives.

Despite these dangers and the terrible terrain the expedition made good progress during May, and by the 25th they were in sight of land. Unfortunately they were also in sight of open water, for the ice was by then becoming increasingly fragmented. The land at which they were gazing over an open seascape was Phipp's Island, beyond which lay another 40 miles of sea-ice, and sea, before their original target, Spitsbergen. Nevertheless the little island on the horizon was an immensely cheering sight for the four men; it had been 15 months since they last saw land.

It was another four days before a member of the party set foot on *terra firma*: four frustrating days on drifting, breaking ice, during which Phipp's Island slipped elusively past. They had missed landing on another small, unnamed island by a mere 50 ft., and there was a time when it seemed that their rubber boat might have to be called into play, and the expedition thus robbed of complete success. On May 29, however, Herbert radioed the news that two of his men, Koerner and Hedges, had just scrambled ashore on Small Blackboard Island to complete the first surface crossing of the Arctic Ocean. The last great journey left on Earth had been completed.

Lone Sailors and Oarsmen

The year saw such a variety of spectacular adventures, bizarre and dangerous stunts, and gruelling records of endurance, that events which only a few years before would have amazed the world occurred almost as commonplace incidents. 1969 was the year of the first single-handed yacht race across the Pacific—a tremendous seafaring competition that was won on April 25 by Eric Tabarly, the Frenchman who had won the single-handed Transatlantic yacht race in 1964. His yacht, *Pen Duick V*, took 41 days to cross the Pacific. On May 12 a 39-year-old American housewife, Mrs. Sharon Adams, set out from Yokohama, Japan, on a successful lone Transpacific sail in her 31-ft. ketch *Sea Sharp II*. She arrived in California on July 25 (75 days later), the first woman to make such a voyage.

The Atlantic, as always, extended its challenge to the human spirit. On January 20 a lone Englishman, John Fairfax, rowed out from Las Palmas in the Canary Islands, his destination Florida, his ambition to become the first man to row the Atlantic singlehanded. Six months later, on July 19, his 23-ft. bright orange craft *Britannia*, specially designed by Uffa Fox, and claimed to be unsinkable, finally touched American soil at the sleepy little resort of Hollywood, on the Miami coast. Lashed to *Britannia*'s bow were some dried shark fins, trophy of a victorious battle with a giant hammerhead that had occurred on his 126th day at sea. Fairfax had been attacked by the shark while scraping barnacles

John Fairfax, first man to row the Atlantic singlehanded, signals to a circling seaplane from his weird, unsinkable craft *Britannia*.

off *Britannia*'s hull, and in true *Boy's Own* fashion had slain the monster with his knife.

Nine days after Fairfax stepped ashore in Florida, a bewildered Irishwoman was hailed

Tom McClean, who rowed the Atlantic from Canada to Ireland in a mere 72 days.

by a bedraggled and exhausted figure with the words: "I've just rowed the Atlantic, can you take me to a telephone?" Tom "Moby" McClean, a 26-year-old paratrooper, had taken just 72 days to row from St. John's, Newfoundland, to the coast of co. Mayo, Ireland. During the 2,000-mile journey he had only two fine days; for the rest it was storm, snow, and ice. The most dangerous part of this amazing row was when, at the end of the voyage, his 20-ft. Yorkshire dory *Super Silver* was flung on to the rocks off the Mayo coast and lashed by Atlantic breakers. The lone rower had to jump out and heave his craft back into the sea to save her. Eleven days before, still about 250 miles from land, he had almost drowned on waking to find the boat awash, at times below the surface. Diving out into the ocean he had tilted her to get water out and it was only after seven hours' bailing

that she was empty. On September 13 another lone Atlantic seafarer, Bill Verity, stepped ashore on San Salvador Island, in the Caribbean, after sailing from Fenit, co. Derry. He had built his 20 ft. wooden craft, *Brendan the Navigator*, on the lines of the medieval Irish boat in which, legend relates, St. Brendan made the crossing in A.D. 550—in order to show that such a voyage was possible. Verity, a Florida anthropologist, took 114 days to sail from Ireland to San Salvador.

Climbers and Fliers

The most incredible climb of the year was accomplished not on any virgin peak, nor by experienced climbers, but by seven blind Africans who conquered the 19,340-ft. Mount Kilimanjaro, the highest mountain in Africa. Their guide was Geoffrey Salisbury, an instructor with the Royal Commonwealth Society for the Blind. A more conventional triumph, but one of great importance to British climbers, was the conquest, at last, of Stone Ulladale, the intimidating 800-ft. cliff on the Hebridean island of Harris. The feature that makes this cliff the greatest challenge in British climbing is the daunting scoop at its northern end which rears 400 ft. with a 150-ft. overhang. Until recently the scoop was considered impossible to climb, but on May 23 a Nottingham school-teacher, Doug Scott, together with Jeff Lepton, Mick Terry, and Guy Lee, all of Nottingham Climbing Club, attacked it, and on May 29 reached the top.

Other notable climbing achievements of the year included, on August 16, the first summer conquest of the north face of the Eiger by the *direttissima* (most direct) by a Japanese team

In the most remarkable climb of the year Geoffrey Salisbury led seven blind African climbers to the top of Mount Kilimanjaro, Africa's highest mountain. Mutual congratulations were exchanged at the summit.

Bivouac of the Japanese team climbing the north face of the Eiger by the *direttissima* route.

which included a woman; the scaling of the 25,300-ft. Tirich Mir, a major Himalayan peak, in July by a British Army team; the first total cross of the Mawenzi—the second highest mountain in Africa—achieved by the Swiss mountaineer, Fritz Lortscher; and the successful Joint Services Expedition to North Peary Land in Greenland, which climbed 16 major peaks, in addition to surveying its northern peninsula.

In the air Dr. Alvin Marks, an American, set up a new record of 14 days for a solo round-the-world flight in a light aircraft on April 17. On September 6 that irrepressible aeronaut Sheila Scott set up a record for a London-Nairobi solo flight of just under 48 hours.

By Foot and Hand

More down-to-earth but even more arduous were the astonishing John o' Groats to Land's End walks by David Ryder and Norman Croucher. Ryder, 21, a polio victim, wearing leg-irons and using crutches, averaged 16 miles a day, from June 21 to August 18. Croucher, 26, on artificial legs (he lost both lower legs in a rail accident), averaged 10 miles a day, from September 18 to December 20. Each walked the 850 miles to raise £1,000 for charity—Ryder for the Chigwell, Essex, Riding School for the Disabled, Croucher for Oxfam. By contrast, Lance-corporal William "Chik" Foster did the walk in 14 days 2 hours 32 minutes, a new record. Bruce Tulloh, the British athletic ace, beat the five-year-old record for the 2,876-mile run across the U.S.A. from Los Angeles, which he left on April 21, to New York, where he arrived on June 25 after 64 days 21 hours 50 minutes on the road, at an average speed of 43·1 miles a day. Another gruelling road record was established on April 28 when Vic Brown of Melbourne smashed the Perth–Sydney road cycling record by covering the 2,798 miles in 11 days 6 hours 47 minutes. It was left to another Australian to achieve perhaps the most friendly feat of 1969: at midnight on July 12 a handshake of congratulation set the seal on Peter Cremonile's successful attempt at the world hand-shaking record. He had shaken a magnificent total of 12,726 hands in 24 hours! Peter had started his marathon bare-handed, but gloves were donned after a fiendish saboteur had stretched out a hand smeared liberally with glue.

Two proud walkers of 1969 were polio victim David Ryder (*left*) on leg-irons and crutches, and Norman Croucher on two artificial lower legs, who despite their handicaps tramped from John o' Groats to Land's End.

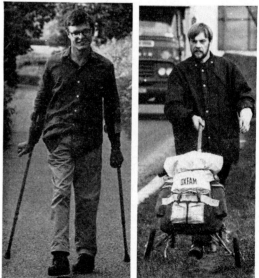

212

R.A.F. entrant Tom Lecky-Thompson rose amidst a swirl of coal dust in a vertical take-off Harrier from St. Pancras in the heart of London...

"Race You to the Top!"

JACK MAXWELL

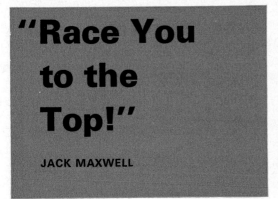

THE *Daily Mail* Transatlantic air race of May 1969 was a bizarre event, paradoxical in its contrasting elements. On the one hand it was a brash, frantic publicity bonanza decked out with contrived zest and jaded superlatives—instant news for the hungry presses and the insatiable TV cameras; on the other, it was the genuine inspiration of some spectacular drama, determined grit, cool daring, humour, and vitality. Certainly the whole affair (the race lasted from Sunday, May 4, to Sunday, May 11) stamped itself upon the texture of the year, inspiring among the cheers several notable boos—mainly from old women and one from that angry old man, John Osborne, who lambasted the race in a letter to *The Times*.

Held in commemoration of the epoch-making, first non-stop flight across the Atlantic by Alcock and Brown in their Vickers Vimy

biplane fifty years before, in 1919, the race attracted some 390 entrants from at least 10 countries, competing for £60,000 in prize money. The competition was divided into 21 different classes according to the whims of the various sponsors. But the rules specified that each competitor had to go from the top of the Post Office Tower in London to the top of the Empire State Building in New York, or vice versa. Any mode of conveyance, any number of vehicles, could be used—provided only that the contestant crossed the Atlantic Ocean by air.

As London's clocks struck eight on the chilly morning of May 4, Anne Alcock, the pretty 18-year-old niece of Sir John Alcock (the pioneer transatlantic aviator), clocked out of the Post Office Tower hotfoot for her chartered DC.-8 jet and Manhattan—and the week-long epic had begun. That same day saw Lt. Paul

... and, on touching down in Manhattan, sped to the Empire State Building by motor-cycle—all set for a record.

Conjugal congratulations for Phantom-borne Peter Goddard, New York to London record-breaker.

Above: Prizewinners Clement Freud and (*right*) Billy Butlin.

Below: Stirling Moss about to board barge-borne helicopter in mid-Thames.

Waterhouse, of the Fleet Air Arm, in a 1,000 m.p.h. Royal Navy Phantom jet, break the world record for an Atlantic crossing and take the lead for the major New York–London award with a sizzling point-to-point time of 5 hours 30 minutes 24·4 seconds. A touch of high drama attended this attempt: as the Phantom touched down at Wisley airfield, Surrey, its pilot, anxious to lop every superfluous second off Waterhouse's time, braked savagely and two of the screaming tyres burst and billowed into flame! Meanwhile, a Wessex helicopter, flying less than 15 ft. behind the jet, came so close as the Phantom halted that its rotor blades sliced the aircraft's nylon brake 'chute! Undeterred, Lt. Waterhouse bounded from the Phantom into the helicopter, was whisked to a building site a scant 50 yards from the G.P.O. Tower, and sprinted for the lift. Fantastic though his time was, it was beaten twice during the week—by his own Naval team mates, Drake and Goddard, both using Phantoms, on Wednesday, May 7, and Sunday, May 11, respectively. Lt.-Cmdr. Goddard's shattering time, clipping nearly 20 minutes off Waterhouse's, was 5 hours 11 minutes 22 seconds, which set the high performance seal on the final day.

Jump-Jet to Manhattan

While the Royal Navy was bent on winning the major award for the New York–London crossing, the R.A.F. concentrated on the London–New York award. On Monday, May 5, Squadron-Leader Tom Lecky-Thompson dashed out of the Post Office Tower and leapt on to the pillion of a motor-cycle bound for St. Pancras station, where, nestling in a disused coalyard, was the revolutionary Harrier jump-jet. Thus, amid a fearsome cloud of coal dust, aviation history was made. It was the first time that a vertical take-off aircraft had left the teeming centre of London bound for the skyscrapers of New York. His time for the crossing was 6 hours 11 minutes 57·15 seconds—good enough to win the £6,000 prize for the fastest westward crossing.

If the high performance prizes went to the armed services with all their advantages of trained personnel, in-flight refuelling facilities, superlative machines, and indulgent taxpayers, the variety of the categories in the race meant that there was still scope for individual effort. Broadly, these various categories included competitors using scheduled airline services; competitors using executive jets (for which an all-important handicap system was adopted to even out the differences between turbo-props and pure jets); and competitors piloting light aircraft.

Some famous names were amongst the contestants. On the first day of the race that veteran of speed, Stirling Moss, sped from the Post Office Tower with a spectacular display of well-rehearsed ground drill. He raced for five minutes through the streets of London clinging to the pillion of a 750 c.c. Norton Commando motor-cycle. At the Waterloo Bridge police-boat depot he leapt from the machine and dived into a moving speedboat as it gathered speed. Leaping from that craft on to a barge moored in mid-river, he scrambled into a Jet-Ranger helicopter and was up and off to Gatwick and a waiting chartered VC-10. Stirling's time of 7 hours 31 minutes 45·63 seconds from point to point, though impressive, was not a prize-winner. Luckier was Sir William (Billy) Butlin, who clinched the £500 London–New York chartered jet award with a time of 11 hours 30 minutes 41 seconds (less 6 hours' handicap).

Mary Rand, the Olympic athlete, *ran* down the street from the Post Office Tower to Warren Street Underground station, where she caught a tube train to Victoria, hurtled up the Thames by launch, and boarded a helicopter at Battersea bound for a chartered DC-8 at Stansted. On landing in New York she used a car and an ambulance to thwart the traffic jams as she sped to the Empire State Building.

Royal Rope Trick

Clement Freud, the dry wit and celebrated gourmet, was, despite his ponderous form, another pillion rider. Whatever injuries this mode of haste inflicted upon the humorist's dignity and person, he had good reason to consider it worth while. With a time of 8 hours 4 minutes 18 seconds he secured the coveted Aer Lingus award for a scheduled passenger flight via Shannon.

A touch of Royal patronage and a hint of the Indian rope trick were provided by Prince Michael of Kent, who cut the odd few seconds off his New York–London trip by swinging Tarzan fashion out of his chartered VC-10 on a rope. He and a team-mate, both serving with the 11th Hussars, might have won the £400 Rothman's award for subsonic aircraft had they not been held up for 45 minutes by air traffic control at Kennedy Airport.

The race abounded with zany personalities and whimsical happenings. Vehicles included a rickshaw, a Roman chariot, a sedan chair, and a balloon. Contestants included a U.S. Navy Commander, who competed *blindfolded*, aided by an uncanny knack—the ability to "see" with his eyes closed! Another American, one Ben Garcia, announced that he intended to

Above: **Mary Rand took the tube** *en route* **for Stansted.**
Below left: **One contestant tried a chariot.**

Above right: **Roller-skating Ben Garcia holding a hunk of his crashed Piper Colt.**

Below: **TV advertisement chimp Tina clocking out.**

AIR RACE PRIZE-WINNERS
London—New York

£5,000 *Daily Mail* and £1,000 British Aircraft Corporation (shortest time overall): Squadron-Leader Tom Lecky-Thompson, R.A.F. (6 hr. 11 min. 57 sec.)

£4,000 Rothmans of Pall Mall (subsonic aircraft): Richard Selph, U.S.A. (7 hr. 6 min. 24 sec.)

£5,000 Aer Lingus (scheduled passenger flight via Shannon): Clement Freud, U.K. (8 hr. 4 min. 18 sec.)

£2,500 *Daily Sketch* (unsponsored personal attempt via Shannon): Edmond Freudman, U.K. (8 hr. 4 min. 21 sec.)

£500 Castle Britannia Group (chartered business jet): Sir William Butlin, U.K. (5 hr. 30 min. 41 sec.—handicap time)

£1,000 London *Evening News* (light aircraft—man): Stephan Wilkinson, U.S.A. (20 hr. 23 min. 31 sec.)

£1,000 *Evening News* (light aircraft—woman): Sheila Scott, U.K. (26 hr. 34 min. 1 sec.)

£2,000 Brooke Bond Tea Ltd. (most meritorious non-winning Commonwealth entry): Miss Valerie Rosario, Air India (7 hr. 15 min. 31.34 sec.)

New York—London

£5,000 *Daily Mail* and £1,000 Vickers Ltd. (shortest time overall): Lieut.-Cmdr. Peter Goddard, R.N. (5 hr. 11 min. 22 sec.)

£4,000 Rothmans of Pall Mall (subsonic aircraft): Peter W. Hammond, U.K. (6 hr. 54 min.)

£5,000 BOAC (direct passenger flight): Dr. Ken Holden, Republic of Ireland (6 hr. 48 min. 33·88 sec.)

£2,500 *Daily Sketch* (unsponsored personal attempt): Miss Susan Scribner, U.S.A. (6 hr. 55 min. 48 sec.)

£500 Grovewood Securities (chartered business jet): Ted Drewery, U.K. (7 hr. 3 min. 5 sec.)

£1,000 *Evening News* (light aircraft—man): Michael Fallon, U.K. (21 hr. 31 min. 57 sec.)

£1,000 *Evening News* (light aircraft—woman): Mrs. Nancy Kelly, U.S.A. (22 hr. 31 min. 57 sec.)

£2,000 Brooke Bond Tea Ltd. (most meritorious non-winning Commonwealth entry): Neil Campbell Stevens, New Zealand (108 hr. 14 min. 38·67 sec.)

Other Classes

£1,000 *Evening News* (best performance in a light aircraft under 5,000 lb.): Miro John Slovak, U.S.A. (175 hr. 42 min. 7·11 sec.)

£5,250 Butlins Ltd. (most meritorious non-winning entries either way by British entrants): David A. Wynne-Davies (44 hr. 3 min. 10·43 sec.); Mrs. Juna Turner (33 hr. 34 min. 13·07 sec.); Miss Patricia Johnson (27 hr. 29 min. 45·69 sec.)

£5,000 Ziff-Davis Publishers (most meritorious non-winning entry either way by an American): William Guinther (22 hr. 13 min. 18 sec.)

£1,000 Blick (fastest Swiss national overall): B. Studer (7 hr. 45 min. 45 sec.)

£1,000 Empire State Building (most meritorious effort by a New York State resident): Nicholas A. Kleiner (10 hr. 55 min. 20·92 sec.)

compete in a tiny Piper Colt that lacked the fuel capacity to take him on the 700-mile hop from Iceland to Shannon. Undeterred, Garcia claimed that he would "climb to a great height and glide"! To cap this pronouncement he also made it known that he was going to "mug up" the art of navigation from a book *en route*. The Canadian authorities refused him permission to take off over the Atlantic and the eccentric aviator, resolute in his ambition to compete, headed for Pennsylvania in an ill-fated attempt to fit long-range fuel tanks. He got as far as a Pennsylvanian chicken farm on which he attempted to land and crashed owing to soft ground. But this was not the end of Ben Garcia's fighting attempt; on May 7 he arrived in London on a scheduled flight, wearing roller skates, prior to setting out again on a return bid the following day in topper and tails! In all he made six scheduled crossings in as many days. Among other competitors were a chimpanzee named Tina, a tortoise named George, and a team of 130 bowler-hatted London business men, whose leader, Ted Drewery, won a prize in the chartered business jet class.

The Daredevil Crossings

The real drama of the race, however, was, as always, provided in the many examples of courage, determination, and endurance. Sheila Scott, the lone female pilot, in her Piper Comanche, *Myth Too*, fought off sleep and the menace of ice. "There was no way I could get rid of it," she said afterwards. "I could see great lumps of it and it was affecting the controls. The radio was out of action and also the air speed indicator." Nevertheless, with a London–New York time of 26 hours 34 minutes 1 second, Sheila won the £1,000 *Evening News* prize for light aircraft (women) and smashed a few records into the bargain.

David Wynne-Davies, at 20 the youngest pilot in the race, and his co-pilot Derek Johnson, took nearly two days to make the journey from New York to London in a little twin-engined Aztec. Their radio failed; their generator broke down; their heater packed up, and—in a temperature of minus 20° C.—between Greenland and Iceland, Wynne-Davies was frostbitten.

Most staggering of all the daredevil crossings was that of Czechoslovakian-born American, Miro Slovak, who took 175 hours 42 minutes 7 seconds from New York to London, but was still in the prize money, with £1,000 for the best performance in a plane weighing under 5,000 lb. This was a 860-lb. Fournier RF 4 *glider* powered by a 36 h.p. Volkswagen *car* engine!

Sport
and
Games

Compiled and edited by

DON WOOD

Editor of *World Sports*

Opening ceremony on September 16, 1969, of the European Athletics Championships, at Karaiskakis Stadium in Athens.

British Sport in 1969

HERE WAS NEVER really any doubt who would take Britain's sports stars of the year awards once July was out. On successive weekends of a summer made for sport, Ann Jones, tennis queen, and Tony Jacklin, golf master, scored what must certainly rank as the most outstanding British victories of the 1960s. In Wimbledon's second year of open tennis, Ann Jones finally won the women's singles title and laid the bogey which had followed her around the centre court for 13 years. While her final triumph came against Billie-Jean King, champion for the previous three years, the title was as good as won two days earlier when Mrs. Jones beat the No. 1 seed Margaret Court in a nerve-tingling semi-final. This was the day when the Birmingham left-hander, seeded No. 4, at last proved that a long-time hard-court specialist could also win on grass.

A week later at Royal Lytham and St. Annes, Scunthorpe-born Tony Jacklin, 25, reaped the benefit of his hard work on the tough U.S. circuit by winning the British Open golf championship—the first home winner of the event since Max Faulkner took the title at Portrush in 1951. For years British golfers have appeared to lack the temperament to win when in commanding positions, particularly when facing the Americans. The year will be remembered not only for the way Jacklin kept his head and a two-stroke lead during a tense last round to win the Open, but also for his fine performances in the tied Ryder Cup match against the U.S.A. Jacklin was over par only seven times in his six unbeaten Ryder Cup games. Who among the millions who saw it on television will forget the struggle with Jack Nicklaus in the last match? One down with two to play, Jacklin eagled the 17th to go into the last hole all square.

An encouraging omen for the future of British golf was the form of a young Scot, Bernard Gallacher, whose season was rather overshadowed by Jacklin's performances. Only 20, Gallacher won three major tournaments and was second in three others, to top the official Order of Merit list and become the youngest to win the Vardon Trophy. The Scot, showing that vital will-to-win, was also the youngest player to take part in the Ryder Cup, and justified the honour by beating the 1968 U.S. Open champion Lee Trevino in his singles match.

The Soccer Scene

With Scotland, Wales, and Northern Ireland all eliminated in the qualifying rounds, England, the holders, will be the only home country representatives among the last 16 (see page 222) contesting the final rounds of the IX World Cup in Mexico in 1970. On form, Wales had little chance in a tough group including Italy and East Germany, but the Scots and Irish ought to have qualified or at least forced a play-off with the teams who topped their respective tables. Scotland, who never seem to produce their known power in important internationals unless they are facing England (preferably at Wembley!), again left their best display until the last vital match against West Germany at Hamburg, and were a little unlucky to lose 3-2. The failure of Northern Ireland to qualify was even more disappointing: their hopes were dashed when Russia succeeded in holding them to a goalless draw at home in Belfast.

Northern Ireland, with the Manchester United idol George Best at his unstoppable best at times, had made the most of the new-style home international championship to knit themselves into a formidable eleven. Playing all the internationals between the four home countries within eight days at the end of the season gave the Scots, Welsh, and Irish the same chance to get their players together for worth-while training sessions as has been enjoyed by England's squad before every match since the arrival of Sir Alf Ramsey as manager. The "championship week" is likely to remain as an end-of-season attraction, but not with the same blanket

218

TV coverage. About 100,000 fewer people attended the six matches than during the corresponding series of games spread over the 1966–67 season. It is not certain however, that the decline should be blamed solely on the presence of the TV cameras: heavy rain swept most of the country during the week, and this combined with a rail strike kept the crowd at Hampden Park, Glasgow, to a record low of 7,483 for the Scotland v. Northern Ireland match.

England, fortunate to have a priority on players not enjoyed by the other home countries, won all their three games to take the championship, and then set off on a fact-finding tour of the Americas as part of manager Ramsey's World Cup preparations. Playing in the afternoon heat and thin air of Mexico City, they were held to a goalless draw. Three days later and several thousand feet lower, a Mexican representative side was beaten 4-0 in Guadalajara. The team journeyed on to Montevideo and beat Uruguay 2-1, and then on to Rio where two goals by Brazil in the closing minutes gave the home side a 2-1 win.

Outstanding club sides of the British 1968–69 season were Newcastle United, who gave north-east soccer a much-needed boost by winning the European Fairs Cup, and Leeds United, who won a long overdue League championship. After many years of so-near-yet-so-far experiences the team, under the astute management of Don Revie and captaincy of Billy Bremner, made sure this season by losing only twice in the League and amassing a record 67 points—one more than Arsenal in 1931 and Tottenham in 1960. In the F.A. Cup, Manchester City, still overshadowing their United neighbours, followed a League title win the previous year by beating Leicester, and in the Football League Cup a Third Division club, Swindon Town, beat the once mighty Arsenal in a dramatic final.

Full Cricket Season

Cricket had a busy year, with all the major Test-playing countries heavily committed except South Africa, who were left without a series when the M.C.C. visit was cancelled following the inclusion of coloured Basil D'Oliveira in the proposed M.C.C. party. On the field, the year saw the West Indies toppled from their unofficial world champion's pedestal. The cracks began to widen in Australia in a series which produced a record run aggregate of 1,764 for one Test between the the two countries (at Adelaide) and saw the flagging West Indies attack concede more than 500 runs in an innings in four of the five Tests and finally lose the series 3-1.

England, badly weakened by the retirement of Ken Barrington, a tragic accident which cost Colin Milburn his left eye, and an injury which kept Colin Cowdrey out of the game for most of the season, confirmed the decline of the West Indies by winning a three-match series which should have been shared. In the third Test at Headingley, the West Indies seemingly had the match in their pockets at 219 for 3, needing only 83 runs to win. But in 16 staggering minutes the cream of their batting had gone, and England scrambled home by 30 runs to win the series.

New Zealand, the season's second visitors, lacked the batting strength to test England, and had an unhappy time facing Kent's left-arm bowling star Derek Underwood, who collected 24 wickets in the three-match series

and £500 in cash awards for his outstanding performances, including a match analysis of 12 for 101 in the Oval Test.

The domestic cricket scene continued to change in look and character, with overseas stars playing a major role in most counties. The year saw the successful introduction of the new Player's Sunday League of one-day matches, in addition to the now well-established Gillette Cup. As crowd-pulling entertainment the one-day match has obviously come to stay, but there remains the nagging doubt that "pop" cricket cannot completely replace the traditional three-day county championship match. If it did so, where would the Test players of the future be groomed?

Welsh Successes

Wales had a good Investiture year in sport. Glamorgan won the county cricket championship for only the second time, and the national Rugby Union team carried off the 1968–69 International championship. The Rugby success proved the value of a new squad coaching scheme under former international Clive Rowlands, and this Welsh lead was soon followed by England, who appointed a first national coach just one year before the England Rugby Union celebrates its centenary.

Wales found during her short close-season tour to New Zealand that there is still a long way to go before the best British XV can match the strength of the powerful All Blacks, but a welcome break-through has been made on the coaching side. This new approach by British Rugby surprised the South African touring side in the autumn more than the anti-apartheid demonstrations that hounded them everywhere they played. Their first-ever defeat by England at Twickenham in December just two weeks after defeat by Scotland found the Springboks struggling to find their usual form.

European Athletics and Swimming

There was no rest for the stars in the two major Olympic sports—athletics and swimming—and in both a well-organised state-sponsored coaching programme reaped a bumper harvest for East Germany. In the new European Cup competition, Britain's men swimmers failed to win an event and were relegated to the B division. The women fared better, finishing fourth.

In the European athletics championships in Athens the British team came third in the final medals table, with 17 medals, behind East Germany (25) and the USSR (24).

This meeting, now held every two years, usually brings out the best in British athletes, especially if they can get the morale booster of a first-day gold. This time it was produced by Paul Nihill in the 20 km. walk. Other individual successes came from John Whetton (1,500 m.), Ian Stewart (5,000 m.), Ron Hill (marathon), and Lillian Board (800 m.). The women's 4 × 400 m. relay team ended an unbeaten season by winning the race of the championships. In a tingling last lap Lillian Board found herself between 8 and 10 yards behind the French girl Colette Besson, and it seemed that the Olympic champion, who beat Miss Board in the Mexico City final, could not be caught. But a rather reckless effort by Miss Besson began to take its toll, and the British girl closed the gap with every stride and snatched victory in a photo finish.

CRICKET

TEST MATCH SERIES OF THE 1969 SEASON

AUSTRALIA v. WEST INDIES 1968-69

Australia won 3; West Indies won 1; 1 drawn

1st TEST: Brisbane, Dec. 6–10, 1968
West Indies won by 125 runs
1st inns.: West Indies 296 (M. Carew 83, R. Kanhai 94; A Connolly 4—60)
Australia 284 (W. Lawry 105, I. Chappell 117; L. Gibbs 5—88)
2nd inns.: West Indies 353 (Carew 71 n.o., C. Lloyd 129; J. Gleeson 5—122)
Australia 240 (Chappell 50; G. Sobers 6—73)

2nd TEST: Melbourne, Dec. 26–30, 1968
Australia won by an innings and 30 runs
1st inns.: West Indies 200 (R. Fredericks 76; G. McKenzie 8—71)
Australia 510 (W. Lawry 205, I. Chappell 165, K. Walters 76)
2nd inns.: West Indies 280 (S. Nurse 74, G. Sobers 67; J. Gleeson 5—61)

3rd TEST: Sydney, Jan. 3–8, 1969
Australia won by 10 wickets
1st inns.: West Indies 264 (C. Lloyd 50; G. McKenzie 4—85)
Australia 547 (K. Walters 118, I. Redpath 80, E. Freeman 76)
2nd inns.: West Indies 324 (B. Butcher 101, R. Kanhai 69)
Australia 42 for 0

4th TEST: Adelaide, Jan. 24–29, 1969
Match drawn
1st inns.: West Indies 276 (G. Sobers 110, B. Butcher 52; E. Freeman 4—52)
Australia 533 (K. Walters 110, W. Lawry 62, K. Stackpole 62, I. Chappell 76, P. Sheahan 51, G. McKenzie 59)
2nd inns.: West Indies 616 (Butcher 118, M. Carew 90, R. Kanhai 80, D. Holford 80, G. Sobers 52; A. Connolly 5—122)
Australia 339 for 9 (Chappell 96, Lawry 89, Stackpole 50, Walters 50)

5th TEST: Sydney, Feb. 14–19, 1969
Australia won by 382 runs
1st inns.: Australia 619 (K. Walters 242, W. Lawry 151, E. Freeman 56)
West Indies 279 (M. Carew 64; A. Connolly 4—61)
2nd inns.: Australia 394 for 8 dec. (I. Redpath 132, Walters 103)
West Indies 352 (S. Nurse 137)

PAKISTAN v. ENGLAND 1969

Series drawn

1st TEST: Lahore, Feb. 20–24, 1969
Match drawn
1st inns.: England 306 (C. Cowdrey 100; Intikhab 4—117, Saeed 4—64)
Pakistan 209 (Asif Iqbal 70; Cottam 4—50)
2nd inns.: England 225 for 9 dec. (K. Fletcher 83)
Pakistan 203 for 5 (Jehangir 68)

2nd TEST: Dacca, Feb. 28–March 3, 1969
Match drawn
1st inns.: Pakistan 246 (J. Snow 4—70)
England 274 (B. D'Oliveira 114 n.o.; Pervez Sajjad 4—75)
2nd inns.: Pakistan 195 for 6 dec. (D. Underwood 5—94)
England 33 for 0

3rd TEST: Karachi, March 6–8, 1969
Match abandoned (riots stopped play)
1st inns.: England 502 for 7 (C. Milburn 139, T. Graveney 105, A. Knott 96 n.o.)

WOMEN'S CRICKET

Australia v. England 1968–69: 3 Tests. All drawn.

New Zealand v. England 1968–69: 3 Tests. England won 2; 1 drawn.

NEW ZEALAND v. WEST INDIES 1969

New Zealand won 1; West Indies won 1; 1 drawn

1st TEST: Auckland, Feb. 27–March 3, 1969
West Indies won by 5 wickets
1st inns.: New Zealand 323 (B. Taylor 124, B. Congdon 85)
West Indies 276 (M. Carew 109, S. Nurse 95)
2nd inns.: New Zealand 297 for 8 dec. (G. Dowling 71)
West Indies 348 for 5 (Nurse 168, B. Butcher 78 n.o.)

2nd TEST: Wellington, March 7–10, 1969
New Zealand won by 6 wickets
1st inns.: West Indies 297 (R. Motz 6—69)
New Zealand 282 (G. Turner 74; R. Edwards 5—84)
2nd inns.: West Indies 148 (R. Cunis 3—36, B. Yuile 3—25)
New Zealand 164 for 4

3rd TEST: Christchurch, March 13–17, 1969
Match drawn
1st inns.: West Indies 417 (S. Nurse 258, M. Carew 91; R. Motz 5—113)
New Zealand 217 (D. Holford 4—66)
2nd inns.: New Zealand (follow on) 367 for 6 (B. Hastings 117 n.o., G. Dowling 76)

ENGLAND v. WEST INDIES 1969

England won 2; 1 drawn

1st TEST: Old Trafford, June 12–17, 1969
England won by 10 wickets
1st inns.: England 413 (G. Boycott 128, T. Graveney 75; Shepherd 5—104)
West Indies 147 (Brown 4—39, Snow 4—54)
2nd inns.: West Indies (follow-on) 275 (R. Fredericks 64)
England 12 for 0

2nd TEST: Lord's, June 26–July 1, 1969
Match drawn
1st inns.: West Indies 380 (C. Davis 103, S. Camacho 67, R. Fredericks 63; Snow 5—114)
England 344 (R. Illingworth 113, J. Hampshire 107, A. Knott 53)
2nd inns.: West Indies 295 for 9 dec. (C. Lloyd 70, R. Fredericks 60)
England 295 for 7 (G. Boycott 106, P. Sharpe 86)

3rd TEST: Headingley, July 10–15, 1969
England won by 30 runs
1st inns.: England 223 (J. Edrich 79; Holder 4—48)
West Indies 161 (Knight 4—63)
2nd inns.: England 240 (Sobers 5—42)
West Indies 272 (S. Camacho 71, B. Butcher 91; Underwood 4—55)

ENGLAND v. NEW ZEALAND 1969

England won 2; 1 drawn

1st TEST: Lord's, July 24–28, 1969
England won by 230 runs
1st inns.: England 190 (R. Illingworth 53; Taylor 3—35)
New Zealand 169 (Underwood 4—38, Illingworth 4—37)
2nd inns.: England 340 (J. Edrich 115)
New Zealand 131 (Underwood 7—32)

2nd TEST: Nottingham, Aug. 7–12, 1969
Match drawn
1st inns.: New Zealand 294 (B. Congdon 66, B. Hastings 83; Ward 4—61)
England 451 for 8 dec. (J. Edrich 155, P. Sharpe 111; Hadlee 4—88)
2nd inns.: New Zealand 66 for 1

3rd TEST: The Oval, Aug. 21–26, 1969
England won by 8 wickets
1st inns.: New Zealand 150 (G. Turner 53; Underwood 6—41)
England 242 (J. Edrich 68; Taylor 4—47)
2nd inns.: New Zealand 229 (B. Hastings 61; Underwood 6—60)
England 138 for 2 (M. Denness 55 n.o., P. Sharpe 45 n.o.)

INDIA v. NEW ZEALAND 1969

New Zealand won 1; India won 1; 1 drawn

1st TEST: Bombay, Sept. 25–30, 1969
India won by 60 runs
1st inns.: India 156 (Wadekar 49; Hadlee 3—17)
New Zealand 229 (Congdon 78; Prasanna 4—97)
2nd inns.: India 260 (Wadekar 40, Nawab of Pataudi 67; Taylor 3—30)
New Zealand 127 (Bedi 6—42)

2nd TEST: Nagpur, Oct. 3–8, 1969
New Zealand won by 167 runs
1st inns.: New Zealand 319 (Dowling 69, Congdon 63; Burgess 89, Bedi 4—98)
India 257 (S. Abid Ali 63, Ambar Roy 48; Howarth 4—66)
2nd inns.: New Zealand 214 (Congdon 57, Venkataraghaven 6—74)
India 109 (Howarth 5—34)

3rd TEST: Hyderabad, Oct. 15–20, 1969
Match drawn
1st inns.: New Zealand 181 (Murray 80, Dowling 42; Prasanna 5—51)
India 89 (Hadlee 4—30, Cunis 3—12)
2nd inns.: New Zealand 175 for 8 dec. (Dowling 60)
India 76 for 7 (Hadlee 3—31, Cunis 3—12)

PAKISTAN v. NEW ZEALAND 1969

New Zealand won 1; 2 drawn

1st TEST: Karachi, Oct. 23–27, 1969
Match drawn
1st inns.: Pakistan 220 (Sadiq Mohammad 69)
New Zealand 274 (Murray 50, Hadlee 56; Nazir 7—99)
2nd inns.: Pakistan 283 for 8 dec. (Younis Ahmed 62, Intikhab Alam 47)
New Zealand 112 for 5 (Burgess 45; Pervez Sajjad 5—33)

2nd TEST: Lahore, Oct. 30–Nov. 2, 1969
New Zealand won by 5 wickets
1st inns.: Pakistan 114 (Howarth 3—34, Pollard 3—27)
New Zealand 241 (Murray 90, Hastings 80 n.o.; Pervez Sajjad 7—74)
2nd inns.: Pakistan 208 (Shafquat Rana 95; Hadlee 3—27)
New Zealand 82 for 5 (Mohammed Nazir 3—10)

3rd TEST: Dacca, Nov. 8–11, 1969
Match drawn
1st inns.: New Zealand 273 (Turner 110, Burgess 59; Intikhab Alam 5—92)
Pakistan 290 for 7 dec. (Shafquat Rana 65, Asif Iqbal 92; Howarth 4—85)
2nd inns.: New Zealand 200 (Burgess 119 n.o.; Intikhab Alam 5—91) Pakistan 51 for 4

INDIA v. AUSTRALIA 1969

Australia won 3; India won 1; 1 drawn

1st TEST: Bombay, Nov. 4–9, 1969
Australia won by 8 wickets
1st inns.: India 271 (Mankad 74, Nawab of Pataudi 95; McKenzie 5—69)
Australia 345 (Stackpole 103, Redpath 77; Prasanna 5—121)
2nd inns.: India 137 (Wadekar 46; Gleeson 4—56)
Australia 67 for 2

2nd TEST: Kanpur, Nov. 16–20, 1969
Match drawn
1st inns.: India 320 (Engineer 77, Mankad 64; Connolly 4—91)
Australia 348 (Walters 53, Redpath 70, Sheahan 114)
2nd inns.: India 312 for 7 dec. (Mankad 68, Vishwanath 137)
Australia 95 for 0 (Lawry 56 n.o.)

3rd TEST: New Delhi, Nov. 29–Dec. 2, 1969
India won by 7 wickets
1st inns.: Australia 296 (Stackpole 61, Chappell 138; Bedi 4—71, Prasanna 4—111)
India 223 (Mankad 97, Mallett 6—64)
2nd inns.: Australia 107 (Bedi 5—37, Prasanna 5—42)
India 181 for 3 (Wadekar 91 n.o.)

4th TEST: Calcutta, Dec. 12–17, 1969
Australia won by 10 wickets
1st inns.: India 212 (Vishwanath 54; McKenzie 6—67)
Australia 335 (Chappell 99, Walters 56; Bedi 7—98)
2nd inns.: India 161 (Wadekar 62; Connolly 4—31, Freeman 4—54)
Australia 42 for 0

5th TEST: Madras, Dec. 24–28, 1969
Australia won by 77 runs
1st inns.: Australia 258 (Walters 102)
India 163 (Nawab of Pataudi 59; Mallett 5—91)
2nd inns.: Australia 153 (Redpath 63; Prasanna 6—74)
India 171 (Mallett 5—53)

GILLETTE CUP FINAL

Lord's: September 6, 1969
YORKS bt. **DERBY** by 69 runs
Yorkshire bt. Norfolk (by 89 runs); Lancashire (7 wkts); Surrey (138 runs); Notts (68 runs)
Derbyshire bt. Somerset (3 wkts); Worcestershire (4 wkts); Glamorgan (9 wkts); Sussex (87 runs)

SHEFFIELD SHIELD

1968-69

	Points
South Australia	52
Western Australia ..	44
Queensland	38
Victoria	28
New South Wales ..	14

COUNTY CHAMPIONSHIP

Final Table

				P	W	L	D	Btg.	Blg.	Pts
Glamorgan (3)	..	..	..	24	11	0	13	67	73	250
Gloucestershire (16)		..	..	24	11	6	8	26	93	219
Surrey (15)		..	..	24	7	1	16	64	76	210
Warwickshire (11)		..	..	24	7	3	14	41	89	205
Hampshire (5)	..	..	..	24	6	7	11	56	87	203
Essex (14)	..		..	24	6	6	12	44	85	189
Sussex (17)		..	..	24	5	8	11	47	88	185
Nottinghamshire (4)		..	..	24	6	2	16	49	75	184
Northampton (13)		..	..	24	5	7	12	47	66	163
Kent (2)	..	..	..	24	4	6	14	35	76	151
Middlesex (10)		..	..	24	3	7	14	40	76	146
Worcestershire (7)		..	..	24	5	7	12	30	62	142
Yorkshire (1)	..	..	..	24	3	6	15	30	77	142
Leicestershire (9)		..	..	24	4	7	13	26	64	130
Lancashire (6)		..	..	24	2	1	21	39	67	126
Derbyshire (8)		..	..	24	3	5	16	20	69	119
Somerset (12)		..	..	24	1	9	14	17	69	96

Figures in brackets indicate 1968 positions.

PLAYER'S SUNDAY LEAGUE

Final Table

				P	W	L	Tie	No Rslt	Pts
Lancashire ..	..	..	..	16	12	3	0	1	49
Hampshire ..	..	..	..	16	12	4	0	0	48
Essex ..	..	..	..	16	11	4	0	1	45
Kent ..	..	..	..	16	9	6	1	0	38
Surrey ..	..	..	..	16	9	6	0	1	37
Gloucestershire ..		..	..	16	8	8	0	0	32
Middlesex ..	..	..	..	16	7	7	0	2	30
Yorkshire ..	..	..	..	16	7	7	0	2	30
Warwickshire ..		..	..	16	6	6	0	4	28
Glamorgan ..	..	..	..	16	7	9	0	0	28
Leicestershire ..		..	..	16	6	7	0	3	27
Worcestershire ..		..	..	16	6	7	0	3	27
Nottinghamshire ..		..	..	16	5	9	1	1	23
Northamptonshire ..		..	..	16	5	9	0	2	22
Derbyshire ..	..	..	..	16	5	10	0	1	21
Somerset ..	..	..	..	16	5	10	0	1	21
Sussex ..	..	..	..	16	3	11	0	2	14

WORLD CUP 1970
Qualifying Matches (16 Groups), 1968–69
EUROPE

Group 1

	P	W	D	L	F	A	Pts
RUMANIA	6	3	2	1	7	6	8
Greece	6	2	3	1	13	9	7
Switzerland	6	2	1	3	5	8	5
Portugal	6	1	2	3	8	10	4

1968
Oct. 12	Switzerland .1	Greece	0
Oct. 27	Portugal .3	Rumania	0
Nov. 23	Rumania .2	Switzerland	0
Dec. 11	Greece .4	Portugal	2

1969
April 16	Portugal .0	Switzerland	2
April 16	Greece .2	Rumania	2
May 4	Portugal .2	Greece	2
May 14	Switzerland .0	Rumania	1
Oct. 12	Rumania .1	Portugal	0
Oct. 15	Greece .4	Switzerland	1
Nov. 2	Switzerland .1	Portugal	1
Nov. 16	Rumania .1	Greece	1

Group 4

	P	W	D	L	F	A	Pts
U.S.S.R.	4	3	1	0	8	1	7
N. Ireland	4	2	1	1	7	3	5
Turkey	4	0	0	4	2	13	0

1968
Oct. 23	N. Ireland .4	Turkey	1
Dec. 11	Turkey .0	N. Ireland	3

1969
Sept. 10	N. Ireland .0	U.S.S.R.	0
Oct. 15	U.S.S.R. .3	Turkey	0
Oct. 22	U.S.S.R. .2	N. Ireland	0
Nov. 16	Turkey .1	U.S.S.R.	3

Group 7

	P	W	D	L	F	A	Pts
W. GERMANY	6	5	1	0	20	3	11
Scotland	6	3	1	2	18	7	7
Austria	6	3	0	3	12	7	6
Cyprus	6	0	0	6	2	35	0

1968
May 19	Austria .7	Cyprus	1
Oct. 13	Austria .0	W. Germany	2
Nov. 6	Scotland .2	Austria	1
Nov. 23	Cyprus .0	W. Germany	1
Dec. 11	Cyprus .0	Scotland	5

1969
April 16	Scotland .1	W. Germany	1
April 19	Cyprus .1	Austria	2
May 10	W. Germany .1	Austria	0
May 17	Scotland .8	Cyprus	0
May 21	W. Germany 12	Cyprus	0
Oct. 22	W. Germany .3	Scotland	2
Nov. 5	Austria .2	Scotland	0

NORTH & CENTRAL AMERICA AND CARIBBEAN

Group 13: Semi-finals

1969
Apr. 20	Haiti .2	U.S.A.	0
May 11	U.S.A. .0	Haiti	1
June 8	Honduras .1	El Salvador	0
June 15	El Salvador .3	Honduras	0
June 27	El Salvador .3	Honduras	2

(play-off in Mexico City)

Final: EL SALVADOR won.
Sept. 21	Haiti .1	El Salvador	2
Sept. 28	El Salvador .0	Haiti	3
Oct. 9	Haiti .0	El Salvador	1

(play-off in Kingston)

Group 14
MEXICO (hosts) automatically qualify.

ASIA AND OCEANIA

Group 15
Sub-group 1: Australia bt. Japan 3–1, 1–1, and S. Korea 2–1, 1–1 ; S. Korea bt. Japan 2–2, 2–0

Sub-group 1a: Australia bt. Rhodesia 1–1, 0–0, 3–1

Sub-group 2: Israel bt. New Zealand 4–0, 2–0

Final: ISRAEL bt. Australia 1–0, 1–1

Group 2

	P	W	D	L	F	A	Pts
CZECHOSLOVAKIA	6	4	1	1	12	6	9
Hungary	6	4	1	1	16	7	9
Denmark	6	2	1	3	10	6	5
Eire	6	0	1	5	3	14	1

1968
Sept. 25	Denmark .0	Czechoslovakia	3
Oct. 20	Czechoslovakia1	Denmark	0

1969
May 4	Eire .1	Czechoslovakia	2
May 25	Hungary .2	Czechoslovakia	0
May 27	Denmark .2	Eire	0
June 8	Eire .1	Hungary	2
June 15	Denmark .3	Hungary	2
Sept. 14	Czechoslovakia3	Hungary	3
Oct. 7	Czechoslovakia3	Eire	0
Oct. 15	Eire .1	Denmark	1
Oct. 22	Hungary .3	Denmark	0
Nov. 5	Hungary .4	Eire	0
Dec. 3	Czechoslovakia4	Hungary	1

(Play-off in Marseilles)

Group 5

	P	W	D	L	F	A	Pts
SWEDEN	4	3	0	1	12	5	6
France	4	2	0	2	6	4	4
Norway	4	1	0	3	4	13	2

1968
Oct. 9	Sweden .5	Norway	0
Nov. 6	France .0	Norway	1

1969
June 19	Norway .2	Sweden	5
Sept. 10	Norway .1	France	3
Oct. 15	Sweden .2	France	0
Nov. 1	France .3	Sweden	0

Group 8

	P	W	D	L	F	A	Pts
BULGARIA	6	4	1	1	12	7	9
Poland	6	4	0	2	19	8	8
Netherlands	6	3	1	2	9	5	7
Luxemburg	6	0	0	6	4	24	0

1968
Sept. 4	Luxemburg .0	Netherlands	2
Oct. 27	Bulgaria .2	Netherlands	0

1969
March 25	Netherlands .4	Luxemburg	0
April 20	Poland .8	Luxemburg	1
April 23	Bulgaria .2	Luxemburg	1
May 7	Netherlands .1	Poland	0
June 15	Bulgaria .4	Poland	1
Sept. 7	Poland .2	Netherlands	1
Oct. 12	Luxemburg .1	Poland	5
Oct. 22	Netherlands .1	Bulgaria	1
Nov. 9	Poland .3	Bulgaria	0
Dec. 7	Luxemburg .1	Bulgaria	3

AFRICA

Group 16
Sub-group 1: Algeria bt. Tunisia 2–1, 0–0
Sub-group 2: Morocco bt. Senegal 1–0, 1–2, 2–0
Sub-group 3: Ethiopia bt. Libya 0–2, 5–1
Sub-group 4: Sudan bt. Gambia 2–4, 4–2
Sub-group 5: Nigeria bt. Cameroons 1–1, 3–2
Sub-group 6: Ghana automatically qualified
Semi-finals
Morocco bt. Tunisia 0–0, 0–0, 2–2 (on toss of coin)
Sudan bt. Ethiopia 1–1, 3–1
Nigeria bt. Ghana 2–1, 1–1

Final
	P	W	D	L	F	A	Pts
MOROCCO	4	2	1	1	5	3	5
Nigeria	4	1	2	1	8	7	4
Sudan	4	0	3	1	5	8	3

1969
Sept. 13	Nigeria .2	Sudan	2
Sept. 21	Morocco .2	Nigeria	1
Oct. 3	Sudan .3	Nigeria	3
Oct. 10	Sudan .0	Morocco	0
Oct. 26	Morocco .3	Sudan	0
Nov. 8	Nigeria .2	Morocco	0

Group 3

	P	W	D	L	F	A	Pts
ITALY	4	3	1	0	10	4	7
E. Germany	4	2	1	1	7	5	5
Wales	4	0	0	4	3	10	0

1968
Oct. 23	Wales .0	Italy	1

1969
March 29	E. Germany .2	Italy	2
April 16	E. Germany .2	Wales	1
Oct. 22	Wales .1	E. Germany	3
Nov. 4	Italy .4	Wales	1
Nov. 22	Italy .3	E. Germany	0

Group 6

	P	W	D	L	F	A	Pts
BELGIUM	6	4	1	1	14	8	9
Yugoslavia	6	3	1	2	19	7	7
Spain	6	2	2	2	10	6	6
Finland	6	1	0	5	6	28	2

1968
June 19	Finland .1	Belgium	2
Sept. 25	Yugoslavia .9	Finland	1
Oct. 9	Belgium .6	Finland	1
Oct. 16	Belgium .3	Yugoslavia	0
Oct. 27	Yugoslavia .0	Spain	0
Dec. 11	Spain .1	Belgium	1

1969
Feb. 23	Belgium .2	Spain	1
April 30	Spain .2	Yugoslavia	1
June 4	Finland .1	Yugoslavia	5
June 25	Finland .2	Spain	0
Oct. 15	Spain .6	Finland	0
Oct. 19	Yugoslavia .4	Belgium	0

Group 9
ENGLAND (holders) automatically qualify.

SOUTH AMERICA

Group 10

	P	W	D	L	F	A	Pts
PERU	4	2	1	1	7	4	5
Bolivia	4	2	0	2	5	6	4
Argentina	4	1	1	2	4	6	3

1969
July 27	Bolivia .3	Argentina	1
Aug. 3	Peru .1	Argentina	0
Aug. 10	Bolivia .2	Peru	1
Aug. 17	Peru .3	Bolivia	0
Aug. 24	Argentina .1	Bolivia	0
Aug. 31	Argentina .2	Peru	2

Group 11

	P	W	D	L	F	A	Pts
BRAZIL	6	6	0	0	23	2	12
Paraguay	6	4	0	2	6	8	8
Colombia	6	1	1	4	7	12	3
Venezuela	6	0	1	5	1	18	1

1969
July 27	Colombia .3	Venezuela	0
Aug. 2	Venezuela .1	Colombia	1
Aug. 6	Colombia .0	Brazil	2
Aug. 6	Venezuela .0	Paraguay	2
Aug. 10	Colombia .0	Paraguay	1
Aug. 10	Venezuela .0	Brazil	5
Aug. 17	Paraguay .0	Brazil	3
Aug. 21	Brazil .6	Colombia	2
Aug. 21	Paraguay .1	Venezuela	0
Aug. 24	Brazil .6	Venezuela	0
Aug. 24	Paraguay .2	Colombia	1
Aug. 31	Brazil .1	Paraguay	0

Group 12

	P	W	D	L	F	A	Pts
URUGUAY	4	3	1	0	5	0	7
Chile	4	1	2	1	5	4	4
Ecuador	4	0	1	3	2	8	1

1969
July 6	Ecuador .0	Uruguay	2
July 13	Chile .0	Uruguay	0
July 20	Uruguay .1	Ecuador	0
July 27	Chile .4	Ecuador	1
Aug. 3	Ecuador .1	Chile	1
Aug. 10	Uruguay .2	Chile	0

EUROPEAN CHAMPIONS' CUP 1968-69

First Round	Second Round	Third Round	Semi-Finals	Final

A.C. MILAN ....4 : 1
Malmo ....2 : 1 — A.C. MILAN ....bye — A.C. MILAN ....0 : 0

St. Etienne ......2 : 0
Celtic ....4 : 0 — Celtic ....5 : 1 — Celtic ....0 : 1 — A.C. MILAN ....2 : 0

Red Star, Belgrade ..bye — Red Star Belgrade ....1 : 1

Waterford ....1 : 3
Manchester Utd. ....7 : 1 — Manchester Utd. ......3 : 0 — Manchester Utd. ......3 : 0

Anderlecht ....3 : 0
Glentoran ....2 : 2 — Anderlecht ....3 : 1 — Manchester Utd. ......1 : 0

RosenburgTrondheim 1 : 3
Rapid Vienna ....3 : 3 — Rapid Vienna ....1 : 0 (won on away goals) — Rapid Vienna ....0 : 0

Real Madrid ....6 : 0
Limassol ....0 : 6 — Real Madrid ....2 : 1

A.C. MILAN..4

Floriana ....1 : 1
Reipas Lahti ....2 : 0 — Reipas Lahti ....1 : 9 — Spartak Trnava ....2 : 1

Steaua Bucharest ..3 : 1
Spartak Trnava ......4 : 0 — Spartak Trnava ......7 : 1 — Spartak Trnava ....2 : 0

AEK Athens ....3 : 0
Jeunesse Esche ....3 : 2 — AEK Athens ....0 : 0 — AEK Athens ....1 : 1

F.C. Zurich ....1 : 3
Akademisk..........1 : 2 — Akademisk ....0 : 2

At Madrid,
May 28, 1969

Valur ....0 : 0
Benfica ....8 : 1 — Benfica ....bye — Benfica ....1 : 3

Manchester City ....0 : 0
Fenerbahce ....2 : 1 — Fenerbahce ....0 : 2 — AJAX AMSTERDAM ..1 : 3 — AJAX AMSTERDAM ..3 : 0

Nuremburg ....1 : 1
AJAX AMSTERDAM 4 : 0 — AJAX AMSTERDAM ..2 : 0 — Ajax won play-off 3–0

AJAX
AMSTERDAM . 1

EUROPEAN CUP-WINNERS' CUP 1968-69

First Round	Second Round	Third Round	Semi-Finals	Final

BARCELONA .....3 : 0
Lugano ....0 : 1 — BARCELONA ....bye.. — BARCELONA ....3 : 2

Altay Izmir.........3 : 1
Lyn Oslo ....4 : 1 — Lyn Oslo ....2 : 0 — Lyn Oslo ....2 : 2 — BARCELONA ....4 : 1

Crusaders ....2 : 2
Norkopping ....4 : 1 — Norkopping ....3 : 2

A.D.O. The Hague .4 : 1
A.K. Graz ....0 : 2 — A.D.O. The Hague ....0 : 1 — Cologne ....2 : 1

Bordeaux ....2 : 1
Cologne ....3 : 0 — Cologne ....3 : 0

BARCELONA ..2

Freja Randers .....1 : 0
Shamrock R........1 : 2 — Freja Randers ....6 : 0 — Freja Randers ....0 : 3 — Cologne ....2 : 2

Rumelingen ....2 : 1
Sliema Wand. ......1 : 0 (won on away goals) — Sliema Wand. ....0 : 2

At Basle,
May 21, 1969

Dunfermline ......10 : 1
Apoel Nicosia .....0 : 2 — Dunfermline ....4 : 0 — Dunfermline ....0 : 0

Olympiakos ....2 : 0
Fram Reykjavik ....0 : 2 — Olympiakos ....3 : 0 — Dunfermline ....1 : 1

Dynamo Bucharest ..bye — Dynamo Bucharest ....1 : 1

F.C. Bruges ....3 : 1
West Bromwich A. ..2 : 0 (won on away goals) — West Bromwich A. ..4 : 0 — West Bromwich A.....0 : 1

SLOVAN
BRATISLAVA ..3

Partisan Tirana ....1 : 0
Torino ....3 : 1 — Torino ....bye — Torino ....0 : 1

Cardiff City ......2 : 2
F.C. Oporto ....2 : 1 — F.C. Oporto ....1 : 0 — SLOVAN BRATISLAVA 2 : 1 — SLOVAN BRATISLAVA 1 : 0

Bor ....2 : 0
SLOVAN BRATIS. ..3 : 0 — SLOVAN BRATISLAVA 4 : 0

INTER-CITIES FAIRS' CUP FINAL

May 29, 1969 Newcastle United (Eng) 3 Ujpest Dozsa (Hung) 0
June 11, 1969 Ujpest Dozsa ....2 Newcastle United ..3
Newcastle won 6-2 on aggregate

WORLD CLUB CHAMPIONSHIP 1969

AC Milan (It) ....3 Estudiantes (Arg) 0
Estudiantes ....2 AC Milan....................1
AC Milan won 4-2 on aggregate

LEAGUE FOOTBALL 1968-69

THE FOOTBALL LEAGUE

Division	Champions	Runners-up	*Relegated Clubs †Re-elected Clubs
One	Leeds United ....67 pts.	Liverpool ....61 pts.	*Leicester City ....30 pts. *Queen's Park Rangers ....18 pts.
Two	Derby County ....63 pts.	Crystal Palace ....56 pts.	*Bury ....30 pts. *Fulham ....25 pts.
Three	Watford ....64 pts.	Swindon Town ....64 pts.	*Northampton Town ....40 pts. *Hartlepools United ....39 pts. *Oldham Athletic ....35 pts. *Crewe Alexandra ....35 pts.
Four	Doncaster Rovers ....59 pts.	Halifax Town ....57 pts. 3rd. Rochdale ....56 pts. 4th. Bradford City ....56 pts.	†York ....39 pts. †Newport ....36 pts. †Grimsby ....33 pts. †Bradford ....20 pts.

SCOTTISH LEAGUE

One	Celtic ....54 pts.	Rangers ....49 pts.	*Falkirk ....18 pts. *Arbroath ....16 pts.
Two	Motherwell ....64 pts.	Ayr United ....53 pts.	

LEAGUE CUP FINALS

Football League
March 15, 1969 (Wembley): Swindon Town....3 Arsenal....1

Scottish League
April 5, 1969 (Hampden Park): Celtic......6 Hibernian......2

INTER-LEAGUE MATCHES
Sept. 4, 1968 (Dublin) Irish ....0 Scottish 0
Nov. 27, 1968 (Belfast) Irish ....0 Football League....1
March 26, 1969 (Glasgow) Scottish ....1 Football League....3

EUROPEAN LEAGUE CHAMPIONS
1968-69
Albania ....Nenduri Tirana
Austria ....Austria Vienna
Belgium..................................Standard Liege
Bulgaria ....CSKA Sofia
Cyprus ....Olympiakos Nicosia
Czechoslovakia ....Spartak Trnava
Denmark ..............................K.B. Copenhagen
East Germany..........................Vorwaerts Berlin
West Germany ....Bayern Munich
Eire ....Waterford
Finland ....Palloseura Turku
France ....St. Etienne
Greece ....Panathinaikos Athens
Hungary ....Ferencvaros Budapest
Iceland ...............................K.R. Reykjavik
Italy...Fiorentina
Luxemburg ....Avenir Beggen
Malta ....Pawla Hibernians
Netherlands ....Feijenoord Rotterdam
Northern Ireland ....Linfield
Norway ....Lyn Oslo
Poland ....Legia Warsaw
Portugal ....Benfica
Rumania ....UT Arad
Spain ....Real Madrid
Sweden.................................Oster Voxjoe
Switzerland...................................Basle
Turkey ....Galatasary
U.S.S.R. ....Dynamo Kiev
Yugoslavia ....Red Star, Belgrade

UNDER-23 INTERNATIONALS
Oct. 2, 1968 (Wrexham) Wales ....1 England 3
Nov. 13, 1968 (Birmingham) England ......2 Netherlands ..2
April 16, 1969 (Coventry) England ......4 Portugal 0
May 22, 1969 (Deventer) Netherlands ..2 England 1
May 25, 1969 (Ostend) Belgium "B"..0 England 1
May 28, 1969 (Funchal) Portugal ......1 England 1

AUSTRALIAN SOCCER 1969
Greek Tour of Australia
Internationals
At Sydney: Australia ....1 Greece 0
At Brisbane: Australia ....2 Greece 2
At Melbourne: Australia ....0 Greece 0
Other Matches
At Melbourne: Victoria ....0 Greece 0
At Sydney: New South Wales ....2 Greece 1
At Adelaide: South Australia ....0 Greece 6
At Perth: Western Australia ....1 Greece 2

State League Premierships
New South Wales	1st Division ....South Coast United	
	2nd Division ....Marconi Fairfield	
South Australia	1st Division ....W. A. Hellas	
	2nd Division ....Port Adelaide	
	3rd Division ....Taperoo	
Western Australia	1st Division ....Azzurri	
	2nd Division ....Perth City	
	3rd Division ....Croatia North Perth	
Queensland	1st Division ....Hellenic	
	2nd Division ....Latrobe	
	3rd Division ....Taringa	

1969 Youth Championships
(Newcastle, N.S.W.)
1st New South Wales
2nd Northern New South Wales
3rd South Australia
4th Victoria
5th Western Australia
6th Tasmania
7th Australian Capital Territory
8th Northern Territory

AUSTRALIAN NATIONAL FOOTBALL
Premiership Teams 1969
Victorian Football League ....Richmond
Victorian Football Association (1st Div.)....Preston
Victorian Football Association (2nd Div.) ..Williamstown
South Australia..............................Sturt
Western Australia..........................West Perth
Tasmania ....North Hobart
New South Wales........................Western Suburbs
Queensland ....Wilston Grange
Canberra ....Manuka

The biggest crowd ever to watch a sporting fixture in Australia—119,165—saw Richmond defeat Carlton to win the Victorian Football League premiership at the Melbourne Cricket Ground on September 27, 1969.

F.A. CUP COMPETITION 1968-69

Third Round

Everton 2	Ipswich Town 1
Coventry City 3	Blackpool 1
Bolton Wanderers 2	Northampton Town 1
Bristol Rovers 1 : 2	Kettering 1 : 1
Sheffield Wedn'day 1 : 3	Leeds United 1 : 1
Birmingham 2	Lincoln City 1
Exeter City 1	Manchester United 3
Watford 2	Port Vale 0
Blackburn Rovers 2	Stockport County 0
Portsmouth 3	Chesterfield 0
Newcastle United 4	Reading 0
MANCHESTER CITY 1	Luton Town 0
Walsall 0	Tottenham Hotspur 1
Hull City 1	Wolverhampton W. 3
Oxford United 1 : 0	Southampton 1 : 2
Aston Villa 2	Queen's Park Rangers 1
Preston North End 3	Nottingham Forest 0
Chelsea 2	Carlisle United 0
York City 0	Stoke City 2
Swansea Town 0	Halifax Town 1
Sunderland 1	Fulham 4
West Bromwich Alb. 3	Norwich City 0
Cardiff City 0 : 0	Arsenal 0 : 2
Charlton Athletic 0 : 2	Crystal Palace 0 : 0
Mansfield Town 2	Sheffield United 1
Swindon Town 0	Southend United 2
Bury 1	Huddersfield Town 2
West Ham United 3	Bristol City 2
Liverpool 2	Doncaster Rovers 0
Burnley 3	Derby County 1
Middlesbrough 1 : 0	Millwall 1 : 1
Barnsley 1 : 1	LEICESTER CITY 1 : 2

Fourth Round

Everton 2	Coventry C. 0
Bolton W. 1	Bristol R. 2
Sheffield Wed. 2 : 1	Birmingham 2 : 2
Manchester U. 1 : 2	Watford 1 : 0
Blackburn R. 4	Portsmouth 0
Newcastle U. 0 : 0	MAN. C. 0 : 2
Tottenham H. 2	Wolverhampton W. 1
Southampton 2 : 1	Aston Villa 2 : 2
Preston N.E. 0 : 1	Chelsea 0 : 2
Stoke C. 1 : 3	Halifax T. 1 : 0
Fulham 1	West Bromwich A. 2
Arsenal 2	Charlton A. 0
Mansfield T. 2	Southend U. 1
Huddersfield T. 0	West Ham U. 2
Liverpool 2	Burnley 1
Millwall 0	LEICESTER C. 1

Fifth Round

Everton 1	Bristol R. 0
Birmingham 2 : 2	Manchester U. 2 : 6
Blackburn R. 1	MANCHESTER C. 4
Tottenham H. 3	Aston Villa 2
Chelsea 3	Stoke C. 2
West Bromwich A. 1	Arsenal 0
Mansfield T. 3	West Ham U. 0
Liverpool 0 : 0	LEICESTER C. 0 : 1

Sixth Round

Everton 1	Manchester U. 0
MANCHESTER C. 1	Tottenham H. 0
Chelsea 1	West Bromwich A. 2
Mansfield T. 0	LEICESTER C. 1

Semi-Finals

Everton 0	MANCHESTER C. 1
West Bromwich A. 0	LEICESTER C. 1

Final

MANCHESTER CITY 1	LEICESTER CITY 0

At Wembley, April 26, 1969

F.A. CHARITY SHIELD
League Champions v. Cup-Winners
August 2, 1969
Leeds United 2, Manchester City 1

INTERNATIONAL CHAMPIONSHIP 1969

(England, Scotland, N. Ireland, Wales)

May 3 (Wrexham)	Wales 3	Scotland 5
May 3 (Belfast)	N. Ireland 1	England 3
May 6 (Glasgow)	Scotland 1	N. Ireland 1
May 7 (Wembley)	England 2	Wales 1
May 10 (Belfast)	N. Ireland 0	Wales 0
May 10 (Wembley)	England 4	Scotland 1

	P	W	D	L	Goals F	Goals A	Pts
England	3	3	0	0	9	3	6
Scotland	3	1	1	1	7	8	3
N. Ireland	3	0	2	1	2	4	2
Wales	3	0	1	2	4	7	1

OTHER INTERNATIONALS 1968-69

(Not including World Cup qualifying matches—see page 222)

1968			
Sept. 10 (Tel-Aviv)	Israel 2	N. Ireland 3
Oct. 16 (Copenhagen)	Denmark 0	Scotland 1
Oct. 30 (Chorzow)	Poland 1	Rep. of Ireland 0
Nov. 6 (Bucharest)	Rumania 0	England 0
Nov. 10 (Dublin)	Rep. of Ireland 2	Austria 2
Dec. 11 (Wembley)	England 1	Bulgaria 1
1969		
Jan. 15 (Wembley)	England 1	Rumania 1
March 12 (Wembley)	England 5	France 0
March 26 (Frankfurt)	W. Germany 1	Wales 1
June 1 (Mexico City)	Mexico 0	England 0
June 8 (Montevideo)	Uruguay 1	England 2
June 12 (Rio de Janeiro)	Brazil 2	England 1

P

SCOTTISH CUP COMPETITION 1968-69

First Round	Second Round	Third Round	Semi-Finals	Final
RANGERS 1				
Hibernian 0	RANGERS 2			
Dundee 1		RANGERS 1		
Heart of Midlothian 2	Heart of Midlothian 0			
Stenhousemuir 0			RANGERS 6	
Airdrieonians 3	Airdrieonians ....1 :3			
Dumbarton 0		Airdrieonians 0		
St. Mirren 1	St. Mirren ....1 :1			RANGERS 0
Aberdeen 3	Aberdeen 2			
Berwick Rangers 0		Aberdeen ....0 :3		
Raith Rovers 0	Dunfermline Athletic 0			
Dunfermline Athletic 2			Aberdeen 1	
Montrose 1	Montrose ....1 :1			
Cowdenbeath 0		Kilmarnock ....0 :0		
Kilmarnock 6	Kilmarnock ....1 :4			At Hampden Park,
Glasgow University 0				April 26, 1969
Dundee United 2	Dundee United 6			
Queen's Park 1		Dundee United 2		
Ayr United 1	Ayr United 2			
Queen of South 0			Morton 1	
Stranraer 3	Stranraer 1			
East Fife 1		Morton 3		
Falkirk 1	Morton 3			CELTIC 4
Morton 2				
East Stirling 2	East Stirling ....1 :0			
Stirling 0		St. Johnstone 2		
St. Johnstone 3	St. Johnstone ....1 :3			
Arbroath 2			CELTIC 4	
Motherwell ....1 :1	Clyde ....0 :0			
Clyde ....1 :2		CELTIC 3		
Partick Thistle ......3 :1	CELTIC ....0 :3			
CELTIC ....3 :8				

AMATEUR FOOTBALL

F.A. AMATEUR CUP FINAL
April 12, 1969, Wembley

NORTH SHIELDS 2   SUTTON UNITED 1

N. Shields bt. Spennymoor Utd 4–1; Coventry Am 3–0; Hendon 2–0 (1–1); Wealdstone 1–0; Skelmersdale Utd 2–1 (1–1) in semi-final.

Sutton Utd bt. Bromley 9–0; Leeds & Carnegie Coll 5–2; Marine 2–0; Leytonstone 3–0; Whitley Bay 4–2 in semi-final.

AMATEUR INTERNATIONAL CHAMPIONSHIP
(England, Scotland, Ireland, Wales)

Sept. 28, 1968 (Charlton)	England 5	Ireland 0
Nov. 9, 1968 (Watford)	England 1	Wales 1
Jan. 11, 1969 (Ton Pentre)	Wales 1	Ireland 0
March 15, 1969 (Portadown)	Ireland 1	Scotland 2
March 28, 1969 (Glasgow)	Scotland 1	England 5
April 5, 1969 (Wrexham)	Wales 1	Scotland 1

	P	W	D	L	F	A	Pts
England...............	3	2	1	0	11	2	5
Wales................	3	1	2	0	3	2	4
Scotland	3	1	1	1	4	7	3
Ireland	3	0	0	3	1	8	0

OTHER AMATEUR INTERNATIONALS

March 9, 1969 (Dublin)	Rep. of Ireland..1	England........1
May 1, 1969 (Montecatini)	Italy 0	England........0

IRISH F.A. CUP

Final: April 23, 1969 (Belfast): Ards 4....Distillery 2.
(Replay after 0–0 in first match, April 19)

F.A. OF IRELAND CUP

Final: April 23, 1969 (Dublin): Shamrock Rovers 4....Cork Celtic 1.
(Replay after 1–1 draw in first match, April 20)

WELSH F.A. CUP

Final: Cardiff (3:2) beat Swansea (1:0), 5–1 on aggregate.

SCHOOLS' AND YOUTH FOOTBALL

SCHOOLS' INTERNATIONAL TOURNAMENT (VICTORY SHIELD) 1969

March 14 (Belfast)	N. Ireland 2	Wales..........1
March 22 (Burnley)	England 0	Scotland 2
March 29 (Cardiff)	Wales 2	England........1
April 15 (Dundee)	Scotland 5	N. Ireland 1
May 17 (Kirkcaldy)	Scotland 3	Wales..........1
May 17 (Newtownards)	N. Ireland 1	England........2

Final Placings: 1st, Scotland (6 pts); 2nd, N. Ireland (3); 3rd, Wales (2); 4th, England (1).

OTHER SCHOOLS' INTERNATIONALS 1969

April 5 (Coventry)	England 5	Netherlands 2
April 19 (Wembley)	England 3	Wales..........0
April 26 (Berlin)	W. Germany 2	England........2
April 29 (Hamburg)	W. Germany 0	England........1
May 16 (Dublin)	Rep. of Ireland ..1	England........6

ENGLISH SCHOOLS TROPHY FINAL

1st leg: Liverpool 3   Swindon 0
2nd leg: Swindon 1   Liverpool 0
Liverpool won 3–1 on aggregate

F.A. YOUTH CHALLENGE CUP FINAL

1st leg: West Bromwich Albion..3   Sunderland 0
2nd leg: Sunderland 6   West Bromwich Albion..0
Sunderland won 6–3 on aggregate

INTERNATIONAL YOUTH TOURNAMENT
(East Germany, May 1969)

Final: Bulgaria 1   E. Germany...........1
(Bulgaria won on toss)

3rd place: U.S.S.R. 1   Scotland 0

HOME INTERNATIONAL YOUTH CHAMPIONSHIP 1969

Feb. 1 (Stranraer)	Scotland 1	England........1
Feb. 28 (Birkenhead)	England........0	N. Ireland 2
March 15 (Haverfordwest)	Wales..........1	England........3
April 12 (Ayr)	Scotland 1	Wales..........0
April 18 (Belfast)	N. Ireland 1	Scotland 1
May 17 (Aberystwyth)	Wales..........4	N. Ireland 2

Final Placings: 1st, Scotland (4 pts); 2nd, England (3); 3rd, N. Ireland (3); 4th, Wales (2).

RUGGER

RUGBY UNION

INTERNATIONAL CHAMPIONSHIP 1969

Jan. 11 (Paris) France ....3 Scotland 6
Jan. 25 (Dublin) Ireland........17 France 9
Feb. 1 (Murrayfield) Scotland ......3 Wales 17
Feb. 8 (Dublin) Ireland........17 England 15
Feb. 22 (Twickenham) England ......22 France 8
Feb. 22 (Murrayfield) Scotland ......0 Ireland........16
March 8 (Cardiff) Wales ....24 Ireland........11
March 15 (Twickenham) England........8 Scotland 3
March 22 (Paris) France ....8 Wales.........8
April 12 (Cardiff) Wales ....30 England 9

	P	W	D	L	F	A	Pts
Wales	4	3	1	0	79	31	7
Ireland	4	3	0	1	61	48	6
England	4	2	0	2	54	58	4
Scotland	4	1	0	3	12	44	2
France	4	0	1	3	28	53	1

University Match
(Twickenham, Dec. 10, 1968) : Oxford..6 Cambridge..9
County Championship
Final (Redruth, March 8, 1969) : Cornwall..9 Lancashire..11
Hospitals Cup Final
(Richmond, March 12, 1969) : St. Bartholomew's..11 Guy's..3
Schoolboys' International
(Cardiff, April 19, 1969) : Wales..3 England..12

AUSTRALIAN STATE CAPITAL PREMIERSHIPS

Sydney Premiership ....Eastern Suburbs
Melbourne Premiership ....Melbourne
Brisbane Premiership ....University
Adelaide Premiership ....Elizabeth
Perth Premiership ....Perth

WELSH TOUR OF AUSTRALASIA 1969

May 31 (Christchurch) New Zealand ..19 Wales 0
June 14 (Auckland) New Zealand ..33 Wales 12
June 21 (Sydney) Australia ......16 Wales 19
June 25 (Suva) Fiji ....11 Wales 31

AUSTRALIAN TOUR OF S. AFRICA 1969

Aug. 2 (Johannesburg) S. Africa........30 Australia 11
Aug. 16 (Durban) S. Africa........16 Australia 9
Sept. 6 (Cape Town) S. Africa........11 Australia 3
Sept. 20 (Bloemfontein) S. Africa........19 Australia 8

FIJIAN TOUR OF AUSTRALIA 1969

July 12 (Melbourne) Fiji ....40 Victoria 8
July 16 (Canberra) Fiji ....17 A.C.T. 12
July 19 (Sydney) Fiji ....31 Sydney 16
July 23 (Tamworth) Fiji ....22 N.S.W. Country ..9
July 26 (Sydney) N.S.W. ....6 Fiji.............5
July 30 (Brisbane) Queensland ...17 Fiji.............16
Aug. 2 (Brisbane) Fiji ....26 Australian XV ..3
Aug. 6 (Goondiwindi) Fiji ....40 Queensland Ctry..21
Aug. 9 (Townsville) Fiji ....44 Townsville D.I. ..11

AUSTRALIAN SCHOOLBOYS IN S. AFRICA

In August–September 1969 a team of 25 Australian schoolboys toured South Africa, playing seven matches—against the schools of Northern Transvaal, Western Province, Eastern Province, the Border, Orange Free State, Griqua, and Transvaal. The Australians won five matches, drew one (with Orange Free State) and lost one (to Griqua Schools). More than 65,000 spectators watched the seven matches.

RUGBY LEAGUE

FINAL TABLE 1968-69

	P	W	D	L	F	A	Pts
Leeds	34	29	2	3	775	358	60
St. Helens	34	27	2	5	669	262	56
Wigan	34	25	2	7	732	368	52
Castleford	34	24	2	8	462	255	50
Swinton	34	23	0	11	503	412	46
Salford	34	19	5	10	573	309	43
Featherstone Rovers	34	21	1	12	523	346	43
Workington Town	34	21	0	13	512	379	42
Leigh	34	19	4	11	447	371	42
Hull Kingston Rovers	34	20	0	14	566	445	40
York	34	20	0	14	477	440	40
Wakefield Trinity	34	19	1	14	473	375	39
Hull	34	18	3	13	494	419	39
Widnes	34	19	1	14	506	434	39
Keighley	34	18	1	15	380	407	37
Oldham	34	18	0	16	479	474	36
Warrington	34	17	1	16	561	546	35
Halifax	34	16	2	16	468	485	34
Bradford Northern	34	16	0	18	525	475	32
Barrow	34	13	1	20	454	559	27
Rochdale Hornets	34	13	0	21	342	485	26
Dewsbury	34	12	1	21	306	430	25
Hunslet	34	11	0	23	439	554	22
Doncaster	34	11	0	23	279	622	22
Huddersfield	34	9	1	24	296	553	19
Batley	34	8	1	25	294	577	17
Huyton	34	8	0	26	273	657	16
Bramley	34	7	0	27	313	575	14
Blackpool Borough	34	7	0	27	382	752	14
Whitehaven	34	6	1	27	360	539	13

Top 16 Play-off Final: Leeds......16 Castleford........14
Players 7-a-side Final: Workington Town....10 Salford....5

INTERNATIONALS

Nov. 7, 1968 (Salford) England ......17 Wales 24
Nov. 30, 1968 (St. Helens) Gt. Britain ....34 France........10
Feb. 2, 1969 (Toulouse) France ....13 Gt. Britain......9
March 9, 1969 (Paris) France ....17 Wales 13
April 17, 1969 (Castleford) England Udr-24.42 France Udr-24..2

CHALLENGE CUP FINAL
May 17, 1969, Wembley

CASTLEFORD ....11 SALFORD 6
Castleford bt. Hunslet 19–7 (1st round), Wigan 12–8 (2nd), Leeds 9–5 (3rd), Wakefield Trinity 16–10 (semi-final). Salford bt. Batley 17–2 (1st round), Workington Town 12–5 (2nd), Widnes 20–7 (3rd), Warrington 15–8 (semi-final).

COUNTY CHAMPIONSHIP

Cumberland ....10 Yorkshire 23
Yorkshire ....10 Lancashire..................5
Lancashire ....24 Cumberland 19
Final Placings: 1st Yorks; 2nd Lancs; 3rd Cumberland
Yorkshire Cup Final: Leeds ....22 Castleford......11
Lancashire Cup Final: St. Helens ....30 Oldham 2

AUSTRALIAN RUGBY LEAGUE 1969

Sydney Premiership ....South Sydney
Brisbane Premiership ....Northern Suburbs

New South Wales Country Competitions

Newcastle .Maitland
Illawarra ..Western Suburbs
Group 1.
  Richmond Clarence
  League   Ballina
  Bonalbo League
      Mallanganee
Group 2.....Nambucca
      Heads
Group 3.....Wauchope
Group 4.....West Tamworth
Group 5.....Guyra
Group 6.....Campbelltown
      Kangaroos
Group 7.....Kiama
Group 8/9...Queanbeyan
      Kangaroos

Group 9/20..Griffith Waratahs
Group 10. ..Oberon
Group 11. ..Dubbo C.Y.M.S.
Group 12. ..Wyong
Group 13. ..Tarcutta
Group 14. ..Baradine
Group 15. ..Brewarrina
Group 16. ..Candelo-
      Bemboka
Group 17. ..Tullibigeal
Group 18. ..Murwillumbah
      Brothers
Group 19. ..Delegate
Group 21. ..Scone

Riviera R.L.—Zone 3
      Wagga Kangaroos

AUSTRALIAN TOUR OF NEW ZEALAND 1969

May 28 Australia ....17 North Island Colts......13
June 1 AUSTRALIA ....20 NEW ZEALAND 10
June 2 Australia ....24 South Island 15
June 4 Australia ....48 Wellington 7
June 7 AUSTRALIA ....14 NEW ZEALAND 18
June 10 Australia ....14 Auckland............15

Sports Personalities of 1969

Left: Jon Erikson (USA), at 14 the youngest boy to swim the Channel (August 11). *Above:* left, Miss H. Yuki (Japan), All-England badminton singles champion; right, Norwegian Dag Fornaes, World and European speed-skating champion.

Above: left, 18-year-old Liz Allan (USA) won four titles in the World water-skiing championships; right, David Broome (GB), European show-jumping champion, on Mr. Softee. *Right:* Ondrej Nepela (Czecho), European figure-skating champion.

| Ivan Mauger (New Zealand), World speedway champion. | Tony Book (Manchester C.), British footballer of the year. | Eddy Merckx (Belgium), Tour de France winner. | Johnny Famechon (Australia), featherweight champion. |

| Ruben Olivares (Mexico), bantamweight champion. | Giacomo Agostini (Italy), motor-cycling champion. | Great Britain's sportsman and sportswoman of the year; golfer Tony Jacklin and Wimbledon winner Ann Jones. |

TENNIS

AUSTRALIAN CHAMPIONSHIPS

Milton Courts, Brisbane, Jan. 20–27, 1969

Men's Singles. R. Laver (Austral) bt. A. Gimeno (Sp), 6–3, 6–4, 7–5.
Women's Singles. Mrs. B. Court (Austral) bt. Mrs. B. King (USA), 6–4, 6–1.
Men's Doubles. R. Emerson & R. Laver (Austral) bt. K. Rosewall & F. Stolle (Austral), 6–4, 6–4 (reduced by consent to three advantage sets).
Women's Doubles. Mrs. B. Court & Miss J. Tegart (Austral) bt. Mrs. B. King & Miss R. Casals (USA), 6–4, 6–4.
Mixed Doubles. Match unfinished: title shared by F. Stolle (Austral) & Mrs. P. Jones (GB) and M. Riessen (USA) & Mrs. B. Court (Austral).

SOUTH AFRICAN CHAMPIONSHIPS

Johannesburg, April 1–12, 1969

Men's Singles. R. Laver (Austral) bt. T. Okker (Neth.), 6–3, 10–8, 6–3.
Women's Singles. Mrs. B. King (USA) bt. Miss N. Richey (USA), 6–3, 6–4.
Men's Doubles. R. Gonzales (USA) & R. Moore (SA) bt. R. Hewitt & F. McMillan (SA), 6–3, 4–6, 6–1, 6–3.
Women's Doubles. Mrs. P. Jones (GB) & Miss F. Durr (Fr) bt. Miss N. Richey (USA) & Miss V. Wade (GB), 6–2, 3–6, 6–4.
Mixed Doubles. T. Okker (Neth) & Mrs. J du Plooy (SA) bt. R. Maud (SA) & Miss V. Wade (GB), 8–6, 5–7, 6–4.

ITALIAN CHAMPIONSHIPS

Rome, April 21–27, 1969

Men's Singles. J. Newcombe (Austral) bt. A. Roche (Austral), 6–3, 4–6, 6–2, 5–7, 6–3.
Women's Singles. Miss J. Heldman (USA) bt. Miss K. Melville (Austral), 7–5, 6–3.
Men's Doubles. J. Newcombe & A. Roche (Austral) bt. M. Riessen (USA) & T. Okker (Neth), 6–4, 1–6 (abandoned).
Women's Doubles. Mrs. P. Jones (GB) & Miss F. Durr (Fr) bt. Mrs. B. King and Miss R. Casals (USA), 6–3, 3–6, 6–2.
Mixed Doubles. Abandoned.

FRENCH CHAMPIONSHIPS

Paris, May 28–June 8, 1969

Men's Singles. R. Laver (Austral) bt. K. Rosewall (Austral), 6–4, 6–3, 6–4.
Women's Singles. Mrs. B. Court (Austral) bt. Mrs. P. Jones (GB), 6–1, 4–6, 6–3.
Men's Doubles. J. Newcombe & A. Roche (Austral) bt. R. Emerson & R. Laver (Austral), 4–6, 6–1, 3–6, 6–4, 6–4.
Women's Doubles. Mrs. P. Jones (GB) & Miss F. Durr (Fr) bt. Mrs. B. Court (Austral) & Miss N. Richey (USA), 6–0, 4–6, 7–5.
Mixed Doubles. M. Riessen (USA) & Mrs. B. Court (Austral) bt. J. Newcombe (Austral) & Mrs. B. King (USA), 7–5, 6–4.

WIMBLEDON CHAMPIONSHIPS

London, June 23–July 5, 1969

Men's Singles. R. Laver (Austral) bt. J. Newcombe (Austral), 6–4, 5–7, 6–4, 6–4.
Women's Singles. Mrs. P. Jones (GB) bt. Mrs. B. King (USA), 3–6, 6–3, 6–2.
Men's Doubles. J. Newcombe (Austral) & A. Roche (Austral) bt. T. Okker (Neth) & M. Riessen (USA), 7–5, 11–9, 6–3.
Women's Doubles. Mrs. B. Court & Miss J. Tegart (Austral) bt. Miss P. Hogan & Miss M. Michel (USA), 9–7, 6–2.
Mixed Doubles. F. Stolle (Austral) & Mrs. P. Jones (GB) bt. A. Roche & Miss J. Tegart (Austral), 6–2, 6–3.

GERMAN CHAMPIONSHIPS

Hamburg, Aug. 5–11, 1969

Men's Singles. A. Roche (Austral) bt. T. Okker (Neth), 6–1, 5–7, 7–5, 8–6.
Women's Singles. Miss J. Tegart (Austral) bt. Miss H. Niessen (W Ger), 6–3, 6–4.
Men's Doubles. M. Riessen (USA) & T. Okker (Neth) bt. J.-C. Barclay (Fr) & J. Fassbender (W Ger), 6–1, 6–2, 6–4.
Women's Doubles. Miss J. Tegart (Austral) & Miss H. Niessen (W Ger) bt. Miss E. Buding & Miss H. Schultze (W Ger), 6–1, 6–4.
Mixed Doubles. M. Riessen (USA) & Miss J. Tegart (Austral) bt. F. McMillan and Miss P. Walkden (SA), 6–4, 6–1.

U.S.A. CHAMPIONSHIPS

Forest Hills, Aug. 28–Sept. 8, 1969

Men's Singles. R. Laver (Austral) bt. A. Roche (Austral), 7–9, 6–1, 6–2, 6–2.
Women's Singles. Mrs. B. Court (Austral) bt. Miss N. Richey (USA), 6–2, 6–2.
Men's Doubles. K. Rosewall & F. Stolle (Austral) bt. D. Ralston & C. Pasarell (USA), 2–6, 7–5, 13–11, 6–3.
Women's Doubles. Miss D. Hard (USA) & Miss F. Durr (Fr) bt. Mrs. B. Court (Austral) & Miss V. Wade (GB), 0–6, 6–4, 6–4.
Mixed Doubles. M. Riessen (USA) & Mrs. B. Court (Austral) bt. D. Ralston (USA) & Miss F. Durr (Fr), 7–5, 6–3.

ALL-ENGLAND JUNIOR CHAMPIONSHIPS

Wimbledon, Sept. 1–6, 1969

Boys' Singles. M. Collins bt. C. Mottram, 1–6, 7–5, 6–1.
Girls' Singles. Miss V. Burton bt. Miss J. Fayter, 6–0, 6–3.
Boys' Doubles. G. Newton & I. Thomson bt. K. McCollum & R. Walker, 6–4, 6–4.
Girls' Doubles. Miss J. Fayter & Miss H. Retter bt. Miss L. Charles & Miss W. Slaughter, 6–1, 7–5.
Mixed Doubles. G. Newton & Miss W. Slaughter bt. J. Feaver & Miss J. Fayter, 6–4, 6–4.

WILLS COVERED COURTS CHAMPIONSHIPS

Wembley, November 17–22, 1969

Men's Singles. R. Laver (Austral) bt. A. Roche (Austral), 6–4, 6–1, 6–3.
Women's Singles. Mrs. P. Jones (GB) bt. Mrs. B. King (USA), 9–11, 6–2, 9–7.
Men's Doubles. R. Laver & R. Emerson (Austral) bt. R. Hewitt (SA) & R. Gonzales (USA), 5–7, 6–3, 6–4, 6–3.
Women's Doubles. Mrs. P. Jones & Miss V. Wade (GB) bt. Mrs. B. King & Miss R. Casals (USA), 6–2, 6–4.

FEDERATION CUP

Women's International Team Championship

Athens, May 19–25, 1969

Semi-Finals

Australia (holders) bt. Great Britain......3–0
U.S.A. bt. Netherlands................3–0

Final

U.S.A. bt. Australia...................2–1
Miss N. Richey (USA) bt. Miss K. Melville, 6–4, 6–3.
Mrs. B. Court (Austral) bt. Miss J. Heldman, 6–4, 8–6.
Miss N. Richey & Miss P. Bartkowitcz (USA) bt. Mrs. B. Court & Miss J. Tegart, 6–4, 6–4.

WIGHTMAN CUP

Cleveland, Aug. 9–11, 1969

U.S.A. bt. Great Britain (holders) by 5 matches to 2, and won the Cup.
Singles. Miss J. Heldman (USA) bt. Miss V. Wade, 3–6, 6–1, 8–6; and bt. Miss W. Shaw, 6–3, 6–4.
Miss N. Richey (USA) bt. Miss W. Shaw, 8–6, 6–2; and lost to Miss V. Wade, 3–6, 6–2, 4–6.
Miss P. Bartkowitcz (USA) bt. Mrs. G. T. Janes, 8–6, 6–0.
Doubles. Miss J. Heldman & Miss P. Bartkowitcz (USA) bt. Miss V. Wade & Miss W. Shaw, 6–4, 6–2. Mrs. P. W. Curtis & Miss V. J. Ziegenfuss (USA) lost to Mrs. G. T. Janes & Miss F. E. Truman, 6–1, 3–6, 4–6.

DAVIS CUP

1. **European Zone "A" Final.** Great Britain bt. S. Africa, 3–2.
2. **European Zone "B" Final.** Rumania bt. U.S.S.R., 4–1.
3. **American Zone Final.** Brazil bt. Mexico, 4–1.
4. **Eastern Zone Final.** India bt. Japan, 5–0.
5. **Winner of 1 v. Winner of 3.** Great Britain bt. Brazil, 3–2.
6. **Winner of 2 v. Winner of 4.** Rumania bt. India, 4–0.
7. **Winner of 5 v. Winner of 6.** Rumania bt. Great Britain, 3–2.
8. **Challenge Round: Winner of 7 v. U.S.A. (holders).** U.S.A. bt. Rumania, 5–0.

Metric Distances   **MEN**   Records at Jan. 1, 1970
(y) = set over longer yards course

Event	World Record	European Record	British Record
Free-style			
100 m	52·2 s, M. Wenden (Austral), 1968	52·9 s, A. Gottvalles (Fr), 1964	53·4 s, R. McGregor, 1967
200 m	1 m 54·3 s, D. Schollander (USA) 1968; M. Spitz (USA), 1969	1 m 56·5 s, H. Fassnacht (W. Ger), 1969	2 m 00·1 s*(y)*, A. Jarvis, 1968
400 m	4 m 04·0 s, H. Fassnacht (W. Ger), 1969	Same as world record	4 m 19·6 s*(y)*, M. Woodroffe, 1969
800 m	8 m 28·8 s M. Burton (USA), 1968	8 m 42·0 s, F. Luyce (Fr), 1967	9 m 05·4 s*(y)*, M. Woodroffe, 1969
1,500 m	16 m 04·5 s, M. Burton (USA), 1969	16 m 32·2 s, H. Fassnacht (W. Ger), 1969	17 m 13·2 s, A. Kimber, 1966
4×100 m	3 m 31·7 s, USA (Z. Zorn, S. Rerych, M. Spitz, K. Walsh), 1968	3 m 34·2 s, USSR (S. Belits-Geiman, V. Mazanov, G. Kulikov, L. Ilyichev), 1968	3 m 38·3 s, GB (A. Jarvis, K. Bewley, M. Turner, R. McGregor), 1967
4×200 m	7 m 52·1 s, USA (S. Clark, R. Saari, G. Ilman, D. Schollander), 1964; USA (G. Ilman, M. Wall, M. Spitz, D. Schollander), 1967	7 m 54·5 s, USSR (V. Bure, S. Belits-Geiman, Anajabev, G. Kulikov), 1969	8 m 11·8 s, GB (K. Bewley, A. Jarvis, J. Thurley, R. McGregor), 1967
Back-stroke			
100 m	57·8 s, R. Matthes (E. Ger), 1969	Same as world record	1 m 02·2 s*(y)*, R. Jones, 1967
200 m	2 m 06·4 s, R. Matthes (E. Ger), 1969	Same as world record	2 m 16·8 s*(y)*, C. Rushton, 1969
Breast-stroke			
100 m	1 m 05·8 s, N. Pankin (USSR), 1969	Same as world record	1 m 09·9 s*(y)*, R. Roberts, 1968
200 m	2 m 25·4 s, N. Pankin (USSR), 1969	Same as world record	2 m 34·3 s, R. Roberts, 1967
Butterfly			
100 m	55·6 s, M. Spitz (USA), 1968	58·0 s, L. Stoklasa (W. Ger), 1968	58·8 s, M. Woodroffe, 1969
200 m	2 m 05·7 s, M. Spitz (USA), 1967	2 m 07·8 s, M. Woodroffe (GB), 1969	Same as European record
Medley			
200 m	2 m 09·6 s, G. Hall (USA), 1969	2 m 13·5 s, F. Wiegand (E. Ger), 1967	2 m 17·1 s M. Woodroffe, 1969
400 m	4 m 33·9 s, G. Hall (USA), 1969	4 m 42·5 s, H. Fassnacht (W. Ger), 1969	4 m 49·5 s, M Woodroffe, 1969
4×100 m	3 m 54·9 s, USA (C. Hickcox, D. McKenzie, D. Russell, K. Walsh), 1968	3 m 56·5 s, East Germany (R. Matthes, E. Henninger, H. Gregor, F. Wiegand), 1967	4 m 03·9 s, GB (R. Jones, R. Roberts, M. Woodroffe, R. McGregor), 1967

WOMEN

Event	World Record	European Record	British Record
Free-style			
100 m	58·9 s, D. Fraser (Austral), 1964	59·6 s, G. Wetzko (E. Ger), 1969	1 m 00·5 s, A. Jackson, 1968
200 m	2 m 06·7 s, D. Meyer (USA), 1968	2 m 08·9 s, G. Wetzko (E. Ger), 1969	2 m 16·1 s*(y)*, E. Long, 1965
400 m	4 m 24·5 s, D. Meyer (USA), 1968	4 m 36·1 s, G. Wetzko (E. Ger), 1969	4 m 45·6 s*(y)*, S. Williams, 1967
800 m	9 m 10·4 s, D. Meyer (USA), 1968	9 m 30·8 s, K. Neugebauer (E. Ger), 1969	9 m 59·3 s, S. Davison, 1968
1,500 m	17 m 19·9 s, D. Meyer (USA), 1969	18 m 11·6 s, N. Calligaris (It), 1969	*None established*
4×100 m	4 m 01·1 s, Santa Clara, USA (L. Gustavson, L. Watson, P. Carpinelli, J. Henne), 1968	4 m 02·6 s, Hungary (M. Patoh, E. Kovacs, A. Gyarmati, J. Turoczy), 1969	4 m 12·5 s, GB (F. Kellock, P. Sillett, S. Ratcliffe, A. Jackson), 1967
Back-stroke			
100 m	1 m 05·6 s, K. Muir (SA), 1969	1 m 07·9 s, C. Caron (Fr), 1964	1 m 08·7 s*(y)*, L. Ludgrove, 1967
200 m	2 m 21·5 s, S. Atwood (USA), 1969	2 m 27·9 s, C. Caron (Fr), 1966; B. Duprez (Fr), 1968	2 m 28·5 s*(y)*, L. Ludgrove, 1968
Breast-stroke			
100 m	1 m 14·2 s, C. Ball (USA), 1968	1 m 15·4 s, G. Prosumenschikova (USSR), 1968	1 m 17·3 s, D. Harris, 1968
200 m	2 m 38·5 s, C. Ball (USA), 1968	2 m 40·8 s, G. Prosumenschikova (USSR), 1966	2 m 47·0 s, S. Mitchell, 1965
Butterfly			
100 m	1 m 04·5 s, A. Kok (Neth), 1965	Same as world record	1 m 07·4 s*(y)*, M. Auton, 1968
200 m	2 m 21·0 s*(y)*, A. Kok (Neth), 1967	Same as world record	2 m 32·7 s*(y)*, M. Auton, 1968
Medley			
200 m	2 m 23·5 s, C. Kolb (USA), 1968	2 m 27·5 s, M. Grunert (E. Ger), 1969	2 m 33·0 s, S. Ratcliffe, 1968
400 m	5 m 04·7 s, C. Kolb (USA), 1968	5 m 14·9 s, S. Steinbach (E. Ger), 1968	5 m 24·5 s, S. Ratcliffe, 1968
4×100 m	4 m 28·1 s, USA (K. Hall, C. Ball, E. Daniel, S. Pedersen), 1968	4 m 34·8 s, East Germany (B. Hofmeister, E. Wittke, H. Lindner, G. Wetzko), 1969	4 m 38·0 s, GB (W. Burrell, D. Harrison, M. Auton, A. Jackson), 1968

DIVING. **European Championships.** Men—Highboard, G. Cagnotto (It); Springboard, K. Dibiasi (It). Women—Highboard, I. Pertmager (Aus); Springboard, U. Knape (Swed).
    British Championships. Men—Highboard, A. Gill; Springboard, A. Roberts. Women—Highboard and Springboard, B. Boys (Can).

EUROPEAN CUPS. Men (Wurzburg)—1. E. Germany (136 pts.); 2. USSR (124); 3. W. Germany (117).
    Women (Budapest)—1. E. Germany (138 pts.); 2. USSR (90); 3. Hungary (82).

PROFESSIONAL CHAMPIONS

Weight	World Champion	European Champion	British Champion
Fly	Efren Torres (Mexico)	Fernando Atzori (Italy)	John McCluskey
Bantam	Ruben Olivares (Mexico)	Salvatore Burruni (Italy)	Alan Rudkin
Feather	Johnny Famechon (Australia)	Tomaso Galli (Italy)	Jimmy Revie
Junior Light	Hiroshi Kobayashi (Japan)		Jimmy Anderson
Light	Mando Ramos (USA)	VACANT	Ken Buchanan
Junior Welter	Nicolino Locche (Argentine)	Bruno Arcari (Italy)	Vic Andreetti
Welter	Jose Napoles (Mexico)	Hans Orsolic (Austria)	Ralph Charles
Junior Middle	Freddie Little (USA)	Gerhart Plaskowy (W. Germany)	—
Middle	Nino Benvenuti (Italy)	Tom Bogs (Denmark)	Les McAteer
Light-Heavy	Bob Foster (USA)	Ivan Preberg (Yugoslavia)	Eddie Avoth
Heavy	VACANT	Peter Weiland (W. Germany)	Jack Bodell

AMATEUR CHAMPIONS

Weight	Olympic Champion (1968)	European Champion (1969)	Commonwealth Champion (1966)	Great Britain Champion (1969)
Fly	R. Delgado (Mexico)	C. Cluca (Rumania)	S. Shittu (Ghana)	D. Needham
Bantam	V. Sokolov (USSR)	A. Dumitrescu (Rumania)	E. Ndukwu (Nigeria)	M. Pinner
Feather	A. Roldan (Mexico)	L. Orban (Hungary)	P. Waruinge (Kenya)	A. Richardson
Light	R. Harris (USA)	C. Cutov (Rumania)	A. Andeh (Nigeria)	H. Hayes
Lt.-Welter	J. Kulej (Poland)	V. Frolov (USSR)	J. McCourt (N. Ireland)	J. Stracey
Welter	M. Wolke (E. Germany)	G. Meier (W. Germany)	E. Blay (Ghana)	T. Henderson
Lt.-Middle	B. Lagutin (USSR)	V. Tregubov (USSR)	M. Rowe (England)	T. Imrie
Middle	C. Finnegan (GB)	V. Tarrasenkov (USSR)	J. Darkey (Ghana)	D. Wallington
Lt.-Heavy	D. Pozdnik (USSR)	D. Poznyak (USSR)	R. Tighe (England)	J. Frankham
Heavy	G. Foreman (USA)	I. Alexe (Rumania)	W. Kini (NZ)	A. Burton

Other Champions: Olympic Light-Fly—F. Rodriguez (Venezuela); European Light-Fly—G. Gedo (Hungary)

MOTOR RACING

World Champion: Jackie Stewart (GB, Matra-Ford)
S. African G.P. Stewart (Matra-Ford)
Spanish G.P. Stewart (Matra-Ford)
Monaco G.P. G. Hill (GB, Lotus-Ford)
Dutch G.P. Stewart (Matra-Ford)
French G.P. Stewart (Matra-Ford)
British G.P. Stewart (Matra-Ford)
German G.P. J. Ickx (Belg, Brabham-Ford)
Italian G.P. Stewart (Matra-Ford)
Canadian G.P. Ickx (Brabham-Ford)
U.S. G.P. J. Rindt (Aus, Lotus-Ford)
Mexican G.P. D. Hulme (NZ, McLaren-Ford)
Sebring 12-hour and Le Mans 24-hour. J. Ickx (Belg) & J. Oliver (GB), Ford GT40
Indianapolis 500. M. Andretti (USA), Hawk-turbo-Ford

MOTOR-CYCLE RACING

World Champions 1969

500 cc. G. Agostini (It, MV-Agusta)
350 cc. G. Agostini (It, MV-Agusta)
250 cc. K. Carruthers (Austral, Benelli)
125 cc. D. Simmonds (GB, Kawasaki)
50 cc. A. Nieto (Sp, Derbi)
Sidecar. K. Enders (W. Ger, BMW)

Isle of Man TT

500 cc. G. Agostini (It, MV-Agusta)
350 cc. G. Agostini (It, MV-Agusta)
250 cc. K. Carruthers (Austral, Benelli)
125 cc. D. Simmonds (GB, Kawasaki)
Sidecar K. Enders (W. Ger, BMW)

SPEEDWAY

World Champion. I. Mauger (NZ)
World Pairs. N. Zealand (I. Mauger & B. Andrews)
World Team. Poland
European Champion. V. Klementiev (USSR)
British League Champions. Poole (Dorset)

CYCLING

World Championships Professionals

MEN

Sprint. P. Sercu (Belg)
Pursuit. F. Bracke (Belg)
Road Race. H. Ottenbros (Neth)
Motor-paced. J. Oudkirk (Neth)

Amateur

Sprint. D. Morelon (Fr)
Pursuit. X. Kurmann (Switz)
Team Pursuit. USSR
Tandem. W. Otto & J. Geschke (E. Ger)
1,000 m Time-Trial. G. Sartori (It)
Team Time-Trial. Sweden
Road Race. L. Mortensen (Den)
Motor-paced. A. Broom (Neth)

WOMEN

Sprint. G. Careva (USSR)
Pursuit. R. Obodovskaya (USSR)
Road Race. A. McElmury (USA)

Cyclo-Cross Championships

World Prof. Eric de Vlaeminck (Belg)
World Amateur. R. Declercq (Belg)
British Prof. J. Atkins
British Amateur. B. Moss

European Classic Winners

Tour of France. E. Merckx (Belg)
Tour of Italy. F. Gimoudi (It)
Tour of Britain. F. den Hertog (Neth)
Milan-San Remo. E. Merckx (Belg)
Tour of Flanders. E. Merckx (Belg)
Paris-Roubaix. W. Godefroot (Belg)
Ghent-Wevelgem. W. Vekemans (Belg)
Amstel Gold. G. Reybroeck (Belg)
Flèche-Wallonne. J. Huysmans (Belg)
Liége-Bastogne-Liége. E. Merckx (Belg)
Henninger Turm. G. Pintens (Belg)
Zürich. R. Swerts (Belg)
Bordeaux-Paris. W. Godefroot (Belg)
Paris-Tours. H. van Springel (Belg)
Tour of Lombardy. G. Karstens (Neth)

British National Championships

Professional Sprint. R. Barnett
Amateur Sprint. R. Whitfield
Women's Sprint. B. Swinnerton
Professional Pursuit. H. Porter
Amateur Pursuit. I. Hallam
Women's Pursuit. C. Barton
Prof. Road Race. W. Lawrie
Amateur Road Race. B. Jolly
Women's Road Race. A. Horswell
Tandem. T. Brockhurst & P. Mugglestone
Amateur 10-mile Track. R. Keeble

British Time-Trial Championships

MEN

25 miles. A. Engers, 54 m 42 s
50 miles. M. Roach, 1 h 53 m 32 s
100 miles. A. Taylor, 3 h 54 m 08 s
24 hours. R. Cromack, 507 miles

WOMEN

25 miles. B. Burton, 58 m 30 s
50 miles. B. Burton, 1 h 56 m 15 s
100 miles. M. Wroe, 4 h 36 m 08 s

HORSE-RACING

Grand National. Highland Wedding (E. Harty)
1,000 Guineas. Full Dress II (R. Hutchinson)
2,000 Guineas. Right Tack (G. Lewis)
Oaks. Sleeping Partner (J. Gorton)
Derby. Blakeney (E. Johnson)
St. Leger. Intermezzo (R. Hutchinson)
Champion British Jockey. L. Piggot, (163 wins)

Australian

Melbourne Cup. Rain Lover
Australian Cup. Dead heat: Cyron—Yootha
Sydney Cup. Lowland
Brisbane Cup. Galleon King
Adelaide Cup. Gnapur
Perth Cup. Jenark
Hobart Cup. Delarus
Caulfield Cup. Big Philou

Records at Jan. 1, 1970   **MEN**   Metric and Field events

Event	World Record	European Record	British Record
100 m	9·9 s, J. Hines (twice), C. Greene, R. Smith (all USA), 1968	10·0 s, A. Hary (W. Ger), 1960; R. Bambuck (Fr), 1968; V. Sapeya (USSR), 1968; V. Borzov (USSR), 1969	10·2 s, M. Campbell, 1967
200 m	19·8 s, T. Smith (USA), 1968	20·3 s, P. Clerc (Switz), 1969	20·5 s, P. Radford, 1960
400 m	43·8 s, L. Evans (USA), 1968	44·9 s, C. Kaufmann, 1960; M. Jellinghaus, 1968 (both W. Ger)	45·7 s, A. Metcalfe, 1961; R. Brightwell (twice), 1964
800 m	1 m 44·3 s, P. Snell (NZ), 1963; R. Doubell (Austral), 1968	1 m 44·9 s, F. Kemper (W. Ger), 1966	1 m 46·3 s, C. Carter, 1966
1,500 m	3 m 33·1 s, J. Ryun (USA), 1967	3 m 36·3 s, M. Jazy (Fr), 1966	3 m 39·0 s, I. Stewart, 1969
5,000 m	13 m 16·6 s, R. Clarke (Austral), 1966	13 m 24·8 s, H. Norpoth (W. Ger), 1966	13 m 29·0 s, R. Taylor, 1969
10,000 m	27 m 39·4 s, R. Clarke (Austral), 1965	28 m 04·4 s, J. Haase (E. Ger), 1968	28 m 06·6 s, R. Taylor, 1969
Steeplechase	8 m 22·2 s, V. Dudin (USSR), 1969	Same as world record	8 m 30·8 s, G. Stevens, 1969
110 m/120 yd hurdles	13·2 s, M. Lauer (W. Ger), 1959; L. Calhoun, 1960, E. McCullouch, 1967, W. Davenport, E. Hall, 1969 (all USA)	Same as world record (Lauer)	13·6 s, D. Hemery, 1969
400 m hurdles	48·1 s, D. Hemery (GB), 1968	Same as world record	Same as world record
4×100 m relay	38·2 s, USA, 1968	38·4 s, France, 1968	39·3 s, GB, 1968
4×400 m relay	2 m 56·1 s, USA, 1968	3 m 00·5 s, W. Germany, 1968; Poland, 1968	3 m 01·2 s, GB, 1968
High jump	7 ft 5¾ in (2·28 m), V. Brumel (USSR), 1963	Same as world record	6 ft 10 in (2·08 m), G. Miller, 1964
Pole vault	17 ft 10¼ in (5·44 m), J. Pennel (USA), 1969	17 ft 8½ in (5·40 m), C. Schiprowski (W. Ger); W. Nordwig (E. Ger), 1968	16 ft 7½ in (5·06 m), M. Bull, 1968
Long jump	29 ft 2½ in (8·90 m), R. Beamon (USA), 1968	27 ft 4¾ in (8·35 m), I. Ter-Ovanesian (USSR), 1967	27 ft 0 in (8·23 m), L. Davies, 1968
Triple jump	57 ft 0¾ in (17·39 m), V. Saneyev (USSR), 1968	Same as world record	54 ft 0 in (16·46 m), F. Alsop, 1964
Shot	71 ft 5½ in (21·78 m), R. Matson (USA), 1967	67 ft 8½ in (20·64 m), H.-P. Gies (E. Ger), 1969	64 ft 2 in (19·56 m), A. Rowe, 1961
Discus	224 ft 5 in (68·40 m), J. Silvester (USA), 1968	223 ft 3 in (68·06 m), R. Bruch (Swed), 1969	189 ft 6 in (57·76 m), J. Watts, 1968; W. Tancred, 1969
Hammer	247 ft 7½ in (75·48 m), A. Bondarchuk (USSR), 1969	Same as world record	223 ft 3½ in (68·06 m), H. Payne, 1968
Javelin	304 ft 1 in (92·70 m), J. Kinnunen (Fin), 1969	Same as world record	268 ft 9 in (81·92 m), J. FitzSimons, 1969
Decathlon	8,417 pts, W. Toomey (USA), 1969	8,319 pts, K. Bendlin (W. Ger), 1967	7,451 pts, C. Longe, 1969
Marathon	2 h 8 m 33·6 s, D. Clayton (Austral), 1969	2 h 10 m 47·8 s, W. Adcocks (GB), 1968	Same as European record
20 km walk	1 h 26 m 45·8 s, G. Agapov (USSR), 1969	Same as world record	1 h 28 m 15 s, K. Matthews, 1960
50 km walk	4 h 10 m 51·8 s, C. Hohne (E. Ger), 1965	Same as world record	4 h 11 m 31·2 s, P. Nihill, 1964

Linear records set in 1969. World—100 yd, 9·1 s (equals) J. Carlos (USA); 440 yd, 44·7 s, C. Mills (USA). British—3 miles, 13 m 04·6 s, R. Taylor; 6 miles, 27 m 10·2 s, R. Taylor.

WOMEN

Event	World Record	European Record	British Record
100 m	11·0 s, W. Tyus (USA), 1968	11·1 s, I. Szewinska (Pol), 1965 & 1968; L. Samotyosova (USSR), 1968	11·3 s, D. Hyman (twice), 1963; D. James, V. Peat, 1968
200 m	22·5 s, I. Szewinska (Pol), 1968	Same as world record	23·2 s, D. Hyman, 1963
400 m	51·7 s, N. Duclos, C. Besson (both Fr), 1969	Same as world record	52·1 s, L. Board, 1968
800 m	2 m 00·5 s, V. Nikolic (Yugo), 1968	Same as world record	2 m 01·1 s, A. Packer, 1964
1,500 m	4 m 10·7 s, J. Jehlickova (Czecho), 1969	Same as world record	4 m 15·9 s, R. Ridley, 1969
100 m hurdles	12·9 s, K. Balzer (E. Ger), 1969	Same as world record	13·5 s, C. Perera, 1968
4×100 m relay	42·8 s, USA, 1968	43·4 s, Netherlands, 1968; USSR, 1968	43·7 s, GB, 1968
4×400 m relay	3 m 30·8 s, GB, 1969; France, 1969	Same as world record	Same as world record (GB)
High jump	6 ft 3¼ in (1·91 m), I. Balas (Rum), 1961	Same as world record	5 ft 10½ in (1·79 m), L. Hedmark, 1969
Long jump	22 ft 4½ in (6·82 m), V. Viscopoleanu (Rum), 1968	Same as world record	22 ft 2¼ in (6·76 m), M. Rand 1964
Shot	67 ft 0¼ in (20·43 m), N. Chizhova (USSR), 1969	Same as world record	53 ft 6¼ in (16·31 m), M. Peters, 1966
Discus	209 ft 10 in (63·96 m), L. Westermann (W. Ger), 1969	Same as world record	171 ft 4 in (52·22 m), R. Payne, 1969
Javelin	204 ft 8½ in (62·40 m), Y. Gorchakova (USSR), 1964	Same as world record	182 ft 5 in (55·60 m), S. Platt, 1968
Pentathlon	5,352 pts, L. Prokop (Aus), 1969	Same as world record	4,731 pts, S Scott, 1969

Linear records set in 1969. World—100 yd, 10·3 s (equals), Chi Cheng (Formosa); Mile, 4 m 36·8 s, M. Gommers (Neth).

BRITISH NATIONAL ATHLETICS LEAGUE
Final Placings
Division 1. 1, Birchfield; 2, Cardiff; 3, Thames Valley. *Relegated:* Polytechnic and Blackheath.
Division 2. 1, Hillingdon; 2, Surrey A.C. (both promoted); 3, Sale. *Relegated:* Notts and Achilles.
Division 3. 1, Woodford Green; 2, Southampton (both promoted).

IX EUROPEAN ATHLETICS CHAMPIONSHIPS

Athens, September 16-21, 1969

MEN

Event	Gold Medal	Silver Medal	Bronze Medal
100 m	V. Borzov (USSR), 10·4 s	A. Sarteur (Fr), 10·4 s	P. Clerc (Switz), 10·5 s
200 m	P. Clerc (Switz), 20·6 s	H. Burde (E. Ger), 20·9 s	Z. Nowosz (Pol), 20·9 s
400 m	J. Werner (Pol), 45·7 s	J. Nallet (Fr), 45·8 s	S. Gredzinski (Pol), 45·8 s
800 m	D. Fromm (E. Ger), 1 m 45·9 s	J. Plachy (Czecho), 1 m 46·2 s	M. Matuschewski (E. Ger), 1 m 46·8 s
1,500 m	J. Whetton (GB), 3 m 39·4 s	F. Murphy (Ire), 3 m 39·5 s	H. Szordykowski (Pol), 3 m 39·8 s
5,000 m	I. Stewart (GB), 13 m 44·8 s	R. Sharafutdinov (USSR), 13 m 45·8 s	A. Blinston (GB), 13 m 47·6 s
10,000 m	J. Haase (E. Ger), 28 m 41·6 s	M. Tagg (GB), 28 m 43·2 s	N. Sviridov (USSR), 28 m 45·8 s
Marathon	R. Hill (GB), 2 h 16 m 47·8 s	G. Roelants (Belg), 2 h 17 m 22·2 s	J. Alder (GB), 2 h 19 m 05·8 s
20 km walk	P. Nihill (GB), 1 h 30 m 49 s	L. Caraiosifoglu (Rum), 1 h 31 m 6·4 s	N. Smaga (USSR), 1 h 31 m 20·2 s
50 km walk	C. Hoehne (E. Ger), 4 h 13 m 32·8 s	P. Selzer (E. Ger), 4 h 16 m 9·6 s	V. Soldatenko (USSR), 4 h 23 m 4·8 s
4 × 100 m relay	France, 38·8 s	USSR. 39·3 s	Czechoslovakia, 39·5 s
4 × 400 m relay	France, 3 m 02·3 s	USSR, 3 m 03 s	West Germany, 3 m 01·1 s †
110 m hurdles	E. Ottoz (It), 13·5 s	D. Hemery (GB), 13·7 s	A. Pascoe (GB), 13·9 s
400 m hurdles	V. Skomorokhov (USSR), 49·7 s	J. Sherwood (GB), 50·1 s	A. Todd (GB), 50·3 s
Steeplechase	M. Zhelev (Bulg), 8 m 25 s	A. Morozov (USSR), 8 m 25·6 s	V. Dudin (USSR), 8 m 26·6 s
High jump	V. Gavrilov (USSR), 7 ft 1½ in	R. Vahala (Fin), 7 ft 1½ in	E. Azzaro (It), 7 ft 1½ in
Pole vault	W. Nordwig (E. Ger), 17 ft 4¾ ins	K. Isaksson (Swed), 17 ft 0¾ in	A. Righi (It), 16 ft 8¾ in
Long jump	I. Ter-Ovanesian (USSR), 26 ft 9¾ in	L. Davies (GB), 26 ft 5¾ in	T. Lepik (USSR), 26 ft 4½ in
Triple jump	V. Saneyev (USSR), 56 ft 10¾ in	Z. Cziffra (Hung), 55 ft 3½ in	K. Neumann (E. Ger), 54 ft 8¾ in
Shot	D. Hoffman (E. Ger), 66 ft 0¼ in	H. Rothenburg (E. Ger), 65 ft 9½ in	H. Gies (E. Ger), 64 ft 10¾ in
Discus	H. Losch (E. Ger), 202 ft 10 in	R. Bruch (Swed), 200 ft 4½ in	L. Milde (E. Ger), 194 ft 8 in
Hammer	A. Bondarchuk (USSR), 245 ft 0 in*	R. Klim (USSR), 238 ft 7½ in	R. Theimer (E. Ger), 236 ft 3½ in
Javelin	J. Lusis (USSR), 300 ft 3¼ in	P. Nevala (Fin), 293 ft 10½ in	J. Sidlo (Pol), 271 ft 11½ in
Decathlon	J. Kirst (E. Ger), 8,041 pts	H. Wessel (E. Ger), 7,828 pts	V. Chelnokov (USSR), 7,801 pts

WOMEN

Event	Gold Medal	Silver Medal	Bronze Medal
100 m	P. Vogt (E. Ger), 11·6 s	W. Van den Berg (Neth), 11·7 s	A. Neil (GB), 11·8 s
200m	P. Vogt (E. Ger), 23·2 s	R. Meissner (E. Ger), 23·3 s	V. Peat (GB), 23·3 s
400 m	N. Duclos (Fr), 51·7 s*	C. Besson (Fr), 51·7 s*	M. Sykopa (Aus), 53 s
800 m	L. Board (GB), 2 m 1·4 s	A. Damm-Nielsen (Den), 2 m 2·6 s	V. Nikolic (Yugo), 2 m 2·6 s
1,500 m	J. Jehlickova (Czecho), 4 m 10·7 s*	M. Gommers (Neth), 4 m 11·9 s	P. Pigni (It), 4 m 12 s
4 × 100 m relay	East Germany, 43·6 s	West Germany, 44 s†	Great Britain, 44·3 s
4 × 400 m relay	Great Britain, 3 m 30·8 s*	France, 3 m 30·8 s*	West Germany, 3 m 32·7 s †
100 m hurdles	K. Balzer (E. Ger), 13·3 s	B. Podeswa (E. Ger), 13·6 s	T. Nowak (Czecho), 13·7 s
High jump	M. Rezkova (Czecho), 6 ft	A. Lazareva (USSR), 6 ft	M. Mracnova (Czecho), 6 ft
Long jump	M. Sarna (Pol), 21 ft 3½ in	V. Viscopoleanu (Rum), 21 ft 2 in	B. Berthelsen (Nor), 21 ft 1½ in
Shot	N. Chizhova (USSR), 67 ft 0¼ in*	M. Gummel (E. Ger), 64 ft 3 in	M. Lange (E. Ger), 60 ft 10¾ in
Discus	T. Danilova (USSR), 194 ft 6 in	I. Muravieva (USSR), 194 ft 4 in	K. Illgen (E. Ger), 192 ft 5½ in
Javelin	A. Ranki-Nemeth (Hung), 196 ft 0½ in	M. Vidos (Hung), 192 ft 11 in	V. Evert (USSR), 185 ft 6½ in
Pentathlon	L. Prokop (Aus), 5,030 pts	M. Antenen (Switz), 4,793 pts	M. Sisiakova (USSR), 4, 773 pts

* New world record.   † West Germany competed only in relay events.

NATIONAL MEDALS TABLE

	Gold	Silver	Bronze
East Germany ..	11	7	7
U.S.S.R.	9	7	8
Britain	6	4	7
France	3	4	0
Czechoslovakia ..	2	1	2
Poland	2	0	5
Hungary	1	2	0
Switzerland	1	1	1
Italy	1	0	3
Austria	1	0	1
Bulgaria	1	0	0
Rumania	0	2	0
Finland	0	2	0
Sweden	0	2	0
Netherlands	0	2	0
West Germany ..	0	1	2
Denmark	0	1	0
Ireland	0	1	0
Belgium	0	1	0
Yugoslavia	0	0	1
Norway	0	0	1

CHANNEL SWIMMERS, 1969

Date	Direction	Name	Time
July 24	France—England	Ronald Fletcher	10 h 24 m
July 28	France—England	Margot Orford	15 h 53 m
August 6	England—France	Barry Watson	13 h 56 m
August 6	England—France	Philip Gollop	14 h 28 m
August 6	England—France	Mervyn Sharp	14 h 29 m
August 6	France—England	Mair Leonard	19 h 45 m
August 11	France—England	Jon Erikson*	11 h 22 m
August 14	France—England	Michael Read	12 h 10 m
August 17	England—France	Haagse Bluf Team	9 h 29 m
August 18	England—France	Peter Elwin Bales	13 h 38 m
September 4-5	France—England	Bolton Dolphins	11 h 25 m
September 6	France—England	John Koorey	10 h 32 m
September 9	France—England	Atina Vidakovic	13 h 20 m
September 10	England—France	Jan van Scheyndal	12 h 47 m
September 13	France—England	Judith de Nys	12 h 15 m
September 16	France—England	Lamorbey Training & Swimming Club	17 h 58 m
September 25	England—France	Thomas J. Hetzell	14 h 54 m
October 4	England—France	Mervyn Sharp	19 h 41 m

*At 14 years 11 months the youngest male Channel swimmer.

Supplied by the Channel Swimming Association.

TABLE TENNIS

World Championships
Munich, April 17–27, 1969

Men's Singles. S. Ito (Jap) bt. E. Scholer (W. Ger), 19–21, 14–21, 21–19, 21–15, 21–9
Women's Singles. T. Kowada (Jap) bt. G. Geissler (E. Ger), 20–22, 21–14, 21–17, 21–8
Men's Doubles. H. Alser & K. Johansson (Swed) bt. N. Hasegawa & T. Tanaka (Jap), 21–19. 17–21 21–8, 21–12
Women's Doubles. Z. Rudnova & S. Grinberg (USSR) bt. M. Alexandru & E. Mihalca (Rum), 17–21, 21–17, 21–15, 16–21, 21–14
Mixed Doubles. N. Hasegawa & Y. Konno (Jap) bt. M. Kono & S. Hirota (Jap), 21–17, 21–19, 21–19
Men's Team (Swaythling Cup). 1. Japan ; 2. W. Germany ; 3. Yugoslavia
Women's Team (Corbillion Cup). 1. USSR ; 2. Rumania ; 3. Japan

English Open Championships
Brighton, Feb. 27–March 1, 1969

Men's Singles. S. Gomozkov (USSR) bt. D. Surbek (Yugo), 21–17, 21–17, 21–12
Women's Singles. Z. Rudnova (USSR) bt. S. Grinberg (USSR), 21–18, 21–11, 21–18
Men's Doubles. S. Gomozkov & A. Amelin (USSR) bt. H. Alser & K. Johansson (Swed), 21–16, 21–14, 13–21, 21–19
Women's Doubles. S. Grinberg & Z. Rudnova (USSR) bt. M. Alexandru & E. Mihalca (Rum), 21–17, 21–15, 21–11
Mixed Doubles. E. Scholer & Mrs. D. Scholer (née Rowe) (W. Ger) bt. A. Amelin & S. Grinberg (USSR), 21–11, 21–11, 21–15

English Closed Championships
Crystal Palace, Jan. 2–4, 1969

Men's Singles. D. Neale bt. C. Barnes, 21–16, 21–16, 21–18
Women's Singles. J. Williams bt. J. Shirley, 14–21, 21–9, 19–21, 21–12, 21–15
Men's Doubles. A. Hydes & D. Neale bt. C. Barnes & D. Brown, 13–21, 24–22, 20–22 21–9, 21–11
Women's Doubles. J. Heaps & P. Piddock bt. L. Radford & D. Simpson, 21–17, 15–21, 21–10, 18–21, 21–13
Mixed Doubles. D Neale & K. Matthews bt. A. Hydes & M. Heppell, 21–17 21–16, 16–21, 21–13

BADMINTON

All-England Championships
Wembley, March 19–22, 1969

Men's Singles. R. Hartono (Indo) bt. Darmadi (Indo), 15–1, 15–3
Women's Singles. H. Yuki (Jap) bt. N. Takagi (Jap), 11–5, 11–5
Men's Doubles. H. Borch & E. Kops (Den) bt. J. Eddy & R. Powell (GB), 13–15, 15–10, 15–9
Women's Doubles. M. Boxall & P. Whetnall (GB) bt. H. Amano & T. Takahashi (Jap), 15–11, 15–11
Mixed Doubles. R. Mills & Miss G. Perrin (GB) bt. A. Jordan & Mrs. P. Whetnall (GB), 15–5, 15–3

Asian Champions. Men : Muljadi (Indonesia) Women : Pang Yuet-Mui (Hong Kong)
Uber Cup (Challenge Round). Japan (holders) 6, Indonesia 1

SQUASH RACKETS

World Amateur Championships (London & Midland clubs). Individual : G. Hunt (Austral).
Team : 1. Australia ; 2. Britain ; 3. Pakistan
British Open Championship. G. Hunt (Austral)
British Amateur Championship. J. Barrington (GB)
British Women's Championship. H. McKay (Austral)

ARCHERY

World Championships
Valley Forge, U.S.A., Aug. 11–20, 1969

Men's Target. H. Ward (USA) ; Team : USA
Women's Target. D. Lidstone (Can) ; Team : USSR
Men's Field. R. Branstetter (USA)
Women's Field. E. Danielsen (Swed)

British Target Championships
Men. R. Matthews, 2,108 pts. **Women.** L. Thomas, 2,120 pts.

ROWING

Henley Royal Regatta
July 2–5, 1969

Double Sculls. D. Oswald & M. Burgin (Grasshopper, Zürich) bt. A. J. Cowley & N. F. Drake (St. Ives) : 3 lengths (7 m 35 s)
Grand Challenge Cup. S. C. Einheit (Dresden, E. Ger) bt. University of Pennsylvania (USA) : ¾ length (6 m 28 s)
Ladies' Plate. A. S. R. Nereus (Holland) bt. Trinity College, Hartford (USA) : 1 length (6 m 55 s)
Silver Goblets and Nickalls Cup. U. Bitterli & U. Frankhauser S.E.E., Lucerne, Switz) bt. R. C. Wait & M. A. Sweeney (Nottingham and Union R.C.) : easily (7 m 56 s)
Prince Philip Cup. D. S. R. Lago (Holland) bt. Hutt Valley R.C. (NZ) : ½ length (7 m 19 s)
Visitors Cup. Eton Coll. bt. Clare Coll. (Camb) : 2½ lengths (7 m 22 s)
Diamond Sculls. H. J. Bohmer (S.C. Dynamo, Berlin) bt. W. B. Tytus (Seattle Tennis Club, USA) : easily (8 m 6 s)
Thames Cup. Leander Club bt. University of Pennsylvania : 3 lengths (6 m 43 s)
Wyfold Cup. London R.C. bt. Trident R.C. (SA) : 2½ lengths (7 m 16 s)
Stewards' Cup. A. S. R. Nereus
Princess Elizabeth Cup. Washington-Lee H.S. (USA) bt. Emmanuel School : 2/3 length (7 m 0 s)

European Championships
MEN
Klagenfurt, Sept. 10–14, 1969

Single Sculls. A. Demiddi (Argentina)
Double Sculls. USA
Coxed Pairs. Czechoslovakia
Coxed Fours. W. Germany
Coxless Pairs. USA
Coxless Fours. USSR
Eights. E. Germany

WOMEN
Klagenfurt, Sept. 5–7, 1969

Single Sculls. G. Shidagite (USSR)
Double Sculls. E. Germany
Coxed Fours. USSR
Coxless Fours. USSR
Eights. E. Germany

Other Events
University Boat Race. Cambridge won by 4 lengths
Doggett's Coat and Badge. Leonard Grieves (26 m 46 s)

Australian
King's Cup, 1969 (Burnett River, Queensland, April 26, 1969). 1. Victoria. 2. New South Wales. 3. South Australia. 4. Tasmania

YACHTING

Class	World Champions	European Champions
Cadet	C. Winters (Belg)	—
Dragon	R. Mosbacher (USA)	A. Holm (Den)
Finn	T. Lundqvist (Swed)	A. Akerson (Swed)
Flying Dutchman	R. Pattison (GB)	—
Hornet	S. Lodge (Austral)	J. Kania (Pol)
Lightning	B. Goldsmith (USA)	S. Bonas (Gre)
Moths	D. McKay (Austral)	J. Faroux (Fr)
Snipe	E. Elms (USA)	—
Soling	P. Elvstroem (Den)	A. von Gruenewald (Swed)
Star	P. Pettersson (Swed)	B. Larsson (Swed)
Tempest	C. Norbury (GB)	—
5-0-5	J. Le Guillou (Fr)	D. Farrant (GB)

Sydney-Hobart Race. Morningcloud (E. Heath, GB)

WATER SKI-ING

World Champions, 1969
Men. M. Suyderhoud (USA). **Women.** E. Allan (USA).

British Champions, 1969
Men. P. Adlington. **Women.** L. Jackson.

HOCKEY

MEN
Home Internationals 1969
Champions: Scotland

Ireland	1	Wales	0
Wales	0	England	1
Scotland	1	Ireland	0
England	0	Scotland	1
Ireland	0	England	2
Wales	0	Scotland	0

Other Internationals

England	0	W. Germany	0
Scotland	1	S. Africa	2
Wales	2	Belgium	1
Wales	0	S. Africa	2
England	1	Netherlands	2
England	1	S. Africa	0
Ireland	0	Netherlands	0

County Championship. Final: Lancs 2, Lincs 0 (after 0–0 draw)

British Clubs' Cup. Final: Cork Church of Ireland 2, Stepps (Scot) 1

WOMEN
Home Internationals
Champions: England

England	2	Ireland	1
Wales	0	Scotland	0
England	2	Wales	1
Scotland	0	England	1
Wales	0	Ireland	0
Ireland	2	Scotland	1

Other Internationals

Ireland	2	W. Germany	0
Netherlands	2	Scotland	1
W. Germany	3	England	2

County Championship. Final: Lancs 1, Herts 1

International Tournament
Lahore, March 8–16 1969

Pool A

	P	W	D	L	F	A	Pts
Pakistan	4	4	0	0	15	0	8
Malaysia	4	2	1	1	4	9	5
Belgium	4	1	2	1	2	4	4
W. Germany	4	1	1	2	2	4	3
Spain	4	0	0	4	1	7	0

Pool B

	P	W	D	L	F	A	Pts
Pakistan B	4	4	0	0	10	1	8
France	4	3	0	1	5	6	6
Australia	4	2	0	2	5	4	4
E. Germany	4	1	0	3	3	7	2
Kenya	4	0	0	4	1	5	0

Semi-finals: Pakistan..2 France..0
Pakistan B..2 Malaysia..0
Third Place: France..1 Malaysia..0
Final: Pakistan..1 Pakistan B..0

Australian Championship
Melbourne, August 1969

1. Western Australia .... 9 pts.
2. South Australia .... 7 pts.
3. { Queensland .... } 5 pts.
   { Victoria .... }
4. Tasmania .... 3 pts.
5. New South Wales .... 1 pt.

BASKETBALL
European Championships
Naples, Sept. 21–30, 1969

1. USSR; 2. Yugoslavia; 3. Czechoslovakia

GOLF
Professional Champions
S. African Open. G. Player (SA)
US Open. O. Moody (USA)
British Open. A. Jacklin (GB)
Canadian Open. T. Aaron (USA)
French Open. J. Garaialde (Fr)
German Open. J. Garaialde (Fr)
Australian Open. G. Player (SA)
Australian Prof. B. Devlin (NSW)
US Masters. G. Archer (USA)
US P.G.A. R. Floyd (USA)
"Piccadilly" Match-play. R. Charles (NZ)
"Alcan" Golfer of the Year. W. Casper (USA)
World Cup. Team: USA (O. Moody, L. Trevino). Individual: Trevino
Ryder Cup. USA (holders) 13..GB 13 (6 halved)

Amateur Champions
British. M. Bonallack
USA. S. Melnyk
Australian. R. Shearer (Vic)
English (match-play). J. Cook
English (stroke-play). R. Foster
British Boys. M. Foster
British Youths. J. Cook
Home Internationals. 1. England; 2. Ireland; 3. Scotland & Wales
European Team. 1. England; 2. W. Germany; 3. Ireland
Walker Cup. USA (holders) bt. GB, 10–8

Women Champions
British Open. C. Lacoste (Fr)
British (stroke-play). A. Irvin
British Girls. J. de Witt Puyt (Neth)
Home Internationals. 1. Scotland; 2. England; 3. Ireland; 4. Wales
European Team. 1. France; 2. England; 3. Netherlands

CANOEING
World Championships
Moscow, Aug. 18–21, 1969

MEN
Canadian Singles.
1,000 m T. Vichman (Hung)
10,000 m T. Vichman (Hung)
Canadian Pairs. 1,000 m Rumania
10,000 m Hungary
Kayak Singles. 500 m A. Tichenko (USSR)
1,000 m A. Chaparenko (USSR)
10,000 m V. Tzarev (USSR)
Kayak Pairs. 500 m Rumania
1,000 m USSR
10,000 m Hungary
Kayak Fours. 1,000 m East Germany
10,000 m Norway
Kayak Relay (4 × 500 metres) USSR

WOMEN
Kayak Singles. 500 m A. Schimanaskaya (USSR)
Kayak Pairs. 500 m USSR
Kayak Fours. 500 m USSR

World Slalom and Wild Water Championships
Bourg St. Maurice, Aug. 1–6, 1969

Slalom.
Single canoe. W. Peters (W. Ger)
Double canoe. France
Single kayak. C. Peschier (Fr)
Single kayak (women). L. Polesna (Czecho)
Double canoe (mixed). Czechoslovakia

Wild Water.
Single canoe. J. Boudehen (Fr)
Double canoe. France
Single kayak. J. Burny (Belg)
Single kayak (women). L. Polesna (Czecho)
Double canoe (mixed). Austria

CHESS
World Championship
Moscow, June 1969

Boris Spassky (12½ pts.) bt. Tigran Petrosian (10½ pts.)

British Champions
Men. Dr. J. Penrose (London). Record 10th win in 12 years
Men under 21. R. G. Eales (Chester)
Boys under 18. C. Cubitt (Gt. Yarmouth)
Boys under 16. M. F. Stean (Kew)
Boys under 14. J. Speelman (London)
Girls under 18. G. Fielding (Huddersfield) and M. McGinn (Glasgow)

Australian Championship
Melbourne, January 1969

First: Shawn Browne (NSW)
Equal Second: { Douglas Hamilton (Vic)
{ Alfred Flatow (NSW)

BRIDGE
World Championship. Italy
European Championship. Italy
British Team Championship (Gold Cup). Scotland
England Team Championship (Crockford's Cup). Mrs. R. Oldroyd, J. Bloomberg, I. Manning, A. Finlay, E. Newman
Women's Team Championship (Whitelaw Cup). Mrs. M. Britt, Mrs. M. Gough, Miss H. Schindler, Mrs. R. Banerjee
Tollemache Cup. Warwickshire
Pachabo Cup. Southern Counties
English Pairs. G. S. Moffat & D. Valley
Life Masters Pairs. E. W. Crowhurst & A. E. Wardman
"Daily Mail" Schools Cup. Kings School, Worcester

ANGLING
World Championship
Individual. R. Harris (GB)
Team. Netherlands

British Championships
Individual. R. Else (Lincs) **Team.** Stoke

POWERBOAT RACING
World Championship
Offshore Races
(Sam Griffith Trophy)

Champion. D. Aronow (USA)
Bahamas 500. D. Aronow (USA)
Wills Trophy. V. Balestrieri (It)
Napoli-Medisima. F. Cosentino (It)
Roseto-Split. V. Balestrieri (It)
Sam Griffith Race. B. Wishnick (USA)
Viareggio-Bastia. D. Aronow (USA)
New York Hennessey. P. Rittmaster (USA)
Dauphin d'Or. France
Gettingloppet. E. Lennart (Swed)
Long Beach Hennessey. D. Aronow (USA)
Cowes-Torquay. D. Aronow (USA)
Deauville. T. Sopwith (GB)
Miami-Nassau. D. Aronow (USA)
Miami-Key West. B. Wishnick (USA)

MODERN PENTATHLON
World Championships
Budapest, Sept. 19–26, 1969

1. A. Balczo (Hung); 2. B. Onichenko (USSR); 3. B. Ferm (Swed)
Team: 1. USSR; 2. Hungary; 3. W. Germany
British Championship. R. Phelps

SHOW-JUMPING

European Championships 1969

Men's Show-Jumping. D. Broome (GB) on Mister Softee

Women's Show-Jumping. I. Kellett (Ire) on Morning Light

European Dressage. Mrs. L. Linsenhoff (W. Ger) on Piaff

Three-day Event. Miss M. Gordon-Watson (GB) on Cornishman. Team : Great Britain

Junior Show-Jumping. B. A. Dufour (Fr) on Mounana. Team : Switzerland

Junior Three-day. Hans-Otto Bolten (Ger) on Lausbub. Team : USSR

Royal International Horse Show
Wembley, July 22-27, 1969

Horse and Hound Cup. Mrs. D. Backhouse (GB) on Cardinal

Philips Stakes. F. Kernan (GB) on Top of the Morning

Moss Bros. Cup. H. Smith (GB) on O'Malley

Country Life and Riding Cup. Miss M. Coakes (GB) on Stroller

King George V Cup. T. Edgar (GB) on Uncle Max

Queen Elizabeth II Cup. Miss A. Westwood (GB) on The Maverick II

John Player Trophy. A. Schockemohle (W. Ger) on Donald Rex

Daily Mail Cup. Miss J. Lefebvre (Fr) on Rocket

Horse of the Year Show
Wembley, Oct. 6-11, 1969

Butlin's Championship. A. Oliver (GB) on Sweep

Philips Championship. A. Oliver (GB) on Pitz Palu

Foxhunter Championship. Miss C. Bradley (GB) on Walkie-Talkie

Daily Telegraph Cup. J. O. Wannius (Swed) on Shalimar

Leading Show-Jumper of Year. T. Edgar (GB) on Uncle Max

Dick Turpin Stakes. Mrs. C. D. Barker (GB) on Brandy Jim

Sunday Times Cup. H. Smith (GB) on Mattie Brown

Ronson Trophy. A. Oliver (GB) on Pitz Palu

WEIGHT-LIFTING
World Championships
Warsaw, Sept. 20-28, 1969

Fly. V. Krishishin (USSR), $743\frac{3}{4}$ lb (337.5 kg)

Bantam. M. Nassiri (Iran), $793\frac{1}{4}$ lb (360 kg)

Feather. Yoshiyuki Miyake (Jap), $848\frac{1}{2}$ lb (385 kg)

Light. W. Baszanowski (Pol), $980\frac{3}{4}$ lb (445 kg)

Middle. V. Kurentsov (USSR), $1,030\frac{1}{4}$ lb (467.5 kg)

Lt.-heavy. M. Ohuchi (Jap), $1,074\frac{1}{4}$ lb (487.5 kg)

Middle-heavy. K. Kangasniemi (Fin), 1,135 lb (515 kg)

Heavy. Y. Talts (USSR) $1,206\frac{1}{2}$ lb (547.5 kg)

Super-heavy. J. Dube (USA) $1,272\frac{1}{2}$ lb (577.5 kg)

GYMNASTICS
European Champions 1969
Men. M. Voronin (USSR)
Women. K. Janz (E. Germany)
British Champions
Men. Stan Wild (Rotherham)
Women. Margaret Bell (Sidcup)

SKATING
World Championships 1969
Men's Figure. T. Wood (USA)
Women's Figure. G. Seyfert (E. Ger)
Pairs. A. Ulanov & I. Rodnina (USSR)
Dancing. B. Ford & D. Towler (GB)
Speed Skating. Men : D. Fornaes (Nor) Women : L. Kauniste (USSR)

European Championships 1969
Men's Figure. O. Nepela (Czecho)
Women's Figure. G. Seyfert (E. Ger)
Pairs. A. Ulanov & I. Rodnina (USSR)
Dancing. B. Ford & D. Towler (GB)
Speed Skating. Men : D. Fornaes (Nor)

BRITISH SPORTSMAN AND SPORTSWOMAN OF THE YEAR 1969
British Sports Writers' Association choice :
Tony Jacklin ; Ann Jones
Daily Express poll :
Tony Jacklin ; Ann Jones
BBC-TV Sportsview Personality poll :
Ann Jones

WINTER SPORTS
World Championships 1968-69
Alpine Ski-ing (World Cup). Men : K. Schranz (Aus). Women : G. Gabl (Aus)

Two-man Bobsledding (Lake Placid, USA). 1. Italy ; 2. Rumania ; 3. Italy

Four-man Bobsledding (Lake Placid, USA). 1. W. Germany ; 2. Italy ; 3. USA

Biathlon (Zakopane, Poland). Individual : A. Tikhonov (USSR). Team relay : USSR

Curling (Perth, Scotland). Final : Canada 9, USA 6

Ice-Hockey (Stockholm). 1. USSR ; 2. Sweden ; 3. Czechoslovakia

Ski-bob (Montana-Crans). Men's Combined : P. Bonvin (Switz). Women's Combined : G. Schiffkorn (Aus)

Snow-karting (La Plagie, Switzerland). Men : L. Negrini (It). Women : S. Salice (It)

Tobogganing (Koenigsee, W. Ger). Men : J. Feistmanti (Aus). Women : P. Tierlich (W. Ger). Men's pairs : I. Schmid & E. Walch (Aus)

European Championships 1969
Two-man Bobsledding (Cervinia). Austria

Four-man Bobsledding (Cervinia). Italy

WRESTLING

| Weight | World Champions | European |
	Free-style	Champions Greco-Roman
Lt.-fly	E. Javadi (Iran)	R. Lacour (W. Ger)
Fly	R. Sanders (USA)	B. Marinko (Yugo)
Bantam	T. Tanaki (Jap)	R. Bjorlin (Fin)
Feather	S. Abdulbekov (USSR)	M. Alacop (Turk)
Light	A. Mohaved (Iran)	S. Damjanovic (Yugo)
Welter	Z. Berishavili (USSR)	E. Tapio (Yugo)
Middle	F. Fozzard (USA)	M. Nenadic (Yugo)
Lt.-heavy	B. Gurevich (USSR)	J. Coark (Yugo)
Heavy	C. Lomidze (USSR)	P. Svensson (Swed)
Super-heavy	A. Medved (USSR)	O. Topuz (Turk)

FENCING

	World Champions	British Champions
Foil	F. Wessel (W. Ger)	M. Breckin
Sabre	V. Sidiak (USSR)	D. Acfield
Epee	B. Andrejewski (Pol)	G. Paul
Ladies' Foil	E. Novikova (USSR)	J. Wardell-Yerburgh

JUDO

Weight	World Champions	European Champions
Light	Y. Sonada (Jap)	Feist (Fr)
Light-middle	H. Minatoya (Jap)	Rudman (USSR)
Middle	I. Sonada (Jap)	Bondarenko (USSR)
Light-heavy	F. Sasahara (Jap)	Snijders (Neth)
Heavy	S. Suma (Jap)	Ruska (Neth)
Open	M. Shinomaki (Jap)	Ruska (Neth)

BILLIARDS
English Amateur Championship. J. Karnehm bt. M. Wildman (holder)

Australasian Championship. Norman Squire (Australia), 5,005 pts, bt. C. McConachy (NZ), 4825 pts.

Australian Professional Championship. N. Squire, 1,618 pts., bt. Warren Simpson, 1,483 pts.

SNOOKER
World Professional Championship. J. Spencer (GB) bt. G. Owen (GB)

Australasian Professional Championship. E. Charlton (Austral) bt. W. Simpson (Austral)

Australian Professional Championship. E. Charlton bt. N. Squire

English Amateur Championship. R. Edmonds bt. J. Barron

The World at Large

Winds of Change Swept the 1960s

THE WIND OF CHANGE—Harold Macmillan's phrase was spoken in 1960—turned into a gale and even a hurricane before the decade ended. Almost all the established leaders—Macmillan himself, Hugh Gaitskell, Churchill, Menzies, Adenauer, Eisenhower, Khrushchev, De Gaulle, Pope John, Nkrumah, Verwoerd, Welensky, the Kennedys, Johnson, Ho Chi Minh—were blown away by death or retirement. The gale dispersed the remnants of the British Empire in a torrent of independence ceremonies. It battered the powerful image of the United States, both at home and abroad. It huffed and puffed at the values of the Western way of life as they had been revered for generations, and hurtled into prominence the Beatles and the whole apparatus of "pop" culture, the rioting of frustrated students, drug obsession, "sick" humour, and the "permissive" society. The world of December 1969 bore little resemblance to the world of January 1960— except for the running sores of the "cold war" and the war in Vietnam.

The 1960s were full of man-made horrors —Mau Mau, the Berlin wall, the Cuba crisis, the assassination of the Kennedy brothers and Martin Luther King, racial rioting, Aberfan, the thalidomide children, the suppression of Czechoslovakia, the Six-Day war, the Nigerian war, and the war of bigots in Northern Ireland. But they were full of honours, too—the incredible venture of men into space from Gagarin to the Apollo 11 and 12 crews on the Moon, the lonely courage of the round-the-world sailors and airmen and airwomen, and the hardy determination of Everest and Eiger climbers, trans-Arctic walkers, trans-Atlantic rowers, underwater-dwellers, cave-sitters, and 14-year-old Channel swimmers. Individuals like these gave the world hope that it was not sliding permanently into a rootless never-land of flower children, drop-outs, hippies, and teeny-boppers.

To the extent that the classical values —honesty, thrift, loyalty, patriotism—gave way to the philosophy of personal self-interest, it was a decade of the spendthrift "ad-mass," to whom material possessions were the only status symbols; the criminal, who if his crime was big enough was, like the participants in the Great Train Robbery, likely to find himself regarded as a hero; and the traitor-spy, who would willingly barter his country's safety for the brief thrill of spending his few pieces of silver. Governments made little effort to support the old pillars of virtue; indeed some joined gleefully in pulling them down, as in Great Britain where gambling was encouraged to run riot, homosexuality and abortion were legalised, theatre censorship was abolished, and adulthood was presented to 18-year-olds. In tune with the times the judiciary hastened to redefine obscenity to allow Lady Chatterley and her imitators a free hearing, and the mass media assiduously followed suit by publishing language, ideas, and pictures that had been taboo since printing was invented. Much of the new freedom was a gain, and this particular wind of change blew away many cobwebs of hypocrisy that had enwrapped the antique values.

It was a decade dominated by youth, which has always rebelled against the *mores* of the previous generation but never so successfully. In France students changed the course of history, and elsewhere they won unheard-of freedom from the authority of parents, pedagogues, and proctors. Their demonstrations against the larger evils of war, racialism, and deprivation, although influential, were less effective. At the end as at the beginning of the decade the shadow of the Bomb overhung their future, for France and Red China had added themselves to the nuclear club and upset the equalised stability of the East-West balance of power. And that other time-bomb—the population explosion —was almost as menacing, despite the invention of the Pill and the loop.

The Churches could make neither head nor tail of the moral and social revolution of the 1960s. Some bishops appeared to abandon theology altogether, while the new Supreme Pontiff, looking sometimes forward and sometimes back, threw the greatest Christian church into a ferment of doubt and disloyalty. Loss of faith was paralleled by a loss of self-confidence; people who no longer knew where they were going retreated ever more deeply from reality into the fantasy world of television, where fact and fiction become almost indistinguishable.

In science alone there were indisputable advances: the biologists and physicists made new sense of the invisible particles that constitute ourselves and our world, the surgeons' skill gave the transplanted organ the chance to save doomed lives, the engineers improved on the materials of the human environment and lifted some of the burdens of industrial serfdom. And the awakening awareness by scientists of their responsibilities for the use made of their inventions was one of the more hopeful signs for the 1970s.

"The Twelve Corners"

DAVID TINKLER gives under this heading a summary of the political history of the nations of the world during 1969. The world is divided into twelve major areas on a geographical basis, and within each section the individual countries are considered in alphabetical order.

1 The United Kingdom

Great Britain

It was a year of three notable failures and one conspicuous success for Harold Wilson's Labour government. The first failure involved the government's attempt at a major constitutional change—the reform of the House of Lords. On February 3, 1969, the Parliament (No. 2) Bill passed its second reading in the Commons with the benign connivance of both front benches, but was opposed by an "unholy alliance" of left-wing Labour Members and right-wing Conservatives. The argument of these strange bedfellows was that the Bill would vastly increase the Prime Minister's already staggering powers of patronage and give any government a built-in, obediently whipped, majority in the Upper House. Michael Foot, Labour Member for Ebbw Vale, attacked the Bill on the grounds that the "reformed" Lords—with its members chosen by party Whips—would be a mere "seraglio of eunuchs." These words appeared faintly ironic to many a commentator who considered that they could be an apt description of the Commons itself. But they reckoned without "backbench power" wielded by an obstinate rump, including Michael Foot and Enoch Powell, which succeeded in a brilliant filibuster until 10 parliamentary days including night and early morning sittings had been fruitlessly expended, and, on April 17, the Prime Minister rose to announce that the government had "decided not to proceed further at this time." The Bill was abandoned in order to give time to the more urgent Industrial Relations Bill—a move to which the unfolding of events lent a smack of heavy irony.

The second failure was the final abandonment of a stringent incomes policy in the face of three years of trade union pressure and the imminence of a general election. On December 11, Mrs. Barbara Castle, Secretary for Employment and Productivity, explained to the Parliamentary Labour Party that the Government intended to drop its powers to delay wage increases after a bridging period designed to avoid an inflationary free-for-all. The same day saw the publication of a new White Paper on prices and incomes which mooted a range of $2\frac{1}{2}$-$4\frac{1}{2}$ per cent for pay rises together with temporary—and milder—delaying powers of at most four months (as opposed to twelve). Mrs. Castle also announced that early in 1970 she would present a Bill creating a new Commission of Industry and Manpower engendered from the union of the Prices and Incomes Board and the Monopolies Commission. The powers of the proposed C.I.M. were unknown as the year ended, but these plans were interpreted by some as heralding the end of wage restraint imposed by legislation and the start of some sort of voluntary policy operating along pious government guidelines.

The most crashing defeat of the year, however, resulted from the much vaunted clash between the Government and the trade unions—which proved the political equivalent of a headlong collision between a pumpkin and a cannon-ball—on the subject of industrial disputes and strikes. On January 17, Mrs. Castle presented to Parliament her White Paper *In Place of Strife—A Policy for Industrial Relations*. Three of her proposals aroused immediate and continuous criticism from trade unions. They were: to impose a 28-day conciliation pause ("cooling-off" period) on unofficial strikes; to enforce the holding of a ballot before a major official strike is decided upon; and, through a new Industrial Board, to impose financial penalties for breach of "cooling-off" orders issued by the Secretary of State. Other proposals in the White Paper included the setting up of a Commission on Industrial Relations, with powers to look into trade union recognition problems, including inter-union disputes, if the T.U.C. was unable to resolve them. The establishment of this Commission took place immediately; George Woodcock gave up the general secretaryship of the T.U.C. to take the post of chairman.

As soon as the text of *In Place of Strife* was known there came ominous reverberations from the unions, particularly from George Woodcock's successor, Victor Feather. But on March 3 the Commons approved the White Paper by a curious 224 votes to 62, the Conservatives and some 40 Labour Members abstaining, and 53 Labour M.P.s and nine Liberals voting against the Government. On March 26 the Labour Party Executive, by a majority of 16 to 5, voted against the Government's

Vic Feather (*left*) led the T.U.C. rout of the Government—championed by Harold Wilson (*centre*) and Barbara Castle (*right*)—over the Industrial Relations Bill, which sought to outlaw "wild-cat" strikes.

plans, and it was revealed (thanks to a leak) that the Home Secretary, James Callaghan, had voted with the majority.

During Chancellor of the Exchequer Roy Jenkins's Budget speech of April 15, he announced that the government planned to go ahead with legislation enshrining "some of the more important provisions" of Mrs. Castle's White Paper. It was not, however, on the floor of the House that the merits or demerits of the proposals were thrashed out, but in a protracted dialogue between Harold Wilson and Barbara Castle on the one hand and the T.U.C. on the other, which finally produced, after weeks of hard bargaining and a special meeting of the T.U.C. held at Croydon on June 5, an agreement whereby the T.U.C. General Council itself undertook to "police" unofficial strikes and inter-union disputes. If it was ignored the T.U.C. was empowered to suspend or expel an erring union. This pious compromise earned instant analysis as "rubber teeth" from press and public. Unofficial strikes went merrily on.

The Government's conspicuous success was with the balance of payments. Over the weekend June 21–22, Roy Jenkins announced that Britain's trade figures had not, as had been thought, been "in the red" all year. A miscalculation, explained the Chancellor, "seems to have started as long ago as 1964, following a change in documentary practice introduced in 1963." The miscalculation, he claimed, meant that since 1964 there had been a consistent underestimate of British export figures of between 1 and 3 per cent. Taking the lower figure, this meant a £10–£11 million a month error. By July it could be seen that, for the first time since 1966, the haunting current account deficit had been laid to rest. From then on it appeared increasingly evident that the Government's stringent measures, the devaluation of 1967, and the export-orientated selective employment tax (raised during April 1969) had brought about a climate in which, at least, the country was not going to be forced deeper into debt. The balance of payments picture for the first three quarters of 1969, from figures available as the year ended was as follows:

	1st Qtr. £m.	2nd Qtr. £m.	3rd Qtr. £m.
Visible trade	−135	−79	+10
Invisibles	+161	+144	+131
Long term capital	−87	+7	+73
Balance	−61	+72	+214

See also Fact Digest under Capital Punishment; Local Government; Pensions.

Northern Ireland

In the last months of 1968 a sequence of events had unfolded that set the scene for the débâcle of 1969. The leader of the Unionist government, Captain Terence O'Neill, held tenuous sway over a cabinet containing such Protestant diehards as William Craig and Brian Faulkner, while beyond the walls of Stormont, Protestant and Catholic extremists were preparing for action. Spurred on by student activists, a number of militant organisations espousing the Catholic cause for civil rights mushroomed, while the traditional organs of the Catholic minority—long dominated by a system of gerrymandering and voting restrictions in local elections based on property—toed an increasingly belligerent line.

In response to these ominous echoes of the past, the Protestant "loyalists" grouped themselves about the leadership of the Rev. Ian Paisley and his henchman, Major Ronald Bunting. November 30, 1968, had seen street battles in Armagh, and, on December 11, 1968, the moderate O'Neill had sacked his Home Affairs Minister, William Craig, who disagreed with the Premier's "soft line" towards civil rights demonstrations. Thus 1969 opened with the beginnings of a split in the Unionist ranks and sectarian violence already rampant on the streets. New Year's Day saw the start of a civil rights march from Belfast to Londonderry stretching over four days and punctuated at intervals by fierce clashes with Paisleyites. The worst of these occurred on January 4 at Burntollet Bridge, near Londonderry, when the 250-strong march was ambushed by Protestant extremists, stoned from both flanks, and attacked from the front: 50 casualties were taken to hospital. When the marchers finally arrived in Londonderry fierce fighting broke out between Catholics and police, which continued sporadically until early morning.

On January 15, O'Neill announced that the Government had appointed an Independent Commission to investigate the disturbances. It was later announced that the distinguished Scottish judge, Lord Cameron, would chair the inquiry. The decision to appoint a Commission led to the resignation of Brian Faulkner, Minister of Commerce. By now the revolt against O'Neill's moderate leadership was growing within the Unionist ranks and, as a result of this split, O'Neill announced, on February 3, the dissolution of parliament and the calling of a general election for February 24, in order that the country could decide on the merits of the rival Unionist wings.

An ironic feature of the campaign was the way press and public opinion polls forecast a massive pro-O'Neill victory. In the event nine of 13 dissident Unionist backbenchers were re-elected, and the pro-O'Neillites generally failed to erode the traditional Unionist vote especially in rural areas. Out of an electorate of 900,000, 559,106 voted. The results were as follows: Unionists, 36; Independent O'Neill Unionists, 3; Nationalists (R.C. opposition), 6; N.I. Labour Party (non-sectarian), 2; Republican Labour, 2; Independents, 3.

Captain O'Neill commented on the results with the words: "I hope this is the dawn of the new Ulster. It hasn't broken as fully as one would have hoped." Just how dim that dawn was can be seen by the result in O'Neill's own constituency: O'Neill, 7,745 votes; Rev. Ian Paisley, 6,331; Farrell (People's Democracy) 2,310.

O'Neill promised some much-needed reforms in March, but further civil rights demonstrations marked the month of April, including two large clashes at Lurgan on April 4, and another at Londonderry over the weekend April 19–20. Meanwhile a spate of bomb attacks on installations occurred, bearing the stamp of the I.R.A., and the Prime Minister announced that key installations were to be placed under guard and that 1,000 "B" specials (an all-Protestant auxiliary armed police force greatly feared by Catholics) were to be mobilised. On April 20 further sabotage took place and the Government announced that London had agreed to make British troops available to guard key installations in Ulster. Next day 1,500 troops were on guard in the Province.

Street ablaze in Londonderry on the night of August 12-13 during savage street fighting between Protestants and Catholics, following the annual Protestant Apprentice Boys' March. British troops restored order on August 14.

On April 23 O'Neill won a narrow victory during a Unionist parliamentary party meeting, which voted, by 28 to 22, to "adopt the principle of universal franchise at the next local government elections." This led to the resignation of the Minister of Agriculture, Major James Chichester-Clark, who disagreed with the timing of these plans. O'Neill himself resigned on April 28, remarking that a new leader "unhampered by personal animosities may have a better chance of carrying on the work I have begun." On May 1, Major Chichester-Clark was elected as the new Unionist leader by the parliamentary party, receiving 17 votes to Brian Faulkner's 16. On May 6 the Government declared an amnesty for all arrested during the recent disturbances, as a result of which Paisley and Bunting (who had been jailed on March 25 on charges arising from the clash of November 30, 1968) were released and 133 charges were dropped, including a case against Bernadette Devlin, the newly elected Westminster M.P. for Mid-Ulster.

The street fighting of the early months of the year proved a mere prelude to the warfare that started with the riots at Londonderry on August 12. These followed the closing stages of the annual Protestant Apprentice Boys' march, when a clash between Protestant and Catholic turned into a battle between the inhabitants of Bogside and the police aided by groups of Protestants. The fighting involved 1,000 policemen armed with water cannon and tear gas, battling with Catholics hurling petrol bombs. Rioting continued during August 13, and only abated with the arrival of British troops the next afternoon.

The violence spread: in Armagh a man was shot dead during fighting between civil rights supporters and Paisleyites; in Belfast the Falls road area became a battleground on which seven people were killed including a boy of nine, many were wounded, and flames engulfed houses and factories. Towards the end of August 15, 400–500 British troops moved into the area and attempted to separate the rival factions. Chichester-Clark and leading members of his Government flew to London on August 19 for talks with the British Government, after which a joint communiqué announced that the British G.O.C. Northern Ireland, General Freeland, was to assume overall responsibility for security opera-

A Catholic youth hurling a petrol bomb during the Londonderry riots August 12-14 which unleashed a storm of sectarian violence across Ulster. On August 15 British troops entered a smouldering Belfast, and the following day saw this typical scene (*right*) in the Falls Road—one of the major trouble spots—as bystanders chatted casually amidst barbed wire, observed suspiciously by armed sentinels.

tions. A few days later General Freeland announced that as the army were fulfilling all riot-control duties, it would be possible to relieve the "B" specials; the latter were assigned the task of guarding installations, and were ordered to place their arms in secure arsenals instead of keeping them in their homes.

By now under the thumb of Westminster, the Northern Ireland Government announced a series of far-reaching measures. These included the appointment of a committee under Lord Hunt to "examine the recruitment, organisation, structure, and composition of the Royal Ulster Constabulary"; the appointment of two British officials to the office of Major Chichester-Clark and the Ministry of Home Affairs; the establishment of a tribunal of inquiry into the riots; an arms amnesty; and a proposal for the setting up of a Community Relations Board. From August 27 to 29 the British Home Secretary, James Callaghan, visited Northern Ireland, and a reform programme was announced following discussions between him and the Northern Ireland cabinet. This proposed: (1) equality of opportunity without regard to religion; (2) protection against the incitement of hatred on the grounds of religion; (3) fairness in the allocation of public authority housing; (4) effective means for the investigation of grievances against public bodies; (5) fair electoral laws. Joint working parties were set up between London and Belfast to thrash out these reforms in detail.

On September 12 the Cameron Report was published. It substantiated Catholic complaints of unfair housing and gerrymandering, and also declared that "there was early infiltration of the Civil Rights Association . . . by subversive left-wing and revolutionary elements."

Tension remained in the Province following the August riots and barricades remained up in the Catholic areas of Belfast and Londonderry—making Bogside a "state within a state"—until troops established a barbed-wire "peace-line" in the Belfast riot area on September 10, tore down the remaining Belfast barricades on September 16, and entered the Bogside on October 12. On October 13 the last Londonderry barricade came down. Further isolated crises and sniping incidents punctuated the strained calm until the year's end, notably rioting in the Shankhill road area of Belfast over the weekend October 11–12, when three people were shot dead and 800–900 British troops were in action. This followed the publication, on October 11, of the Hunt Report, after which sweeping police reforms were accepted in principle by the Northern Ireland Government. The Inspector General of the Royal Ulster Constabulary resigned, and Sir Arthur Young, City of London police commissioner, was appointed chief of police. Among police reforms was the disbanding of the "B" Specials and their replacement by a part-time military force under General Freeland. The strict limitation of weekend drinking hours also seemed to have a calming effect.

2 Countries of Western Europe

Austria
On May 29, 1969, the Austrian Minister of Education, Dr. Theodor Piffl-Percevic, resigned on an issue of principle. The government had received a mammoth petition signed by 340,000 (6·78 per cent of the electorate) demanding that the proposed introduction of a ninth school year in secondary schools—a major plank in the educational policy of the ruling People's Party—should be abandoned. While the cabinet backed down, deciding that the measure should be postponed for five years to "prepare for the reform," Dr. Piffl-Percevic, who was opposed to the petitioners' demands, stuck by his principles and resigned from the government. On the same day Herr Karl Pisa, State Secretary for Information, resigned in order to take up the post of deputy secretary-general of the People's Party with the task of preparing the party for the general election due on March 1, 1970.

On November 30 the Foreign Ministers of Austria and Italy, meeting in Copenhagen, agreed on a four-year timetable for implementing Italy's plan for greater autonomy for the 150,000 German-speaking South Tyroleans in the Alto Adige region that Austria ceded to Italy after the First World War.

Belgium
Following the crisis of 1968—when bitter rioting between French-speaking and Flemish-speaking Belgians brought down the government and threatened to tear the country asunder—Belgium's political stew simmered gently throughout 1969 without boiling over. The one threat to the uneasy equilibrium afforded by the delicate checks and balances of the coalition government, came

on January 21 with the tragic death, following a car crash, of the deputy Prime Minister M. Joseph Merlot. The compromise coalition government had taken months to construct and had involved a painstaking distribution of power among the rival linguistic and political factions. M. Merlot was not only the senior Socialist in the coalition, but the key figure in the arrangement whereby of the 29 government positions 15 should be held by Flemish-speaking and 14 by French-speaking Ministers. He was from Wallonia, in the French-speaking south, and was the leader of the 13 Socialists in the Government. Fears that M. Merlot's death would lead to a crisis proved unfounded, however, and his weight on the political see-saw was made up by appointing the Minister of the Budget, M. André Cools, as Vice-Premier, on January 27, while M. Edmond Leburton entered the cabinet as Minister of Economic Affairs. The "language war" received the attention of both Flemish- and French-speaking politicians, including extremists, on September 18, when it was agreed in Brussels to set up a 28-man working party in an effort to resolve this bitter issue.

On September 10 the Belgian government dealt a blow to the already slow move towards the full economic integration of the Common Market, when it postponed the adoption of the added value tax until January 1, 1971.

Denmark
The month of May saw Denmark rocked by a financial crisis in the wake of wheeler-dealing on the international

exchange markets sparked off by the departure of President de Gaulle and the widespread anticipation that the Deutschemark was to be revalued upwards. Danish reserves had plummeted from the equivalent of £166 million in December 1968 to a mere £79½ million by April 30, 1969. During the first few days of May the drain continued unabated, and on May 10 the bank rate was raised from 7 per cent to a record 9 per cent—the highest in Europe. Further squeeze measures included sharp tax increases on petrol and car licences, higher railway fares, dearer post and telegraph charges, and the introduction of a state lottery. The Government announced that its 1969–1970 expenditure would be cut by 1 per cent, and approached the International Monetary Fund for a stand-by loan of $45 million, which they were granted, together with a loan from the Germans of DM 235 million (£24 million).

The Danes overwhelmingly rejected their government's proposal to lower the voting age from 21 to 18 in a referendum held on June 24, 1969.

Finland

The most important item to emerge from the Finnish Parliament during 1969 was the decision, taken on May 9, to cut the voting age from 21 to 20. Otherwise the significant events of the year were conducted behind the scenes. For example, the powerful Finnish Communist party (which is represented in the Coalition Government) split down the middle and waged a bitter internal battle during the year. It was the familiar duel between "moderates" and "hardliners," the former led by the party chairman, Aare Saarinen, who condemned the Russian invasion of Czechoslovakia, and the latter by Taisto Sinisalo, leader of the Stalinists. At the beginning of April the "moderates" purged the party's Central Committee of "hard-liners" and thus flung down the gauntlet, which was readily plucked up by Sinisalo with a call for the party to wreck the parliamentary programme, call strikes, and resort to "extra-parliamentary opposition" in order to create a "revolutionary condition." The moderate wing is committed to the Coalition's national economic recovery programme which over the previous two years had pulled Finland out of debt, reduced unemployment, and raised the standard of living.

During 1969 the Finnish Government, which finds it expedient to keep on good terms with the U.S.S.R., was hawking the Russian-initiated plan for a European defence conference about the capitals of Europe and North America. It was not surprising therefore that Helsinki became the venue of the Strategic Arms Limitation Talks (SALT) between Russia and the U.S.A., the preliminary session of which lasted from November 17 to December 22 and could possibly herald a slowing-down of the arms race between the two nuclear giants. The SALT talks are to continue in Vienna, on April 16, 1970.

France

It was the year de Gaulle finally left the Elysée Palace following the rejection—by 53 to 47 per cent—of a referendum that he had elevated into a vote of confidence in himself. In the wake of the student and worker riots of May 1968 and the Gaullist triumph in the subsequent June general election, the new Cabinet, under the premiership of Couve de Murville, set about the task of drawing up reforms, vaguely promised in the Gaullist campaign. The key word in these deliberations

Exit de Gaulle: the French President resigned following his defeat in the April referendum, and—during the subsequent presidential elections—decamped to Ireland.

was "participation"—a concept culled from the students themselves, which exercised a singular fascination on the President who, in some mystical fashion, saw it as a panacea for the world's new ills. France has always had a highly centralised power structure and it was on this that the government turned, with the axe of "participation" clasped firmly. Reform was to involve devolution: powers were to be snatched from the Paris bureaucrats and handed to the regions. Throughout the last six months of 1968 these vague ideas were taking practical shape, soundings were taken, the minds of provincial mayors were pumped, and the pumpings were gazed upon with the reverence due to oracular pronouncements. By September 1968 the new proposals had solidified enough for the President to outline them and announce that they would be the subject of a referendum. Briefly they were as follows:

(1) The country's 21 economic regions were to be given constitutional status and each was to have a Regional Council comprising the area's National Assembly Deputies, councillors elected by the local councils-general and municipal councils, and "socio-professional" councillors chosen by representative organisations such as trade unions and professional bodies. These councils were to elect officers to be responsible for "affairs within the competence of the region."

(2) The Senate—France's second legislative chamber—was to be reformed in line with the new wonder doctrine, and in the process lose its effective power.

(3) The line of Presidential succession—in the event of death or incapacity—was to be shifted from the President of the Senate to the Prime Minister.

These three basic issues comprised the bill to which the electorate could say either "Oui" or "Non." Since most Frenchmen found the first part of the deal attractive and the other two less so, the idea of a single reply to the three proposals was unpopular. Nevertheless, the cabinet decided on April 27 as the date for the referendum, and mounted a massive campaign in favour of their proposals. Even more significant was the way in which the President threw his personal prestige behind the campaign. In a television broadcast on March 11—speaking at a time of industrial deadlock following the collapse of talks between the government and the unions on March 5—he first alluded to attempts to wreck the economy by enemies who wished to "shut our people in the totalitarian prison" and then intoned the magic word *Participation*. Every individual was to participate in his own destiny, and the proposals enshrined in the reform bill held the salvation of the individual and of France.

He went even further to identify himself with the new ideas in another broadcast of April 10, in which he unequivocally stated that he would resign if the bill was defeated in the referendum. In another, a mere two days before the voting, he warned that he would resign "if I am disavowed." In the early hours of April 28 the voting trend was unmistakably disavowing, and the General sent a communiqué to Paris from his country house at Colombey-les-Deux-Eglises stating: "I am ceasing the exercise of my functions as President of the Republic. This decision takes effect at noon today." Thus the President of the Senate, Alain Poher, stepped into the interim presidency and a presidential election was called for June 1.

While the parties deployed for this second battle, the rejected de Gaulle, feeling that the election would go more smoothly without his shadow over the proceedings, decamped to a remote hotel in a distant quarter of faraway Ireland, from which he intermittently emerged like an owl into the daylight to be mobbed by representatives of the world's press who were roosting in bars and perched up trees in the vicinity. Meanwhile seven aspiring candidates stomped the hustings: the beetle-browed Georges Pompidou, the Gaullist candidate and de Gaulle's protégé, who had been Prime Minister from 1962 to July 1968 when, following the general election, the President had called on Couve de Murville to form a government while sending Pompidou an ambiguous letter telling him to hold himself ready for higher things; Alain Poher, acting President and a member of the *Union Centriste*; Gaston Defferre, the mayor of Marseilles, campaigning under the banner of the Socialist party (the non-Communist left was in fact hopelessly split over Defferre's candidature, moderates supporting him, leftists advocating an alliance with the Communists and a single left-wing candidate); Jacques Duclos, veteran leader of the powerful French Communist party; Michel Rocard, candidate of the small extreme left-wing P.S.U. (*Parti socialiste unifié*); Alain Krivine, a Trotskyist; Louis Ducatel, a millionaire industrialist and former Radical Party Paris city councillor, who stood as a non-party candidate. The only two with a chance were Pompidou and Poher.

The result of the first ballot, on June 1, expressed in percentages of the total of votes cast was as follows: Pompidou 44·6; Poher 23·3; Duclos 21·27; Defferre 5·01; Rocard 3·61; Ducatel 1·26; Krivine 1·05. According to the 1962 constitution Pompidou and Poher qualified to contest a second ballot, while the other candidates were eliminated. On June 2 the Communists announced they had advised their supporters to abstain from voting since each candidate was as bad as the other, and both represented the *grande bourgeoisie*. The result of the second ballot, on June 15 (again expressed in percentages of the total votes cast), was: Pompidou 58·21, and Poher 41·78. There was an abstention rate of 31·14 per cent of the electorate.

The new President assumed office on June 20, and his cabinet—led by Jacques Chaban-Delmas—reflected his response to tension within the party and the nation. Gaullist hard-liners had to be satisfied, while an authentic break with the past had to be effected to please the country at large. The unbending Michel Debré, the

General's Foreign Minister, was eased into the Ministry of Defence, and the rest of the cabinet was composed of 12 Gaullists and seven independent Right and Centre men. The choice emphasised Pompidou's wish for a more moderate foreign policy and greater fiscal restraint.

On August 11 the French franc was devalued by 12½ per cent. It had been hit hard by the disturbances of 1968, and was only saved from devaluation in November of that year by the fact that de Gaulle would not hear of it. (His handling of France's fiscal problems was described at the time by Chaban-Delmas, then President of the National Assembly, as "amazing trapeze gymnastics performed at first with a net, later without a net, and now with scarcely a trapeze.") Rumours of an upvaluation of the West German mark in May 1969 sent a massive flight of speculators' funds over the frontier. Nevertheless the August devaluation came as a surprise not only to the French but to the international exchange markets. Next, "squeeze" measures to arrest inflation were brought into play, the most important of which was the introduction of machinery to regulate prices and severe penalties for infringements of the price freeze. The Government discussed the effects of devaluation on wages with the unions on August 12–13, and although the general reaction from the Left was hostile, the talks went on through the year and some progress was made.

The Common Market agricultural problems during the year bore special reference to France, particularly after devaluation, by which French farmers would have received relatively more francs for their produce. Thus the E.E.C. units of account (which are the fixed common market agricultural exchange units valued as equal to the gold value of one U.S. dollar) were suspended for three days, August 8–11, while the Six met for consultation. The outcome was that the Common Market agricultural price system was suspended for up to two years.

The difficulties within the Gaullist ranks that Pompidou had borne in mind when forming his administration led to an open split in September, with Debré publicly urging policies more in line with the true spirit of Gaullism. Nevertheless, all the signs were that in foreign policy there was a less eccentric line. Pompidou capitulated to the demands of France's E.E.C. partners when they met at the Hague at the beginning of December, and agreed to the start of negotiations on British entry; while on December 5 it was announced that France was to resume her place in the Western European Union which she had abandoned following a diplomatic row with London in February.

West Germany

The general election of September 28 held the key to West German politics during 1969. The various major issues facing the country—its attitude to East Germany; whether or not to put pressure on the French over the U.K.'s aspirations to join the Common Market; the pros and cons of the nuclear non-proliferation treaty; and, above all, the question of the Deutschemark—were all matters that divided the two partners of the coalition government (the Christian Democrats and the Social Democrats), and thus the answers had to be delayed until after the election.

Meanwhile late February and early March saw a small-scale Berlin crisis. In order to clear the decks for the forthcoming election, the head of state, President Heinrich Lubke, had announced on October 14, 1968—

his 74th birthday—that rather than sit out his full term of office until September 1969, he would resign on June 20, thus enabling the German electoral college to meet to choose his successor early in the year. For the fourth successive time the venue chosen for the meeting of the college was West Berlin. Predictably the East Germans protested—with extreme prolixity and vehemence—to Bonn, Washington, London, and Paris. Predictably their protests were ignored, and predictably the U.S.S.R. waded in to support the German Democratic Republic. Thus Warsaw Pact armed forces "manoeuvres" near the city coincided with the convening of the college on March 4, and for a week beforehand road traffic to and from the West was harassed, the roads blocked on eight occasions. Nevertheless, the crisis was muted and there is no doubt that the Russians, anxious not to wreck their hopes for a European defence conference, held East Germany on a tight rein. By a narrow majority the college chose the Social Democrat Party's candidate, Gustav Heinemann—Minister of Justice in the coalition —who became President on July 1.

The rumbling wrangle within the coalition over the mark led to an open split between the Finance Minister, Herr Strauss, and the Economics Minister, Professor Schiller, in April. Basically Schiller and the Social Democrats opined that the Deutschemark should be up-valued to take the heat out of Germany's economic boom, which they predicted would lead, if unchecked, to massive inflation. The Christian Democrats, however, considered that German prosperity depended on a low mark and high exports. The April dispute, with pro-posed up-valuations of between 8 and 10 per cent championed or decried by the rivals—coinciding with the fall of de Gaulle—led to a rush of speculation on the international exchanges and a huge flight of funds into West Germany.

Thirteen parties took the field for the General Elec-tion, but of these only five were of importance: the conservative Christian Democrats, led by Chancellor Kurt-Georg Kiesinger; the Christian Social Union— the Bavarian wing of the Christian Democrats—led by the dynamic Finance Minister, Franz-Josef Strauss; the Social Democrats, led by Foreign Minister Willy Brandt; the Free Democrats, an assortment of liberals led by Walter Scheel; and the National Democratic Party (N.P.D.), the ultra-right-wingers known to the press as "neo-Nazis," led by Adolf von Thadden. Of these four groups (counting the C.D.P. and the C.S.U. as one) the two uneasy partners of the coalition were the main con-testants, each aiming at an overall majority in the Bundestag or, failing that, an alliance with the Free Democrats.

The Socialists, however, entered the fray with a better image than on previous occasions. Like the British Labour Party, the S.D.P. has assigned Marx to the archives and the cloth cap to a peg in the attic. Led by the reliable figure of Brandt, and, above all, with three years in the coalition behind them, they were a force to be reckoned with. Much publicity attached itself to the campaign of the N.P.D., harassed by youthful demon-strators who dogged the footsteps of Thadden as he stumped the country.

The Bundestag has 518 members (including 22 non-voting M.P.s from West Berlin), of whom 248 are elected directly from constituencies and 248 by proportional representation of votes cast. Each elector has two votes— one for a candidate and one for a party. Thus a party

Leading figures in the West German elections of September 28: *(left to right)* Franz-Josef Strauss, the Bavarian "strong man"; Walter Scheel, leader of the Free Democrats, who opted to enter a coalition with the Social Democrats following the elections; Kurt-Georg Kiesinger, erstwhile Chancellor and leader of the conservative Christian Democrats; and Willy Brandt, leader of the Social Demo-crats and, following the elections, Chancellor.

without constituency members can still return M.P.s, if it commands at least 5 per cent of the total votes. Com-mentators were especially interested to see if the N.P.D. could break the 5 per cent barrier into the Bundestag. In the event the result of the September 28 polling was as follows (with previous seats in brackets): C.D.U./ C.S.U. 242 seats (245); S.P.D. 224 seats (202); F.D.P. 30 seats (49); N.P.D. nil (nil). As expected, the F.D.P. held the balance between the two major parties, and elected to form a coalition with the Socialists. Thus, on October 21, Willy Brandt became Chancellor of the Federal Republic.

He announced that the new Government had four immediate aims: (1) to stabilise the economy; (2) to initiate reforms in education and science; (3) to begin talks with the Polish government with a view to opening diplomatic relations; (4) to prepare the ground for signing the nuclear non-proliferation treaty. The new administration turned swiftly to these tasks, and on October 24 the mark (which had been allowed to float during the election) was revalued upwards by $8\frac{1}{2}$ per cent. On November 28 West Germany formally denounced the manufacture, aquisition, and use of nuclear weapons by signing the nuclear non-proliferation treaty through its ambassadors in Washington, Moscow, and London. Chancellor Brandt's avowed policy of seeking an easing of East-West tension was given prac-tical application earlier that month when significant negotiations were opened with both Russia and Poland on the mutual renunciation of force, and, in December, an agreement was signed with the Russians by which a pipeline will take Soviet natural gas to West Germany. As the year ended, however, it appeared that—despite a much-publicised exchange of friendly letters between the East and West German heads of state—there was little basis for negotiations between the two.

The new Chancellor made his mark as a major protagonist on the international stage at the summit talks of the Common Market countries held at The Hague from November 30 to December 2, when he bearded the French President on the question of Britain's application to join, protracted the talks far into the night, and at last forced a French agreement to the opening of negotiations with Britain before the end of June 1970.

Gibraltar

It was a dramatic year for the Rock, with mounting Spanish pressure culminating in an October crisis, while, within, an unedifying feuding match was waged by local politicians following the July elections. October 1, 1969, was the date set by the U.N. for the termination of Gibraltar's colonial status. Spanish moves started in January, with an extension of territorial waters from 6 to 12 miles, and were stepped up following May 30, when Gibraltar's new constitution came into force. This scrapped the existing Legislative Council and City Assembly, replacing them by an elected House of Assembly. Reacting to the constitutional proclamation, Madrid completely closed the Spanish border, barring 4,838 Spanish workers from their jobs in Gibraltar and cutting the Rock's labour force by one-third. On June 27, Spain severed another link with the mainland when she stopped the ferry from Algeciras. The Gibraltarians went to the polls for the first time under thier new constitution, on July 30. The result was inconclusive: the Gibraltar Labour Party, led by Sir Joshua Hassan, for many years Chief Minister, obtained seven seats, one short of an overall majority in the 15-seat Assembly. The chief opposition party, led by Major Robert Peliza, won five seats, and the remaining three were held by Independents led by the former Deputy Chief Minister, Peter Isola. Sir Joshua was called on to form a government, but failed to cement a coalition with the Independents. Major Peliza was then summoned, and succeeded.

As September drew to a close, Spanish activity intensified, and on October 2 the telephone link with the mainland was cut. Then the crisis suddenly shrank: in the last week of October (which saw the departure from the Spanish government of the Foreign Minister, Señor Castiella), a considerable easing of tension was observed, although Señor Lopez Bravo, the new Foreign Minister, made it clear that Spain was not softening her attitude.

Republic of Ireland

The Irish went to the polls on June 18 for the first time under the new electoral reforms that have increased the number of constituencies from 38 to 42 and shaken up the boundaries. Some 75 per cent of the electorate turned out to vote, and the ruling *Fianna Fail* gained an absolute majority for the first time since 1961. The largest Opposition party, *Fine Gael*, also made gains, while the Independent and Labour ranks shrank. The final results were: *Fianna Fail* 75 seats; *Fine Gael* 50; Labour 18; Independent 1.

The Irish Government's reaction to the Ulster crisis was full of sound and fury, and eyebrows were raised throughout the world as Prime Minister Jack Lynch appeared intent on pouring oil on the flames. In August, at the height of the chaos in the North, Irish units, officially designated as "field hospitals," moved up to the border, thus further inflaming the passions of Protestant militants in Belfast. At the same time the Dublin government (backed by, oddest of all bed-fellows, the Kremlin) was making abortive calls for U.N. intervention and suggesting a joint Anglo-Irish peace-keeping force that would have brought Republican troops into Ulster and have inevitably caused a blood-bath. This apparently ham-handed handling of a delicate sutuation was seen by shrewd observers of the Dublin scene as some sharp trimming not merely to luff inflamed public opinion, but, it was alleged, to spike the guns of a militant faction bidding for power within the cabinet.

Italy

A year of chaos due to riots and strikes provided an apposite background for the collapse of the Christian Democrat–Socialist Coalition in July. It had long been an axiom of Italian politics that the powerful Communist Party was unacceptable in a coalition dominated by the Christian Democrats. The Socialists, however (who had disciplined their left wing in order to accept this axiom and enter the government in 1963), discovered in the elections of 1968 that their appeal was on the wane, and their left wing, led by the Party General Secretary (and Deputy Premier of Italy) Francesco de Martino, began to make overtures to the Communists. As a result the Socialists split and their representatives in the administration resigned. Under Italian protocol this meant that the Prime Minister, Mariano Rumor, also had to resign—in other words the Government fell. Rumor, as leader of the Christian Democrats (the largest party in parliament), was asked to form another government—which he managed to do by August 6, although without a parliamentary majority. The Christian Democrats themselves were wracked by internal divisions, and during the year some eight factions were discernible in their ranks: each was represented in the new Government. The feuding Socialists pledged themselves to support the Government, but how long they would deem themselves able to honour this promise was open to question. One factor helped to keep them firm: if the new Government had fallen the Socialists would almost certainly have lost ground to the Communists in the subsequent general election.

Meanwhile, anarchy prevailed in the country as a whole: students marched; workers fought; prisoners rioted; public servants withdrew their labour; and waves of strikes rippled constantly across the industrial scene, growing in intensity as the Christmas deadline for the signing of three-year contracts (affecting the pay of some five million workers) approached. A climax to a year of violence and disruption was reached on December 12, when a bomb exploded in a crowded Milan bank, killing 14 people and injuring many more. An anarchist was later arrested by police.

On November 28 the Chamber of Deputies passed, after a stormy three-year passage through committees, a controversial bill to introduce divorce in a limited number of cases. The bill, which was attacked by the Church and opposed in the Chamber by Christian Democrats, Monarchists, and neo-Fascists, was another cause of dissension in a year of distressing violence and hatred in Italy.

Norway

Norway's four-party coalition held on to power in the general election of September 7–8, although losing four seats, while the Labour opposition gained six. This gave the Conservative, Liberal, Centre, and Christian People's parties (which had campaigned on a united front) a majority of two in the 150-seat Storting. The extreme left wing Socialist People's Party (formed from a Labour Party splinter in 1961) lost both its seats. Some 81 per cent of the electorate voted, and the final result was as follows: Labour 74; Conservatives 29; Centre Party 20; Liberals 13; Christian People's Party 14. Hr. Steen, Vice-Chairman of the Norwegian Labour

Strikes, riots, and demonstrations marked the year in Italy. Here supporters of the Divorce Bill wave their slogans in Rome during June. The Chamber of Deputies eventually passed this controversial bill, thus for the first time allowing divorce in a limited number of cases.

Party, declared the results "a clear triumph" for his party. Nevertheless, the vote confirmed the opposition role of Labour, which had been first ousted from office in 1965 after 30 years of almost continuous rule.

On September 29, the prices of most consumer goods were frozen at their level of January 1969. This was to prevent shopkeepers from increasing their prices before a 20 per cent value-added tax comes into force in January 1970. The new tax, which replaces a 14 per cent general purchase tax, will affect watches, sports equipment, refrigerators, furniture, washing machines, machinery, and building materials.

Portugal
The two great questions that faced the people of Portugal during 1969 under their new Prime Minister, and virtual dictator, Marcello Caetano (who had succeeded his mentor Dr. Salazar in September 1968, following the latter's brain operation) were: (1) would there be any slackening of the regime's iron grip at home prior to the elections for the 130 seats of the Lower House of Assembly in October; (2) what hopes were there that the long-standing colonial war in Africa would end, or, at least, die down?

Under Dr. Salazar elections had been considered nothing more than elaborate farces by those opposed to the regime, and were usually boycotted by Opposition candidates. Much had been mooted, however, concerning Professor Caetano's "liberalism" and it was generally believed that the autumn elections would be held in reasonably fair conditions. Thus it came as a sudden shock when, in August, the government dealt a blow to Opposition plans for success in the forthcoming general election, by declaring that the Democratic Electoral Commissions—which the Opposition were setting up in each constituency to mobilise their campaign—were illegal. In the event the "free elections" were more liberal than under Salazar, but the results were a foregone conclusion; a massive return of National Union candidates. The new members, however, had an average age of 48, compared with the previous average of 57. On November 19 it was announced that Portugal was to disband her secret police.

Meanwhile the colonial war dragged on, a constant drain on the far from affluent—though potentially rich—nation. The war claims a reputed 130,000 men and one half of the national budget. Throughout 1969, however, all the signs were that the military problems in Africa were, at least temporarily, under control (see Portuguese Africa) and lent some substance to the Portuguese claim that her troops in Africa were mainly occupied in engineering and policing activities.

Spain
Spain is a monarchy with a vacant throne—as proclaimed by El Caudillo, Generalissimo Franco, in 1947, when he announced that should he ever become incapacitated or die the Regency Council should appoint a king or regent. This "law of succession" was duly approved by a referendum in that year. That is why Royalist politics are still of significance in Spain, and assumed particular importance during 1969. In May, the Carlists—supporters of the exiled Prince Carlos Hugo of Bourbon-Palma, a pretender with only an outside chance—took to the streets and later to their heels. Meanwhile the son of the late King Alfonso XIII, Don Juan, was ensconced over the border in Lisbon patiently waiting for the call. On July 22, however, Franco announced in the Cortes that the succession would bypass the claims of Don Juan and alight on the head of his son, Prince Juan Carlos. This young prince had long been Franco's protégé, and has been groomed for eventual succession.

With the succession settled, Franco had next to decide which group among his supporters was to inherit political power. Two contending wings had to be considered: the die-hard leadership of the Falange, and the rising group of technocrats that constitute the Catholic organisation known as *Opus Dei*. The latter enjoyed the mentorship of the Vice-President, Admiral Luis Carrero Blanco, and the leadership of "the Brain," 48-year-old Planning Minister Laureano Lopez Rodo. Franco decided that the technocrats should inherit, and a massive cabinet reshuffle took place on October 29, which involved the dismissal of 13 of the old guard, including the Falangist leader, Jose Solis, and the

Prince Juan Carlos, named as Franco's eventual successor, swearing the oath of allegiance in the Spanish Cortes.

Foreign Minister, Dr. Fernando Maria Castiella. The new Foreign Minister was Señor Gregorio Lopez Bravo, former Minister of Industry. The reshuffle, which firmly placed the mantle of succession on the technocrats (Carrero Blanco was re-appointed Vice-President), was hailed by Spaniards as "Carrero's coup."

On June 20 the Spanish and American governments agreed, after months of haggling, on the extension of American leases on bases in Spain for a further 18 months, and on June 30 Spain handed over the small North African colony of Ifni to Morocco. On March 28, a "general and total amnesty" for all crimes committed during the civil war was declared. This proclamation was issued to mark the 30th anniversary, on April 1, 1969, of the ending of the war.

Sweden

On September 26, Tage Erlander, Prime Minister of Sweden, resigned after holding office for 23 uninterrupted years—he was the world's longest-serving democratically elected prime minister. His successor, Olof Palme, on October 1 was unanimously elected chairman of the ruling Social Democratic Party, thus automatically becoming Prime Minister. The new prime minister is said to be somewhat to the left of Erlander, whose friend and protégé he is. Nevertheless he was only following through a plan hatched under his predecessor when, shortly after taking office, he announced that Sweden was to give £15 million in aid to North Vietnam. Washington retorted that the U.S. State Department was considering whether this act constituted "aid to America's enemies." Sweden replied, somewhat glibly, that she was giving the aid because she considered that the war was over.

The importance of Washington's attitude to the new Swedish government's policy stems from the fact that the Americans could withhold some £200 million of credits for airlines and shipyards.

Czechoslovakia

Following the Russian invasion of August the previous year, 1969 saw the final dissolution of the liberal reforms of the "Dubcek era" and a wave of purges that ousted from office all those remotely associated with them and ushered in pro-Russian "hard-liners." A new Federal Constitution came into law with the new year, by which the country now consists of a federation of the Czech Socialist Republic and the Slovak Socialist Republic—as ordained by legislation passed in October 1968.

Far-reaching though these constitutional changes were, there occurred on January 16 a tragic event far more in tune with the mood of the year: the suicide in Prague by self-immolation of Jan Palach. Palach, a 21-year-old philosophy student at the Charles University, died on January 19. A letter found near him explained that his suicide was an anti-Soviet gesture and alleged that unless certain repressive measures were lifted others were pledged to follow him. The news of his death had a profound effect on the nation, and on January 25 he was buried amidst national mourning. Over half a million people, from all over Czechoslovakia, stood for hours in the rain waiting for his cortege to pass, and thousands had filed past his coffin at its lying-in-state.

On March 28 rioting broke out in Prague following a Czechoslovakian victory over the Russians in an ice hockey match. Jubilant crowds thronged the streets, rampaged through the Soviet airline offices in Prague, and stoned Russian barracks. The Russians seized on the demonstrations as an excuse for the first violent turn of a screw that was to tighten inexorably as the year advanced. Measures taken to placate the Kremlin included the suspension of three liberal journals and the inception of a new censorship code banning all unfavourable references to the Russians.

Moscow was still not satisfied, and on April 17 Alexander Dubcek was at last removed from his high office and Gustav Husak took over as First Secretary of the Party. The new man, dubbed "Husak Rusak" (Husak the Russian) by Czech wits, an austere, tough, but patriotic individual—believed to be fairly "liberal" in his heart of hearts (indeed, he had spent nine years in the old dictator Novotny's prisons) but a "realist"—was at first not altogether unwelcome since it was thought that he would be more likely to stand up to the Russians than his weaker predecessor. Dubcek's 21-man Presidium (the ruling committee of the Party) was also scrapped and replaced by a new 11-man Presidium reflecting a careful balance of power: it contained two liberals, Svoboda and Dubcek; the latter was made President (Speaker) of the Federal Assembly, merely an

Tear gas billowed among demonstrators in Prague, Czechoslovakia, on August 20—a mere prelude to the rioting that next day celebrated the first anniversary of the Russian invasion. The violence heralded a further twist to the repressive screw that tightened inexorably in 1969.

honorary post. Smrkovsky, the hero of the liberals, was dropped from the Presidium after a ritual recital of "errors." Two "conservatives" were included, and the remainder, including the new party boss, were "realists" —liberals in theory, Russia's stooges in practice. The changes ushered in a series of repressive measures. All forms of protest were forbidden; purges ousted liberals from the Central Committee of the Party; some 20,000 "control and revision" committees were established to purge the bureaucracy; the Student Union was disbanded; and the press was muzzled.

Tension mounted as the anniversary of the invasion, August 21, approached. On August 19 came the first clash when crowds in Wenceslas Square were met by edgy police and troops wielding truncheons, firing water cannon, and driving armoured cars. The next day saw even bigger crowds in the square—some 10,000—and again flailing truncheons, armoured cars, and water cannon came into the crowd. Some 320 were arrested, and two were killed. The "Day of Shame" itself began calmly. Public transport, shops etc., were boycotted; bouquets of flowers were showered upon the grave of Jan Palach; and at noon to the wail of car horns and factory hooters the country ground to a standstill. At least 50,000 people, jammed into Wenceslas Square, raised their hands in the victory salute, and stood silent for 15 minutes. They then began chanting "Husak is a traitor, Husak is a traitor!" Immediately the police were busy lobbing tear gas grenades, and, as people panicked, they found their way blocked by troops and police who dashed among them clubbing indiscriminately. The demonstrators retaliated by erecting barricades which were swept aside by the tanks that next careered into the square, followed by police with dogs. Some 1,377 were arrested.

The following month saw a renewed burst of propaganda aimed against Dubcek and the liberals, and on September 28 the cabinet was dissolved and Prime Minister Cernik appointed a new one consisting entirely of "hard-liners." Liberals "resigned" from the National Councils, and the Prague City Communist Party Committee was also purged. Dubcek himself was sacked from the Presidium and from his post of President of the Federal Assembly, while Smrkovsky (along with 29 other liberals) was kicked off the Party Central Committee and dismissed from his job as Vice-President of the Federal Assembly. By the year's end the two National

Councils had been thoroughly purged, a number of judges had been ousted, innumerable journalists sacked, and Dubcek was to be sent ignominiously to Turkey as Czechoslovakian ambassador. Meanwhile, as morale sagged throughout the country, the economy sagged in response. Some 30,000 Czechs and Slovaks left the country illegally during the year for a new life in the West.

East Germany

While the Warsaw Pact countries in general were feeling their way towards conciliation with the West during the year—spurred on by Russian fears of war with China and encouraged by the new government in West Germany—Walter Ulbricht's face was at first set firmly against rapprochement. The East German media refrained from chronicling the start of trade negotiations between West Germany and Russia on December 8, and on December 17 Otto Winzer, the East German Foreign Minister, warned Russia and other Pact members against concluding non-aggression agreements with Bonn. Nevertheless, negotiations went forward between the West Germans and both the Russians and the Poles on non-aggression pacts, and Russia, Poland, and Czechoslovakia were all keen for more West German trade and credits. Indeed the Russians signed a £140 million natural gas pipe-line deal with the West Germans in December. Significantly the 1,500 miles of pipe-line (which will bring the West Germans a 20-year supply of methane) will bypass East Germany and run into Bavaria via Czechoslovakia. At the end of the year Ulbricht sent a feeler to Dr. Heinemann, the new president of West Germany, indicating willingness to discuss better relations. But this was seen in Bonn as a tactical ploy to gain recognition of the German Democratic Republic (East Germany) from the West Germans. (For a report of the Berlin crisis of March 1969, see under West Germany, p. 245.)

Poland

The Polish "anti-Zionist" campaign came to an abrupt end during February as a result of the fall of the Minister of the Interior, General Mieczyslaw Moczar, a "hard-liner" who had been riding high as the leader of the anti-Semitic, nationalistic "Partisan" movement. It is alleged that the general overreached himself by planning a palace revolution within the top leadership of the Polish Communist party against the Gomulka regime, and had actually gone so far as to "bug" Gomulka's office. The student demonstrations of March 1968 had led to a split in the Polish United Workers' (Communist) party, with Moczar's "Partisan" faction swooping on the riots—some student leaders were Jews—as a pretext for a violent anti-Semitic campaign. Not only is there a long history of virulent anti-Semitism in East Europe, but Jews dominated the Polish Communist party just before and after the War (in 1939 over 20 per cent of Party members were Jews), and they are therefore popularly associated with the imposition of Russian-backed Stalinism. Moczar, a fervent nationalist, hoped to use these feelings to undercut the Party leadership of Gomulka, whose wife is Jewish.

A great change occurred in East Europe during the last months of the year when the Poles responded to West German overtures for peaceful co-existence, and on December 22 Poland approved a plan for talks with West Germany aimed at "normalising" relations between Bonn and Warsaw.

Rumania

Rumania followed a dogged and dangerous foreign policy during the year in the teeth of Russian opposition. The rift with Russia was best symbolised by President Nixon's visit to Bucharest on August 2 on his "world tour" following the first moon landing. The visit, although fleeting, was a conspicuous success for the American President. Cheered by thronging crowds waving the Stars and Stripes, Nixon danced the traditional Rumanian hora, and received backslaps—and kisses from pretty girls.

Scarcely had he departed when the delegates to the Tenth Congress of the Rumanian Communist Party began to assemble at Bucharest. Presumably to avoid any comparisons between his welcome and that of Nixon, Mr. Kosygin stayed in Moscow, sending instead Konstantin Katushev—at 42 a rising star in the Kremlin, and Russian party secretary in charge of dealings with foreign Communist Parties—a man described as possessing the toughness of two Molotovs. Rumania's leader Ceausescu began the conference with a marathon speech, attacking, by implication, the Russian invasion

Nixon visited Rumania in August at the invitation of President Ceausescu (right), a fraternal exchange that was viewed coolly in the Kremlin.

of Czechoslovakia. Katushev replied with an attack on "bridge building" to the West which had only one purpose, he maintained: "to drive a wedge between the socialist countries." He went on to justify the invasion and warn, also by implication, that the same thing could happen to Rumania.

Soviet Union

Russia's long-standing ideological quarrel with China erupted during the year in a series of battles arising from border disputes which were seen by some as the first clashes in a major conflict between the two Communist giants. It was this looming danger of a full-scale war in the East that led to a Soviet policy of rapprochement with the West and consolidation among her Warsaw Pact allies.

The Sino-Soviet border dispute concerned territories seized from the Chinese during the 19th century. The first of these is the area regulated by the treaties of Aigun (1858) and Peking (1860) by which the Czar extended his authority over 230,000 square miles of the Maritime Kray Region north of the River Amur and 150,000 square miles east of the River Ussuri, thus giving to Russia a coastline in the Far East where she built the great port of Vladivostok. This chunk of former Chinese territory, although it had never been settled by the Chinese, who had only acquired it in the 17th century, remained a nagging ache in Sino-Soviet relations. The second area of tension is the border between the Chinese autonomous region of Sinkiang and the Soviet Republic of Kazakhstan.

It was in early March that news of battles between Russian and Chinese troops on the frozen Ussuri was proclaimed to the world by the Russians. On March 2 fighting lasting several hours involved at least a battalion on each side, and vitriolic propaganda battles waxed loud. Following this crisis, troop movements on both sides intensified: it was reported that 5 million Chinese troops were being mobilised to reinforce the border, while Russia had an estimated 1½ million troops massed on the border by June, mostly along the Trans-Siberian railway east of Irkutsk. Moreover, Russia stepped up the building of border missile sites, thus threatening Manchuria and, more significantly, China's nuclear research and testing grounds at Lop Nor, in Sinkiang. June 11 saw a large-scale battle involving tanks at the Dzungarian Gates—a mountain border pass only 250 miles from the Chinese nuclear base, in the Taklamakian desert, Sinkiang. The border province of Sinkiang, which constitutes a sixth of the total area of China, abounds in mountains and deserts but not in population—about 8 million inhabit the province, and of these only 3 million are Chinese, the rest comprising 14 tribes all resenting rule from Peking. During 1969 the Chinese were still without missiles for their nuclear bombs and the temptation for the Russians to strike over the border and take Sinkiang, including the Chinese nuclear research base, was strong. Indeed some observers were surprised that no such move had been taken by the year's end.

Following the death of Ho Chi Min, a Chinese delegation led by Chou En-lai swooped in and out of Hanoi on September 5, pointedly avoiding the Russians. But intermediaries appear to have arranged a meeting between the two sides, for Kosygin and Chou met briefly in Peking on September 11, and abortive border talks began in late October. The situation, however, was still deteriorating as the year ended.

The threat of war in the East not only gave Russia added incentive to strengthen the bonds between the Kremlin and other European Communist capitals (and international Communist parties), but also gave her a handy drum to beat in order to marshal that support— and also to drown any faint cries concerning her invasion of Czechoslovakia the previous year. This task was generally attended with success. Although the Moscow-initiated World Communist Meeting of June saw Russia's Czechoslovakian policy condemned by the leading West European Communist Parties and also by Rumania, the majority of the delegates were tripping over themselves in their hurry to justify the invasion.

Détente with the West, initiated during the year (see under West Germany), led to the Strategic Arms Limitation Talks (SALT) with the Americans in Helsinki which started during November (see under Finland and U.S.A.). But inside Russia, all the signs pointed to the tightening of repressive measures against intellectual freedom and also against minorities such as the Crimean Tartars, Jews, and Christians. It was the attacks on literary freedom that received the most publicity in the West, in a year that saw the defection of Kuznetsov (see p. 169) and the expulsion of Solzhenitsyn (author of *The First Circle* and *Cancer Ward*) from the Russian Writers Union.

White-clad Russian soldiers patrolling the snow-bound Sino-Soviet border in the Far East during March, following skirmishes over the frozen Ussuri River. The menace of possible war with China brooded over the year, leading to a Soviet policy of rapprochement with the West.

4 The Eastern Mediterranean

Albania
Since 1961 the Communist state of Albania has pursued an anti-Soviet line, backed firmly by Peking. She is therefore unique in Europe, shunning contact with both Eastern and Western blocks. During 1969, Chinese engineers and military experts were engaged in the construction of a missile base in Scutari. This was part of a scheme for six similar bases designed to control the entrance of the Adriatic as part of a Chinese-Albanian defence system, set up as a direct result of Albanian fears of growing Russian naval power in the Mediterranean. The Albanian government, led by Enver Hoxha, first secretary of the Albanian Communist Party, believes that the Russians are planning to reoccupy their old submarine base on the island of Sazami, off the Albanian coast near Valona, which they abandoned in 1961. Chinese engineers were also busily engaged in modernising the country's medieval communication system, and in instructing revolutionary students from Western universities in Maoist thought and insurrection tactics.

Greece
On April 19, the Prime Minister, Mr. Papadopoulos, announced the restoration of three Articles of the Constitution that had been previously suspended. They related to the "sanctity of the home," the right of assembly, and the right of association. (Nine Articles of the Constitution remained suspended.) He also announced that dismissed officials up to a certain rank were to be reinstated, and that the cases of all those under house arrest were to be reviewed. On May 10, unofficial strikes were banned. On October 3, the Prime Minister announced further liberalising measures, including more freedom for the press; no arrests without warrants—

except in cases involving public order and security; and the limitation of the jurisdiction of military courts to cases of treason, sedition, and espionage. The measures were not enough, however, to satisfy the Council of Europe, which was expected to suspend Greece from membership when it met in Paris in early December. The Greek Foreign Minister, Pinayotis Pipinelis, forestalled this move, however, by announcing on December 12 that Greece would withdraw from the Council.

On June 6, Alexandros Panagoulis—who had been sentenced in November 1968 for his unsuccessful attempt to kill Papadopoulos—escaped from prison, but he was recaptured three days later.

Israel
Entrenched firmly in Egyptian, Jordanian, and Syrian territory overrun and occupied during the Six-Day War of 1967; successfully waging a protracted commando and aerial war on these three fronts; and rebuffing the U.N.'s pious instructions, Israel sat out the year. On February 26, Levi Eshkol, the Prime Minister, died in Jerusalem, and on March 2 the Labour Party Ministers of the Labour-dominated coalition met and chose Mrs. Golda Meir, matriarchal 71-year-old, who had erstwhile been Foreign Minister, as his successor. She became Israel's fourth Prime Minister on March 17. Before this decision the world's press had buzzed with rumours concerning Eshkol's likely successor, with the name of the Defence Minister, General Dayan—hero of the 1967 war—on the lips of pundits from Tel Aviv to Golders Green. But Mrs. Meir—who at the time of her appointment was regarded by the world as a mere stop-gap— impressed her personality upon the national and inter-

General elections took place in Israel and Turkey during October 1969. *Left:* Some 10,000 Arabs braved terrorist threats and voted in the Jerusalem municipal election that was held concurrently with the Israeli general election on October 28. *Right:* An elderly Turk casting his vote in the Turkish elections of October 12, which were marked by violence in some areas.

national scenes. Indeed, by the time the general election was held on October 28 she completely dominated the short campaign. Sixteen parties contested the election and the seats, as expected, were not startlingly different from the previous parliament and confirmed the *status quo*. Braving terrorist threats, some 10,000 of the 34,000 Arabs eligible voted in the Jerusalem municipal elections that took place at the same time. Thanks largely to their votes, the moderate Mayor, Teddy Kollek, was returned for a second term, despite a Zionist campaign against him.

On the international scene Israel found herself in semi-isolation, thanks to Russia's clear pro-Arab line and Western equivocations. In June Mrs. Meir visited London, where she was stonewalled, and in September, Washington, where she asked for aid and arms and believed herself welcome. In late December the Israelis were staggered by American peace proposals calling for Israel's withdrawal from occupied Egyptian territory, and from most of the occupied west bank of the Jordan. The proposals were flatly rejected by the Israeli government. Graver still was the lack of response in Washington to Mrs. Meir's requests for arms and aid. America had previously been Israel's firm friend in the West, while other nations concerned with Arab markets and Russian influence, were more cool. France was particularly so, still refusing to hand over fighters and warships already paid for by the Israelis before the war. It was thus a considerable boost to Israeli morale when five gunboats previously sold by the French to the Israelis but placed under embargo, slipped out of Cherbourg at Christmas and headed for the Israeli port of Haifa. Whether this exploit was facilitated with French connivance was uncertain as the year ended, but Paris "suspended" two generals and asked the chief Israeli arms negotiator in France to leave.

On August 21, the Al Aqsa mosque in Jerusalem, an important Moslem shrine, was set alight. Although an Australian (claiming to be King of Jerusalem) was later arrested, the Arab powers seized on the fire to try to drag non-Arab Moslem states into a holy war with Israel. A Moslem summit held at Rabat in September failed in this design (see under Morocco and India), and as the year ended another Rabat conference—this time an Arab summit—afforded the Israelis some grim delight as their enemies demonstrated once again their

hopeless disunity. To rub this in and, above all, to humiliate Nasser still further, massive waves of Israeli jets screamed into action against Egyptian and Jordanian ground targets over Christmas, destroying ground-to-air missile sites built by the Russians in Egypt. The greatest triumph occurred on Boxing Day when Israeli commandos actually captured, cut up, and carried away by helicopter an entire Russian-built radar station, of advanced and secret design, from Ras Ghareb, on the Gulf of Suez.

Turkey

The real power in Turkey resides with the Army, and the President Mr. Sunay, a former general, while never directly interfering in the administration, exercises an absolute power of veto over the government. On May 21, after a week of crisis, Prime Minister Demiral prevented this *de facto* military control from becoming *de jure* (tanks were actually rolling into Ankara), when he managed to persuade his ruling Justice Party's Senate to withdraw a constitutional proposal to restore political rights to the Democrats—who were ousted by an army coup in 1960.

The general election of October 12 resulted in a convincing majority (253 of the 450 seats) for the conservative Justice Party. An important feature of the election was that extremist opposition parties did badly, and a basic two-party system appears to have been established, with the left-of-centre Republican People's Party winning a respectable 147 seats. The poll was marked by violent clashes in some rural areas, and four people were killed.

Yugoslavia

The ninth congress of the League of Communists of Yugoslavia, held in Belgrade, March 11–16, 1969, was boycotted by all the Warsaw Pact countries except Rumania. President Tito's introductory speech dwelt on the rift with Russia and attacked, by inference, the Soviet invasion of Czechoslovakia. Speaking again to the Congress, on March 12, Tito announced that a 15-man Executive Bureau was to be set up as the leadership of the League of Communists and its policy-making committee. Yugoslavia thus became the first Communist country to abolish the Central Committee, which in other Communist countries constitutes the supreme authority. The Congress ended on March 16 with the creation of the new Executive Bureau, the election of a new Presidium, the re-election of Tito as Party President, and the adoption of new, more liberal party statutes, which allow party members to hold minority opinions.

The trend in Yugoslavian affairs symbolised by these new Party statutes suffered a set-back on December 15, however, when Tito lashed out at "enemies of all

colours" and "protagonists of factional strife" within the Party. The President's remarks were seen as heralding a major purge in the million-strong Yugoslav Communist Party, affecting all ranks. A check-up of party cards in January 1970 would, it was announced the same day, result in the dismissal of all members "hindering the implementation of the party's programme."

5 The Arab World

Algeria

The most significant event in Algeria in 1969 was a natural catastrophe—the devastating floods that hit the country in October (see The Violence of Nature, p. 134.) The political events comprised a welter of political trials, the most important of which resulted in the passing of a death sentence on Amirat Slimane, a former member of the provisional government, on April 8 (fortunately for Slimane, he was in exile in Paris during the trial and was sentenced in his absence); a visit from the Soviet President the same month; a ban on begging in June; a Pan-African conference in July; and an oil-pact with Libya in December, under which the two countries agreed to exploit their oil resources mutually.

Egypt (United Arab Republic)

"The six-day war has not ended: the two-, three-, or even four-year war is still continuing. We are at war with Israel." Thus spoke President Gamal Nasser towards the end of July, and his words were apposite. Throughout 1969 a war of words spiralled in unison with an escalating pattern of raid and counter-raid, foray and reprisal, between Israel and the surrounding Arab countries. The Suez Canal celebrated its centenary as a blocked and inadequate moat between the Egyptians and their enemies entrenched in the Sinai desert and the Gaza strip—a permanent reminder of Arab defeat and impotence. Another reminder was an increasingly important phenomenon—the Arab guerrilla movements. Following the ignominious defeat of 1967, which emphasised once again the incompetence of the regular Arab armies, Arab guerrilla groups recruited basically from Palestinian refugees and independent of any individual Arab government, mushroomed in strength and influence. During 1969, eleven rival groupings of these Fedayeen (men of sacrifice) were in existence, of which seven were loosely aligned under the leadership of one Yasser Arafat, leader of Al Fatah. The guerrillas were active behind the enemy lines, committing acts of terrorism within Israel, and attacking Israeli offices and airliners throughout the world, but their real significance lay not in their military prowess, which is negligible, but in their heroic charisma which won them the awe-struck admiration of the Arab masses and particularly the Arab young. At the funeral of Egypt's chief-of-staff, Lt.-Gen. Abdel Monem Riad, who was killed by an Israeli shell during an artillery duel on March 9, 1969, some 100,000 mourners bayed "Gamal, Gamal to the canal!" This was a significant manifestation of an anti-Nasser, pro-guerrilla feeling in the country.

Mob leaders, students, and other dissident groups (including cells of the illegal Communist Party) served to force the President towards an increasingly belligerent

stance. The situation was complicated by the Russians who, having at tremendous cost (some £800 million) re-equipped Egypt's shattered defences, had no wish to see another full-scale war in which their protégé would not only be defeated, but once again lose most of its military hardware. On the other hand, it is probable that the Kremlin saw in the pro-guerrilla swing a chance to topple the regime and put in a puppet government of their own. At the same time, the large number of Russian technicians and advisers in the country (estimated at about 10,000) were unpopular. But Nasser was able to step in and quash any Russian plans without inflaming public opinion against him, which he did in September, by demanding that the Russians recall their ambassador, and by ousting those he distrusted from the civil service and the armed forces and replacing them with more reliable material. As the year ended the influence of the armed forces was again strong, and the President was hanging on to power with their support, plus that of his vast secret police.

In foreign policy Egypt recognised during the year both East Germany and the N.L.F. in South Vietnam—clearly at the behest of her dangerous mentors in Moscow and, following the Syrian "coup" of February 28, patched up her long-standing quarrel with that nation. The efforts of the U.N. Middle East mediator, Gunnar Jarring, to bring Israel and the Arabs to negotiate were more or less ignored by both sides, as were those of the Big Four—U.S.S.R., U.S.A., U.K., and France—whose emissaries met intermittently with a similar purpose, much to the amusement of cynical observers, since not only do those governments provide arms for the contestants, but could be said in fact to be waging a war by proxy through them. Nasser enjoyed his fair share of the international limelight, playing host to a meeting of the Arab League in September and hitting the headlines with seven weeks of ill-health in the autumn, during which time the machinery of government is reported to have turned more smoothly in his absence. As the year ended those given to crystal-gazing were predicting that the incompetence and corruption of the country's top-heavy bureaucracy, the mood of fatalistic despair in the armed services, the disillusionment of the middle classes, and the desperation of the intellectual young might well combine to bring about the fall of the Egyptian President before another year was out. (See also under Israel.)

Iraq

The hideous spectacle of hanged corpses publicly exhibited on gibbets in the centre of Bagdad on January 27 set the year's sordid tone for President Bakr's Baathist

Members of the Action Organisation of Arab guerrillas photographed in the Jordan valley. The increasing political significance of the various Arab guerrilla groups within the Arab world was a feature of 1969.

regime in Iraq. Eleven men, including nine Iraqi Jews, had been hanged at dawn following a secret trial before a "revolutionary court," charged with alleged espionage for Israel. Three others were publicly hanged in Basra on the same day. It was also announced that a further 65 "spies" would be brought to justice. The executions took place in a singularly inappropriate carnival atmosphere: televised pictures of the swinging corpses were relayed across the nation, as thousands thronged the streets and under their official cheer-leaders demonstrated against Israel, Zionists, and fifth columnists. It was only the start of a wave of executions that occurred intermittently throughout the year as the regime turned to the familiar policy of witch-hunting and terrorising to secure its position. The ruling party made open use of armed thugs; countless arrests and murders were perpetrated; youths armed with automatic weapons and dignified with the title "National Guard" roamed the streets by night; and houses were requisitioned in residential areas in order to house them so that they could the better scrutinise the residents' movements. Minority groups, particularly Christians, Persians, and, of course, the 3,000 or so Iraqi Jews lived in constant fear and, following skirmishing on the Persian border, many Persians were expelled in April and May (see Persia).

Among important personages languishing in gaol was the former Prime Minister, Dr. Bazzazz, who was reported to have been brought to secret trial during July. The regime had originally hoped to present Dr. Bazzazz on television in one of the familiar screen "confessions." On November 27 it was announced that he had been sentenced to 15 years in jail on charges of conspiracy. Simultaneously came the news of six more death sentences for spying, bringing the total of executions of this type for the year to at least 60.

Rebel Kurds, who were active in the early part of the year, received an offer of full autonomy on May 24. But since the offer merely reiterated a provision of the constitution (which Bakr had proclaimed in 1968) it is doubtful if the offer was worth the paper it was written on. Following the military semi-coup in Syria, Syrian-Iraqi relations improved and a defence pact between the two countries was signed (see Syria). But after agreement with Israel to raise their respective envoys to embassy status, Iraq (together with Syria and the Sudan) broke off diplomatic relations with Bucharest.

Jordan

As one of those nations adjacent to Israel, and indeed occupied in part by the Israelis, Jordan was plagued throughout the year by both skirmishes with the enemy and the activities of Arab guerrilla groups operating from her territory. King Hussein as a monarch, a pro-Westerner, and a man who is known to favour negotiations with Israel, was held in contempt by the Fedayeen and also by influential sections of his own subjects. In the early months of the year a crisis between the Jordanian army and the free-booting guerrillas loomed, but by August the regulars had gained the whip-hand. It was announced that a system of passes was to be introduced for commando irregulars using the Jordan Valley, and Al Fatah and other Fadayeen groups were stopped from setting up rocket sites in Jordan. Commandos were to operate only in enemy territory. This tough line stemmed from cabinet changes made in July, which saw the departure of pro-guerrilla ministers and two of Hussein's most trusted henchmen moved to top positions. These were his uncle, General Nasser ben Jamil, who became Commander-in-Chief of the Forces, and General Rasoul al Kailani, who became Interior Minister.

The King visited the U.S.A. and the U.K. during April with a six-point peace plan which, although achieving nothing tangible, proved a successful propaganda move. While in London he is alleged to have had a secret meeting with the Israelis, which was presumably fruitless. In New York he addressed the U.N. with his proposals—which could have been a carbon copy of the Security Council resolution of 1967 calling for Israeli withdrawal from territories seized during the 6-day war.

Following the burning of the Al Aqsa Mosque in Jerusalem on August 21, President Nasser's call for an

Arab summit was taken up eagerly by King Hussein, and a series of meetings were initiated, some merely of ceremonial value (such as the "Islamic" summit, which took place in September) but others of more practical moment. The meeting of the Arab League Defence Council in November, and various unofficial conferences between Egypt, Syria, Iraq, and Jordan, could lead to closer co-operation between the four, even to a unified military command and certainly a co-ordinated strategy for the battle which is inevitable and imminent.

On October 6 it was announced over the Amman radio that an extremist right-wing coup had been foiled on October 3—the day that the King returned from the Islamic summit at Rabat. Those behind the plot were members of the fanatical Tahrir (Freedom) Party, which is banned throughout the Arab world. The chief plotter, Shaikh Taqieddin (who founded the party in the 1930s), is believed to have eluded arrest. (See also under Israel.)

Lebanon
No better example of the Palestinian Fedayeen guerrillas tendency to threaten Arabs as much as Jews can be afforded than the turbulence that reigned in the Lebanon during 1969. Operating from bases in Arab states, contemptuous of their hosts' sovereignty, and drawing immense popular support, they constitute a threat to any Arab leadership inclined towards peace with Israel. Anxious to avoid a repetition of the massive reprisal raid that took place at Beirut airport on December 28, 1968, Lebanon attempted to stop the Fedayeen from raiding Israel across her south eastern border. In mid-April a Lebanese army patrol attempted to stop a party of Al Fatah near the border, and were fired on for their pains. The incident sparked off a chain of events that led to the downfall of the Government.

There are some 160,000 Palestinian refugees living in the Lebanon. A mob of 11,000 stormed police barricades and stoned security forces at Sidon. Troops fired into the crowd, and three of the rioters were killed. Immediately the rioting spread, and students, refugees, and opposition supporters crammed the streets of Beirut. While the Prime Minister, Rashid Karami, tried unsuccessfully to coax Yasser Arafat (who was in Amman) to appeal to the rioters to stop, the *Voice of Al Fatah* (a Cairo-based radio station) was urging the populace to rise. On April 23 the country was placed under a state of emergency and a curfew was imposed on the major cities. Rioting continued, however, until some 17 had been killed and 115 wounded. The following day the cabinet resigned. The Prime Minister, speaking just before his resignation, declared that the country was split into two camps, one claiming that commando action *should* be carried out from the Lebanon whatever the consequences, and the other disagreeing. He emphasised that no government could take either side without splitting the country down the middle. As no one else could form an administration, Karami's government remained in office on a caretaker basis. The state of emergency was lifted on April 28 and the curfew on May 4. But in the same week units of the Lebanese army battled with guerrillas of the Syrian-backed Al Saiqa who had infiltrated into the south, and two days later an army spokesman said that clashes were provoked daily by the guerrillas.

The tension between the military and the Palestinian irregulars simmered on throughout the year, erupting again in October. On October 21 Syria, which backed the guerrillas, closed its borders with the Lebanon, and it was alleged in Beirut that Syrian troops were massing on the border. Meanwhile the guerrillas claimed that they had 7,000 rebels ready to throw into the fight, but proved in the event to be better wielders of words than of weaponry. Negotiations involving Cairo finally brought about a truce on November 2 which was not in fact observed, but on November 4 it was reported that some form of agreement had been reached between the belligerents, and it was rumoured that the Lebanese authorities had made concessions to the guerrillas, At all events, a cease fire was established, and the guerrillas were observed pulling out of villages on the Lebanese-Syrian border, which they had occupied during fighting. Some 90 captured guerrillas were released by the army in exchange for one jeep—an indication of the way in which the battle had gone. It is probable that under the terms of the agreement guerrillas will be able to pass through Lebanese territory but not to set up permanent bases.

The cosmopolitan character of the country, with its influential Christian community and its legendary commercial prowess, makes Lebanese politics especially delicate, and it was not until November 25 that Karami, who had resigned again on October 22, was finally able to announce that he could form a new government—a three-party coalition of the National Liberal Party, Phalange, and National Block. The sole N.L.P. representative resigned the following day, but this did not appear to endanger the coalition. (See also under Israel.)

Libya
In the early hours of September 1, while the aged King Idris was abroad, the army rolled into Tripoli, seized power with a perfectly executed coup, and the Kingdom of Libya was transformed overnight into the Libyan Arab Republic. Although the move took the world by surprise, Libya had been ripe for a coup for some years. The King was an enfeebled 79 and his heir, Crown Prince Hassan Rida, a nonentity; the country was flanked by the Socialist regimes of Algeria and Egypt; and, above all, over the past decade vast oil wealth had been tapped—on a par with that of Saudi Arabia or Iran. Nevertheless, observers had not expected a move until the death of the King since he is the father of the nation and the religious leader of the powerful Moslem sect, the Senussi.

Immediately following the coup, Idris—who was at a Turkish spa—decamped to Greece where he announced that he would not abdicate (although he had offered to do so five years previously). His heir remained in Libya and announced his support for the revolution. The first communiqué broadcast by the military, on September 1, said that: (1) all legislative institutions of the former regime were abolished and M.P.s sacked; (2) the Revolutionary Council was the only authority responsible for the affairs of the Libyan Arab Republic, and any failure to obey it would be severely punished; (3) the Council would build up a revolutionary and undoctrinal Socialist state; (4) the Council attached importance to the unity of all developing countries; (5) the Council stood for freedom of religion and the ethical values of the Koran.

The coup appeared to have been organised by young army officers led by Captain (later Colonel) Moamer al Kadhafi, and on September 2 the former chief of staff,

King Idris of Libya symbolically upturned by students sacking the Libyan embassy in Syria after the September coup that ousted the ageing monarch.

General Shams-ed-Din el Senussi, and the Director of security, General Salem Ben Talib, were thrown into prison. Public reaction to the revolution was calm and generally in favour. On September 8 the new government was announced: the new Prime Minister was Dr. Mahmoud Soliman al Maghrabi, a left-wing lawyer, but the anonymous members of the Revolutionary Council remained in supreme authority. September 10 was a day of activity on the part of the new government: journalists were prohibited from publishing the names or photographs of the mysterious Revolutionary Council; Yasser Arafat, leader of the Palestinian Al Fatah guerrillas, arrived in Tripoli for talks; and all wages were raised by 100 per cent—apart from those of the Government. The country's airports, which had been closed at the outset of the revolution, were opened again, but only foreigners were allowed to leave and only Libyans to enter. On September 21 the junta banned the English language from official use, and at the beginning of December declared that the veil was to be abolished.

The new Libyan leaders assured the British, American, and French ambassadors that foreign plant would not be nationalised—some 40 foreign oil companies operate in the country—but were adamant that the British and Americans should quit their Libyan military bases, including the vast U.S. airbase at Wheelus Field, near Tripoli. Also in the balance was a vast sale of British arms to Libya. The £150 million worth was to comprise 200 Chieftain tanks and an anti-aircraft missile system. While the long-drawn-out negotiations for this sale were still in progress, it was unexpectedly announced on December 19 that the French would be supplying Libya with £166 million worth of tanks and Mirage fighters. The news came as a shock to Britain who only a few days before had amicably agreed to evacuate her military bases in Libya by March 1970—all the more bitter when it was learned that France would be given a "watching brief" over the evacuated U.K. and U.S. bases.

A counter-revolutionary plot was reported to have been foiled and scotched on December 10.

Morocco

Rabat—the capital of Morocco—was the venue for two important conferences during 1969. The first was the Islamic summit held in late September, in which Arab zealots hoped to involve Iran and Pakistan in the Arabs' quarrel with Israel after the firing of the Al Aqsa mosque (see Israel)—and failed. The only lasting political significance of this meeting was that attending the snub delivered to India (see under India). Of more importance was the fifth Arab summit conference, which was held in Rabat from December 20 to 23 when it broke up in chaos. The summit saw bitter strife between South Yemen and Saudi Arabia over their border dispute (see under South Yemen); the delegations from Syria and Iraq walked out in protest against President Nasser's "high-handed attitude"; and Nasser himself stormed out on the final day, after telling the assembled heads of state to stop talking and start fighting. The Egyptians spelt out a plan for the "mobilisation of the Arab nations" which laid down the exact part to be played by the 14 nations of the League. These proposals were unpopular, to say the least: Kuwait and Saudi Arabia refused to increase their already massive cash contributions to Egypt and Jordan, and President Boumédienne of Algeria poured scorn on Egypt's military capacity.

King Hassan II paid a private visit to Madrid during June for talks with Franco, and Spain formally handed over her small North African colony of Ifni to Morocco on June 30.

Saudi Arabia

An attempted coup was reported to have been thwarted in Saudi Arabia during June. It was said that the plot against King Faisal had been hatched among young army officers, and junior officers certainly formed the majority of the 200 arrested. The coup was organised by the Arab National Movement and the Harakat al Qaumiyin al Arab—both left-wing Arab nationalist organisations—and its aims were to assassinate the King and his brother, Prince Sultan, Minister of Defence, and seize the capital Riyadh, Dahran, the old centre, and Jidda. It was later alleged that the C.I.A.—the American intelligence organisation—had infiltrated the plotters and given away the plot to the regime. As the year ended it was generally believed that the political situation within Saudi Arabia was still simmering dangerously, and that another attempt at a coup was imminent. During October there was a massive flight of capital from the country. (See also South Yemen.)

South Yemen

Aden and the former Emirates of the South Arabian Federation now form the People's Republic of South Yemen. As the year began this infant Arab state was run by President Qatan al-Shaabi, the N.L.F. leader, together with a general command of forty revolutionaries. On June 22, however, a five-man Presidential Council assumed power following the President's resignation. This followed a power struggle between extremists and moderates inside the N.L.F. (National Liberation Front). This feud had come to light a week previously, when Muhammad Ali Haithem, Minister of the Interior, was sacked, thanks to the machinations of Faisal Abdul Latif, who had become Prime Minister a short time before. From the resulting rumpus Haithem emerged triumphant as one of the five members of the Presidential Council.

The country is tucked firmly under the wing of the Kremlin; Russian diplomats and technicians abound and Russian naval ships use the harbour. The government persists in propaganda attacks on sultans and sheikhs, feudalists and reactionaries, imperialists and colonialists, much to the chagrin of some of her rich and influential neighbours, particularly Saudi Arabia. Partly as a result of this, South Yemen receives no aid from rich Arab states and the economic plight of the country is desperate. The closure of the Suez Canal has reduced shipping calls by 80 per cent, and only one half per cent of the country's 112,000 square miles is cultivated. At the end of November South Yemen's troops crossed the frontier with Saudi Arabia and seized the oil-rich Wadiyeh oasis. There followed a ten-day battle in which they were defeated. On November 28, 36 foreign firms, including all foreign bank branches, were nationalised.

Syria

A feud between two factions within the ruling Baath party in Syria led to a curious coup on February 28, 1969. A "nationalist" wing within the party were hot in favour of a more belligerent policy towards Israel, but were opposed by the Prime Minister, Dr. Nureddin Atassi, and the "progressives," who opined that the country's economy should be the government's priority. The disagreement was particularly fierce on the question of the establishment of a joint military command with Jordan and Iraq. In January the "progressive" Damascus Radio broadcast propaganda against the Iraqi regime—which the "nationalists" interpreted as a deliberate ploy to wreck the alliance with Iraq. On February 24, Al Fatah bases near Damascus were bombed by the Israelis, and the Prime Minister is alleged to have blamed the chief of staff, Maj.-Gen. Mustapha Tlass—who, with Gen. Hafez el Assad, the Defence Minister, led the zealots—for sending only five fighters to attack the Israeli aircraft. Tlass and Assad replied by ordering troops and tanks to surround government offices, police stations, and the radio station. Party leaders then ordered them both to appear before them for a dressing down, but the pair refused. There followed a month of confusion during which it appeared that the "nationalists" had the support of the armed forces, and the "progressives" the support of the press, the party machine, and the radio station (which, although under guard, continued to broadcast in favour of the Premier's faction).

On the initiative of the Algerian president a compromise was patched up on March 7, and, although it was an uneasy one, it endured. On April 27 a nine-man Baathist Political Bureau was announced in which the "nationalists" outweighed the "progressives." On May 1 a provisional Constitution (the brain child of Dr. Atassi) was proclaimed, stating that Syria would be a democratic, popular, and one-party Socialist republic in which the supreme power would be the People's Assembly. At the end of the same month a new government was formed which, at General Assad's suggestion, contained four ministers who were not Baathists. (See also under Lebanon and Israel.)

Tunisia

President Habib Bourguiba's pragmatic regime turned sharply to the right on September 8 with a massive cabinet reshuffle. The right turn was a response to the stubborn opposition put up by the peasants to the government's heavy-handed co-operativisation of agriculture, and the minister behind this campaign, Ahmed ben Salah, was bereft of his economic portfolios. A congress of the ruling Destour Socialist Party that was to have met in October to confer the Premiership on Salah was postponed.

It was not only the peasants' opposition to his policies that led to Salah's fall; the economic effects of co-operativisation had caused concern to the World Bank, and it is alleged that it was an attempt by Salah to conceal an unfavourable World Bank report threatening to cut off loans if the policy went ahead, that led to his dismissal. He remained in the cabinet, however, as Minister of Education. The Libyan coup of September 1 may have also played a part in the swing, the President deeming it no time to indulge in unpopular policies. On December 7, the Tunisian National Assembly approved an amnesty law which set free all political prisoners. Some 43 people were affected, mostly Communists, Trotskyists, and Baathists arrested after riots at Tunis University in March 1968.

Floods hit the country in the autumn: for 38 days in September and October torrential rain inundated whole towns, killing some 600, destroying 70,000 homes, making 300,000 homeless, drowning 1,000,000 livestock, and ravaging crops, and setting the country back an estimated five years in its struggle towards economic salvation (see The Violence of Nature, p. 134). Despite the floods the general and presidential elections took place on November 2. As Tunisia is a one-party state, the ruling party was returned to office, and the President was elected to a third—and final—term.

Yemen

There was very little fighting in the six-year-old civil war during 1969, although Sada, in Northern Yemen, the last big town held by the Royalists, was taken by the Republicans on September 6. Following the defection of Sheikh Qussem Munasser on November 7, 1968, Royalist tribesmen were reported to be tired of the conflict and to be settling down with their new tractors and barns, bought with mercenary fees. At the end of October, however, the Imam's troops were reported to be advancing on Sada—thanks to a decision made not by that Royal personage, but by King Faisal of Saudi Arabia. This latter monarch was irritated by the Yemeni government's refusal to renounce the mooted plans for unity with revolutionary South Yemen. Such plans, however, were very much in the realm of fantasy, for the two Yemens were at daggers drawn.

In the first two months of the year many Royalist and other exiles took advantage of the government's policy of reconciliation and returned to the country. This enraged some left-wingers and one Major Wahab, threatened to lead a revolt. He was shot while resisting arrest. As a result clashes between army factions blazed from January 27 to 30.

On March 17 a National Convention met to draw up a constitution for Yemen. Twelve seats were reserved for South Yemenis, but the N.L.F., as expected, refused to participate. Eventually this constitutional committee is expected to produce a quasi-democratic constitution on the principle of one man, one vote, and one party. On March 23, the Prime Minister, General Amri, resigned, which he is apt to do at the drop of a fez—this was his seventh resignation—but on April 3 he bowed to

President Iriam's request to form a new government. The latter lasted only until July 8, when he resigned both the Premiership and the command of the Armed Forces, on "health" grounds. It is thought that the reason behind this ultimate resignation was the opposition to his policies among a powerful group of left-wing army officers. Two left-wingers tried unsuccessfully to form governments, then Mr. Khorshumi, an ex-Minister of Public Works, succeeded in forming an administration on September 2.

On July 25 the last senior member of the Royal family still in the country and exercising authority, Prince Abdullah bin Hassan, was murdered. The Prince had quarrelled with both Royalists and Republicans.

6 Africa South of the Sahara

Botswana
The landlocked republic of Botswana continued to be used as a thoroughfare by African terrorists seeking to infiltrate into white-controlled South Africa, South West Africa (mandate of South Africa), and Rhodesia, much to the embarrassment of the government.

On October 18, Botswana went to the polls in the country's first elections since independence. The 196,000 voters had a choice of four parties, but, as expected, Sir Seretse Khama's ruling Democratic party was returned with a handsome majority.

Central African Republic
On April 12 President Bedel Bokassa (who came to power following a military coup on January 1, 1966) announced that a counter-coup organised by Lt.-Col. Alexandre Banza had been foiled. Banza had organised the coup by which Bokassa himself had come to power, and was for some time the President's right-hand man. Their relationship cooled, however, and Banza found himself demoted a rung or two on the political ladder— to Minister of Health and commander of paratroops. On April 10, the disenchanted Colonel is alleged to have appeared at a military camp at Kasaï, near Bangui, the capital, where he ordered the military to arrest members of the Government. They arrested him instead, and documents containing detailed plans of a plot and for setting up a new government were found in his pocket. The luckless revolutionary was found guilty of treason by the standing military court and shot in the early hours of April 12.

Chad
By the end of 1969 some 2,000 French troops were estimated to be in Chad "stiffening" President Tombalbaye's units employed against rebel Arab tribes in the north. These Arabs form the 3,000-strong Chad Liberation front, FROLINA, which the French troops have orders to crush by April 1970. Chad is of strategic importance as the hub of the French sphere of influence in Africa, and was said to be used as a staging-post for ferrying arms to Biafra.

Congolese Republic
During June violent rioting erupted at Lovanium University, near Kinshasa (spreading to other Congolese seminaries) when students rampaged with Molotov cocktails and portraits of Mao. Some six of them were killed in clashes with the forces of law and order, and later 30 students were jailed—five of them for 20 years. Lovanium University was closed down until August 8, when it reopened with promises of "student participation," and all student political organisations were banned apart from the youth movement of the ruling M.P.R. More important was the simultaneous announcement that since the M.P.R. was the "embodiment of the will" of the Congolese nation it was "unnecessary" to refer to any other Congolese party. In other words, during 1969 the M.P.R., contrary to the constitution, in effect declared a one-party state.

Dahomey
On December 10, 1969, Dahomey had its fifth coup in six years, when President Emile Zinsou was shot and wounded by soldiers at his seaside palace. He was hauled

President Zinsou of Dahomey who was shot, wounded, and bundled into a car by mutinous military on December 10. This was Dahomey's fifth coup in six years.

into a car and never seen again. The Chief of Staff, Lieut.-Colonel Maurice Kouandete, announced that the President had been ousted for failing to fulfil his mission of national reconciliation.

The real reason for the military coup, however, was that Zinsou—who was wrestling with an annual deficit— planned to cut down the army as one of his many economy measures.

Equatorial Guinea
Equatorial Guinea, the small, part-mainland, part-island ex-Spanish colony that consists of Rio Muni, a mainland province wedged between Cameroon and Gabon, and the island of Fernando Po, off the Nigerian coast, started its first full year of independence disastrously with violent events surrounding an attempted coup on March 5. During the last week of February President Francisco Macias Nguema stirred up a wave of racial unrest when, in a series of speeches, he attacked "Spanish exploiters" and demanded the removal of one of the three Spanish flags fluttering over the Spanish consulate-general in Bata. When the Spanish ambas-

sador failed to comply Macias ordered troops of the National Guard into the consulate and the offending flag was duly hauled down and committed to the flames. A Spaniard was killed in the fracas. In the atmosphere of confusion, with large numbers of Europeans leaving the country, the Foreign Minister, Atanasio Ndongo Miyone, and Equatorial Guinea's U.N. Ambassador, Saturino Ibongo, arrived in Bata and attempted to persuade the President to stop his inflammatory broadcasts—which were inciting members of the youth movement to attack whites. When the President refused Ndongo rallied some units of the National Guard, blew up the radio station, and moved into the President's office. Troops loyal to the President counter-attacked, and it is alleged that when Ndongo saw his supporters melting away he attempted suicide by leaping from an upstairs window. He was shot by troops surrounding the building. Ibongo was arrested and is variously reported to have poisoned himself in prison or to have been beaten to death by other prisoners. Some 18 others, arrested in a purge following the attempted coup, were said to have had their legs broken and to have died of gangrene.

Meanwhile anarchy prevailed, rival African factions clashed, and those Europeans who had not fled the country sought sanctuary in the barracks of the small Spanish force, the *Guardia Civil*. On March 9 President Macias appeared in public and blamed the Spanish government for the whole affair. A delegation from the Organisation for African Unity arrived in Bata and, on March 20, flew to Madrid in an attempt to persuade the Spaniards to halt the flow of Spanish citizens from their ex-colony. This request was given a cool reception. Meanwhile a U.N. mission that had arrived in Bata on March 10 managed to arrange an orderly evacuation of Spanish troops and civilians.

Despite chagrin in Madrid over President Macias's conduct, the Spanish government agreed to mitigate the economic effects of the unfortunate episode with a grant of 400 million pesetas (£2,400,000).

Ethiopia

Although Ethiopia continued to play a leading part on the world's stage as the senior and most distinguished of the black African nations, the country was in a far from healthy state. While the Somali border troubles smouldered on, the struggle with Eritrea was brought into focus in March when an Ethiopian Airways airliner was sabotaged at Frankfort airport by members of the Arab Liberation Front on behalf of the people of Eritrea, which federated with Ethiopia in 1952. About 70 per cent of Eritrea's 1,500,000 population are Muslims who want independence from the Christian government in Addis Ababa. Eritrean guerrillas receive arms and training from Syria, Algeria, Egypt, and Saudi-Arabia. (See also under Somali Republic.)

Ghana

During April a crisis of a dramatic order stirred the nation. The military council that had ruled Ghana since 1966 had seized power because of the extravagance and, above all, the wholesale corruption of the Nkrumah regime. Lt.-Gen. Joseph Ankrah, the new head of state, and his National Liberation Council pledged themselves to stamp out this corruption and indeed, they did so. But on April 2 came the announcement that Ankrah himself had been accused of receiving money from foreign sources and, admitting his guilt, had resigned. His successor was Brigadier Afrifa, an austere and, at 33, youthful officer who had served as Finance Minister. Commentators observed that a further reason for Ankrah's sudden exit could be connected with the fact that he planned to run as a candidate in the elections that were to take place later in the year (when the country was scheduled to return to civilian rule). Afrifa, however, was an ardent supporter of the former Leader of the Opposition, Dr. Busia, one of the chief candidates for the premiership—whose chances were all the rosier once Ankrah was discredited.

Following the return to civilian rule in Ghana, Dr. Kofi Busia became the new prime minister after the general election of August 29.

The change in leadership did not affect the proposed return to civilian rule and, following the lifting of the ban on partisan politics on May 1, some 15 parties stepped into the light of legality. The political dust settled about the feet of two leading contenders for power—Dr. Busia, former leader of the opposition United Party and a voluntary exile during the excesses of the Nkrumah regime, and Mr. Gbedemah, who was Nkrumah's Finance Minister until the "Redeemer" took exception to him in 1961, when he fled the country. The election campaign thus emerged as a fight between Busia's Progress Party and Gbedemah's National Alliance of Liberals (N.A.L.).

The general election was held on August 29, and the military government went to great lengths to guarantee fairness and calm; a distinguished judge headed the election commission, the ballot boxes were triple-sealed, acid baths were provided for destroying unused ballots, an estimated 16,000 troops guarded polling stations, and all bars were closed. An impressive 60 per cent of the 2,300,000 registered voters went to the polls, and the result was an equally impressive victory for the Progressives, who won 105 seats in the National Assembly to the N.A.L.'s 29. Thus after 15 years in opposition, seven of them in exile, Dr. Kofi Abrefa Busia, became Prime Minister of Ghana and officially assumed power on October 1. Under the new constitution thrashed out by a Constituent Assembly inaugurated on January 6, 1969, no Ghanaian government can set up a one-party state or interfere in any way with the legal political activity of Ghanaian citizens.

Another article of the new constitution states that anyone found guilty of misusing funds cannot sit in Parliament for the next five years. Under this provision a successful legal action was taken by Mr. Awoonor-Williams (the defeated Progressive candidate in the opposition leader's Keta constituency), and Mr. Gbedemah (who is alleged to have received £17,109 illegally under Nkrumah) was barred from his seat on November 24.

The year ended on a sombre note as Ghana began a massive expulsion of aliens. Of a population of eight million, some two million were aliens—40 per cent of them under 14 years of age. A large proportion of these were expelled at two weeks' notice following the announcement, on October 23, that the influx of foreign nationals was to be checked. Mid-November saw a "National Crusade for the Protection of Ghanaian Enterprises" and a call for the inspection of residence permits and the expulsion of aliens not in possession of them by December 2. Police and public joined in the campaign with enthusiasm—and persecution sparked off a mass exodus. It is estimated that some 60,000 Africans, mainly Nigerians, were driven from the country by the "National Crusade".

Kenya

A scandal, a murder, and a threat marked themselves indelibly upon the year in Kenya. The scandal involved gratuities estimated to total about £1 million paid to ministers and assistant ministers from public funds without the consent of parliament. This was revealed when the Government presented its estimates to the house in June, and tried to rush through a request for an extra £41 million for what it called expenses. The "expenses" included large tax-free hand-outs to ministers and their deputies. The house was outraged, and the Government only calmed it by using their ablest debater, Tom Mboya (a leading politician of the ruling KANU party and Minister for Economic Planning and Development). With a skilful speech, on June 27, he succeeded in mollifying the house. Eight days later he was assassinated while shopping in Nairobi. The murderer was later caught, sentenced, and executed, but not before constantly reiterating the words "Look for the big man, why don't you go and get the big man?" He had been a supporter and party worker for KANU, and had in the past worked for Mboya himself; the motive for the killing is therefore a mystery.

The affair, however, is complicated by that inevitable African menace, tribalism. Mboya was a Luo, one of Kenya's two main tribes, but he was a member of the predominantly Kikuyu Kenya African Nation Union (KANU). The ruling party has always been distrusted by Kenya's 1,300,000 Luos, who tolerated it largely because of the prominence of Mboya. With Mboya's murder (at the hands of a Kikuyu) the Luos became entrenched more than ever behind their tribal chief the leader of the Opposition Kenya's People's Union, the left-wing Oginga Odinga. The violence that accompanied Mboya's lying-in-state and funeral (involving the stoning of President Kenyatta's car) illustrated the strong tribal feeling that the murder both intensified and brought to light.

As if all this were not enough, evidence came to light during August and September that the Kikuyu were engaged in widespread oath-taking ceremonies. The Kikuyu is the largest tribe in Kenya (2 million strong) and is headed by President Jomo Kenyatta. It was largely responsible for the Mau Mau movement and the struggle for independence, during which Kikuyu ritual oath-taking became notorious for barbarity. The practice declined once Kenyatta assumed power, but its sudden resurgence during the last six months of 1969 indicated that powerful elements within the tribe are working for solidarity in preparation for a struggle ahead, presumably a tribal one. Throughout August and

Although Kenya became a one-party state during 1969, a wide choice of candidates was offered in the December 6 primary elections.

September influential voices were raised in condemnation of the ceremonies, particularly after September 21 when a church elder who had refused to take an oath was beaten to death while his wife and two other elders were beaten up. The Government was determined to hush up the affair, and at the end of September three British journalists, who had been reporting news of the oath-taking were ordered out of the country.

On October 27, Oginga Odinga was placed under house arrest following clashes at Kisumu, on the shores of Lake Victoria, the previous weekend. Some 70 people had been injured in the disturbances, in which President Kenyatta's escort opened fire on a hostile crowd closing in on his car. The Kenya People's Union was blamed for the affair and described in the National Assembly as "a subversive organisation backed by foreign staff and funds."

With Odinga in detention and the K.P.U. banned, the government announced the first parliamentary elections since independence. Although the country was a one-party state, feverish electioneering went on throughout Kenya during November as hundreds of hopeful candidates campaigned for the first stages of the election, the primaries held on December 6, hoping to win a KANU ticket which would automatically send those selected into the National Assembly—as there was to be no polling on January 3, 1970 (the official date for the general election) under the terms of the new one-party system.

The primary elections brought about a massive change in the composition of the Assembly, with two out of every three existing M.P.s (including five members of the Cabinet) voted out and the average age of members lowered considerably. On December 20 those elected in the primaries were formally nominated to the National Assembly. President Kenyatta's new 23-man Cabinet, announced at the year's end, contained six new members, and several of the "old guard" were excluded.

Nigeria

The Nigerian civil war continued its apparently interminable course during 1969. Throughout the year peace initiatives from such quarters as the Commonwealth Conference, the Organisation of African Unity, the Pope, former president Azikiwe, and the governments of Ethiopia and the United Kingdom, were rejected by one side or the other, and bitter disputes raged over mercy flights to the break-away province of Biafra. The military stalemate that had developed during the last months of 1968 was broken in April 1969 with the capture of the Biafran capital, Umuahia, by Federal troops, and the subsequent re-capture by the Biafrans of Owerri, which had fallen in September 1968. During February and March disturbing reports that Federal aircraft were bombing civilian targets in rebel territory caused considerable concern in the West—particularly in the U.K., which supplies arms to Lagos. This concern led to a debate in the Commons and the announcement that Harold Wilson would go to Lagos to discuss "the prospects for progress in reaching a settlement" with the Nigerian President, General Gowon. This he did, arriving on March 27 and leaving Nigeria on March 31. His visit had no observable effect.

Federal monopoly of the air was dented at the end of May when a quixotic Swedish Count, Gustav von Rosen, formed a minute air force for the rebels, consisting of five second-hand light aircraft fitted out with rockets and long-distance fuel tanks. These attacked Nigerian airfields at Enugu and Benin, destroying planes on the ground.

Meanwhile, the mercy airlifts into beleaguered Biafra, especially those of the Red Cross, were the subject of a protracted dispute. Biafra was entirely dependent on supplies by air for its arms (mainly from France and South Africa) and food from charitable organisations. The Federal authorities were concerned that mercy flights should not aid the Biafran war effort by providing disguises for gun-runners, and fought a persistent battle for control and inspection of such flights with the Red Cross. Following the shooting down of a Red Cross plane over Uli Ihialo (a Biafran airstrip) on June 5 and the subsequent halting of Red Cross flights, aid to Biafra slowed down to a mere 100 tons per week—one fifth of the amount required—and by mid-September it was estimated that some 1,000 Biafrans were dying daily.

Biafran military strategy during 1969 included aerial and commando attacks on oilfields, designed to encourage the oil companies (Gulf, Phillips, Shell, B.P., and Italian Agip Nucleare) to put pressure on the Federal Nigerians to negotiate. Although some Italian personnel were killed in a raid in May, and 18 others captured, sentenced to death, and later released after an outcry in Italy, this policy was unsuccessful, and by the year's end, the Federal government was reported to be preparing for a massive battle on three fronts—which, commentators were cautiously predicting could bring the terrible conflict to an end.

Portuguese Africa

Angola, Portuguese Guinea, and Mozambique are neither sovereign states nor colonies but overseas "provinces" of Portugal. In April 1969 these territories received a visit from Dr. Caetano, the new Prime Minister of Portugal, who arrived on a tour to rally the faithful prior to the general election of October 26 (see Portugal). This was the first time a Prime Minister had visited any overseas provinces while in office, and Caetano's trip was seen as a reassurance to the provincial populations after the eight years of bitter warfare against nationalist guerrillas, and as a symbol of the stability that the Portuguese military claimed for these areas.

On February 3, 1969, Dr. Eduardo Mondlane, president of FRELIMO—the African guerrilla movement for the liberation of Mozambique—was assassinated (by a time-bomb planted in a book) at a house near Dar-es-Salaam, Tanzania. It is believed he was murdered not by an agent of the Portuguese but either by dissidents within the ranks of FRELIMO or by one of two rival Mozambique guerrilla organisations. Dr. Mondlane, a cosmopolitan African educated in Portugal and the U.S.A., was an ex-professor of sociology at Syracuse University. He had a white American wife and drew much of FRELIMO's financial backing from within the U.S.A. As far as the Communists were concerned he preferred Moscow to Peking. This pro-West, pro-white attitude earned him the distrust of certain elements among his own followers, and the implacable enmity of the two rival organisations, CORREMO (backed by Peking) and *União Nacional Africana de Rumbezia*, who claimed that he was an agent of the Portuguese secret police.

While the guerrilla leaders squabbled in Tanzania, the Portuguese authorities in Beira, Mozambique, announced that on March 20, 1969, Lazaro Kavandame, the guerrilla leader of the Macondes (a warlike tribe, whose warriors still file their teeth to sharp points, living on both sides of the Tanzanian border in an area reported by the Portuguese Chief of Staff, in September 1968, as the only remaining hot-bed of terrorism in Mozambique) gave himself up. He stated that the Macondes wanted peace and were prepared to return to their villages. The Portuguese agreed to an amnesty and to improvements in the Maconde area. In November reports coming from Dar-es-Salaam suggested the complete disintegration of the FRELIMO leadership and that the ideological and tribal divisions splitting the leadership had penetrated to the fighting lines.

On August 4, a triumph for the Portuguese took place when Rafael Barbosa, the president of the central committee of the PAIGC—the Portuguese Guinea guerrilla organisation—swore an oath of loyalty to Portugal, together with 91 other political prisoners.

Rhodesia

In 1969 Rhodesia finally broke irretrievably with the United Kingdom and formalised the breach that had existed since the declaration of U.D.I. in 1965. In a broadcast on May 20, Ian Smith, the Prime Minister, declared that hope of a negotiated settlement had ended because of the U.K.'s "increasingly intransigent attitude," announced that a White Paper containing proposals for a new constitution would be published the next day, and stated that there would be a referendum on June 20 on whether or not Rhodesia should become a republic under the terms of that White Paper. The main points of the White Paper were as follows. (1) The existing constitution contained "objectionable features," principally those that provided for eventual African rule and the inevitable domination of one race by another, and failed to guarantee that government would be retained in responsible hands. (2) The Head of State should be chosen by an Executive Council consisting of the Prime Minister and other Ministers, and should serve a renewable term of five years and have limited powers. (3) The Legislature should consist of a House of Assembly and a Senate, the former consisting initially of 50 non-African (defined as European, Coloured, and Asian) and 16 African members, but as the African contribution to the national exchequer rose so would the number of African parliamentary seats, to a maximum of 50. (4) The franchise qualifications should be: for Europeans an annual income of £900, or the ownership of property worth £1,800, or at least four years' secondary education together with an annual income of £600 or property worth £1,200; for Africans, an annual income of £300, or property worth £600, or two years' secondary education and an annual income of £200 or property worth £400. The nomination of Africans for non-African seats or *vice versa* should be prohibited. Of the 16 African members eight should be elected by the old African A and B roll voters operating on a new common African roll, four from Matabeleland and four from Mashonaland. The other eight African M.P.s should be elected by chiefs and headmen through a system of electoral colleges. (5) All land in Rhodesia should be divided into reserved European and African areas, totalling 44,900,000 and 45,200,000 acres respectively, with 6,400,000 acres of national land.

The referendum of June 20, in which those on the existing voters' rolls took part, gave the government a victory: 81 per cent voted for its proposal to sever all ties with the British Crown, and 73 per cent for its constitutional proposals. The exact figures were: for the Republic 61,130, against 14,372; for the new constitution 54,724, against 20,776. Following the referendum the British Foreign Secretary, Michael Stewart, announced the closure of the British Residual Mission in Salisbury and Rhodesia House in London, and the forthcoming resignation of Sir Humphrey Gibbs, Governor of the colony—thus severing diplomatic contact with the would-be republic. During late August, shortly after the words of Rhodesia's new national anthem had been chosen, came the news that the small 600-strong Tangwena tribe was preparing passive resistance to the Government's attempts, under the Land Apportionment Act, to evict them from the remote eastern highland area they regarded as their homeland. The extraordinary saga that this led to, involving the eviction and return of the tribe, continued into the autumn. On September 11,

Rhodesian premier Ian Smith speaking in support of the June 20 referendum in which 81 per cent voted to sever all ties with the British Crown, and 73 per cent approved of the new constitutional proposals.

the new constitution, following closely the provisions of the White Paper accepted in the June referendum, was at last published as a Bill. It was attacked by the opposition Centre Party and also by the right-wing Republican Alliance, but nevertheless became law on November 29, 1969, and Rhodesia will declare herself a republic when parliament is dissolved during 1970—and the next parliament will be elected under the new constitution.

Somali Republic

Although peopled largely by nomads and created by the union of British and Italian colonies, Somalia enjoys a religious and ethnic unity rare in Africa, which is the main reason why democracy survived there until October 1969. In the elections of March 25 the ruling Somali Youth League, led by Muhammad Haji Ibrahim Egal, was returned to power with its majority cut slightly to 73 out of the 123 parliamentary seats. The nomadic Somali herdsmen inhabit large areas of adjoining Kenya, Ethiopia, and French Afar and Issa Territory, and ever since independence in 1960, the eventual unification of these areas has been a guideline of Somali policy, with small-scale border wars waged on both Kenya and Ethiopia. On becoming Prime Minister in 1967, Egal had toned down Somali militancy, believing that more positive results might be achieved by peaceful diplomacy. As a result a cease-fire with Kenya was agreed upon, bringing to an end four years of fighting, and, on February 21, 1969, at a meeting of Egal and Kenyatta in Nairobi, Kenya agreed to lift the state of emergency in her North Eastern province, to grant an amnesty to all political offenders connected with the border dispute, and to allow refugees to return from Somalia. The situation on the Ethiopian border however, remained tense throughout the year, despite an official cease-fire.

Following the March elections, Somalis began a bout of soul-searching. President Abdel Rashid Ali Shermarke hit out at bribery, and on July 1 (Independence Day) he called on constitutional experts from all over the world to suggest improvements to the Somali constitution. "We are sure," he said, "that whoever has the cause of representative democracy in Africa at heart . . . will not fail to respond to our appeal." Submissions were to be printed and then evaluated at a conference to be held in 1970. But on October 15 President Shermarke was shot by a member of his own police force in Las Anod, in drought-stricken northern Somalia. Six days later the military seized power and Prime Minister Egal was thrown into jail. On October 21, the leader of the leftist military junta, General Fiyad, proclaimed that his revolutionary council would support all those in "illegally occupied territory," a phrase traditionally used for North Eastern Kenya and the Ogaden region of Ethiopia.

South Africa

The most significant events in South Africa during 1969 were the Gandar-Pogrund trial; the introduction of the new "BOSS" security laws; and the split in the ruling Nationalist Party. On July 11, after an eight-month trial, Laurence Gandar, editor-in-chief of the Johannesburg newspaper the *Rand Daily Mail*, was fined R200 (£117) on charges of publishing false information, and Benjamin Pogrund, the paper's senior reporter, received a six-month jail sentence, suspended for three

Major-General Nimeri (*right*) seized power in the Sudan during May, making left-winger Abu Bakr Awadullah prime minister. Friendship waned, however, and Awadullah was sacked in October.

years. Four years previously, in July 1965, Pogrund had written and Gandar had published a series of four articles alleging brutality in the treatment of prisoners at the Cinderella Prison, Boksburg.

Despite opposition, the Government went forward with its legislation to give sweeping powers to the new Bureau of State Security, known as BOSS. Under the BOSS laws it will be an offence to publish or communicate any information concerning military, police or security matters which could be in any way interpreted as prejudicial to the safety of the state.

Prime Minister Vorster announced in August 1969 that the New Zealand rugby team, due to compete in South Africa in 1970, would be allowed to bring Maori players. Immediately a storm was unleashed from the right wing of the Nationalist Party, led by Dr. Albert Hertzog. The right, which accused Vorster of "weak, vacillating, and opportunistic leadership," had for some time been affronted by the government's "outward-looking" policy, whereby trade agreements have been made with black African states; also by the policy of encouraging European immigration at the rate of 50,000 a year, regardless of the fact that most immigrants are Southern European Roman Catholics who, it fears, will soon outnumber the Afrikaners; and, probably, by the decision in May to give the go-ahead for television, anathematised by Hertzog. As a result of the clash between Vorster and Hertzog, the latter was expelled from the party in September, and in October founded a new one, the Reconstituted National Party. Following the Prime Minister's September decision to hold an early general election the parties began active preparation for the poll, which will take place early in 1970.

Sudan

The Republic of the Sudan, the largest country in Africa in land area, had a military coup in May that ushered in a left-wing, Nasser-like regime. The coup was sparked off by a crisis in the coalition government of Muhammad Ahmed Mahgoub caused by the healing of a split between the right and left wings of the two-million strong Umma Party. The Umma right, led by Imam el Hadi el Mahdi, was already represented in the government, but with its new-found unity the party as a whole

was set to bring down the government, and it seemed certain that Dr. Sadiq el Mahdi—leader of the progressive wing of the Ummas—would be the next prime minister of the Sudan. (The Umma party, incidentally, is the political organisation of the Mahdist sect that killed Gen. Gordon at Khartoum in 1885.) The squabbling and horse-trading that attended this crisis served to lower public estimation of the coalition even further. Nevertheless it came as a surprise when, on Sunday May 25, a military junta headed by Col. Jaafar al-Nimeri seized power in an allegedly bloodless coup Nimeri (who promoted himself to Major-General immediately) made a left-wing civilian, the former Chief Justice Abu Bakr Awadullah, the Sudan's figurehead premier, and the country was re-named the Sudan Democratic Republic. All political parties except the Communists were outlawed, and the General commented: "We have tried liberal democracy in the Sudan. It failed, and we will never go back to it."

The new Prime Minister claimed that the regime was "socialist but not extremist"—except on the Israeli question—but when his new cabinet was announced eight of its 24 members turned out to be die-hard Communists. Among the junta's first actions were the recognition of East Germany and the dispatch of a mission to Moscow to raise arms. At home vague warnings on the nationalisation of "local capital with imperialist connections" were issued, and leading politicians, including Dr. Sadiq el Mahdi, the Umma leader, were arrested to face trial for "treason." In June General Nimeri set about tackling the major internal problem in the Sudan—the 14-year-old civil war between the 9 million-strong Arab north and the three southern provinces inhabited by 4 million pagan negroes. On June 10, Nimeri outlined a plan for southern regional autonomy, and ordered the army to help build up the south's economy. The situation in the south (which had been fairly quiet for a year before the coup, owing to exhaustion and lack of external backing for the rebels) was reported to have improved, thanks to this initiative. However, thanks to the regime's militant anti-Israeli policy, arms began to flow into the rebel areas and tension returned. The military had become increasingly disenchanted with the Communist members of the cabinet, and on October 28 Major-General Nimeri took over as prime minister himself and formed a new 25-man cabinet.

Swaziland

This tiny African kingdom entirely surrounded by South Africa celebrated its first year of independence on September 6, 1969. To mark the occasion Princess Alexandra opened the new £146,000 Houses of Parliament at Lobomba. Although the second smallest sovereign state in Africa, Swaziland is potentially rich: the soil is fertile, the land is full of minerals, and there is water in abundance. Foreign capital, however, vital for developing these resources, is slow in coming in, depite vigorous efforts to attract it on behalf of the Swazi government. King Sobhuza II and his premier, Prince Makhosini Dlamini, were also harrying Whitehall during 1969 over the long-standing question of Swazi claims for compensation for land alienated during British rule.

Uganda

A highlight of 1969 for Uganda, a largely Catholic country, was the visit of the Pope, July 31-August 1. Over a million African pilgrims plodded the dusty roads that wind through the bush to Kampala to welcome him

Three East African leaders met in Nairobi at the start of a year that was to prove momentous for each of them. Both Presidents Kaunda of Zambia (*left*) and Kenyatta of Kenya (*centre*) found themselves faced with mounting tribal tensions, while Prime Minister Egal of Somalia (*right*) was thrown into jail following the assassination of the Somali President and a military coup in October.

on the first appearance in Africa of any Pope. The political situation, however, was tense, as it has been since the army mutinies of 1964 and the Buganda rising of 1966. The internal equilibrium of the country is ruthlessly maintained by the shrewd and tough government of President Milton Obote, but reports emerging from Kampala suggested that friction was increasing between the Acholi and Langi tribes, who between them form Obote's support and fill most of the important positions. Meanwhile, the Baganda tribe, who in the main oppose the regime, brooded under repeated states of emergency. The first week of 1969 saw the gates of Luzira Prison, Kampala, close behind Princess Victoria, sister of the exiled Kabaka of Buganda, better known as "King Freddie" (who died in London during November). The incarceration of the princess represented one more political prisoner for Uganda, one more act of repression against the former kingdom of Buganda, and one more manoeuvre by Obote to preserve the peace in his dangerously divided land. The government's mail-fisted response to the threat of internal disorder has resulted in repression and high taxes which have lost it the support of the middle classes. One incident that particularly repelled educated people was the arrest of Mr. Mayanja, a leading Opposition M.P. and a former Minister of Education in the Kabaka's government, and of Rajat Neogy, editor of the respected magazine *Transition*. Charged with sedition, they were acquitted when they appeared before a magistrate on February 1, but were re-arrested following their release. On September 7, the leader of the opposition Democratic Party, Benedicto Kiwanuku, who was Uganda's first Prime Minister, was arrested at his house near Kampala. This arrest was also under the emergency regulations. On December 19, President Obote was shot in the jaw by a gunman as he left a political meeting in Kampala. The President was not badly injured by the assassination attempt, and was reported to be on the road to complete recovery as the year ended.

Uganda has some 40,000 Asians who retained their British citizenship when the country became independent from British rule. It was made clear in a White Paper published in January that, like the Kenyan Asians, they would eventually have to leave the country.

Zambia

It was a dramatic and somewhat hysterical year for Zambia. Throughout 1969 reports emerged from Lusaka that members of President Kaunda's ruling United

National Independence Party (U.N.I.P.) were persecuting Jehovah's Witnesses and supporters of the opposition party, the African National Congress. By June it was estimated that some 2,000 Witnesses were homeless and deprived of their livelihoods. This aggression reflected a gnawing insecurity within the ruling party; the popularity of the opposition was growing while U.N.I.P. itself was seething with an internal power struggle. The prevailing mood, quickened by rejection at provincial elections, was intensified further by a referendum on June 17. Although the government won a majority of votes (giving it the power to abolish any clause in the constitution on a two-thirds parliamentary majority—a measure instigated to permit the seizure of land from absentee landlords without paying compensation), it received a rebuff when voters in the Mumbwa district staged a general boycott, defying an explicit warning by the President made only the day before. A month later a judicial crisis occurred when Judge Ifor Evans, hearing an appeal, quashed sentences on two Portuguese soldiers convicted of crossing into Zambia from Angola, on the grounds that the offence was "trivial," that the punishment (a fine of £2,000 or two years in prison) was "unlawful and excessive," and that the verdict "did not redound to the credit of the Zambian authorities." Bowing to the hot winds of nationalism within U.N.I.P., the President lambasted the all-white High Court, reversed its decision, and demanded to know whether the courts were "defending our interests or foreign interests." Chief Justice Skinner replied that it was "one of the functions of the Judiciary to criticise actions of the Executive—when the need arises." As a result Messrs. Skinner and Evans were forced to barricade themselves inside a room in the Lusaka High Court as 500 rioting youths—members of the uniformed Zambia Youth Service—tried to batter down the door. Following this affair a number of judges, including Skinner and Evans, left the country, and white residents in Zambia were uneasy.

On August 11, the President announced, to wild cheering from the national council of U.N.I.P., that he intended to nationalise Zambia's £500 million copper industry, inviting the Anglo-American Corporation and the Roan Selection Trust to offer his government 51 per cent of the shares in the country's six copper mines and one lead and zinc mine. This measure, the President maintained, was to "put Zambian business firmly in Zambian hands, just as political power is in Zambian hands." Nevertheless it was interpreted as a political rather than an economic gesture, intended to spike the guns of Vice-President Kapwepwe, a militant nationalist, who was making a play for the leadership within the party supported by the 800,000-strong Bemba tribe.

This power struggle, with its tribal roots and all that they bode in disruption and civil strife, is believed to be the nagging, unspoken factor behind President Kaunda's uncharacteristic behaviour during the year, including his attack on the judges and his failure to arrest the High Court rioters. By nationalising the mines, the President bought time from Kapwepwe and his fire-brands, but the question remained—how long? During the last week of August, Kapwepwe came out into the open by resigning, in the hope that a wave of popular acclaim would sweep him into Kaunda's chair. The gambit failed. The president declared a state of siege (on the grounds of tribal tension) and took personal control of U.N.I.P., suspending its constitution and sacking all the members of its central committee, including Kapwepwe. Then, in a political master-stroke, the President called upon the erstwhile Vice-President to withdraw his resignation in the interests of national unity. Kapwepwe could not fail to respond to this plea without appearing unpatriotic, yet, by stepping back into the Number Two position, he admitted that Kaunda was still Number One.

7 Southern Asia

Afghanistan

Afghanistan's five-year-old democratic constitution continued to function lethargically during 1969. Although general elections took place in the autumn, the country has not yet adapted itself to the democracy that King Muhammed Zahir himself initiated in 1964. The main trouble continues to be the quality of the rump of members returned to the Shura—hide-bound back-woodsmen whose faces are set firmly against change and who take refuge from their responsibilities in inertia. The result is that, although the basic framework for a modern democratic state has been provided, a democratic ethos and legislative code remain non-existent. The most glaring example of apathy is the failure to form cohesive political parties, which means that the real division of power exists only between the King and his ministers and the Shura as a whole. Meanwhile, economic development is going forward apace and with it a new, youthful, and educated class is emerging, impatient with its torpid elders. Afghanistan's meagre sense of national identity is being eroded by this economic advance, which tends to enrich the dominant Pathans—particularly in Kabul, the country's capital and Pathan centre—and by-pass the Uzbegs, Hazaras, Tajiks, Turkomen, and other tribal minorities.

Mr. Kosygin, the Russian Prime Minister, arrived in Kabul on June 26 for a four-day official visit and talks with the King.

Ceylon

The year saw the start of an imaginative scheme concerning the 2,300,000 young people of Ceylon. On April 26, 1969, the Prime Minister, Dudley Senanayake, inaugurated a National Youth Service at Kota Vehera—the legendary birthplace of the 12th-century Sinhalese King Parakrama Bahu the Great. The plan links a youth unemployment problem with the need for rapid economic development. Youths and girls are encouraged to volunteer their labour, and under the scheme receive nominal pay of Rs.3 per day's work and credits which, after a year, entitle each worker to a place in a residential training centre where he or she will be trained for a career.

India

For years pessimistic pundits have forecast the imminent collapse of India into absolute chaos, and during 1969 (the year in which people all over the world celebrated the centenary of Gandhi's birth) the prophets of doom were given much encouragement by the antics of Indian politicians. The most significant were those that brought about a split in the ruling Congress Party. This behemoth of a political organisation—so closely identi-fied with India's struggle to independent nationhood—is synonymous with stable and democratic government in India. This is because it is the only party competent to govern, the Indian Communist parties (all three of them) being unbelievably inept, and other opposition parties fixed in narrow regional or religious grooves. The Congress Party is, however, an organisation of such massive and protean proportions that it is wracked by constant internal squabbles. During 1969 a power struggle developed about the two poles of party patron-age: the party organisation on the one hand, and the parliamentary wing on the other. The crisis began in May when the two factions fell out over the choice of the party's nominee for the presidential chair of Dr. Zakir Husain who died on May 3. Members of the party organisation (the old guard of veteran Congress men headed by the party president, Mr. Nijalingappa, and known collectively as the "Syndicate") allied with the Deputy Prime Minister, Mr. Mororji Desai, were ranged behind the official party candidate, while the Prime Minister, Mrs. Indira Gandhi, and the broad majority of Congress M.P.s backed Varahagiri Venkata Giri, an independent, who—after an unedifying if dramatic display of infighting—was finally elected. An open breach in the Party was averted at this stage only by a hastily concocted resolution of unity.

Mrs. Gandhi's sudden July decision to nationalise the banks proved a shrewd tactical ploy. Both wings of Congress profess a socialist ideology, but the "Syndicate," infuriated at the arbitrary manner in which the decision was taken, and anxious lest a half-baked measure should damage India's fragile economy, sprang to the attack. On the other hand, by publicising the move as an economic panacea, Mrs. Gandhi strengthened her position by appearing as the darling of the masses valiantly fighting a hide-bound party machine. Encour-aged by her success, Mrs. Gandhi made a bid to capture control of the party machine by calling a convention of party delegates. This move was an unconstitutional gauntlet swished across Mr. Nijalingappa's cheeks, as

The year saw India's ruling Congress party divide into two disputing wings: one led by the Party President, Mr. Nijalingappa (*left*), leader of "the Syndicate"; the other by the Premier, Mrs. Indira Gandhi (*right*).

only he—as party president—had the right to convene such a meeting. The "Syndicate," however, had a trick in its fist, and, following a frenzy of plotting, they "expelled" the Prime Minister from the party for refusing to obey party discipline and embarking on a "personality cult." The acid test of the rival claims came with the reassembling of parliament at the end of November, after the summer recess, when the battle-lines reformed on the floor beneath the vaulted ceiling of the Lok Sabha (the Lower House of the Indian parliament). As expected, the mass of Congress M.P.s ignored the "Syndicate's" edict and re-elected Mrs. Gandhi as their leader. The rebel minority, however, was large enough to lose the government its parliamentary majority. Mrs. Gandhi commanded the votes of only 210 of the 282 Congress M.P.s in the 522-seat house, thus requiring another 52 votes for a majority. The 43 Communists rallied to her banner, somewhat to her embarrassment, and so did the 25 Dravidian Advancement Party M.P.s (a regional faction seeking southern autonomy), and 23 independents. The 60 "syndicated" Congress members took their places on the opposition benches in alliance with the 42 right-wing Swatantra Party members. And there matters stood as the year ended. On December 26, Mr. Jagjivan Ram, Food Minister and unofficial leader of India's 75 million Untouchables, was elected president of the Prime Minister's wing of the Congress Party.

Meanwhile, other events had occurred significant to the nation. Mid-term elections had taken place in the states of Bihar, Pondicherry, Punjab, Uttar Pradesh, and West Bengal in February. A United Front, headed by the left-wing Communist Party of India (Marxist), won an overwhelming victory in West Bengal; the new state government, however, was unable to preserve order in the face of Maoist disruption. The Naga rebellion petered out during 1969, and in May the rebels were reported to have given up fighting. President Nixon arrived (on his Asian tour) for talks with Mrs. Gandhi on July 31. Bloody religious rioting occurred in Ahmedabad September 18–28, following allegations that Muslims had slaughtered holy cattle; some 1,000 people died—mostly Muslims. India fell flat on her face while bathed in the limelight of the international stage on September 25. This followed the Government's insistence that it should be represented at the Islamic summit conference

held at Rabat to discuss the burning of the Al Aqsa mosque in Jerusalem, on the ground that India has a 60-million Muslim minority. An Indian delegation was present on the opening day of the conference but, at the insistence of the Pakistanis, was asked to leave on the second.

Iran (Persia)

A border dispute between Iraq and Persia rumbled through the year, erupting occasionally into skirmishing. The critical area was the Shatt-al-Arab, the muddy river that oozes between Persia and Iraq from the confluence of the Tigris and Euphrates before disgorging into the Persian Gulf. The dispute concerned the 1937 treaty between the two countries by which the whole waterway was defined as Iraqi territory. A joint commission should have been set up under the terms of this treaty, to improve pilotage and dredging, but it never materialised. On April 19, Persia denounced the 1937 treaty, maintaining that Iraq had violated it over many years by unilaterally collecting river tolls without giving a share to Persia. Persia further announced that her ships would no longer pay river tolls to the Iraqis or fly the Iraqi flag—another provision of the treaty—and insisted that the border should be moved from the eastern bank to the middle of the river.

During April and May, army units dug themselves in between the date palms on either side of the river, gazing defiantly at each other down the barrels of their guns. Overhead screaming Persian Air Force jets festooned the cloudless sky with vapour trails, while Persian warships escorted cargo ships down river to the Gulf as a sprinkling of Iraqi M.T.B.s (minus torpedoes) darted warily among them.

This unreal and somewhat trivial quarrel was aggravated tragically by Iraq's expulsion of large numbers of Persians living in Iraq. By mid-May over 15,000 had been driven over the Persian border, some of whom had never before seen Persia. The condition of many of these refugees indicated that they had been deported at a moment's notice with great brutality. Some had scars and broken limbs, and there were hordes of terrified children. On May 12 the Persian government protested to the U.N. Security Council at these expulsions.

Tension in the Gulf is generated basically by the preparations for the power struggle that will come to pass when the British finally withdraw from the area in 1971. Thus the border problem could well smoulder on until a larger conflict decides which power shall fill the vacuum. Meanwhile Persia stepped up its secret aid to Mustafa Bargani's Kurdish rebels, who launched a new campaign in northern Iraq during the year.

On April 2, Persia broke off relations with Lebanon because of that country's refusal to extradite a former Persian deputy premier wanted for embezzlement.

Pakistan

The political storm that had gathered over the head of President Ayub Khan and his regime during 1968 broke out with a savage violence that engulfed the first three months of 1969. The year began against a backcloth of student riots in protest against the alleged corruption, nepotism, and incompetence of the regime, while the enigmatic ex-Foreign Minister and leader of the left-wing People's Party, Zulfiqar Ali Bhutto, kicked his heels in jail following his arrest on November 13, 1968, under the emergency regulations that had been in force since

February saw the release from jail of Mr. Bhutto, the most important of the various opposition leaders who were in full cry during the violent convulsions that hit Pakistan during the first three months of 1969.

the 1965 war with India. Mr. Bhutto had been charged with inciting students to violence during the riots that began in October 1968 in West Pakistan and which, by December 1968, had spread to the deprived East. Pakistan is, of course, divided into two segments separated by Indian territory, and the poorer East, jealous of the relative prosperity and influence of the West, nurses a powerful movement for secession. Sheikh Mujibur Rahman, president of the Awami League (a popular Eastern autonomist movement), had been in jail since May 1966.

On January 8, 1969, eight of the more conservative of the various dissident parties within the country joined together to form a Democratic Action Committee and issued an eight-point programme for sweeping constitutional reforms. Their main demand was for the abolition of the curious system of indirect representation by which the President, the National Assembly, and the provincial Assemblies were elected through a college of popularly elected "basic democrats"—these village elders and landlords were all too easily bribed or browbeaten. They also called for the lifting of the state of emergency; for an autonomous East Pakistan; and for a free press. Meanwhile the scale of street rioting was increasing, especially after January 20 when police in Dacca opened fire on about 5,000 demonstrating students armed with hockey sticks and staves, killing one student and injuring many others. There followed 10 days of wide-scale street-fighting and strikes that brought the country to a state of chaos—until on February 1 President Ayub Khan announced in a broadcast that he would invite "representatives of responsible political

parties" to discuss the demands made by the Democratic Action Committee. This offer was received coolly by the opposition, who refused to meet the President until the state of emergency was lifted and all political prisoners released. Thus Ayub Khan was forced into releasing Mr. Bhutto, Sheikh Rahman, and some 200 other political prisoners. He lifted the state of emergency on February 17, and on February 21 announced that he would not stand for re-election as President.

The situation cooled down following the President's February broadcast, but on February 14 a general strike, called for by the Democratic Action Committee, sparked off another wave of violence, particularly in the East, where a political agitator had been shot while allegedly attempting to escape from a police escort. The rioters' attention was especially focused on the "basic democrats," one of whom was beaten to death on February 21, and many of whom resigned. Mob rule prevailed in Dacca, the largest city in the East, while in the West the newly released Bhutto entered Karachi to triumphant cheering (and a gun battle between the police and his supporters) on February 17. When the talks between the President and his opponents finally began on February 26, Bhutto together with Maulana Bhashani (an 83-year-old Maoist with a considerable following among the peasants) refused to attend, but Sheikh Rahman was present. Although the talks produced an agreement to hold elections for a democratic parliament with a universal adult franchise, they failed to deal with the problems of East Pakistan. This failure led to an inevitable return to violence—this time on a still bloodier scale. During March the forces of law and order in the East retreated before the mob until the toll of vigilante murders of government officials and "basic democrats" swelled to over 200. In the West, workers in hundreds of factories went on strike for higher wages, paralysing the country's economy. Throughout the whole débâcle, the various parties of the opposition showed themselves blind to their responsibilities and rent by faction. By March 25, Ayub had to admit that affairs were beyond the government's control and handed the country over to the army. General Yahya Khan, the chief-of-staff, declared martial law and the tanks rolled on to the streets, bringing a sharp return to order and ushering in a precarious peace. Five days later Yahya took over as President.

For the remainder of 1969 President Yahya headed a military junta, making occasional announcements that the army intended eventually to hand power back to the civilians, and on November 28 finally declared that general elections for a National Assembly would be held on October 5, 1970.

8 Countries of South-East Asia

Burma

Early in 1969, U Nu, the ousted Prime Minister of the civilian government, sacked by the military in 1962, managed to slip into exile by feigning illness and convincing the regime that he needed medical treatment abroad. He thereupon stumped the capitals of the world fluttering the banner of Burmese democracy and, as the year ended, was ensconced in Bangkok plotting

the overthrow of the regime of strong-man Ne Win. Rebels continue to operate among the hill tribes, some aided by the Chinese, and 133 Burmese soldiers were reported killed during the first eight months of the year. The army, however, is reputed to have gained the upper hand against "White Flag" Communists in the Pegu Yoma mountains, north of Rangoon.

Cambodia

March 1969 saw a significant move on the part of the Cambodian Head of State, Prince Norodom Sihanouk, when he decided to resume diplomatic contact with the U.S.A.—which he had broken off four years previously, ostensibly because American and South Vietnamese troops were violating Cambodia's borders. Cambodia shares a border with South Vietnam and many of the ramifications of the Ho Chi Minh trail—the main North Vietnamese supply route to South Vietnam—pass through the country, as do Communist supply routes to South Vietnam from the sea. It is estimated that the North Vietnamese and the Viet Cong have three divisions in Cambodia, and the Prince became increasingly concerned about their presence during the year, particularly as President Nixon began the slow American withdrawal from Vietnam.

Indonesia

It was the year in which the Papuans of West Irian, former Dutch New Guinea, were supposed to exercise their right of self-determination in deciding their future relationship with Indonesia, as stipulated in 1962 by the U.N. Since April 1968, a U.N. official had been responsible for recommending the form that the act of self-determination should take. Indonesia, however, ignored his recommendation that a plebiscite should be held, and in July, 1,025 "people's representatives" were chosen by the Indonesians and, by a mixture of brow-beating and bribery, there was a unanimous vote in favour of continued Indonesian administration. Thus in effect Indonesia annexed West Irian. Meanwhile, in Djakarta, President Suharto's government and the main political parties were wrangling throughout the year on the framing of bills preparing for a return to democracy and a general election due to be held in July 1971.

Laos

Until 1969 the civil war in Laos followed an annual routine with the Communists waging an offensive in the spring and lying low in the monsoon season; while the rains beat down, the Government forces—with aerial superiority—gained the upper hand and recaptured territory lost in the spring. The Communist Pathet Lao, however, continued fighting into the monsoon season during 1969, and in June, backed by seven North Vietnamese battalions and some light tanks, they attacked and captured the important government garrison at Muong Soui (on the north-western edge of the Plain of Jars).

Some 40,000 North Vietnamese troops were estimated to be in the country during the year, mostly guarding the Ho Chi Minh trail, and the Government forces are "stiffened" with several thousand Thai troops, all wearing Royal Laotian uniforms, and at least 1,000 American "advisers."

Malaysia

On May 13, 1969, violent race riots erupted in Kuala Lumpur. Mobs of Malays, wearing white headbands (to signify an alliance with death) and armed with swords and daggers, rampaged through Chinese areas, burning, looting, and killing, while Chinese (and some Indians) armed themselves with guns and raided Malay villages. The government claimed that only 104 died in the clashes, but Western observers put the death toll at around 600, mostly Chinese. Malaysia's ethnic melting

President Marcos voting for himself in the Philippines presidential elections of November 11.

pot comprises 4,300,000 Malays, 3,400,000 Chinese, and 1,000,000 Indians and Pakistanis. The violence followed elections on May 10, in which Chinese opposition parties bit deep into the Alliance Coalition majority, thus rocking the fragile racial balance of the Malaysian power structure. This inflamed Malay nationalists and the riots began, spreading rapidly despite a 24-hour curfew declared immediately by the Government.

As the crisis continued the Tunku and his deputy Prime Minister Tun Abdul Razak suspended parliament, and formed an all-powerful National Operations Council run by Razak, who thus became the man really ruling the country. The Council banned all newspapers for a week, launched a series of arrests of alleged Communists and fellow-travellers, and was still wielding power as the year ended. In the months that followed the rioting, the situation went back to normal, although fierce undercurrents of hostility remained. While these perhaps irremediable tensions weakened the country, there came reports of growing Communist strength and activity along the Malaysia-Thailand border. (See also under Singapore.)

North Vietnam

Following the death of President Ho Chi Minh on September 3, there was much speculation about his successor. The main political figures in Hanoi were Le Duan, First Secretary of the Party; Pham Van Dong, Prime Minister; Truong Chinh, chairman of the National Assembly; and the victor of Dien Bien Phu, General Giap, Minister of Defence. On September 23 the National Assembly elected Ton Duc Thang, the 81-year-old Vice-President, as acting President, but no announcement was made concerning the successor to the chairmanship of the central committee of the Communist party (Vietnamese Worker's Party) which had also been held by the late President. Le Duan, however, appeared to have emerged as the leading politician in the country, being named first among the Vietnamese leaders at Ho's funeral, delivering the oration, and reading Ho's political testament.

The Paris peace talks dragged on through the year and so did the fighting in the South (see under South

Jungle h.q. of the N.L.F. "provisional revolutionary government" of South Vietnam announced in June.

Vietnam); the American bombing pause that started on November 1, 1968, continued.

Philippines

In the November elections President Marcos became the first Filipino President ever to be elected for a second term. The elections passed off serenely by Filipino standards—a mere 50 people were killed in bullet-zipping fracases between enthusiastic partisans. Nevertheless, as a number of ballot boxes were still unaccounted for days after the election, it was not mere pique that inspired the defeated Liberal, Sergio Osmeña Jr., to vouchsafe the opinion that this was "the dirtiest election yet." Marcos began the withdrawal of Filipino troops from Vietnam during the year—largely because of lack of funds.

Singapore

Singapore celebrated its 150th anniversary during 1969 and Princess Alexandra, representing the Queen, attended an anniversary dinner given by premier Lee Kuan Yew on August 8.

On June 19–20 representatives from Singapore, Malaysia, Australia, New Zealand, and the U.K. met in Canberra to discuss the defence problems of Singapore and Malaysia after the withdrawal of British forces in 1971. The talks were not greatly constructive in practical terms (it had already been established that a small Australian and New Zealand presence would remain in the area), and overshadowing them was the pledge of Mr. Edward Heath, leader of the British Opposition, to reverse the British decision to withdraw when, and if, he comes to power.

South Vietnam

1969 was the year in which the South Vietnamese learnt that they were eventually going to be left on their own. As the year ended the Communist North Vietnamese and their allies the N.L.F. still maintained 25,000 regular troops and guerrillas in the country, with tens of thousands more just over the frontiers. Meanwhile, the forces of South Vietnam's American allies were being reduced at the rate of 10,000 a month, and South

Vietnamese troops had begun to bear the brunt of the fighting. Indeed, for some months American casualties had averaged only one quarter of those of South Vietnam.

Following the massive Communist Tet offensive of 1968, in which thousands of Viet Cong and Northern assault troops hurled themselves against the major cities of the South and in doing so destroyed many American illusions and lost the cream of their men, the Communists retreated to their jungle strongholds in Cambodia and Laos and "safe" areas of South Vietnam, where they lay low. The "lull" lasted until March 1969, when one week after the Buddhist new year another Tet offensive was launched. This was not as massive as the previous one, but the Communists concentrated on mortar and rocket attacks with one aim in mind—American casualties—to emphasise their spectacular psychological victory of 1968 and thereby influence the growing antiwar feeling of the American public. As a result, 1,140 American soldiers were killed in the space of three weeks. The Allies responded with two large-scale counter-offensives, but otherwise relied on increasingly mobile tactics, with especial emphasis on patrolling infiltration routes, while the South Vietnamese government intensified its "pacification" programme—fortifying villages—aiming to have 90 per cent of the population in "safe" areas by the year's end.

A spate of peace proposals and counter-proposals marked the year. On May 8 the National Liberation Front (the South Vietnamese Communists) at the Paris peace talks brought out a peace plan, which was followed by proposals from President Nixon on May 14. Basically the N.L.F. called for the immediate withdrawal of all American and allied troops and the setting up of a provisional coalition government in South Vietnam, while the U.S.A. and South Vietnamese governments insisted on the simultaneous withdrawal of North Vietnamese and American troops and elections organised by President Thieu's government. On July 11, President Thieu proposed international supervision of South Vietnamese elections in which the N.L.F. would be free to take part.

On June 8, at a meeting between the American and South Vietnamese Presidents on the Pacific island of Midway, Nixon announced the first big withdrawal of American troops from Vietnam in line with his policy of "Vietnamising" the war (see under U.S.A.). The largest number of American troops in South Vietnam during 1969 was 543,054 on February 20. On June 8 the withdrawal of 25,000 was ordered; on September 16, 35,000 more men were ordered to be withdrawn; and on December 15, Nixon ordered a further 50,000 out. As the year ended it was announced that American casualties in Vietnam over the previous nine years had exceeded 40,000. The toll for 1969 dropped sharply, from 14,592 in 1968 to 9,365.

A land reform programme was announced by Thieu's government during July, by which tenant farmers (i.e. the peasants) were given the land they tilled free. This was seen as a ploy to beat the Communists at their own game. It involved paying landowners $400 million in compensation, 10 per cent of which was provided by Washington. Following Thieu's July announcement that he would be prepared to contest elections with the N.L.F., observers mooted the possibility of his increasing the number of civilians in his government to court popularity. It was therefore a surprise when in August he sacked his civilian Prime Minister Huong Tran Van and replaced him with General Khiem Tran Thien, Minister of Police and Pacification. Thieu must have considered efficiency more important than popularity.

Thailand

On February 10 Thailand went to the polls after more than a decade of military rule. The rights of free speech and political assembly—banned under martial law—were restored and a profusion of parties blossomed. Field Marshal Thanom's government formed its own party—the United Thai People's Party—which contested each of the 219 seats of the House of Representatives. The results, however, cannot have pleased the Field

Marshal, for the regime lost all 21 seats in the twin cities of Bangkok and Thonburi to the main opposition party, the Democrats. The results were as follows: U.T.P.P. 75 seats; Democrats 56; Democratic Front 7; Economist United Front 4; Other parties 5; Independents 72.

Since under the Thai Constitution all important matters are decided by the Senate—the 164-man upper house—members of which are appointed by the government, the regime merely suffered a rebuff at the polls rather than a death blow. Communist guerrillas were active on polling day to a certain extent and several people were killed in remote regions. At least a thousand guerrillas were active within Thailand during 1969, particularly near the border with Malaysia.

9 The Far East

China

Throughout 1969 Peking was proclaiming the imminence of war with Russia and, although this was a distinct possibility (see under Soviet Union), the propaganda value of the danger was exploited to unify the country after the three years of the tumultuous cultural revolution. It also served to intensify the vast compulsory migration in which massive numbers of city dwellers were being moved to China's remote border regions. Reports imply that the regime plans to reduce the population of cities like Shanghai and Canton by one third. Forced migrants include students, teachers, bureaucrats, doctors, and engineers, as well as unemployed youths. The aims behind the scheme include Mao's idea that intellectuals should acquire a proletarian attitude through manual labour, but it is also a way of ridding the cities of unemployed and the factories of surplus labour. The scheme appears, moreover, to have strategic implications, as decentralising China should boost the nation's capacity to resist invasion and enable it to survive nuclear devastation of cities. Despite glowing propaganda describing joyous intellectuals abandoning their "moribund" books for the shovel, the campaign was somewhat unpopular with those forced to leave the cities for the rural joys of Inner Mongolia, Sinkiang, or Manchuria. Even so some 10 million had been moved by the year's end.

The ninth congress of the Chinese Communist Party—the first since 1958—was held in strict secrecy, April 1–24, and 1,512 delegates attended. Three communiqués unfolded the proceedings, which included a Central Committee report read by the Vice-Chairman of the party, Marshal Lin Piao (who was named as Mao's successor during the year). The Party's constitution was revised, and a new Central Committee and Presidium were elected. A point of major significance was that Chairman Mao, who had been declared dead by some Western and Russian observers, was present and appeared on a newsreel film of the affair. The question of whether or not the Great Helmsman was alive or dead, healthy or ailing, was one that fascinated China-watchers during 1969. Mao almost certainly has a number of doubles; indeed it is alleged that at one time during 1969 he was reported in two places at once. Moreover, observers saw a sudden diminution in the

praises sung to Mao during September, which might have indicated that the Chairman was gravely ill or even dead.

The composition of the new Presidium crystallised the results of the power struggle that went parallel with the cultural revolution. Of the 10 women on the 176-strong Presidium, five are the wives of top Peking leaders, including Chiang Ching, Mao's fourth wife, ex-film actress, revolutionary termagant, and, according to some, the real power in the country. Another new Politburo member was Mao's son-in-law Yao Wen-yuan, who is married to a daughter of Chiang Ching by a previous marriage. The wife of Lin Piao, Minister of Defence and heir to Mao, is also in the new politburo.

Lin Piao's report to the congress emphasised the ideological split between China and the Soviet Union. He reaffirmed Lenin's assertion that capitalism made war inevitable (a maxim rejected by the Russians, and long a bone of ideological contention between the two Communist giants), and proclaimed once again that the "class struggle" must go on after the end of capitalism—the philosophy behind the notorious cultural revolution. Despite this, the signs were that during 1969 the Chinese leaders were moving towards "normalisation."

Among delegates at the ninth Chinese Communist Congress in April, were (*left to right*) **Chairman Mao; his declared successor, Lin Piao; Prime Minister Chou en Lai; and** (*far right*) **Mao's wife Chiang Ching.**

Hong Kong

For some 16 years the question of abolition of concubinage had been aired by luminaries in Hong Kong, but it was not until late July 1969 that plans were announced by the colonial government to outlaw it—thus abandoning the pledge, enshrined in the Sino-British treaty of 1843, to preserve the marriage codes of the Ching Dynasty. A draft bill appeared in that month that will deny the legitimacy and remove the automatic right of succession of a concubine's offspring. Rich Chinese are wont to keep a number of such girls—often chosen by their wives—under their roofs, and will, of course, continue to do so on a *de facto* basis.

On October 2, Wong Chack, the Communist journalist, and the remainder of the 13 Communist newspapermen still in jail following rioting in 1967, were released. As a result a number of British citizens held in China were set free, including Anthony Grey, Reuter's Peking correspondent, who had been under house arrest since July 21, 1967.

North Korea

Increased North Korean belligerence marked the year. On April 15 a U.S. Navy E.C.121 reconnaissance aircraft with a crew of 31 was shot down some 90 nautical miles off the North Korean coast, and on August 17 an American helicopter disappeared. There was also a marked increase in infiltration from the North across the border into South Korea, and on April 25 a short, sharp border skirmish was reported. During the year the North Korean leader Kim Il Sung intensified his already fervid efforts to establish himself as a living legend on the international scene. Jealous of the fame of Mao Tse-tung and Ho Chi Minh, Kim launched a world-wide publicity drive. On November 3 raised eyebrows could be witnessed ascending from behind copies of the London *Times*—and august organs of similar ilk elsewhere in the West—as readers were surprised to observe a bizarre, full-page advertisement proclaiming the revolutionary virtues of Kim: "Korea has produced the hero of the 20th century," and plugging his "long-awaited" biography. Experts wondered how strong the link was between the upsurge of North Korea's provocative military activity and Kim's apparent megalomania.

South Korea

While President Park Chung Hee of South Korea was increasingly concerned during the year with the upsurge of North Korean bellicosity, proclaiming in August that he feared another war was approaching, he was concerned at home with ensuring that he should be able to stand for a third term in office despite the constitution. Government moves to enable him to do this inspired a number of student riots—notably those of June 30 and July 1, in which some 385 were injured—but on October 8 the undeterred Park announced that a national referendum would be held on October 17 to determine whether the constitution could be changed to enable him to run for a third term in 1971. On October 19 the results of this poll showed 65·1 per cent support for the proposal, and the returns showed that 75·9 per cent of the country's 15,048,925 voters went to the polls.

On November 3, three South Koreans, including a former Cambridge post-graduate law student, were sentenced to death in Seoul after being found guilty of spying for the North.

Japan

The political highlight of 1969 for Japan was the general election of December 27. The parties contending for office comprised the ruling Liberal Democrats (LDP); the main opposition party, the Japanese Socialists (JSP); Komeito, the political wing of a militant Buddhist sect; the Japanese Communist Party; and an insignificant offshoot of the JSP, the Democratic Socialists. LDP was hot favourite to stay in power, but, thanks to intense intra-party strife, pundits were especially interested in forecasting the exact measure of the predicted victory, as the Prime Minister, Mr. Sato, would almost certainly be ousted by one of his lieutenants if LDP merely scraped home. Those factors weighing against LDP with the electorate included rising prices (there had been a general rise of 6 per cent during the year), a housing shortage, and heavy taxes. A point in favour was Sato's diplomatic triumph in Washington from November 19 to 21, when he managed to persuade the Americans to agree to hand back the island of Okinawa by 1972. Okinawa has remained in the hands of the Americans since the war, a fact which has rankled with many Japanese, particularly the legion of rabid student demonstrators, and feelings concerning the island ran high, especially since nerve gas leaked from weapons there in July 1969. The main plank in the LDP platform, however, was the government's highly impressive economic record—with a rapidly expanding economy, full employment, and the parallel evolution of a massive bourgeois class. The JSP, racked with internal ideological conflicts, adopted a somewhat Utopian stance for a serious contender, with a call for total disarmament. The Japanese-American Security Treaty—due for renewal in 1970—was the major election issue as far as foreign policy was concerned.

The most curious of the major parties was Komeito, which campaigned on a "clean government" platform. This party is the political arm of the Soka Gakkai, a seven-million-strong, semi-religious, strength-through-joy, oriental version of Moral Rearmament. Highly unified, and ploughing a religious, middle-of-the-field furrow, the Komeito had entered political life with a spectacular capture of 25 seats in the elections of 1967.

In the event the government won an overwhelming victory, increasing its number of seats from 272 to 288; the JSP dropped dramatically from 134 to 90; the Communists made a striking gain at JSP's expense, from

Leaders of the Japanese Liberal Democratic party cheering the December election victory which returned them to office with an enlarged majority. In the centre is Eisaku Sato, party president and Prime Minister.

4 to 14; and Komeito rocketed upwards from 25 to 47. One major factor which told against the JSP was the party's strong association with the violent student riots that kept Japan constantly in the world's headlines during 1969. These demonstrations have long lost any public sympathy since students began throwing fire bombs, killing bystanders, and disrupting commuter trains. The Japanese "protest movement" is one of the most bizarre features of the country, and one that was virulently active during the year.

10 Australia and New Zealand

Australia

Elections for the Federal House of Representatives were held throughout Australia on October 25, 1969; 499 candidates contested the 125 seats. The Prime Minister and leader of the Liberal Party, Mr. Gorton, in his policy speech on television, pledged, among other things, a start on a naval base in Western Australia, a reduction in tax on lower and middle-income earners, a five-year plan for the development of water resources, and the building of a nuclear reactor on the south coast of New South Wales. His coalition partner, the leader of the Country Party Mr. McEwen, emphasised the needs of the man on the land and promised to fight for new provisions for country living and industry. The policy of Mr. Whitlam, leader of the Labor Party, included the withdrawal of all Australian troops from Vietnam before the end of June 1970; the signing of the nuclear non-proliferation treaty; the abolition of conscription; and reforms in education, health, and housing.

Although the voting showed a pronounced swing to the Labor Party this was not strong enough to unseat the Government, and the Liberal-Country Party coalition was returned to office with a majority of seven. The state of the parties in the new House was: Liberal Party 46 seats, Country Party 20, and Labor Party 59. Shortly afterwards Mr. Gorton's position as leader of the Liberal Party was challenged, first by Mr. Fairbairn, at the time Minister for National Development, and secondly by Mr. McMahon, then the Federal Treasurer. Mr. Gorton survived the challenge to continue as party leader and Prime Minister. Mr. McMahon was elected deputy leader of the Party. A few days later Mr. Gorton announced his cabinet, which included Mr. McEwen as Deputy Prime Minister and Minister for Trade; Mr. McMahon as Minister for External Affairs; and Mr. L. Bury as Treasurer.

As a result of general elections for Tasmania's House of Assembly on May 10, 35 years of Australian Labor Party government in that State—and the only Labor government in the Commonwealth—came to an end. The A.L.P. won 17 seats, the Liberal Party 17 seats, and the Centre Party one seat. The Centre Party representative, Kevin Orchard Lyons, son of Joseph Lyons who was Prime Minister of Australia 1932–39, had broken away from the Liberals in 1968 to form the Centre Party. Both major groups energetically sought support from the Centre Party to form a government, and after lengthy deliberation it decided to throw in its lot with the Liberals. On May 26 the Governor swore in the Liberal-Centre Party government with Walter Angus Bethune as Premier and Minister-in-charge of the Hydro-Electric Commission, and Kevin Lyons as Deputy Premier, Chief Secretary, and Minister for Tourists. Mr. Bethune replaced Eric Reece, who had been Premier for nearly eleven years.

Elections for the Queensland Legislative Assembly's 78 seats were held on May 17, and the Country Party–Liberal Party coalition was returned to power. The Country Party won 26 seats (the same number as in the previous House), the Liberal Party 19 (also the same as previously), and the Australian Labor Party 31 (a gain of 4). One seat was won by the Democratic Labor Party, and one by an independent. In the long campaign preceding the election the government's promises included a few tax concessions, some liquor reform, an increase in Housing Commission loans, extension in textbook allowances, and certain incentives for industry in country centres. The Australian Labor Party, led by Mr. Houston, promised wide liquor reform with Sunday trading in Brisbane, measures to deal with exploitation and damage of the Great Barrier Reef, and action in connection with Australian participation in overseas companies developing Queensland's resources. On May 28 the Premier and leader of the Country Party, Mr. J. Bjelke-Petersen, announced his cabinet. It included the leader of the Liberal Party, Mr. G. Chalk, as Treasurer, and five other Liberals. The remaining six cabinet posts were filled by Country Party members.

The 1969–70 Federal Budget brought down by the Treasurer, Mr. W. McMahon, on August 12 included no tax changes, and contained some provisions that would tend to increase spending rather than limit it. There were many increases in social service benefits, substantial subsidies to private schools, and a significant easing of the pension means test. Pensions were increased over a wide range of categories, and the Budget also included a new allowance of $5 a week for people of 80 years or more who receive approved personal care or live in hostel-type accommodation, and free health insurance for families with an income of less than $39 a week, and for migrants for their first two months in Australia. In the field of education, the Budget provided for yearly subsidies to non-government schools at the rate of $35 for each primary pupil and $50 for each secondary pupil, increased funds for Teachers' Colleges, and an increase in the number of Commonwealth scholarships to Universities and advanced colleges. Rural aid included a rise in the superphosphate subsidy, and a revised formula for financing wool research and promotion whereby the levy on growers will be reduced for three years from 2 to 1 per cent. The allocation for foreign aid was increased by $13,000,000 to $150,000,000, of which Papua–New Guinea will receive $96,000,000. The money allowance for aid to aborigines was nearly doubled, and considerable amounts were given to research and cultural aid. The only higher impost in the Budget was in Air Navigation charges for domestic airlines, which were increased by 10 per cent. Surprisingly the Budget allowed for a decrease in defence spending of about 5 per cent, but the Treasurer explained that this did not amount to a reduction in the defence effort.

In spite of very severe drought in Queensland and other difficulties in certain rural industries, the Australian economy went from strength to strength during 1969. Minerals provided the most spectacular features of the growth, and some dramatic developments were announced in that sector. In January a contract for the sale of 85 million tons of coal, over 13 years, from the Bowen Basin of Central Queensland was signed in Tokyo. At the time it was the largest contract ever negotiated by the Japanese steel industry, and it is believed to be a world record for a coal transaction. In April, Japanese and U.S. business interests concluded a contract for the supply of 87 million tons of Robe River (W.A.) iron ore pellets over 21 years, and for 36 million tons of crushed ore over 15 years; and later in the year it was announced that as a result of another long-term contract with Japan, Hamersley Holdings, with its vast operation at Mount Tom Price, W.A., and a proposed one at Paraburdoo in the same region, would become the largest iron-ore producer in the world. Other highlights of the booming mineral industry were the announcement of plans to increase the production of copper in South Australia and at Mount Isa, and of bauxite in North Queensland, and a report of new findings of nickel in Western Australia.

Success in the mineral industry tended to obscure the difficulties experienced in pastoral and farming activities. Although seasonal conditions were generally good in south-eastern Australia and production was on a high level, working costs and uncertainty of markets caused a good deal of concern. The 1968–69 wool clip sold at auction reached a record of 5,207,105 bales, and sheep figures at 176,200,000 also created a record. But the average price of greasy and scoured wool was 44.67 cents a lb., a price that left little profit for the grower. Production of wheat also ran into high figures, but the doubtful international demand clouded the horizon. The dairy industry faced a bleak future. In the Queensland drought cattle and sheep losses were severe. Sugar and grain crops also suffered badly. Nevertheless the overall picture of Australia's trade was bright. The export of manufactured goods continued to expand, and even the most cautious authorities were confident of a continued growth in the economy during 1970.

Bruce Pratt

New Zealand

Several milestones in New Zealand history were passed in 1969, which was also a year of significant economic advance. It was the 200th anniversary of Captain Cook's first voyage of discovery to New Zealand, paving the way for the country's settlement by Britain, and the event was suitably celebrated. After the National Export Year in 1968, trade figures in 1969 produced a record: for the first time exports soared beyond the $1,000 million mark. Of this, meat exports alone accounted for more than $300 million, another record figure.

Manufacturers, too, in this almost wholly primary producing nation, achieved production records, with exports doubled and running at an annual rate in excess of $100 million. Advances in the industrial sphere, in fact, provided the most spectacular results or show of potential. There were positive discoveries of both oil and minerals, and although the commercial possibili-

ties of most of the finds have yet to be fully assessed, stock exchange prices shot up to high levels. Applications for prospecting licences came from all over the world, notably from Australia, Japan and North America.

Meanwhile, solid foundations were laid for vastly increased industrial activity in years to come. Agreement was reached with Comalco of Australia and two Japanese firms to build an aluminium smelter at Bluff at a cost of $92 million; and the country's first steel plant at Glenbrook, south of Auckland, began production using iron sands from west coast beaches.

New exports have included seemingly unlikely items such as aircraft—types used mainly for aerial top-dressing, and the small Airtourer which has interested countries abroad for both civilian and air force training. In addition, the prototypes of two New Zealand-made cars—one with a rotary engine—have reached the test stage, with production possible in 1970 for both home and export markets. It was also decided to allow trout farming and deer farming to serve markets abroad for trout and venison. Oyster farms established now number 20.

The Kapuni natural gas pipeline from Taranaki to the two main cities, Auckland and Wellington, was completed, and natural gas will soon serve North Island homes and industry. The computer system for banking was completed, and the country became the first in the world to have all its banks computer linked.

Further progress was made towards the eventual aim of abolishing import licenses needed for certain goods and changing to a system of tariffs which will be regulated as required to give protection for local industry. To carry on the work of the 1968 National Development Conference it was decided to set up a National Development Council, and a New Zealand Export Corporation, with government help, was established to find new markets and sell new products overseas. There was further progress in co-operation between Australia and New Zealand through the free trade agreement.

While the huge wool stockpile—wool bought in at auction because of low prices in 1967 and 1968—was considerably reduced during 1969, the year ended with prices again weakening and prospects somewhat clouded. A severe drought towards the end of the year also caused concern among many farmers who were forced to sell stock early because of feed problems. But other farm products were finding buoyant markets, meat, fruit, and canned and frozen vegetables leading the way. The boom in tourism also gathered pace, with a big increase in people from abroad filling the new hotels and motels at resorts.

Emigration, however, exceeded new arrivals, and this led to skilled-labour shortages in some sections of industry. The Government raised the quota for its sponsored and assisted immigration schemes to help counter the net outflow of population.

As the general election in November drew near, it emerged that New Zealand had achieved its first balance of payments surplus in 20 years; and the return of Mr. Holyoake's National Party Government for its fourth successive term was due mainly to the country's undoubted rise in prosperity after the depression and devaluation of two years before. The Government's working majority, however, was reduced. Just before the election, the voting age, and the age at which people are allowed in hotel bars, was lowered to 20.

The country's preoccupation with the effect of British entry into the Common Market led to several ministerial visits to Europe, headed by the Prime Minister and his deputy, Mr. Marshall. Mr. Marshall was able to get recognition among the Six and Britain that permanent rather than transitional arrangements are needed for New Zealand produce in Britain.

Achievements in sport included an overseas tour of the cricket team, led by Graham Dowling, which for the first time ever won a test series—against Pakistan. New Zealand's world cricket ranking rose from 7th to 4th. New Zealand won a rugby Test series against Wales; Ivan Mauger was again world speedway champion; a New Zealand crew won the One-Ton Cup for yachting in Rainbow II; and Cliff Tait flew round the world in the smallest plane ever to circumnavigate the globe, the New Zealand-made Airtourer.

W. M. Elliott

11 North America

Canada

Some international feathers were ruffled on April 3, 1969, when Prime Minister Pierre Trudeau announced a proposed reduction of Canadian troops serving in Europe as part of the NATO alliance. The cuts were ostensibly part of the major "re-think" of Canadian foreign policy promised by the premier during the 1968 election campaign. Some commentators on Canadian affairs, however, considered that the decision had been made to appease growing domestic criticism of the rising amount of expenditure on defence (a sixth of the national budget). The proposals were put into effect on June 2, when it was announced in the House of Commons at Ottawa that Canada's 6,000-man armoured brigade in Europe would be replaced by a "smaller mobile armed force," and that six squadrons of Starfighters were to be withdrawn.

Other traditional allegiances were questioned during the year. During October the Duke of Edinburgh, while visiting Ottawa, remarked that if Canadians felt that it was time to sever their links with the monarchy it should be done amicably, thus sparking off a debate within the country on Canada's future relations with the United Kingdom. The same month saw a wildcat strike on the part of a force of Canada's legendary Mounties in Montreal on October 7, where, for a day and a night,

looting, fire, and violence reduced the city to anarchy. Student unrest was a feature of the year, particularly in Montreal, where student disruptions and destruction cost the city an estimated $11 million and hit the world's headlines when demonstrators at Sir George Williams University sacked and almost destroyed the computer centre on February 11.

United States of America

The low-pitched keynote of the first year of Richard Nixon's term as 37th President of the United States was struck in the inauguration speech of January 20, 1969, when he said: "To lower our voices would be a simple thing ... in these difficult years, America has suffered from a fever of words—from inflated rhetoric that promises more than it can possibly deliver ..." Much of what made 1969 a better year than had been expected— there were no ghetto riots and somewhat less hysteria on the campuses—was this damping down of the political fires by the new President.

Three main problems faced the Nixon government: the war in Vietnam; the cities, with their problems of race, crime, and poverty; and, less dramatic but no less menacing, inflation. Nixon's policy in Vietnam was outlined in a communiqué issued following his June 8 meeting with President Thieu of South Vietnam on the Pacific island of Midway, and also in speeches during the year (notably a broadcast of November 3, in which Nixon appealed to the American public for support for his Vietnam policies and first used the phrase "the silent majority" to describe those in favour of them). He pledged the complete withdrawal of all U.S. ground combat forces and their replacement by South Vietnamese on an orderly timetable depending on (1) the scale of enemy activity, (2) the progress of the Paris peace talks, and (3) the progress in training South Vietnamese troops. Following the Midway talks, he ordered the withdrawal of 25,000 men, and on September 16 and December 15, 45,000 and 50,000 respectively were ordered out.

Nixon made a tour of Asia, following the Apollo 11 success, from July 25 to August 3, in which he briefed friends and allies on his Asian policy—which was not to intervene in Asian wars unless an ally was invaded by a nuclear power. He visited the Philippines, Indonesia, Thailand, India, Pakistan, and finally Rumania. Following his inauguration, he had visited Western Europe from February 23 to March 2, calling on Brussels, London, Bonn, West Berlin, Rome, and Paris.

American troops began the slow pull-out from Vietnam during 1969. These Marines left for home in August.

In the U.S.A. 1969 saw the emergence as a political force of the middle-of-the-road "silent majority."

On April 14 Nixon outlined his domestic programme in a written message to Congress which included the following plans: (1) 7 per cent increase in social security benefits to counteract the rise in the cost of living, and long-term measures involving a complete overhaul of the complicated U.S. welfare schemes (August saw amplification of this vague proposal—with, as a main theme, plans to link relief of the able-bodied unemployed to manpower-training schemes); (2) a tax credit system designed to encourage investment in the cities, particularly the ghettos; (3) plans to feed back some Federal funds into local government; (4) improvements in transport—to be financed by user charges; (5) a stringent anti-crime drive, involving massive increase in crime-fighting funds; (6) Post Office reform. These proposals were not over-ambitious, but complied with the Nixon nostrum: "to propose only legislation that we know we can execute once it becomes law." Inflation prompted a rigorous honing of former President Johnson's budget for the fiscal year 1970—starting on July 1, 1969. One department, however, did receive an increase—Justice which got an extra $16 million, most of which went to the F.B.I. to finance their unrelenting war on the Mafia.

One expensive decision made by the President, after a prolonged public controversy during February and March, was to go ahead with a "modified" version of Johnson's proposed A.B.M. (anti-ballistic-missile) shield. Defence Secretary Laird unleashed some classified information in support of this decision, to the effect that Russian missiles of this type were already under way. Moreover, Nixon had pledged during the election campaign of 1968 to keep the U.S.A. ahead in the arms race. Nevertheless 1969 saw some parity between the two nuclear giants—which led to the SALT (strategic arms limitation talks) between them at Helsinki in November–December. On November 25, the President renounced the use of all methods of biological warfare, and announced that stockpiles of such material were to be destroyed.

The year saw a significant shift of emphasis within the fabric of American life. Hysteria was toned down, and the new administration first identified, then communed with, and finally mobilised its power base—the "silent majority." This shift of emphasis away from the liberals, the dissenters, the minorities, and, above all, the blue-blooded "limousine liberals" of the "Eastern establishment" was a political master-stroke. It was engineered by one of the most curious of the actors in the political arena—Vice-President Spiro Agnew. He started the year as the political equivalent to a music-hall mother-in-law and ended it as presidential material, thanks first to his attacks on the anti-war demonstrators, and, secondly and more significantly, to his assault on the slanted slickness of TV news media. Agnew entered the polemical fray against the first anti-war "Moratorium" of October 15, in which millions demonstrated peacefully against the Vietnam war. An even more massive Moratorium was held later, November 13–15, which saw tens of thousands marching in Washington from the Arlington National Cemetery to the Capitol, bearing coffins containing the names of American soldiers killed in Vietnam.

On October 19, at New Orleans, Agnew waded in with some mouth-filling invective directed at the Moratorium supporters, whom he described as "an effete corps of impudent snobs." Those politicians who supported them were dubbed "ideological eunuchs whose most comfortable position is straddling the ideological fence." On a successful tour of the South, Agnew continued his lambasting: militant students and their ilk could, he claimed, "be separated from our society with no more regret than we should feel over discarding rotten apples from a barrel." While these outbursts enraged the liberals, they were like balm to the souls of those soon to be identified as the silent majority. Even more popular was the Vice-President's attack on America's powerful TV current affairs commentators whom he castigated, a month later, as a "small and unelected élite" purveying "instant analysis and querulous criticism."

The liberals, the Democratic party, and the "Eastern establishment" had suffered a body-blow in July when the surviving Kennedy brother, Senator Edward Kennedy—the heir to the Kennedy mantle and its claim on the presidency—was involved in one of the most baffling and damaging scandals of American history. The Senator's car had been revealed by the dawn light of July 19, submerged in the muddy waters beneath Dike Bridge, near the coastal town of Martha's Vineyard, Mass. Trapped inside was the drowned body of one of the Senator's youthful aides, Mary Jo Kopechne. The Senator's inadequate, even conflicting, explanations of the accident, and especially the damning fact that—while admitting that he was the driver and that he had swum clear of the wreck—he had failed to call either police or fire brigade immediately, gave rise to unpleasant rumours and theories on a nation-wide scale. At the year's end a secret inquest on the dead girl was about to begin, but by then a thousand commentators had already officiated at a thousand inquests on Edward Kennedy's presidential hopes.

275

A significant aspect of the American scene was the revelation of the alleged "Pinkville" incident—the supposed killing by American troops of all the inhabitants, including women and children, of the South Vietnam village of My Lai on March 16, 1968—which shocked the rest of the West, yet was received almost philosophically by the American public. An opinion poll taken at the year's end showed that two-thirds of all Americans believed that press and TV had made too much of the affair. The silent majority had spoken.

12 Latin America and the Caribbean

Argentina

The image of peace and progress assiduously displayed by the military-backed government of President Juan Carlos Ongania since 1966 suffered a rude tarnishing during 1969. Riots that began in late May spread rapidly on a nation-wide scale and culminated in a blood-bath in Cordoba, where the army fought street battles against workers and students in which 20 people are estimated to have died. On May 30 a general strike occurred which, together with threats of further stoppages, laid bare the bitter divisions within Argentine society: a working-class divided into three hostile camps —one in league with the military government; a militant student body; and a vocal left-wing element within the Roman Catholic Church. President Ongania reacted to the crisis by declaring martial law on May 21, and by sacking his cabinet on June 5 and appointing a new one.

As the regime had brought stability in the economic field and allowed the press and the judiciary to function fairly freely, the various elements opposed to it were motivated only by a vague (if violent) frustration, fostered above all by the aloof paternalism and pallid personality of the President. Following the appointment of the new cabinet, however, the unnerved regime became highly repressive, various magazines and newspapers were closed down, and on September 17 the army "pacified" the small southern town of Cipoletti following trouble arising from a trivial local dispute.

Bolivia

On April 27, 1969, President René Barrientos of Bolivia was killed in a helicopter crash. He was succeeded by the Vice-President, Siles Salinas, but the latter did not have long to prove himself, for in the small hours of September 26 a deft and bloodless military coup ousted the constitutional government and Siles was dispatched to exile. The new military regime, under the former C.-in-C., General Alfredo Ovando, corresponded to the increasingly familiar Latin American pattern—that of a "revolutionary" (that is to say, nationalistic and overtly leftish) junta, bidding for left-wing support and taking an anti-American stance.

Brazil

The military regime that has ruled Brazil since seizing power from the ineffectual President Goulart in 1964 has steered Latin America's largest nation along the rugged path leading from bankruptcy towards economic salvation. Celebrating the fifth anniversary of the coup, President Arturo da Costa e Silva was able to announce that the rate of inflation had been cut from 87 per cent in 1964 to 24 per cent in 1968. Moreover, thousands of new jobs and homes had been created, and new shipyards and factories built. Economic success, however, has been achieved at the cost of a repression that has been increasingly resented. If bankruptcy, graft, and incompetence made the new military broom welcome in 1964, efficiency and economic progress have destroyed its *raison d'être*, and during 1969 the view prevailed that it was time for the military to step down. The President, in the teeth of powerful opposition from his supporters, decided to bow (somewhat stiffly) to this general feeling, and announced that on September 7, 1969, he would publish a democratic constitution. These plans, however, were scrapped only a week before the proposed date of their publication, when the 66-year-old president suffered a stroke that left him paralysed and unable to speak. An interim triumvirate of service chiefs took over, quietly side-stepping the claims of the nominal Vice-President, and on October 7 it was announced that General Emilio Garrastazo Medici was to be the new president of Brazil. Da Costa e Silva died soon afterwards.

On September 4, Brazilian "urban guerrillas" kidnapped the American ambassador, C. Burke Elbrick, and held him captive for 77 hours, only releasing him after the government had capitulated to their demands for the release of 15 political prisoners.

Chile

In the congressional elections of March 1969—the last elections before the presidential campaign of 1970—the ruling Christian Democrats suffered a sharp rebuff. The "democratic left"—as the Christian Democrats are described by their leader, President Eduardo Frei—lost 27 of its 82 seats (and its overall majority) in the 150-seat lower house, while the right-wing Nationalists leapt from 8 seats to 34. The reasons for the anti-government swing included inflation, high taxes and various natural catastrophes occurring within Frei's six-year term (during 1969, for example, Chile was suffering from the worst drought since records began there). But when, on October 21, President Frei had to declare a two-day state of siege after an army regiment in Santiago had mutinied over low wages, the nation rallied solidly again behind the government.

Colombia

In March President Carlos Lleras Restrepo announced that the government was concerned about growing anarchy; throughout the country, students, disaffected workers and armed guerrilla bands were clashing with police. The President summoned the commanders of 11 army brigades to Bogotá for instructions on putting down the disorder. At the end of May, however, students launched the inevitable riot, when the indefatigable roving U.S. envoy, Nelson Rockefeller, arrived in Bogotá.

On May 26, 1969, the five Andean countries— Colombia, Ecuador, Peru, Bolivia, and Chile—signed an agreement which set up an Andean common market.

Cuba

There was no Christmas in Cuba in 1969, the festival being postponed to July 1970 in order not to interrupt the sugar harvest. This bizarre juggling of the calendar was connected with President Fidel Castro's ambitious goal for a 10-million-ton crop. Previously the sugar harvest was from January to March, but the "1970 harvest" was started in July 1969 to extend for a full year, even though that entails cutting unripe cane and hacking down part of the 1971 crop. A million Cubans (an eighth of the total population) are taking part in this massive harvest, but it is doubtful if Castro's target will be achieved since it is more than double the average yield. As bread rationing had been imposed in May, many were wondering why some of the effort could not have been granted to grain. The answer is that Castro needs sugar to export to Russia in return for Soviet economic aid and machinery. In July there was some consternation amongst sun-bathers in Florida following the news that a squadron of Soviet warships was steaming towards Cuba. But this naval visit was only the Russian response to President Nixon's announcement that he planned to visit Bucharest.

Havana exercises an attraction to aerial hijackers akin to that wielded by Mecca upon the minds of fanatic Wahhabis, and in 1969 scores of commandeered American passenger aircraft were forced to touch down on Cuban tarmac. On February 11 it was announced that the Cuban and U.S. governments had reached an agreement whereby all hijacked American airliners diverted to Havana would be allowed to return immediately to the U.S.A. with their original passengers.

El Salvador

Those cynics who maintain that sport is less a means to international goodwill than a source of dissension had their philosophy fortified by the notorious "Soccer war" that raged briefly between the two Central American states of El Salvador and Honduras during July 1969. The immediate cause of the conflict was tension generated during football matches played between the two states in the qualifying rounds of the World Cup. On June 8 the El Salvador team played away in the first leg, losing 1–0. This, and the fact that Salvadoran supporters in Tegucigalpa (the Honduran capital) complained bitterly of ill-treatment, led to an atmosphere of intense hostility when the Honduran team arrived in San Salvador (capital of El Salvador) the following week for the second leg. Honduras lost 3–0 and their supporters were subjected to insult, rape, and injury. Reports of these incidents on Honduran radio inflamed the people of Honduras, and Salvadoran immigrants living in Honduras were attacked and their property burnt. In this atmosphere of mutual hostility, with large numbers of Salvadorans resident in Honduras pouring back over the border, the play-off between the two teams took place on neutral ground in Mexico City. El Salvador won 3–2, and this disgrace intensified Honduran bullying of the remaining Salvadorans in Honduras, which led to serious border incidents.

The situation deteriorated over the next ten days, and on July 14 President Sanchez of El Salvador ordered a full-scale attack on Honduras. The small Salvadoran army moved over the Honduran frontier, while the air force of six Second World War Mustangs dropped a few bombs, to no great effect. The next morning the Honduran air force (consisting of 11 old Corsairs) launched a reprisal attack, bombing oil tanks at the Salvadoran ports of Acajutla and Cutuco. On the ground, the Salvadoran army, equipped with light tanks, mortars, and bazookas, and led by a colonel with the dashing soubriquet of *El Diable*, swept a machete-wielding Honduran army over the Guatemalan border and seized the provincial capital of Nueva Ocotepeque, in S.W. Honduras. On the 18th a ceasefire was negotiated by the Organisation of American States and the fighting petered out into sporadic skirmishing. By the end of the month it had stopped altogether, and by August 7 the occupying Salvadoran troops had withdrawn from Honduran soil. The C.A.S. peace-making team estimated that some 2,000 had been killed on both sides, but it is doubtful whether losses were in fact so heavy.

The underlying causes of this curious affair derive from economic stresses. El Salvador, the smallest independent state on the American continent, is over-populated, with a density of 137 people per square kilometre, while Honduras, five times the size, has population of only 2,360,000, representing a density of only 20 per square kilometre. Moreover Honduras is fertile, and for many years its empty plains and valleys have drawn Salvadorans from their overcrowded country—where 90 per cent of the land is in the hands of 1 per cent of the population. This large-scale Salvadoran immigration (much of which was illegal) led inevitably to resentment among Hondurans and to the mood of mutual hatred which the football episodes turned to actual war.

Guyana

Scarcely had the rumpus of the general election of December 16, 1968, died away—leaving the air over Georgetown loud with accusations of ballot-rigging—when the "ranchers' revolt" erupted in the remote Rupununi grasslands. Political allegiances in Guyana follow racial divisions, with the opposition People's Progressive Party led by the Marxist Cheddi Jagan supported by the country's East Indians, and the governing People's National Congress Party, led by the dapper sophisticated figure of Forbes Burnham, the organ of the Negroes. Far to the south east, separated from the machinations of the metropolis by miles of wild jungle and desolate mountains, lie rich cattle lands watered by the Rupununi river, farmed by American Indians, and presided over by their half-caste "chieftains", hot-headed cattle barons of British and American descent known as the "white ranchers." The ranchers had never been able to acquire proper title to their lands, and lived in fear of the day when the government would dispossess tham in favour of Negro and East Indian smallholders from the coast. Various signs made it appear that that day was approaching. So the cattle moguls rallied their American Indian cowboys and gambled on revolt, calculating that one of the most significant facts of Guyana's political life—that neighbouring Venezuela claims over half of the country—might swing events in their favour. The rebellion was planned to the last detail, and it seems certain that the ranchers received help from the Venezuelan government, particularly in training. On January 2, the rebels went into action in the small town of Lethum, gunning down police, seizing the police station and the post office, and sabotaging the airstrip. But thanks to a tip-off, the government had flown troops into nearby Mauari that same day, and after a short, sharp battle they nipped the insurrection in the bud. By January 4 the fighting was over.

Another border dispute—this time in the south, involving land claimed by the former Dutch colony of Surinam—developed into a crisis in August when Guyana army patrols found an airstrip built by Surinam in the disputed territory. The offending Surinamese were chased over the border and the diplomatic row that broke out involved Surinam's European mentors, the Dutch.

Sir David Rose, Governor-General of Guyana since 1966, was tragically killed in London on November 10, when 40 tons of scaffolding collapsed, crushing his car. On February 23, 1969, the Prime Minister, Forbes Burnham announced that Guyana would become a republic on February 23, 1970.

Haiti

It was a harrowing year for Dr. François Duvalier, dictator of the Republic of Haiti. The country which occupies the western part of the Caribbean island of Hispaniola or Santa Domingo, has a population of some 4½ million Negroes ruled with a rod of iron by "Papa Doc", the president for life, and his army of sinister henchmen, the Tonton Macoute. Rumours circulated, during May that Duvalier was seriously ill, having suffered a major heart attack on May 8, complicated by hepatitis, and for several weeks they were lent credibility by the mysterious seclusion of the president. Meanwhile it was said that his daughter Marie Denise had become the power behind the throne in Port-au-Prince. The health, affections, and whims of President Duvalier are of immense political significance in Haiti, since he holds absolute power and has always refused to name a successor. Thus the news of his illness acted like a match to the country's explosive political atmosphere. On June 2, while the president was still apparently confined to bed, a battalion of Haitan troops attacked and killed 20 communists in Port-au-Prince, and two days later a rebel plane flew over the capital, dropping incendiary bombs in the courtyard of "Papa Doc's" palace. However, by July 2, when Nelson Rockefeller (President Nixon's special envoy to Latin America and the Caribbean) arrived in Port-au-Prince, Duvalier was well enough to appear briefly in public, although he appeared to be in bad shape, silent, stooped, and trembling. It seemed that the President for life might soon be out of office, but at the year's end he was still there.

Honduras

The "football war" between this Central American republic and its neighbour El Salvador is described under El Salvador (p. 277).

Panama

On December 15 an abortive coup was staged by officers of the National Guard while Brig.-Gen. Omar Torrijos was visiting Mexico. Early on December 16 Torrijos returned to Panama, rallied loyal officers, secured the guard headquarters in Panama City, and jailed the leaders of the revolt, Col. Ramiro Silvera and Col. Amado Sanjur.

Peru

A prolonged diplomatic row between Peru's military junta—which, had seized power in October 1968—and the U.S.A. rumbled through the year, to the irritation of Washington, the delight of the U.S.S.R. and the political advantage of the military regime, which played on anti-American feeling to consolidate its position and distract the people from economic troubles at home. The quarrel arose from the Peruvian seizure of an American company's oilfields, offering a mere $54 million compensation, while the Americans claimed $120 million. The seriousness of the dispute was magnified by the fact that, unless fair compensation was paid within six months of the take-over (i.e. by April 9, 1969), Washington was bound by U.S. law to stop American economic aid to Peru. This aid amounts to $34 million a year in cash and $45 million in preferential tariffs for Peruvian sugar, on which 350,000 Peruvian sugar workers are dependent. In an attempt to find an alternative market, and also to forestall the withdrawal of American aid, the junta embarked on a pro-Soviet foreign policy, and in February exchanged ambassadors and signed a two-year trade pact with Russia. Peruvians hoped, no doubt, that anxiety in Washington over this left-turn would manifest itself in aid. The gambit failed, however, and only by backing down and, in March, entering into negotiations over the oil compensation did General Velasco and his junta preserve their $79 million per annum.

Meanwhile a more violent dispute with the U.S.A. raged over fishing rights. Peru claims a 200-mile limit to its territorial waters, and during the year a number of American tuna boats were seized (and/or fired on) by the Peruvian navy. As a result the U.S.A. suspended the sale of arms to Peru—a measure that was only revealed in May, although it had been first put in force in February at the time of Peru's seizure of the first American boat.

At home the new regime, faced with gigantic economic problems, instigated a sharp "squeeze," as a result of which unemployment rose until, by May, 10 per cent of the Peruvian labour force was estimated to be out of work. But the regime did appear willing to tackle the fundamental weakness of the country's predominantly agrarian economy. Peru has one of the most antiquated and unfair land distribution systems in Latin America, under which 0·1 per cent of the population owns 60 per cent of the land, while peasant smallholders, representing 83 per cent of the population, own a mere 5·8 per cent. On June 25 it was announced that the government was to embark on a land reform programme involving the break up of the country's vast agricultural estates to create new peasant co-operatives. Among foreign landowners to feel the pinch of this new agrarian law was President Nixon's envoy Nelson Rockefeller who, in May, had already felt the nudge of a Peruvian cold shoulder when the junta cancelled his visit as "inopportune."

St. Kitts—Nevis—Anguilla

A Caribbean "comic opera" involving an invasion by British troops and wild tales of Mafia infiltration and Black Power was played out to an incredulous world on the tiny island of Anguilla during 1969. In 1967, while wrapping up some of the last remnants of Empire into convenient packages for independence, Britain had granted associated statehood to a number of small Caribbean islands, including a group of three—St. Kitts, Nevis, and Anguilla—in which St. Kitts was the dominant partner. The backward island of Anguilla, which harboured a traditional hostility towards St. Kitts, resented this position and declared itself independent in June 1967, deporting the St. Kitts-based police force and demanding direct links with the United Kingdom. As

Associated States have full control over their internal affairs, Great Britain being merely responsible for their defence and foreign relations, London found itself in a difficult situation, for the legal guardian of Anguilla's internal affairs was the government in St. Kitts headed by Robert Bradshaw, a man particularly hated by Anguillans. For two years the Foreign Office delayed taking any effective action.

Meanwhile the islanders, following a referendum in January 1968, had set up their own seven-man council, headed by "President" Ronald Webster, a dollar millionaire and Seventh Day Adventist lay preacher. The Foreign Office reacted by dispatching an official, Anthony Lee, to sort matters out. He was on the island a year to no great effect, and in February 1969 the islanders held a second referendum in which they voted (by 1,739 to 4) to set up an independent republic. Whitehall was by now somewhat rattled, and there sallied forth one William Whitlock, a junior minister in the British government. He arrived in (and departed from) Anguilla on March 12, 1969. In that day quite a lot happened to Mr. Whitlock. Having read out proposals for the re-instatement of Anthony Lee as commissioner and the appointment of an advisory committee to help him, he retired to lunch. During the meal armed Anguillans set up a road-block near by. Mr. Whitlock laid down his fork and stalked out to see what was afoot. He was met by a party of toughs and an agitated "President," who declared himself "very annoyed" with the proposals. A few shots that were then let off into the air put Mr. Whitlock literally to flight. His arrival home was accompanied by hair-raising allegations that "Black Power was rampant," that "a number of armed characters were running the island," that the island was "completely dominated by a gangster element," and that "subversive elements" from the U.S.A. were influencing the conduct of Ronald Webster. Even the Mafia was mentioned. Many greeted these notions with scepticism, but not the British Government. Thus, on March 19, 200 British troops and police launched a dawn attack on the island, arriving by frigate to a burst of flash bulbs from the world's press assembled on the beach to welcome them. The Anguillan "defence force," with their much-publicised reconditioned cannon, did not put in an appearance.

British military occupation of Anguilla lasted some six months, ending on September 14. It was punctuated by a few angry demonstrations, a trouble-shooting guest-appearance by Britain's U.N. ambassador Lord

Hymn-singing Anguillan matron blandly observed by British policemen.

Caradon (who patched up a vague seven-point agreement with the self-styled "President" on March 31), the removal of Anthony Lee as commissioner, and the eventual mollification of "President" Webster. When the paratroopers left the island about 80 Royal Engineers remained to work on road projects, a primary school, and a jetty. Meanwhile, on May 22, Foreign Secretary Michael Stewart and Mr. Bradshaw, meeting in London, had agreed that a commission should be appointed to study the problem and seek a solution acceptable to all sides.

Uruguay

On March 2, 1969, the Uruguayan government surprised the populace by capitulating to parliamentary pressure and ending the state of emergency that it had imposed on June 13, 1968, when the country was in the grip of an economic crisis aggravated by striking unions and industrial unrest. All detained trade union leaders and militants were released from gaol. But the respite was short-lived. On June 24, in a desperate attempt to end a prolonged campaign of strikes, President Jorge Pacheco Aceco again placed the country under a state of emergency. This repressive response to industrial action, and the absence of constructive measures to deal with the factors making for discontent, could spell the end of democracy in Uruguay.

A touch of Latin bravado lit the political scene in September, when Adolfo Aguirre Gonzalez, Dean of the University School of Architecture in Montevideo, who had been detained for four weeks without trial under the special security measures, sent his seconds to the Minister of the Interior to challenge him to a duel. The Minister, however, declined to meet the don on the "field of honour."

On April 23, Uruguay was one of five South American countries to sign, in Brasilia, a treaty for the economic integration and joint development of the River Plate basin; Argentina, Bolivia, Brazil, Paraguay, and Uruguay pledged themselves to co-operate on the development of the basin's principal rivers and agree on a joint system of navigation.

Venezuela

Following his narrow victory (by a margin of only 0·8 per cent) in the presidential elections of December 1968, Rafael Caldera, on assuming office in March 1969, set out to make good his election promise of el cambio (change). His victory over the right-wing Democratic Action party had outraged a number of military men, and rumours that the army planned a coup prompted the new president to swift action. He appointed new loyal commanders to key units and "sacked" the army's number one general by making him an ambassador in Central America. Caldera then held out the olive branch to the 300 or so Castro-backed guerrillas operating a terrorist campaign in the mountains, by offering them an amnesty, legalising the Communist Party, freeing political prisoners, and curbing the secret police. In the field of foreign affairs, the new government dropped Venezuela's previous policy of severing diplomatic relations with all countries under overt military rule and, as a result, recognised Peru, Panama, and Argentina. Venezuela also opened diplomatic relations with Russia, where she wants to sell oil. In June the visit of the U.S. envoy to Latin America, Nelson Rockefeller, was "postponed" because of threatened anti-American violence.

Diesel-electric express travel (*above*) between Sydney, N.S.W., and Melbourne, Victoria, became possible in 1962. From March 1970 through trains between Sydney and Perth, Western Australia, will run twice a week.

As if alert to the advice of the Red Queen in *Through the Looking-Glass*, Australia is learning to "run at least twice as fast," because "Now *here*, you see, it takes all the running *you* can do to stay in the same place." The pressures of modern life make Lewis Carroll's remark uncomfortably apt everywhere. But no country is literally faster on the move than Australia, thanks to big transport developments on land, by sea, and in the air.

1970 will see the realisation of an Australian dream of many years. From March 1 it will be possible to cross the entire width of the continent by railway, from Brisbane in the east to Perth and Fremantle in the west, on a uniform gauge of 4 ft. 8½ in. Railway construction in Australia began in the 1850s; some lines were built by private firms, but most by the governments of the various Colonies. Shortsightedly, each Colony decided on the gauge which would best serve its own interests, without any regard to what its neighbours were doing. So, for reasons of economy, Queensland and Western Australia settled on the narrow gauge of 3 ft. 6 in.; New South Wales alone opted for the standard 4 ft. 8½ in.; while Victoria and South Australia went further with a wide gauge of 5 ft. 3 in., in the latter Colony supplemented by certain 3 ft. 6 in.-gauge lines.

Thus when in later years the various Colonies had extended their lines to one another's borders, the only two which could work through trains between their systems were Victoria and South Australia; at every other frontier there had to be a troublesome and expensive changing of trains by passengers, and, still worse, the transshipment of all freight from one gauge to the other. The last straw was that, when the Commonwealth Government carried out the tremendous task of laying its 1,051-mile main line across the great waterless region of the Nullarbor Plain from Kalgoorlie in Western Australia to Port Augusta in South Australia, it chose the 4 ft. 8½ in. gauge, different from that of either of the States which the line linked.

After the opening in 1917 of the Transcontinental line, anyone wanting to travel from Brisbane to Fremantle, across the continent, would first have to change at Wallangarra from the Queensland 3 ft. 6 in. gauge to the 4 ft. 8½ in. New South Wales gauge, over which he would travel to Sydney and on to the New South Wales–Victoria border at Albury. Here would come another change, to the Victorian 5 ft. 3 in. gauge, over which he would travel through Melbourne and Adelaide until he reached Terowie, from which a tiresome little 3 ft. 6 in.-gauge stretch intervened, requiring two changes before he found himself in the Transcontinental train at Port Augusta. One further change still remained, from the Transcontinental 4 ft. 8½ in. to the 3 ft. 6 in. Western Australia gauge at Kalgoorlie. So there were five changes for passengers and freight before the journey would be complete.

Standardising the Gauges

The first improvement was the extension in 1930 of the New South Wales 4 ft. 8½ in.-gauge coastal line north-eastwards from Kyogle, near the Queensland border, into South Brisbane, eliminating one change. Next, the short 3 ft. 6 in. stretch in South Australia between Terowie and Port Augusta was cut out by extending the Transcontinental line southwards from Port Augusta to Port Pirie, on the South Australian 5 ft. 3 in. system. In 1958 there followed the very important task of extending the 4 ft. 8½ in. track from Albury to Melbourne alongside the 5 ft. 3 in. line, and in 1962 for the first time a really fast through service between Sydney and Melbourne was started. But by far the biggest task, brought to completion in 1968, was that of the Western Australian Government Railways in laying a 4 ft. 8½ in.-gauge track over the 437 miles from Kalgoorlie to Perth and Fremantle, partly by conversion of the existing 3 ft. 6 in.-gauge line but very largely by entirely new construction. In November 1968 for the first time a railway wagon could be loaded on Brisbane, Queensland, and delivered at Kewdale, near Perth, by means of a bogie exchange at Dynon near Melbourne. And on June 13, 1969, the first standard-gauge passenger train left Port Pirie on its 1,515-mile journey to Perth.

The longest through passenger service without change across Australia will be from Sydney to Perth and Fremantle. This cannot pass through Melbourne and Adelaide, as the gauge is still 5 ft. 3 in. west of Melbourne, but it takes a much shorter route from Sydney westwards to Broken Hill. From here the former 3 ft. 6 in.-gauge line westwards to Port Pirie has been converted to 4 ft. 8½ in., so completing the link.

The interest of a through journey on the Sydney–Perth express needs no emphasis. In the days of steam the run of over 1,000 miles across the waterless Nullarbor Plain presented considerable difficulties, and locomotives had to be provided with tenders of considerable size in order to carry enough water. The advent of diesel traction has changed all that. But, despite the straightness of the Transcontinental line—it includes the longest dead straight, 297 miles, of any railway in the world —the difficulties of maintenance in desert conditions make it necessary to keep maximum speeds within strict limits. Even so, gauge unification and the use of the Broken Hill route have made possible a cut of a whole day in the journey time between Sydney and Perth.

The length of the journey—2,459 miles—is about the same as that across Canada. The 12-coach "Indian-Pacific" trains will carry 52 first-class and 96 second-class passengers, everything possible being done to keep them comfortable and amused during the 60-hour journey. Indeed, the air-conditioned Transcontinental is like a first-class travelling hotel. One-berth and two-berth sleeping cabins convert to private sitting-rooms by day. Each car has hot and cold showers. High-class meals are served in the luxurious dining saloon, and their cost is included in the fare. The first-class lounge car, with its smoking compartment, music saloon, and ladies' lounge, is a social centre for passengers. There is a cafeteria club car. Similar standards are found in the Southern Aurora, Spirit of Progress, and Intercapital Daylight between Sydney and Melbourne; the Overland between Melbourne and Adelaide; the Brisbane Limited between Sydney and Queensland's capital; and the Sunlander on its 41-hour journey from Brisbane to Cairns.

Australian railway techniques in general are highly developed. Victoria largely pioneered, with flash-butt welding in 1935, continuous rails. Electronic systems handle signalling,

Club car on the Southern Aurora express between Sydney and Melbourne—a standard long-distance amenity.

Young skiers in the "disco" car of the Thredbo Express en route to the Mt. Kosciusko snows.

safety precautions, and train control. Computers have taken over many operations. Containers, new to shipping, have been moved by rail for more than 20 years in Australia; specialised rolling stock with high-speed bogies was developed for them.

Over 250 miles of new standard-gauge railway have been added to Australia's 25,000 miles of track to develop the huge iron-ore deposits in Western Australia's north-west. Up to three diesel-electric locomotives, each 70 ft. long and developing 3,600 h.p., are being used to haul 24,000-ton ore trains. In the Northern Territory, 311 miles of line from Larrimah to Darwin have been rebuilt for iron-ore development at Frances Creek. In Queensland, rail extensions are helping coal-field development. Trains hauled by three diesel locomotives are carrying increasing tonnages over a new 112-mile line from the central Queensland open-cut mines at Moura and Blackwater to Gladstone, for export to the factories and power stations of Japan.

Typical scene of the outback: road and air transport meet at Ayers Rock, Northern Territory.

Australia has a higher proportion of city and suburban dwellers than almost any other country, and increasing strains are being placed on city transport. In the Sydney metropolitan area 177 miles of electrified track handle 245 million passenger journeys a year. The city's underground system is being extended. Late in 1968 construction of a twin-tunnel line began for the Eastern Suburbs railway which will extend more than seven miles under Kings Cross and east through Rushcutters Bay. Eventually it will reach Bondi Junction. So far Sydney is the only capital with a "tube" system, but Melbourne plans a two-mile underground circuit with four sets of single tracks in four separate tunnels, to join up with existing main rail arteries. Perth, too, considered a "tube," but decided against it.

Some $A2,000 million is tied up in Australian railways—the southern hemisphere's biggest industrial investment. They employ 122,000 people earning $A370 million a year. Passenger and freight revenue is $A500 million a year. ($A1 = 9s. 3d. sterling.) Locomotives, rolling stock, and components are almost entirely Australian-made.

The railways are catering for specialised travelling groups. In New South Wales the Thredbo International Express was introduced in 1967 in the Kosciusko snow season for young skiing enthusiasts. About four trains a season carrying swinging, dancing young Sydneysiders on a lively night journey to Cooma in the Australian Alps. Each train is made up of second-class sitting cars, one first-class sleeping car, a "disco" car with beat band, and a buffet car. Motor coaches pick up the passengers at Cooma for the snowfields at Smiggin Holes and Thredbo.

Transport by Road and Air

The various modes of transport have become increasingly interdependent in Australia with its vast distances, vital overseas markets, and skyrocketing tourist industry. The result is increasing co-ordination of rail, road, and sea services, coupled with vigorous road modernisation and new road construction. Australia is spending $A500 million a year—more than 2 per cent of her total expenditure—on road construction, of which the Commonwealth Government finances about a third. Over the next five years the Government will spend on roads 67 per cent more than over the past five.

In the air Australia, one of the "flyingest" nations because distances are great and flying conditions almost ideal, continues to be expansionary. Qantas, Australia's international airline, will take delivery of its first

$A40 million "jumbo" Boeing 747 jet about August 1971, probably for the Pacific route; and it hopes to have one on the Kangaroo route to Britain by early 1972. At present its front-line fleet is 21 Boeing 707s. In 1968 Qantas flew 30 million miles, and carried nearly 493,000 passengers and more than 14,000 short tons of freight.

To handle the huge jumbo jets with their 350 passengers, a 13,000-ft. runway is to be built at Sydney's international airport. Extensions to be completed in 1970 will bring the total cost of the airport to $A100 million. A $A50 million airport is being built at Tullamarine, 12½ miles north-west of Melbourne. City and airport will be linked by a $A5,100,000 freeway. Tullamarine, like other major airports, will be equipped with the latest landing systems, navigational aids, and cargo handling facilities. The Australian Department of Civil Aviation exercises strict supervision and provides the most modern equipment in the interests of flying safety. Australia's airlines are the world's safest. Their record is 1 passenger killed for every 1,000 million miles flown, compared with 2½ on U.S. airlines, 7½ on British, 8½ on French, and a world average of 7.

Domestic air lines provide a growing network of services. Australians "hop on a plane" almost as Londoners "hop on a bus." During the year ending June 30, 1969, the domestic services carried a record 5¼ million passengers (a 10 per cent increase over the previous year) and about 98,000 short tons of freight and 11,000 tons of mail. Air freighting comes into its own when speed is essential—for instance, for carrying highly perishable goods. Qantas has opened up a trade in Sydney rock oysters to Singapore, Kuala Lumpur, Bangkok, and other south-east Asian cities; also in highly perishable emulsions for colour films. But all sorts of things fly by Qantas, from tiny transistors to not-so-tiny motor cars and race horses.

Revolution in Cargo-Carrying

Sea cargoes are very important to an island continent with all its State capitals on the coast. Here big changes began in 1969 with the introduction of containerisation. This requires specially constructed ships on the decks of which standardised aluminium containers are stacked and fastened. The cargo is above deck instead of below, permitting much quicker loading and unloading, quicker "turn-round," and less time in ports. A new container terminal at White Bay, Sydney, turns ships round in 36 hours as compared with 21–30 days for ordinary ships handled by

Part of the expressway road linking Sydney with the mining and heavy industry centre of Newcastle.

old methods. A 4,000-ton general cargo used to take 200 men about a week to unload; the same cargo containerised can be unloaded by 15 men in eight hours. Wool—Australia's main export—can be shipped in highly compressed bales by container at an estimated saving of 43 cents a bale. On five million bales that's a lot of money.

New container terminals are being built in most major ports. Sydney, handling 15 million tons of cargo a year, has two container berths in operation and another four planned. Near-by Botany Bay may be developed as a second port at an estimated cost of $A75 million over 20 years; container berths would be prominent there. Melbourne, handling 12 million tons of cargo a year, has three container berths and plans another five.

The world's biggest container ship, *Encounter Bay*, owned by Overseas Containers Ltd., opened the first container shipping service between Europe and Australia in March 1969. She was the first of five 29,000-ton container

General-cargo container ship loading with her own cranes at Melbourne before a run to Fremantle.

283

ships that will operate OCL's Europe–Australia run. She was followed within weeks by *ACT1*, first container ship of Associated Container Transportation Ltd. It was announced in April 1969 that the Australian Government would buy container ships outright, instead of on a preliminary charter of five years, as had been previously intended. In a joint venture with Associated Container Transportation (Australia) Ltd., the Government is entering the business of overseas shipping to Britain and Europe. The Government-owned Australian National Line was formerly confined to coastal shipping, but now the Government is operating Australian-crewed vessels in its own right overseas. By doing this it can join appropriate "conferences"—organisations of ship owners—and help to keep down charges for freights vital to Australia's competitive position as a trading nation.

The climax of the container-ship saga came on October 27 when the formation of a gigantic international container-ship consortium for the Australian trade was announced. The combine, representing virtually the entire national interest in that trade of Great Britain, France, W. Germany, the Netherlands, Italy, and Australia, will be called Australia Container Service (A.C.S.) and will begin to operate in August 1970. The 14 large container-ships owned by 13 different shipping lines will become a single fleet worth, with its equipment, between £100 million and £150 million; a fully integrated service, with computerised controls, will operate 5–10-day sailings between three or four European and three Australian ports. The reaction of Scandinavian shipowners to the formation of a cartel from which they were excluded was immediate; the next day they ordered five big container-roll-on ships for delivery in 1972–73, for use on the Australia run, and also announced that they will be forming their own consortium, to operate from July 1970.

The Australian National Line is taking part in a joint venture with the K Line of Japan: each is to operate one container ship and one roll-on roll-off vehicle-and-container ship on a fortnightly service. The first ANL container ship for this service, the 11,000-ton *Australian Enterprise*, inaugurated the Eastern Searoad Service in September 1969, and the second, *Australian Searoader*, was commissioned in October, followed in November by the Japanese container ship *Hakozaki Maru*. Two ships of the Australia–Japan Container Line, owned by British and Swedish interests, will join this trade. A full container service to Japan is expected by the end of 1970.

Australian Enterprise and *Searoader* were built in Japan, but Australia is herself building container ships for the coastal trade. The container ship *Kanimbla*, built at Whyalla in South Australia for Associated Steamships Pty. Ltd., opened a service between Australian States in March 1969. This 13,000-ton ship carries 530 20-ton containers, has a special propeller which makes her independent of harbour tugs, and is of advanced design. Latest ship to join the Bass Strait ferries to Tasmania is *Australian Trader*, launched in July 1969. *Brisbane Trader*, built in 1969, is on the Melbourne–Brisbane run, and *Sydney Trader*, latest of these ships, plies between Melbourne and north Queensland ports. All these ships were built in Australia.

The world's largest roll-on roll-off passenger-vehicle-cargo vessel, the 12,000-ton *Empress of Australia*, which plies between Sydney and Tasmania, one of the longest open-water voyages sailed by such ships.
All photos in this article by Australian News and Information Bureau

Alphabetical Guide to 1969

Names in the News 1969

Agnew, Spiro Theodore (born 1918). When in August 1968 Mr. Nixon named "Ted" Agnew as his running mate in the forthcoming presidential election most Americans looked at one another in surprise and the TV comedians had a field day, asking each other "Spiro *Who?*" Mr. Agnew was almost unknown outside his native state of Maryland, of which he had been Governor for a year and a half. But by the time Nixon won the election and Agnew became Vice-President, the Republican party propagandists had made him better known, and better liked, among the voters. During 1969 he emerged as the spokesman of the "silent majority," the mass of decent, law-abiding patriotic Americans. His life story is of the popular American "rags-to-riches" type. Born in Baltimore on November 9, 1918, to a Virginian mother and a Greek immigrant restaurant-keeper who shortened his name from Anagnostopoulos to Agnew, as a boy he had a comfortable home, but the depression of the 1930s reduced his father to selling vegetables on the streets. But the boy was kept at school and sent to Johns Hopkins University, where he studied chemistry. He kept himself by working in an insurance office, where he met his wife, Elinor Isabel Judefind, known as "Judy."

After marriage in 1942 Agnew served in the U.S. Army in Europe for four years, and later was called up for the Korean war. Meanwhile he studied law, taking his degree in 1947, and becoming a successful lawyer, busy in local affairs. In 1962 he was elected manager of Baltimore county and in 1967 Governor of Maryland. He was particularly active in civil rights legislation and introduced the first Governor's Code of Fair Practices, which guaranteed equal rights for all in state government jobs in Maryland. A golfer and pianist in his spare time, Mr. Agnew has four children—three daughters and a son.

Spiro "Ted" Agnew, U.S. vice-president.

Field Marshal Earl Alexander, in 1943.

Alexander of Tunis, Earl (1891–1969). Field Marshal Earl Alexander of Tunis, one of the outstanding British generals of the Second World War, died on June 16, 1969, at the age of 77. He was born Harold Rupert Leofric George Alexander on December 10, 1891, the third son of the 4th Earl of Caledon, and educated at Harrow and Sandhurst. In 1911 he joined the Irish Guards. He fought in France during the Great War, in which he was three times wounded, won the D.S.O. and M.C., and rose to the command of a battalion by the age of 25. From 1934 to 1938 he commanded a brigade in India, leading it on two campaigns on the North-West Frontier. On the outbreak of the Second World War he went to France in command of the 1st Division, and commanded the last corps on the beaches of Dunkirk, scouring the area on foot and in a small boat to satisfy himself that "no one was left behind." After the outbreak of war with Japan he was sent out to command the British troops retreating in Burma and led them through the jungle to the Assam frontier. In 1942, while passing through Cairo on his way home, he was made commander-in-chief in the Middle East. Thus he was responsible for the general strategy of the successful African campaign, starting with Alamein, fought by his brilliant lieutenant Montgomery. Alexander himself, as deputy commander-in-chief to Eisenhower, conducted the final campaign in North Africa, culminating in the victory at Tunis in May 1943. There followed the conquest of Sicily and the Italian campaign, with the offensive at Cassino (1944) which led to the liberation of Rome. At the end of the war, Alexander retired from the army to become Governor-General of Canada. He was by then a field marshal and had received a G.C.B. (1942), and the highest honours of the U.S.A., the U.S.S.R.,

Greece, and Poland. He was a popular governor-general, and his term was twice extended, although cut short in 1952, when he entered Churchill's government as Minister of Defence until 1954. He had been created a Knight of the Garter in 1946 and awarded an earldom, and had been appointed a member of the Privy Council of Canada in 1952. Lord Alexander's memoirs were published in 1962.

Anne Elizabeth Alice Louise, H.R.H. Princess (born 1950). In a year that saw the Royal Family increasingly in the news, Princess Anne exerted her own new and considerable influence. In the world of fashion she was voted, in one poll, the second best-dressed woman in the world, after the Duchess of Kent (the men put Anne first). This was only a year or so after some women journalists had been condemning the drabness of her clothes. The American fashion writer who a year before had written that she had no sense of dress now called her a "proper British bird." Most noticeable were her hats, so successful that British milliners were hard at work turning out hundreds of copies.

Aged 19 on August 15, one year out of school, Princess Anne played her full part in public life. Her first solo public engagement was on March 1, with a St. David's Day visit to the Welsh Guards at Pirbright to distribute leeks. She launched her first ship in May, a 250,000-ton tanker, the biggest built in Britain, at Wallsend. For the first ever trip by a woman to a North Sea gas production platform she wore a highwayman style hat and a red trouser suit. She opened research laboratories, hospitals, student hostels, old folks' homes. At a luncheon she created a royal precedent by naming nine West End clothes stores at which she had been a customer. Assured, poised, and confident, she could switch easily from playing guest at a dolls' tea party (when visiting a girls' home in Edinburgh) to driving a 50-ton tank at 20 m.p.h. across country, over steepish jumps (when she visited the 14/20 King's Hussars, as colonel-in-chief, at Paderborn in Germany). She astonished her troops by her shooting with a Sterling sub-machine gun and her handling of a whole range of army vehicles; they played her back into her helicopter afterwards with "Oh, You Beautiful Doll." Her other driving feats included taking a lorry on to a skid pan, manoeuvring a double-decker bus, and taking over the controls of a Trident airliner. But she was most at home on a horse, although occasionally, unabashed, she came off. She took first prize in a novice class at the Windsor Park Horse Trials, and then took on Olympic Games riders elsewhere, by no means disgracing herself. In

Princess Anne—the milliners' delight of the year.

the Horse of the Year Show she managed to qualify for a combined championship event, coming ninth. But perhaps her high spot as a horsewoman was when she showed her style on a Lipizzaner stallion at the Spanish Riding School in Vienna during the state visit to Austria.

Ansermet, Ernest (1883–1969). Ernest Ansermet, the redoubtable founder of l'Orchestre de la Suisse Romande and its conductor for forty years, died in Geneva on February 20, 1969, at the age of 85. He was born at Nevey, Switzerland, on November 11, 1883, and educated at Lausanne where he became professor of mathematics (1905–09). Music, however, was exercising an increasingly powerful influence on him, and while yet a professional mathematician he was studying with Denereaz at Lausanne. In 1910 he took up music as a career when he became conductor of the Montreux orchestra. This post he held for four years before becoming conductor of the Geneva Symphony Orchestra 1915–18. It was during these years that he first met Diaghilev and began an association with Russian ballet that gave him an international reputation. With his founding of l'Orchestre de la Suisse Romande in 1918 there began the years of his preeminence in Swiss music. His name was associated with modern music, particularly that of Stravinsky, and his career testified to that enigmatic link between music and mathematics, as his clear mind rejoiced in and expanded the complex abstractions of modern scores.

Appleton, George Most Rev. (born 1902). When George Appleton was commissioned on March 10, 1969, at Lambeth Palace as Archbishop in Jerusalem a surprising new turn was given to a long career of varied appointments. Since 1963 he had been the popular Archbishop of Perth, Western Australia. Before that he was briefly Archdeacon of London, with a canon's stall in St. Paul's Cathedral. Before being installed in this grand fashion he had been working among drug addicts and among men of many faiths in an ancient church near Liverpool Street Station, hard by London's East End.

That work itself was a great change from what had gone before. He had been for several years the general secretary of the Conference of British Missionary Societies and at the heart of a good deal of ecumenical work during a key period. His own missionary work was given in Burma in the years 1927–46; for part of the time he was Archdeacon of Rangoon. Here he developed a deep knowledge of Buddhism, and one of his best known books, *On the Eightfold Path*, is about the Christian encounter with that faith. He has also won world-wide acclaim in Christian circles as the author and compiler of very popular books of prayers.

Asquith of Yarnbury, Baroness (1887–1969). Lady Asquith of Yarnbury, better known as Lady Violet Bonham Carter, was the daughter of H. H. Asquith, the Liberal prime minister, and mother-in-law of Jo Grimond, Liberal leader from 1956 to 1967. By her death on February 19, 1969, one of the last links between the present Liberal party and the party of Gladstone was broken. Born on April 15, 1887, the only daughter of Asquith's first marriage, and educated at Dresden and Paris, she was five when her father became Home Secretary in the last Gladstone ministry of 1892, and 18 when he became Chancellor under Campbell-Bannerman. In April 1908, he assumed the premiership only to be ousted eight years later in the cabinet crisis of December 1916 when Lloyd George seized power. For twelve stormy years after this, a political civil war was waged within the Liberal ranks in which Lady Violet proved herself a staunch partisan

on her father's wing. "It must have been," wrote Winston Churchill, "one of Asquith's greatest human joys in his dusk to find this wonderful being he had called into the world armed, vigilant, and active at his side." In 1915 she had married Sir Maurice Bonham Carter, her father's private secretary, by whom she had two sons and two daughters. Her début in active politics took place in 1920 when she fought beside her father in his famous election contest at Paisley. It was here that she first attracted public notice for her brilliant gift of oratory. It is unfortunate that this gift never carried her into the House of Commons where she would have sparkled at her brightest; but her party's star had paled and sunk by the time she made her two unsuccessful attempts to seek election, at Wells in 1945 and Colne Valley in 1951. "Lady Vi" was twice president of the Women's Liberal Federation and once of the Liberal party organisation; since 1945 she had been a governor of the Old Vic, from 1941 to 1946 a governor of the BBC, and, in 1947, a member of the Royal Commission on the Press. A well-known and respected speaker on television and a doughty writer in newspapers and magazines, she entered the House of Lords with a life peerage as Lady Asquith of Yarnbury in the county of Wiltshire, on December 23, 1964. A year later she published *Winston Churchill as I Knew Him*, an account of a friendship that had extended over many years.

Ayub Khan, Mohammed (born 1907). For ten years, until his resignation from the presidency of Pakistan on March 25, 1969, Ayub Khan brought paternalist qualities to his position as "strong-man ruler." For most of those ten years there was an untinged flavour of success about him and Pakistan, as he and his country became ever more closely identified. He came to power, in October 1958, in a bloodless military coup, on an anti-corruption, anti-smuggling, and anti-black-market platform, when Pakistan was on the verge of chaos and demoralisation. Massive economic and social reforms were initiated. No one could deny the stability he brought to the country, for a time at least, by economic changes and the adroitness with which he managed to secure relations beneficial to Pakistan, with Russia, China, and the U.S.A. Yet in his resignation speech he admitted: "the situation is fast deteriorating, the administrative institutions are being paralysed. Self-aggrandisement is the order of the day . . . The economy has been shattered. The wheel had gone full circle. Much had happened to alienate him from the army, from which he came. His sons had left the army and grown rich. There was growing usury. In 1965 he had taken Pakistan into a war with India that it could not win, and accepted a ceasefire when his soldiers believed they were on the point of inflicting a severe set-back on India.

West Pakistan the move was against his personal rule and for a parliamentary system. In East Pakistan it was against him as a vehicle for West Pakistan domination. General Yahya Khan, commanding chief of the armed forces, took over responsibility and declared martial law.

Six feet three inches in height, with a personality as commanding as his physique, with perfect English, flavoured with the military expressions of his generation, and a clipped moustache, Ayub Khan was the complete product of Sandhurst—where he went when he was 19. He was born on the North West Frontier, in Rehana, on May 14, 1907. In the Second World War he commanded a battalion with distinction in Burma. His military rise was phenomenal: colonel 1947, major-general 1948, adjutant-general 1950, general and commander-in-chief 1951, minister of defence 1954–55; then supreme commander and president 1958, promoting himself to field-marshal 1959. As the first commander-in-chief of the Pakistan army he thoroughly reorganised it. Maximum austerity and efficiency were his guiding principles, and when he assumed the presidency by proclamation he brought to the reform of the country the principles used for reforming the army. By 1961 he had convinced British and other observers that Pakistan had the best rule she had enjoyed since independence. He failed to restore parliamentary government, inventing a system of democracy of his own, in which councils at various levels from village to cabinet passed on his instructions. But despite his military origin, his was a civilian rule. It improved country life with land reform, weeded out inefficient officials, suppressed black-marketing, checked inflation, and achieved economic development. But, in the end, it was military ineffectiveness that brought him down; he never survived the inconclusive end to the 1965 war with India.

Barbirolli, Sir John (born 1899). As chief conductor of the Hallé from 1943 to 1969, Sir John Barbirolli led the orchestra back to a position of pre-eminence among the world's orchestras. When he took it over "Charles Hallé's band" had fallen on troubled days, many of its members were in the forces, and its home, the Free Trade Hall in Manchester, had been destroyed in an air raid. He scoured England for musicians; his first trombonist was a woman from a Salvation Army band, and the story that he looked especially for the flat-footed, rejected by the military, has some truth. The modern Hallé is as much his creation as it is Sir Charles Hallé's, but his devotion to it meant that he had to forego many opportunities to indulge in his greatest love, conducting opera in the great opera-houses. When, in 1969, he changed from conductor-in-chief to conductor-laureate, he remained available for important concerts, but was able

Sir John Barbirolli, of the Hallé.

to take other engagements. His début at Rome, in April, conducting *Aïda* was a triumph, although it was akin to an Italian producing Shakespeare at the Old Vic.

Sir John, despite his name—his father was an Italian and his mother French— was London-born, indeed Cockney-born as occasional asides at concerts showed. He was born on December 2, 1899, over a baker's shop in Southampton Row. Later his parents moved to Drury Lane, near Covent Garden. At the age of 11 he performed a cello concerto, on a half-size cello, at Queen's Hall, and by 16 he was the youngest member of Henry Wood's orchestra there. At 25 he founded and conducted a small chamber orchestra. In 1926 he was invited to join the panel of conductors of the British National Opera Company, and ten years later, on the recommendation of Heifetz, he was appointed to succeed Toscanini as conductor of the New York Philharmonic. Sir John was knighted for his services to music in 1949. In 1960 he accepted an invitation to succeed Leopold Stokowski as conductor-in-chief of the Houston Symphony Orchestra, Texas. This meant three months a year in Texas, but that did not affect his connection with the Hallé. "They are bone of my bone," he once said of the Hallé players, "they will always be my orchestra."

Betjeman, Sir John (born 1906). Romantic, reactionary, High Church crank, or genial commentator on popular attitudes to class and sex, religion and art? Betjeman is probably both; certainly he has been an unmistakable original voice in poetry since the last war. He received a knighthood in the birthday honours of 1969. His starriest year previously was 1960, which brought him the Queen's gold medal for poetry, a C.B.E., and publication of his autobiography in verse, *Summoned by Bells.* By writing from rooted if exasperated attachment to seaside lodgings, restored churches, and railway stations, and by his affectionate satire on the life of the

inter-war years, this laureate of suburbia steadily claimed a public. *Selected Poems* gained the Heinemann award for 1948; *Collected Poems* followed ten years later. "A Subaltern's Love-Song," one of the most appealing lyrics of our time, has been set to music (by Donald Swann); while the brief ode "Christmas" is always effective when read aloud. Another following was attracted by the Shell guides to various counties, of which Betjeman was part-author. Broadcasting on Victorian architecture, he had the authority of a Royal Fine Art Commissioner to weigh against the aura of a roguish cherub. His bent for literature was probably fortified by finding T. S. Eliot as one of his schoolmasters at Highgate and C. S. Lewis as his tutor at Magdalen College, Oxford; between those phases he was educated at the Dragon School and Marlborough. For cutting out a career a period in the family firm of glass-makers and woodworkers seems to have been a false start; and war-time jobs as U.K. press attaché in Dublin and a civilian at the Admiralty now read like some eccentricity fit for gentle satire in his own verse. He married Penelope, daughter of Field-Marshal Lord Chetwode.

Boult, Sir Adrian (born 1889). In his 80th year, laden with the honours of the world, the doyen of British conductors was admitted to the exclusive circle of Companions of Honour in the New Year's honours of 1969. This recognition came as Sir Adrian was rehearsing yet another programme of all-English music, and only weeks after he had conducted a concert to mark the tenth anniversary of the death of his old friend and colleague Vaughan Williams. The lives of the two men, twin apostles of the British musical revival, had run together since they first met when Boult was a member of the Bach choir at Oxford performing Vaughan Williams's *Sea Symphony.*

Born at Chester on April 8, 1889, and brought up near Liverpool, Boult was intended for his father's business. But even as a small child he would reach up to the piano keys, and by the time he went to Westminster School at the turn of the century, he was buying musical scores and taking notes on Henry Wood's technique at his Sunday concerts. He graduated in music at Christ Church, Oxford, where he was president of the University Music Club, before entering the Leipzig Conservatorium to study under Artur Nikisch, who he has admitted was one of the great influences on his work. Boult's first public appearances in Liverpool were followed by an appointment to the musical staff of the Royal Opera House, Covent Garden. But war intervened and German-speaking Boult went as a linguist to the War Office, where he worked with the late Lord Woolton. In 1918 he used his savings to give four concerts in the Queen's Hall, among the works he conducted being the Vaughan Williams *London Symphony.* "The composer, who was in uniform, came to my office and sat among piles of boots to amend the score," Boult recalled.

For the next eleven years he taught young conductors at the Royal College of Music, at the same time giving concerts, conducting for Diaghilev, and taking music to London's East End. From 1924 to 1930 he was conductor of the City of Birmingham Orchestra, and from 1928 to 1932 of the Bach Choir.

His 21-year association with the BBC began in 1929 as Director of Music. In 1930 he took over the BBC Symphony Orchestra which he brought up to world standard, always playing, where he could, the music of English composers. In 1937, four years after his marriage, he was knighted after conducting the Coronation music at Westminster Abbey. The London Philharmonic, his last major engagement, he conducted from 1950 to 1957, with tours of the U.S.A. and Canada and the first British orchestral visit to Russia in 1956. In his later years he went back to teaching and individual concerts.

Braddock, Mrs. Bessie (born 1899). Known to innumerable Liverpudlians as the "workers' champion" and also, in one famous Parliamentary exchange, described by Quintin Hogg as his favourite pin-up, Bessie Braddock announced the approaching end of her parliamentary career, after 24 years, because of ill-health. The announcement that she would not fight another election came just after her 70th birthday, from a hospital bed, where she was under-going treatment for nervous exhaustion.

Her political outlook had been formed in the struggles of the unemployed in Liverpool early in the century. Just three weeks after her birth on Sept. 24, 1899, she was taken, wrapped in a shawl, to her first political meeting, where her mother addressed striking dockers. After the First World War she joined the Communist Party and was one of its principal workers in the North-East. But she resigned in 1924 because, she said, she found Communism itself a

Mrs. Bessie Braddock retired.

tyranny. Elected to the Liverpool City Council in 1930, she gave her attention chiefly to housing, hospitals, and maternity and child welfare. During the Second World War she was a full-time member of the Liverpool ambulance service and rose to be deputy divisional ambulance officer. In 1945 she fought the Liverpool Exchange division, the seat of Liverpool's financial life, and won it for Labour. Because she campaigned continually for outsize clothes for women she was regarded herself as an Amazon. Her vital statistics for most of her Parliamentary career were 50—40—50, and she weighed 15 stone, later reducing to $13\frac{1}{2}$, but she was only 5 ft. 2 in. tall. A firm advocate of boxing, convinced that if it was put on every school curriculum it would help to reduce delinquency, she once gave Floyd Patterson, world heavyweight champion, lunch at the Commons; on another occasion she almost stopped proceedings in the House when she took Marlene Dietrich there. She was the first woman M.P. to be suspended, when she refused to resume her seat in a debate after waiting eight hours for her turn—nothing annoys a woman more than missing her turn, she said. Only her illness cheated her of the chairman-ship of the Labour Party in 1969.

Brandt, Willy (born 1913). Probably one of the most popular political events of the year was the election of Willy Brandt as Chancellor of West Germany on October 21, 1969, when the members of the Bundestag voted him into office by 251 votes to 235. After the general election on September 28 it seemed likely that the outgoing Chancellor Kurt Kiesinger would again head a Christian Democrat-Free Democrat coalition. His Christian Democrats had 242 seats, while the Social Democrats led by Brandt had 224 seats. But the Free Democrats with 30 seats decided to give their support to Brandt, and he became the first Social Democrat Chancellor for 39 years.

Willy Brandt was born on December 18, 1913, at Lübeck. He was illegitimate and had an unhappy childhood. He became active in Socialist youth organi-sations and joined the Social Democratic party at 17. When the Nazis came to power in 1933, he escaped to Norway only hours before the Gestapo came to arrest him. He worked as a journalist in Norway and, when German forces occupied that country, in Sweden. In Stockholm the exiled Norwegian govern-ment granted him Norwegian citizenship since he had been deprived of his German nationality. During this period he kept in touch with the German resistance movement, and was strongly influenced by the theories of Swedish social democracy.

When the war ended Brandt returned to West Germany as a Scandinavian press correspondent. He was elected to the Bundestag in 1949. Chief editor of

Willy Brandt, German Chancellor.

the *Berliner Stadtblatt*, 1950–51, he was elected to the Berlin House of Represen-tatives in 1950 and later became its president. In 1957 he became chief burgomaster of West Berlin. His defiance of the threats and pressure of East Germany and Russia brought him great admiration from his own countrymen and from all the Western bloc. He was able to use his office as a springboard for the Chancellorship. Twice, in 1961 and 1965, he stood unsuccessfully. In 1964 he became chairman of the Social Democratic party. In the autumn of 1966 Brandt persuaded his party to join the other two parties under Kiesinger in a grand coalition and himself became Foreign Minister and Vice-Chancellor. He devoted his efforts to reducing tension between East and West and encouraging exchanges between the two halves of Germany.

Caro, Anthony (born 1924). The stockbroker's son who managed to shake up, yet again, the shell-shocked world of sculpture followed Matisse and Van Gogh into London's Hayward Gallery, and was made a C.B.E. in the New Year honours, in 1969. Leading critics had called him "the best sculptor in the world" and "the best English artist since Turner," but Caro, artist in rusted nuts and bolts and steel tubing, remained an enigma to many of his fellow-country-men. A product of Charterhouse School and Christ's College, Cambridge, where he read engineering, he went into the Navy before moving into sculpture via the Royal Academy Schools. He was first noticed for his small bronze figures during the two years, 1951–53, when he was assistant to Henry Moore. Leaving Moore, he plunged into the tough artistic market-place of the St. Martin's School of Art, London, as a two-days-a-week teacher. From this and from meetings with David Smith, Kenneth Noland, and Clement Greenberg during a visit to America in 1959, evolved the uncompromising originality which saw beauty in junk metal and could create art from wire mesh. In 1963 Caro stunned London with an exhibition at the Whitechapel Gallery. There followed shows at Emerich Gallery, New York, in 1964 and 1966, at the Washington Gallery of Modern Art in 1965, and at top galleries in Canada, Switzerland, Holland, and Venice. His early steel pieces, "Midday" and "Sculpture Seven," were among the 45 vast, welded girder works, weighing up to $2\frac{1}{2}$ tons, at the 1969 Hayward Gallery Show. Married in 1949, Caro has two sons.

Chichester-Clark, Major James (born 1923). After taking over from his distant cousin, Captain Terence O'Neill, as Prime Minister of Northern Ireland in the spring of 1969 and receiving a unanimous vote of support from the Unionist Party, Major Chichester-Clark found himself in office during the most troubled summer the province had known for more than a generation. At the end of the summer, with British troops maintaining law and order, the "B" Specials of the Ulster police force disbanded, and promises given about a quicker pace of reform, he was beset from two sides of his party. A liberal non-sectarian faction attacked his conservatism, but it was a die-hard group, objecting to the reforms, particularly to the disbanding of the Specials, which defeated him in his own constituency, where a bus-conductor ousted him from the position of vice-chairman of his branch in Castledawson, co. Londonderry.

Born on February 12, 1923, educated at Eton, and commissioned in the Irish Guards in 1942, Major Chichester-Clark had an Army career until 1960. For two years he was A.D.C. to the Governor-General of Canada, the late Field-Marshal Earl Alexander. With a family tradition of public service—his young brother, Robert, is a Westminster M.P.—he virtually inherited the South London-derry Stormont seat, and was returned unopposed in 1960. Three years later he was appointed an assistant Government whip and, shortly afterwards, chief Government whip. In October 1966 he became leader of the House and in May 1967 Minister of Agriculture. Prime Minister O'Neill's wish to introduce the one-man-one-vote principle in local government saw Major Chichester-Clark resigning his ministerial office, not, he pointed out, because he was opposed to the principle but because he disagreed with the timing. Shortly afterwards Capt. O'Neill resigned, and Major Chichester-Clark was elected leader in his place, by a majority of one vote over the other candidate Brian Faulkner, a former deputy prime minister, and became Prime Minister on May 1, 1969.

Clark, Kenneth Mackenzie, Baron (born 1903). If Britain proposed to appoint a Minister of Fine Arts, the choice for most electors would be narrowed to one. The diplomat among propagandists, always eager to embrace the State or other institution as a patron of art; the administrator, youngest-ever director of the National Gallery, who later allowed chairmanship of the Independent Television Authority to overlap that of the Arts Council; the professor whose lectures at Oxford after the war were the most popular on his subject since Ruskin's, and who captured the vast television audience with many talks on art and in 1969 with a theme no less demanding than "Civilisation"; the authority of world repute on Leonardo da Vinci and Piero della Francesca, also zealous champion of Graham Sutherland and Henry Moore: all were embodied in the profound, polished, and persuasive Kenneth Clark, who, knighted in 1938 and a Companion of Honour since 1959, was raised to life peerage in the birthday honours of 1969.

Clark was a product of Winchester and Trinity College, Oxford, whence he went to study under Bernard Berenson in Florence. From running the department of fine art at the Ashmolean, Oxford, he was called to the National Gallery in 1934. Staying throughout the war, he helped to brighten bombed London by exhibiting in special prominence a "picture of the month," and by devising with Myra Hess the lunch-time chamber concerts that became legendary. Simultaneously he was surveyor of the King's pictures. He was welcome on the BBC Brains Trust, and did publicity for the Ministry of Information. Clark's earliest important book was *The Gothic Revival* (1929); lectures given at Oxford were reprinted as *Landscape into Art*; and many treatises and essays with challenging titles—*Moments of Vision, The Nude, Looking, A Failure of Nerve*—have maintained him as a foremost interpreter of how art can add to the pleasure of living. Naturally he became a denizen of Albany in Piccadilly, while Saltwood Castle, near Folkestone is his residence.

Coia, Jackomo Antonio (born 1898). Jack Coia, an architect celebrated for his churches, received the Royal Gold Medal for Architecture on June 17, 1969. He was born in Wolverhampton on July 17,

Jack Coia, honoured architect.

1898, the child of a Neapolitan street musician and his wife Ernestina, a Florentine circus dancer, who were on their way, on foot, from Italy to Glasgow. Soon after his birth, the trek north continued, with the baby in a crib resting on the street organ by which the family earned its living. Coia was educated at St. Aloysius College, Garnethill, and received his vocational training at Glasgow's School of Architecture from 1917 to 1923. A travelling scholarship took him abroad for a short time, and on his return he joined the staff of a London practice before returning to Scotland in 1927 to take up a partnership with W. A. Kidd and a teaching post at the School where he had trained.

Through the practice of Gillespie, Kidd, and Coia, he has undertaken almost every type of commission, but he has an international reputation for modern church architecture, and his churches include: St. Anne, Glasgow (1936); St. Columba, Glasgow (1937); St. Patrick, Greenock (1938); St. Columcille, Rutherglen (1939); St. Peter in Chains, Ardrossan (1940); St. Paul, Glenrothes (1957); St. Mary of the Assumption, Bo'ness (1958); St. Mary of the Angels, Camelon (1959); St. Patrick, Kilsyth (1965); Our Lady of Good Council, Dennistoun (1966). He has also designed hospitals (Bellshill); schools (Cumbernauld, Glasgow, and Bellshill); housing (Cumbernauld, East Kilbride, Dunbarton); colleges (Beardsden, Cardoss); student residences (University of Hull); and exhibitions. In 1953 the firm's design for Murray Flats, East Kilbride, won the Saltire Award. In 1963 they received an R.I.B.A. Bronze Medal for St. Bride's, East Kilbride, and since the creation of the R.I.B.A.'s Architecture Awards, in 1966, they have won a regional award each year. Coia's work resolves the problems of space, light, and function with an inevitable simplicity. The play of light on volume, and the rich textures which he displays with basic building materials, help to make him the greatest living Scottish architect.

Compton-Burnett, Dame Ivy (1884–1969). This novelist, regarded by many as one of the greatest figures in English fiction, and by others as unreadable, died, aged 85, on August 27, 1969, in her South Kensington flat, her home for 30 years. The daughter of a doctor, she was born in Pinner, Middlesex, on June 5, 1884, shared a classical education with her brothers, and went on to take a degree at Holloway College, London. Her first novel *Dolores*, published in 1911, was totally unlike all her future work, and in later years she preferred not to speak of it, omitting it from her 18 published works listed in "Who's Who." In 1925 she wrote *Pastors and Masters,* the first of her highly stylised novels, the plots of which were related almost entirely in dialogue with almost no description of places or people. Even the titles she chose—*Men and Wives* (1931), *A House* *and Its Head* (1935), *Daughters and Sons* (1937), *A Family and a Fortune* (1939), *Elders and Betters* (1944), and the rest—had an individual stamp, indicating to her devotees that they would again be led into the world of some undefined Edwardian era where, in a large country house, over cups of tea served by a well-ordered staff, the members of an upper-class family would talk. They spoke mostly about themselves, expressing their thoughts as though alone, and in this way Dame Ivy revealed the terrible secrets of incest, madness, and murder which always lurked beneath the civilised façade. It is surprising that, with such themes, she should have been essentially a comic writer, but her wit in commenting on the follies of the world led her to be called one of the funniest writers of the century.

She continued to write all her life, publishing her last book, *A God and His Gifts*, in 1963. Several of her novels were adapted for radio, for which they are eminently suitable. She did not receive recognition from either critics or the general public until late in life, but then her admirers became legion. In 1951 she was appointed C.B.E.; in 1956 she received the James Tait Black Memorial Prize for *Mother and Son*; in 1967 she was made Dame of the British Empire; and in 1968 she became a Companion of Literature. Dame Ivy was a small, neat, courteous woman, always immensely interested in people, and seemingly untouched by fame. What lasting mark she has made on literature only time can reveal, but it is certain that none who read her can be indifferent to her originality.

Maureen "Little Mo" Connolly-Brinker.

Connolly-Brinker, Maureen (1934–1969). "Little Mo," the former tennis champion who won her first Wimbledon as a girl of 18, died of cancer in Dallas, Texas, U.S.A., on June 21, 1969. In 1951 she took the world of tennis by storm when, aged 16, she beat Doris Hart, then the reigning Wimbledon champion, in a semi-final of the American championships at Forest Hills, which she went on to win. In the three years following this

triumph she achieved every crown in women's tennis, completely dominating the scene at a time when it bristled with players of outstanding calibre, such as Doris Hart, Shirley Fry, Louise Brough, and Margaret Du Pont. She won the women's singles title at Wimbledon in 1952, and retained it for three years. She also held the American title for three years running (1951–1953). In 1953 she achieved a unique record—the "grand slam," winning the Australian, French, Wimbledon, and American championships. Her success was due to an intense competitive spirit and the incredible driving power of her ground strokes, particularly her backhand. To this solid base, experience added skills and subtleties at the net, until not only was she the greatest of her contemporaries but—with Suzanne Lenglen of France and fellow Californian Helen Wills Moody—one of the three greatest women players of all time. In 1954, at the pinnacle of her fame, Little Mo's tennis career was tragically cut short by a riding accident in which she broke a leg. She was not then 20. Thereafter she remained close to the game as a coach, and as the moving spirit of the Maureen Connolly–Brinker Foundation in Dallas for coaching and encouraging young players. In 1955 she married Norman Brinker, a businessman and a member of the American Olympic show-jumping team, and between her coaching commitments and bringing up two little girls, she joined him in business ventures in Texas and California as a restaurateur.

Cosgrove, Sir Robert (1884–1969). Few men have a greater record of public service to Tasmania than Sir Robert Cosgrove, who died in Hobart on August 25, 1969. As Labour Premier of the State from 1939 to 1947 and from 1948 until his retirement in 1958, he guided it through a difficult period, and subsequently gave generously of his time to various public organisations. Robert Cosgrove was born at Tea Tree, Tasmania, on December 28, 1884, and was educated locally and at St. Mary's Boys' School, Hobart. On leaving school he entered the grocery business, but quickly became interested in politics. In 1919 he was elected to the Tasmanian House of Assembly for Denison, and from 1934 to 1939 was Minister for Transport and Agriculture. In the last-named year he became Premier, beginning a Tasmanian record term in that position. His continuity in office was interrupted in 1947 when allegations in Parliament of improper transport practices resulted in a Royal Commission and his vacating the premiership. He was cleared of the charges, and was re-instated as Premier in 1948, assuming also the portfolio of Education. He retired in 1958 as the result of ill-health, and in 1959 was created K.C.M.G. Sir Robert was an energetic supporter of the development of Tasmania's hydro-electric resources, and as Minister for

Education he raised the school-leaving age from 14 to 16.

Billy Cotton, great entertainer.

Cotton, Billy (1899–1969). The band-leader who was known to millions by his raucous cry "Wakey-Wakey" followed by the thunderous opening bars of *Somebody Stole My Girl*, died of a heart attack on March 25, 1969, while watching a heavyweight prizefight at Wembley Pool. As English as roast beef and Yorkshire, as cockney as a whelkstall in Wapping, Billy Cotton had for some forty years occupied a unique niche in the texture of British life, thanks to his never-ebbing popularity on radio and television. He was born on May 6, 1899, in the city of Westminster. As a stripling of fifteen he joined the colours as a drummer in the Royal Fusiliers and saw service in the Dardanelles. He later lied about his age, joined the Royal Flying Corps, and was commissioned before returning to civvy street. Flinging himself headlong into the crazy '20s, he achieved distinction as boxer, footballer, and racing driver, but, most brilliantly of all, as the leader of one of the big bands that typified the era. He began his musical career as a drummer in a dance band and by 1928 was broad-casting as the leader of his own band. His style and format was that of the big-band comedy show which reached a highwater mark in the 1930s and which, in Billy Cotton's case, proved the formula for durable success. He introduced the *Billy Cotton Band Show* on television in 1956 and followed this up with the *Wakey-Wakey Tavern*. His latest series, *Billy Cotton's Music Hall* ran from May to July, 1968, and he was due to appear with a new series in the spring of 1969. Despite his success as a showman Billy Cotton found time for his sporting activities until late in his career. As a racing driver he was a well-known figure at the old Brooklands track and at the ripe age of 50 he finished sixth in the British Grand Prix at Silverstone. In 1962, at the age of 64, he was nominated show-business personality of the year by the Variety Club of Great Britain, but soon afterwards he was taken seriously ill and forced to give up work for three months. It was typical of the man that he scorned to retire after this setback and, still in harness and living life to the full, died in his boots at a boxing match.

Cousins, Frank (born 1904). The dominant personality in British trade union affairs for over a decade, Frank Cousins retired, in the autumn of 1969, from the leadership of Britain's largest union, the Transport and General Workers'. The following day he started on his full-time "retirement" job as chairman of the Community Relations Commission, a post he had held in a part-time capacity for nine months. His departure from the T.G.W.U. meant he also ceased to be a member of the General Council of the T.U.C. after fifteen years, broken only by the two years when, as Minister of Technology, he had tried to put into effect Harold Wilson's proposals for revitalising British industry.

Born on September 8, 1904, in Bulwell, Notts, Cousins left school at 14 to go down the pits. In the depression of the 1930s he changed his job, became a lorry driver and a T.G.W.U. man, and by 1939 was an organiser in the union's road transport section. In 1948 he became national secretary of that section, and in 1955 the union's assistant general secretary. He was still virtually unknown outside the union when he was voted general secretary in 1956, following such men as Arthur Deakin and Ernest Bevin. Asked whether he would follow Deakin or Bevin, he replied "I stand on the Cousins line." This, the Labour movement soon learned, was the line of an old-fashioned Socialist. The most politically minded of trade union leaders, with considerable physical presence and a fine platform manner, with the backing of his 1½ million-strong union, he was from the start a thorn in the side of the Conservative government, and soon killed the idea that trade unions would accept wage restraint. He also harried the Labour Party leadership over the issue of unilateral renunciation of nuclear weapons, and won a notable victory over the party leader, Hugh Gaitskell, in 1960, although the vote was reversed at the next Congress. His fight to keep the basic principle of public ownership as stated in the famous Clause Four of the party programme also saw him in conflict with the party leadership of that time. But the Wilson leadership was more to his liking, and he secured leave of absence from the T.G.W.U. to start the Ministry of Technology. He could not, however, reconcile his membership of the government with his opposition to its prices and incomes policy and to what he felt was a lack of Socialism in both home and foreign policy. In March 1966, his union declined to collaborate with the Prices and Incomes Board in an inquiry into busmen's pay, and in July he resigned from the government. Back in the secretaryship of the T.G.W.U., he soon left Parliament, despite pressure to remain as leader of the militant left-wing Labour M.P.s.

Crompton, Richmal (1890–1969). Richmal Crompton Lamburn, who as Richmal Crompton created the character of William, one of fiction's most endearing rebels, died on January 11, 1969, at the age of 78. A clergyman's daughter, she was born on November 15, 1890, and educated at St. Elphin's School, Darley Dale, and at the Royal Holloway College, London. On graduating she became a classics mistress at her old school and in 1917 moved to Bromley High School where she stayed for seven years. It was during these years that her short stories began to appear in magazines; they included one, in 1921, for *Home Magazine* in which the famous William made his début. After a bout of polio she gave up teaching and devoted herself entirely to writing. Her first book, *Just William,* appeared in 1922. Although Richmal Crompton wrote some 40 adult novels—including *The Old Man's Birthday* (1934), *Narcissa* (1941), and a trilogy *The Wildings*—it was to William that she owed her reputation and wealth. The leader of the outlaws was immensely popular from the outset; close to 9 million copies of his various adventures have been sold in English language editions alone. This astounding popularity stems from the books' genuine appeal to both child and parent, achieved, in large measure, by the restricted scope of Miss Crompton's canvas, and the skill with which she pictured the middle-class suburban milieu inhabited by familiar individuals. Gentle satire at the expense of these characters amused the adult, while the child's interest was intensified because the adventures were credible and the protagonists easy to identify with.

Bernadette Devlin, M.P. at 21.

Devlin, Josephine Bernadette (born 1947). A member of Parliament at 21, an impassioned speaker against the Ulster government, the fiery rouser of spirits on the barricades of Bogside in Londonderry in the summer riots, this member of the "fighting Devlins" family found herself in a Maid of Orleans role in the civil rights movement. But the delight which many people, particularly women journalists, expressed at her appearance at Westminster in April, just before her 22nd birthday, was overtaken by the abuse which her later activities at Londonderry aroused. The Speaker of the House of Commons was asked to take action against her and was shown a photograph of her, dressed in jeans and sweater, breaking stones, allegedly for use as missiles. He could take no action against an M.P. for activity outside the House, he said; but in Ulster a whole series of charges were levelled against her : more than a dozen summonses were presented to her on her return from a fund-raising trip to the U.S.A. In December she was found guilty on three counts, but released on bail pending appeal.

Born on April 23, 1947, at Cookstown, co. Tyrone, she made her first political gesture at the age of 12, reciting revolutionary writings from 1916, in a talent contest which she won. Her father died when she was 9, and her mother when she was 19. After she had taken part in civil rights marches in 1968 which fell foul of the Ulster police, her educational career—working for a psychiatry degree at Queen's University, Belfast—gave way to politics. She first shook the Unionists by polling 5,812 votes to the 9,195 cast for Major James Chichester-Clark in South Derry in the Northern Ireland general election in February. Then, in April, she won the Mid-Ulster seat in the Westminster parliament, defeating the widow of the former M.P. In November she published her autobiography, *The Price of My Soul.*

Dornier, Claudius (1884–1969). Professor Claudius Dornier, the famous German aeronautical engineer, died at Zug, Switzerland, aged 85, on December 5, 1969. He was born on May 5, 1884, and educated at Munich Technical University. One of the world's first experts on flying boats, Dornier produced (1929) the giant Do-X transatlantic airliner capable of carrying 170 passengers. As proprietor and director of Dornier-Werke for 50 years he played a major part in the German war effort during the Second World War. His Dornier 17 was nicknamed the "flying pencil" because of its long slender lines. The Dornier bombers formed the spearhead of the German Luftwaffe that destroyed so many cities in the early years of the war. The Dornier 217, a high-wing monoplane, fitted usually with two 1,600 h.p. B.M.W. radial engines, had a wing span of 62 ft. 5 ins., and the fuselage (56 ft. 6 ins. long) held a four-man-crew, heavy armament, and up to 5,550 lb. of bombs. It was one of the most-feared sights in the skies of Europe for five years. Dornier was an honorary senator of Munich Technical University; senator of the Lilienthal Association for Aeronautical Research; and member of the German Academy for Aeronautical Research.

Douglas of Kirtleside, William Sholto, 1st Baron (1893–1969). Marshal of the Royal Air Force, Lord Douglas of Kirtleside, great war commander and shrewd airline chairman, died on October 30, 1969. He had a distinguished career in the R.A.F. and during the Second World War became chief of Fighter Command and of Coastal Command. He played a decisive part in overcoming the threat of enemy submarine attacks during the later stages of the war. Afterwards he ran British European Airways for 15 years, and saw the number of passengers increase from half a million to six million a year. Throughout his career he showed extraordinary powers of analysis and judgement.

William Sholto Douglas was born on December 23, 1893, at Oxford. He was educated at Tonbridge School and Lincoln College, Oxford. He joined the R.F.A. in 1914, transferring to the R.F.C. and qualifying first as an observer and later as a pilot. During the 1914–18 War he won the M.C., D.F.C., and Croix de Guerre, and was mentioned in dispatches three times. After a brief period as test pilot with Handley Page, he returned to the R.A.F. and by 1938 was Assistant Chief of the Air Staff. In the Second World War he took over Fighter Command from Lord Dowding after the Battle of Britain had ended; next he followed Lord Tedder as Chief of Middle East Command, organising heavy attacks on the ships that carried Rommel's supplies from Italy to North Africa; and in 1944 he took over Coastal Command and the direction of the Battle of the Atlantic. At the end of the war Douglas became Chief of British Air Forces in Germany and supervised the disarmament of the Luftwaffe in the British zone. He joined the board of B.O.A.C. in 1948, but left it the following year to become chairman of B.E.A., which he made into Europe's leading airline. He was raised to the peerage in 1948.

Eisenhower, Dwight David (1890–1969). Dwight D. Eisenhower, one of the best loved and most admired Americans of the twentieth century, commander-in-chief of the Allied armies of liberation in North Africa and in Europe in the Second World War, and 34th President of the U.S.A., died on March 28, 1969, after a series of heart attacks that had kept him in the Walter Reed military hospital, Washington, for 10 months. It was Eisenhower's organising capacity and, above all in a war waged by a coalition of powers, his ability as a conciliator that made him of inestimable value to the Allied cause in the Second World War. The personal charm and integrity that appeared to radiate from him won the loyalty and respect of all his distinguished, often testy, subordinates — tactical commanders such as Montgomery and Patton, men of superior experience and unbounded confidence in their own genius, and overworked staff officers,

Dwight David Eisenhower died in March. *Top:* Allied c.-in-c., with Montgomery and Tedder. *Lower:* left, U.S. President, with Khrushchev; right, golfer, in his electric car.

representing diverse shades of national pride and petty jealousy. It was again the personal qualities of good humour, reasonableness, and shining "goodness" that brought him his political success. He was not a partisan politician; the American people voted for him in unprecedented numbers as a "good guy," a leader who symbolised all the old American virtues and who came, as he put it himself, "from the heart of America," the Middle West.

"Ike," as he was called from his schooldays, was born on October 14, 1890, at Denison, Texas, and from the age of two was brought up in Abilene, Kansas, in a close-knit Mennonite family whose German ancestors had emigrated to the New World in 1732. His deeply religious parents instilled into him and his four brothers the simple and pious traditions of nineteenth-century rural America. He was undistinguished at school and at West Point, the U.S. military academy, where in 1915 he graduated 61st in a class of 164. Posted to San Antonio, Texas, he met his future wife Mamie Geneva Doud, member of a wealthy Denver, Colorado, family. They were married on July 1, 1916, and had two sons; the first died in infancy, and the second, John Sheldon Doud Eisenhower

followed his father into the army and was appointed U.S. ambassador to Belgium in 1969.

Eisenhower was not sent to Europe in the First World War, but his promotion was rapid and his career distinguished. By 1929 he was assistant to the Secretary of War in Washington, where he attracted the attention of General MacArthur, then the Army's Chief of Staff. When MacArthur went to Manila in 1935, as military adviser to the Philippines, he took Eisenhower with him as his assistant. With the outbreak of war in Europe in 1939, Eisenhower returned to Washington, where he became chief of the war plans division. In June 1942 he was appointed to the command of the American forces in the European theatre and flew to London to plan the invasion of North Africa. His talent for organisation and sure grasp of logistics led to his appointment as Allied Commander-in-Chief, North Africa, even though he had never led troops in the field. The invasion of Algeria and Morocco went smoothly, but the subsequent campaign involved bitter fighting and some setbacks; finally, linking up with the British Eighth Army under Montgomery, who had advanced from Egypt across Libya, Tripoli, and Tunisia, the Allies forced the surrender of the German-Italian army of 250,000 men in May 1943.

The invasion of Sicily and Italy followed. Meanwhile the date of the invasion of France was settled and Eisenhower was appointed supreme commander of the operations. His conduct of operations following the Normandy landings on D-day, June 6, 1944, has been the subject of criticism. Montgomery wanted to attack on a narrow front into the heart of Germany, but Eisenhower was in favour of advancing on a broad front. He has also been condemned for failing to press on to Berlin and Prague before the Russians, although there is evidence to suggest that this decision was not his to make and that the post-war map of Europe had already been agreed on between Stalin, Churchill, and Roosevelt. Whatever the tactical arguments, Eisenhower's military colleagues always spoke of him in the highest personal terms. "I would not class Ike as a great soldier in the true sense of the word," wrote Montgomery in his memoirs, ". . . but he was a great supreme commander—a military states-man." De Gaulle said of him : ". . . it was chiefly by method and perseverance that he dominated the situation. By choosing reasonable plans, by sticking firmly to them, by respecting logistics, General Eisenhower led to victory the complicated and prejudicial machinery of the armies of the free world." He received the unconditional surrender of the German high command at his h.q. in Rheims on May 7, 1945.

For the next two years Eisenhower served as U.S. Army Chief of Staff. In 1948 he retired to become president of Columbia University, but relations between the free world and the Soviet Union were at that time falling apart, and with the formation of NATO in 1949 he was recalled to lay the groundwork for this alliance and take supreme command of NATO forces. While he was still engaged in this daunting task in Paris, movements developed in the U.S.A. to draft him for the presidential nomination of both major parties. Although he was not in favour of generals taking to politics, he disclosed, in January 1952, that he had a Republican voting record— a statement tantamount to saying he would agree to run for the presidency as a Republican. Resigning from his NATO appointment, he returned to America in June 1952, and engaged first in a successful and lively contest with Senator Robert A. Taft for the Republican nomination, and second (with Senator Richard M. Nixon as his running mate) in an equally vigorous and successful campaign against Governor Adlai E. Stevenson of Illinois, the Democratic candidate, for the presidency. He defeated Stevenson again in 1956, when Eisenhower was given a second term by the biggest popular vote recorded at that time.

Eisenhower was not the ineffectual president that he seemed. Nevertheless a number of factors served to emphasise that impression. His health was suspect : he suffered a heart attack in 1955 and a stroke in 1957, and had to undergo an intestinal operation. More important was his idealistic, somewhat old-fashioned conception of his office ; he saw it as the president's duty to reign above the partisan intrigues of party politics. This, together with the military way in which he organised his staff, delegating power and thus to some extent insulating himself from his responsibilities, gave an appearance of aloofness to his presidency. Again his refusal to countenance any hint of gerrymandering or to use his considerable powers of patronage to ease legislation through Congress proved a stumbling block to his administration's power to put policy into action, particularly for his programme of domestic reforms. Nevertheless he persuaded Congress to set up a Civil Rights Commission and to pass the Civil Rights Acts of 1957 and 1960 to protect minorities' right to vote; and in 1957 he sent Federal troops to support the courts' decision to desegregate the schools at Little Rock, Arkansas.

In foreign affairs certain formidable achievements remain : a creditable peace in Korea in 1953 ; the creation of SEATO ; and an American guarantee to Formosa which effectively saved the island from an invasion from mainland China. He conceived it to be in the U.S.A.'s interests to demand the cessation of the Israeli–British–French invasion of Egypt in the Suez "incident" in 1956, and in the following year announced the "Eisenhower doctrine," which promised U.S. assistance to any Middle East country threatened by Communist aggression. It was, however, a source of great disappointment to him that his most treasured hope, the establishing of a better relationship with the U.S.S.R., was unfulfilled. At a summit conference in Geneva in 1955 he made his "open skies" proposal for the observation from the air of all countries' warlike preparations. When this failed he ordered espionage flights by U-2 planes over the U.S.S.R., and it was the shooting down of one of these that caused a second summit conference in Paris in 1960 to break up when Khrushchev returned home in anger. Following this, Eisenhower's protégé, Vice-President Richard Nixon, was defeated at the presidential election in November 1960 by Senator John F. Kennedy, the Democratic party candidate.

Eisenhower continued to be active in public life for some years after leaving the White House, but chiefly filled the role of a benevolent father-figure of the nation while playing golf, reading his Bible, and keeping an eye on the price of corn at his beloved farm at Gettysburg. Kings and presidents attended his lying-in-state and funeral service in Washington, but he was buried in the simple churchyard at Abilene where he had grown up.

Levi Eshkol, Israeli premier, died.

Eshkol, Levi (1895–1969). Levi Eshkol, Prime Minister of Israel, died in Jerusalem on February 26, 1969, at the age of 73. He was an early pioneer of the modern state of Israel, arriving in Palestine as a youth of 19 from Russia. He had been born to a Jewish family living in Oratovo, a Ukrainian railway junction near Kiev; and had come under the influence of the Zionist movement in his teens. Fired with the vision of a Jewish independent state in Palestine, he sailed for Jaffa in 1914 and trekked inland on foot, eventually joining a group engaged in establishing small Jewish settlements in the barren stony hills near Jerusalem. During the Great War Eshkol served with the 40th Royal Fusiliers of the Jewish Legion in the British Army under Allenby, in which he began his long association with his friend, mentor, and later bitter enemy, David Ben-Gurion. After the war a bout of malaria finished Eshkol's hopes of a farming career, and he became actively engaged in politics as an official of Hapoel Hazair, a Zionist labour party. When the Nazis came to power in Germany Eshkol was sent to Berlin as a Zionist representative responsible for helping the transfer of German Jews and their property to Palestine. In 1944 he returned to Tel Aviv, where Ben-Gurion appointed him to the high command of the Hagana, responsible for the party finances and founding secret arms factories. On Israel's independence in 1948 he became director-general of the Defence Ministry in Ben-Gurion's government.

It was the conciliatory aspect of Levi Eshkol's personality that led to his advance to the premiership on Ben-Gurion's retirement in 1963. In the feuding arena of Israeli party politics the cohesive force of this amiable statesman proved the most valuable contribution of his ministry. He not only made concessions to political rivals in the cause of unity but presided over an Israel that saw the unification of her three workers' parties into the new Israel Labour Party. These concessions earned him the

Victor Feather, acting general secretary of the Trade Union Congress.

implacable enmity of his former friend Ben-Gurion, and the feud that developed between the two men was one of the most tragic developments of his career. Another was the infighting in his closest political associates on the eve of the Six-Day War in 1967, when his colleagues compelled him to relinquish his defence portfolio to the more bellicose General Dayan.

Feather, Victor Grayson Hardie (born 1908). Victor Feather, who succeeded to the mantle of the beetle-browed George Woodcock when he became acting general secretary of the T.U.C. on March 1, 1969, moved constantly in the political limelight during the following June as one of the protagonists in the struggle attending the Government's attempt to outlaw wildcat strikes. It was Feather who led the steadfast, and victorious, trade union opposition to the proposals, routing the combined forces of Harold Wilson and Barbara Castle, and emerging from the fray with the reputation of a man of iron.

He was born in Bradford on April 10, 1908, and named after the famous socialists Victor Grayson and Keir Hardie. His father, who, as these names suggest, was an ardent socialist and pacifist, died at the age of 47, leaving his wife and four children to live on grants from the Board of Guardians. It was against this background that the youthful Feather, working as a Co-op van boy at 12s 6d a week, imbibed his socialism from—ironically—Barbara Castle's father, Frank Betts. He was employed by the Co-op from 1923 until 1937 when he joined the staff of the T.U.C. He was a member of the T.U.C. delegation to Russia in 1943 and he assisted in the post-war re-organisation of the Greek trade unions in 1945 and of the Berlin trade unions in 1949. Ten years later he gave the benefit of his experience to the trade union movements of India and Pakistan. He was made a C.B.E. in 1961. He has published *Trade Unions, True or False* (1951); *How do the Communists Work?* (1953); and *Essence*

of Trade Unionism (1963). A formidable lobbyist and a man dedicated to the trade union movement—having turned down the general secretaryship of the Labour Party—Vic Feather is destined to remain a leading public figure until he retires on his 65th birthday in April 1973.

Ferguson, Sir John Alexander (1881–1969). With the death of Sir John Ferguson at Roseville, Sydney, on May 7, 1969, Australia lost one of her most distinguished citizens and scholars. As judge of the New South Wales Industrial Commission for 17 years, as an elder of the Presbyterian Church for 57 years, and as a trustee of the Public Library of New South Wales for 34 years, he worked tirelessly for the community, while as compiler of the *Bibliography of Australia* he created a reference work of lasting value. Comprising seven volumes, the *Bibliography* lists and describes, in the first four volumes, every pamphlet, record, and book concerning Australia published anywhere from 1784 to 1850. The last three volumes record the same material from 1850 to 1900, but on a selective scheme. An eighth volume will record Sir John's addenda to vols. 5, 6 and 7, and in addition will contain a comprehensive index to those volumes. Appropriately all volumes have been published by Angus & Robertson, whose managing director is Sir John's eldest son.

The eldest son of a Presbyterian minister, John Ferguson was born at Invercargill, New Zealand, on December 15, 1881. Following his father's appointment to St. Stephen's Church, Sydney, in 1894, he attended William Street Superior Public School in that city. Subsequently he studied at the University of Sydney, where he took honours in classics, logic and mental philosophy, and law. He was admitted to the bar in 1905, and practised in the Court of Industrial Arbitration, later the Industrial Commission. In 1936 he was appointed judge of the Commission, a position that he filled until retirement in 1953. During his term he was largely responsible for a marked improvement in the conditions of industrial workers in such matters as sick leave, long service leave, and better hours and wages. He was knighted in 1961. Sir John was a noted authority on Australiana, and the Ferguson Room in the National Library, Canberra, named in his honour, houses his very valuable collection of rare Australian and Pacific works.

Flint, Sir William Russell (1880–1969). Russell Flint, doyen of British water colourists, died on December 27, 1969, at the age of 89. He was born in Edinburgh on April 4, 1880, the eldest son of Francis Wighton Flint, an artist and designer. Educated at Daniel Stewart's College, Edinburgh, and the Royal Institution School of Art, Edinburgh, he began his artistic career by serving a six-year apprenticeship to a lithographic artist. In 1898 he held his first exhibition of

Russell Flint, popular British artist.

water colours in Edinburgh, and two years later, aged 20, arrived in London. Here he worked for a while illustrating medical textbooks, but in 1903 he joined the staff of the *Illustrated London News* where he worked as an artist until 1907. He next struck out as a painter in oil and water colour and was some way along the road to fame when the First World War broke out. He served first in the R.N.V.R. and later as an officer in the R.A.F. Following the war he established himself as a successful artist and engraver, becoming a regular exhibitor at the Royal Academy and elsewhere, and was elected R.A. in 1933.

Flint held innumerable one-man exhibitions—chiefly at the galleries of the Fine Art Society. His style embraced English, Scottish, and Provençal landscapes, idealistic nudes, and graceful figure compositions—all of which tended to raise the critical hackles of critical hacks, who intoned piously on his lack of depth, mere skill, and sugary sweetness. Such carping, however, missed the true significance of Russell Flint's talent: he was one of the last British masters of the brush who had enormous popular appeal and, what is more, he was not afraid of embracing popular media. He was active in the field of typography, book illustration, posters, and even menu cards.

Among Flint's book illustrations are the Riccardi Press edition of the *Canterbury Tales; One Hundred and Eleven Poems by Robert Herrick;* and albums of nudes—*Models of Propriety,* and *Minxes Admonished.* His pictures hang in many galleries and museums in the United Kingdom, the U.S.A., Canada, and Australia. He was knighted in 1947.

Garland, Judy (1922–1969). The mercurial singer and film star who made her name as a child star in *The Wizard of Oz* and who was cheered or jeered off many a stage in the course of her tragic career, died of an overdose of drugs in London on June 22, 1969, at the age of 47. She was born in 1922 at her father's vaudeville theatre, in Grand Rapids, Minnesota, her original name being Frances Gumm. At 30 months she made

Judy Garland as the world likes to remember her—in *The Wizard of Oz*.

her first appearance singing *Jingle Bells*, and while still a child she appeared regularly as part of her mother's act, which was billed as the Gumm Sisters. Mrs. Gumm played the piano and her three daughters sang. It was during such a performance in 1935 that Frances was spotted by her mentor, Louis B. Mayer (the final M of M.G.M.), who was struck by her vivacity and talent. As Judy Garland she appeared in two minor musical films, but was then forgotten until she sang a special number at a birthday party in honour of Clark Gable, one of Mayer's favourite stars. The song, *Dear Mr. Gable*, received such an overwhelming response that Mayer put her straight into *Broadway Melody of 1938*, and followed this by starring her with Micky Rooney in *Thoroughbreds Don't Cry* and later *Love finds Andy Hardy*.

It was *The Wizard of Oz* that established her as an international star in a role she received only because Shirley Temple was not available. The impact of this whimsical fantasy was so powerful that, no matter to what extent her later life was scarred by age, neurosis, or drugs, she remained linked inexorably in the public mind with the little Kansas farm girl who tripped down the yellow brick road hand-in-hand with the Tinman, the Scarecrow, and the Cowardly Lion. Judy was 17 when she made *The Wizard of Oz*, which brought her an Academy award and established her song "Somewhere Over the Rainbow" as a classic of the age. From 1939 to 1950 she starred in a number of films, of which the best were *For Me and My Gal* (1941), *Girl Crazy* (1943), *Meet Me in St. Louis* (1944), and *Easter Parade* (1948). In 1949, however, the instability that was to mark her future began to show : she had a breakdown and Mayer lost patience with her, there was a blazing quarrel, and Judy Garland left M.G.M. to pursue her career as a stage and cabaret singer, making only occasional films, such as *A Star is Born* (1955) and *Judgment at Nuremberg* (1961).

Her private life was tragic ; married five times, she suffered a number of nervous breakdowns and became addicted to amphetamines and sleeping tablets. Sometimes she would fail to arrive for a show, or arrive late, or dry up and stalk off the stage to the accompaniment of boos. Yet she was one of the most magnetic stars of all time ; everything was forgiven when her theme song "Somewhere Over the Rainbow" evoked with each wistful note the tristful link between lost youth and the land that never was.

Gilroy, Norman Thomas, Cardinal (born 1896). The creation of Cardinal Gilroy as K.C.B.E., announced in the 1969 New Year's honours list, was a widely approved tribute of respect to a notable Roman Catholic churchman. The first Australian-born Cardinal, he is famous for his uncompromising adherence to high moral principles, his genial presence, and his ability to fill with great distinction a high ecclesiastical office and, at the same time, remain close to the people whom he leads. Norman Gilroy was born at the Sydney suburb of Glebe on January 22, 1896, and received his early education at Marist Brothers' College, Kogarah, Sydney. On leaving school he joined the Postal Department and was stationed successively at Sydney, Bourke, and Narrabri, N.S.W. During the First World War he joined the

Cardinal Archbishop Gordon Gray.

Naval Wireless Transport Service, and was present at the Anzac landing of April 25, 1915. On returning to Australia he resumed duty with the Postal Department at Lismore, N.S.W., but resigned in 1917 and was adopted as an ecclesiastical student by Dr. Carroll, Bishop of Lismore. He began studies for priesthood at St. Columba's College, Springwood, N.S.W., and in 1919 went to Rome as a student of the Urban College of Propaganda, being ordained priest in 1923 and graduating in the following year. From 1924 to 1931 he was secretary to the Apostolic Delegate, and from 1931 to 1934 secretary to the Bishop of Lismore and chancellor of the dioceses. In December 1934 Dr. Gilroy was appointed Bishop of Port Augusta (South Australia) ; he was translated in 1937 to Sydney as coadjutor archbishop, and succeeded to the see of Sydney in March 1940. On February 18, 1946, he was created and proclaimed Cardinal. The conferring of a knighthood on a Cardinal is without known precedent. It caused some questioning in Catholic circles, some members feeling that it was inappropriate for a Prince of the Church to accept the honour. But His Eminence described the knighthood as "a gracious honour, gratefully accepted as a tribute to the Catholic people of Australia through me."

Gray, Gordon Joseph, Cardinal (born 1910). The nation-wide welcome given throughout Scotland to the elevation to the Sacred College of Cardinals of the Most Rev. Gordon Gray, Roman Catholic Archbishop of St. Andrew's and Edinburgh since 1951, was tribute both to the happier relations between the Churches in these ecumenical days and to the personal character and popularity of the man on whom the honour was bestowed. Not since the 15th century has any Scot serving in his native land received this honour. The fact that Scotland has a small Roman Catholic community compared with those on whose leading prelate the cardinal's hat has traditionally been conferred, made the raising of Monsignor Gray to the College more obviously a recognition of his personal worth. The new Cardinal has been to the forefront in developing warmer relationships with the national Church of Scotland (which is Presbyterian in character), and numbers many of the leaders of that Church among his personal friends. Cardinal Gray is 59, born on August 10, 1910. He went to Holy Cross Academy, Edinburgh, and trained for the priesthood at St. John's Seminary, Wonersh. All his service as priest and bishop has been given in his native land—in St. Andrews, Hawick, and Aberdeen. His elevation to the Archbishopric at the age of 41 was an earlier recognition of his calibre.

Gropius, Walter (1883–1969). An architect who built less in materials than in ideas, Gropius was a pioneer of the

Walter Gropius, *Bauhaus* **founder.**

doctrine that art should be wedded to technology, with designer and craftsman alike conscious of being socially responsible. Cosmopolitan in the range of his influence, he spent in Germany his first 50 years from birth in Berlin to voluntary exile from Nazi persecution. London was his home for three years during which he was partner to Maxwell Fry; he revisited it in 1968 to open an exhibition recalling his brain-child, the *Bauhaus*. The U.S.A. gave him a professorship at Harvard in 1937; he settled in that country, and at Boston, on July 5, 1969, he died.

The *Bauhaus* was inaugurated at Weimar in 1919, but after six years of official hostility transferred to Dessau. A building composed of two interlocking Ls, strictly cubic and banishing curves, it was an institute dedicated to practising the ideals of its founder, teamwork in design and construction, and an almost reverent regard for the intrinsic qualities of steel, concrete, and other materials. Outstanding creators like Kandinsky, Klee, and Moholy-Nagy were instructors there. Already before the 1914 war, in which he served as an airman, Gropius had enunciated a policy for housing the industrial masses. He had devised for a shoe-last factory at Alfeld a structure that now seems prophetic, with huge areas of glass in a classical framework; and his hall of machinery at a Cologne exhibition included circular staircases.

Gropius was the architect (with Fry) of the Impington Village College in Cambridgeshire, and became a consultant for the Monico site at Piccadilly Circus. In America a team he headed called Architects Collaborative is credited with a graduate centre at Harvard, offices in Chicago, a housing estate in Pittsburgh, and also the U.S. embassy building in Athens.

Hagen, Walter Charles (1893–1969). This American golfer, who died aged 76 on October 6, 1969, at Traverse City, Michigan, where he had spent 30 years in retirement, was the outstanding professional competitor between the

wars, winning more titles than anyone except the amateur Bobby Jones. Among them were the British Open four times (1922–24–28–29), the American Open in 1914 and 1919, and perhaps most convincingly the match-play championship of his country four times running from 1927, and five times in all. Hagen's supremacy was founded on his short game—mid-irons, pitches, bunker shots, and putting. Confidence, not to say truculence, of demeanour—"Who's going to be second?"—must have helped to undermine some opponents, and also drew admiring crowds, who forgave him for an occasional shattering defeat, as when Archie Compston beat him by 18 and 17 in a 72-hole challenge match (just before Hagen's third British Open) or George Duncan triumphed by 10 and 8 in the Ryder Cup the following year. In that event he played every time before the 1939–45 War, being captain in 1937. Whatever career he had adopted Hagen would undoubtedly have been some kind of showman; sartorially, epigrammatically, prankishly, he attracted the spotlight, to become "the nearest thing to royalty most Americans had ever seen." The first golfer to make a million dollars (and to spend as much), he more than anybody lifted the financial status of his profession. He also raised it socially; granted his mastery of what was later called gamesmanship, his performance was always perfectly mannered.

Hall, William George Leonard, 2nd Viscount (born 1913). On May 22, 1969, the Postmaster General announced in the Commons that Viscount Hall had been appointed chairman of the new board of the Post Office Corporation, with a salary of £15,000 a year. Lord Hall, who succeeded to his father's viscounty in 1965, was born at Penrhiwceiber, Glamorgan, on March 9, 1913, and educated at Christ College, Brecon, the University of Wales, and University College Hospital, London. He began his career as a doctor, was appointed deputy medical officer of

Walter Hagen—a 1929 photograph.

health at Merthyr Tydfil in 1938, and served during the Second World War as a naval surgeon lieutenant-commander. He came into contact with the world of business when he joined the Powell Duffryn Group as their principal medical officer in 1945. A year later his career shifted from medicine to administration and he joined the company's executive. By 1950 he was a director of Duffryn Subsidiaries and his career as a tycoon and financial wizard was launched. Having been chairman and director of various companies, in 1962 he became a director of African, Asian, and Middle East investments in the International Finance Corporation, an offshoot of the World Bank, and the next year its adviser for special projects. Immediately previous to his appointment as head of the new, independent Post Office, he was a member of the advisory committee to the board of the Nuclear Power Group and British director of the Chase Selection Fund, of Boston. Lord Hall is married with two daughters. His hobbies include shooting and walking, and he is a qualified wireless operator.

Sir Paul Hasluck, Australian gov.-gen.

Hasluck, Sir Paul Meernaa Caedwalla (born 1905). On February 10, 1969, it was announced simultaneously in London and Canberra that Sir Paul Hasluck would become Governor-General of Australia following Lord Casey's retirement at the end of April. At the same time the Queen created him G.C.M.G. The choice of Sir Paul was widely approved, the only dissent coming from those who thought it unwise that a serving cabinet minister should be appointed to the position, but Hasluck himself sought a separation of three months from active political life before taking up the new appointment.

Paul Hasluck was born on April 1, 1905, at Fremantle, Western Australia, and educated at Perth Modern School and the University of Western Australia, where he gained his M.A. For some years he served on the literary staff of the *West Australian*, and in 1939–40 was lecturer in history at his old university. In 1941 he joined the Department of External Affairs and subsequently became counsellor in charge of the Australian mission to the U.N. at New York, Australian representative on a number of international bodies, and a delegate to the U.N. General Assembly. He resigned in 1947, and in the following year was appointed reader in history at the University of Western Australia. As a member of the Liberal Party, Hasluck in 1949 was elected M.H.R. for the Western Australian electorate of Curtin, a seat he occupied until, in February 1969, he resigned following the announcement about the Governor-Generalship. He was Minister for Territories 1951–63; for Defence 1963–64; and for External Affairs from 1964. In his last office he held many other important positions and travelled widely. He was chairman of SEATO ministerial council and of ANZUS ministerial council in 1966, and of the economic commission for Asia and the Far East, 1968; and leader of the Australian delegations to the U.N. General Assembly in 1964, 1966, and 1967, to ECAFE conferences in Wellington, Manila, New Delhi, Tokyo, and Canberra, to Colombo plan conferences in London and Rangoon, to SEATO conferences in London, Washington, Canberra, and Wellington, to ASPAC meetings in Seoul, Bangkok and Canberra, and to five-power defence meetings in Kuala Lumpur during 1964–68.

Sir Paul is a historian and poet who has added materially to Australian literature. He contributed a volume—*The Government and the People 1939–41*—to the official war history of Australia, and his other publications include *Our Southern Half-Castes* (1938), *Into the Desert* (1939), *Black Australians* (1942), and *Workshop of Security* (1948). Lady Hasluck is also a distinguished author, who has concentrated chiefly on Australian social history.

Heath, Ted (1902–1969). One of the biggest figures in the light music world of the post-war years, "Mr. Music," "King of Swing," band leader and showman, Ted Heath died on November 18, 1969. For nearly twenty years he led the most popular big jazz band in Britain, taking part in innumerable broadcasts and one-night stands, making many hit records, and successfully touring the U.S.A. several times. An ex-busker, he used to boast that he had played the trombone outside almost every pub in London.

Ted Heath was born at Wandsworth in 1902. His father, who led a local brass band, taught him to play most of the brass instruments. After playing the tenor horn at the Crystal Palace at the age of 7, Ted switched to the trombone and at 16 formed a street band with five other boys. He busked in London for two years until Jack Hylton gave him his first break at the roof night club of the Queen's Hall. Later he played the trombone in the bands of Bert Firman,

Ambrose, Sidney Lipton, and Geraldo. In 1945 he formed his own band from some of the best musicians in Britain, who quickly became popular for their attack, precision, and "swing." In 1953 the band won the accolade of an appearance at a Royal Variety Performance. In 1956 an exchange arrangement with the Stan Kenton Orchestra broke a 20-year embargo on visiting bands to the U.S.A. Several other tours followed, and sales of records rocketed both there and in Great Britain. Ted Heath was always keen to encourage young talent, and some of the singers who worked with him, such as Dickie Valentine and Lita Roza, became well-known names in their own right.

Heinemann, Gustav (born 1899). West Germany's first Socialist head of state since the collapse of the Weimar Republic 40 years before was elected to office in March 1969 despite a massive Soviet blockade of the election city, Berlin. Born at Schwelm an der Ruhr, the son of a sick fund director for the Krupp works at Essen, Heinemann served briefly in the First World War before studying law at five universities. He became a doctor at both Marburg and Münster. In 1926 he married and, with his wife Hilda, printed illegal pamphlets in the basement of his Essen home during the Third Reich. He channelled his anti-Nazi activities into the Confessional Church, of which he became a prominent member. In 1949 he left the Rheinischen Stahlwerke where he had worked for 31 years, to found the Christian Democratic Union in the British occupation zone. Minister of the Interior in Adenauer's first government, he resigned in 1950 in protest against the rearmament of West Germany, which he said should stay neutral.

Sonja Henie, at the height of her fame.

Heinemann founded a new All German People's Party in 1952, but after the party had gained only 5 per cent of the 1953 poll disbanded it three years later. In 1957 he was back in the Bundestag on the Social Democratic ticket, and he rapidly established himself as the party's legal expert and a focus for cold war opposition. Minister of Justice in 1966, he was a keen advocate of East-West detente. When he became President he threatened to resign if the country took control of atomic weapons or if the death penalty were restored.

Henie, Sonja (1912–1969). No one did more to turn ice skating into a sport for the watching multitude than this Hollywood star who died on October 12, 1969, while on a flight from Paris to her native Norway. Probably no more sparkling performer on the rink has yet been seen. She really cut out two separate careers, before and after 1936. There was the girl who, starting before her own crowd at Oslo in 1927, won ten successive European figure-skating championships —a feat without parallel—and three Olympic titles running, at St. Moritz, Lake Placid (N.Y.), and Garmisch. Her art was always expanding with the introduction of more elaborate choreography, for she had been trained to dance; she recorded later, in her autobiography *Wings On My Feet*, that seeing Pavlova in London was what had determined her to blend ballet with skating. In 1936 she turned professional; Hollywood claimed her full-time and made her a millionaire. Never aspiring as an actress, she remained a skater in her pictures, although a critic of her first film, *One in a Million*, found her heroine "satisfactorily blonde, dimpled, and ingratiating." It was a smash-hit, and *Thin Ice* and *My Lucky Star* raised her, according to one magazine, to third place among leading money-makers in the cinema. In 1941 came *Sun Valley Serenade*, perhaps her best-remembered film. Another of her enterprises was to stage the Hollywood Ice Revue for 13 years without a gap from 1938. A keen collector, with her third husband, Niels Onstad, a shipping magnate, she founded a museum of modern art in Oslo, which they opened in 1968.

Ho Chi Minh (1890–1969). The President of North Vietnam and revered elder statesman of the Communist world, died in Hanoi on September 3, 1969, aged 79. He is believed to have been born on May 19, 1890, at the village of Kim-Lien in the Nghe-an province of Vietnam, the youngest child of a minor Vietnamese official who had been sacked by the French and who supported his family as a travelling healer. Ho's given name was Nguyen Tat Thanh, but he used innumerable pseudonyms throughout his revolutionary career (Ho Chi Minh translates as "he who enlightens"). He was educated at a French mission school and became an elementary school-teacher before embarking on his

Ho Chi Minh, N. Vietnam leader.

travels as a steward aboard a French liner in 1912. He was a sailor for some years before arriving in London where he worked as a pastry-cook in the kitchens of the Carlton Hotel. By the end of the 1914—18 war Ho was in Paris, by now totally immersed in politics. The treaty of Versailles saw him vainly pacing the corridors of the palace hoping to meet President Wilson in order to persuade him to use his influence towards an independent Vietnam. It was at this time that Ho, already a member of the French Socialist party, formed the Inter-Colonial Union, a group of colonial nationalists resident in Paris. In 1920, at the Socialist Congress in Tours, Ho voted for the Third International and became a founder member of the French Communist Party. This took him to Moscow two years later, where he stayed for three years studying at the "Toilers of the East" University.

In 1925 he was a member of a Russian mission to China, where he formed the Vietnamese Revolutionary Youth League, an organisation which contacted Vietnamese nationalists and sent them to Russia for training and indoctrination. In 1927, when the Nationalist government of China turned on the Communists, Ho returned to Russia. By 1930 he was in Hong Kong where he founded the Vietnamese Communist Party. In 1931 he was arrested there; Stafford Cripps pleaded his case before the Privy Council and secured his release. Little is known of his movements during the next decade, but in 1941 (in China) he formed the Communist - dominated Vietnamese nationalist movement, the Viet Minh. Arrested by the Chinese in 1942, he languished in prison for a year before being released to spy in Vietnam during the Japanese occupation. With the end of the Second World War, Ho manoeuvred and intrigued against the Chinese occupation force, the returning French, and non-Communist Nationalists. In September 1945 he proclaimed the Democratic Republic of Vietnam in Hanoi, and there followed the fierce Indo-Chinese war, which culminated

with the defeat of the French in the battle of Dien Bien Phu. At the subsequent Geneva conference, Soviet and Chinese pressure forced Ho to agree to the partition of Vietnam into North and South, and North Vietnam became a Communist state under his presidency. Ho was a man remarkable for his political expertise and absolute ruthlessness. Outwardly calm and charming—the epitome of his role of "Uncle Ho"—he did not shrink from ordering the massacre of many anti-Communist Vietnamese following partition. During the struggle to capture the South, involving the bitter war against the Americans, the ageing Ho was chiefly a figurehead, but one that was an abiding inspiration to his followers in the field.

Holyoake, Keith Jacka (born 1904). In a year when the much prophesied "disaster" of British Common Market membership seemed likely to come about, its leading Commonwealth opponent, New Zealand Prime Minister Keith Holyoake, became a Freeman of the City of London and won a general election. It is the pride of this stocky fourth-generation New Zealander to trace his ancestry back to Civil War Royalist clergy, a 17th-century Rugby headmaster, and a founder of the British co-operative movement George Jacob Holyoake. Since he became Prime Minister in 1960, Holyoake's main energies had been devoted towards retaining the powerful tie with Britain—and building up a new alliance with neighbouring Commonwealth countries and the U.S.A. British entry to Europe, he said in January 1969, would suddenly cut off New Zealand markets. In February he pledged that New Zealand forces would remain in Malaysia and Singapore after the British withdrawal.

The third child of a family of seven, Holyoake was taken away from school at the age of 12 to follow the plough barefoot on his father's small farm. Educated by correspondence courses, he entered politics through the Farmers' Union, and at the age of 28, by then a successful sheep farmer, he entered Parliament. When the right-wing National Party returned to power in 1949 he became deputy prime minister and took on the thorny Ministry of Agriculture. In 1960 he led his party back to power against the Socialist Walter Nash. Married with two sons and three daughters, he is a gifted mimic and striking orator, although his TV performances have been criticised as "pompous." In May, despite hints that he might retire, Holyoake won a massive vote of confidence in his party, and in the general election on November 29 the National party won a fourth consecutive term in power by a narrow majority.

Horne, Kenneth (1907–1969). Kenneth Horne, the urbane pedlar of pun and witticism, star of such effervescent radio shows as *Much Binding in the Marsh*,

Beyond our Ken, and *Round the Horne,* and also chairman of *Twenty Questions,* collapsed and died while officiating at a television award presentation ceremony on February 14, 1969. The son of a leading Congregationalist minister, he was born on February 27, 1907, and was educated at St. George's, Harpenden, and Magdalene College, Cambridge. On leaving Cambridge he embarked on a successful business career with Triplex Glass, and only drifted into his true vocation as a comedian while serving with the R.A.F. during the war (he reached the rank of wing-commander). Together with Richard Murdoch he had a vast war-time audience glued to the radio every week for the now legendary *Much Binding in the Marsh.* His comic persona was that of the benign innocent abroad. It was a technique that ideally suited his role as a master of ceremonies ushering the action from scene to scene, and also his most distinctive comic device, the *double entendre.* Despite his success as a broadcaster Kenneth Horne continued his association with the business world (he was chairman of Chad Valley, the toy manufacturers, and of several other companies) until 1958 when he suffered a severe stroke and was forced to reduce his activities. It was while he was lying dangerously ill that he worked out the idea for *Beyond Our Ken,* which became an incredible success, with 10 million listeners, a vast radio audience for the television era. Shortly before his death Kenneth Horne had branched into television comedy with *Horne a Plenty,* and a new radio series of *Round the Horne*—the show that had evolved from *Beyond Our Ken*—had been planned for the autumn of 1969. At his death he left £67,000.

Horsbrugh, Florence, Baroness (1889–1969). The first woman to be a Conservative cabinet minister, Florence Horsbrugh died in Edinburgh on December 6, 1969, at the age of 80. She was born on October 13, 1889, the daughter of Henry Horsbrugh of Edinburgh, and educated at Lansdowne House, Edinburgh, and St. Hilda's, Folkestone. On leaving school she launched herself into a career of public service, receiving the M.B.E. for her work in canteens during the 1914–18 war. In 1931 she was elected Conservative member for Dundee, a seat she held until ousted in the Labour landslide victory of 1945. In 1936 she became chairman of the departmental committee on Adoption Societies and Agencies, and later she drew up a private members' bill which passed into law—the Adoption of Children (Regulation) Act 1939. Also in 1936 she became the first woman ever to reply to the Speech from the Throne in the House of Commons. Shortly before the outbreak of war she was appointed parliamentary secretary to the Ministry of Health and played a large part in the evacuation of children to escape the blitz. She re-entered the House in 1950 as member for Moss Side,

Manchester. She was in the Conservative government as Minister of Education, 1951–54, and, on leaving this post, was made D.B.E. She remained in the Commons until 1959, when she was given a life peerage.

Among her many "firsts" Florence Horsbrugh was the first woman to receive the honorary diploma of the Royal College of Surgeons, Edinburgh, and, in the Lords, the first woman to act as one of the three lords commisioners who constitute a Royal Commission. She never married. In person she spoke with a mellow contralto (once praised by Baldwin), and had a spinsterish, bespectacled, exterior, behind which were a keen mind and a warm heart.

Jacklin, Anthony (born 1944). The putt went in, with two to spare against Bob Charles who had finished, with other recent champions behind. It "released the heartiest cheer in British golf for two decades" as at Royal Lytham on July 12, 1969, the Open championship was won by a native player for the first time since Max Faulkner's victory in 1951. Tony Jacklin, from Scunthorpe by birth but professionally from Potters Bar, had achieved four rounds in 280 without a six on his card. Besides collecting £4,250 as a prize, he changed gear that day in his drive to riches and fame; the American impresario who managed his affairs said the event might be worth half a million pounds. Britain's young hope, a slight dark-haired figure, usually looking cheerful as well as determined on the links, was familiar to non-golfers by the chance that, in the course of his record-breaking last round of 64 that won the Dunlop Masters tournament in 1967, viewers on television were aware before the player that his tee shot to the 16th had finished in the hole. That autumn he played in the Ryder Cup against the U.S.A., scoring 2 points in foursomes as partner to David Thomas. Then on the American circuit his whole game was tightened until he overcame any nervousness at the prospect of winning. A professional since 1962, Jacklin first competed in the Open in 1963; he took the assistants' championship twice running, and in 1966 began to carry off titles overseas. With a success in top company at Jacksonville in 1968, he clearly reached world class. After the 1969 Open he came third in the Masters and contributed 5 points out of a possible 6 to Britain's tie in the Ryder Cup. He was chosen Sportsman of the Year by the British Sports Writers Association, and the *Daily Express* poll.

Jones, Mrs Ann (born 1938). After years of so-near-yet-so-far experiences, the amazingly consistent Birmingham girl finally laid a bogey when she won the Wimbledon singles title in 1969 to record Britain's first victory in the event since Angela Mortimer's 1961 success. She was voted Sportswoman of the Year by the British Sports Writers

Association, and the *Daily Express* poll, and was chosen BBC-TV Sportsview personality. The record-books did not suggest that the left-handed Mrs. Jones would be the one to end Billie-Jean King's three-year reign as Wimbledon champion. Seven times in ten years Mrs. Jones had reached the Wimbledon semi-finals, and on the only occasion that she survived the hurdle—in 1967— she lost to Billie-Jean in two sets. Wimbledon 1969 brought an end to the jinx that had seen her triumph in almost every tennis-playing country except her own. On the hard courts of Europe her concentration had brought her the French title twice and Italian once, and twice she had finished runner-up in the U.S. championships.

Born on October 17, 1938, Ann Haydon was a table-tennis star in her teens and was runner-up three times in the world championships. Switching to lawn tennis she reached the Wimbledon semi-finals for the first time in 1958, and won her first major title—the French—in 1961 when seeded only sixth. The same year she finished runner-up in the U.S. championships, but she had to wait several years before she was to add match-winning confidence to her game. She recalls an invaluable spell spent with the late Maureen Connolly, three times Wimbledon champion, who convinced Ann that more successes could come with a more positive approach when a game seemed to be slipping away. On tour with the first of the contract professionals (she signed a two-year contract in April 1967), Ann is always accompanied by her husband, "Pip," a former Warwickshire L.T.A. president whom she married in 1962, and a plentiful supply of steel rackets. Some experts believe that her switch to new-style racket in 1968 added considerably to the power of her play.

Jones, Aubrey (born 1911). In the summer of 1969 Aubrey Jones declined an offer of a two-year extension of his contract as Chairman of the National Board for Prices and Incomes, and joined the International Publishing Corporation as a full-time director and the prospective deputy chairman when his P.I.B. contract expires in the spring of 1970. Under Jones the Board laid the foundation of a system which was being copied in places as far away as Canada and Uruguay. Despite lack of "teeth" and failure to maintain the $3\frac{1}{2}$ per cent norm, it had kept wage increases down to a figure 1 per cent lower, it was generally accepted, than they would otherwise have been, and had restrained prices by possibly a larger amount.

Born in Merthyr Tydfil on November 20, 1911, a miner's son, a scholarship winner, and a favourite pupil of Harold Laski at the London School of Economics, where he took a first class honours degree, Aubrey Jones was a journalist and then an Army intelligence officer before becoming a Conservative

M.P. After a succession of ministerial posts in the 1950s he entered industry. When the P.I.B. was formed in 1965 he was the only suggested chairman acceptable to both employers and unions, and he took the post although its salary of £15,000 meant a personal sacrifice—he was then chairman of the £20 million Staveley Industries group. In its task of investigating and reporting on cases referred to it by the Government, the Board had no powers beyond that of calling evidence and, of course, persuasion. Despite this and the opposition of some unions, including the giant Transport and General Workers Union, 70 per cent of its reports were accepted and their recommendations followed. Although chairman of a government board, Aubrey Jones was outspoken in criticism of official policies when he felt it was necessary. Once he said that Selective Employment Tax had done little in its intended task (making workers move from non-productive to productive work), but it had raised prices. In 1968 he declared that the incomes policy as it was operated was unfair, and that his work was being inhibited by the Monopolies Commission. After the announcement of his intended departure from P.I.B. a "superboard" was set up to oversee monopolies, prices, and incomes.

Juan Carlos, H.R.H. the Prince of Spain (born 1938). On July 22, 1969, General Franco in a speech to the Cortes in Madrid proposed that Prince Juan Carlos should be his successor, and, at a moment of his choosing, become King of Spain. As was expected, the Cortes overwhelmingly approved the proposal. The Prince, who was given the title Prince of Spain, pledged his unswerving allegiance to Franco and his regime on the following day. Born in Rome on January 5, 1938, Juan Carlos is the eldest son of Don Juan of Bourbon and Battenberg, who has himself never ceased to lay claim to the throne of Spain. The Prince has been carefully trained for his role. He began his formal education in Madrid at the age of 10, and in 1950 moved to San Sebastian where his education continued under the direction of a university professor. When he was 16 it was decided that he should enter the Services, and he went to Spain's foremost army school in Saragossa; this course completed, he served in the navy at the Marine Academy and at the age of 19 he continued his Service training at the Air Force Academy. By the time he was 22 the Government had sent him to every part of the country to acquaint him with local conditions, and he had also received advice from experts on social, industrial and economic affairs. Prince Juan Carlos is tall (6 ft. 2 in.), is admired for his looks, is a keen sportsman particularly good at karate and athletics, and has a flair for languages. He married Princess Sophie, sister of King Constantine of Greece, in 1963, and has three children.

Boris Karloff. *Left,* as himself, Mr. Pratt, English gentleman; *right,* in his greatest role, Frankenstein's monster.

Karloff, Boris (1887–1969). The exotic screen name of this film star was borrowed from its actual owner, his maternal grandfather. He himself was born prosaically Pratt: whether Charles Edward or William Henry went before it reference books dispute. Thoroughly English, he retained that nationality, and spent near London the first 21 and the last 10 years of his life, which ended at Midhurst, Sussex, on February 3, 1969. Few performers can have been so universally identifiable as was Boris Karloff: to pre-war filmgoers he was simply "the monster." Rising to instantaneous fame in 1931 with his portrayal of the inhuman creation of Frankenstein, he ran a gruesome gamut in pictures with titles like *The Mummy, The Ghoul, The Old Dark House, The Isle of the Dead, The Grip of the Strangler.* At his mildest he was a crack-brained inventor or creaking butler. But such horrors curdled blood and froze spines in the most pleasurable way, even for youngsters, while serious critics noted how Karloff's art sprinkled on his most frightful figures the dew of pathos. "He gives the monster a soul," wrote one. Away from the feats of make-up entailed by his impersonations, the man was unrecognisably contrasted. Born at Dulwich, he was educated at Merchant Taylors' and Uppingham Schools, threw up an intended diplomatic career, and sailed to Canada, appearing as a touring actor at Kamloops, British Columbia, in 1910, and arriving at the Hollywood studios six years later. On stage he scored successes in *Arsenic and Old Lace, The Linden Tree, The Shop at Sly Corner, The Lark,* and in a record run of *Peter Pan.* He enchanted children with gentle tales read on the radio, and adored gardening and watching cricket.

Kennedy, Joseph Patrick (1888–1969). Joseph Kennedy, father of President Kennedy and Senators Robert and Edward Kennedy, died on November 18, 1969, after eight years' partial paralysis from a stroke. He will be remembered as the inspiring patriarch of a large and talented family, and also as something of a *bête noire* to those concerned with Anglo-American relations, thanks to his war-time stance as an advocate of American isolationism—first as the U.S. ambassador to the Court of St. James, and later, following his resignation in 1940 (and before Pearl Harbour), as a leading publicist of that cause within the U.S.A.

He was born into a Boston-Irish family on September 6, 1888. His father was a leading local Democrat and the owner of the saloon which formed the centre of the Boston-Irish Democratic circle. Educated in Boston schools and at Harvard—where he graduated in 1912—Joseph Kennedy started his career as a bank examiner and within a year borrowed enough money to buy a controlling interest in the Columbia Trust Company of Boston, of which he became president. The following year he married Rose Fitzgerald, daughter of "Honey Fitz" Fitzgerald, Democratic mayor of Boston. During the 1914–18 war, while manager of a shipbuilding yard, he first met Franklin D. Roosevelt, who was then Assistant Navy Secretary. After the war Kennedy's shrewd speculations on Wall Street built him a massive fortune until by 1930 he was reputed to be worth $5 million. It is also reputed that he dipped deep into that sum in aid of the Democratic campaign of 1932 and that it was only because of his reputation on Wall Street that he was not rewarded with high office when Roosevelt formed his administration in 1933. The following year, however, he was appointed chairman of the Securities Exchange Commission—to loud protests from many Democrats. But he was a success in the post, only resigning from it in 1935 in order to re-organise the Radio Corporation of America. Kennedy was active in the Roosevelt camp during the 1936 presidential campaign, bringing out a book, *I'm for Roosevelt,* and was appointed chairman of the Maritime Commission in 1937. His opposition to the fiscal policies of the New Deal led to a cooling of his enthusiasm for the administration; nevertheless, in 1938 he was appointed U.S. ambassador in London.

Knox-Johnston, Robin (born 1939). In his yacht *Suhaili* the first man to sail single-handed round the world non-stop arrived in Falmouth to a tremendous ovation on April 22, 1969. Born in Richmond of Ulster stock on St. Patrick's Day 1939, he went to Berkhamsted school. At 17 failure in A-level physics frustrated his ambition to join the Royal Navy as an officer cadet, and he opted to go to sea as a merchant navy cadet, joining the British India Steam Navigation Company's training ship *Chindwara.* As one would expect from a non-stop circumnavigator, Knox-Johnston is a man of obstinate individuality. At school he enjoyed the most individual sports, such as boxing, running, and swimming, and as a cadet aboard the *Chindwara* he endured a night lashed between two davits on deck, and an hour locked in the steam room— indignities inflicted upon him by his contemporaries for his failure to submit to adolescent ritual. At the end of four years on the *Chindwara,* Robin passed his mate's ticket and was posted to the Indian coast. As a boy of 14 he had built a canoe; now he planned to build a yacht, and in 1964 he started work on *Suhaili* in a Bombay boatyard. He adapted a Norwegian design and paid for the building month by month out of his pay, doing a lot of the work himself. Meanwhile he passed his master's ticket and became a chief officer on the London–Africa run. When *Suhaili* was completed he sailed her from India to England together with one of his younger brothers, Christopher, and a friend Heinz Fingerhut. After a year on the liner *Kenya* he heard about the *Sunday Times's* non-stop round-the-world solo yacht race and obtained indefinite leave from his employers in order to compete. The course of his voyage is described in pages 207–208. The title of the book he published about his adventures is *A World of My Own.*

Lane, Sir Allen (born 1902). The founder of Penguin Books, and managing director of that famous firm for 34 years, retired on April 23, 1969. That date was deliberately chosen by Sir Allen, for it was not only St. George's Day and Shakespeare's birthday, but also the 50th anniversary of the day he first entered publishing. This was when, on leaving Bristol Grammar School at 16, he joined his uncle, John Lane, of The Bodley Head. He had a thorough apprenticeship in every aspect of publishing from packing parcels to a directorship at 21. His most notable achievement at The Bodley Head was the publication of the first English edition of *Ulysses* by James Joyce. The book had been originally published in Paris, and copies sent to England had run foul of the authorities, hundreds of volumes being burnt as obscene. Lane went to Paris, bought a copy, addressed it to himself in London, and wrote all over the parcel: "This contains a copy of *Ulysses* by James Joyce." It arrived without interference by the Customs, and, taking this as a

Allen Lane, father of "Penguins."

favourable omen, The Bodley Head published and were not damned!

Allen Lane's great innovation in the field of publishing was, of course, the revolutionary idea of publishing good books—reprints or new writing—in enormous editions at ludicrously low prices—that is to say, he was responsible for the advent of the quality paperback. In 1935, as managing director of The Bodley Head, he discussed this brainchild with a number of leading lights in the book trade; they all shook their heads and told him such a plan could never succeed. Lane, however, was undeterred: he resigned from The Bodley Head in 1936 and formed Penguin Books Ltd. as a private company, with a nominal capital of £100. He set up an office in the crypt of a disused church in the Euston Road, and there, surrounded by tombs, he procured publishing rights, hired printers, and organised the distribution of the first ten Penguins (all priced at 6d.). A new era in publishing had commenced. Lane was knighted in 1952.

Lewis, John Llewellyn (1880–1969). John L. Lewis, a titan in the American labour movement and, for four decades, the driving force of the United Mine Workers of America, died in Washington on June 11, 1969. Born in Lucas, Iowa, on February 12, 1880, the son of an immigrant Welsh miner, he entered the pits as a boy of 14, and had mined coal in Colorado, copper in Montana, silver in Utah, and gold in Arizona by 1911 when he went to work for Samuel Gompers, president of the American Federation of Labour.

Lewis became president of the Mine Workers in 1920, starting his 40 years in the post by almost destroying the union by adding his own blunders to the prevailing slump. Only by diverting the attention of his members with a Communist witch-hunt did he survive into the years of his fame. Then, as a potent demagogue of demonic visage, garnished by eyebrows like a pair of eagle's wings, he expressed in sonorous rhetoric his

autocratic will—dedicated to the advancement of the American worker.

Having seen Union membership dwindle in the decade 1920–1930, Lewis marked the Roosevelt era by embarking on a recruiting campaign which built up the Mine Workers into a disciplined force of 450,000—over which he held despotic sway. There followed the legendary years during which Lewis was responsible for galvanising unskilled labour, thus earning the hatred not only of employers but also of the craft-oriented American Federation of Labour. Lewis broke with the A.F.L. and was a founder, and first president, of the Congress of Industrial Organisations which sought to organise the unskilled and semi-skilled. The C.I.O.'s spectacular success represented a profound change in American labour relations and cemented Roosevelt's "new deal" for the manual labourer. After a tempestuous career, Lewis retired in 1960, accepting the title "President Emeritus" of the Mine Workers. The miners also gave him a pension of $50,000 a year, a Cadillac, and a chauffeur. When he died they honoured him appropriately by walking out of the pits for a four-day period of mourning.

Lindsay, Norman Alfred William (1879–1969). The death of Norman Lindsay at Springwood in the Blue Mountains of New South Wales on November 21, 1969, closed the career of an Australian who was remarkable for his creative skill, output, and versatility. As a painter in water-colour and in oils, as an etcher, illustrator (especially in line) and cartoonist, and as a maker of model ships he displayed a genius of rare quality, and as a writer for both children and adults he has an established position in Australian literature. Much of his work departed from conventional standards—his novel *Redheap*, published in 1931, was banned in Australia for nearly 30 years, and his picture of the Crucifixion, bought by the Melbourne Art Gallery, caused such a torrent of protest that it was removed from the walls. On the

John L. Lewis, U.S. labour leader.

other hand, his children's story, *The Magic Pudding* (1919), became an Australian classic and has been published in many editions.

Norman Lindsay was born at Creswick, Victoria, on February 23, 1879, and educated at Creswick Grammar School. At 16, he was engaged to draw illustrations for the *Hawklet*, a sporting gossipy paper published in Melbourne. Transferring to Sydney, he became in 1901 chief cartoonist of the Sydney *Bulletin,* a position he was to occupy for a number of years. At the same time he gave much attention to other forms of art, and his work was included in the Exhibition of Australian Art held in London in 1923. He illustrated in line and wash drawings Theocritus, Boccaccio, and Casanova, as well as Hugh McCrae's *Satyrs and Sunlight,* Leon Gellert's *Songs of a Campaign,* and "Banjo" Paterson's *The Animals That Noah Forgot.* As a writer Lindsay was also prolific. In addition to those already mentioned his publications included *A Curate in Bohemia* (1913), *Creative Effort* (essays on life and art, 1920), *Saturdee* (1932), *The Cautious Amorist* (1934), *Age of Consent* (1938), and *The Cousin From Fiji* (1945). Shortly before his death he presented a large part of his art collection to Melbourne University, leaving the balance to the National Trust of Australia on condition that it was preserved at his own home at Springwood.

Lutyens, Elisabeth (born 1906). Still controversial after 30 years as a composer, the grande dame of modern British music at last received official recognition with a C.B.E. in 1969. Uncompromising as a pioneer, the eternal explorer and experimenter, she was yet able to say, as critics sought to understand her latest work: "Now everybody under 30 uses 12 tone." Born in London, the third daughter of the architect Sir Edwin Lutyens, she studied music in Paris, but only after playing the violin on and off outside her mother's bedroom door for six months to prove her dedication to music. In 1932 her unorthodox approach startled the fashionable audience at a Savoy Theatre matinee of her ballet *The Infanta's Birthday.* On the night of the performance she became engaged to a young radio singer Ian Glennie. The marriage broke up during the Second World War. By 1939 Miss Lutyens was already established in the forefront of the *avant garde* with a surrealist ballet, *Les Trois Arts,* and several string quartets to her credit. In 1943 she produced *Salute to Orchestra,* and in 1945 one of her best known works *The Pit.* In 1959 she wrote *Quincunx for Orchestra* and *Music for Orchestra I, II* *III.* In 1961 followed her *Symphonies for Solo Piano, Wind, Harps, and Percussion.* By 1967, when her *And Suddenly It's Evening* opened the new Queen Elizabeth Hall in London, the critics were on her side. In 1942 she married the president of the International Society for Contemporary Music, Edward Clark, who died in 1962. Of her four children she said: "Each child takes five years out of professional life."

Macdonald, Malcolm John (born 1901). After a life-time in the service of the British Empire and Commonwealth, in a host of jobs around the world, earning the title of "Our Man Anywhere," Malcolm Macdonald retired in 1969 with the Order of Merit. He overcame two of the worst disabilities a politician could face—being the son of a premier (the late Ramsay Macdonald) and changing sides in the House, when he followed his father out of the Labour Party into the National Government in 1931. Despite that he remained continuously in office under nine premiers, from his father to Harold Wilson. In that time he was once a Minister, an Ambassador Extraordinary, a Commissioner-General, and a Governor, twice a Secretary of State, a Special Representative and a Special Envoy, and three times a Governor-General and a High Commissioner.

Born in Lossiemouth on August 17, 1901, he entered Parliament in 1929, and was quickly recognised as one of the best orators in the House. A speech he made in 1940 as Secretary for the Colonies, on the Palestine settlement scheme, was commended for its mastery of detail and lucidity as one of the greatest in living memory. From 1931, when he was Under-Secretary for the Dominions, and 1935, when as Colonial Secretary he was the youngest member of the cabinet, he had only one spell of office in home affairs. That was in 1940, as Minister of Health during the "blitz," with responsibility for the evacuation programme. After several war-time years as Governor-General of Canada he went to the Far East as the first Governor-General of the Malayan Union and Singapore. In his role of roving trouble-shooter east of Suez, he was High Commisioner of India from 1955 to 1960, co-chairman of the International Conference on Laos in 1961, and co-chairman of the Geneva Conference in 1962. Chou En-lai, China's premier, once described him as "the only capitalist I can trust." When Kenya looked like flaring up into another Congo, he moved there in 1963, and from then was Britain's special representative in the whole continent. Some of the stiffer-necked colonial officials might frown at pictures of him walking between bare-breasted native girls or officiating at some function wearing little more than bathing trunks, but he gained the trust of many African national leaders, who also respected him as a shrewd negotiator, combining an almost oriental placidity with an ability to see the other man's point of view.

Marciano, Rocky (1923–1969). Rocky Marciano, former undefeated world heavyweight champion boxer, was

tragically killed in a plane crash 30 miles east of Des Moines, Iowa, U.S.A., on the eve of his 46th birthday. The toughest of heavyweights, he will always be remembered as the man who never lost a professional contest, for he fought and won 49 fights, 43 of them inside the distance. Born Rocco Marchegiano on September 1, 1923, in Boston, Mass., the son of a poor immigrant cobbler, he first thought of taking up boxing after a brawl with an Australian serviceman in a Swansea public house. After he had taken two punches on the chin he knocked out the Australian with a single right-handed punch. He changed his name when he turned professional in 1947, and although always a crude fighter learned how to defend himself against opponents much taller than his 5 ft. 11 in., and heavier than his 13 stone 4 lb. It was in October 1951 that he met the former world champion, Joe Louis, and made his name by beating him in the tenth round. After four more victories he fought Joe Walcott for the world title on

Rocky Marciano, undefeated "champ."

September 23, 1952, and although Walcott managed to knock him down in the first round, in the thirteenth Marciano knocked Walcott out with a sledge-hammer right-hander to the head. His last fight was against Archie Moore before a crowd of more than 61,000. Many believed that in Moore he had met his match, but although Moore knocked him down in the second round—for only the second time in Marciano's boxing career—he was up at the count of three, and proceeded to win the fight after giving Moore a terrible pounding. In 1956 Marciano retired from boxing and, although he received tempting offers to do so, he never returned. This man, whose place in boxing history is assured, vicious and tough in the ring, was one of the gentlest and mildest outside it.

Martin, Basil Kingsley (1897–1969). Kingsley Martin, the patriarch of left-wing journalism, who died in Cairo on February 16, 1969, began his celebrated editorship of the *New Statesman* in 1931

and presided over it, ate, drank, and slept with it for 30 influential years. The marriage of an obscure, dissenting academic to a paper of much the same credentials was hardly auspicious. By the deft and vigorous string-pulling of those famous Fabians the Webbs, Martin had been hoisted into his editorial chair from the crowd of dons and writers snuffing the gentle airs of Bloomsbury; the paper was a dull testament to liberal values: nothing in either record was remarkable. Yet by miraculous alchemy Martin infused the pages of the *New Statesman* with his obsessive, vehement, oddly melancholic personality—a tone that exactly reciprocated the bitter mood of his potential readership, the left-wing intelligentsia of the 1930s. Under his control the paper's circulation leapt from 15,000 in 1931 to 30,000 in 1939 and to about 90,000 by the end of the Second World War. He attracted contributors of outstanding calibre—both Harold Wilson and Barbara Castle wrote for the paper—and the *New Statesman* became compulsory reading at Cabinet level in many western countries.

Kingsley Martin was born on July 28, 1897, the son of a Unitarian minister; he was educated at Mill Hill and Magdalene College, Cambridge, where he read history, and in between served as a hospital orderly in France in 1914–18. From 1923 to 1927 he was an assistant lecturer in political science at the London School of Economics before joining the staff of the *Manchester Guardian* as a leader writer. Besides his work as a journalist Martin was the author of a dozen books all of which are compelling reading, immensely stimulating and stamped with his personality. These were for the most part either history or polemics such as *The Triumph of Palmerston* (1924); *French Liberal Thought in the Eighteenth Century* (1929); *The Magic of Monarchy* (1937); and *The Press the Public Wants* (1947). But he also wrote a biography of Harold Laski, and two volumes of autobiography. *Father Figures* and *Editor*.

Maschwitz, Eric (1901–1969). Writer and producer of many successful musical comedies and a pioneer of radio and television, Eric Maschwitz died on October 28, 1969. He had delighted audiences both before and during the Second World War with tuneful, charming, and somewhat nostalgic shows. *Balalaika* ran for 570 performances, and *Carissima* twelve years later for almost 500 performances. But the things for which he will be remembered in both Britain and America are the lyrics of "These Foolish Things" and "A Nightingale Sang in Berkeley Square."

Eric Maschwitz was born in Birmingham on June 10, 1901. He was educated at Repton school and at Caius College, Cambridge. In 1926 he joined the BBC and for six years was editor of *Radio Times*. In 1933 he became Director of Variety. He started the popular magazine programme "In Town Tonight," which had enormous audiences for many years. In 1937 he resigned, feeling that he needed "refuelling." He then concentrated on his musicals, for which he generally wrote both music and lyrics. After the success of *Balalaika* in 1936, *Paprika*, which was also set in eastern Europe, failed at first, but was later revived successfully with Binnie Hale in the lead and with a new title, *Magyar Melody*. In 1939 he produced the revue *New Faces*. During the war Maschwitz was a lieutenant-colonel in the Intelligence Corps and in this capacity went on a mission to North and South America. But he kept his hand in on his stage work: *Waltz Without End* was produced in 1942. It was based on the life of Chopin and was not a success. But in 1948 *Carissima*, for which he wrote particularly charming lyrics, had a good run.

In 1958 Maschwitz returned to the BBC as television Head of Light Entertainment, and in 1961 he became Assistant and Adviser to the Controller of Television Programmes. In 1963 he went over to ITV and Rediffusion appointed him producer in charge of special projects. He wrote a number of novels. But his most delightful book is his autobiography, *No Chip on My Shoulder*, the title of which sums up his attitude to life.

Maxwell, Ian Robert (born 1923). A former East European refugee from Nazism, with the bare minimum of formal education, Robert Maxwell built in the post-war years one of the world's largest empires in scientific book and journal publishing, the Pergamon Press. But at a shareholders' meeting in October 1969, he lost control of it to an American firm, Leasco, which earlier in the year had put a £25 million valuation on it in a take-over bid that was later withdrawn. Maxwell had bought Pergamon, then a small textbook firm, in 1951 for £13,000, convinced that there was a market for inexpensive scientific textbooks quickly produced. But he did not confine himself to textbooks. He was

one of the first publishers to realise that there was a market, industrial and academic, which had to have the latest scientific information and was not too concerned about the cost. Apart from his defeat over Pergamon, Maxwell had other disappointments during the year. His £34 million attempt to take over the *News of the World* failed in face of a merger proposal from the Australian newspaper magnate, Rupert Murdoch, and his later offer to buy the *Sun* newspaper from the International Publishing Corporation was also outbid by the Australian.

Born Jan Ludwig Hoch in Slatinske Doly, a Czechoslovakian village just over the border from Rumania, on June 10, 1923, he started school at 8, left at 10 and, at 15, had joined a Czech under-

Tom Mboya, assassinated in Kenya.

ground movement in the struggle against Hitler. He gave a false age to enlist in the Czech army, fought in France, and arrived in Britain in 1940. He returned to France in the Normandy landing as a sergeant, was commissioned in the field for his powers of leadership and outstanding bravery, and, the day after taking over his platoon in the West Surreys, won the Military Cross. His intellect is as undoubted as his bravery, and was shown not only by the way he mastered the complications of the business world to become a multimillionaire but also by his command of nine languages. Those languages helped him in his intelligence work with the occupation authorities in Germany at the end of the war and then, as a civilian, for the Foreign Office in Berlin. He won the Buckingham parliamentary seat for Labour in 1964 and retained it with an increased majority in 1966. Married to a cousin of Couve de Murville, the French statesman, he has eight children. When a son, a brilliant scholar, suffered severe head injuries in a car crash he founded the Robert Maxwell Fund for Brain Research.

Mboya, Thomas Joseph (1930–1969). Tom Mboya, the Kenyan Minister of Economic Planning, and one of the

founders of the modern state of Kenya, was shot dead by an assassin while shopping in Nairobi on July 5, 1969. He was born on August 15, 1930, the son of a sisal worker, and educated at the Holy Ghost College, Manju, the Royal Sanitary Institute's Medical Training School, where he qualified as a sanitary inspector, and Ruskin College, Oxford. After working for a short time (1951–52) for the Nairobi city council he became involved in political and trade union affairs, joining the Kenya African Union, and becoming general secretary of the Kenya local government workers' union. From 1953 to 1962 he was general secretary of the Kenya Federation of Labour, a post in which he wielded great power and influence, and in 1960 he became general secretary of the Kenya African National Union—the ruling party of Kenya—where his abilities as an organiser proved invaluable. Mboya was Minister of Labour (1962–63) and, following independence, Minister of Justice and Constitutional Affairs (1963–64), before receiving the Economic Planning portfolio. As the most prominent Luo in the Kikuyu-dominated K.A.N.U. party Tom Mboya had an importance in the Kenyan political scene that went beyond the limits of his exceptional political talents. He was an example of a man indisputably following political rather than tribal loyalties; in that, he was apparently ahead of his time. He married in 1962, and published *Freedom and After*, 1963.

Meir, Golda (born 1898). Into the able hands of this grey-haired 71-year-old grandmother was committed the peace of the Middle East and possibly the world in March 1969. Israel's fourth premier, Mrs. Meir took office as incidents escalated along the borders with Egypt, Syria and Jordan. Born in Kiev, she was taken at the age of 8 to the U.S.A. with her family. After graduating at a teachers' training college in Milwaukee, she became drawn to the Jewish homeland and in 1921 joined the slow trickle of Jews heading for Palestine.

Robert Maxwell, M.P. and publisher.

Israel's premier, Mrs. Golda Meir.

From 1921 to 1924 she worked at the Merhavia co-operative settlement as a labourer in the fields. Then she shifted to a building firm owned by Histadruth, the Jewish Labour Federation, where her organising talents won her a place in 1926 on the Women's Labour Council. Two years later she was secretary to the executive. During the Second World War she was a member of the Palestine government's economic council, and in 1946 she went to work in the Jewish Agency political department, of which she became head when other Zionist leaders were arrested during the post-war terrorism.

Israel was born in 1948 and Mrs. Meir, now a leading member of the Labour Party, was appointed her country's first envoy to the U.S.S.R. She returned in 1949 and joined the Cabinet as Minister of Labour. But it was as Foreign Minister, which post she took in 1956, that she became a world figure. During ten years she established the links with the "third world" of Africa and Asia that were to stand her country in good stead during the six-day war of 1967. In 1966, "to have a rest," she became political head of the Labour Party. It was a rest that ended in the premiership, on the death of Mr. Levi Eshkol. Mrs. Meir is known affectionately as "the only brave man in the government," for her courage is legendary. In 1948, disguised as an Arab, she slipped through the lines to visit King Abdullah in a bid to stop the Arab-Israeli war. In 1957 she saved the life of Ben-Gurion during a bomb attack. In 1969 she needed all her bravery.

Mies van der Rohe, Ludwig (1886–1969). One of the acknowledged founders of modern architecture, Ludwig Mies van der Rohe died in Chicago on August 17, 1969, aged 83. Ludwig Mies—he added his mother's surname when he began to practise as an architect in 1912—was born at Aachen, the son of a master mason. As an apprentice in his father's yard Mies learnt the use of stone and, already a skilled mason and draughtsman, he went to Berlin in 1905 to work for the furniture designer, Bruno Paul, to learn the use of wood. In 1907 he built his first house, in the 18th-century manner, and in 1908 started work in the architect Peter Behrens' office where he met Walter Gropius and Le Corbusier. His work was interrupted by the 1914–18 war, in which he served as an enlisted man. On his return his work broke away from formal classicism and became original and daring: in 1919 he exhibited designs for steel and glass skyscrapers which revolutionised architecture, and led to his being commissioned to design the German pavilion for the 1929 international exhibition at Barcelona, hailed as one of the greatest buildings of the 20th century. Mies succeeded Gropius as director of the *Bauhaus* at Dessau in 1930, but closed the school in 1933. In 1937, because of disagreements with the Nazis, he

Ludwig Mies van der Rohe died.

emigrated to the U.S.A. to become director of the department of architecture at the Illinois Institute of Technology, Chicago. He took American citizenship in 1944.

The stark beauty of his designs bore out the truth of his maxim "Less is more." Among them are the bronze-towered Seagram Building, New York; glass and metal apartment buildings on Lake Shore Drive, Chicago; and the New National Gallery, Berlin. In 1968, in conjunction with Lord Holford, Mies designed a controversial 290-ft.-high glass and steel tower for a site opposite the Mansion House in the City of London. His honours included the R.I.B.A. gold medal.

Miles, Sir Bernard (born 1907). The knighthood conferred on this actor-manager in the birthday honours of 1969 had been predictable from the success of his Mermaid Theatre. This pioneer modern playhouse with open stage recalling Elizabethan originals, the first theatre of any kind built in the City of London for 300 years, was opened by the Lord Mayor at Puddle Dock, Blackfriars, on May 28, 1959. Miles adapted from Fielding for the occasion a musical romp,

Bernard Miles was knighted.

Lock Up Your Daughters, which drew the town for months and was transferred to the West End and more than once revived. His open-plan theatre had been conceived in 1951, when he set out the garden of his North London home to produce *Dido and Aeneas* (with Mesdames Flagstad, Teyte, and Coates to sing). For a season in 1953 he transferred stage and tiring house into the Royal Exchange.

As a performer Bernard Miles has so excelled in the dialect of old codgers and rough diamonds that the notion became current of his being a countryman bred. In fact his birthplace lay no deeper in rusticity than Uxbridge; he attended its county school, also Pembroke College. Oxford, and was briefly a schoolmaster, People would overlook that the sinister visage and gritty voice suited to a sensational Iago with the war-time Old Vic, or to Long John Silver—a character of whom he seems to have taken lease in perpetuity—could be discarded for the urbane Inquisitor of *Saint Joan* or the languid, cultured Uncle Vanya. From first professionally entering as a messenger in *Richard the Third* in 1930, Miles explored the universe of make-believe, in provincial repertory as often as in the West End, helping to build or paint scenery, or to look after properties, whenever not acting. He portrayed rural types in music halls and on records. In the cinema this stalwart supporting player touched a peak as part-author, co-director, and star of the whimsical *Tawny Pipit.*

Murdoch, Keith Rupert (born 1931). Already the most impressive newspaper tycoon in Australia, Rupert Murdoch invaded Great Britain to great effect in 1969, acquiring control of one paper that was a national institution and revivifying another that was on the point of collapse. The son of the late Sir Keith Murdoch, a notable journalist, war correspondent, and newspaper proprietor, he was born at Melbourne on March 11, 1931, and educated at Geelong Grammar School, and at Oxford. During his school and university days he had little liking for sport, but showed a keen interest in politics and international affairs. In 1952, while he was at Oxford, his father died, leaving his son an important interest in News Ltd., a publishing company founded in Adelaide in 1922. Rupert's energy and ability had a far-reaching effect on the organisation. Today it publishes 14 major Australian newspapers, including *The Australian* (national), *The News* (Adelaide), *The Daily Mirror* (Sydney), *Truth* (Melbourne), *Sunday Truth* (Brisbane), and *The Sunday Times* (Perth); and owns, or has substantial interests in, numerous magazines, trade journals, television and radio stations, country and suburban newspapers, commercial printers, and establishments for the production and distribution of books and records. Murdoch founded *The Australian* in 1964 with the object of giving

Rupert Murdoch, with the first issue of his new *Sun* newspaper.

Australia a national newspaper. Originally produced in Canberra, it is now based on Sydney, and is printed simultaneously in Melbourne and Brisbane. Ever since its inception *The Australian* has observed a high standard of journalism and news presentation.

In the autumn of 1968, when Robert Maxwell made a take-over bid for the British Sunday newspaper, the *News of the World*, the owning family, the Carrs, called on the assistance of Murdoch and News Ltd. to fend it off, and in January 1969 he was appointed to the board. In the same month a majority of *News of the World* shareholders voted in favour of linking up with News Ltd., and in June Murdoch was appointed chairman of the organisation. Almost immediately he turned his attention to the *Sun*, the former *Daily Herald*, "official" daily organ of the trade union movement and Labour party, which the International Publishing Corporation (*Daily Mirror* group) had failed to rescue from approaching closure. After lengthy discussions with the trade unions Murdoch's offer for the *Sun* was accepted, and in November it appeared in a new tabloid form and lively dress that made it a formidable rival to the *Daily Mirror*.

In 1967, Murdoch married Miss Anna Tory, who made her own impression on London during the year.

Nabarro, Sir Gerald (born 1913). Ebullient, bewhiskered, broadcasting bureaucrat-baiter—as he and others see him—Nabarro has created many furores. But the biggest was over his claim, in February 1969, that he had "irrefutable evidence" that the cost of car licences was to leap from £25 to £35 in the April Budget. He had lseen the printed forms, he said. A Select Committee inquired if there had been a Budget leak but reported no foundation for the allegation. At the

Budget Chancellor Roy Jenkins told the Commons that the decision not to increase car tax was in a Treasury minute of December 31, 1968. But Sir Gerald still claimed victory in his campaign—car tax had not risen.

Born on June 29, 1913, in London, he left school at 14, joined the army at 15 (the King's Royal Rifle Corps because they recruited small men—he is 5 ft. 5 in.), and rose to staff-sergeant instructor. When 24 he turned to civilian business and, equally quickly, rose from labourer to manager and director. After a short spell back in the army as a lieutenant, his activities in running a factory were thought more important. He became an M.P. in 1950 and soon earned the nickname "Kidder from Kidderminster" for his persistent questioning. He has been a thorn in the side of every Chancellor of the Exchequer, especially spotlighting taxation anomalies, but he has had constructive success too, chiefly his Clean Air Act of 1956. He runs several

Sir Gerald Nabarro raised a storm.

companies, in publishing, machine tools, unit trusts, advertising, and marketing, is a governor of Birmingham University, made 968 speeches in one year (1967) before going down with tonsillitis, and drives 30,000 miles a year in his five cars, registered NAB1 to NAB5.

Newby, Percy Howard (born 1918). P. H. Newby, Controller of BBC Radio 3, was the winner of the first £5,000 Booker prize (see Fact Digest) for writing the "best novel of 1968," *Something to Answer For.* Born in 1918 at Crowborough, Sussex, in the house of Sir Arthur Conan Doyle, Newby was educated at Hanley Castle Grammar School, Worcester, and St. Paul's College, Cheltenham. He was called up in July 1939 and went to France with the R.A.M.C.; he came home, via St. Nazaire, in June 1940, and after a spell in Britain was sent to the Middle East. After the war he remained in that area, teaching English at the Fuad I University in Cairo, and it was there that he wrote his first novel, *A Journey into the Interior* (1946). It earned him a Rockefeller Foundation Atlantic Award in Literature, and this success persuaded him to give up teaching and return to England as a full-time writer. For three years he pushed a lonely pen before deciding, in 1949, that a writer's solitary life was too remote and joined the BBC. The previous year Newby had received the Somerset Maugham Prize for *Agents and Witnesses* and spent some time travelling in France and Italy; later a Smith-Mundt Fellowship allowed him to travel extensively in the U.S.A.

His literary mentors are Conrad and Dickens, and it was particularly the massive and dramatic impact of *Something to Answer For* in an English literary scene that is increasingly insipid that impressed the judges on the Booker panel. Other books of his include *Spirit of Jem* (1947); *Mariner Dances* (1948); *The Snow Pasture* (1949); *Maria Edgeworth* (1950); *The Young May Moon* (1950); *The Novel, 1945–50* (1951); *A Season in England* (1951); *A Step to Silence* (1952); *The Retreat* (1953); *The Picnic at Sakkara* (1955); *Revolution and Roses* (1957); *Ten Miles From Anywhere* (1958); *A Guest and His Going*(1959); *The Barbary Light* (1962); *One of the Founders* (1965).

Oldham, Joseph Houldsworth (1874–1969). Dr. J. H. Oldham, who died on May 16, 1969, at the age of 94, managed to be one of the most influential Christian leaders of the 20th century without ever being widely known to the general public. Only the fact that since 1961 he had been honorary president of the World Council of Churches outwardly signified the stature of this slim very deaf Scotsman who trained for the Presbyterian ministry but was never in the event ordained. He gave full-time life-long service to the Churches as an Anglican layman. Perhaps no man did more to create the modern ecumenical movement and so to transform the relationships between the Churches of the world. He was secretary of the great World Missionary Conference held at Edinburgh in 1910, from which that movement is usually held to date. He became the first ecumenical "civil servant," by acting as secretary of the International Missionary Council that sprang from that conference. Even in 1920 he was envisaging "something like a world league of Churches," and his work helped to bring it about. He was one of the first Christians to see the immense importance of an emergent Africa, and it has been suggested that modern Kenya as a multi-racial society could not have come into being without Oldham's work. He saw, too, the significance of the rise of Hitler and other dictators, and by the great conference on "Church, Community, and State" held at Oxford in 1937, and attended by churchmen from all over the world (but *not* from Nazi Germany), prepared Christians for the holocaust that was coming. In war-time Britain Oldham produced a *Christian News-Letter* which had great influence in clarifying the kind of society towards which Christians ought to work.

Paisley, Ian Richard Kyle (born 1926). Militant leader of the extreme Protestants of Northern Ireland, Rev. Ian Paisley came out of Belfast prison and to within an ace of toppling the then prime minister of Ulster, Captain Terence O'Neill, at the 1969 general election. He went on to lead marches, demonstrations, and protests during the whole of the new "troubles," preaching against Roman Catholicism and those who would, he said, "destroy the constitution of Northern Ireland." Television news programmes made an international figure of this "ancestral foghorn of beleaguered anti-Popery" (*The Times*'s memorable phrase), and he made his mark, too, in the U.S.A., where he flew as a counter-blast to Bernadette Devlin's successful visit a few weeks before.

Born at Ballymena, co. Antrim, Paisley went to the local Academy and served in the R.A.F., merchant navy, and Ulster police before studying theology at colleges in Belfast, Wales, and the U.S.A. A formidable Bible scholar, he was ordained by his father, a Baptist preacher, in 1946, and in 1951 formed the "Free Presbyterian Church of Ulster," of which he became the self-styled Moderator. His doctorate of divinity was awarded by the Bob Jones University of Greenville, South Carolina. Early meetings in a shabby brick hall in Belfast's working-class Protestant districts brought a membership of 1,000 by 1961. Eight years later the numbers had swelled to an estimated 10,000, and Paisley built the largest mission hall in the world, a £500,000 cathedral-type church (see page 129). As the ecumenical movement grew, his 6-foot 17-stone frame became a natural rallying point for Protestants rejecting the Catholic embrace. Soon his

Lord's Day services at the Ulster Hall, Belfast, were drawing capacity 1,600-strong crowds; in 24 churches throughout Ulster, 15 of his ministers preached the word. In 1966 Paisley made headlines by trying to gatecrash the Archbishop of Canterbury's meeting with the Pope in Rome; the Italian police returned him to London. The same year he served three months in jail for refusing to be bound over. In January 1969 he succeeded in disrupting a service at St. Paul's attended by Cardinal Heenan, but in June he failed to enter Switzerland to protest against the Pope's visit to the Geneva headquarters of the World Council of Churches. In jail for unlawful assembly, he emerged under the general amnesty of May 6. By now his activities had become as much political as religious: in O'Neill's own constituency he had won 6,331 votes to Captain O'Neill's 7,745 in the general election in February, and he had rejoiced when his slogan "O'Neill must go" was borne out by the Prime Minister's resignation in April.

Papen, Franz von (1879–1969). "The Fox," as he was universally called—a cunning intriguer whose plots almost always went awry through oversight or misjudgement—von Papen was the former German chancellor who, believing he had frustrated Adolf Hitler's rise to power, actually placed him in the saddle in 1933. He died on May 2, 1969, having evaded all the just consequences of his acts and outlived all the other historic characters of the immediate pre-war period. A typical representative of the German landed gentry and a Roman Catholic, von Papen was born on October 29, 1879, in Westphalia, entered the army at 19, and at 26 married the daughter of a rich Saarland industrialist. The outbreak of the First World War in 1914 found him military attaché at the German embassy in Mexico. Transferred to Washington, he set up an espionage and sabotage network which was soon unmasked and its author was deported.

Having won the Iron Cross on the Western Front, he was sent to assist Germany's ally Turkey to raise rebellion in British-held territory in the Middle East and Africa, but again his plans failed.

During the 1920s von Papen, through his associations with the landed gentry, the industrialists, and the army, made himself a Centre party leader in Prussia, and in 1932 he became Chancellor (prime minister) of Germany. He failed, however, to win party support and was soon replaced. Thereupon he entered into an unholy alliance with Hitler, leader of the fiercely active though still small National Socialist (Nazi) Party, mistakenly believing that in a coalition the forces of the right could contain Hitler's fire. On the ill-fated January 30, 1933, the coalition was formed: Hitler was Chancellor, von Papen Vice-Chancellor, and the Nazi leaders Goering and Frick were in the cabinet. The Nazis seized their opportunity: the Reichstag was burnt down and the Communist party outlawed; a falsified election in March "confirmed" them in power; mass arrests and concentration camps were instituted. Von Papen was ousted, and in the "purge" of June 30, 1934, he was lucky to escape alive. Yet a month later "the Fox" was exercising his talent for intrigue as Hitler's ambassador in Vienna in preparation for the take-over of Austria in March 1938. His reward was the war-time German embassy in neutral Turkey, where he was plotting again from 1939 to 1944. He it was who employed the famous spy "Cicero" who, having obtained the post of valet to the British ambassador, photographed many Allied secret documents. After the war, von Papen was put on trial before the Nuremberg war crimes tribunal, but was acquitted. A German denazification court sentenced him to eight years in a labour camp, but he was released almost at once. He lived out the rest of his life uneventfully and comfortably, writing his own accounts of his devious life in his Memoirs (1952) and in *The Collapse of a Democracy 1930–33* (1968).

Franz von Papen (*left*), with German Nazi leader Adolf Hitler in 1934.

Payne, Jack (1900–1969). This famous British band-leader and impresario died on December 4, 1969. It was as the first director of the BBC Dance Orchestra that he shot to fame in 1928, and for the next four years he worked for the Corporation, broadcasting some 30,000 tunes, before handing his BBC baton to Henry Hall. Payne was born in Leamington, into a musical family—it is on record that his mother was a star of the local madrigal society— but it was during the Great War, while serving in the Royal Flying Corps, that he founded a mess dance band and found his vocation. After the war (inspired by the success of Paul Whiteman in the U.S.A.) he formed a highly successful professional band and etched his name indelibly on the era of the big dance band in Britain, along with Ambrose, Geraldo, Debroy Somers, and Jack Hylton. Payne did not stay in the big band business for long after the Second World War, but turned to theatrical production and other interests; but he preserved some links with popular music, and his face was familiar to the British TV public of the late 1950s and early 1960s. As a businessman Payne was not a great success, and in 1965 he went bankrupt with liabilities of £48,000. He was married to Peggy Cochrane, the pianist and singer. "Say It With Music" was Jack Payne's signature tune, and millions remember with pleasure how it ushered in their daily ration of the popular tunes of the late 1920s and early 1930s.

Pevsner, Sir Nikolaus (born 1902). While looking every inch the European scholar he is, big round spectacles gleaming below high brow and balding dome, Pevsner has so thoroughly absorbed the culture of his adopted country that a knighthood in the birthday honours of 1969 was felt to be in appreciation of a British expert on art who had built a career by combining four branches—as historian, lecturer, journalist, and encyclopedist. His life story from an academic home in Germany to a Victorian terrace house in Hampstead shows an astonishing curve, with what must have seemed utter nadir in 1940. Born on January 30, 1902, and educated at Leipzig, he became known there and at sister universities as an authority on baroque art. Jewish ancestry induced him in 1933 to emigrate from Göttingen, landing in England possessed of 10 marks. He taught Italian at the Courtauld Institute, then spent four years studying industrial design with Gordon Russell. The war reduced this bookish alien to navvying after air raids in Kentish Town and firewatching at Birkbeck College. There on duty he wrote in manuscript and from memory his *Outline of European Architecture*, a continuing best-seller. After the war, Penguin Books rehabilitated Pevsner. He was chosen as their art editor and put in charge of a 50-volume history; he undertook virtu-

Nikolaus Pevsner was knighted.

ally single-handed the monumental series on *The Buildings of England*, still unfinished after 20 years because Pevsner will tackle only one county each spring and another each autumn, visiting personally every place he describes. He edited the *Architectural Review*, became a Royal Fine Art Commissioner, and was chairman of the Victorian Society. The R.I.B.A. bestowed on him its gold medal for architecture. As Slade professor of fine art at Cambridge, 1949–55, he drew audiences so large that the examination schools were needed to hold them, and he was retained for a weekly lecture after the appointment ended. He was made C.B.E. in 1953. Complete naturalisation was implied by the theme of his Reith lectures for the BBC in 1955—*The Englishness of English Art*.

Phillips, Montague Fawcett (1885–1969). This well-known composer of many well-loved ballads died at Esher on January 4. 1969, at the age of 83. Born in London on November 13, 1885, he studied at the Royal Academy of Music where he distinguished himself and carried away many prizes for composition and organ playing. He became famous with the production of his light opera *The Rebel Maid* in 1921. Although this romantic and imaginative show enjoyed great success, Phillips concentrated on concert rather than theatre music. In his youth, while still practising as an organist, he composed over 150 songs that enjoyed and retain considerable popularity; they included *Sing, Joyous Bird; April is a Lady; Wake Up!; The Dawn Has a Song; O Ship of My Delight;* and *Sing Merrily To-day*. Indeed his talent was for light music and his serious work failed to establish his reputation, although his Symphony in C minor; the *Charles II* overture; *The Death of Admiral Blake* (for baritone, chorus, and orchestra); Piano Concerto (No. 2) in E; and the *In Praise of My Country* overture were notable for technical skill. His Shakespearean Scherzo (1942) and Sinfonietta for orchestra (1946) were more successful, with complementary

technique and emotional content. Montague Phillips, who was professor of harmony and composition at the Royal Academy of Music, was married to the well-known light operatic soprano Clara Butterworth.

Pompidou, Georges (born 1911). Following his success in the French presidential elections Georges Pompidou, de Gaulle's protégé assumed the office of his mentor on June 20, 1969. The bushy-browed president was born on July 5, 1911, in the small village of Montbouif, in the department of Cantal, in the South West of France, the son of a schoolmaster and a schoolmistress. Pompidou's father, whose academic ambitions had been frustrated by the First World War, was intensely ambitious for his son, and to this paternal drive the youthful Georges added an intellect of the first order. A model pupil, he studied at both the *Ecole Normale Supérieure,* (emerging first from France's most exacting competitive examination) and the *Ecole Libre des Sciences Politiques.* He became a teacher in Marseilles and Paris. On the liberation of France in 1944 he joined General de Gaulle's staff as educational adviser, but in 1946 left education for banking, joining the house of Rothschild. During this period he published an anthology of French poetry with an introduction of great style and scholarship.

Pompidou regularly visited de Gaulle in retirement at Colombey-les-deux-Eglises, and when the General returned to power in 1958 he was appointed *Directeur de Cabinet,* chief private political secretary to the President. Four years later, in April 1962, when at 50 he was still almost unknown to the French public (and not even a member of the official Gaullist party), de Gaulle told him "I am making you Prime Minister of France, and you have no right to refuse." But after the 1968 elections, held in the wake of the student-worker riots, in which the Gaullists romped home, the General made Couve de Murville his Prime Minister and sent the surprised Pompidou

President Georges Pompidou.

a letter informing him that he should hold himself "ready to accomplish any mission and assume any mandate which one day the nation might entrust to you." This ambiguous statement perhaps indicated that Pompidou's were the shoulders on which de Gaulle wished his mantle to descend.

Portman, Eric (1903–1969). This British stage and film actor died, aged 66, on December 7, 1969, at his Cornish home. He was born on July 13, 1903, in Yorkshire, and, on leaving Rishworth School, worked as a shop assistant in a Leeds store. The youthful Portman, however, nursed theatrical ambitions and became a leading member of the Halifax Opera Society. This led, in 1923, to his joining Robert Courtneidge's Shakespeare Company while it was playing at the Grand Theatre, Leeds. The following year saw his first professional speaking part at the Victoria Theatre, Sunderland, and his arrival in London with the company in *The Comedy of Errors.* In 1925 he won fame in *White Cargo,* and he then remained in contemporary plays for two years before joining the Old Vic. Portman's reputation as a Shavian actor was established in 1929 when he played the brooding Undershaft in Shaw's *Major Barbara,* at Wyndham's Theatre. During the 1930s he was one of the leading actors in London and New York, and he made his name in films during the war with *49th Parallel, One of Our Aircraft is Missing, We Dive at Dawn,* and *Millions Like Us.*

After the war Portman had great West End successes in Terence Rattigan's *The Browning Version* and *Separate Tables,* and Graham Greene's *The Living Room.* During the 1950s he disappeared from the London scene and was in the U.S.A. for eight years exclusively. On his return he failed to regain his former niche in the West End, although he continued to work until 1968, when his doctors advised him to retire.

Potter, Stephen (1900–1969). This British humorist, biographer, versifier, and inventor of Gamesmanship, died on December 2, 1969. He was born in Clapham on February 1, 1900, and educated at Westminster and Merton College, Oxford, where he read English. On taking his degree, he was for a while secretary to Henry Arthur Jones, the dramatist, and in 1926 he became a lecturer in English at London University. His pen was not idle: his first novel, *The Young Man,* came out in 1929; learned papers on his two literary hobby-horses, D. H. Lawrence and S. T. Coleridge, followed, together with the edited letters of Mrs. Coleridge, *Minnow Among Tritons* (1934), and the *Nonesuch Coleridge.* Having summed up his experience as an English don in the aptly titled *The Muse in Chains* (1937), he entered the BBC as a writer-producer. Here he remained throughout the war,

specialising in programmes of a literary flavour and documentaries concerning the conflict. It was in 1946 that he brought out the highly successful *How* series with Joyce Grenfell. The following year (during which *How to be good at games* was broadcast) saw the promulgation of the concept with which his name is synonymous, in his book *Gamesmanship.* From this inspired invention stemmed a mint of coinings by himself and others—including (thanks to Adlai Stevenson) "brinkmanship" to describe the foreign policy of John Foster Dulles. Gamesmanship is adequately explained by the book's sub-title—*The Art of Winning Games Without Actually Cheating. Lifemanship* (1950) inspired the film *School for Scoundrels* in which, thanks to a course in *One-Upmanship* (1952) from Alastair Sim, Ian Carmichael surmounted diffidence to achieve scoundrelhood and outbounder Terry Thomas.

Other books of Stephen Potter's include *Potter on America* (1956); *Supermanship* (1958); an autobiography, *Steps to Immaturity* (1959); *Anti-Woo* (1965); *The Adventures of a Clasperchoice* (1964); and *The Complete Golf Gamesmanship* (1968).

Prichard, Katharine Susannah (1883–1969). This distinguished Australian writer, whose career covered more than 60 years, died at Greenmount, Western Australia, on October 2, 1969. Many of her works had been published in other countries, and translated into a number of languages, including Russian and Chinese. Katharine Prichard was born at Levuka, Fiji, on December 4, 1883, and was taken to Australia in infancy. She spent part of her childhood in Tasmania, and was educated at South Melbourne College. For a time she worked as a governess in Australian country areas, gathering experience that later formed the background of her novels. Moving to London, she worked for six years as a free-lance journalist, contributing to English and French periodicals. In 1915 she won Hodder and Stoughton's £1,000 prize in an all-British novel competition with her work *The Pioneers.* Returning to Australia, she devoted the rest of her life to writing novels, many with a West Australian background. They include *Black Opal* (1921), *Working Bullocks* (1926), *The Wild Oats of Han* (1928), *Haxby's Circus* (1930), *Intimate Strangers* (1937), *Potch and Colour* (1944), *Child of the Hurricane* (1964), and *Subtle Flame* (1967). Her trilogy *The Roaring Nineties* (1946), *Golden Miles* (1948), and *Winged Seeds* (1950) have for their scene the goldfields of Western Australia from the first rush to the organised commercial development of today. Probably her best-known work is *Coonardoo* (1929), which tells the tangled poignant story of a western cattleman's love for an aboriginal girl. In the 1940s Katharine Susannah Prichard was described by a noted

American literary critic as "unquestionably the most important living fiction writer of Australia," an opinion that is widely held. Radical in her outlook, she was a foundation member of the Australian Communist Party and a member until her death. In 1919 she married Capt. Hugh Throssell, V.C., who died in 1933.

Rayne, Sir Max (born 1918). The "shy millionaire" who gave away a £2 million fortune to help others was knighted in the 1969 New Year honours after a decade of silent good works. It was not until he was revealed as the man who gave the nation £225,000 to save Cézanne's *Les Grandes Baigneuses* from going abroad in 1964 that the property tycoon began to emerge as a leading philanthropist. The son of an immigrant Jewish tailor from Poland, Max Rayne was born in the East End of London. He went to grammar school on a scholarship before joining his father's business, studying law by night at University College, London. During the Second World War he served with the R.A.F. It was in 1947 when he and his father bought a house in Wigmore Street for their business, disliked it, and sub-let it that Rayne realised the tremendous profit potential of property. "I was already interested in building. It's rather a masculine thing to want to build something," he said later. "So it was easy to drift into property." His first investment of £1,250 produced a colossal £900,000 profit. In 1948 he founded the British Commercial Property Investment Trust and joined the board of the Sanitas Trust. As the post-war building boom swept him upwards, Rayne did not forget his origins. Two years after becoming chairman of the London Merchant Securities financial octopus in 1960, he launched the Max Rayne Foundation to channel his philanthropy. In his £70,000 home in Hampstead he kept a sculpture of a lonely child, made at a displaced persons' camp, "to keep one in his place." Among his recorded gifts were £100,000 to St. Anne's College, Oxford; £750,000 to St. Thomas's Hospital, London, of which he became a governor in 1962; and, to celebrate his parents' golden wedding in 1967, £50,000 for a block of old people's flats in Wandsworth. He married his second wife, the former Lady Jane Vane-Tempest-Stewart sister of the Marquis of Londonderry and friend of the royal family, in 1965. A daughter was born the following year.

Refshauge, Sir William Dudley (born 1913). The announcement in August 1969 that Major-General Sir William Refshauge had been appointed chairman of the executive board of the World Health Organisation added another mark of esteem to an Australian medical man who has given outstanding service to his country and his profession. Refshauge was born on April 3, 1913, and educated at Scotch College, Melbourne, and

Melbourne University. His interest in the Australian army began in 1930, when he enlisted as a member of the Scotch College cadet corps. He joined up at the outbreak of the Second World War, and was a regimental medical officer, a commander of field ambulances, and finally director of medical services with the 7th Division. In seven years with the A.I.F. he served in the Western Desert, Greece, Crete, Wau-Mubo, Salamaua, Ramu Valley, and North Borneo. He was awarded the O.B.E. in 1944, and was mentioned in dispatches four times. After the war he was in civil practice until February 1948, when he became medical superintendent of the Royal Women's Hospital, Melbourne, until 1951. In May of that year he returned to the army as deputy director-general and major-general in 1955, when he was also appointed honorary physician to the Queen. In 1960 he became Commonwealth Director-General of Health. He was created C.B.E. in 1959, and knighted in 1966.

Richardson, Victor York (1894–1969). "Vic" Richardson, who died at Adelaide on October 29, 1969, was one of the greatest all-round sportsmen that Australia has produced, and his high standard of conduct in all fields was in keeping with his physical powers. Known best as a cricketer, he also excelled in Australian National football (in which he captained South Australia), in lacrosse, baseball, basketball, and tennis. He was born at Adelaide on September 7, 1894, and educated at Kyre (now Scotch) College in that city. He first played cricket for his State in 1919, and for Australia during the English tour of 1924–25. He was vice-captain of the Australian team that toured England in 1930, and acted in the same capacity during the turbulent English visit of 1932–33. He led Australia in South Africa during 1935–36, and South Australia in Sheffield Shield competitions for several seasons. In first-class cricket he scored 10,714 runs at an average of 37.5 runs per innings, and at the same time proved himself one of the finest fieldsmen of his day. During the Second World War Richardson served with the R.A.A.F. in Australia and India. In 1954 he was awarded the O.B.E. for his services to cricket. In later years his authoritative, well-expressed radio commentaries on cricket gained him a large and appreciative audience.

Rose, Lionel (born 1948). An Australian aboriginal, boxing champion Rose capped a career of notable "firsts" when he was named Australian of the Year 1968 and thus joined a distinguished group which has included Sir Macfarlane Burnet, Joan Sutherland, Sir John Eccles, and Sir Robert Helpmann. The award went to an aboriginal for the first time to provide apt national recognition for the first-ever world-title success by a member of his race in any sport.

Born the eldest of eight children near

Lionel Rose, "Australian of the Year."

Drouin in the Gippsland district of Victoria on June 21, 1948, Rose was the son of a fair-ground fighter who, even though he boxed sometimes a dozen times a day when business was brisk, found it hard to provide for his family. Lionel admits he had little time for school and often skipped the long trek to class. He started work at 14 in a timber mill and began taking his first interest in boxing at the Warragul Youth Club. Under the instruction of Frank Oakes he ran up a series of victories in amateur bouts, won the amateur national flyweight championship in 1964, and appeared a certainty for the Tokyo Olympics team until he was beaten in the trials. About the same time Rose's father died and, needing extra cash to help support the family of nine, Lionel turned professional under the management of Jack Rennie. His first "pro" fight brought him only a £25 purse, but within two years he had arrived on the Australian fight scene by winning the national bantamweight championship from Noel Kunde when only 18 years of age. Rose moved on to the world scene a few months before his 20th birthday when as a late substitute he shocked the boxing world by winning the world bantamweight title from the Japanese holder, Masahiko "Fighting" Harada, on points in Tokyo. The victory brought Rose a hero's civic welcome through the streets of Melbourne, and an M.B.E. Rose journeyed to Tokyo again to defend his title against Takao Sakurai in July 1968; made another title defence in Los Angeles against Chucho Castillo later the same year; and defended the title for the third time against Britain's Alan Rudkin in March 1969 in Melbourne. He finally lost the title to the Mexican Ruben Olivares in Los Angeles in August 1969.

Russell, Charles (1906–1969). The famous white jazz clarinettist "Pee Wee" Russell died in Alexandria, Virginia, on February 16, 1969, at the age of 62. "You take each solo like it was the last one you were going to play in your life," he once said referring to his inimitable,

unorthodox solo flights. "If you miss, you miss. If you get lucky, you get lucky—but you take a chance. With it goes plenty of mistakes, but the more you try the luckier you are." Bizarre invention, growls, grunts, squeaks, fluttering runs, and odd angular sounds were the rich harvest of this adventurous philosophy which fascinated jazz listeners for over 40 years. Although he was usually heard with Dixieland bands, his solos were so idiosyncratic they defied categorisation and were considered by some to be a significant break with tradition. "He does with musical phrases just what Joyce did with words," the jazz critic Carlton Brown once wrote. "He breaks them up, violently rearranges their structure and accustomed order, and puts them together into fascinating new patterns." In the early days of jazz Pee Wee played with Bix Beiderbecke in St. Louis, the city of his birth, moving to Chicago in 1926, the time of jazz's great flight north. In 1927 he moved to New York to play with Red Nichols. Despite his Dixieland tag, during his long career Russell was associated with the big bands of Paul Specht and Bobby Hackett, and with such names as Thelonious Monk, Jimmy Giuffre, and Duke Ellington.

Saud, Ibn Abdul-Aziz (1902–1969). Ex-King Saud of Saudi Arabia, who died in Athens on February 23, 1969, presented to Western eyes the bizarre figure of a medieval prince decked out with the expensive trappings of 20th-century technology. One of the legends told of him is that he used to select concubines from his well-stocked harem by means of closed-circuit television. Such staggering contrasts in feudal whim and modern means typified the man, all-powerful ruler of a backward state squandering incredible wealth provided by that lifeblood of the machine age—oil. Second of the 32 sons of King Ibn Saud, he was born in Kuwait (1902) where his family was living in exile after being driven by the Turks out of their Kingdom of Nejd. Soon after Saud's birth his father succeeded in recapturing Riyadh,

Ex-King Saud of Saudi Arabia.

the dynastic capital, from which he went on to conquer most of the Arabian peninsula. By 1926 he had driven the Hashemite family from the throne of the Hejaz, and in 1932 he formed the combined kingdom of Saudi Arabia. Prince Saud was groomed to succeed his father: in 1933 he was made Crown Prince and later Viceroy of Nejd and commander-in-chief. When Ibn Saud died in 1953 Saud assumed the throne. While following his father's domestic policy of strengthening alliances among Arabian tribes by making numerous marriages—yet keeping the Koranic law by which no man can have more than four wives at a time—he was at the same time led by expediency to join the despised republics of Egypt and Syria in the Arab solidarity bloc, in 1956. His friendship with Nasser was shortlived, however, and when civil war broke out in the Yemen (1962) the two rulers were at war by proxy, with Saud supplying the Royalists and Nasser sending his army in to support the Republicans. Despite his massive oil revenues Saud was unable to bring financial stability to his kingdom and in 1958 he was forced by family pressure to hand over executive power to his able half-brother Crown Prince Faisal. Saud came back to power in 1960, but after a further crisis he recalled Faisal in 1962, and by 1964 had conceded all power to him. Dogged by bad health, Saud spent most of his remaining years seeking medical treatment in various Western countries.

Sheppard, David Stuart (born 1929). Nomination to a bishopric before one's fortieth birthday is rare; within fourteen years of ordination, scarcely paralleled; and no one else has worn the mitre after an England cricket cap. In September 1969 Sheppard succeeded as Bishop of Woolwich when the Right Rev. John Robinson became dean of Trinity, Cambridge. Sheppard had spent eleven years as warden and chaplain of the Mayflower Family Centre, a non-denominational settlement at Canning Town in dockland; and declared he would go on dwelling in a working-class

David Sheppard, bishop of Woolwich.

district, so as not to become a Church bureaucrat. In earlier days he had been a curate in Islington, but never in charge of a parish. Sheppard was born at Reigate, attended preparatory school at Bognor, went on to Sherborne, and, after army service, to Trinity Hall, Cambridge. County cricket, for Sussex, he started as a schoolboy, and he skippered the university eleven in 1952, also heading the national batting averages. Next season he led his county. Then came theological studies at Ridley Hall, ending in ordination in St. Paul's Cathedral at Michaelmas 1955.

Sheppard's diffuse international career of 22 Test matches, beginning against West Indies in 1950, included a tour of Australia while an undergraduate. "Wisden's" prediction that he might captain England was fulfilled on Pakistan's visit in 1954 when Sir Leonard Hutton was twice unfit to play. Recalled against Australia in 1956, "the Rev" made 113 in "Laker's match." Australia saw him once more, opening the innings throughout the 1962–63 series and compiling another 113. Outspoken whenever he suspected racial discrimination, Sheppard refused to play against the 1960 cricketers from South Africa since *apartheid* had governed their selection; and in 1968 tried to censure the M.C.C. committee over its delayed choice of Basil D'Oliveira for an intended tour there. In the autobiographical *Parson's Pitch*, 1964, he expressed his views on ministry and sport alike.

Short, Hugh Oswald (1883–1969). The youngest of the three famous Short Brothers died on December 4, 1969. Horace, Eustace, and Oswald, scions of a Derbyshire family, formed the first British aircraft manufacturing company in 1908. Eustace and Oswald had started making balloons in London in 1898, and later built airships at Bedford. Horace joined them in the manufacture of aircraft—under licence from the Wright Brothers—first at Leysdown, Sheppey, and later at Eastchurch. After their first six planes, Moore-Brabazon approached them for a plane with which he could compete in the *Daily Mail* competition for the first circular mile flight in a British machine. When he won the prize (1909), Short Brothers had arrived. In 1914 they moved to Rochester, where they concentrated particularly on seaplanes and flying boats. After the First World War, they were early in the field with the use of aluminium alloys, and led the way in stressed-skin construction. By 1924 Horace was dead and by 1932 Eustace, and Oswald was in full control. With the designer Arthur Gouge he produced the Singapore military plane and the Sarafand. But Short became increasingly involved with administration, and the design of the successful commercial flying boats Calcutta, Empire, and Golden Hind was Gouge's responsibility. From the Empire flying boat evolved the famous Sunderland, which the R.A.F.

flew during the Second World War and afterwards until 1960. The four-engined Stirling bomber was another Short machine. The firm moved to Belfast after the war.

Sir Osbert Sitwell died in May.

Sitwell, Sir Osbert (1892–1969). Sir Francis Osbert Sacheverell Sitwell, the mannerist and connoisseur whose brilliant persiflage and literary baroque placed him upon an ornate and polished plinth far above the vulgar currents of the age, died at his villa in Italy on May 4, 1969. It was during the 1920s that the three Sitwells — Edith, Osbert, and Sacheverell—exploded like squibs among the ankles of the Philistines. Possessed of talent, breeding, and wealth, equipped with a flair for sensational remarks and the cultivation of personal eccentricity, the trio became renowned for exotic aesthetics and extravagant gestures. Sir Osbert, with his bitter verse and biting novels, was perhaps the most gifted of the three, and the one whose work is most likely to find favour with posterity.

He was born in London on December 6, 1892, the eldest son of Sir George Sitwell, Bt., whom he succeeded in 1943, and was educated, as he said, "during the holidays from Eton." He entered the army in 1911 and fought in France with the Grenadier Guards during the First World War, publishing his satirical war poems under the pseudonym of "Miles." In 1916 he collaborated with his sister Edith on a book of poems, *Twentieth Century Harlequinade.* The tone of his contribution was continued in *Argonaut and Juggernaut,* 1919; *The Winstonburg Line,* 1919; *Out of the Flame,* 1923; and *England Reclaimed,* 1927. As a novelist, *Before the Bombardment,* 1926, founded his reputation, and *The Man Who Lost Himself* confirmed it. His chef-d'oeuvre, however, remains his five exquisite and elaborate volumes of autobiography *Left Hand, Right Hand!* (1945), *The Scarlet Tree* (1946), *Great Morning* (1948), *Laughter in the next Room* (1949), and *Noble Essences* (1950). Sir Osbert was made C.B.E. in 1956 and C.H. in 1958. He was unmarried and lived during his old age at Montegufoni, near Florence.

Boris Spassky, chess champion.

Spassky, Boris (born 1937). Spassky became chess champion of the world on June 17, 1969. Three years earlier he had qualified to challenge the holder, Tigran Petrosian, but in a match of 24 games he narrowly failed to dethrone him and had to survive a series of eliminating contests before mounting a fresh challenge in Moscow in April 1969. Spassky began badly by losing with the white pieces; but after 8 games he was two up, and after 16 level. Then he gained three successive wins as white, interspersed with one draw and one defeat. The event ended, ironically on Petrosian's 40th birthday, at 12½–10½ in the challenger's favour. Critics crowed at the victory of the inventive combinations of Spassky over Petrosian's mastery of solid positions, for they thought the champion had become unexcitingly defensive. But Spassky spoke of the enormous strain such a long-drawn duel imposes; it would be fairer, he thought, to decide the title, as players of other games do, by a briefer series of tournaments. As matters stand, he will hold the championship until 1972.

This elegant Leningrad journalist of suave and methodical manners became famous beyond his own country as a youthful prodigy at chess. The English grand master Harry Golombek, opponent at a congress in 1953, predicted in print that Spassky would turn out the world's best. He was then ahead of his older contemporary Mikhail Tal (born 1936), a mercurial genius who preceded him to the chess pinnacles of the U.S.S.R. and, in 1960, of the world. A celebrated game between them in 1958, won by Tal after Spassky had refused a draw, seemed decisive for the immediate future of both, but in the long view was apparently not. Spassky was a decade in maturing, though he frequently performed on top board for the U.S.S.R. against other nations.

Stokes, Donald Gresham, Baron (born 1914). "Mr. Export" became "Lord Export" in January 1969 when Sir Donald Stokes, the former Leyland apprentice who rose to control nearly half of Britain's motor industry, was honoured with a life peerage for selling abroad. The son of the Plymouth, Devon, traffic manager, Stokes was born on March 22, 1914, and educated at Blundell's School and the Harris Institute of Technology, Preston. He had just started a student apprenticeship with Leyland Motors when the Second World War broke out and he joined up. Selling was already fascinating him more than production techniques and when he left the army, a R.E.M.E. colonel, at the end of the war he went to Leyland's then chief, Sir Henry Spurrier, and laid before him a blueprint for exporting. In 1946 he was made export development manager for Leyland and in 1950, aged 35, general sales and service chief. "It's no use making things," he said, "if you can't sell them. I'm not ashamed to tell my friends that I'm a salesman." By 1954 he was a member of the board. In 1960, when he became managing director of the Scammell lorry subsidiary, production was doubled. The Standard-Triumph

Lord Stokes, British-Leyland boss.

firm was taken over in 1961; in 1966 the prestige Rover company, followed. By then Stokes had been managing director of Leyland for three years. Already the Stokes export coups had become legendary. He had sold buses to Cuba and lorries to China in the teeth of American opposition, cut the Motor Show to clinch an export deal with the Shah of Persia, travelled a daunting 100,000 miles a year. In 1965 he became Sir Donald, though his workmen, many of whom he knew by their Christian names, persisted in calling him "God."

It was in January 1968 that Stokes came to the top of the heap. British Motor Holdings, makers of Austin, Morris, MG, Riley, Wolseley, Jaguar and Daimler cars, merged with the heavy-vehicle-oriented Leyland group. The £900 million a year giant, employing 200,000 men, became the third largest motor company—after Volkswagen and Fiat—in the world outside the U.S.A. Stokes was deputy chairman and managing director. When chairman Sir George Harriman of B.M.H. retired a year later with output up 16 per cent, Stokes took charge. "The economic miracle is just around the corner," he said. "A five per cent increase and we've got everyone licked."

Taylor, Robert (1912–1969). Spangler Arlington Brugh, who, as Robert Taylor, followed in the footsteps of Valentino as the last of the great Hollywood matinee idols, died, aged 57, in Santa Monica, California, on June 8, 1969. He was born at Filley, Nebraska, and educated at Doane College, Nebraska, and Pomona College, California, where he took a degree in liberal arts before becoming a medical student. While acting in a college production of *Journey's End* he was spotted by an M.G.M. talent scout and given a screen test and a contract. Thus began Taylor's long association with Metro-Goldwyn-Mayer which lasted 27 years—his entire acting career—and established a Hollywood record. Although he claimed to have no acting ability and to owe his success wholly to his good looks, he was, if not a brilliant performer, at least a competent one. Moreover his career spanned the age of the "personality star" when studios built up elaborate mystiques around the characters of their celebrities, and the films were merely the packages in which the stars were sold.'

He began with *Andy Hardy* (1934) and soon established himself as a leading romantic star in musicals, drama, and light comedy. During the war years he turned to more dramatic roles, in war films and melodramas such as *Waterloo Bridge* with Vivien Leigh, and *Undercurrent* with Katharine Hepburn. The post-war revival of the costume epic proved a boon to Robert Taylor whose powerful physical presence enabled him to dominate the screen where shorter, less glamorous actors were lost. He starred in such costumed romps as *Ivanhoe, Quo Vadis,* and *Quentin Durward.* In 1954 he married Ursula Thiess, the German actress (a first marriage was dissolved in

Robert Taylor, Hollywood idol.

1951), who was at his besdide at the time of his death. He had been seriously ill since the removal of a lung in October 1968. Others among Robert Taylor's better known films are: *Johnny Eager, Bataan, Song of Russia, Knights of the Round Table, A House is not a Home,* and *Return of the Gunfighter.*

Traven, B. (1890?–1969). A shroud of romantic mystery surrounds the identity of the famous writer who signed himself B. Traven and who died in Mexico City on March 26, 1969. For B. Traven, author of *The Treasure of the Sierra Madre,* never revealed his identity. This eccentricity inspired bizarre guesses: some believed him to be the reincarnation of Jack London; others that he was a bankrupt Hohenzollern princeling, a refugee Bavarian socialist, an Austrian archduke, an American negro on the run, a leper, an explorer of the Arctic, the bastard son of the Kaiser, or a millionaire industrialist who wrote to salve his conscience. It was indeed not the neurosis associated with luxury but the stresses of poverty that provided Traven with his themes. His books were tough, raw, packed with action and the cry of human misery: sickness and death stalked their pages. In 1947 an incident occurred which was to lead to his almost certain identification. In that year Warner Brothers began filming *The Treasure of the Sierra Madre* and the director John Huston met a man in Mexico City who claimed to be Traven's "agent," Hal Croves, a translator from Acapulco. Huston was convinced that Croves was in fact Traven. The translator disappeared only to be rediscovered by a Mexican reporter who, when checking Mexican immigration records, found a Berick Traaren Torsvan who had been born in Chicago on March 5, 1890, the son of Scandinavian parents. The journalist succeeded in tracking down this individual and by bribing a servant came into possession of a letter with a royalty payment for B. Traven.

Besides *The Treasure of the Sierra Madre,* B. Traven also published *The Bride of the Jungle, The Death Ship, The Rebellion of the Hanged, The General, White Rose, The Creation of the Sun and the Moon,* and some short stories.

Tshombe, Moise Kapenda (1919–1969). Moise Tshombe, negro politician extraordinary, at one time self-styled president of the Congo's secessionist province of Katanga, and later premier of the re-united Congo itself, died under mysterious circumstances in detention near Algiers, the news being announced on June 30, 1969. He was born on November 10, 1919, at Musumba, near the Katangan provincial capital then called Elisabethville. His father, a successful African businessman, was over-indulgent to his son, who acquired expensive tastes—particularly for champagne and women—and a vigorous flamboyance of character. Educated at a Methodist mission school, he entered his father's business—a chain of stores and

an hotel—which he inherited in 1951 and soon dissipated. Declared bankrupt, he turned to politics, sat as a member of the Katangan provincial council, and in 1959 was a founder and president of the Katangese party Conakat. One of the African leaders summoned to Brussels in January 1960 to a round table conference to plan an independent Congo, he argued in favour of a loose confederation. On June 30 independence came, and with it chaos: the army mutinied, law and order broke down, tribal conflict prevailed, and Tshombe, then provincial president of Katanga, seized his chance and declared the richest of the country's six provinces independent. The Congo government (then led by Kasavubu as president and Patrice Lumumba as premier) was unable to take effective measures against him and called in the United Nations.

Nevertheless Katanga maintained its precarious secession for three years until overwhelmed by the last of three onslaughts by U.N. troops in January 1963, when Tshombe fled to Spain. Eighteen months later, the Congo was in such a state that President Kasavubu, with the support of General Joseph Mobutu, asked the former rebel to return as prime minister. As premier of the Congo, Tshombe fought to prevent the disintegration of the country he had previously torn asunder. In elections held in 1965 his party polled well and received a small majority in the legislature, but Kasavubu, jealous of his own position, dismissed him. Chaos returned until in November a military coup led by Mobutu ousted Kasavubu, and Tshombe again packed his bags and went into exile in Spain. Here he dabbled in business ventures and plotted his return to Congo politics until July 1, 1967, when a plane in which he was travelling was hijacked over the Mediterranean and flown to Algiers where he was imprisoned. The Mobutu regime had sentenced him to death in absentia, and the Algerian government hesitated to hand him over but at the same time was unwilling to let him go free. A certain

Moise Tshombe, Congolese rebel.

suspicion was attached to his death after two years' incarceration, for it was announced on the very anniversary of the date originally proposed by the Mobutu regime for his execution. But an autopsy performed by eleven surgeons under a professor from Marseilles pronounced that Tshombe had died of a heart attack.

Victoria Eugénie (Ena), Ex-Queen of Spain (1887–1969). The former Queen Ena of Spain, consort of the last Spanish monarch the late King Alfonso XIII, died in Lausanne, Switzerland, on April 15, 1969. A grandchild of Queen Victoria, she was born at Balmoral on October 24, 1887, the daughter of Princess Beatrice, Victoria's youngest child, and Prince Henry of the house of Battenberg (changed to Mountbatten in 1917). The young princess was christened Victoria Eugénie Julia Ena. This last name, by which she was known to the family, was a mistake: her mother had written the Gaelic name *Eua,* which was misread. She made her debut in London in 1905, as delectable a maiden as any that were at that moment on the European royal

Victoria Eugénie, ex-Queen of Spain.

marriage market. Her charms were first felt by the Russian Grand Duke Boris; he was, however, forestalled by one of even greater rank and fortune. The young king Alfonso of Spain was at that time touring the monarchies of Europe with a list of eligible princesses in his pocket. Although Victoria Eugénie did not figure on it, once he had met her no other would do. They were married in Madrid on May 31, 1906. A bitter incident marked the occasion. As they passed down a thronged sun-soaked street, a bomb concealed in a bouquet of flowers tossed by an anarchist from a balcony towards the happy couple exploded near their open carriage and killed 18 people. The couple were unhurt, but it was an omen. Sadness was to haunt Queen Ena's life. Alfonso's amatory indiscretions were soon the subject of comment; two of her sons suffered from that dreadful "royal disease" haemophilia (both died in motoring accidents), and another prince was afflicted with deafness and a disorder of speech; above all in 1931 Spain became a republic. On April 14, 1931, Alfonso fled from Spain, and on the following day his Queen departed with more dignity, by royal train and British warship. From this time the royal exiles lived apart, and on her estranged husband's death, in 1941, Victoria Eugénie made her home in Lausanne. The Spanish government granted her a life annuity in 1955. In 1968, at the age of 80, the ex-Queen entered Spain for the first time since her husband's fall, for the christening of her great-grandson Prince Felipe. A cheering crowd of 15,000 monarchists greeted her arrival in Madrid, a regal, erect, remote example of the *ancien régime.*

Voroshilov, Klimenti Yefrimovitch (1881–1969). Marshal Voroshilov, Red Army general and former President of the Soviet Union, died on December 3, 1969. "Klim" Voroshilov was born on February 4, 1881, in the village of Verkhne, Dnepropetrovsk. He started work at 7, first in the mines and later as a shepherd, and first went to school at 13, leaving two years later. At 18, working as a crane operator in an iron foundry, he led the first strike ever known in the Lugansk district, for which he was dimissed. Thus he embarked upon his political career, under the pseudonym of Plakhov. He joined Lenin in 1905 and met Stalin about 1908. Following the October revolution of 1917, his military career commenced as chairman of the committee for the defence of Petrograd. His first operation was a massive retreat with 15,000 soldiers and 30,000 refugees, some 650 miles to Tsaritsyn. Here he was appointed commander of the Tenth Army against the counter-revolutionary "White Russians." In 1925 he became Commissar for Naval and Military Affairs and a member of the Politburo. In May 1940 he was made a deputy premier and chairman of the Committee of Defence. Thus he had to bear responsibility for the lack of Russian preparedness when the German attack came in 1941, and he was sacked by Stalin, who took over himself, sending Voroshilov to the front. On Stalin's death in 1953 Voroshilov became chairman of the Praesidium of the Supreme Soviet—in effect President of the Soviet Union—a post which he retained until 1960.

Wickberg, Erik (born 1904). On July 23 the 45 members of the 1969 High Council of the Salvation Army met in London to elect the movement's new leader and, at the first ballot, chose Erik Wickberg as their ninth—and first non-British—General. General Wickberg was born in Sweden, the son of Salvation Army officers whose work took the family first to Germany, where he spent his boyhood, and then to Switzerland, where he spent his youth. Educated in Berne, and later at the Salvation Army's International Training College in London, he was appointed to Scotland after his commissioning in 1925. He

returned to Germany as a member of the staff of the Army's training college, but in 1934 came back to London where he served in the overseas department of international headquarters. At the outbreak of the war he was transferred to Sweden to undertake vital liaison work with the Salvation Army territories cut off from headquarters. He also trained post-war relief teams ready to move in at the heels of the troops to those countries desolated by the conflict.

In 1948 Wickberg was appointed to Switzerland as second-in-command of Salvationist operations; five years later he returned to Sweden in a similar capacity, and, within another four years, he was back in Germany in full command of the German Salvation Army, which was rebuilding itself after the war. In 1961 he became the Army's chief of staff (second in command), moving once more to London, where he worked closely with the two preceding Generals. Eight years in that post, with the responsibility for arranging two High Councils and heavy involvement in the movement's vast centenary celebrations, were an ideal preparation for ultimate command. General Wickberg married in 1932 and has four children.

Wilde, Jimmy (1892–1969). A legend in British boxing, world flyweight champion from 1916 to 1923, Jimmy Wilde died in hospital at Cardiff on March 10, 1969. A frail-looking figure, pale and thin, he possessed a powerful punch that earned him the nickname of "the ghost with a hammer in his hand." The official record books credit him with 125 victories over 12 years, of which 76 were won inside the distance; but in all he is said to have had 864 fights. He lost only four official bouts, and was knocked out only once, when he lost his world title to Pancho Villa in New York in June 1923. At 7 stone 5 lb., his usual weight, he has been described as "pound for pound, the greatest boxer who ever lived"; he certainly defeated many men whose weight greatly exceeded his. Probably no

Jimmy Wilde, by Tom Webster.

British boxer earned as much fame or affection as Jimmy Wilde, but he remained a quiet and unassuming character. Older sports fans will associate him particularly with the *Daily Mail* sports cartoonist Tom Webster, who delighted over many years in depicting Wilde's spidery frame in action; indeed, Webster's caricature of Wilde was more of a public image than Wilde's own figure.

Jimmy Wilde was born at Pontypridd, Glamorganshire, and began work in a South Wales coalmine at the age of 13. He soon left the pit for the boxing booth, and at 19 already had a following. He won the British flyweight title in 1916 by beating Joe Symonds, and later in the same year became world champion when he defeated the American nominee Young Zulu Kid. In 1917 he won the Lonsdale belt outright. He had had no fights for over two years and was out of condition when Pancho Villa knocked him out in the seventh round of his last bout. In retirement Wilde took up sporting journalism and was a regular, but often unrecognised, ringside spectator at big fights until two years before his death.

Williams, Hugh Anthony Glanmor (1904–1969). Hugh Williams the actor-playwright died in London, aged 65, on December 7, 1969. He was born on March 6, 1904, educated at Haileybury and R.A.D.A., and embarked on his theatrical career at the Liverpool Playhouse. He was there for just under three years before achieving success—via West End comedies, an Australian tour with Irene Vanbrugh, and a tour of the U.S.A. The 1930s saw him an established name in the West End in such productions as *Dear Octopus, Grand Hotel, Pride and Prejudice,* and *The Green Bay Tree.*

It was not however, until 1956 that London was to discover that Williams wielded a writer's pen. While "resting"—following serious roles in *The Cocktail Party* in New York, and *The Seagull* in London, and light comedy with *Affairs of State* and *Book of the Month*—he collaborated with his wife, Margaret Vyner, the actress, and created *Plaintiff in a Pretty Hat,* which was successfully produced during that year. Williams, like most actor-authors, wrote himself a good part in this comedy, that of a sophisticated peer, a type that was to reappear in the next offering but one, *The Grass is Greener,* which was a huge commercial success as a film starring Cary Grant. In between, the husband and wife team had written *The Happy Man.* Having found this conjugal talent, the pair exercised it liberally with a success that stemmed from the fact that they were among the last exponents of the sort of elegant comedies that appealed to the middle-aged, middle-brow, but still theatre-going audience. Hugh Williams starred with Joan Greenwood in *The Irregular Verb to Love,* and with Susan Hampshire in

Past Imperfect. The Flip Side was not graced by the co-author's presence but was nevertheless a hit, as was—and indeed is—*Charlie Girl*. Other recent "Williamses" shows include *Let's All Go Down the Strand* (1967) and *His and Hers* which opened at the Apollo only a week before his death, with Hugh Williams playing the lead.

Winchell, Walter (born 1897). The reporter who fathered the American gossip column and at his peak commanded an audience of 25 million, howed himself off the front pages in 1969. He retired, as he had lived, in the centre of a big news story, but this time the victim was his own son, Walter, 33, who had shot himself through the head the previous Christmas Day. Winchell was heartbroken.

The Winchell story began in New York where as a song and dance man at the end of the First World War he began writing gossip articles between acts for *Vaudeville News*. His unerring news sense took him on to the staff in 1922. And as prohibition arrived with its attendant gangsters and racketeers, so, for America, did Walter Winchell. In 1929 he went to work for the great Hearst newspaper chain. The figure in the snap-brimmed hat patrolling New York in a car with a police radio appealed to the imagination of the time. His coined words, such as "making whoopee," "pash" for passion, and "shafts" for legs, passed into the language on both sides of the Atlantic. At its peak his column was syndicated to 1,000 newspapers, and his annual income exceeded £200,000 for many years. His radio programme was eagerly listened to. He was not only a gossip writer, but a newsman of the first order. In 1939 Louis Buchalter, the most wanted man in America, surrendered himself to Winchell, and he announced the murder of gangster Vincent Coll before it happened, and told a disbelieving America that Roosevelt would run for a third term. One of his last "incredible" prophecies was that Jacqueline Kennedy would marry Aristotle Onassis.

But in the 1950s, when Winchell lined up with Senator McCarthy, the clouds had begun to gather. His column became a little querulous, or "tetchy" as he might have said, and newspapers began to drop it. While he was still a legend, Winchell laid down his pen.

Woodcock, George (born 1904). The quiet-spoken leader of eight million British trade unionists moved on to become, it was hoped, the nation's key industrial peacemaker in 1969. He ended 33 years of union activity with a triumphant opposition to the Labour government's threat of jail discipline for unofficial strikers before becoming chairman of the new Commission for Industrial Relations in March. Born on October 20, 1904, at Bamber Bridge, Lancs, he went to Brownedge elementary school, starting work at the age of 12 as

George Woodcock left the T.U.C.

an 8s.-a-week cotton weaver. In 1927, after eleven years in the mills, he won his way through Ruskin College and New College, Oxford, to a 1st class honours degree in philosophy and political economy. The young man with the bushy eyebrows who had dreamed of playing football for Preston North End was on his way to the top. In 1934 he joined the Civil Service, but after two years moved on to one of the key back-room jobs of the Trade Union Congress, secretary to the research and economic department. Throughout the Second World War his was the guiding hand behind the strategy of Walter Citrine which gave the unions commanding power in the economy when the Attlee government was returned in 1945. Two years later Woodcock had his reward. He became assistant general secretary at Congress House. Now he was living in a three-bedroomed "commuter's" house at Epsom where his wife Laura, whom he married in 1933, was a member of the borough council, soon to become mayor. Promotion came again to Woodcock in 1960 when he became general secretary of the T.U.C., the voice of organised Labour. Shrewd, logical, never given to flights of oratory, he won respect from both wings of his sprawling movement. It was he who in 1964 broke the log jam of the seamen's strike which threatened the nation's economy, and three years later successfully toned down government proposals for compulsory wage restraint. The good wishes of all followed him to his new appointment in 1969.

Woolf, Leonard Sidney (1880–1969). Publisher, author, editor, one-time Civil Servant, and a former member of the circle of intellectuals known as the Bloomsbury group, Leonard Woolf died on August 14, 1969, at Rodwell, Sussex. The son of a Q.C., he was born on November 25, 1880, and educated at St. Paul's School and Trinity College, Cambridge. While he was at Cambridge he met a daughter of Sir Leslie Stephen, whom he married in 1912 and who became more famous than her husband, as Virginia Woolf. She died in 1941.

From 1904 to 1911 Woolf served in the Ceylon civil service, and then devoted himself to writing, publishing his first work *The Village in the Jungle* in 1913. In 1917 he and his wife founded the Hogarth Press, which printed her novels, T. S. Eliot's *The Waste Land,* and many other early works of later distinguished authors. Becoming increasingly interested in politics Woolf was an active member of the Fabian Society, and also served as honorary secretary on international and imperial affairs committees of the Labour party. From 1923 to 1930 he was literary editor of *The Nation,* and from 1931 to 1959 joint editor of *The Political Quarterly.*

Leonard Woolf's distinctive and engaging style of writing was most evident in his autobiographical works, *Sowing, 1880–1904* (1960), *Growing, 1904–11* (1961), *Beginning Again, 1911–18* (1964), and *Downhill All the Way, 1919–39* (1968). The fifth volume, *The Journey not the Arrival Matters, 1939–1969,* was published after his death. He continued to write into his old age, and in 1965, shortly before his 85th birthday, was awarded the £1,000 W. H. Smith prize for *Beginning Again.*

Wyndham, John (1904–1969). John Beynon Harris, who, under various *noms de plume,* notably that of John Wyndham, was a distinguished science fiction writer and the creator of such classics as *The Day of the Triffids, The Kraken Wakes,* and *The Chrysalids,* died on March 11, 1969, at the age of 65. Like so many young writers the youthful Harris followed various trades: after leaving Bedales School in 1921 he worked at farming, commercial art, and advertising. He began writing in earnest in 1925, quickly breaking into American pulp magazines, but it was not until after the Second World War that he found fame and fortune as John Wyndham with *The Day of the Triffids.* Besides his three major works he also published *The Midwich Cuckoos, Trouble with Lichen, Chocky,* and two collections of short stories *The Seeds of Time* and *Consider Her Ways.* The magnetic blend of fantasy and realism of these books, together with the chastity of Wyndham's style and the subtlety of his characterisation, earned him the accolade of a place in the English Literature curriculum of many secondary schools. Unlike his literary mentor H. G. Wells, Wyndham was fundamentally an optimist who had a deep sympathy for his human characters as they battled with extra-terrestria forces. Man, he believed, was merely an accident with no right to expect security, but, with the help of courage and, above all, of reason he could endure and survive any shattering of his social order. In the days of his fame Wyndham, a shy, retiring man who shunned publicity, was seldom seen or photographed. He was, nevertheless, by no means a recluse and had many friends, and was for some years on the governing board of the P.E.N. Club.

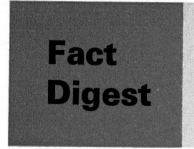

Fact Digest

In this "little encyclopedia" of the year will be found several hundred short articles on topics of importance that came into prominence during 1969 but are not considered in detail in the other main sections of the Year Book. The items are arranged in alphabetical order throughout.

Aberfan, South Wales. Details of the Coal Board's plan for the complete removal of the seven Aberfan coal tips were given in February 1969. At the cost of about £1 million, the 2,600,000 tons of colliery waste will be removed to the comparatively flat top of the hillside overlooking Aberfan, and deposited in a series of six terraces, no more than 45 ft. high at any point, out of sight of Aberfan and nearby villages. The material will be removed either by conveyor belt or by heavy earth-shifting vehicles, and the scheme will take between two and three years. After the tips have been removed the land will be planted with trees and hedges, and seeded, so that eventually sheep will be able to graze there.

On June 6 the Prime Minister opened new primary and junior schools built to replace the one destroyed in the 1966 tip disaster.

Abortion. The Secretary of State for Social Services stated on June 16, 1969, that the total of abortions notified in England and Wales between April 27, 1968, when the Abortion Act came into operation, and May 27, 1969, was 41,496. Of this number 16,650 (40·1 per cent) operations were carried out in approved places; 101 (0·2 per cent) in other places; and 24,745 (59·6 per cent) in National Health hospitals. A total of 1,827 were performed on the ground of risk to the woman's life; 29,954 because of risk of injury to her physical or mental

health; and 690 because of risk to the mother's health and of abnormality in the child. Up to Dec. 31, 1968, 1,103 women (5 per cent) on whom abortions were performed gave their usual residence as being outside the U.K., the Isle of Man, and the Channel Islands. Provisional death registrations for all forms of abortion between April 1, 1968, and March 31, 1969, totalled 42.

On Dec. 5, 1969, the State parliament of South Australia passed the first law to legalise abortion in Australia. It allows abortion in cases where two doctors certify that childbirth could endanger the medical or physical health of the mother or produce a seriously handicapped child.

Accidents. Statistics given by the World Health Organisation on March 12, 1969, showed that in 1966, the latest year for which complete figures were available, Australia had the world's highest death rate from car accidents (28·3 deaths per 100,000 population). The second highest was Austria, with 28 deaths per 100,000; then came West Germany, with 27·9; the U.S.A., with 27·1; Canada with 27; France, with 24·9; Finland, with 24·4; Venezuela, with 22·5; Denmark, with 22·4; Switzerland, with 21·6; New Zealand, with 21·2; Netherlands, with 21; Japan, with 18·2; Sweden and West Berlin, with 17·6; Northern Ireland, with 17·2; Portugal, with 15·7; England

and Wales, with 15·5; Scotland, with 15·3; Puerto Rico, with 15·1. Lower figures included Norway, with 12·9; Bulgaria, with 12·7; Ireland, with 12·2; Greece, with 11·8; Spain, with 11·4; Israel, with 10·8; and Poland, with 9·1. Another WHO report (published in January 1969) stated that, in the world as a whole, one death by road accident occurs every 2½ minutes.

United Kingdom. Although the volume of traffic increased by 4 per cent over 1967, the totals of road deaths, casualties, and accidents in 1968 were all lower than for any of the five previous years. During 1968 there were 264,000 accidents involving personal injuries (5 per cent fewer than in 1967); total casualties numbered 349,208 (a reduction of 6 per cent); deaths totalled 6,810 (a reduction of 7 per cent); and serious and slight injuries fell by 6 per cent. In the first 9 months of 1969 (to Sept. 30), however, the figures increased again, to 5,133 deaths (a 5·6 per cent increase over the same period of 1968); 65,737 seriously injured (an increase of 1·6 per cent); and 185,275 slightly injured (a decrease of 0·8 per cent).

Australia. During 1968, 3,074 people were killed in road accidents in Australia, and more than 30,000 were injured, the highest road toll ever recorded. More people than ever before were killed in New South Wales, South Australia, Tasmania, and Western Australia, while Victoria's figure was only 3 below the record of 977 killed in 1966. Queensland's annual figures dropped by 32, and the Northern Territory's by eight. In 1969, the total rose again, by 3 per cent, to 3,521. In Queensland the number of deaths rose by 78 over the 1968 figure, and in Victoria by 47; in Northern Territory and the A.C.T. the number doubled. Small decreases were recorded in N.S.W., South Australia, Western Australia, and Tasmania.

Germany. Road deaths in West Germany during 1968 decreased by 1·7 per cent, although the number of cars increased. The number of deaths in 1968 was 16,600, compared with 17,000 in 1967.

U.S.A. At least 55,225 people were killed and 1,980,000 injured in nearly 4 million traffic accidents in the U.S.A. in 1968, according to estimated figures published by the U.S. National Safety

Aberfan. The two new schools—infants and junior—which replace that destroyed in the disaster of October 1966 were opened on June 6, 1969.

Council on Jan. 2, 1969. The figures represent a 4 per cent increase over those for 1967. In the 70 years since it first appeared on the roads of the U.S.A. the motor car claimed its two millionth American victim on Sept. 12, 1969. This is five times the number of dead killed in all the wars in which the U.S.A. has participated since 1899, including the war in Vietnam up to Sept. 1.

Japan. In Japan the record number of 16,258 people were killed in traffic accidents during 1969, according to a report published on Jan. 6, 1970.

Factories. The 1968 annual report of the chief inspector of the U.K. Factory Inspectorate, published on Oct. 1, 1969, showed that the total of 312,430 accidents reported in 1968 was 2·8 per cent higher than that for 1967. The number killed rose from 564 in 1967 to 625 in 1968. It was estimated that 171 of these deaths were due to failure by management to take practical precautions; this figure compares with 113 in 1967 and 100 in 1966. But, although in over a third of the fatal accidents in factories the employer had broken statutory regulations, no precautions could have prevented about half the total number of accidents, for they included many caused by sheer chance, by momentary clumsiness, or by the worker's own neglect.

Farms. According to figures given by the Royal Society for the Prevention of Accidents nearly 10,000 accidents were reported among farm workers in Great Britain during 1969, 431 of them fatal. Since 1956 over 1,600 people have died as a result of farm accidents, the largest single cause being tractors overturning. Between 30 and 50 farmers and farm workers are killed in this way each year.

Adelaide, South Australia. An international award for the "most outstanding construction project completed in Australia in the last ten years" was given to the building contractors for the Australian Mutual Provident Society branch office building in Adelaide in May 1969. The judging panel, who considered finishing time, construction problems, job, management, and quality of workmanship, as well as good design and planning, found that not only was the A.M.P. project completed early, but the contractors also successfully dealt with a multitude of constructional problems, including underground water and the proximity of high density traffic areas. The award, valued at $A600, consisted of a leather bound wallet containing a gold plaque and a vellum scroll.

In September 1969 a grant of $A200,000 from the Federal government towards the cost of the Adelaide Festival Theatre was announced. The money will help to meet the approximately $A300,000 needed to make up the balance of the costs of the theatre.

Adelaide. The Australian Mutual Provident Society's building won an award for the most outstanding construction project in Australia in the last 10 years.

Adrenalin. This hormone, secreted by the adrenal or suprarenal glands, has been successfully used by doctors at St. Vincent's Hospital, Melbourne, Australia, to treat the post-operative condition known as pulmonary embolism. The treatment was based on work done by researchers in the medical department of Sydney University. The condition, due to a blood clot in the pulmonary artery of the lung, is common among patients kept in bed after a surgical operation or after childbirth; clots tend to form in the leg and break away, moving round the body until they settle near the heart or lungs. The Australian researchers found that a clot in the pulmonary artery causes the lung to release histamine (a chemical substance formed at the site of any injury), which, if insufficiently balanced by increased adrenalin secretion, has harmful effects on heart, lungs, and blood vessels, causing collapse and sudden death. Injection of additional adrenalin counters these effects by blocking the action of histamine, and can save the lives of 75 per cent of severely affected patients.

Alcoholism. A World Health Organisation survey, published in February 1969, gave figures of the number of people who died from alcoholism in 1965. They showed that alcoholism killed more people in France than in all the other major western industrialised countries put together, for in that year 5,816 died in France; 1,665 in the U.S.A.; 626 in West Germany; 608 in Japan; 385 in Italy; and 82 in Britain. The French alcoholism death rate was 12 per 100,000 population, compared with the U.S. figure of 1·4 and England and Wales's 1. Death rates in the Scandinavian countries

per 100,000 population in 1965 were Sweden 9, Norway 3, and Finland 2; no figure for Denmark was available. The death rate per 100,000 for those who died of cirrhosis of the liver, frequently caused by excessive drinking, during 1965 were: France 34·2, Portugal 30·4, Chile 29·9, Austria 26·9, Italy 22·9, West Germany 22·5, U.S.A. 12·8, Denmark 7·5, Sweden 6·3, Norway 4, and Finland 3·4.

Italy. The results of a four-year survey into alcoholism in Italy, conducted by two professors of medicine at a Rome hospital, were published in September 1969. They showed that about 17 per cent of Italians are alcoholics, and that workers and peasants account for 72·4 per cent of the incidence rate. The professors said that anyone who drinks more than a litre of wine a day must suffer from excessive drinking habits, even though there is no apparent physical harm.

New Zealand. The Alcoholism and Drug Addiction Act, 1966, came into force on Jan. 1, 1969. Recognising alcoholism as a health rather than a penal problem, it provides procedures for dealing with alcoholics similar to those relating to the mentally ill, the chief provision being that persistent drunkards and drug addicts may be detained for up to two years without conviction.

Scotland. In proportion to population Scotland has four times as many alcoholics as England, according to a report by Glasgow's alcoholism council on June 11, 1969. There are 50,000 alcoholics in Glasgow—half the total number of alcoholics in Scotland—which means that one person out of 20 in the city is an alcoholic.

Aldeburgh Festival. The £176,000 Maltings opera house and concert hall at Snape, near Aldeburgh, which was opened by the Queen in 1967, was gutted by a fire on June 7 after the opening day of the 1969 Festival. Musical instruments destroyed included a £2,000 piano belonging to Benjamin Britten, founder and principal artistic director of the festival. The next day it was announced that the festival would continue, the Maltings performances being transferred to Blyburgh church. On Aug. 21 it was stated that the Maltings will be rebuilt on a much larger scale. The building is to be extended to the south, and rehearsal rooms and a recording room added. There will be better facilities for staging opera, and an off-stage workshop.

Alginates. These are compounds of alginic acid, which is extracted from seaweed. They have a large number of uses as thickeners, emulsifiers, gels, stabilisers, film- and filament-formers, blood-clotters, and fire-proofers. The world's second largest alginate industry is situated at two places on the W. coast of Scotland—Girvan, Ayrshire, and Barcaldine, Argyll — where Alginate Industries Ltd. have operated factories

Aluminium. The world's longest all-aluminium pedestrian bridge—210 ft. long and 11 ft. wide—crosses a 4-lane highway at Birmingham, Michigan, U.S.A. Its prime purpose is to provide a link between two adjoining golf courses.

and laboratories since 1941. Extensions to the Girvan works were opened in 1969. The Falkland Islands in the S. Atlantic are a possible site for new works.

The seaweed, gathered on the foreshore of the Scottish coast, in the Hebrides, Orkneys and Shetlands, and Ireland, or imported from Norway and S. Africa, arrives already dried at the plant, is ground to powder, treated in a series of vats and pipes with chemicals, water, and acid in some partially secret processes, and emerges as a white fibrous substance.

This substance is dried again and mixed with different chemicals to produce the various alginate compounds. The latter are used in ice-cream, soups, cosmetic creams and toothpastes, jellies, ceramics, beer, soft drinks, insecticides, emulsions, polishes, sausage casings, coated and washable papers, photography, surgical dressings, stockings, and other products. The current world production of alginates amounts to 15,000 tons a year, worth over £10 million. It is said that the Falkland Islands could provide raw material enough to increase production tenfold.

Antibiotics. On Nov. 20, 1969, the U.K. Minister of Agriculture announced that the government had accepted the recommendations of the Swann Report that antibiotics of value in human medicine should no longer be used as growth-promoters in animal feeding-stuffs. He said that he was concerned that an "indiscriminate use of antibiotics might result in the development of organisms transmissible to man which would be resistant to treatment." The report of the committee chaired by Prof. Michael M. Swann, Principal and Vice-

Chancellor of the University of Edinburgh, on the "use of antibiotics in animal husbandry and veterinary medicine" was published on the same day. It stated that the general use of penicillin, chlortetracycline, and oxytetracycline constituted a risk to human and animal health because of the development of resistant bacteria strains. It recommended that these antibiotics should be administered to animals only if prescribed by a vet, and stated that tylosin, which tends to cause resistance against related antibiotics, and the sulphonamides should also be available only on a vet's prescription.

Anti-Missile Defence. In March 1969 President Nixon announced his approval of the setting up of an anti-ballistic-missile defence system in the U.S.A. No attempt will be made to provide defence for urban populations; the system will be deployed to defend only American strategic centres—air force bases, missile launching stations, etc.—with the addition of Washington, D.C., site of the central command. The system consists of highly refined radar of two kinds, and missiles which will be sent up to destroy enemy missiles before they reach their targets. "Perimeter acquisition radar" (PAR), the first stage, detects the on-coming enemy missile and warns the target of its approach; "missile site radar" (MSR) then takes over and tracks the enemy missile; finally the anti-missile missiles are launched from sites between the perimeter and the target and are guided on to the enemy missile. The system, which will comprise 12 defence bases (shown on the map in page 319), can be completed in six or seven years, at a cost of 6,000 million U.S.

dollars. As a beginning, it will be installed to protect the air force bases at Malmstrom, Montana, and Grand Forks, N. Dakota.

Architecture Awards. The 1969 winners of the world's leading award for architecture—the Sir Patrick Abercrombie award by the International Union of Architects—were the Greater London Council team who planned London's new riverside town, Thamesmead. When the award was announced on May 28, 1969, it was stated that 31 schemes from various countries had been considered by the panel of judges, who included architects from Italy, France, and the Soviet Union; they praised the Thamesmead design for its "human values, aesthetic expression, and modern techniques." Up to now the Abercrombie award has been made every two years, but it will in future be made every three years.

The 1969 Royal Gold Medal for Architecture given by the Queen on the recommendation of the council of the Royal Institute of British Architects—the highest award for architecture in Britain—was awarded in January to Jack Coia, senior partner in the firm of Gillespie, Kidd, and Coia, of Glasgow (see Names in the News, p. 290).

The R.I.B.A.'s own awards for 1969 were announced on June 30. The winning designs included three schools, two university buildings, a computer centre, a research station, a swimming pool, and the first private house to win an award. In the North-west, South-east (outside London), and Wales, no awards were given. The winners were:

Northern: Gas Council engineering research station, Killingworth, Northumberland (Ryder, Yates and Partners, Killingworth).

Yorkshire: Computer Centre, Leeds (Braithwaite and Jackman, Leeds, for Yorkshire Bank).

West Midlands: Charford County Secondary School, Bromsgrove (Richard Sheppard, Robson and Partners, for Worcester Education Committee).

East Midlands: Lincoln Estate, Corby (John Stedman, chief architect, Corby Development Corporation).

Eastern: St. Alban's Abbey Gateway School, St. Albans (Richard Sheppard, Robson and Partners, for the school governors).

South-Western: Creek Vean, a private house at Feock, Cornwall (Richard Rogers, Norman Foster, Wendy Foster, for Mr. and Mrs. Marcus Brumwell). See p. 156.

Southern: Christ Church Gallery, Oxford (Powell and Moya, London).

London: Swimming Baths, Putney (Powell and Moya, for Wandsworth Council).

Scotland: Pathfoot Building, University of Stirling (Robert Matthew, Johnson-Marshall and Partners, Edinburgh).

N. Ireland: Collegiate School for Girls, Enniskillen (Shanks and Leighton, Belfast, in association with H. M. Jones, Fermanagh county architect for Fermanagh County Education Committee).

In May the South-eastern Society of Architects, one of the regional bodies set up by the R.I.B.A., announced a new type of architectural award. It will be given to the building which, after being in use for at least five years, is judged to have worn the best and proved the most successful in occupation.

The U.K. Civic Trust announced in February 1969 the winners of its 1968 competition for architectural design. The awards are made triennially in successive years for county boroughs, county council, and Greater London Council areas. In 1968 there was a record number of 1,400 entries; 82 awards were made, and 180 schemes carried out in the county council areas were commended. The awards are divided into three: Group A, for schemes in areas of architectural interest or natural beauty; Group B, for new buildings in other areas; and Group C, for landscaping schemes which contribute to good surroundings. The winning designs covered an extremely wide range, from a crematorium to a suspension bridge, and the Trust's report praised the general welcome departure from the dull monotony of the box design prevalent during the early 1960s.

The 1969 R. S. Reynolds memorial award, made by the American Institute of Architects for a significant work of architecture in which aluminium is a main element, went to Boyd Auger a London architect and engineer, for his design for a 200 ft.-high pyramid-shaped space-frame structure, the Gyrotron, formed of aluminium tubes and built in Montreal for Expo 67. The building enclosed a theatre in which spectators were taken for a ride round the sets. Apart from the U.S.A., Great Britain is the only country to have won the Reynolds award twice since it was first given in 1956.

The Prince Philip prize for Australian design was won in 1969 by a plastic house designed by Transtar Villas (Australia) Pty. Ltd. The house, 14 ft. by 24 ft., is encased on a single sheet of moulded plastic $2\frac{1}{4}$ in. thick, and is dustproof, moisture resistant, and termite resistant. It can stand up to 80 m.p.h. winds. It was announced in November 1969 that Robin Boyd of Melbourne had been awarded the Australian Institute of Architects' Gold Medal, its highest honour, in recognition of his outstanding contributions to architecture. Mr. Boyd designed the Australian Expo 70 pavilion.

Ardines, Spain. The discovery of Stone Age cave paintings at Ardines, on the Asturian coast of northern Spain, not far from the small port of Ribadesella, was announced in January 1969. Described as being comparable in importance with the historic finds at Altamira and Lascaux, the paintings were found in April 1968 by a group of students exploring caves, the original entrance to which lay about 100 ft. below ground and had been blocked by landslides for many centuries. Some of the paintings, which show reindeer, stags, horses, and a bison, are more than 6 ft. long and are reported to be in good condition.

Armed Forces. Figures published on Feb. 25, 1969, showed that in 1968 the number of naval recruits was about 3,000 less than in 1967. On Jan. 1, 1969, the total strength of the Royal Navy and Royal Marines was 76,964, compared with 81,053 on Jan. 1, 1968. At the end of February 1969 the Royal Navy possessed only 144 operational ships and 60 in reserve. The 144 include minesweepers and submarines, but exclude survey vessels and depot and support ships. In 1968 operational ships numbered 166. Army and R.A.F. recruiting, on the other hand, showed a slight increase.

A scheme to give interest-free loans to help servicemen and women in the last 12 months of service to buy homes was introduced on July 1, 1969. A loan, which will be recovered from the

recipient's terminal benefits on retirement or discharge, can be up to £1,250 for an officer and £755 for a sailor, soldier, or airman. The money is intended to cover the deposit, legal expenses, and surveyors' and land registration fees entailed in buying a house on which a building society, local authority, recognised bank, or insurance company is willing to advance a mortgage of about 85 per cent.

It was stated in the House of Commons on March 5, 1969, that 1968 was the first year in this century in which no United Kingdom soldier, sailor, or airman was killed in military action anywhere in the world.

Arnhem, Battle of. The 1969 pilgrimage to Arnhem, on the 25th anniversary of the tragic failure of the operation by the 1st Airborne Division and the Polish Parachute Brigade to secure a bridgehead over the Rhine at Arnhem, Netherlands, in a nine-day battle in September 1944, was the last of these annual occasions. Organised by the Airborne Security Fund for survivors of the battle and next of kin of those who died in it, the pilgrimages have taken place for many years, the pilgrims being the guests of the Dutch people. The 400 veterans of the battle were led in 1969 by the 1944 commander of the 1st Airborne Division, Maj.-Gen. Robert Urquhart, and other officers who commanded troops in the action. Queen Juliana and Prince Bernhard took part in the ceremonies, which included on Sept. 17 a procession of Arnhem veterans and residents, with a three-minute silence and a wreath-laying ceremony at the memorial to the fallen, (1,200 British and Polish soldiers). The pennant from General Urquhart's army vehicle, captured by the Germans and stolen from them by a Dutch schoolboy, was returned to the General by the boy, now a man in his 30s. A visit was made to a farm where the 10th Parachute (Volunteer) Battalion owns a flock of sheep descended from two given to the hungry men during the battle which they could not bring themselves to kill.

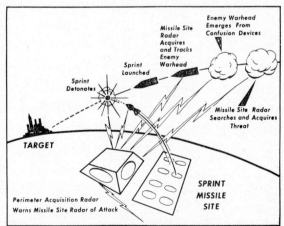

Anti-Missile Defence. *Above:* the sites to be defended and the location of "perimeter acquisition radar" and "missile site radar" installations. *Right:* how the radar will spot the danger and the Sprint missiles will attack.

Art Awards (Australia). Four of Australia's most important prizes for painting were awarded on Jan. 14, 1969. The Archibald prize went to William Pidgeon, of Sydney, who had won the award on two previous occasions. The Wynne prize went to Laurence Scott Pendlebury, of Melbourne; the Pring prize to Margaret Stern, of Sydney; and the Sulman prize to Timothy Ferrier, also of Sydney. The 1969 Portia Geach memorial award, worth $A2,000, made annually for the best portrait of any person distinguished in the arts, sciences, or letters, painted from life by a woman artist resident in Australia, went to Mrs. A. R. Lakeman of Sydney, for her portrait of fellow artist, Guy Warren. Winners in 1967 and 1968 were Bettina McMahon of Sydney, and Jo Caddy of South Australia. The 1969 Blake prize for religious art was won by Eric Smith, for a series of 12 poster-size paintings illustrating the Apostles' Creed. It was the fifth time this Sydney artist has received the $A1,000 award.

The Sydney sculptor R. Robertson-Swann was announced the winner of the $A3,000 first prize in the Comalco invitation award for sculpture in aluminium on Oct. 2, 1969. He and five other sculptors were invited to design a model for a free-standing work of sculpture for a public urban space. The winning entry was a 10-ft.-high 35-ft.-long abstract aluminium sculpture with suspended levels. A month later Robertson-Swann won the $A5,000 Transfield art prize for his "Sydney Summer."

Art Awards. The 1969 Otto Beit Medal of the Royal Society of British Sculptors went to John Poole for his steel "Wizened Christ" for St. Dunstan's R.C. church at King's Heath, Birmingham. The award is given to the best work shown in the Commonwealth outside London.

Art Sales. Following the purchase in November 1968 by the National Gallery for £150,000 of a Duccio painting, "Virgin and Child," which had been bought at auction in March 1968 for £2,700, it was announced by the President of the Board of Trade that an investigation into the alleged existence of a dealers' ring would be made. On March 18, 1969, it was stated in the House of Commons that the evidence given in this investigation would not be published. The Minister said that the inquiries, which took the Board's two investigators as far as Italy, had not disclosed any evidence which could form a basis of criminal proceedings. He said also that a study of prices at sales at leading London art auctions during the past two years suggested that rings had not operated there, and that dealers competed freely. The British Antique Dealers' Association urged that the evidence should be published, finding the Minister's decision "very unsatisfactory," and the Ombudsman in June criticised the Board of Trade for giving the impression that it was taking an active part in investigating the sale of the Duccio painting when in fact it did not hold its enquiry until after the time limit for legal proceedings had elapsed.

Protests were raised during the year against the continued large export of art treasures from Australia, which is one of the few countries that have no legislation to prevent such loss. In 1967–68, the last year for which figures are available, art works worth over $A2 million were sold and taken abroad, mostly to the U.S.A.

During the 1968–69 auction season, which ended on August 1, 1969, Sotheby's total was £25,082,520, a world record for any auction house, and £4½ million more than the previous record figure in the 1967–68 season. Sotheby's Parke-Bernet galleries in New York increased their sales by more than 60 per cent to £15 million. During the 1968–69 season the company held 448 sales in London; 174 in New York, at Parke-Bernet; 11 in Toronto; 4 in Florence; two in Scotland; and one each in Colorado and San Francisco.

Christie's also increased their sales during the year to a record total of £15,239,661, an increase of 21 per cent on 1967–68. The company held 300 sales during the year, including the first it had held in Switzerland and Tokyo. The Tokyo sale, on May 27, was the first foreign auction to be held in Japan. It took place at the Bijutsu Club, and closed circuit television was used, as well as a telephone link with London. The proceeds, which totalled £812,652, included the highest sum ever paid at auction for a single piece of porcelain—£25,698 for a 14th-century 15-inch-high Chinese blue-and-white jar. Christie's also took part in the first direct telephone link-up art auction to be held in Australia. This took place on March 18, when a sale of 160 works by Australian painters was

held in the main Christie's auction room in London. Australian art dealers and collectors were able to bid by telephone from the Wentworth Hotel, Sydney, and the Windsor Hotel, Melbourne. Artists whose works were sold included Arthur Boyd, Charles Conder, Sir William Dobell, Donald Friend, Sydney Nolan, and Sir Arthur Streeton. The highest price, $A20,000, was fetched by "The First Government Residence, Melbourne 1837," painted in 1880 by J. A. Panton from a contemporary sketch—a primitive of purely historical interest. At the beginning of October 1969 Sotheby's held, for the first time, three days of public auctions in Tokyo. The total proceeds, were about 711 million yen (£812,000), the highest price being £39,900 for a Renoir nude, "Andrée assise."

On April 29, 1969, the biggest fine arts deal ever made was signed in London between a British export company, Maple-Leblanc, and a multi-million pound Japanese trading organisation, Marubeni-Iide Co. Ltd. Maple-Leblanc agreed to supply the Japanese company with items of fine art of value amounting to £2 million during 1969. It is expected that this amount will escalate to at least £10 million a year, and cover a wide range of goods, including British furniture, sculpture, works by contemporary British artists, reproduction of world-famous works of art, and all varieties of antiques.

The largest auction of old masters to be held in any country for several years raised a total of £1,133,160 at Sotheby's, London, on March 26. It was the third highest total for a sale of this nature, and the highest for an old master sale without the benefit of a major Rembrandt oil. Eight world auction records for individual artists were set, including £105,000 for Canaletto's "Prato della Valle, Padua." The total was exceeded at Christie's on Dec. 5 when a sale of old masters fetched a total of £1,348,441, a European auction record. But in this sale the works sold did include a Rembrandt—a portrait of an old man, believed to be the artist's father—which fetched 300,000 gns.

Among other record prices reached during the season were: 17,000 guineas for Sir Alfred Munnings's "The Whip" (Christie's, April 18); £46,000 for a family group by Arthur Devis (Sotheby's, March 12) and £48,000 for another work by the same 18th-century British artist (Sotheby's, June 18); 28,000 guineas for John E. Ferneley Senior's painting of the Ferneley children (Christie's, June 20); $A32,000 for Charles Conder's "Box Hill" (Australia, March 7); £87,000 for Vlaminck's "Le Pont sur La Seine à Chatou" (Sotheby's, July 2); 1 million French francs (about £83,000) for Sisley's "Bords de Seine à Fort-Marly" (Paris, June 16); £58,000 for a drawing of a stag-beetle 5⅝in. by 4½ in. by Dürer (Sotheby's, June 26), the record price for any drawing; £409,500 for a work by Tiepolo, and £483,000 for a Rembrandt self-portrait (Christie's, June 27). In

Art Sales. *Left:* Rembrandt's portrait of an old man, sold for £100 in 1877, fetched £315,000 in 1969. *Right:* Hans Baldung's "Temptation of Eve" bought for £224,000.

November a circular miniature by Holbein the Younger, only $1\frac{1}{2}$ in. across, was sold at Sotheby's for the record price of £21,000.

"The Temptation of Eve" by the 16th-century German artist Hans Baldung, which measures $25\frac{1}{4}$ in. by $12\frac{3}{4}$ in., was sold at Sotheby's on Dec. 3, 1969, for £224,000. This hitherto unknown work had been hanging in the home of an Edinburgh couple, who decided to dispose of it to raise the deposit on a new car.

Art Thefts. On March 11, 1969, seven paintings worth £125,000 were found to have been stolen from the London flat of Lord Rockley, City banker and art collector. The most valuable was a seascape by Van de Cappelle purchased in 1967 for £65,000. Others were a flower still-life by Verendael valued at £20,000, and "Detail from Italian Landscape" by Jan Both valued at £10,000. Little hope was held of recovering these works, but on May 6 they were found, apparently undamaged, hidden in the roof of Honor Oak crematorium. Also recovered ten days after its theft was an oil by Watteau valued at between £150,000 and £200,000, which had been stolen from Sir John Soan's Museum, Lincoln's Inn Fields, London, on March 26. A collection worth about £300,000, and including six works by Picasso, was stolen from the home of Sir Roland Penrose in Kensington, London, during the Easter week-end. The most valuable painting was Picasso's "Weeping Woman," valued at between £60,000 and £80,000; the other stolen paintings included works by Braque, Chagall, Chirico, and Miro. All were found by demolition workers stripping an empty shop in Ealing, West London, on July 2. Less fortunate was Lord Sainsbury, from whose London house seven paintings, including a Sickert and a Bernard, two Picasso lithographs, and a quantity of Georgian silverware were stolen in August 1969; the provisional total value

of these articles was more than £100,000. On Feb. 17, 1969, paintings worth about £100,000 from a touring exhibition of the Edward James collection were stolen from the Cumberland House Museum in Southsea, Hampshire. The paintings, which included a Rembrandt and a river scene by Corot, were recovered in a police raid on cars in a seafront car park in Southsea on Oct. 20.

Art Thefts. Picasso's "Weeping Woman" stolen and recovered in 1969.

Asthma. A drug, disodium cromoglycate, sold under the name of "Intal," and developed by Fison's Pharmaceuticals Ltd., was reported in February 1969 to provide great relief for those suffering from allergic asthma. A preventive drug, which must be taken before an attack, it was developed after analysing a Middle Eastern weed, *khellin,* and the isolation of its compounds. Work on these led to the synthesis of a group of chemicals called cromones, one of which was "Intal." The drug is taken as a powder by inhalation, and has proved helpful in treating the allergic asthma to which children are especially prone.

Athletics. A National Athletics League in three divisions, with six clubs in each division, run on a promotion-relegation basis, came into operation in the U.K. on May 10, 1969. The 18 clubs were: Division I—Birchfield, Blackheath, Brighton and Hove, Cardiff, Polytechnic, Thames Valley; Division II—Achilles, Edinburgh Southern, Hillingdon, Notts, Sale, Surrey; Division III—Belgrave, Bristol, Croydon, London, Southampton, Woodford Green. Other meetings were held on August 23 and September 13. At the end of each season the bottom two clubs in each division are relegated and replaced with the top two clubs of the next lower division, the bottom two clubs in Division III being replaced by the two leading clubs in a qualifying competition. See Athletics tables (at the foot of page 232).

Auctions. The Auctions (Bidding Agreements) Act, designed to prevent illegal rings operating at auctions, came into force in the U.K. on Nov. 23, 1969. It strengthens the Act of 1927 by providing a maximum penalty of two years' imprisonment and/or a fine for the offence of inducing someone for a consideration not to bid at an auction sale, or of agreeing to accept a reward for not bidding. It also rules that anyone convicted of taking part in an auction ring may be banned from attending an auction sale for up to three years. The 1927 Act ruled that the maximum penalty for operating auction "rings" was a fine of £400 and/or 6 months' imprisonment, and also that, since the offence was only subject to summary trial, proceedings could not be brought more than 6 months after the offence. The new Act extends the period to 5 years from the date of the offence, and within 3 months of the Attorney General's certifying that evidence justifying proceedings came to his knowledge, and allows the offence to be tried on indictment.

Australian of the Year. This award is given annually to the Australian who has brought the greatest honour to his country during the year. The 1968 award, announced in Melbourne on Jan. 17, 1969, went to the world bantamweight boxing champion, Lionel Rose, the first aboriginal to receive it. There were 28 other candidates for the 1968 award, including the athlete Ron Clarke and the entertainer Rolf Harris.

Automobile Association. The uniform of A.A. patrolmen, which had for 50 years been khaki, underwent a complete change in May 1969. The modern double-breasted unbelted jacket of the new uniform is dark olive-green in colour, and the white cap cover has been abolished. The outfit includes a reversible reflective waistcoat which can be put on for safety reasons to make the patrolman more easily visible when he is attending a breakdown.

x

Avonmouth, Bristol. Work began in August 1969 on a 4,550-ft.-long bridge, with a main river span of 570 ft., which will form part of the southward extension of the Birmingham–Bristol–Exeter Motorway (M 5). Of steel structure with concrete piers and abutments, and with dual 36-ft.-wide three-lane carriageways, the bridge is expected to take three years to complete.

b

BACCHUS. This is the name of a diving system devised by the British Aircraft Corporation, derived from the initial letters of British Aircraft Corporation Commercial Habitat Under the Sea. It was shown for the first time at the international oceanology exhibition at Brighton in February 1969. BACCHUS comprises a series of modules that can be joined together to make two-, four-, or six-man units which can be lowered to depths of 600 ft. and operate independently of surface help for more than a week, or with ship support, "almost indefinitely." The system is designed to support saturation diving techniques (diving to extreme depths for such prolonged periods that the diver's body tissues become saturated by his breathing mixture). BACCHUS will, it is claimed, provide life support for divers working on mining, salvage operations, and pipeline maintenance, and will also act as a transportable underwater base for oceanographic engineering and scientific projects. Once it is positioned on the sea bed divers will be able to operate outside without restriction and move in and out with only one decompression session at the completion of the operation.

Baikal, Lake, Eastern Siberia. It was announced in February 1969 that the forests round this lake, the largest freshwater lake in Asia, and the deepest inland water in the world, had been designated as a protected zone. Steps are being taken to clear the lake, the rivers flowing into it, and its shores of the debris of the timber industry, and no future industrial building round the 12,000 sq. mile lake is to be allowed unless complete absence of any kind of industrial pollution can be guaranteed. The lake contains 1,200 different kinds of animals and plants, 80 per cent of which are found nowhere else.

Ballet Competition. At the end of the first Moscow international ballet competition, held June 11–23, 1969, at the Bolshoi Theatre, Moscow, the French dancers, Francesca Zumba and Patrice Bart from the Paris Opera, were awarded joint first prize with the Russians Nina Sorokina and Yuri Vladimirov. No silver medals were awarded, but bronze medals went to Yukido Yasuda and Jun Tanaka of Japan, graduates of the Tokyo ballet

school; and to two Soviet pairs from Leningrad, Natalia Bolshakova and Vadim Gulyayev, and Lyudmila Semenyaka and Nikolai Kovmir. In the solo competition the ballerina's gold medal went to Malika Sabtrova from Soviet Tajikistan; the silver to Loipa Aranjo of Cuba; and the bronze to Irina Dzhandieri, of the U.S.S.R. In the male dancers' contest the gold medal went to Mikhail Baryshnikov, of the U.S.S.R.; and silver medals were awarded to Hideo Fukagawa of Japan, and Helgi Thomasson of the U.S.A.

Banking. In March 1969 the Commonwealth Bank in Sydney, Australia, introduced a new electronic savings bank system which links the teller's box direct to a computer. The system, known as on-line banking, uses the computer as a huge ledger whose memory contains details of every transaction by each customer. The teller, who has a special terminal inside his booth, transmits details of each transaction to the computer, which instantly stamps the customer's pass book, entering items such as outstanding deposits, interest, child endowments, or pension payments.

Bantry. Statue of St. Brendan the Navigator unveiled on May 6, 1969.

Bantry, Ireland. On May 6 a statue of St. Brendan the Navigator was unveiled in Bantry to mark the offical opening of the Gulf Oil terminal at Whiddy Island in Bantry Bay. The 21-ft. copper statue of the Irish seafaring saint, presented to the town by Gulf Oil, faces the wide bay with outstretched arms.

Basle, Switzerland. The airport which Swiss Basle shares with the French city of Mulhouse about 20 miles away was enlarged during 1969 to allow the handling of 2,500 passengers per hour. The third largest airport in Switzerland (after Zürich and Geneva), it is one of the very few dual-nationality airports in the world. The approach road forks after a few yards, one fork leading into the Swiss road system and the other into the French.

Bath, Somerset. A report on the city of Bath, published on March 10, 1969, was one of four studies commissioned by the government and local authorities on the protection of historic centres of towns and cities from traffic and other pressures of the 20th century. A similar report on York appeared on Feb. 14 (see York) and on Chester on May 23 (see Chester). The report said that Bath, with nearly 3,000 buildings classified as architecturally important, presents serious organisational problems. As leases run out at varying dates, and administration of Corporation land is divided, improved estate management methods should be introduced. The report urged that a major programme of converting historic buildings into hostel accommodation for university students should be put in hand. The cost of acquisition and conversion was put at £109,000, and it was estimated that university grants would total £75,000. It stated that in the buildings which were studied basements were found to be damp, and roofs and gutters were in poor condition, and that excessive traffic was spoiling the environment of the city.

Beds. In line with the current trends towards the westernisation of living habits in Japan, more Japanese now sleep on beds in preference to the traditional tatami floor. This fact was given by the Japanese Economic Planning Agency in a survey published in April. It said that the diffusion rate of western-style beds rose to 19 per cent in 1968, which meant that there is one bed in every five households.

Beer. The U.K. Monopolies Commission, asked by the Board of Trade in 1966 to investigate the question whether there is a monopoly in the supply of beer for retail sale in licensed premises, produced its report on April 28, 1969. The Commission found that elements of monopoly do exist in the "tied house" system, by which public houses and off-licences owned by brewers mostly sell only their owners' products. Brewers own 78 per cent of public houses and 30 per cent of off-licences in the U.K. (in England and Wales the figures are 86 per cent and 34 per cent respectively), and over 90 per cent of the average tied house's sales of beer are of its owner's brands. Because it prevents competition this system operates against the public interest, and is detrimental to efficiency in production, wholesaling, and retailing, the Commission declared, but the monopoly can be broken only by changes in the licensing laws. Accordingly it recommended that any retailer should be allowed to sell alcoholic drinks for consumption on or off his premises, so long as his character and premises meet certain minimum standards; the enforcement of those standards should be done by local authorities and government departments, in place of the present licensing of premises by local justices. In addition

Belfast. The world's largest Goliath crane, 460 ft. wide, is used to lift prefabricated ship sections into place at Harland and Wolff's new yard.

to considering the monopolistic aspect of the matter, the Commission took into account evidence submitted by the Consumer Council which found that "what people really want is a kind of popular catering establishment that will serve meals or drinks or both as the customer desires."

Consumption. The chairman of the U.K. Brewers Society said in February that an estimated 1,131 million gallon output of beer in 1968 was the highest peace-time total since 1918. The increase over the 1967 figure was 27 million gallons.

Belfast, Northern Ireland. The first 600 ft. of Harland and Wolff's new £15 million shipbuilding dock here came into use in May 1969, when the first section of the first of two 253,000-ton tankers ordered by Esso was laid down. The dock, which is the only one in the U.K., will not entirely replace the traditional slipways, but its operation serves enormously to decrease costs. A 200,000-ton tanker built in the dock costs £500,000 less than one built on a slipway. The saving is in time. On a 100,000-ton bulk carrier, slipway work requires 50–60 man-hours per ton of steel throughput; the dock reduces this to below 40 man-hours per ton on a large tanker. By 1972 it is expected that at least three large ships per year will be built in the Belfast dock. Steel fabrication plant is necessary to service the installation, and this was under construction in 1969; when it is completed Harland and Wolff's annual steel throughput will increase from 55,000 tons in 1969 to 110,000 tons in 1971. Shipbuilding docks have been responsible for the success of Japanese yards in recent years; Harland and Wolff's dock will be one of the few in the world outside Japan capable of building the 400,000-ton and 500,000-ton tankers that are expected to be ordered in the near future.

To mark Northern Ireland's 50th anniversary, which will be celebrated in 1971, a new leisure centre is to be built in Belfast. The centre, which is intended to serve the whole of Northern Ireland, will comprise a concert hall, a swimming pool, a sports hall, and a restaurant, with ancillary accommodation. The planning will be flexible, allowing for later extensions to include, for example, an art gallery and theatre. In March 1969, when the government's decision to build the centre was announced, it was stated that it was hoped that the foundation stone would be laid in 1971. The Belfast Corporation has agreed in principle to siting the centre on the west bank of the Lagan near Albert Bridge.

Benjamin Franklin Medal. It was announced in January that Dr. Louis Booker Wright, the historian and director of the Folger Shakespeare Library, Washington, U.S.A., had been awarded the Royal Society of Arts Benjamin Franklin Medal for 1969. This award has been made since 1962 in alternate years to a citizen of the U.S.A. and one of the U.K. who, in contributing to the encouragement of arts, manufactures, and commerce, has advanced Anglo-American understanding.

Bikini, Marshall Islands. The first party of this atoll's original 167 inhabitants, evacuated in 1946 so that nuclear bomb tests could be held there, returned to Bikini in October 1969. Numbering about 30, they started the rehabilitation of the atoll by planting coconut, bread-fruit, and pandanus trees. A party of Americans had been working since February on clearing away debris and repairing the airstrip. Although 23 nuclear bomb tests were carried out there between 1946 and 1958, radioactivity in Bikini now is only one-fifth of what it is in mainland U.S.A., where the average lies between 10 and 20 microroentgens.

Binney Medal. The 1968 Binney memorial awards for acts of bravery in support of law and order, instituted to commemorate Capt. Ralph Binney R.N., who was killed in a single-handed attempt to prevent the escape of smash-and-grab thieves in the City of London on Dec. 8, 1944, were announced in December 1969. The top award, the Binney Memorial Medal for Bravery, went to David Davies, aged 75, a retired teacher, of Beckenham, Kent, who helped security men when an attempt was made to rob them of £10,000. Although the raiders squirted ammonia in his face he continued the struggle. Nineteen people received Certificates of Merit.

Birds. The publication *British Birds* for January 1969 recorded two new bird species in the British Isles. One is a brown thrasher, seen at Durlston Head, Swanage, Dorset, in November 1966; this is a North American species never previously recorded in Europe save for one unauthenticated report from Heligoland in 1836. The other new British bird is the Royal tern, another American species, seen at Shellness Point, Kent, in July 1965.

The Royal Society for the Protection of Birds announced in April that a new nature reserve for the rare black-tailed godwit is to be established. Before 1829 this wader nested regularly in the Eastern counties of England, but it became a table delicacy, and did not again become a regular breeder in the U.K. until a few years ago.

Births. According to the U.K. Registrar-General's provisional figures for England and Wales, published in February 1969, there was a fall in the birthrate in 1968 for the second year in succession. The number of live births in 1968 was estimated at 819,000, about 13,000 or 1·6 per cent fewer than in 1967. This compared with a drop of 18,000, or 2·1 per cent, between 1966 and 1967. The number of illegitimate births, however, continues to rise. During 1967, the latest year for which figures are available, there were almost 70,000, which was 8·4 per cent of all live births for the year. In 1957 there were 35,000, only 4·8 per cent of the total. The Registrar-General's report in April 1969 said that the trend towards more illegitimate babies was on the increase among women of all age groups under 35.

Another report from the Registrar-General, in June 1969, showed that Northern Ireland had a higher birth rate and a lower death rate than any other part of the British Isles. In the December quarter of 1968 the number of live births was 7,710, giving an annual rate of 20·5 per 1,000 population. Comparative rates for England and Wales, Scotland, and Eire were 15·9, 17·4, and 19·5 respectively. Deaths in Northern Ireland numbered 3,804, equivalent to an annual rate of 10·1 per 1,000 population. Comparative rates for England and

Wales, Scotland and Eire were 11·7, 12·1, and 10·4 respectively.

West Germany. According to figures given by the Federal Statistics Office on Feb. 25, 1969, the birth rate in Germany has been declining since 1964. Between 1945 and 1964 the rate rose continuously to reach 18·2 live-born babies per 1,000 inhabitants; preliminary figures for 1968 showed that the rate had fallen to 16·1 per 1,000 inhabitants.

U.S.A. The birth rate in the U.S.A. fell from 17·9 births per 1,000 population in 1967 to 17·4 in 1968, the lowest ever recorded. But as the large number of women born shortly after the end of the Second World War will soon enter their major child-bearing years, the birth rate is expected to rise during the 1970s.

Blind (persons). A new method of enabling the blind to see was brought a step nearer to realisation in 1969. The principle is the by-passing of the eyes to bring about direct stimulation of the vision area of the brain. In 1968 two London doctors, by successfully implanting 80 electrodes in the brain of a blind patient, enabled her to experience the sensation of sight. In November 1969 an American eye research scientist, Dr. Herbert Schummel, of the Albert Einstein College of Medicine, New York, gave details of a similar but more sophisticated device which, he said, should be ready for testing on human beings in three or four years' time. It involves the transmission of electronic signals from the lenses of miniature television cameras to tiny wires implanted in the brain. Prototype versions will be worn on the forehead like a miner's lamp, or as a badge attached to the jacket, but Dr. Schummel stated that within five to ten years it may be possible to create television cameras small enough to fit into the eye sockets.

The world's first pair of "sonar spectacles," worth £1,500, were developed in 1969 by a team headed by Prof. Leslie Kay in New Zealand. The spectacles are an improvement on the hand-held sonic "torch" which emits a narrow beam of ultrasonic waves that are reflected by objects in the user's path and produce sounds in hearing-aid-type earphones. Three tiny receivers in the bridge of the spectacles pick up the echoes and transmit them through tubes to the earpieces. A blind New Zealander, in London for a physiotherapy course, made his way unaided through the streets wearing the spectacles in November 1969. A month before, the U.K. National Research Development Corporation's annual report had stated that prototypes of the "spectacles" had been made, but said that they were unlikely to be available for general use in Great Britain for several years. A team at Nottingham University had produced similar "spectacles" in February.

In February an art exhibition for the blind was held in Zürich, Switzerland. Visitors were able to appreciate the works through feeling the contours and shapes of the exhibits.

Bluff, New Zealand. An agreement was signed at the beginning of September 1969 with the New Zealand Government in Wellington for an Australian and Japanese consortium to finance the building of an aluminium smelter at Bluff, South Island. To produce initially 73,000 tons of aluminium a year, it is planned to expand production to 100,000 tons a year, and later to over 200,000 tons. Fifty per cent of the capital is to come from Comalco of Australia, and two Japanese partners, Showa Denko and Sumitomo Chemicals, each providing 25 per cent. The first stage of the smelter, which will handle alumina from ore mined in Australia, will cost $A50 million; it will be completed late in 1971.

Bollinger Prize. The 1969 award of this $US 5,000 (£1,785) American prize for poetry which is presented every two years by the Yale University Library, and carries great prestige, was announced in January. The joint recipients were Karl Shapiro, professor of English at the University of California, and John Berryman, English professor at the University of Minnesota. The award is usually given to one poet, but on this occasion the three judges could not decide between John Berryman's volume of new poems *His Toy, His Dream, His Rest,* and Karl Shapiro's "continuing achievement represented in *Selected Poems."* Previous poets who have received the prize, which comes from a trust created by Paul Mellon, the banker philanthropist, and is named after Bollinger, Switzerland, where he lived after graduating from Yale, include Archibald McLeish, W. H. Auden, E. E. Cummings, Robert Frost, and Robert Penn Warren.

Bonn, West Germany. The W. German capital city more than doubled its population in May 1969 when it was allowed by Parliament to annex ten neighbouring communities on both sides of the Rhine. Best known of the annexed places is Bad Godesberg, Bonn's next-door neighbour, a wealthy town where most of the foreign embassies are situated and many well-to-do professional people reside; the others include Duisdorf, Oberkassel, and Holzlar. After the annexation Greater Bonn's population became 300,000; previously it was 140,000.

Booker Prize. This annual prize of £5,000 and a trophy was awarded for the first time in April 1969. Given by Booker McConnell Ltd., an industrial and commercial firm, in co-operation with the Publishers' Association, the prize went to P. H. Newby for *Something to Answer For,* the best novel, in the opinion of the judges, published between Dec. 1, 1967, and Nov. 30, 1968. The judges, Dame Rebecca West, Stephen Spender, Professor Frank Kermode, David Farrer, and their chairman W. L. Webb, literary editor of *The Guardian,* considered 62 novels, which they short-listed to six before judging Mr. Newby the winner. The prize is open to novels written in English by citizens of the British Commonwealth, the Republic of Ireland, and the Republic of South Africa, and published for the first time in the U.K. by a British publisher between the above mentioned dates each year. See also p. 306.

Boson. The intermediate boson is a hypothetical transitory atomic particle, the existence of which has been postulated to account for some inconsistencies in the theoretical "weak interaction" between atomic particles. (The weak interaction is an assumed fourth natural force by which interactions between matter can be explained: the other three are electrical force, gravitation, and the "strong interaction" between atomic particles.) The establishment of the

Blind. At an art exhibition for the blind at Zürich, Switzerland, blind visitors enjoyed the works by sense of touch.

Bonn, W. Germany. The Bonn Centre, opened on November 25, 1969, includes a hotel, theatre, cinema, swimming pool, shops, offices, restaurants, and four embassies.

existence of the boson became a possibility in 1969 after the invention at CERN (the European Centre for Nuclear Research) in Geneva of a new device—"intersecting storage rings"—in which beams of protons can be made to collide with an energy 60 times greater than that obtained in an ordinary proton accelerator.

Bosporus. This narrow strait between the Black Sea and the Sea of Marmara, which separates Europe from Asia, will in 1972 be bridged for the first time if plans made by the Turkish government come to fruition. Designs for a bridge to cross the Bosporus from Ortakoi near Istanbul to Beylerbey near Uskudar were made in 1968 by the British firm of Freeman Fox and Partners. The bridge, longer than Freeman Fox's Severn and Forth bridges, which it will closely resemble, will be a suspension bridge supported by twin towers over 500 ft. high. The cost will be over £70 million, which will be repaid by tolls in 15 years. The bridge is expected to carry 7½ million vehicles a year, compared with the 4½ million transported at present by ferries between three crossing points. An extension across the Golden Horn, the inlet that divides Istanbul from its north-eastern suburbs, is included in the plan.

Bothair, South Celebes, Indonesia. Australian and Indonesian archaeologists during excavation work on the southern tip of this island during 1969 found remains of a civilisation which may be up to 3,000 years old. They uncovered combs, metal spearheads, ancient coins, bones, and pottery inscribed with zigzag motifs. Similar work by a Dutch team in the area in 1929 indicated that such relics may be from the Tuala civilisation, an aboriginal tribe dating back about 2,000 years.

Bougainville, Solomon Islands. Bulldozers started clearing work on the Australian-owned Arawa plantation here in the autumn of 1969 as part of a project to build a new town for a proposed copper mine. A site is being cleared for a hospital to cost about $A1 million, which will supplement the relatively small hospital at Kieta. The proposed township will provide homes, shops, offices, and other amenities for a population of about 8,000 Europeans.

Boundary Commission. Reports of the boundary commissions for England, Wales, Scotland, and Northern Ireland were published on June 19, 1969. Recommended changes in parliamentary constituencies would increase the present total of 630 members of parliament to 635. Additional seats, proposed for areas of England where the electorate is overlarge, were one each for Bedfordshire, Berkshire, Buckinghamshire, Cheshire, Northamptonshire, Oxfordshire, Staffordshire, East Sussex, West Sussex, and Worcestershire; and two each for Essex, Hampshire, Hertfordshire, Kent, Surrey, and the North Riding of Yorkshire. Reductions in the number of constituencies were proposed for Greater London (11), co. Durham (2), Lancashire (2), Norfolk (1), and the West Riding of Yorkshire. Major alterations were proposed in 322 of the existing 630 constituencies, and minor changes in a further 88, the aim of the commissions being to avoid constituencies with more than 80,000 or fewer than 40,000 electors. The Commission for Wales recommended that there should continue to be 36 members of parliament, that the two Rhondda constituencies in Glamorgan should be amalgamated, and that there should be a boundary adjustment in Monmouthshire.

Although the date fixed by law required the boundaries to be redrawn by

Nov. 1, 1969, the Home Secretary said in the House of Commons on June 19 that there would be no general revision of boundaries before the next general election (except in Greater London), as account must be taken of the radical boundary changes advocated by the Maud commission on local government (see Local Government). Nevertheless, on Nov. 12 the government bowed to opposition pressure and introduced orders implementing the Commission's recommendations, as they were required to do by law, but instructed Labour M.P.s to vote against them, and the recommendations were rejected by a majority of 53.

In a white paper published on July 2 the government announced that the 73 local councils in Northern Ireland are to be replaced by 17 new area authorities, for which around 400 councillors will be elected in 1971. Belfast and co. Fermanagh are the only two authorities to remain largely the same. It was also stated that legislation will be introduced to set up an independent commission to review ward boundaries and electoral divisions within each new area.

Boys' Clubs. Figures given in the U.K. National Association of Boys' Clubs annual report for 1968–69, published in September 1969, showed an increase in membership of nearly 4,000 in the year. This brought the total membership to 168,854 boys, 80 per cent of whom are between 14 and 20 years of age. The Association's administrative officer said that the increase in membership was due to the increased popularity of outdoor activities.

Breakwater. Details of a new type of floating breakwater, designed by Col. H. S. Hasler with the support of the National Research and Development Corporation to save the lives of those on drilling rigs and in other exposed sea situations, were given in August 1969. The breakwater consists of a shallow pontoon about 20 times as long as its width, which is moored to lie broadside on to advancing waves. Flexing is limited by a tubular superstructure, and rolling minimised by an outrigger. Most previous designs have consisted of a large vertical surface to combat wind and waves. The Hasler breakwater is not only cheaper but also easier to moor.

Breathalyser. A London police report published on June 10, 1969, stated that the number of drivers in the city who were required to take a breath test rose steadily during 1968, and the number of positive tests increased to 71·5 per cent over the last nine months of the year compared with 55·8 per cent in the first three months. The average number of tests in 1968 was 28 a day.

"Brief Lives." On May 27, 1969, the actor Roy Dotrice established a record at the Criterion Theatre, London, with his 104th appearance in *Brief Lives*, a solo dramatisation of the gossip of John Aubrey (1626–97), the English antiquary. No other one-man show had run for so long uninterrupted, and the occasion was marked by the presentation of a bronze bust by Sir John Gielgud to Roy Dotrice. The previous record for a solo performance was held by Ruth Draper, who played 100 consecutive performances at the Haymarket Theatre, London, in 1949.

Brighton, Sussex. The Brighton Marina scheme, for which planning permission was given in September 1966, received a setback on March 17, 1969, when the Brighton Corporation Bill was defeated by four votes on second reading in the House of Commons. The Bill was designed to empower Brighton town council to acquire land compulsorily for new roads to provide access to the proposed marina. The £14 million marina is to occupy 35 acres on the Brighton sea front under the cliffs at Black Rock, and will include a casino, night club, hotels, and restaurants. Unless access roads can be provided the whole project is jeopardised. A town poll was held in December on the question whether the town council should reintroduce the Bill during the next session of Parliament; only one eighth of the electorate voted, 9,461 votes being cast for the reintroduction of the Bill and 5,422 against.

Brisbane, Queensland. Trolleybuses ran for the last time in Brisbane on March 13, 1969, when the last ones were replaced by diesel-engined buses. Brisbane's 36 trolleys had been operating since 1951. All the remaining trams in the city were also replaced by diesel buses on April 14; on the day before (a Sunday) thousands turned out to say farewell to the trams with a last ride for a souvenir 20-cent ticket.

"Britain 1969." This handbook, prepared by the Central Office of Information and published in January 1969, gave a picture of the average British household. Families are revealed as demanding high standards of home comfort, with a sharp rise in central heating and wall-to-wall carpeting, while four families in five are prepared to do their own home decorating. The general level of nutrition is high and still rising. The average Briton's weekly food consumption in 1967 included nearly 5 pints of milk and cream; over 3 ounces of cheese; over 36 ounces of meat, poultry, and bacon; over 20 ounces of sugar and preserves; over 105 ounces of fruit and vegetables; 40 ounces of bread; 6 ounces of butter; and 7·6 ounces of sweets and confectionery. Tea remains the most popular drink.

More than four in five British households have a vacuum cleaner; two in five a refrigerator; over half a washing-machine; nearly all an electric iron; one in three an electric hair-drier; two in five an electric blanket; and about one in five an electric toaster. Less than one per

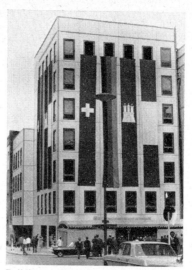

Building. The completed block in Hamburg erected in one week-end.

cent of homes now have a resident servant, and fewer than one in 600 an au-pair girl.

Other facts given in the 500-page book are: that photography is the most popular hobby, in terms of money spent; that about a million and a half enter competitions in the hope of winning a house, a car, or a holiday; and that at least 31 million people take an annual holiday, half of them travelling by car.

British Hydrocarbons Company. This is the tentative name, announced on July 23, 1969, for a new Gas Council subsidiary designed to increase state participation in the British offshore search for natural gas and oil. The new company will concern itself with the exploration and marketing of both products, and will initially confine its activities to the Irish Sea, but may later extend them to the North Sea.

British Standard Time. The U.K. Ministry of Transport gave on Feb. 3, 1969, the first offical analysis of road accidents related to the change to British Standard Time in 1968. Comparing November 1968 with November 1967, the figures showed that during the darker 7 a.m.–9 a.m. period there were 181 more fatal and serious accidents in 1968, but in the lighter 4 p.m.–6 p.m. there was a decrease of 232. In the morning period during weekdays in 1968 there were four fewer fatal and serious casualties to child pedestrians aged 5–14 than in 1967, but in the 4 p.m.–6 p.m. period there were 17 more. These figures were affected by the fact that November 1968 contained one more weekday than November 1967.

The Home Secretary announced in June 1969 that a social survey of the views of the public on British Standard Time will be made on behalf of the government after the winter of 1969–70. Results of the survey, including the

number of accidents in the winter of 1968–69 and 1969–70 will be given to parliament before the end of 1970. A decision will then be taken whether the British Standard Time Act, which ends in 1971, should be made permanent.

Buddhism. The Japanese lay movement of Sokagakkai began work on the construction of a £41 million temple on the slopes of Mount Fuji early in 1969. According to Sokagakki it will be the largest religious building in the world.

Building. A record in building construction was put up in Hamburg, W. Germany, in the summer of 1969 when a 7-storey office block with ground-floor shops was erected from prefabricated parts in one week-end (65 hours 41 minutes 23 seconds, from dawn on a Friday to 2.41 a.m. on the following Monday). By means of a 100-ft. crane a team of 30 men fitted, welded, cemented, and installed the units, which weighed up to 8 tons, at the rate of one every 10 minutes 8 seconds. Decorators and fitters moved into each floor as soon as its ceiling was in place, and at the end of the operation the building was ready for occupation in every detail. As well as walls and ceilings, lifts and lift-shafts, complete toilets (including mirror and lighting), doors and even shop fronts bearing the shopkeepers' names in neon lights had been prefabricated during a year's preparatory work. By conventional methods construction would have taken at least 5 months.

Bulldozers. A Japanese company has developed an underwater bulldozer, claimed to be the first of its kind in the world. At a public demonstration of the vehicle early in 1969, it ran under the water at 2 m.p.h., excavating and levelling portions of the sea bottom. The bulldozer is driven by a power unit floating on the surface; a diesel engine operates a hydraulic pump, and the pressure generated by it is transmitted by a high pressure hose to the bulldozer at the sea bottom to run two hydraulic driving motors and one hydraulic cylinder for operating the blade. In shallow water where the bottom can be seen from the surface, the vehicle is driven by a single operator, who mans the floating power unit; but when the sea is too deep for the movement of the bulldozer to be observed from the surface, the operator is directed by signals from a diver on the sea-bed.

Burlington, Ontario, Canada. The Canadian federal government is proceeding with the construction of a major water-research centre here, to be known as the Canada Centre for Inland Waters. The centre, which should be completed in 1972, will enable chemists, biologists, engineers, physicists, geologists, economists, and sociologists, to work together on studies of pollution, quality of water, currents and water circulation, changing water-levels, flooding, shore erosion,

Some New Bridges of 1969

This three-level crossover at Pierre, South Dakota, U.S.A., took 2 years to build and cost 2 million U.S. dollars.

Left: Denmark's first big suspension bridge, 3,300 ft. long, will span the Little Belt between Jutland and Funen. *Right, upper:* in this pipeline bridge across the Danube near Vienna, the cable supports are at an unusual angle; *lower*, the Kingston Bridge over the Clyde at Glasgow, seen here under construction, is 470 ft. long and carries a 10-lane carriageway.

The longest bridge in Europe, over the entrance to Cadiz Bay, Spain, was opened on October 28, 1969. See page 328.

sedimentation, ice-formation, and biological factors, as well as their economic and social effects. The centre will have all the necessary marine facilities and service buildings, and will also include a marine research laboratory, hydraulics laboratory, and a water-quality pilot plant which will help to improve treatment methods for industrial wastes and sewage. The Burlington site was chosen mainly because of its strategic location on the lower Great Lakes, and its proximity to major sources of water-pollution from industrial and urban complexes on both sides of the international boundary.

Byron. On May 8, 1969, Lord Byron, who died in 1824, was given his place in Poets' Corner in Westminster Abbey, London, at last receiving the official blessing of the Church of England. Permission for his commemoration in the Abbey had previously been refused on several occasions because of his character and morals, but, as the Dean of Westminster said in his address: "When this easily criticised man turned to poetry he became another man." The white marble floor memorial, with an inscription in gold lettering, was unveiled by Dr. William Plomer, president of the Poetry Society, and the Poet Laureate, Cecil Day-Lewis, laid a wreath of laurel and red roses.

Cabora Bassa. This is the name of a dam, the largest in Africa, which is to be built across the Zambesi in the province of Tete in the Portuguese territory of Mozambique. After two years' delay, contracts with a South African-led consortium were signed on Sept. 19, 1969, and preliminary work began shortly afterwards, about a year later than intended. The site is 200 miles from Salisbury, Rhodesia, and only 60 miles from the Rhodesian border. A power transmission line, 800 miles in length, from the dam into South Africa is part of the scheme, which will cost £150 million to complete. Tete is one of the provinces of Mozambique where guerrilla war by the Frelimo (liberation movement) against the authorities is at its fiercest.

Cadiz, Spain. A £3,500,000 bridge across Cadiz Bay, which took eight months to build, was opened on Oct. 28, 1969. The 11,000-ft. bridge, the longest in Europe, cuts across the entrance to the bay, and reduces the distance between Seville and Cadiz from 86 to 62 miles. The bridge will play an important part in the economic development of S.W. Spain.

Calcutta. The most important commercial city in India and its leading port, Calcutta in the last 20 years has had to face the possible loss of this position

through the silting up of the Hoogly river on which it stands. This has been due to a severe reduction in the amount of water flowing from the Ganges into its distributaries in India—the Bhagirathi and Hoogly—simultaneously with an increase of flow into the Padma, its third distributary, which is in East Pakistan. The change in the flow of the Ganges waters, which has been observable over centuries, has now reached such a pitch that the Bhagirathi and Hoogly receive no water at all except during the three months of the monsoon floods. The solution to the problem is the diversion of Ganges waters into the Bhagirathi and Hoogly, and to this end a 7,366-ft.-long barrage across the Ganges was begun in the early 1960s at Farakka, about 200 miles north of Calcutta; it was scheduled for completion in 1971, but will be completed one year earlier. From this a 25-mile-long feeder canal leads into the Bhagirathi near Jangipur, where another barrage is being built across the Bhagirathi itself as a regulator of the monsoon floods. The increased flow into the Hoogly should scour away the silt, and also reduce the severity of the bore tides which now frequently sweep up that river to the danger of shipping. East Pakistan has objected to the diversion of waters which she uses for irrigation, but Indian engineers claim that ample water will continue to flow into the Padma and the lower reaches of the Ganges and its delta, and that there will be a reduction in the flood danger to East Pakistan.

Cambridge, University of. In June 1969 the University voted for the inclusion of a new social services tripos in its syllabus. Voting on the decision, which had caused much controversy, was 461 to 332. The new tripos will require the appointment of three additional lecturers at a combined salary of £6,000 a year, and a library costing £10,000.

The first woman proctor at Cambridge was appointed on May 9, 1969. A married woman of 26, director of studies in history at Girton, she was given charge

of maintaining discipline among girl undergraduates. She was succeeded by another Girton don, a 38-year-old crystallographer, in August.

It was announced in April that the Wren Library at Trinity College is to be restored by the same craftsmen as did the restoration work on King's College Chapel. The work, which is expected to take two years, at a cost of about £120,000, will include the replacing of defective stonework and structural timbers.

Canals. Plans for enlarging Britain's 1,400-mile "amenity" canals to create canal-side marinas capable of accommodating large numbers of small craft were announced in April. Between £50,000 and £100,000 is to be spent on each of these marinas which are intended to rival the Norfolk Broads in popularity among boating enthusiasts and holiday-makers. Work on the first at Nantwich on the Shropshire Union Canal, and on the second at Banbury on the Oxford Canal, started during 1969. Two other sites are in the River Severn area, at Purton, Glos. and Upton-on-Severn. Private holiday and boating firms are to be encouraged to widen their interest in the canals, and facilities for boat hire and mooring, boat sales, repair yards, and other amenities are to be provided. It is possible to cruise for about 1,600 miles on Britain's canals without travelling over the same stretch of water twice.

Cancer. Provisional figures for cancer death rates in England and Wales in 1968 were given on May 17, 1969. There were 2,583 per million population for males, and 2,063 for females, an increase of 52 and 32 per million respectively on the 1967 figure.

The results of research by the Tobacco Research Council into the possible risk of cancer to cigar smokers were published in July 1969. They contradicted the previously held theory that cigar smoking is less likely to cause lung cancer than cigarette smoking. During the experiments, which were conducted at the

"Cardentity." *Left:* **machine used for engraving numbers.** *Right:* **number engraved on rear window.**

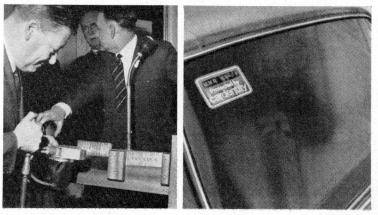

Car Ferry. New B.R. Isle of Wight ferry carries 48 cars and 400 passengers.

the first year, and that the figure will increase to a maximum of 50,000 cars per year.

Car Ownership. Statistics in the U.K. Ministry of Transport's 1968 annual report, published in August 1969, showed that the number of households with one car rose from 28 per cent in 1961 to 43 per cent in 1968; during the same period the number of households owning two cars trebled—to 6 per cent. Since 1958 road traffic had doubled to 118·4 thousand million vehicle miles on Britain's 172,188 miles of road, 1 per cent of the roads carrying 16 per cent of the total vehicle mileage. The average annual mileage driven in passenger cars rose from 8,100 miles in 1967 to 8,200 miles in 1968. In 1958 consumer spending on cars and motor-cycles was £769 million; in 1968 it had risen to £2,347 million. In 1968 there were 10,816,100 private cars on the roads (out of a total of 14,804,700 vehicles), compared with 10,227,400 in 1961, 1,744,282 in 1926, and 17,810 in 1904. The number of motor cycles, scooters and mopeds in 1968 was 1,228,000.

The 1966 sample census, in which questions were asked for the first time about car ownership and garaging, showed that in that year over 7 million households had no car, 5,914,000 had one car, 867,000 had two cars, and 162,120 had three or more cars.

Car Sales (Australia). The figures for new car sales in 1968 in Australia were published in April 1969. The home-grown Holden topped the list with 31·5 per cent (an increase of 3·2 per cent over 1967). Second were Ford's with 18·9 per cent (a decrease of 1·6 per cent); third Chrysler with 9·7 per cent (a decrease of 0·9 per cent); fourth Morris with 7·8 per cent (a decrease of 1·8 per cent); fifth Toyota (Japan) with 7·5 per cent (an increase of 1·2 per cent); sixth Austin with 4·1 per cent (an increase of 0·1 per cent); seventh Volkswagen with 3·6 per cent (a decrease of 1·6 per cent); eighth Datsun (Japan) with 3·5 per cent (an increase of 0·6 per cent). In sales of station wagons Holden's were again first with 49·5 per cent (a decrease of 4 per cent); second Ford's with 20·3 per cent (a decrease of 0·7 per cent); third Chrysler with 15·4 per cent (an increase of 0·6 per cent); fourth Toyota with 4 per cent (an increase of 1 per cent); fifth Datsun with 3·2 per cent (same as 1967). Altogether Japanese car sales were 14·6 per cent of the total (an increase of 3 per cent), and station wagon sales 8·9 per cent (an increase of 1·8 per cent); the actual Japanese figures were 45,352 cars and 5,212 station wagons.

Casey Station, Antarctica. This station, which replaced the Wilkes station occupied by Australian expeditions since 1959, was opened in February 1969. It takes its name from Lord Casey, the former Governor-General, as the Aus-

Council's Harrogate laboratories over a two-year period, three products were used—a small cigar, a standard plain cigarette, and a cigarette made from cigar tobacco—and the tar deposits collected from an automatic smoking machine were painted on mice three times a week. Although the cigar smoke dosage used was lower than the cigarette smoke dosage, there was a statistically significant increase in cancer in mice dosed with cigar smoke condensate over that in mice painted with cigarette tar. No difference in cancer development among mice treated with tars from plain and cigar-based cigarettes was shown.

Canoeing. In what was thought to be the largest ever single expedition of canoes in the world, and was certainly the biggest on an English river, more than 280 canoeists took part over Whitsun in a 100-mile canoe test on the River Severn, organised by the National Association of Boys' Clubs. The canoeists, from boys' clubs throughout Great Britain, left Leighton Bridge, outside Welshpool, Montgomeryshire, on May 23, and arrived at Worcester on May 26.

Capital Punishment. On Dec. 16, 1969, in a division in the House of Commons in which 532 M.P.s took part, there was a majority of 158 for making permanent the Murder (Abolition of Death Penalty) Act, 1965. On December 18 the House of Lords followed the Commons' lead, and defeated by a majority of 46 an amendment to prolong the abolition "experiment." These votes, in effect, meant that no one will ever again be executed in Great Britain for murder, although in theory, death remains the statutory penalty for certain offences such as piracy, treason, and mutiny with violence.

"Cardentity." This is the name given to an entirely new method of reducing the theft and resale of motor vehicles, demonstrated for the first time in London on Feb. 5, 1969. The simple idea is to engrave the registration number of a car on all its side and rear windows; only by replacing each window can the registration number be removed, and this task is likely to deter would-be thieves. Engraving takes only 10–15 minutes, requires no special skill, and will be available at leading garages throughout the U.K. at a charge of £3.

Cardiff. The U.K. Minister for Sport announced in March that the Government had agreed to give a grant of up to £600,000 for a Welsh national sports centre at Cardiff. Local authorities will be invited to contribute to the running costs of the centre, which is being built and administered by the Central Council of Physical Recreation. Construction started in June, and is expected to be completed in the spring of 1971.

Car Ferry. British Rail announced in April 1969 that its existing passenger service between Heysham and Belfast is to be developed as a drive-on drive-off car and passenger ferry by the summer of 1970. The new service will provide extra capacity for expanding car tourist business between England and Northern Ireland, but it will continue to carry a substantial number of passengers travelling by train or other public transport, as well as Post Office mail and rail express parcels. The scheme includes building new terminal installations at each port. The two ships already on the route, the *Duke of Argyll* and the *Duke of Lancaster*, will be converted to single-class vessels capable of carrying 110 cars and 1,200 passengers each. It is estimated that 29,000 cars will use the service during

tralian government wished to make some recognition of his contribution towards fostering Australian activities in Antarctica. The new station is about one mile from Wilkes station.

Castlewellan Forest Park. This park, extending over 1,000 acres of the Mourne Mountains in co. Down, Northern Ireland, was opened to the public on April 1, 1969. Among its attractions for visitors are a lake well stocked with trout, a pony-trekking trail, woodland walks, picnic sites, and viewpoints. It also includes the Annesley Garden Arboretum which contains many rare and exotic trees. This is Northern Ireland's third forest park, the others being at Tollymore in co. Down, and Gortin Glen in co. Tyrone.

Cathode Ray Tube. A new type of cathode ray tube, claimed to be the first of its kind in the world, was announced by the instrument-making division of the British Rank combine early in 1969. The tube is made of high purity alumina ceramic, which is tough enough to withstand vibrations and shocks that shatter normal glass tubes. The tubes will be of particular use in display panels in supersonic aircraft, and probably in computer-control systems for machine tools.

Census. In a voluntary test census—a "trial run" for the official 1971 census—held on April 27, 1969, in High Wycombe, Nottingham, and Huddersfield, and in Dumbarton, Kelso, and the Isle of Lewis, 200,000 householders were asked new questions on amount of personal income, employment during the previous 12 months, mode of travel to work, number of G.C.E. "A" level passes, and for married women under 60 their children's dates of birth. Questions on the date of entry into the U.K. and parents' place of birth were intended to identify immigrants and their children. Scots were asked if they can speak, read, or write Gaelic. Other questions concerned access to accommodation, e.g. whether it is necessary to pass through another household in order to reach one's own.

Central Heating. News of an electrical central heating system which can be installed simply by applying a conducting paint to the interior surfaces of walls was given in May 1969. Developed in Britain, the paint forms the heating element, and is linked to the electricity supply by two strips of adhesive aluminium foil which run round behind the picture-rail and skirting board. The system runs on electricity at 40 volts, and a transformer is needed to adjust the household supply to that voltage. The paint is blackish in colour, but ordinary paint can be applied to cover it; it is expected to cost little more than any top quality decorative paint. Because the heat comes from its entire surface, one treated wall should provide adequate

warmth for a whole room. After a demonstration of the new system on a 10 ft. by 8 ft. section of a wall at the Paint Research Station, Teddington, on May 7, it was stated that only a rough estimate for the total cost of equipment and installation could be given; it was thought, however, that it would be in line with conventional electrical central heating systems, viz. about £150–£200 for a three-bedroomed semi-detached house. The most expensive item is the transformer, which costs £60–£100.

Channel Tunnel. The U.K. Minister of Transport announced on July 22, 1969, that a site at Cheriton near Folkestone, Kent, had been chosen for the British terminal of the Channel Tunnel, if and when the British and French governments agree on its construction. This site, rather than alternatives at Sellindge, Sevington, and Marsham, was preferred by the Kent county council. A railway passenger station will be built at Saltwood, near Cheriton, and a railway cargo yard will operate at either Sevington or Stanford.

Charlemagne Prize. This annual prize given since 1950 by the city of Aachen, West Germany, for outstanding contributions to European unity, was awarded in 1969 to the High Commission of the European Community (Common Market) for its "exalted service" for European unity and its work for the Coal and Steel Community, the Common Market, and Euratom. This was the first time that an institution rather than an individual had received the prize.

Chemical Elements. The synthesisation of a new chemical element, No. 104, was announced by radiation laboratory scientists at the University of California,

Chicago. John Hancock Centre, 100 storeys high, was occupied in 1969.

Berkeley, on April 15, 1969. Discovery of the element was claimed in 1964 by Russian scientists who believed they had created it by bombarding plutonium with neon and suggested the name kurchatovium for it. But the Russian discovery has never been generally accepted. The American synthesisation was brought about by bombarding the man-made transuranic element californium with carbon ions. Element 104 decayed, after a half-life of 4 seconds, into nobelium. Element 104 is the first to be found of a new family of elements—the transactinide elements—beyond the man-made transuranic elements Nos. 93–103. With 104, entrance is made to a different part of the periodic table drawn up and predicted by Mendeleev.

Chester. A report on the city of Chester, commissioned jointly by the Ministry of Housing and Local Government and the local authorities, was published on May 23, 1969. Based on a survey of the 200-acre central area of the city, the report says that the present 375 buildings listed as of architectural importance should be increased to 508. At least 28 of these are in an advanced state of decay, and the report says that £50,000 should be spent on their restoration. Of 142 buildings in need of permanent repair, 51 also needed conversion. Reconditioning and repair would require a public and private outlay of £1 million; a further £600,000 ought to be spent on a 10-year repair and improvement programme on 229 historic premises. The report suggested that a national Historic Towns Corporation should be formed and given powers to acquire, restore, convert, and dispose of valuable historic buildings. Under the existing system funds available from the central government were inadequate to deal with this task, and it was unreasonable to expect local authorities to foot the bill alone. See Bath; York.

Chicago, Illinois, U.S.A. Occupation of the 100-storey, 1,107-ft.-tall John Hancock Centre, which towers above the surrounding buildings, took place during 1969. Spires on top of the Centre form bases for TV antennae which will add another 349 ft. to its height. Half of this, the world's largest office-and-residential building, will be occupied by business, parking, and office facilities, and the other half by residential apartments.

Children in Care. Home Office statistics, published on Jan. 30, 1969, showed that the number of children in the care of local authorities in England and Wales in 1968 fell by 47 to 69,358, the first annual drop for nine years. In 1968 there were 75,518 children in the care of local authorities and voluntary organisations, compared with 79,996 in 1966 and 78,648 in 1959. The average weekly cost of maintaining a child in local authority care was £7. 6s. 2d., compared with £6. 14s. 2½d. in 1966–67.

Churchill Memorials. *Top:* **stained glass screen at Dudley, Worcs, shopping centre.** *Lower, left:* **Sir Robert Menzies and Lady Spencer-Churchill at unveiling of statue at Westerham, Kent;** *right:* **Lady Churchill unveiling statue in the Commons.**

by stone on the campus of Westminster College, Fulton, Missouri, U.S.A., was dedicated as the Winston Churchill Memorial and Library. The ceremony was attended by Lord Mountbatten, Mrs. Christopher Soames (Sir Winston's daughter), Gen. Mark Clark as President Nixon's representative, and many diplomatic and academic dignitaries. It was at Fulton in 1946 that Sir Winston made his famous "Iron Curtain" speech. The removal of the Wren church had been agreed by Church, Parliament, and L.C.C. in 1963; dismantling began in 1965. All the stones were marked and numbered before being shipped across the Atlantic and through the St. Lawrence Seaway and the Great Lakes to St. Louis.

An 8-ft.-high bronze statue of Sir Winston Churchill by Oscar Nemon was unveiled on the village green at Westerham, Kent, on July 23, 1969, by Sir Robert Menzies, who succeeded Sir Winston as Lord Warden of the Cinque Ports. The statue, which weighs half a ton, stands on a plinth of white marble from the Adriatic island of Brac, given by Marshal Tito and the Yugoslav people in recognition of the help Sir Winston gave their country during the war. The people of Westerham, which is two miles from Chartwell Manor, Churchill's home from 1922 until his death, raised £7,000 to pay for the statue. Another statue by Oscar Nemon, presented by the "British Association of Monaco," was unveiled on Great Britain Avenue, Monte Carlo, on May 19, 1969. The ceremony was attended by Princess Grace and Prince Rainier of Monaco, Christopher and Mrs. Soames, and the sculptor. On Dec. 1, 1969, Lady Spencer-Churchill unveiled Oscar Nemon's £11,000 bronze statue of Sir Winston Churchill in the members' lobby of the House of Commons. The 7 ft. 5 in.-high statue, weighing a little less than a ton, stands on a 3 ft. 5 in. plinth on the left-hand side of the Churchill Arch, so called because it was from here that Churchill, in May 1941, saw the ruins of the bombed Chamber. A large coloured glass screen, 39 ft. by 10 ft., commemorating Winston Churchill, in the new shopping precinct named after him at Dudley, Worcs, was unveiled on Sept. 8, 1969. Consisting of 17 separate panels, the screen shows Sir Winston seated and surrounded by the Parliament buildings, St. Paul's Cathedral, and his books and paintings; some panels show the three armed services in action. The screen was the work of the artist Edward Bainbridge Copnall.

A new walk in Bedgebury Forest, Kent, was named Churchill Wood Walk when it was opened to the public on June 26. At the ceremony Winston Churchill, Sir Winston's grandson, planted a Lawson cypress of a variety named after Sir Winston. This planting was part of the Forestry Commission's jubilee celebration.

The 1969 Winston Churchill Fellowship Awards were announced on Feb. 11. The 86 men and women who

Chimneys. The highest chimney in the world is to be built by the International Nickel Company of Canada to serve their smelter complex at Copper Cliff, Ontario. When the new 1,250-ft. stack is completed, ground concentrations of sulphur dioxide will cause no damage, because gases from the smelter will be emitted at high velocity, temperature, and altitude, and will thus be dispersed and diluted. The new chimney is a part of INCO's air pollution control plans for the smelter, which also include the installation of two new electrostatic precipitators and the enlargement of existing ones.

The tallest chimney in Europe, 850 ft. high, was completed at the Drax power station, near Selby, on May 16, 1969. It contains a lift in its centre for maintenance work. The Drax power station, which will burn 4 million tons of coal to produce almost 2,000 megawatts, will begin to make electricity in 1971. Cost of construction is £1¼ million.

Cholera. A further increase in this disease was reported in a World Health Organisation statement published in April 1969. The number of cases rose from 23,201 in 1967 to 28,941 in 1968—a 25 per cent increase.

Chronometers. It was announced in June 1969 that marine chronometers used in ships of the Royal Navy for navigational timekeeping since 1825, when the hydrographic service pattern chronometer was made general issue to all ships wearing the White Ensign, had been withdrawn. In future the Royal Navy is to use a high-grade Swiss lever watch as a replacement for the massive chronometer; kept in a similar wooden box, its dial is 2½ in. in diameter compared with its predecessor's 4½ in.

Churchill Memorials. On May 7, 1969, the City of London church of St. Mary Aldermanbury, reconstructed stone

received the awards were chosen out of 5,761 applicants who submitted projects for world travel. The award winners included an underwater photographer whose project was to go to Aldabra Atoll in the Indian Ocean to attempt to photograph a coelacanth; a fireman whose plan was to go to Germany and Russia to study fire safety laws and publicity for safety methods; and a road patrolman who wanted to go to Japan in order to study Japanese methods of dealing with the hazards of motorway driving.

Church of Scotland. The first woman minister, Miss Catherine McConnachie, aged 66, was ordained on March 27, 1969, at St. Mary's, King Street, Aberdeen, where she was previously a deaconess. The General Assembly decided in May 1968 to admit women to the ministry on the same terms as men.

The hymnary revision committee reported to the General Assembly in May 1969 that their new hymn book was complete and is likely to be published in 1971. The committee has commissioned 30 new tunes by modern composers. The new hymn book will be used also by the United Free Church of Scotland and by the Presbyterian Churches of England, Wales, and Ireland.

Church Service. A new simplified service of Holy Communion for optional use in Anglican churches was published in August by the standing liturgical commission of the Church of England in Australia, set up in 1966. The service incorporates the new translations of the Lord's Prayer, Gloria, and Creed prepared by the International Consultation on English Texts, and introduces a shortened and simplified version of the General Confession prepared by the commission itself. The five divisions of the service are defined as introduction, ministry of God's word, intercession, Lord's Supper, and dismissal.

Church Unity. Twenty representatives of twelve denominations met in early May 1969 at a joint working group of the Australian Council of Churches and the Roman Catholic Church in Australia in an attempt to find sufficient agreement on the theology of the Eucharist, Mass, Holy Communion, or Lord's Supper, to allow the preparation of an experimental common service for all churches. Joint chairmen of the four-day meeting were the Anglican archbishop of Melbourne and the R.C. archbishop of Hobart, Tasmania. The Roman Catholic view of the Mass as a sacrifice was agreed to by the other churches, after it had been explained that the word "sacrifice" meant no more than that the Mass presents in symbolic manner the death of Jesus on the Cross and a means whereby participants offer themselves in sacrifice to His service. With regard to transubstantiation, the Conference was content to state that Christ is truly present

through the Holy Spirit at every celebration of the Eucharist, but the manner of His presence cannot be precisely defined.

The proposed union of the Church of England and the Methodist Church failed to come to pass in 1969. Although on May 6 the Convocations of Canterbury and York gave a two-thirds majority to entry upon stage one of the process, a referendum of Anglican clergy a month later showed that only 63 per cent were willing to take part in the proposed Service of Reconciliation, and at the crucial meetings on July 8 there was only a 69 per cent majority of Anglicans in favour of the scheme of union, although a 77·4 per cent majority in favour was shown by the Methodists. Since a two-thirds majority on both sides had been accepted as necessary, the scheme was considered defeated. The actual voting at the Methodist Conference on July 8 was 524 in favour and 153 against; and at the Anglican Convocations 263 in favour and 116 against. See also pp. 128, 129.

The Vatican announced on Oct. 11, 1969, that the Roman Catholic Church and the Church of England had set up a permanent joint commission to discuss steps towards Christian unity. The first meeting of the commission will take place at Windsor in January 1970.

Cinema Attendance. Figures given by the U.K. Board of Trade in July 1969 showed that the total number of admissions to cinemas in 1968 fell to 237·3 million, 10 per cent lower than the 1967 figure. The number of cinemas open at the end of 1968 was 1,631, compared with 1,736 in 1967. Takings, however, rose from £57·6 million in 1967 to £57·7 million in 1968, the average price of admission having been increased by 58 per cent.

Cliveden. This Thames-side house at Taplow, Bucks, the former home of the Astor family, was given to the National Trust in 1942 with a £232,000 endowment by the second Victor Astor. He made it a condition that it should be let to an Anglo-American interest. When his son died in 1966 the house was offered unsuccessfully by the Trust to three trade unions as an educational centre. Early in 1969, Stanford University, California, U.S.A., negotiated a 21-year lease, in order to use Cliveden as a British campus of the University. The first 80 students moved into the house at Easter. The house will still be open to visitors three days a week, and the gardens five days a week, from April to the end of October.

Coastal Command. On Nov. 27, 1969, R.A.F. Coastal Command (formed in 1936) was officially disbanded, its responsibilities being transferred to command and control of R.A.F. Strike Command. From Nov. 28 Strike Command assumed Coastal Command's tasks of maritime reconnaissance, anti-submarine warfare, and search and rescue.

Coast Erosion. Plastic "seaweed" laid off shore to build up a sand bank.

Coast Erosion. An experiment to halt coast erosion at Walberswick, Suffolk, was undertaken during the summer of 1969, when 30,000 lb. of artificial seaweed (made of plastic) was laid off the beach. Over an area of some 500 yards by 40 yards the "seaweed" was anchored about 10 yards off shore. It was expected that a barrier of sand would build up on the "weed" and prevent further loss of land. The plastic ribbon weed was manufactured by Imperial Chemical Industries Ltd.

Coins and Coin-Collecting. Highlight of 1969 for coin collectors was the issue in Britain on October 14 of the new 50p cupro-nickel coins to replace the 10s. banknotes. Midway in size between the florin and the half-crown, the 50p coin is in an unusual shape known as an "equilateral curve heptagon," having seven sides and a constant breadth but no common centre. The obverse of the coin has the portrait of Queen Elizabeth II by Arnold Machin, R.A., already in use on coins of a number of other Commonwealth countries. The reverse, designed by Christopher Ironside, ensures that Britannia's long career on British coins will not end with the old sterling currency; she first appeared on Roman coins minted for use in Britain during the second century A.D. and she reappeared in 1672, when new copper coins were minted for King Charles II. She now enters the decimal era. Another step towards decimalisation was taken on August 1, when the halfpenny ceased to be legal tender. During 1967 and 1968 almost 146,500,000 halfpennies were minted, all of them dated 1967, so that even in mint condition they are likely to remain common coins. The sterling halfpenny is not to be replaced by a decimal equivalent.

Throughout 1969 half-crowns were also gradually withdrawn in preparation for their demonetisation on January 1,

Coins. *Left:* obverse of Fiji's five decimal coins introduced in January 1969. *Right:* Jamaica's 20 cents, showing blue mahoe trees. Jamaica went decimal in Sept.

Souvenir medallions struck in 1969. *Left to right:* Prince of Wales, to commemorate the Investiture; Presidential art medal of the three Apollo 11 astronauts, commemorating the first Moon landing; Jamaican souvenir dollar, showing Alexander Bustamante (premier 1962–67); Sophocles medallion produced by the Paris Mint.

1970. Just over 33,050,000 half-crowns were minted during 1967 and 1968, all of them dated 1967, so that collectors should have no difficulty in finding specimens in mint condition. Like the sterling halfpenny, the half-crown is not being replaced by a decimal coin.

Britain's change to a decimal currency is compelling a similar change in Commonwealth countries which have been using sterling. In Fiji the change was made on January 13, 1969, when five decimal coins became legal tender. On the obverse each had Arnold Machin's portrait of Queen Elizabeth II and the reverses, designed by J. Kenneth Payne, showed traditional Fijian objects—a tanoa, or wooden bowl used at ceremonial banquets (bronze 1 cent), a palm-leaf fan (bronze 2 cents), a lali or wooden drum (cupro-nickel 5 cents), a throwing club (cupro-nickel 10 cents), and a whale's tooth (cupro-nickel 20 cents). In addition, a souvenir cupro-nickel 1-dollar coin with the Fijian coat-of-arms on the reverse was issued for sale to collectors. The Fijian dollar is the equivalent of approximately 9s 6d sterling.

Jamaica changed to a decimal currency on September 8, 1969. Five decimal coins were issued, each bearing the Jamaican coat-of-arms on the obverse. The reverses, designed by Christopher Ironside, featured national symbols—a spray of ackees, a popular Jamaican fruit (bronze 1 cent), a crocodile (cupro-nickel 5 cents), lignum vitae, the "wood of life" tree (cupro-nickel 10 cents), the blue mahoe tree (cupro-nickel 20 cents), and the doctor-bird or swallow-tail humming-bird (cupro-nickel 25 cents). A souvenir cupro-nickel 1-dollar coin with the portrait of Sir Alexander Bustamante, first Prime Minister of independent Jamaica, also was issued for sale to collectors. The Jamaican dollar is equal to 10s. sterling. Bermuda, changing to decimal currency on February 6, 1970, has chosen a dollar equal to the American dollar, at 8s. 4d. sterling. The Republic of Ireland also announced that it plans to change to a decimal currency on the same day as Britain, February 15, 1971. Coins identical in size and metal with the British coins, but with traditional Irish designs, have been prepared (see p. 341).

Some of the important events of 1969 were commemorated by special medallions produced and marketed by private firms. Collectors had a wide choice of souvenir medallions of the American landing on the Moon, most designs featuring the lunar module or the portraits of the three astronauts. In Britain the investiture of the Prince of Wales was the occasion for several firms to produce souvenir medallions with portraits of the Prince and views of Caernarvon Castle or fiery Welsh dragons on the reverse. The Paris Mint continued to delight collectors with its regular issues of large medallions designed by prominent French artists. Among them was a striking portrait of the Greek dramatist Sophocles, by Pierre Turin; others portrayed Napoleon Bonaparte, the American novelist Jack London, and, to mark the 60th anniversary of his historic cross-Channel flight in 1909, the French aviator Louis Blériot.

For collectors of older coins one of the major events of the year was the sale at Sotheby's London auction-rooms on July 14 of some of the treasure recovered from the wreck of H.M.S. *Association*. The flagship of Admiral Sir Cloudesley Shovell, who had commanded a squadron attacking the port of Toulon, the *Association* was wrecked with four other warships off the Scilly Isles during her homeward voyage in October 1707. The treasure, most of it recovered by a team of underwater divers led by Roland Morris, a Penzance restaurant-owner, ranged from French cannon more than 9 ft. in length to rings, a toothpick case, and thousands of coins. Many of these last were Spanish 8 reales, the silver "pieces of eight" renowned in pirate stories; but there were also hundreds of British coins of Charles II, James II, and William III, some in very fine condition and others badly eroded by their 260 years under the sea. Among the more expensive coins were a Portuguese gold 4,000 reis of 1689 which realised £150, and a William III guinea of 1701 which realised £95. The most expensive modern British coin of the year, however, was a 1933 penny sold at Glendining's London auction-rooms for £2,600 and re-sold by the purchaser a few hours later to a Birmingham collector for about £3,000. **C. W. HILL**

Colchester, Essex. A new theatre, the Mercury, hexagonal in shape, is to be built for repertory in Colchester, it was stated in May 1969. Construction will be complete by mid-1971. Adjustable stage and seating will allow different shapes of stage and auditorium to be adopted, but even the seats farthest back will be only 60 ft. from the stage. Audiences of from 420 to 500 will be accommodated. The cost, estimated at £200,000, will be found by public subscription (£60,000), from the Colchester borough council (£60,000), and from the Arts Council (£80,000).

Cologne, W. Germany. At Melaten, a suburb of Cologne, a new Roman Catholic church, built in the style of a medieval castle, was nearing completion at the end of 1969. Designed by Prof. Gottfried Böhm and dedicated to Christ's Resurrection, it cost £150,000.

Comets. Professor Vladimir Radievsky, of the Gorky Training Institute, U.S.S.R., believes that the sources of comets are concentrations of cosmic dust which form in front of hot stars moving through interstellar space. Details of the theory were published in February. Dust particles forming in front of a star with a surface temperature of 15,000–20,000°C. become concentrated, and, as the particles grow in size the gravitational force becomes greater than the repulsive force, so that bodies are formed which go into elongated orbits round the star. If the theory is correct, stars moving towards the earth should look only half

Cologne. "Fortress" church at Melaten, designed by Prof. Gottfried Böhm, architect of the church in p. 159.

as bright as those moving away from the earth, the dust cloud in front acting as a light absorbing screen. To test the theory, about a thousand class B stars were examined, and when the average brightness of those known to be moving away was compared with the average brightness of those approaching the earth, the ratio proved to be almost exactly two to one.

Coming of Age. Lord Denning, Master of the Rolls, ruled in the U.K. Appeal Court on June 19, 1969, that young people aged 18 and over were to be allowed to bring Common Law civil actions on their own account. He rejected the notion that an infant was, in law, in the custody of his parents until the age of 21. See also Family Law Reform Act; Representation of the People Act.

Composers. The first copy of a survey of Australian composers and their work was presented to Dorothy Dodd, president of the Australian Fellowship of Composers, on Oct. 2, 1969. The survey, sponsored by the Commonwealth Assistance to Australian Composers' Advisory Board, took $2\frac{1}{2}$ years to complete, and cost nearly $A30,000. It includes a catalogue of 46 selected Australian composers, including John Antill, George Dreyfus, Peter Sculthorpe, and Felix Werder, and a bibliography of their works and scores, recordings, recorded talks given by them, and a historical review of musical composition in Australia.

Continental Drift. This theory, supported by most modern geologists, that continents once joined together have been carried apart by convection currents in the earth's mantle, has found its most obvious justification in the shape of the continents of Africa and South America. The east coast of South America would fit so well into the west coast of Africa that it seems clear that, some 200 million years ago, these continents were indeed joined together as part of the land mass which theoretical geologists call Gondwanaland. New studies in 1969 by American oceanologists have shown that if, instead of the coastline, the continental shelf at 1,000 fathoms is taken as the margin, the "fit" between continents is even more exact. On this basis the continents of Australia and Antarctica also fit together almost exactly, if Tasmania is placed in the mouth of the Ross Sea and S.W. Australia is laid alongside the Knox Coast. Australia–Antarctica was also probably part of Gondwanaland. A discovery made in 1969 by a team of U.S. scientists near the South Pole goes far to confirm the theory. They reported in December to the National Science Foundation, Washington, D.C., that they had found the fossil remains of a reptile, *Lystrosaurus,* of the Triassic period 200 million years ago, in the Alexandra Range west of the

Continental Drift. Africa, India, Australia, Antarctica, and South America may have fitted together (*left*) **and drifted apart to their present positions** (*right*).

Beardmore Glacier in Antarctica. Other remains of *Lystrosaurus* have been found in Africa, and the supposition is that Antarctica must have been joined to Africa in pre-Triassic times, since this reptile could not have swum across a large expanse of open sea. The existence in Antarctica of coal deposits, which contain the remains of large trees, indicates that the region must once have been warmer than now, and the discovery there in 1968 of a single fossil fragment of a salamander-like amphibian, found also in near-by continents, also tends to bear out the theory.

Cook, Captain James. On Jan. 11, 1969, an American expedition from the Academy of Natural Sciences, Philadelphia, found six $5\frac{1}{2}$-ft. cast-iron cannon jettisoned by Capt. Cook on the night of June 10, 1770, after his ship, the *Endeavour* had run on to coral off the Great Barrier Reef of Australia. The research team of seven went to the reef to find samples of rare fish, but were accompanied by a group of laymen searching for the cannon, undeterred by the fact that at least ten previous scientific expeditions and other search parties had failed to find them. The expedition hired a helicopter and a 30-ft. boat, and equipped themselves with a magnetometer. The electronic sensors of this device picked up a trace of metal in 10 fathoms of water, about 12 miles off Cookstown, and led divers to the cannon. The cannon were so heavily encrusted with marine growth that they had first to be preserved in salt water, and then washed in fresh water for several months before being exposed to air, but they were found to be in exceptionally good condition, having been protected from erosion by the coral crust. The trademark on them showed that they were made about 1760. The director of the Philadelphia Academy said that although their future was undecided, it was probable that one would go to Philadelphia, and the rest to Australian museums.

Coral Sea Islands Territory. This new territory, consisting of a number of small scattered islands lying beyond the Great Barrier Reef east of the Queensland coast, was created a Federal Territory by a bill

introduced in the Australian parliament on May 29, 1969. The territory has only three inhabitants—meteorologists stationed on an island in the Willis group. A lighthouse has been erected on Bougainville Reef, beacons operate on Frederick Reef and Lihoo Reef, and there is an unmanned weather station on Cato Island. The bill was prompted by the desirability of having a framework of administration for the islands in view of the possibility of oil exploration on the continental shelf. The courts of Norfolk Island will have jurisdiction in the territory.

Countryside Commission. This British statutory body was set up by the Countryside Act of 1968 to undertake the functions of the National Parks Commission and to assume further responsibilities for "keeping under review all matters relating to the provision and improvement of facilities for the enjoyment of the countryside in England and Wales, the conservation and enhancement of its natural beauty, and the need to secure public access for open-air recreation." The first chairman of the Commission is Baroness Wootton. The members are assisted by a committee for Wales on matters affecting Wales and Monmouthshire. A separate Countryside Commission for Scotland was set up by Act of Parliament in October 1967 and formed in 1968.

The Commission for England and Wales took over responsibility for the ten National Parks already established, for 25 "areas of outstanding natural beauty," and for the eleven long-distance footpaths and bridleways so far approved. The National Parks are Brecon Beacons, Dartmoor, Exmoor, Lake District, Northumberland, North Yorks Moors, Peak District, Pembrokeshire Coast, Snowdonia, and Yorkshire Dales. The areas of outstanding natural beauty so far designated are: Anglesey, Cannock Chase, Chichester Harbour, Chilterns, Cornwall, Cotswolds, Devon East, North and South, Dorset, Forest of Bowland (Lancs), Gower, Hampshire East and South, Isle of Wight, Kent Downs, Lleyn, Malvern Hills, Norfolk Coast, Northumberland Coast, Quantock Hills, Shropshire Hills, Solway Coast, Surrey Hills, Sussex Downs, and Dedham Vale on the

Container Ships. *Left, upper:* car carrier and container ship *Atlantic Causeway* opening on Dec. 3, 1969, a new service between the U.K. and the U.S.A.; *lower, Transcontainer I,* first ship on the British and French railways Harwich–Dunkirk service carries 194 containers. *Right:* launching in May of *Australian Enterprise,* built at Kobe, Japan (see page 284).

Essex-Suffolk boundary. The long-distance footpaths and bridleways are: Offa's Dyke Path, Pembrokeshire Coast Path, Pennine Way, South Downs Way, South West Peninsula Coast Path (in 5 sections), Yorkshire Coast and North Yorks Moors Path, and North Downs Way from Farnham, Surrey, to Dover, Kent. Of these, negotiations for rights of way along the entire length have been concluded for only two paths—the Pennine Way and North Yorks Moors (Cleveland Way).

Country Parks. In addition, the Countryside Commission is the central source of reference and advice on the setting up by local authorities of Country Parks, picnic sites, and camping sites with the aid of government grants. The purposes of the new Country Parks are to make it easier for town dwellers to enjoy leisure in the open without travelling too far and thus adding to congestion on the roads, to ease the pressure on places attractive by reason of their remoteness or solitude, and to reduce the risk of damage to the countryside by people settling for a few hours at any spot that takes their fancy. The Countryside Act defines a Country Park as "a park or pleasure ground for the purpose of providing, or

improving, opportunities for the enjoyment of the countryside by the public." The Commission has narrowed this description to "an area of land, or land and water, normally not less than 25 acres in extent, designed to offer to the public, with or without charge, opportunity for recreational activities in the countryside." To qualify for the Commission's recommendation for a grant a Country Park must be readily accessible for motor vehicles and pedestrians, and provided with minimum facilities such as car park, lavatories, and a supervisory service (litter collection, information office, enforcement of byelaws). If it includes a waterway, facilities for sailing, boating, bathing, and fishing should be provided. If approved by the Commission the provision of facilities and the cost of the acquisition of the land rank for a government grant of 75 per cent. Country Parks are to be distinguished by a symbol (see page 336) at their entrances, on wardens' badges, etc.

The first Country Parks to be approved by the commission are: (1) the Wirral peninsula park (Cheshire county council) chiefly along the line of the old West Kirby to Hooton railway line, providing a

varied long distance walk or a series of shorter round walks, the old railway stations and goods yards being used for car parks and picnic sites (estimated cost £200,000), partially opened in 1969; (2) the Elvaston Castle estate (Derbyshire county council and Derby city corporation), 390 acres of woodland, parkland, and farmland, about 6 miles S.E. of Derby (purchase price £128,000, and initial development cost £34,000), mostly to be opened by early 1970; (3) Beacon Fell (Lancashire county council), an isolated 873-ft. hill comprising 269 acres of moorland, conifer plantations, and farmland 8 miles N. of Preston and $3\frac{1}{2}$ miles from the M6 motorway (purchase price £9,250, and initial development cost £5,600), possibly to be opened in 1970; (4 and 5) Cotswold Water Park (Glos and Wilts county councils), two water-filled gravel pits at Ashton Keynes and two at Fairford, providing 700 acres of water in all, later to include 3,000 acres in near-by lakes; (6) Barton Farm (Wilts county council), farmhouse, tithe barn, and 24 acres at Bradford-on-Avon, opened in 1969.

Picnic Sites. The Countryside Act empowers local authorities to provide

Countryside Commission. The standard symbol for Country Parks.

picnic sites for motorists and others using the roads "where a Country Park is not justified but something better than a lay-by is needed by the family who want to stop for a few hours, perhaps to picnic, or to explore the footpaths, or simply to sit and enjoy the view and the fresh air" (White Paper, *Leisure in the Countryside*, 1966). To qualify for the Commission's recommendation of a government grant of 75 per cent a picnic site has to be an area generally between 1 and 25 acres, in attractive surroundings, close to a properly drained and surfaced car park, with provision for removal of litter; the provision of lavatories and water supply is desirable but not compulsory. The sites are of two types—transit sites (for short breaks for rest and refreshment on a long car journey) and recreational sites (for day-trippers from near-by towns, as places to settle in for a few hours rather than as stopping-off places). Most of the latter are located in National Parks, Country Parks, Forest Parks, commons, beaches, or historic houses with grounds; facilities to be provided could include bench seats, tables and chairs, refreshment and shelter huts, and fireplaces. The first eight official picnic sites were named on May 1, 1969; three are in co. Durham, two in Sussex, and one each in Suffolk, Cheshire, and Carmarthenshire. They vary in size from 1 acre near Tow Law, Durham, to 26 acres on Sugar Loaf Mountain, near Llandovery, Carmarthenshire.

Cricket. In a book, *The Story of Continental Cricket,* published in September 1969, the authors claim that the game probably originated in Scandinavia, being brought to England by the Jutish invaders from Denmark in A.D. 400. The original Scandinavian game, mentioned in the Icelandic sagas, was *Knattleikr,* played with wooden bats and ball and some violence.

On Sept. 4, 1969, the Australian Cricket Board of Control announced an experimental change in the l.b.w. rule, intended to reduce "pad play" and kicking the ball away. The new rule states that a striker is out l.b.w. when any part of his person, except his hands, intercepts the ball . . . which in the opinion of the umpire would have hit the

wicket, provided that either (a) the ball pitched in a straight line between wicket and wicket, or (b) the ball pitched outside the batsman's off stump, and in the opinion of the umpire, *he made no genuine attempt to play the ball with his bat.* On the same day the Board, which elected Sir Donald Bradman as chairman, announced that three experimental rules used in Australia for some years are now law: 1. Only two fieldsmen can be stationed behind square leg; 2. No more than five fieldsmen can be placed on the leg side; 3. The new ball is due after 65 eight-ball overs. In England's tour of Australia in 1970–71 six Test matches will be played, including the first ever played in Perth, Western Australia. The Captain Cook bicentenary celebration match will be the New South Wales v. M.C.C. fixture in Sydney in November 1970.

The John Player Sunday League for English and Welsh county cricket clubs started on the first Sunday of the season April 27, 1969. The playing rules of the competition, decided at Lord's on Dec. 9, 1968, are:

(1) Matches start at 2 p.m., with a 10-minute tea interval at 4.20 p.m. or between innings, and close at 6.30 p.m., extended to 6.45 p.m. if four overs or less remain to be bowled.

(2) Each team bowls 40 overs if the match is uninterrupted. If the first 40 overs are not completed by 4.10 p.m., the over in progress is completed, the innings is closed, and the side batting second is limited to the same number of overs. Should the start be delayed or cricket suspended, the overs are adjusted so that both sides have the same number if possible. A minimum of 10 overs each is necessary for a definite result; if the allotted overs are not completed and the side batting second has not been dismissed, the scores of the teams at the highest comparable number of balls received decides the result.

(3) No player may bowl more than eight overs, and a bowler's run-up is limited to 15 yards.

(4) A win scores 4 points; a tie 2 points each; and no result 1 point each. If points are level at the end of the season, the best run-rate decides positions in the table.

Since no charge for admission may be made on Sundays, the public are made temporary members (for the day) of the club on payment at the turnstiles of a nominal membership fee. The John Player tobacco and cigarette company sponsoring the League provided cash for the following prizes:

To the winning side in each match: £50
To the League champions: £1,000
To the runners-up: £500
To the third place side: £250
For the fastest 50 of the season: £250
For every six-hit: one share in £1,000 pool at end of season
For bowlers taking four or more wickets in a match: one share in £1,000 pool at end of season.

See further Cricket tables (p. 221).

On June 10, 1969, the Wrigley Co. Ltd. inaugurated a project designed "to stimulate and encourage an interest in the playing of cricket by the young and the achieving by them of a greater proficiency and skill in the game." The Wrigley Cricket Foundation is to give £10,000 a year, initially for the next five years, to further these aims. The money will be used for coaching courses, visual aids, and the organisation of representative school and youth matches. In 1969 a number of courses for coaches were held, young cricketers from Devon, Kent, London, and Yorkshire attended coaching sessions, and work was started on an instructional film on bowling. In 1970 it is proposed to explore the possibility of a colour feature film of the history of the game.

Crime. Figures issued by the Home Office in August 1969 showed that during 1968 crime in England and Wales rose by 6·8 per cent, compared with the exceptionally small increase of 0·6 per cent in 1967. Indictable offences in 1968 totalled 1,289,000, compared with 1,207,354 in 1967. The major increases were: 1·4 per cent in convictions for violence against the person; 12·4 per cent in convictions for robbery; 14 per cent in persons found guilty of receiving; 28·7 per cent in persons convicted of fraud and false pretences. During 1968 nearly 1,600,000 people were found guilty of offences, but almost two-thirds were for motoring and traffic offences. The number of offences cleared up by the police was nearly 42 per cent.

Murder. A Home Office report, "Murder 1957 to 1968", published on Nov. 6, 1969, gave figures showing the number of murders committed in the U.K. since the Murder (Abolition of the Death Penalty) Act came into force in 1965. In 1964, the last full year before the Act took effect, the total number of murders known to the police was 135. In 1965 the number remained at 135, falling to 122 in 1966, but rising to 154 in 1967, and 148 in 1968. These totals include "abnormal" murders, in which the suspect was found insane or committed suicide. In 1964 there were 59 of these; in 1965, 58; in 1966, 34; in 1967, 64; and in 1968, 52. The number of murders by shooting by normal people was 10 in 1965 (13 per cent of the total number of murders); 10 in 1966 (11·4 per cent); 11 in 1967 (12·3 per cent); and 10 in 1968 (10·4 per cent). These figures compared with 4 in 1957 (7 per cent), and 3 in 1964 (3·9 per cent). The report also showed that there had been a considerable rise in convictions for murder by stabbing, reaching a total of 30 in 1968. The report stated that the risk of being murdered in England and Wales, 3 per million of the population, was the same in 1968 as in 1959, for, although there were more murders, there was a corresponding increase in population. It said that murder remained mainly a

Council of Industrial Design Awards 1969

The Duke of Edinburgh's prize for elegant design was won by the Chubb cash dispenser (*left*), which allows a customer to draw £10 by inserting a coded card into the machine: designed by Jack Howe. *Above:* "Concentric," a five-colour mercerised satin cotton fabric designed by Cathryn Netherwood for Heal Fabrics Ltd.

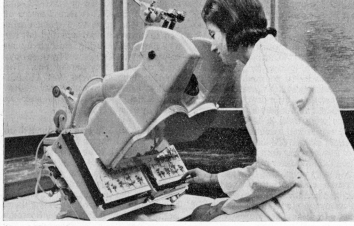

Above: The comparascope made by Vision Engineering Ltd., which superimposes the images of objects placed side by side beneath it, is invaluable for the visual checking of such things as printed circuit assemblies. *Right:* Aluminium-legged restaurant chair designed by Robert Heritage for Race Furniture Ltd., for the *QE2*.

Left: Bed reading light designed by Robert Heritage for Concord Lighting International Ltd. *Right:* the "K Major" diesel engine by Mirrlees National Ltd. develops 70 per cent more power than earlier models for the same weight and size.

All photos by courtesy of the manufacturers and the Council of Industrial Design.

"family" crime, due largely to rage, quarrels, jealousy, and revenge. From 1957 to 1968, 11 policemen and one prison officer had been murdered on duty, three of them victims of "abnormal" murder. Figures showing a steady increase in crimes of violence since 1957 were also included in the report. In 1957 there were 10,960 cases, rising to 23,470 in 1964, and to 31,850 in 1968.

Theft. A survey of loss by theft in 1968, published by the *Security Gazette* on Sept. 18, 1969, showed that property to the value of £50,900,000 was stolen in the U.K., of which only £9 million worth was recovered. These figures refer only to indictable offences known to the police—and many thefts are not reported to the police—and exclude fraud and stolen motor vehicles recovered within one month. The figures for England and Wales only were £47 million, with £8 million worth recovered. In the Metropolitan Police District the losses amounted to over £22 million, of which £2,300,000 worth was recovered. All these were record figures for the U.K., representing a 6·3 per cent increase in losses over 1967, and a 1·7 per cent increase in goods recovered.

London. The crime figures for London during 1968 showed that, while indictable offences increased by 0·8 per cent compared with 1967, there were considerable reductions in some of the more serious crimes, including a 15 per cent drop in burglaries, a 16·2 per cent decrease in breaking into shops and offices, and a 5·1 per cent fall in cases of robbery and assault with intent to rob. But two offences increased in number to the highest total ever recorded: larceny in dwelling houses increased by 1,025 over the 1967 figure, and fraud by 946. There were 57 murders (three more than in 1967) and 89 cases of attempted murder (29 more). 28·4 per cent of indictable offences were cleared up, compared with 24·3 per cent in 1967; the clear-up rate for murder was 96·5 per cent, and for manslaughter and infanticide 92·3 per cent. The London commissioner of police said in June that there had been a "disturbing" increase of 17 per cent in the number of indictable crimes in which firearms were used; in robberies and assaults with intent to rob the increase was 31 per cent.

Provinces. Figures given in the Chief Inspector of Constabulary's report for 1968 showed that crime in the provinces climbed to a record total of more than one million indictable offences, an increase of 8·54 per cent over 1967. The chief increases were: 11·25 per cent in crimes of violence against the person; 4·51 per cent in sexual offences; 13·83 per cent in robbery; 13·94 per cent in shopbreaking; 4·8 per cent in house-breaking; 2·64 per cent in burglary; 18·14 per cent in fraud and false pretences; 18·31 per cent in malicious damage; 15·47 per cent in receiving; 12·35 per cent in forgery; and 13·62 per cent in thefts of motor vehicles. The

number of crimes solved by the police increased from 46·25 per cent in 1967 to 46·6 per cent in 1968. Violence against the police rose from 4,000 cases in 1964 to 6,700 in 1968, an increase of about 67 per cent in the 5-year period.

U.S.A. A report by the Federal Bureau of Investigation in August 1969 stated that the chance of an American becoming the victim of a serious crime had nearly doubled since 1960; in 1968 more than one American in 50 was the victim of murder, rape, assault, burglary, robbery, or car theft. These crimes increased by 17 per cent in 1968, and had increased by 122 per cent since 1960. In 1968 a murder was committed every 39 minutes; forcible rape every 17 minutes; aggravated assault and robbery every 2 minutes; car theft every 41 seconds; larceny every 25 seconds; and burglary every 17 seconds. Of the 13,650 murder cases reported to the police in 1968, 54 per cent of the victims, and 60 per cent of those arrested on suspicion of murder, were negroes. Serious crimes committed by juveniles also rose; of 491,882 suspects arrested during the year, 263,390 were under the age of 18. About 75 per cent of those arrested for robbery were under the age of 25, 56 per cent under 21, and 33 per cent under 18. Arrests for drug offences increased by 64 per cent in 1968; violent crime increased by 19 per cent, robbery by 30 per cent, forcible rape by 15 per cent, murder by 13 per cent, aggravated assault by 11 per cent, larceny by 21 per cent, car theft by 19 per cent, and burglary by 14 per cent. Firearms were used in 8,900 murders, 65,000 aggravated assaults, and 99,000 robberies; since 1964 murder with the use of a firearm has risen by 71 per cent.

More than a quarter of all the murders in 1968 were committed by a relative of the victim, and more than one half of those involved the wife or husband, the wife being the victim in 54 per cent of cases. In cases of lovers' quarrels leading to murder, women were the victims in 51 per cent of the cases, but in "romantic triangles" 90 per cent of the victims were men. Sixty-four policemen were killed in 1968.

The increase in serious crime took place in all areas and regions, for there was an 18 per cent increase in large cities, 17 per cent in the suburbs, and 11 per cent in rural areas. In the metropolitan areas of New York, Los Angeles-Long Beach, San Francisco-Oakland, Baltimore, and Miami, the volume of crime was almost twice the national rate. Just over 20 per cent of serious crimes were solved by the police in 1968, 7 per cent fewer than in 1967.

New York. Violent crime in New York increased in 1968 by 35 per cent over 1967. According to the police department the chief increases were: 21·3 per cent in murder; 51·4 per cent in muggings (bag or wallet snatching, usually with assault); and 6 per cent in assaults. Arrests for murder increased by 28·5 per cent, with 35 per cent—the

largest increase—among those under 16. But rape showed a decrease of 3·4 per cent on 1967. Crimes against property also increased during the year: by 15·5 per cent in burglary, and by 33·1 per cent in car thefts. There were about 500 reports of robbery for every 100,000 persons living in New York during the first nine months of 1968. On a per capita basis the city ranks fourth among the ten largest U.S. cities in reported robberies. Washington, D.C., heads the list with 750 robberies reported for every 100,000 people, and Philadelphia was at the foot of the list, with 140 robberies for every 100,000 residents.

Criminal Injuries Compensation Board. The annual report of this U.K. body, set up in August 1964 to assess the amounts of state compensation to be paid to victims of criminal violence, was published in October 1969. In the year ending March 1969 the Board paid £1,672,958 to victims of crimes of violence, making a total of £4,317,000 paid to 12,232 victims since it was set up. In 1968-69 there were 6,437 applicants, compared with 5,316 in 1967–68, and 3,312 in 1966–67. A record award of £30,000 was made to a woman who had to have her right arm and left leg amputated after being crushed by an empty coal wagon released by three boys on a closed colliery railway line. The previous highest award was £15,580 made in 1965–66 to a university student who suffered brain damage after an attack by a gang of youths.

Criminology. It was announced on May 30, 1969, that a National Institute of Criminology is to be set up in Australia by the Commonwealth government to undertake research, the collation and analysis of statistics, and the training of officers in the investigation of criminal activities and means of combating them. At the same time a Criminology Research Council and Fund will be created jointly by the Commonwealth and the States. The Council, with representatives from the States, will evaluate research needs and allocate money from the fund to specific projects. The creation of these bodies reflects increasing official concern at the rising crime rate in Australia. New Zealand and Singapore may later be invited to participate in the scheme of research.

Cruft's Dog Show. The 1969 Cruft's was held on Feb. 7 and 8 at Olympia, London. The Queen attended on the opening day, the first reigning monarch to visit the Show. A total of 7,786 dogs competed, compared with 7,017 in 1968. The 1969 supreme champion was an Alsatian, Hendrawen's Nibelung of Charavigne, and the reserve champion was Lochranza Strollaway, a cocker spaniel. Two Briards, shaggy black French sheepdogs sometimes called "doormat dogs," a breed never before shown at Cruft's, took between them all

Cruft's. 1969 supreme champion, Alsatian Hendrawen's Nibelung of Charavigne.

the "firsts" in the classes for non-sporting dogs of any variety.

Cublington, Bucks. Construction of an airport at this place near Wing, Bucks, one of the four sites short-listed by the Roskill commission, would mean that at least 7,500 acres of mainly agricultural land would be lost. The commission, which gave this information on April 28, 1969, said that about 1,200 people live within the area covered by the site. Estimates showed that noise from the operating of a four-runway airport would be "intrusive" to 16,300 people; "intrusive and annoying" to 10,900; and "annoying" to a further 7,200. There were no serious problems in constructing an airport, although, because of the undulating terrain, preparation costs of the site would be larger than normal. The proposed airport would offer employment to 65,000 people when working at the full four-runway capacity, which was unlikely before the mid-1990s, when the total number of passengers using it could be over 100 million.

At the public inquiry in July 1969 the county architect and planning officer said that at least 148 villages would be affected if this site was chosen. Three would have to be demolished; life in 12 more would be rendered intolerable by noise; at 52 more it would be made difficult; and at 81 more it would be changed for the worse. Many buildings of architectural and historical interest would be destroyed, and the present rural and peaceful nature of a very large area would be altered. The county's medical offices of health listed 24 hospitals and 38 nursing and welfare homes and mental health hostels which would be affected by noise. Lord

Campbell of Eskdale, chairman of the Milton Keynes Development Corporation, said that the airport would disrupt and delay the planning and building of the new city of Milton Keynes, which, in any case, could not house the large work force the airport would require.

Cyclamates. The sale of these artificial sweeteners was banned by the U.S. government on Oct. 18, 1969. The ban followed reports by government scientists that prolonged doses of cyclamates given to rats and chicken embryos caused deformities and cancer. It was emphasised that there was no evidence that cyclamates could cause cancer in humans. On Oct. 19 it was announced in Sweden, Denmark, and Finland, that all products containing cyclamates would be withdrawn from the domestic market. On Oct. 21 the Canadian Minister of Health announced that cyclamates would be phased out, and on Oct. 23 the U.K. government stated that no food or drink containing the substances is to be sold after Jan. 1, 1970. On Dec. 22 it was stated that in Spain from April 1, 1970, the use of cyclamates will be subject to government authority.

Darwin, Northern Territory, Australia. The Australian government announced in June 1969 that it had agreed in principle to the setting up of a community college here. The type of college proposed will be unique to Darwin, for

not only will it provide for technical training at all levels but it will also incorporate coaching and tutorial facilities for students taking university courses. Adult education facilities also will be provided, including classes for older people who wish to continue their secondary education after leaving school. Consideration is also to be given to providing modified courses for aborigines who wish to further their education.

It was announced in October 1969 that preliminary work will soon start on a new $A9 million rock and earth-filled dam on the Darwin river, 19 miles south of Darwin. It will supply up to 20 million gallons of water a day to the city, enough for about 100,000 people.

D-Day. To commemorate the 25th anniversary of the D-Day landings of June 6, 1944, when British, American, and Canadian troops landed on the Normandy beaches to begin the liberation of Europe, veterans of the invasion returned there on June 5, 1969. On "Omaha Beach" where the American First Division suffered 3,000 casualties there were services of dedication, attended by General Omar Bradley and other senior American commanders, at which the flags of America, Britain, Canada, France, Norway, Belgium, and Holland were unfurled. The official British contingent of 1,000 men set up a tented camp overlooking Ouistreham beach, the scene of bitter fighting, and on June 6 a parade was held here with a fly-past of some 1944 vintage aircraft. Ceremonies were also held at Bayeux, at Le Hamel, and at Pegasus Bridge, where General Gale, commander of the Sixth Airborne Division, men from which were the first to be dropped on D-Day, laid a

D-Day. General Sir Richard Gale, commander of the Sixth Airborne Division in 1944, at Benouville, Normandy, on the 25th anniversary of the Normandy landings.

wreath. The ceremonies ended on June 7 with a march past of all the Allied representatives.

Deafness. A physicist at Stanford University, U.S.A., himself deaf, has developed a device which enables deaf people to use the telephone. It consists of a box coupling a teletype and a telephone line. When a deaf person places the receiver in the coupler and then dials the number of another deaf person a flashing light tells the recipient that there is a call for him. The ensuing conversation consists of messages typed by the two people and recorded on the teletype machines. A quick-flashing light shows on the caller's box if the number is engaged and a slow flash if there is no reply. When these details were given in February it was stated that, because of the cost of the teletype machines, the device was being used on only a limited scale. See also p. 102.

Deaths. The U.K. Registrar-General's quarterly return, published in September 1969, for the first time contained an analysis of deaths registered in England and Wales. This showed that of the 576,788 deaths registered in 1968—some 34,000 more than in 1967—non-violent deaths totalled 554,045, and violent deaths 22,743. Five per cent fewer males, and under 1 per cent fewer females died violently in 1968 than in 1967, the total reduction of 3 per cent being due mainly to a reduction in deaths from road accidents. In 1968 traffic accidents caused 6,249 deaths, compared with 7,098 in 1967 and 7,363 in 1966. The 7 per cent increase in non-violent deaths in 1968 was attributed to the severe weather at the beginning of 1968; in 1967 the same period was unusually mild. Deaths from respiratory diseases, such as pneumonia, bronchitis, and influenza, rose by 24 per cent over the 1967 figure to 84,755 in 1968; deaths from heart diseases, especially coronary thrombosis, rose by 7 per cent, to 138,562; deaths from cancer rose by 2 per cent, with a marked increase in lung cancer among women; and deaths from various types of stroke rose by 4 per cent.

Further evidence of the effect of weather was provided in figures prepared by the Registrar-General, and interpreted by a medical expert on nutrition and body temperature on May 15, 1969. They showed that between 60,000 and 90,000 people die of cold in Great Britain every year. From 1964 to 1967, on average 60,000 more died during the 6 cold months than during the 6 warm months of each year. They were chiefly old people dying from respiratory and circulatory diseases. In Great Britain modern "glass and concrete" blocks become very cold because of the absence of double glazing. The expert believed that people living in centrally heated homes have a life expectation five years longer than those who live in cold, draughty houses, and he instanced one

Decimal Currency. Although the rest of the U.K. will have to accept the seven-sided 50 p coin, the Isle of Man decided to retain a note for this value.

assurance company that offers a 10 per cent reduction in life assurance premiums to persons living in centrally heated homes.

A survey of M.P.s elected between August 1945 and the end of 1967 showed that an M.P. has a better than average life expectation. Out of the 1,418 M.P.s 467 should have died according to the death rate of the whole population, but only 296 did so; 97·2 would be expected to die from heart attacks, but only 81 did so; 94·6 would be expected to die from cancer, but only 54 did so. On the other hand, 15·5 deaths from suicide or accident would be expected, while the actual number was 24. Labour M.P.s showed a higher death rate than Conservatives and were more prone to heart attacks; but more Conservative than Labour M.P.s died from strokes. The survey, carried out by Dr. G. Pincherle of the Institute of Directors' Medical Centre, was published in May 1969.

Australia. The death rate in Australia in 1968 was nearly 5 per cent higher than in 1967, according to figures given by the Bureau of Census and Statistics in Canberra in September 1969. The 1968 figure was 9·1 deaths per 1,000, compared with 8·69 deaths per 1,000 in 1967. The male death rate in 1968 was 10·07 per 1,000, compared with the female death rate of 8·11. Various forms of heart disease were far ahead of all other causes of death, and more than 3,000 died from road accidents.

Decimal Currency. During 1969 the Decimal Currency Board produced several more of its series of booklets concerning the adoption of decimal currency in the U.K. scheduled for Feb. 15, 1971. Because only sixpence and multiples of sixpence have exact decimal equivalents, all other sums will have to be converted, and the Board described three methods of conversion: one for converting money references in contracts and agreements, another (less exact) for shopping, and a third (less exact still) for use in banking and accounting.

For the first, conversion will be on the basis that a £sd penny is worth five twelfths of a decimal penny. In converting, say £18 4s. 6d. by this method the pounds remain the same; 4s. 6d. = 54d. Multiply 54 by $\frac{5}{12}$. Answer is 22½p. Thus the amount is expressed as £18·22½.

The shoppers' conversion table (or "new halfpenny" conversion table) involves a rounding up of some amounts and a rounding down of others. Since the same number of prices are rounded up as are rounded down, gains and losses cancel themselves out. The shoppers' table is as follows:

£sd		£p	
1d	..	½p	a rounding up by 0·2d
2d	..	1p	a rounding up by 0·4d
3d	..	1p	a rounding down by 0·6d
4d	..	1½p	a rounding down by 0·4d
5d	..	2p	a rounding down by 0·2d
6d	..	2½p	(exactly equal)
7d	..	3p	a rounding up by 0·2d
8d	..	3½p	a rounding up by 0·4d
9d	..	4p	a rounding up by 0·6d
10d	..	4p	a rounding down by 0·4d
11d	..	4½p	a rounding down by 0·2d
1s	..	5p	(exactly equal)

By the above table also £18 4s. 6d. converts to £18·22½.

In banking and accounting the new halfpenny will be ignored. The table for use in these operations, called the "whole new penny" conversion table, is:

£sd		£p	£sd		£p
1d	..	0p	1/1	..	5p
2d	..	1p	1/2	..	6p
3d	..	1p	1/3	..	6p
4d	..	2p	1/4	..	7p
5d	..	2p	1/5	..	7p
6d	..	3p	1/6	..	7p
7d	..	3p	1/7	..	8p
8d	..	3p	1/8	..	8p
9d	..	4p	1/9	..	9p
10d	..	4p	1/10	..	9p
11d	..	5p	1/11	..	9p
1s	=	5p	2s	=	10p

By this table £18 4s. 6d. converts to £18·23, and is thus worth ½p (1·2d.) more. When this table is used to convert a sum of money, the largest even number of

Decimal Currency. The Republic of Ireland will go decimal on the same day as the U.K. Above are designs for the reverses and obverse of the new Irish coins.

shillings in it should first be converted (by multiplying by 5), and the rest, which must be an amount between 1d. and 1s. 11d., should be converted by reference to the table.

Example: To convert 17s. 7d.

(a) Convert 16s. ($\times$ 5)   = 80p
(b) Convert 1s. 7d. (by table) = 8p
                             ——
                        88p or
                        £0.88

The introduction of the "whole new penny" table was effected by legislation (the Decimal Currency Act 1969); the shoppers' table has no legal force.

In preparation for the change to decimal currency the $\frac{1}{2}$d. coin ceased to be legal tender on Aug. 1, 1969, and the half-crown on Jan. 1, 1970. The 50p coin was introduced on Oct. 14, 1969, to replace the 10s. note; 120 million of these 7-sided coins were put into circulation. The decision not to replace the 6d. coin with a decimal 2$\frac{1}{2}$p coin was reversed by the House of Commons in April 1969, was re-established during the report stage of the Decimal Coinage Act in May, but was reversed again in Feb. 1970.

The Changeover Period. During the "changeover period," which will last from Feb. 15, 1971 (D Day), for about 18 months, both £sd and £p coins will be legal tender. At the end of the period, circulating shillings and florins will continue to be legal tender (for 5p and 10p), but all other £sd coins will be demonetised. During the period when both coinages are legal tender, the 1969 Act provides that a coin of either currency may be treated as being a coin of the other currency of equal value, viz. 1d. will equal $\frac{5}{12}$p, 3d. = 1$\frac{1}{4}$p, 6d. = 2$\frac{1}{2}$p, 1s. = 5p, 2s. = 10p, and similarly $\frac{1}{2}$p = 1·2d., 1p = 2·4d., 2p = 4·8d., 5p = 1s., 10p = 2s., 50p = 10s.

Legal Tender Limits. After D Day bronze (copper) coins (at present legal tender for amounts up to 1s.) will be legal tender for amounts up to 20p (4s.); the legal tender limit for the nickel-brass 3d. bit will be raised from 2s. to 20p (4s.),

and that for cupro-nickel coins from £2 to £5. The 50p coin (10s.) will be legal tender up to £10.

There will be no changeover period for banks, which will go straight into decimal currency during the four days Feb. 11–14, 1971, when they will be closed. When they reopen on Feb. 15 they will operate in decimal currency only, although still accepting and providing £sd coins. On and after D Day all bills of exchange, cheques, and promissory notes must by law be drawn in decimal currency. Postdated cheques, money orders, postal orders, National Savings warrants, and orders for welfare payments, etc., drawn earlier in £sd will be converted by the whole new penny table. Bank balances of all kinds will be similarly converted.

The Republic of Ireland will introduce decimal currency on the same day as the U.K. There will be six Irish decimal coins: three cupro-nickel coins (for 50 new pence, 10 new pence, and 5 new pence) and three bronze coins (for 2 new pence, 1 new penny and $\frac{1}{2}$ new penny), as in the British system. The new coins will

all be round, with the exception of the 50 new pence coin, which will have seven equal curved sides as in the British design for this value.

Defence (U.K.). The 1969 defence estimates, published on Feb. 20, showed a reduction of £5 million from the previous year's figures—the first decrease in 10 years. The 1968 figure was £2,271 million, and the 1969 estimate £2,266 million. The latter figure represents less than 6 per cent of the gross national product, as against 7 per cent in the years up to 1965. Among other points made in the White Paper were the inadequacy of recruitment (10,000 below the target figure in 1968–69), resulting in the extension for a further 5 years of liability to call-up of the Army General Reserve; the continuing withdrawal from east of Suez and support for Nato; the shift of the nuclear deterrent from V bombers to Polaris submarines; the formation of a consortium of the U.K., West Germany, Italy, and the Netherlands to design and build a new swing-wing multi-role combat aircraft (MRCA), and the decision to give no more orders to Cammell Laird, Birkenhead, but rely entirely on Vickers, Barrow-in-Furness, for the future construction of nuclear-powered fleet submarines. (The fourth of this class of submarine, H.M.S. *Churchill*, was launched in December 1968, and three more are under construction.) The Royal Navy scrapped 39 ships during 1968–69. The cost of cancelling the order for the American F-111 aircraft was £16 million net.

On the withdrawal from the east-of-Suez theatre, the White Paper reported that the Singapore dockyard was formally handed over in December 1968 to the Singapore Government to be run on a commercial basis. By April 1969, 33,000 fewer people in S.E. Asia were working for the Services, including 21,000 British servicemen. By April 1969, 5,500 servicemen were withdrawn from Malaysia and Singapore, and the

Derrick Barge. The "Ingram Derrick Barge No. 7," the biggest barge ever built in Australia, came into use in 1969 for offshore rig construction and pipelaying. It is 401 ft. long, and the derrick can lift 600 tons.

Diving Suits. New Swedish diving suits can be inflated to give buoyancy and provide insulation that preserves body heat in the coldest waters.

Brigade of Gurkhas were reduced by 1,500. As part of the amalgamation of regiments, the Royal Scots Greys will be merged with the 3rd Carabiniers (Prince of Wales Dragoon Guards) in 1971.

At the time of the White Paper's publication British forces were deployed round the world as follows: 246,000 in Great Britain, 59,600 in Europe, 17,500 in the Mediterranean and Near East, 51,500 in the Middle and Far East, and 37,000 elsewhere. A total force of 340,000 officers and men will be necessary after all reductions and withdrawals have been carried out, and this will require the recruitment of 35,000 men each year.

Diving Suits. New Swedish diving suits which are inflated with air as insulation against icy waters and to give any buoyancy required were demonstrated in August 1969. Made of quarter-inch-thick neoprene bonded on both sides to stretch nylon, a suit has enough elasticity to be blown up to grotesque proportions. When the garment is deflated it allows the diver exceptional freedom of movement, as well as keeping him completely dry. For underwater swimming the buoyancy of the small volume of air needed for insulation and comfort is counterbalanced by lead weights, and the diver can regulate his rate of ascent or descent by operating air exhaust and inlet valves.

Divorce. On its third presentation to Parliament the Divorce Law Reform Bill completed its passage through the U.K. House of Commons on June 13, 1969, after a sitting lasting 24 hours 11 minutes, when the third reading was carried by 109 votes to 55. A private member's bill introduced by Alec Jones, Labour M.P. for Rhondda West, with government support, it was most actively sponsored by Leo Abse, Labour M.P. for Pontypool, who had introduced a similar bill in 1963. The Bill abolished the conception of the matrimonial offence as the sole grounds for divorce, and substituted the principle of the "irretrievable breakdown" of a marriage. In effect it offers divorce by consent of both partners on evidence of two years' breakdown, and by one partner (without the other's agreement) after five years'. The Solicitor-General stated that the Divorce Reform Bill would not become law until a new bill to deal with the disposition of the matrimonial home and property, and to incorporate the proposals of the Law Commission on financial provisions, had been passed.

The Law Commission published its report, "Financial Provision in Matrimonial Proceedings," on Sept. 23, 1969. It outlined reforms to improve the provisions for divorced wives and their children, placing responsibility for securing these upon the courts. The proposals' aim is that the divorced wife and her children should be in the position they ought to have been in had the marriage not broken down, and the report said that the courts ought to take into account the family's standard of living, the conduct of the spouses, the wife's contribution to the home, and her loss of entitlement to a widow's pension. In practice this means that the courts will be allowed to transfer a half share in the home to the divorced wife in recognition of the fact that her housework and child-caring form a contribution towards the financial assets of a family. The report also advised greater use by the courts of powers to award lump-sum payments, but declared that periodical payments to a divorced wife should cease on her remarriage and that payments for a child should cease on his 16th birthday. Finally the report called for the abolition of the right to claim damages for adultery,

enticement, seduction, and harbouring of a spouse or child. The report included a draft bill to implement its provisions, which will come into force on Jan. 1, 1971, at the same time as the Divorce Law Reform Act.

Domesday Book. This public record of England is to be republished in facsimile, edited by Prof. V. H. Galbraith, the world authority on the Domesday Book. When this was announced in July 1969 it was stated that the 1,700 pages of the Great and Little Domesday, the unabbreviated survey of the eastern circuit Essex, Norfolk, and Suffolk, will be reproduced in a separate volume for each county, and that there will also be about six volumes of reprints of existing printed Domesday books, including the Exon Domesday, the unabridged survey of the south-western circuit which is preserved in Exeter Cathedral. It is hoped that the first volume will be published in 1970.

Domestic Servants. Figures published by the Registrar-General in January 1969 showed that in the whole of England and Wales there were 810 families with three or more domestic servants in 1966. Out of about 15 million households, 58,300 employed a total of 64,510 servants. The number of men in service was 4,210, and of the 60,000 women employed 8,000 were married.

Driving Schools. The U.K. Minister of Transport said on Feb. 4, 1969, that from Aug. 1, 1970, it will be illegal for anyone to give professional driving tuition unless he is registered with the Ministry as an approved driving instructor. But provided no payment is involved relatives and friends will still be free to teach learners.

Driving Tests. A major change in the U.K. driving test laws came into force on June 2, 1969. From that date motorists who take their tests on cars with automatic transmission will have to take a second test on a car with a clutch and manually operated gearbox before being allowed to drive one of the latter type. The existing Group 1 licence, covering cars and heavier vehicles was split into two groups: 1A, those with manual gear boxes; 1B, those with automatic transmission. Drivers who pass the 1A test may drive 1B cars. Drivers who had passed their test before June 2, 1969, were unaffected by these changes in the law. The new regulations also stipulated that during a driving test candidates cannot take a test on a dual-controlled vehicle unless the second control has been put out of action, and that examiners can ask a candidate to show his driving licence.

Learner drivers in Tacoma, Washington became the first drivers in the U.S.A. to be examined and licensed by electronic machines instead of by human examiners when a system called METER (Machine Examination, Teaching, Evaluation, and Re-education) started in 1969. The system does not involve the use of a car, for the examination is conducted with simulators, resembling driver's car seat, complete with steering wheel, brakes, and other controls. Various road situations, including dangerous incidents, are shown on a film screen placed in the same position as the windscreen, and the applicant is tested on his responses to these situations. The system enables 16 tests to be given in an hour instead of three by the conventional method.

Drug Addiction. A report given to the U.N. Commission on Narcotics in Geneva on Jan. 14, 1969, showed that there is a world-wide increase in drug-taking. The report said that there had been a definite increase in the use of cannabis among the youth of Western Europe and other developed countries, with the U.K. holding first place in illicit traffic in the drug. There was also an increase in the use of new drugs such as LSD, and a significant rise in the abuse of barbiturates and heroin in Persia, Hong Kong, Thailand, and other Far Eastern countries.

A report on the drug cannabis indica (Indian hemp, hashish, marijuana, or "pot") by the U.K. Home Secretary's Advisory Committee on Drug Dependence, prepared by a sub-committee under the chairmanship of Baroness Wootton of Abinger, was published on Jan. 8, 1969. Its main recommendations were that: possession of a small amount of cannabis should not normally be regarded as a serious crime to be punished by imprisonment; unlawful possession of cannabis without knowledge should not be an "absolute offence" to which there is no defence; the law should be altered so that occupiers and landlords would be guilty of allowing premises to be used for smoking cannabis only if the premises were open to the public, the managers of such premises being liable only if they knew cannabis was being smoked there; and new legislation should separate the control of the "soft" drug cannabis from laws controlling "hard" drugs of addiction such as heroin and other opiates. The report also proposed that the existing maximum penalties for using cannabis (a £1,000 fine and 10 years' imprisonment on indictment, and a £250 fine and 12 months' imprisonment on summary conviction) should be reduced to 2 years' imprisonment and an unlimited fine on indictment, and a £100 fine and four months' imprisonment on summary conviction. The committee rejected the suggestion that, in the light of present knowledge of the drug and its effects, cannabis smoking should be made lawful, and said that in the sense that it was a potent drug having as wide a capacity as alcohol to alter mood, judgment, and functional ability, it was a "dangerous" drug. In terms of physical harmfulness, however, the committee regarded it as much less dangerous than the opiates, amphetamines, and barbitu-

rates, and probably no more and possibly less dangerous than alcohol. The report was received with widespread antagonism, and the Home Secretary announced on January 23 that the government had no intention of introducing legislation to reduce existing penalties for the possession, sale, or supply of cannabis. But the subject was by no means regarded as closed, for the Home Secretary's advisory committee on drug dependence set up two further sub-committees on drugs: the first, under the chairmanship of Baroness Wootton, to examine the use and misuse of amphetamine and similar stimulant drugs, as well as completing a study of LSD; and the second, under the chairmanship of William Deedes, Conservative M.P., to review the powers of arrest and search by police in relation to cannabis and other restricted drugs.

Statistics given in a Home Office report published on August 4, 1969, showed that the number of *known* drug addicts in the U.K. in 1968 rose by more than 60 per cent over the 1967 figure. Of the 1968 total of 2,782, 1,775 were in the 15–23 age group, and 2,240 were addicted to heroin. Convictions for drug offences concerned with heroin, cocaine, opium, and cannabis rose by 40 per cent in 1968 to 4,836, and there were 2,957 convictions for misuse of drugs such as amphetamines and hallucinogens. 1968 was the first year in which doctors, under the Dangerous Drugs (Notification of Addicts) regulations, were required to notify particulars of addicts receiving attention. The report admitted that information on obtaining drugs from illicit sources is incomplete, and that the total number of addicts in Britain cannot be estimated.

A report on the second year's work of the Chelsea, London, drug addiction treatment centre, run by the National Addiction and Research Institute, was published in January 1969. It stated that a narcotic drug, physeptone, was proving successful in weaning addicts from hard drugs. First used in the U.S.A., where it is known as methedone, physeptone is a substitute drug which, taken orally in liquid form, kills the craving for hard drugs such as heroin and cocaine.

Australia. The Minister for Customs told the Senate on Sept. 12, 1969, that drug addiction in Australia was increasing at the rate of 80 per cent each year. A national committee on drug abuse, made up of representatives from Federal and State health departments and other government authorities, had been set up under an agreement made in February. The Minister for Health said on Nov. 4, 1969, that a nation-wide system to monitor the movement of narcotics and other drugs of dependence within States and between States would come into operation during January 1970. Initially concerned with narcotics, the system will involve regular reporting by importers, local manufacturers, formulators, and wholesalers, of all transactions involving narcotic substances.

Drunkenness. A report on drink offences during 1968, made by the Christian Economic and Social Research Foundation from information given by more than 50 chief constables was published in April 1969. It showed that pedestrian drunkenness offences in England and Wales rose from 83,992 in 1962 to 70,499 in 1966, and to 78,500 in 1968. Since 1960 police proceedings against motorists for alleged offences relating to drink and drugs had increased in about the same proportion as the number of vehicle licences. The total number of offences for 1968 was thought to be about 20,000, compared with 12,000 in 1967. The percentage of drivers under the age of 30 involved in alleged drunken driving cases rose from 31·5 per cent in 1962 to 49·2 per cent in 1968, accounting for 50 per cent of convictions; while offences by people over this age fell from 68·5 per cent to 50·8 per cent. The report said that purchases, or attempted purchases, of intoxicating liquor by people under the age of 18 rose by 7 per cent, from 2,481 in 1967 to 2,651 in 1968. The police district with the highest figure reported was Durham, with 466 cases. During 1968, in spite of the increased duty levied on wines and spirits in the Budget, consumption of beer and wine rose by 2 per cent and 4 per cent respectively over the previous year, while consumption of spirits fell by 2 per cent.

In June the same Foundation published a booklet, "Ten Years of Advertising Alcohol," which showed that in the U.K. the £911 million spent by the public on alcohol in 1958 had risen to £1,585 million in 1967. The Foundation declared that more than £25 million was spent on advertising alcohol in 1967, an increase of £9 million compared with 1958. It also reported that more people were spending a greater proportion of their income on alcoholic drinks than previously, with a corresponding rise in drunkenness; this was particularly evident among young people, among whom the incidence of proved drunkenness (nearly 18·8 per cent in 1959) had risen in 1967 by over one-third to 25·3 per cent.

A Wiesbaden doctor, Wolfram Kuhnau, and a team of Swiss chemists announced in February 1969 that they had developed a pill which speedily reduces the alcohol level in the blood, so that those who have had too much to drink regain sobriety soon after taking it. The pill was put on sale in Switzerland during 1969, but is to be given a further year of testing before being put on the German market for general sale.

Dublin, Ireland. A new £1 million car-ferry terminal at St. Michael's Wharf, Dun Laoghaire, was officially opened on April 14, 1969. The main feature is a pier 575 ft. long and 70 ft. wide. One of the two principal buildings is a 300-ft.-long three-level passenger building on the pier accommodating, at first-floor level, all

Duke of Edinburgh Awards. Two sets of girl twins received "golds" in February 1969—the Flatterses (*left*) and the Ellertons.

Boy twins—John and Timothy Yeoman—received "golds" in December.

passengers travelling without cars, and on the other a 144 ft.-square car-customs hall, with 12 customs examination bays. This building also houses the various administrative offices. Car-loading ramps situated on each side of the pier allow two vessels to berth simultaneously. The terminal is illuminated by 80-ft.-high lighting masts, designed to throw a bright, virtually shadowless light over the whole assembly area. The new terminal has a capacity for 1,200 cars each day.

Duchamp, Marcel. All the obituary notices of this famous unconventional painter, the "father of modern art," chronicled the accepted "fact" that after 1923 he painted no more, retiring to the enjoyment of chess and conversation until his death on Oct. 1, 1968. But after his death it was discovered that he had been for 20 years secretly painting the walls and ceiling of a rented room in New York. The work is entirely enclosed and can be viewed only through a hole cut in one wall. The whole room was in April 1969 removed to the Philadelphia Museum. The subject of the work was reported in May to be "the relationship between a love-goddess and the male sex," the same as the subject of Duchamp's last known work, the "Large Glass."

Duke of Edinburgh Awards. Changes in the Duke of Edinburgh's Award Scheme were announced in February 1969. The boys' scheme which started in 1956, and the girls', which followed in 1958, originally tended to develop separately, but they are now fully integrated into one scheme. The age range has been raised to 21 for all awards, thus giving more time for those under pressure at their work. While the bronze, silver, and gold stages remain, the new conditions are designed to encourage direct entry at whichever stage is most appropriate to

the individual. The emphasis on service is now more on the practical side, encouraging those with adequate training or briefing to do voluntary work. At the gold stage, in the "design for living" section a more adult look was introduced, and young people of both sexes are now able to take part in activities such as cooking or hair-styling, previously exclusive to young women. In the "interests" section, which offers a choice of over 200 hobbies covering the arts, crafts, and general leisure pursuits, the new conditions give greater freedom of choice and the opportunity of changing the interest first chosen.

When these changes were announced it was stated that since the inception of the scheme the total number of entrants had been estimated at 601,000; the awards gained had totalled 232,000, including 19,300 gold awards.

Duncan Report. The U.K. review committee on overseas expenditure, consisting of Sir Val Duncan, chairman of Rio Tinto-Zinc, Sir Frank Roberts, former ambassador to NATO, Russia, and West Germany, and Andrew Shonfield, the economist, set up in August 1968 to review British representation overseas, in view of Great Britain's changing international role, published its report on July 16, 1969. The government accepted in principle the proposals made by this independent committee, which included: the streamlining of the diplomatic service and the recruitment of more specialists trained in commerce and economics who will be able to help British businessmen abroad more effectively; the seconding of promising diplomatic career men to industry for a period, and the bringing in of businessmen to spread their experience and knowledge through the service; the closing or reduction of smaller overseas missions in the "outer area" including some parts of Africa, Asia, and Latin

America; the formation of a task force of commercially trained diplomats who can be sent to any country where they are needed; and the focusing of British commercial diplomacy on Western Europe (and the Common Market), the U.S.A., Canada, Australia, and New Zealand. The committee recommended a 50 per cent reduction in information services, which would fall mainly on the British Information Service and BBC foreign-language broadcasts, and a one-third reduction in the number of Service attachés and defence staff in British embassies and legations.

Dunnage. Inflated rubber bags in use as dunnage (wedges between cargo items) in place of the conventional wooden variety. Called the Uniroyal Shor-Kwik dunnage bags, the rubber bags can bear a pressure of 10 lb. per square inch. They are here seen wedging rolls of paper en route from Canada to the U.S.A.

Electric Cars. *Left:* The Italian "Urbanina," powered by a 24-volt battery, seen at the Turin Motor Show in November. *Right:* Enfield Automotive's four-seater runs for 35 miles on one battery charge; its top speed is 40 m.p.h.

Dysart, Fife, Scotland. The restoration and preservation of the birthplace of one of Australia's foremost explorers, John McDouall Stuart (1815–1866), and the erection of a museum alongside the house, were announced by the Kirkcaldy corporation in March 1969. Personal relics (and also financial assistance) from Australia are expected. Stuart, son of an army captain, went to South Australia in 1838 and, as a survey draughtsman, accompanied Charles Sturt's expedition to the centre of Australia in 1844–45. In 1858 and 1859 he made expeditions into the interior, and in 1860 on an attempt to cross the continent from south to north he reached what are now called the MacDonnell, Murchison, and McDouall ranges, but had to return to Adelaide. Another attempt at a south-north crossing in Jan.–Sept. 1861 failed, but Stuart succeeded at his third attempt in Oct. 1861–July 1862, reaching the Timor Sea near where Darwin now stands. On the return journey (July–Dec.) he and his party suffered terrible privations which, with the strains imposed by his earlier journeys, undermined his health. Returning to Great Britain in 1864, he died in London two years later.

Eisenhower Memorials. The National Trust of Scotland said in April that it was planning the reconstruction of one of the rooms in Culzean Castle on the Ayrshire coast as a memorial to Pres. Eisenhower. After the Second World War the General was presented with the life gift of a flat in the Castle, as part of Scotland's thanks to him for the victory. The room, complete with government-issue blotter, maps, and chairs used by the General, is to be opened to the public in June 1970.

The seat of the Marquess of Ailsa, the Castle, which was built in 1777, was given to the National Trust in 1945.

Eisteddfod. The Royal National Eisteddfod was held at Flint at the beginning of August 1969. The Crown went to Dafydd Rowlands, lecturer in Welsh at Trinity College, Carmarthen, for his poem on a wide variety of themes, including Vietnam, Prague, and Biafra. The Bardic Chair went to James Nicholas, a Pembrokeshire schoolmaster, for his poem "The Call," written in strict Welsh metre and inspired by the sculptures of Henry Moore. The Prose Medal was awarded to Emyr Jones, a headmaster of Abergele, and the second prize to Dr. John Rowlands, the novelist.

ELDO. Failure continued to dog the European Launcher Development Organisation's Europa 1 rocket. The 1969 launching took place at the Woomera rocket range in South Australia, on July 3. As in 1968, the British first stage and the French second stage on the 104-ton missile worked perfectly, but the German third stage failed. The launching was a test flight to place an Italian satellite into a polar orbit.

Electric Batteries. A new charging process for nickel-cadmium batteries, reducing the recharging time from hours to minutes, has been developed by the McCulloch Corporation, Los Angeles, U.S.A., who demonstrated the process in September 1969. It is a special pulse-charging system in which the battery is short-circuited for microsecond periods between a series of very high current charging pulses. This causes gas layers on the plate surfaces to break up, while spot concentrations of the high charge current are avoided. Not only is the battery charged in about 15 mins., but its performance is improved, and there is no danger of overcharging. Batteries for

electric shavers, tape recorders, radios and other small electrical appliances can all be recharged with a unit about the size of two cigarette packets. As it has particular value for the recharging of car batteries this new development could well speed the development of the electric car.

Electric Cars. At a New York exhibition by the Institute of Electrical and Electronics Engineers in March 1969 three new electric car prototypes were put on show. The Gulton-American Motors station wagon, using standard re-chargeable nickel-cadmium batteries, has a range of 100 miles at 30 m.p.h. and a top speed of 60 m.p.h. To recharge completely depleted batteries takes 15 minutes. The weight of the car with batteries is 4,000 lb. New higher energy batteries under development should reduce this to 2,000 lb., including 300 lb. of batteries; a top speed of 70 m.p.h. would be possible, but a wholly depleted battery would need a recharge time of 2 hours. For this car an electronic method of using the energy of the vehicle's own impetus to control its speed and apply its brakes has been devised. The second car shown was a converted Renault Dauphine powered by four long-life silver-zinc "Silvercel" batteries weighing about 400 lb. Range on one charge is 150 miles, and top speed is 60 m.p.h. The third exhibit was the Alden Starr car system for carrying passengers or cargo through airports, hospitals, shopping centres, etc.; it consists of a chain of small electric cars capable of 60 m.p.h., travelling along a special track at intervals spaced out by computer-controlled signals.

Enfield Automotive launched Britain's first passenger city car, the Enfield "465", on Oct. 31, 1969. The car is a four-seater, just over 9ft. long and 4 ft. wide, with a turning circle of 18 ft., a top speed of 40 m.p.h., and a range of about

Electron Microscope. The first commercial million-volt electron microscope to be built in Europe was constructed in 1969 at Harlow, Essex, by A.E.I. Scientific Apparatus Ltd. for the U.K. Atomic Energy Authority.

35 miles. It has a built-in device for recharging the batteries overnight, and its running costs should amount to about 4d a mile. It will be sold in Britain in 1970 for about £550.

Electricity, Consumption of. Figures given in July 1969 by the Electrical Development Association showed that Norway leads the world in the consumption of electricity. In 1966, the last year for which comparable figures were available, Norway had an average consumption of more than 11,000 units of electricity per head. Following Norway in per capita consumption rates were Canada with 7,000 units a year; Sweden with 5,500; U.S.A. with 5,200; Australia with 3,500; New Zealand with 3,400; and the U.K. with 3,000. In consumption rates per household, New Zealand ranked second to Norway with 6,200 units a year, followed by Sweden with 6,100; Canada with 5,900; U.S.A. with 5,300; Australia with 3,500; and the U.K. with 3,400.

Electricity, Generation of. A power-station building programme for the early 1970s, costing over £400 million, was sanctioned by the U.K. government during October 1969. It covers four new power stations: one at Heysham, Lancs, and one at Sizewell, Suffolk, to be nuclear-powered, of the advanced gas-cooled reactor type, bringing the number of this type under construction to six; one at the Isle of Grain, at the mouth of the Thames, to be oil-powered; and one at Drax, near Selby, Yorks, to be coal-powered. Heysham was the first station for which tenders were invited, and building will start there in the

spring of 1970; tenders for the Isle of Grain station, and finally for Drax and Sizewell together, were invited later.

"Eleven-Plus." The U.K. National Foundation for Educational Research, in a report published on May 5, 1969, said that more than half the 162 local education authorities in England and Wales had dropped English and Arithmetic from the "eleven-plus" examination and that 104 authorities intended to abolish the examination altogether (four of them before 1970). The report said that the number of authorities giving an English test had fallen from 120 in 1964 to 62 in 1968. A verbal reasoning test, however, remained almost universal.

Elizabeth Farm House, Parramatta, N.S.W. It was announced in July 1969 that this stone farmhouse, Australia's oldest home and the birthplace of the nation's wool industry, is to be restored to its original condition and preserved. The house, built in 1793, stands in five acres of parkland at Parramatta, about 14 miles west of Sydney, and was originally the home of John Macarthur, who used Merino sheep from South Africa and Britain to start the Australian wool industry. In 1968 the Elizabeth Farm Museum Trust was formed, and in October of that year it purchased the property for $A50,000 from the Swann family, who had owned it since 1904. The restoration work is expected to cost a further $A50,000, and various organisations have promised financial support. When the work is completed the house will be refurnished with Macarthur family heirlooms. The house figured in *Historic Homesteads of Australia*, commissioned by the Australian Council of National Trusts, a monumental work published in October 1969.

Emigration and Immigration. The results of the 10 per cent sample census made in Great Britain in April 1966, as far as they reflect the number of immigrants and their way of life, were published in June 1969. About 1,200,000 of the population originated from the mostly coloured "new Commonwealth" countries, but this figure includes about 425,000 dependent children, of whom 74 per cent were born in Britain. In 1966 there were 480,000 males and 373,000 females living in Britain who had been born in the "new Commonwealth," and 58,000 males and 67,000 females who had been born in the "old Commonwealth" (Australia, Canada, and New Zealand). About half of all immigrants lived in the south-east, two-thirds of the "new Commonwealth" immigrants in the six major conurbations. Forty-three per cent lived in Greater London, 8·6 per cent in the outer metropolitan area, and 10 per cent in the West Midlands. On living conditions the report showed that of the 326,000 households in which the head or spouse was born in a "new Commonwealth"

country about 118,000 shared a dwelling, and of this number 43,000 did not have the exclusive use of a stove or sink. Of the total 70,000 "old Commonwealth" households more than 8,000 shared a dwelling, and 1,250 of this number had to share a stove and sink. Rather less than half the "new Commonwealth" immigrants (156,000 households) owned their own homes, compared with half the "old Commonwealth" immigrants (35,000 households); and 30,000 from the "new Commonwealth" lived in council-owned property, compared with 11,000 from the "old Commonwealth." In most of the "new Commonwealth" households there were two, three, or four people; in 30,400 there were six; and in 14,500 there were eight or more. Unemployment in both "new" and "old" Commonwealth was 3 per cent.

Other figures obtained in the 1966 sample census, published on Sept. 2, 1969, showed that 1,080,000 men born outside Britain were employed in the country in 1966. Of these, 7 per cent were employers and managers, compared with 10 per cent employers and managers in the population as a whole. Six per cent were professional workers, compared with 4·5 per cent; 26 per cent skilled manual workers, compared with 32 per cent; and 31 per cent semi-skilled and unskilled manual workers, compared with 23 per cent.

In November the figures of babies born to coloured immigrants in Inner and Outer London, and in some other areas, during March and April 1969 were officially published. The proportion of the total number of births varied from one third in Lambeth and Brent and one quarter in Islington, Haringey, and Ealing to one tenth in Camden and Tower Hamlets and one thirteenth in Lewisham, one fifteenth in Barnet, and one nineteenth in Enfield. One fifth of all babies born in Hammersmith, Wandsworth, Newham, Waltham Forest, Bradford, Slough, and Warley were coloured, but only one fourteenth in Leeds.

Figures included for the first time in the U.K. Registrar-General's quarterly report, published on September 24, 1969, showed that Britain's peak net loss in population since 1965 was 63,000 in 1967, compared with 19,000 in 1968. In 1967 approximately 56,000 people emigrated to Canada (compared with 34,000 in 1968), and 13,000 emigrated to New Zealand (compared with 6,000 in 1968). The number emigrating to Australia was approximately 76,000 in each year. Emigration to South Africa was 16,085 in 1968, and 18,811 in 1969. In 1967–68, 87,000 immigrants came into Britain from the "new Commonwealth" countries, and 17,000 returned home; in 1966–67 the figures were 66,000 and 21,000. In 1968, 15,000 immigrants entered Great Britain from Australia, Canada, and New Zealand (compared with 17,000 in 1967) and 25,000 returned home (compared with 12,000 in 1967). In both 1967 and 1968 the number of emigrants in "the professional and managerial groups" was 55,000, but the immigrants in this group dropped from 17,000 in 1967 to 15,000 in 1968.

According to figures given by the U.K. Ministry of Technology in April 1969 the "brain drain" from Great Britain is increasing. The net migration of scientifically qualified people reached 5,000 in 1967, compared with 3,600 in 1966. Most of the 5,000 were engineers and technologists, but the number included 1,400 scientists, double the number who left in 1966. The number of engineers migrating to the U.S.A. appeared to have fallen, but the number going to Commonwealth countries showed a steady increase.

Australia. The record number of 175,000 settlers arrived in Australia in 1968–69. This was 15,000 more than the hoped-for figure. Of the 118,400 who arrived under assisted passage arrangements, 73,500 came from Great Britain, and the balance largely from continental Europe. The total of assisted newcomers from Britain was another record, the previous highest being 70,750 in 1965–66. Arrivals under the special assistance programme, mostly from Northern Europe, totalled 15,300. Scandinavian countries alone provided 4,900 of this figure—more than three times the number in the previous year. Settlers who travelled without financial assistance from the Australian Government numbered more than 57,000. Over 3,500 Americans settled during the year, a 27 per cent increase over the previous year. An official survey into the migration of scientists between 1961 and 1967 showed that Australia had gained 351 more than she had lost.

Australia granted citizenship by naturalisation to 9,790 Asians between July 1, 1956, and December 31, 1968. They included 6,162 Chinese; 2,130 Australian-protected persons; 900 Japanese; 228 Indonesians; 107 British-protected persons; 202 Burmese; 188 Filipinos; 36 Thais; 14 Koreans; 18 Vietnamese; 3 Afghans; and 2 Cambodians. An additional 1,077 Asians, who were already British subjects, acquired Australian citizenship by registration since July 1, 1964.

The Federal Immigration Department announced in August 1969 that it is arranging six-week "crash" courses to teach English to professionally qualified migrants to Australia who are unable to speak the language. Five or six courses a year are planned, to be held in Melbourne and Sydney, and any migrant may volunteer for it.

The Minister for Immigration announced in October 1969 that Australia plans to take at least 10,000 refugees from Czechoslovakia as migrants during the 1969–70 financial year—double the number taken in the previous year. The Minister also announced on Nov. 30 that from Jan. 1, 1970, no assisted migrant arriving in Australia on official

transport will be required to pay more than $A25 towards passage costs, and no contribution would be asked for any child under 19 years of age. This concession will be available to migrants from 25 countries.

New Zealand. The Minister of Labour announced in April 1969 that New Zealand would try to double her immigration from Great Britain to meet the demand for skilled workers. The government had decided to try to recruit up to 2,500 immigrants from the U.K. under the subsidy scheme during the twelve months ending March 31, 1970, and up to 500 under the assisted-passage scheme. For the first time, professional workers, technicians, and those with skills above tradesman level are eligible for sponsorship under the subsidy scheme, and employers' contributions under the scheme by air passage are reduced by about one-third. Each year approximately 16,000 people emigrate to New Zealand from the U.K.; nearly one quarter travel under the assisted passage scheme, while the remainder pay their own fares.

Enzymes. These complex ferments, essential to life, are secreted by body cells and act as catalysts in chemical changes in proteins and other bodily substances. American research chemists announced on Jan. 17, 1969, that they had succeeded in producing the first laboratory-made enzyme, synthetic ribonuclease. This enzyme plays an essential role by breaking down ribonucleic acid (RNA) in the nuclei of cells. The synthesis was achieved by two groups of scientists, using different methods and working independently, at the Rockefeller University in New York, and at the Merck, Sharp, and Dohme Research Laboratories in New Jersey. Their historic achievement marks another step towards the treatment of several diseases believed to be caused by malfunctioning enzymes, and to a better understanding of enzyme action.

Epping Forest, Essex. The Epping corporation announced in February 1969 that a school of woodland appreciation is to be built in the forest, under the management of the Field Studies Council. Up to 100 children a day will be taught the fundamentals of biology and applied ecology there. It is also intended to use the centre for week-end adult education, teachers' training courses, and natural history societies.

Equal Pay. Mrs. Barbara Castle, Minister for Employment and Productivity, told the Labour party conference at Brighton on Sept. 29, 1969, that the Government would introduce an equal pay bill in the next session of Parliament. By the end of 1975, it will be illegal to discriminate against six million working women with regard to rates of pay. The bill will make it illegal for an agreement to lay down special rates for men and

women workers; illegal to give men and women different pay in the same establishment for doing similar work; and illegal for an employer to pay different rates on ground of sex after a job evaluation survey. Where unions and employers fail to agree, the matter will be referred to a tribunal empowered to give a ruling binding in law. The implementation of this pledge on equal pay for women will add to Britain's national wage bill a sum stated to be between £600 million and £800 million annually.

Australia. After a test case hearing brought by the Council of Trade Unions which lasted several months, the Federal Arbitration Commission announced on June 19, 1969, that Australian women workers are to receive equal pay. The pay scale of women doing work of the same nature as men is to be increased in stages from 85 per cent of the male rate on Oct. 8, 1969, to 100 per cent by January 1972. But the decision covers only Federal pay awards, which union officials said would affect only 50,000 out of 1,200,000 women. Prior to the decision most Federal and State awards contained a 25 per cent differential between male and female rates. The Commission stated that work essentially or usually performed by women should not be paid for at the same rate as men.

Erasmus Prize. The 1969 Erasmus prize, the Dutch award given annually to persons or institutions who have contributed most to European thinking on cultural and social subjects, was awarded to the French Roman Catholic philosopher and author Gabriel Marcel, and to the German nuclear expert and professor of philosophy Carl-Friedrich von Weizsaecker. The two men received the prize, which when shared is increased from 100,000 to 150,000 guilders (£17,370), from Prince Bernhard at Rotterdam on Oct. 27, 1969.

Estate Agents. Estate agents became members of a properly registered and regulated profession for the first time in Great Britain in 1969 when the U.K. Estate Agents Council published a register of members and a code of conduct. The code is enforceable through a disciplinary committee, under a legally qualified chairman, which has power to recommend suspension or reprimand and, in extreme cases, removal of a name, from the register. The code, which applies only to the buying, selling, or letting of land or buildings by registered estate agents in England, Wales, and Scotland (not Northern Ireland), forbids the taking of commission or other payment from anyone other than a client without prior disclosure to the client; failure to make full disclosure where a conflict of interest might arise; seeking instructions in an "oppressive or unconscionable" manner; publishing particulars of a property without ensuring their accuracy; accepting instructions without ensuring the

Eurovision Song Contest. The 1968 winner Massiel (*centre*) with 1969's four equal firsts: *left to right,* Lennie Kuhr, Frida Boccara, Salome, Lulu. This was the first of of these contests to end in a tie.

client understands the terms and conditions; failure to point out the desirability of taking legal advice about a contract; and misleading advertising of services. The council also forbids, except in Scotland, the drawing up of any contract or document connected with sale or letting except for tenancies not exceeding three years. The code was published on February 5, and the register, containing the names of 11,000 estate agents, later in the same month. No person on the register can carry on business as an estate agent unless he has deposited an insurance bond for a minimum of £20,000. This is to allow the Council to make good any loss by a client caused by fraud or dishonesty.

The U.K. Monopolies Commission published its report on estate agents on February 25. While accepting that estate agents' services in connection with the buying, selling, and letting of unfurnished dwellings "may be expected to operate against the public interest," it found no grounds for stating that agents' profits are "demonstrably excessive." Nevertheless, it recommended that the main professional estate agency bodies should no longer publish a fixed scale of charges for house sales, and that rules preventing or discouraging competition should be withdrawn. It also considered it important that the formation of the register of estate agents should not lead to restraint on entry into the business.

Eurovision Song Contest. The 1969 contest, held in Madrid on March 29, was a tie for the first time, Britain, France, Spain, and the Netherlands sharing first place. The British entry, "Boom Bang-a-Bang," was sung by Lulu; Frida Boccara, for France, sang "Un Jour, Un Enfant"; Lennie Kuhr, of the Netherlands, sang "De Troubadour"; and Salome, for Spain, sang "Vivo Cantando."

Expo 70. The Japanese reported in August 1969 that preparations for Expo 70, the next international exhibition, which is due to open on March 15, 1970, were making smooth progress, with rapid construction work on several of the pavilions; in Osaka port an "Expo pier," capable of accommodating 30,000-ton passenger ships, had been completed, as well as the expansion work on Osaka international airport. The number of nations who had definitely decided to participate in the world fair had reached the target figure of 70. Sixty-three nations took part in Expo 67, which was held in Montreal, Canada.

Canada's pavilion at Expo 70 will be a pyramidical structure in four sections the outside walls reflecting the sky in a surface of mirrors. As it is estimated that 50 per cent of the visitors to Expo 70 will be under 25 years of age particular attention is being paid to young people's interests. Some of the attractions will be a magic-carpet tour of Canada through time and space, by the use of sound and

Expo 70. Model of the French pavilion.

British pavilion, supported by four double pillars.

Rotating "Global Vision" pavilion, a Japanese design.

Rubber-covered vinyl cloth makes the Fuji group pavilion.

colour; a National Film Board production shown on a triangular screen; an exhibition of Japanese and Eskimo art illustrating the affinity of the two cultures; a display of Canadiana mounted in a school bus painted in psychedelic colours; background music composed by The Collectors, a well-known pop group from Vancouver, who use electronic instruments; and, during "Canada week," the National Ballet, the Royal Canadian Police musical ride, and the Canadian musical *Anne of Green Gables*. In addition, there will be continuous performances by professional entertainers on the open-air stage of the pavilion.

The West German pavilion will consist of a large fluorescent dome, the Music Auditorium, with four adjacent low cylindrical theatres about 100 ft. in diameter and 25 ft. high, accommodating an audience of 600–800. The first will present German geography, industry, nature, people, and art; the second will provide music; the third will be devoted to health and pharmacy; the fourth, showing "Sound and Pictures," will contain examples of sound recording and transmission and optical instruments and glass.

The largest lift in the world will be installed in the Hitachi pavilion. Completed at the Hitachi works in Mico, Japan, during the summer of 1969, this lift is a double-decker, and is capable of moving 260 people at a time.

Falmouth, Cornwall. A £15 million expansion scheme for Falmouth docks was announced in April 1969. The project includes a dry dock large enough for super-tankers which, together with improvements to the deep-water approaches and berths, will make it the largest ship repair yard between Southampton and South Wales.

Family Law Reform Act. This Act of the U.K. Parliament, enacted on July 25, 1969, implemented the main recommendation of the Latey committee on the age of majority that had been established in 1965 and had reported in July 1967. This was that the legal age of majority in England and Wales should be reduced from 21 to 18. This means that at 18 people are allowed to marry without parental or judicial consent, are free to make binding contracts, are no longer liable to be made wards of court, and are allowed to be blood donors, to make valid wills, to act as trustees or personal representatives, to acquire homes and obtain mortgages, to take part directly in litigation, and to apply for passports without parental consent. The Act also provides that those under the age of 18 shall be called "minors" rather than "infants," and that persons over the age of 16 can give consent to medical and dental treatment. The Act further laid down that illegitimate children have the same right as legitimate ones to share estates in the event of intestacy, and also that blood tests can be made and submitted as evidence in civil proceedings where paternity is in dispute in England and Wales. The Act did not cover the Government's declared intention to reduce the minimum voting age from 21 to 18, which was effected by the Representation of the People Act.

Felixstowe, Suffolk. An ambitious £12 million expansion plan is to be undertaken at the privately owned Felixstowe docks, in spite of the long-term threat of nationalisation. When Felixstowe obtained parliamentary approval for big container and oil berth containers in 1968, it was not included among the first ports to be nationalised.

Fenland. Plans for a fishing and boating centre on a 45-acre island site on the borders of Cambridgeshire and Suffolk near the village of Isleham, Cambridgeshire, were announced in September 1969. The estimated cost of the centre, designed to attract "the young businessman," is £200,000. Including about 100 chalets, a restaurant, shop, boatyards, and a picnic area, the project is intended to provide a holiday centre where fishing, cruising, and birdwatching can be enjoyed in peaceful surroundings.

Film Awards. The 1968 awards ("Oscars") of the American Motion Picture Academy of Arts and Sciences were announced in April 1969. *Oliver!*, the British musical, was named best picture of the year, and took six Oscars, including those for best art direction (by Sir Carol Reed), best direction, best musical score, and best sound. For the first time in 37 years the best actress award was shared—by Katherine Hepburn for her part in *The Lion in Winter* and Barbra Streisand for her part in *Funny Girl*. Other awards were:
Best actor—Cliff Robertson, for his part in *Charly*.
Best supporting actor—Jack Albertson, for his part in *The Subject was Roses*.
Best supporting actress—Ruth Gordon, for her part in *Rosemary's Baby*.
Best cinematography—*Romeo and Juliet* (Franco Zeffirelli), which also took the award for best costume design.
Best film editing—*Bullitt*.
Best foreign language film—*War and Peace* (Russia)
Best song—"The Windmills of Your Mind," by Michel Legrand, in *The Thomas Crown Affair*.
Best special visual effects—*2001: a Space Odyssey*.
Best screenplay—*The Lion in Winter*, which also took the award for best original score for a non-musical film.

Best story and screenplay—*The Producers*.
In special production fields the awards were:
Features—*Young Americans*. This award was later withdrawn because the film was released in 1967, and given to *Journey into Self*.
Short subjects—*Why Man Creates*.
Cartoons—*Winnie the Pooh and the Blustery Day* (Walt Disney).
Live action subjects—*Robert Kennedy Remembered*

The 1968 awards of the British Film Academy were announced on March 26, 1969. Five of the 18 awards was taken by *The Graduate*, judged the best film, which gained the best direction award for Mike Nichols, the best film editing award for Sam O'Steen, and the best screenplay award for Calder Willingham and Buck Henry, and gave Dustin Hoffman the most promising newcomer award for his performance in it. Other awards were:
United Nations Award—*Guess Who's Coming to Dinner*.
Best specialised film—*The Threat in the Water*.
Best animated film—*Pas de Deux*.
Robert Flaherty Award—*In Need of Special Care*.
Best cinematography—Geoffrey Unsworth, for *2001: a Space Odyssey*.
Best art direction—Tony Masters, Harry Lange, and Ernie Archer, for *2001: a Space Odyssey*.
Best costume design—Danilo Donati, for *Romeo and Juliet*.
Best sound track—Winston Ryder, for *2001: a Space Odyssey*.
Best actress—Katherine Hepburn, for her performances in *Guess Who's Coming to Dinner* and *The Lion in Winter*.
Best supporting actress—Billie Whitelaw, for her performances in *The Twisted Nerve* and *Charlie Bubbles*.
Best actor—Spencer Tracy, for his performance in *Guess Who's Coming to Dinner*.
Best supporting actor—Ian Holm, for his performance in *The Bofors Gun*.
Anthony Asquith Memorial Award for original film music—*The Lion in Winter* (music by John Barry).

The Writers' Guild of Great Britain awards for 1968 were presented on March 5, 1969. These were:
British original screenplay—David Sherwin, for *If . . .*
Best British screenplay — *Charlie Bubbles*.
Documentary or short script—Peter Baylis, for *Sea-born Treasure*.
Comedy screenplay—Peter Ustinov and Ira Wallach, for *Hot Millions*.

Film Festivals. At the Cannes festival in May a total of 275 films were on view. Apart from the 30 in competition and 13 in the "critics' week," there were an extra 60 in the "directors' fortnight" and another 140 shown on organised "national days." "Special screenings" made up the rest. The Grand Prize went to the British film *If . . .*, directed by Lindsay Anderson. Vanessa Redgrave was awarded the prize for best actress for her portrayal of the title role in the British film *Isadora*, and the best actor prize went to Jean-Louis Trentignant for his performance in the French film *By Night with Maud*. Other awards were :

Best director—Glauber Rocha (Brazil), for *Antonio das Mortes*.

Best first work—Peter Fonda, for *Easy Rider*.

Best production—shared equally between *Antonio das Mortes* and the Czech *Chronique Morave*.

Short features—the Rumanian *Chant de la Renaissance* and the French *Pince à Ongles*.

At the 1969 Berlin International Film Festival, Yugoslavia won the Golden Bear prize for the year's best film with a world première showing of *Rani Radoci*, directed by Zelimir Zidnik. Yugoslavia also took a Silver Bear prize in the short film category with *Presadjivanje Osecanja* (Transplantation of Feeling). The Golden Bear for the best short subject film went to the Canadian *To See or Not to See*, directed by Bretislav Proja. The Silver Bear award for best direction went to Peter Zadek (West Germany) for *I am an Elephant, Madame*. Other Silver Bear awards went to *Greetings*, an American entry ; Italy's *Un Tranquillo Posto di Campagna* (A Lonely Place), starring Franco Nero and Vanessa Redgrave, for the best colour photography ; Sweden's *Made in Sweden*; and the Brazilian *Brazil Anno 2000*. The International Association of Film Critics gave a special award to the French film *Erotissimo*.

At the Moscow Film Festival, held in July 1969, the Italian entry *Serafino*, the Soviet entry *Until Monday*, and the Cuban entry *Lucia* shared first place in the full-length feature film category. The best actor awards went to the British Ron Moody for his part as Fagin in *Oliver !*, and to the Polish Tadeusz Lomicki for his performance in *Pan Wolodiewski*. The best actress awards went to Irina Petrescu of Rumania for her part in *Woman for a Season*, and the Argentinian Anne Maria Picchio for her part in *A Strip of Sky*. In the short film category the prizes went to *The Road to the Frontline* (South Vietnam) ; *Youth of the World* (U.S.S.R.) ; and *Test of Violence* (Great Britain). Silver prizes were awarded to the French entry *Play Time*; the Yugoslavian *When You Hear the Bells*; the Hungarian *Children from Pal Street*; and the Bulgarian *Threads of the Rainbow*.

The British boy actor Mark Lester received a silver prize for his performance in *Run Wild, Run Free*. The gold prize in the children's films category went to the Soviet film *Winter Morning*. The prize for a fairy tale for children went to the Rumanian entry *Youth That Does Not Age* ; the prize for a children's comic film to the East German *Peppi, the Long Stocking*; and the prize for an animated cartoon for children to the Polish *Adventures of a Merry Wanderer*. Special awards went to Sir Carol Reed for his direction of *Oliver !*; to Ivan Pyriev, of the U.S.S.R., for his direction of *The Brothers Karamazov*; *Diary of a German Woman* (West Germany) directed by Annelie and Andrew Thorndike ; the Yugoslavian *The Birch Trees*; the West German *The Apple*; and the American *Why Man Creates*. The U.S. entry, *2001: a Space Odyssey*, won the prize for special cinematic techniques.

It was announced on April 29 that in future no prizes will be awarded at the Venice film festival, which was held during the last two weeks of August. The director said that prizes at this festival, the world's oldest, had become pointless because no jury could decide which film among so many completely different styles deserved the highest award. The only "prize" is now the invitation to show a film at the festival.

Fire-Fighting. The world's first aircraft designed for "water bombing" forest fires, the Canadair CL-215, developed at a centre in Montreal, was tested in the early summer of 1969. When reports of a forest fire are received the plane flies to a lake near the fire and by skimming along the water at 70 m.p.h. scoops up its full load of 6 tons into its storage tanks in 12 seconds. When fighting a fire 100 miles from base the CL-215 can make 75 pickups and drops in one day with only one refuelling. France and Canada have ordered 30 of the aircraft.

The prototype of a device which will allow aerial fire spotters to see through dense smoke was shown to delegates attending a bushfire research conference in Canberra in July. Developed in Australia by the Department of Supply, and based on the detection of infra-red rays, the device can be used to reconnoitre large fires in rough country, and to locate spot fires thrown ahead of a main fire and obscured under a smoke pall.

Fires. The Chief Inspector of Fire Services in a report published on July 1, 1969, said that estimated financial loss by fires in England and Wales during 1968 reached a record £100 million (an 11 per cent increase over the 1967 figure). The number of fires to which fire

Fire-Fighting. *Top:* the world's first "water bomber," used in Canada to extinguish forest fires. It scoops up as much as 6 tons of water from the surface of a near-by lake and pours it out through 32 nozzles set in a pipe along the trailing edge of its wing. *Lower: left,* Japanese "self-dowsing" helmet keeps firemen cool ; water pours from a narrow pipe in the rim. *Right,* "light water foam" forms a film over burning fuel from a blazing plane.

brigades were called increased from 173,180 in 1967 to 188,045 in 1968, and the number of malicious false alarms rose from 38,305 in 1967 to 45,552 in 1968. During 1968, 682 members of the public lost their lives and 3,668 were injured as a direct result or indirect result of fires, and 789 were rescued from hazardous situations. Three firemen were killed and 327 injured. More than three-quarters of the deaths from fire occurred in the home.

Fisheries. The world's largest fishing factory and mother ship, the *Vostok*, was under construction in Leningrad during 1969. The 43,400-ton ship, with 26,000-h.p. engines capable of 19 knots, will carry 14 small fishing vessels on her deck. Her 10,000-ton fuel tanks will allow her to stay at sea for four months. All processing operations will be carried out on board. Facilities for the crew, equal to those of a passenger liner, will include a cinema, library, reading rooms, and swimming pool.

Fish-Fowl Farms. The U.N. Food and Agriculture Organisation described in June 1969 a 10-year experiment in Hungary for increasing the productivity of poor quality land. Large ponds or small lakes, varying in size from a few to several hundred acres, are excavated by bulldozers to a depth of 4 ft., filled with water, and stocked with freshwater fish (usually carp and eels) and ducks, which are fed from mechanical dispensers. When they are mature the fish and birds are caught, killed, and sent to market, the pond or lake is drained, and maize, rice, and other crops are planted on its bottom, which has been so richly fertilised by fish and duck droppings that yields are 15–20 per cent higher than from normal soil. After the crop harvest the pond or lake is refilled with water and restocked with fish and ducks, and the process is repeated on a 3- or 5-year cycle. Hungary, which has no coastline, derives 80 per cent of its fish production from such ponds, while the ducks and eels are exported.

Florey Memorial. On Feb. 13, 1969, an appeal for a minimum of $A300,000 was launched in both Australia and Great Britain for a fellowship scheme to provide a living memorial to the Australian scientist, Lord Florey, famous for his work on penicillin, who died on Feb. 21, 1968. The fellowships will be post-doctoral in the biochemical sciences in Australian and British institutions, and will promote the reciprocal movement of young scientists between the two countries.

Flying Doctor Service. Founded by Pres. Kaunda in 1966, the Flying Doctor Service in Zambia is second only to Australia's in size. With six aircraft, it is manned by eight doctors, eight nurses, and a dentist. This small band dealt with 50,000 patients in 1968, flying 600 of them to hospital.

It was stated in November 1969 that aircraft of the Royal Flying Doctor Service in Australia had flown $1\frac{1}{2}$ million miles from April 1968 to April 1969. This was an increase of half a million miles over 1967–68. During the 1968–69 period the service treated 65,000 patients.

Foot-and-Mouth Disease. After Britain's worst foot-and-mouth epidemic which lasted from Oct. 25, 1967, until June 4, 1968, causing approximately 211,850 cattle, 108,300 sheep, and 113,700 pigs to be slaughtered at a cost in compensation of over £26 million, a committee under the chairmanship of the Duke of Northumberland was set up to report on ways of reducing the risk of the introduction of the disease into the U.K. The first part of their report, published on May 1, 1969, recommended a complete ban on imports of carcase beef and beef offal from territories where the disease is endemic, or, alternatively, that these imports should be limited to boned-out beef, and beef offal processed in such a manner as to destroy the foot-and-mouth virus. The report also recommended the continuance of the ban on imports of mutton, lamb, and pig meat from countries or areas where the disease is endemic, and that imports of mutton, lamb, and pig offal from such areas should be limited to offal processed in a manner that destroys the virus. The U.K. Minister of Agriculture promptly announced that these recommendations had been accepted by the Government; a complete ban on beef imports from countries where the disease is endemic was not imposed, but imports are now limited to boneless beef and specially processed offal.

On Oct. 20, 1969, the U.K. Ministry of Agriculture announced stronger measures to control the disease once it has broken out. Whereas under the previous regulations restrictions were applied only where animals were suspected of having had contact with the disease, the new regulations impose restrictions on the premises where such animals are kept and control the movement of vehicles and materials, including milk, and slurry spraying on the farm. Tankers transporting milk produced in an infected area must now have a filter on the air outlet of the tanks. Farm sales in an infected area are no longer permitted, but, to prevent the disruption of trade, the movement of animals from one infected area to a slaughterhouse in another will be allowed when it is necessary. The new rules represent the first major revision of the regulations since 1931.

Football. The Lang Report on Crowd Behaviour at Football Matches was published on Dec. 17, 1969. The report was produced by a working committee of football administrators, players, police, and representatives of the Home Office, the Scottish Home and Health Department, and the Sports Council, under the

chairmanship of Sir John Lang, which was set up in 1968. Among the remedies for soccer hooliganism suggested in the report were sterner punishments by magistrates; modernisation of grounds, including increased seating instead of standing accommodation; the stationing of police on the terracing as well as round the ground, and the use of available police to encircle the pitch at the end of a game; the segregation of young people from other spectators; the provision of an official detention room at all grounds; and greater self-control by the players, including unquestioning acceptance, both on the field and after the game, of referees' decisions.

Forsyte Saga, The. The BBC television serial in 26 parts of John Galsworthy's series of novels had become the most successful of all TV serials when it ended its second showing in Great Britain on March 2, 1969. First shown on BBC-2 in 1967, when it had an audience of $1\frac{1}{2}$ million, it was repeated on BBC-1 on Sunday evenings in 1968–69 before average audiences estimated at between 12 and 17 million. The serial, which cost £300,000 to make, had by March 1969 been sold to 27 countries, comprising 15 in the Commonwealth, 7 in Western Europe, 4 in Eastern Europe (including the U.S.S.R.), and Mexico. In some countries where it was shown millions of people changed their living habits in order to be sure of seeing each episode, and alterations were made in the timing of church services, concerts, sports events, and public meetings. Such British actors as Kenneth More (Young Jolyon), Nyree Dawn Porter (Irene), Eric Porter (Soames), Susan Hampshire (Fleur), and Margaret Tyzack (Winifred), although already well known, became international stars of the first rank. The producer was Donald Wilson and the director David Giles. A third showing of the serial began on BBC-1 in January 1970.

Fossils. New Zealand geologists discovered in 1969 the richest deposit of fossil animals yet found in Antarctica. The find was made in Victoria Land in Australian Antarctic territory, 150 miles from Scott Base. Twelve scattered sites yielded hundreds of pounds of rock containing fish fossils, among which were the remains of an air-breathing fish that lived over 350 million years ago. It is possible that the earliest land animals were descendants of this fish. Its almost perfect lower jaw could not be removed from the site by its discoverers, but it will be extracted and brought to the Australian Museum by future parties. (See also under Continental Drift.)

Bones of a pre-historic condor with an 18-ft. wingspan, believed to be the largest bird fossil ever found, were discovered in the Anza-Borrego desert, a State park in California, U.S.A. Dr. Theodore Downs, a Los Angeles county museum geologist, announcing the discovery in February 1969, said that the condor, which was probably flying more than one million years ago, has been named *Tera tornis (incredibilis)*.

Dr. Dale Russell, of the palaeontology division of the Canadian National Museum of Natural Sciences, said in March 1969 that fossil bones discovered in Alberta in the summer of 1968 belonged to the ancient reptile *Saurornithoides*, a small (8-ft.-long) dinosaur which roamed western Canada about 75 million years ago. Dr. Russell believes that the dinosaur weighed about 100 lb, walked on two legs, so that its front limbs were free to grasp objects, and had a thin skin and eyes about twice the size of those of a human, with keen stereoscopic vision. Bones belonging to the "skull-cap" showed that the brain capacity of *Saurornithoides* was much greater than that of dinosaurs many times as large. This meat-eating reptile was less intelligent than a dog, but probably more intelligent than ostriches and other large birds, and had a brain "about seven times larger than any living reptile of comparable bodyweight."

Two important fossil finds in Australia were announced in October. In the first, the bones of a whale belonging to the Miocene age, 15–35 million years ago, were unearthed in a disused quarry at Colac, about 100 miles S.W. of Melbourne. The bones, regarded as among the most important zoological finds ever made in Australia, comprise the head, including a 5 ft. upper jawbone, and the first vertebrae. The remains were well-preserved by the clay surrounding them. The second occurred in Central Queensland, where remains of the oldest land animals ever found on the continent were located at a site near Rolleston. The remains, about 210 million years old, are of reptiles which appear to have been up to 5 ft. in height, and to have run on their hind legs. Amphibian remains were also found. At a second site, south of Blackwater, in a new open-cut mine, an equally exciting find of an abundant layer of fish about 230 million years old was reported.

Foulness, Essex. The Roskill Commission gave site information details of Foulness, one of the four sites shortlisted for London's third airport, on May 5, 1969, when the local enquiry opened at Southend. It was stated that an airport there could meet air-traffic needs for the next 20 years, and more, and that its cost would be £255 million less than the other three on the short list (Cublington, Bucks, Nuthampstead, Herts, and Thurleigh, Beds). As the Foulness site would be on reclaimed land no agricultural land would be lost by the construction of the airport itself, but some land—half of which was "medium to good"—would be lost by urbanisation proposals and by the construction of road and rail links. The safety factor of aircraft approaching over water was stressed. The hazard to aircraft from birds would constitute no

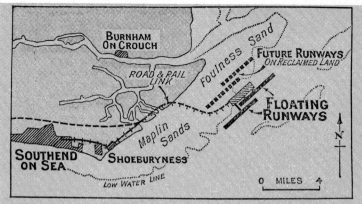

Foulness, Essex. Plans for turning the mud wastes of Foulness into an airport and/or a seaport poured out in 1969. The one shown above, prepared by two firms of consulting engineers on behalf of Shell U.K., was for a "seadrome", a floating airport of 5 million square yards with two runways 2½ miles long made of reinforced concrete filled with buoyant expanded polystyrene.

special risk; to meet objections that the feeding grounds of a number of species of birds would be destroyed, plans could be made to provide feeding grounds and refuges elsewhere. It was a fact, however, that the area's cockle industry would be badly affected. A survey, ordered by the Commission, into air-traffic flow (published on Dec. 24) showed that, assuming Foulness to be the only site compatible with the continued operation of Luton airport, it would suffer less airport-regulated air-traffic control delays than other sites, and would also give small benefits in terms of aircraft route mileage and flying time.

To meet the requirements of airport traffic a separate railway line mainly along existing lines was proposed from the airport to King's Cross, London, with a travel time of 59 minutes, and there would also have to be a new motorway. A county planner with the Essex county council said that more people were affected by "unreasonable" noise from aircraft using Southend airport than would be affected by a four-runway airport at Foulness, although nearly 20,000 more people would be affected by "moderate" noise.

All the chief local authorities in South East England are in favour of building the airport at Foulness. The standing

Foulness. The Thames Aeroport Group proposed to create an airport and a seaport, an industrial complex, a new town, and direct road and rail links to London, by reclaiming 50 square miles of the Maplin and Foulness sands. This—the most expensive of the projects—would entail an expenditure of £1,800 million.

Faster and Bigger

Aviation made significant strides into the future during 1969 with the appearance of the aircraft that will dominate the skies during the 1970s: the supersonic transports and large-capacity jets. As the year began, headlines across the world proclaimed the successful maiden flight of the Russian supersonic airliner, the Tupolev TU-144, which blasted into the air on December 31, 1968, and—despite persistent rumours that the prototype had crashed—was reported to have torn through the sound barrier on June 5. The Anglo-French supersonic transport Concorde (*above*) first left the tarmac on March 2, at Toulouse. During June both British and French prototypes were seen in the air at the Paris Aero Show, and on October 1 the plane first exceeded the speed of sound.

Meanwhile, the giant 231-ft., 300-ton Boeing 747 (*below*)—capable of thrusting 490 passengers through the sky—made her maiden flight on February 9, near Seattle. The "Jumbo-Jet" later ran into engine trouble, but nevertheless made her first transatlantic flight (from Seattle to Paris) in June, and her first passenger flight, carrying journalists, in December.

The aviators who contested the 12,000 miles B.P.-R.A.C. England–Australia Air Race braved almost every aerial hazard. On the first leg severe icing was reported, and one competing aircraft– a Shrike Commander flown by American Bernard Perner and Australian K. Dodd– was lost without trace. Sheila Scott flew into an aeronautical nightmare on the Singapore-Darwin leg when, radio and flying aids awry, her Piper Comanche was hurled off-course by monsoon storms. The 8-leg race was divided geographically into two sections, with a break over Christmas and New Year at Adelaide. Dust-storms and gale-force winds marked the final flight to Sydney. Over 20 main trophies and prizes were awarded, the racing aircraft being divided into three principal classes: (a) single-engined aircraft powered by piston; (b) unsupercharged twin-engined aircraft; (c) aircraft powered by supercharged piston or pro-peller turbine engines. First over the finishing line was a Cessna 310 flown by Australians Jack Masling and Graham Williams who were placed second overall on handicap, winning a prize of $A5,000. The enterprise formed part of the 200th anniversary celebra-tions of Captain Cook's landing on Australia in 1770, and also marked the 50th anniversary of the first England–Australia flight by Ross and Keith Smith and their two mechanics, November 12–December 10, 1919.

The Smith brothers' Vickers Vimy—the first plane to fly from England to Australia, 1919.

Some of the 70 starters on the tarmac—58 completed the race; 8 retired; one went missing; one crash-landed; and two were disqualified.

Sir Francis Chichester started the race at 10 a.m. on December 18, 1969, at Gatwick.

Jean Batten's (left) longstanding England–Australia record eluded Sheila Scott (right), prizewinner for the best all-woman crew.

Overall winners were William Bright and Frank Buxton (GB) who won $A25,000. They flew a Britten-Norman Islander.

conference on London and South East Regional Planning, the authorities' representative body, said in July that Foulness has major advantages on economic, planning, and aircraft noise grounds over other possible sites, and offers the best prospect of benefit to industry; the overall population requirement of 400,000 for the airport would fit in well with development in south Essex.

A new consortium, the Thames Estuary Development Co., formed by the Port of London Authority and Southend Oil Wharves, with the co-operation of the merchant bankers Lazard Bros. and Hambro's, announced on Feb. 13, 1969, a £130 million project to re-shape the Thames estuary and incorporate London's third airport. The consortium wants to investigate the possibility of reclaiming 30,000 acres (46 sq. miles) of Maplin Sands, near Southend, for the airport and for a seaport for super-tankers and giant container ships. The use of reclaimed land for the airport would, it was stated, save 10,000 acres of farmland. Noise would not be a great problem as aircraft would take off and land over the sea. A service of 150 m.p.h. trains from King's Cross could be provided. Initially the consortium is to make a two-year feasibility study; but even if the Government and the Roskill Commission do not favour a third London airport at Foulness, the plan for port development there will still go ahead.

Details of another plan for developing the Foulness site were published in March. This scheme was produced by Thames Aeroport Group, and not only includes plans for an airport and seaport, but envisages a new town on the south bank of the river Crouch. It proposes building four runways in pairs separated by 6,000 ft. and staggered by half a mile, so that aircraft can land and take off over the water well clear of populated land. A deep-water port would be formed by the dredging of a 4-miles-square area, and on the adjoining land an industrial estate with access to the docks and the airfield would be built. Airport employees and their families, who would number up to 100,000, would live partly in the expanded borough of Southend, and partly in the proposed new town. Access to the airport would be by rail (the Fenchurch Street–Southend line), by a new motorway, and by a fast transit monorail system. The overall cost of the scheme was estimated at £1,800 million.

Yet another scheme for Foulness was described in September. This is a proposal to float London's third airport on the sea. The "seadrome" scheme, which was prepared by two firms of consulting engineers on behalf of Shell U.K., suggests a floating airport complex measuring 5 million sq. yds., incorporating two runways $2\frac{1}{2}$ miles by 330 yds. A platform of reinforced concrete, buoyed up with expanded polystyrene, would be moored by stainless steel cables attached to piles driven into the sea bed in such a way as to allow both longitudinal and

lateral movement with the rise and fall of the tide. The platform would comprise all the areas of aircraft movement—runways, aprons, and taxi-ways. Variable ramps would link the floating platform to the land.

Foyers, Loch Ness, Scotland. The construction of an £11 million hydro-electric and pumped-storage power station here was authorised by the Secretary for Scotland on Feb. 20, 1969. At off-peak periods water will be pumped from Loch Ness to an upper reservoir at Loch Mohr, formed by the adaptation of three existing dams; and when needed to meet peak load demands water will be drawn from there to operate the generators. The natural flow of water from a catchment area of 98 sq. miles will be tapped to operate conventional hydro-electric generators. When completed the station will have an installed capacity of 300,000 kW, enough to supply a city the size of Dundee.

Gaming. When the new U.K. Gaming Act comes into force on July 1, 1970, roulette with a zero, which gives the house an automatic advantage, will be permitted in licensed gaming clubs. The only other bankers' games allowed will be blackjack, baccarat, craps, chemin de fer, and punto banco. The Gaming Board have found that clubs made excessive profits on blackjack and craps, and to prevent this the rules are modified to remove "mug options." Baccarat, punto banco, and chemin de fer are allowed in their traditional form, but in the last named the bank must be circulated. Gaming clubs are allowed to open only between 2 p.m. and 4 a.m., with closing times restricted to 3 a.m. in Inner London, and 2 a.m. elsewhere on Sundays.

Bingo clubs are separately controlled under the Act. Sessions for which charges are made are not permitted to take place more frequently than once every two hours, and no one may be charged more than 10s in a session. This sum includes admission and participation charges, but excludes stake money and money paid for taking part in prize bingo. During any session no one can be charged more than three times for card bingo. Bingo clubs are allowed to open from 2 p.m. to 11 p.m. with an hour's extension on Saturdays.

Gamma Ray Star. The observation of the first gamma ray star was reported in September 1969 by two groups of physicists, one Australian, the other American, using balloons flown from Parkes, New South Wales. Gamma rays (high frequency X-rays) should be formed in the same situation as cosmic rays and, because they are not so much

deflected by magnetic fields in space, could point directly to the origin of cosmic rays. The sources of cosmic rays have been sought since their discovery more than 50 years ago. The observations were made by instruments flown by balloons in February. Both groups, one from the University of Melbourne, the other from Case Western Reserve University, Ohio, detected a point source of gamma rays, but could only place it to within a patch of sky measuring about 6 degrees by 4 degrees, too indefinite for it to be located by other astronomical techniques. Astronomers were puzzled, however, because the instruments failed to detect other gamma rays reported in 1967 by the American OSO-3 satellite to be coming from a larger section of the sky in the direction of the centre of our own galaxy.

Garden Island, Tasmania. Because this island, in the centre of the river Tamar in the port of Launceston, was preventing the movement of large ships in the river at low and ebb tides, it was removed during 1969 as part of a multi-million dollar expansion scheme. First, by open quarrying it was excavated to a depth of 50 ft., and the surrounding area was then removed by blasting and excavation with a bucket crane. The Tamar, the longest navigable river for big ships in Australia, has abundant industrial sites with deep-water berths up-river from Garden Island. Large smelting works are already operating on its banks, and a thermal power station and a wood chip plant are under construction. The removal of the island will allow ships of up to 55,000 tons deadweight to use the port by 1971.

Genetics. A significant advance in genetics seemed likely from observations at Cambridge and Bristol Universities, reported simultaneously in December. Work with bacteriophages (viruses which are parasites on bacteria) showed that there are spaces between the genes, that these spaces are made up of the same nucleic material, RNA, and that there is a similarity in the order of the chemical units making up the RNA at key points along the spaces. The spaces may perform the function of switching the genes into action, resulting, in the case of these viruses, in the production of the proteins needed for their reproduction from the bacterium's own cell contents. Advances in the treatment of both viral and bacterial diseases could result from this discovery. At Cambridge a young American woman scientist, Dr. Joan Argetsinger Steitz, split the nuclear structure of a virus, R17, possessing three genes, into three fragments, each consisting of an initiating space and part of its appropriate gene. Her technique was to protect specific points along the viral RNA with cell particles from the bacterium—this was done by starving the virus of chemicals required by the different genes—and then eat away the unprotected parts

George Cross and Medal. Recipients of the awards for bravery in 1969 included: (*left to right*) Barbara Jane Harrison (George Cross), BOAC air stewardess, who gave her life saving passengers from a blazing Boeing 707 at London Airport; and George Medallists Major Stewart Roy Skelton of the Royal Army Catering Corps, Major Michael Hoskins of the Royal Engineers bomb disposal squad, Detective-Constable Philip Williams, and Sgt. James Hall Matchett of the Welch Regiment.

with enzymes. At Bristol the work was done by Drs. J. Hindley and D. H. Staples, working with a different virus, Q-beta. Dr. Hindley was a member of another team, headed by Dr. C. Weissmann of Zürich, who reported working out in detail the chemical structure of the first tenth of the RNA molecule of Q-beta.

George Cross and Medal. The award of the George Cross to Barbara Jane Harrison, aged 22, an air stewardess who died in a fire aboard a BOAC Boeing 707 at London Airport (Heathrow) on April 8, 1968, was announced in August 1969. Miss Harrison, whose devotion to duty in her efforts for the passengers was praised in the citation, was overcome while trying to save an elderly cripple.

Awards of the George Medal made during 1969 were as follows:

February. Major Stewart Roy Skelton, aged 40, of the Army Catering Corps, for his rescue in November 1968 of a 16-year-old girl from an attacker armed with a knife, from which he received a deep wound in the chest.

March. Sgt. James Hall Matchett, of the Welch Regt., who rescued three injured policemen from a minefield on the Hong Kong border, in December 1967.

May. Major Michael Hoskins, aged 30, of the Royal Engineers bomb disposal squad, for "cold-blooded bravery" in September 1968, when he risked his life to defuse a 250-lb. American bomb in a petrol depot in Brunei.

August. Two police detectives, Det. Constable Philip Williams, aged 32, and Det. Sergeant John Whaton, aged 30, for their part in the ambush and arrest of a team of armed bank robbers in May 1968.

September. Staff Sgt. James Barber of Liverpool, New South Wales, for heroism when an ammunition dump blew up in Vietnam in February.

Ghent, Belgium. A new canal encircling the north, west, and south of Ghent was officially opened in November 1969. Work had begun in 1951. The canal is $13\frac{1}{2}$ miles long, 15 ft. deep, and 68 ft. wide at the bottom and about 162 ft. wide at the surface. It is crossed by 21

road bridges and 6 rail bridges, and there are 6 sluices and 3 weirs along its length. A two-lane road is to be built beside the canal to form a bypass round Ghent, to link up with the Brussels-Ostend and Antwerp-Ghent-Courtrai-Lille motorways. The canal has eliminated the use of several smaller canals in the centre of the town, and these will probably be filled in and used either as city motorways and underground parking lots or for an underground tramcar network.

GHOST. This is the code name for a meteorological programme (Global Horizontal Sounding Technique), jointly carried out by the U.S.A. and New Zealand, for releasing a large number of constant level balloons to drift round the Southern Hemisphere recording and transmitting weather data. The first trial balloons were released in New Zealand in 1966. It was reported in March 1969 that the programme is to be enlarged so that within 10 years between 5,000 and 10,000 of the balloons will be afloat at various levels between 20,000 ft. and 80,000 ft. above the earth. The balloons are made of mylar, an exceptionally strong synthetic substance, and filled with helium. They vary in diameter from 7 to 30 ft., and in weight from 2 to 20 lb.

Glasgow. In June 1969 plans for a three-stage development of the terminal buildings at Glasgow Airport, Abbotsinch,

were approved, and work started on the first stage in the autumn. This stage, involving the extension of the northern apron and of the central pier to provide five more aircraft stands, is due for completion by the spring of 1971, at a cost of £645,000. Work will then start on a second £390,000 stage, consisting of a linear extension of the present building, with the addition of a satellite pier (first of its kind in Great Britain) to house 12 additional aircraft, to be completed in 1974. A third stage will involve the installation of airbridges. The whole scheme will enable the terminal to handle up to 5 million passengers a year.

Gove, Northern Territory, Australia. Nabalco Pty. Ltd. announced on June 18, 1969, that a $A15 million, 60,000-kW power station is to be constructed here. To be built in two stages and intended for completion by 1973, as well as supplying the large volume of power needed to refine bauxite into alumina it will have the capacity to meet the needs of a modern town of 3,500 to be built at Gove.

"Great Britain." News that this 126-year-old iron merchant ship, built in Bristol to the design of the engineer Isambard Kingdom Brunel, launched in 1843, and abandoned in the Falkland Islands in 1886, is to be sailed back to England in 1970, was given in October 1969. At the time of her launching the

Ghent. The new canal, opened in November 1969, that encircles three sides of this Belgian city, is crossed in its $13\frac{1}{2}$ mile length by 27 bridges. Two of these elegant structures are seen here. All the bridges are of similar construction.

320-ft. ship was the largest ship afloat; the first all-iron ship driven exclusively by propeller, she was also the first ship able to lower all masts in a head wind; the first to be fitted with a remote electric log showing speed and distance on the bridge and in the lounge; and the first to have a double bottom and water-tight bulkheads. On her last trip in 1886, from Penarth to Panama, she was partially dismasted in a gale while rounding the Horn, and beached off the Falklands. The rescue operation has been made possible by Jack Hayward, who in May 1969 gave the National Trust £150,000 to buy and preserve Lundy Island. He offered a similar sum in order that the *Great Britain* can return to her birthplace.

Gulf Stream. A team of six scientists, headed by Dr. Jacques Piccard, took the long-heralded first close-up view of the Gulf Stream on an expedition in the summer of 1969. Their voyage began on July 14 off the coast of West Palm Beach, Florida, in the 50-ft. 147-ton mesoscaphe (middle-depth underwater vessel), *Ben Franklin*, and ended on August 15 when it surfaced 310 miles south of Nova Scotia. In 31 days the vessel drifted 1,444 nautical miles with the powerful current, at an average speed of 2 m.p.h. At the beginning of the expedition the submarine had an average speed of 1·5 knots, but, as it moved past the Virginian coast, the scientists were surprised to find that the speed increased to an average of 3 knots. They reported to a surface escort ship by radiophone each day; they had to surface once when a cross-current carried them off course, but were towed back and immediately re-submerged.

During the voyage they measured the speed of the Gulf Stream, its temperature, and salt content, and photographed the sea bed, made acoustical measurements, and observed marine biological phenomena. They found that the floor of the continental shelf is more undulating than they had expected, and at one point observed uncharted coral formations 100 ft. high. Although they saw jellyfish—one 30 ft. long with tentacles 4 in. thick in some places—swordfish, a few squid,

tuna, porpoises, and sharks, all the experts expressed surprise at the comparative absence of marine life and lack of the deep layer of plankton in the Gulf Stream; they considered the high temperature of the water to be the cause. They also found that the Gulf Stream is far more turbulent than had previously been believed.

One of the main objects of the expedition was to learn how men live together in a confined space for a long period of time; this is of particular interest in view of the likelihood that teams of astronauts will have to spend long periods in manned satellites. An expert from NASA recorded the sleep and rest periods of the crew, and checked the activity of viruses, bacteria, and other micro-organisms parasitic upon man.

Havre, Le. Work, begun in 1967, on the construction of the largest sea-lock in the world was still in progress at Le Havre, the French port at the mouth of the Seine, in 1969. Large enough to hold two big ocean liners side by side, the lock will be 1,300 ft. long and 218 ft. wide. It will accommodate giant ships of 200,000 tons and more, with a draught of 65–70 ft.

Haydock, Lancs. At this place near the junction of the M6 motorway and the East Lancs Road the largest inland oil storage terminal in Europe was opened by Princess Alexandra on June 12, 1969. Owned by the Shell-Mex and BP Group, it has a capacity of 60 million gallons and will handle nearly 500 million gallons a year. The distribution point for service stations and industrial establishments in East and North Lancs, the terminal can load over 150 vehicles in two hours.

Hearing Aids. The U.K. Hearing Aid Council Act 1968, which came into force on Dec. 29, 1969, set up the Council as a statutory body and requires that all dispensers of privately purchased hearing aids and their employers shall be

registered with it within six months. The Council's first task is to draw up standards of competence and codes of practice for dispensers and their employers.

Heart Surgery. An artificial heart, designed by an Oxford surgeon, Dr. Kenneth Reid, was described on May 13, 1969. It would replace the patient's heart while it was removed for repairs, instead of the large heart-lung machine used at present to maintain circulation during heart operations. After repair, the artificial heart would be removed and the patient's own heart replaced; thus rejection problems, which bedevil heart transplants, would not arise. Dr. Reid's artificial heart, which is the same size as a natural heart, is flexible on all surfaces and circulates the blood in a natural way. Dr. Reid's work was done at the Nuffield department of surgery at the Radcliffe Infirmary.

Heart Transplants. In an article in the British medical publication *The Lancet* of May 9, 1969, Dr. Denton Cooley of Houston, Texas, who has performed more heart transplant operations than any other surgeon, said that the operation prolonged the average patient's life by only 37 days. The average survival time of 15 transplant patients was 111 days, including a 22 days' wait after a patient was deemed suitable for the operation until a donor was found. The average survival time of patients for whom no suitable donor could be found in time was 74 days. The difference of 37 days does not justify the general use of the operation, he concluded, although it should be continued in order to gain knowledge and experience.

Helicopter. Another page was added to aviation history when, on June 29, 1969, a twin-engined helicopter completed a flight of 11,000 miles from England to Point Samson in Western Australia. The helicopter—a Westland Wessex 60—travelled over approximately the same route as that followed by the aviators Ross and Keith (later Sir Ross and Sir Keith) Smith, who flew the first aeroplane from England to Australia in 1919. The Westland flight is believed to be the longest single journey ever made by a helicopter, and occupied 22 days. It flew over France, Italy, Greece, Lebanon, Syria, Jordan, Saudi Arabia, the Arabian Gulf, Pakistan, India, Burma, Malaysia, Singapore, and Indonesia to Western Australia. A British crew flew the helicopter to Calcutta where it was handed over to an Australian-based crew. The aircraft was brought to Australia to service drilling rigs up to 200 miles off shore.

Highway Code. A new U.K. Highway Code, published on Feb. 25, 1969, contains more paragraphs and illustrations and has references to 150 rules compared with 94 in the previous (1959)

Gulf Stream. The mesoscaphe *Ben Franklin*, in which six scientists led by Dr. Jacques Piccard drifted underwater 1,444 miles in 31 days, carried along by the Gulf Stream from Florida to 310 miles south of Nova Scotia.

edition. The Code contains an expanded section on motorway driving, and certain roadcraft changes are incorporated. Changes in legislation and the adoption of the metric system by the U.K. will require another new edition by 1973.

On Feb. 9 a new highway code came into force in France, modifying 118 of the 300 articles in the old code which dated from 1954, and adding 34 new ones. One new rule, which came into force from April 15, forbade new drivers to exceed 90 kilometres an hour (56 m.p.h.), during the first year after passing their test, and obliged them to display a disc bearing this figure on the rear of their vehicles. Drivers of heavy vehicles have to undergo a medical examination every five years from the time they obtain their licence, and not, as under the previous code, from the age of 35. All drivers will be given a medical examination if charged with an offence involving loss of licence, or if involved in an accident which causes personal injuries. Accelerating when about to be overtaken, and failing to dip one's headlights before an on-coming car, were added to the list of offences for which a licence can be revoked. Infringement of the ordinary speed limit, however, was made punishable by revocation of licence only if committed in dangerous circumstances, e.g., in narrow streets, at crossroads, or at night.

Holidays. The results of a special survey into the holiday habits of the British people in 1968, carried out by the British Travel Association, were published in March 1969. The survey showed that there were more than 35 million holiday-makers, and that total holiday spending, including fares, reached a record figure of £890 million. Of this sum, £570 million was spent in Britain (£10 million more than in 1967), and £320 million abroad (about £20 million more than in 1967). Of those people spending holidays in Britain the most popular choice was the South West, which attracted a fifth of all holiday-makers. Next came the South with 16 per cent; Wales with 13 per cent; Scotland with 11 per cent; the North West with 11 per cent; the South East with 10 per cent; the East with 8 per cent; the North and North East with 8 per cent; the Midlands with 7 per cent; and London with 3 per cent. Some holiday-makers stayed in more than one region.

Of all main holidays 62 per cent were started in the months of July and August, 18 per cent in June, 11 per cent in September, and 4 per cent in May. Seventy-five per cent were taken at the seaside, 11 per cent in mountain or moor country, and 7 per cent by lake or riverside. The average length of main holidays was just over ten nights, and second or additional holidays lasted on average just over seven nights. Un-licensed hotels, guest houses, and boarding houses accommodated 23 per cent of main holiday-makers, and

licensed hotels 14 per cent; 25 per cent stayed with friends or relatives. Nearly a third of all holiday-makers stayed in caravans, rented flats or villas, or holiday camps, or went camping. Sixty-six per cent travelled to their destination by private car; 16 per cent by bus or coach, and 14 per cent by rail. The average cost of the main holiday spent in Britain was £20 per person, compared with £19 in 1967.

Of the 5 million who went abroad in 1968, half went on package or inclusive holidays, and 54 per cent travelled from Britain by air. The most popular country was Spain, which attracted 30 per cent of the total; next came France, Italy, and Eire, with 10 per cent each; Austria with 7 per cent; and Switzerland and Germany with 6 per cent each. Hotels and motels accommodated 56 per cent of all holiday-makers abroad; 21 per cent stayed with friends or relatives. Of the 34 per cent who travelled abroad by car two-thirds took their cars with them from Britain. The average length of holidays abroad was 14·8 nights, and the average cost per person £62.

Holt Memorial. In March the Australian Prime Minister, John Gorton, opened the Harold Holt Memorial Swimming Centre in the Melbourne suburb of Malvern. The centre, which cost $A600,000, has five pools, including two enclosed, one heated, one Olympic pool, and a diving pool. Prime Minister Holt, a keen swimmer, disappeared while swimming off Cheviot Beach, Victoria, on Dec. 17, 1967.

Hong Kong. On June 26, 1969, a consortium headed by Costain Civil Engineering Ltd. was awarded an £18½ million contract for the construction of a mile-long tunnel under Hong Kong Harbour. Work on the tunnel, which will link the island of Hong Kong with the mainland of Kowloon, started in September 1969 and is due for completion in 1972. The tunnel is to be constructed by the immersed tube method, which involves lowering prefabricated sections into trenches dredged in the harbour bed. Each section will consist of twin tubes, 34 ft. in diameter and 350 ft. long, constructed of a steel shell reinforced concrete lining, and the ends sealed with steel bulkheads. Ballast for sinking will be provided by concrete poured into the gap between the tubes. The finished tunnel, which will be the longest of its type in Asia and, it is believed, the longest twin steel tube tunnel in the world, will have two 22 ft. carriageways for motor traffic.

Honours. The 1969 New Year honours list contained 686 names, 129 being of women. One-third of the honours went to local services, including 34 awards to teachers, 14 to police, and 14 to nurses. There were 59 awards for contributions to the export drive, compared with 43 in January 1968. The home Civil Service

list contained 153 names, and only 10 C.B.E.s were awarded for the whole of the Civil Service. Life peerages were conferred on Sir Learie Constantine, member of the Race Relations Board and governor of the BBC; Professor P. M. S. Blackett, O.M., C.H., President of the Royal Society; Sir Saville Garner, first head of the combined Diplomatic Service; and Sir Donald Stokes, chairman and managing director of British Leyland Motor Corporation. Among those receiving knighthoods were Prof. Michael Woodruff, first man in Britain to transplant a human kidney; Lew Grade, Associated Television, for services to export; Christopher Cockerell, inventor of the hovercraft; the millionaire financier Max Rayne, for services to the arts; Dr. Israel Brodie, former Chief Rabbi, for services to British Jewry; and Jack Cohen, chairman of the Tesco supermarket chain. Sir Adrian Boult, the conductor, Michael Stewart, Foreign and Commonwealth Secretary, and John McEwen, Australian Deputy Prime Minister, were made Companions of Honour.

The composer, Elizabeth Lutyens, received the C.B.E.; and Tom Arnold, the theatrical manager, the singer Vera Lynn and Cliff Michelmore, the BBC TV personality, received the O.B.E. Sportsmen and sportswomen who received recognition included R. M. Kelly, chairman of Celtic Football Club, who was awarded a knighthood for services to Scottish football, and Henry Cooper, boxing champion, and Mike Wenden, Australian Olympic swimming champion, who received the O.B.E. M.B.E.s went to five of Britain's Olympic gold medallists: boxer Chris Finnegan, hurdler David Hemery, marksman John Braithwaite, and yachtsmen Rodney Pattison and Iain Macdonald Smith. Mrs. Ann Haydn Jones, lawn tennis player, and David Bryant, world bowls champion, also received this honour. The honours list included the first appointment of a Roman Catholic nun as a D.B.E.—Sister Mary Regis, a convent school headmistress.

In June the birthday honours list conferred life peerages on Sidney Bernstein, chairman of Granada, Sir Kenneth Clark for services to the Arts, Sir Robert Lowe Hall, former principal of Hertford College, Oxford, and economic adviser to the government from Nov. 1953 to May 1961, and Sir Paul Gore-Booth, former head of the Diplomatic Service. The 34 new knights included John Betjeman, poet and author; Alec Issigonis, technical director of the British Leyland Motor Corporation Ltd.; German-born Ernst Chain, professor of biochemistry, University of London; Leonard Crossland, chairman of Ford Motor Co. Ltd.; Hector McNeil, chairman of the Export Council for Europe; Bernard Miles, founder and artistic director of the Mermaid Theatre; the German-born Professor Nikolaus Pevsner, for services to the history of art; John David Bates,

NEW HOTELS

With the world-wide growth of tourism most great cities are spawning large new hotels to accommodate visitors. Above is the new Hotel Aurora on the north shore of Lake Balaton, Hungary's most popular summer resort; it has 240 rooms. Below is an artist's impression of the 47-storey 1,108-bedroom Keio Plaza in Tokyo, due to be opened in 1971. At right, the upper two models are of a new international centre in Paris: at La Porte Maillot (the high building is a 1,000-room hotel); and a riverside 870-room hotel being built on the site of the derelict d'Orsay railway station. Four 20-storey buildings, with a common lobby area, form the Four Ambassadors, at Miami (*right*). At bottom is Prague's first "botel" or hotel boat, a floating home for 180 guests called the Albatross.

chairman of the Australian Tourist Commission; Robert Lusty, managing director of the Hutchinson publishing group; and Arthur George Weidenfeld, chairman of the publishing house of Weidenfeld and Nicolson. Sir John Barbirolli was made a Companion of Honour, and the same honour went to Dr. Eric Williams, Prime Minister of Trinidad and Tobago, and to Sir Allen Lane, retiring chairman of Penguin Books.

The Prime Minister's list contained 718 names, but there were only 108 women among them. Three were created Dames Commander of the British Empire: Dr. Mary Cartwright, mathematician and former Mistress of Girton College, Cambridge; the novelist Daphne Du Maurier; and the actress Anna Neagle. Sporting personalities honoured included Robin Knox-Johnston, first man to sail single-handed non-stop round the world (C.B.E.); footballer Bobby Charlton (O.B.E.); cricketer Basil D'Oliveira (O.B.E.); Derek Rogers, rugby player (O.B.E.); Jonah P. Barrington, squash rackets champion (M.B.E.); and Bernard Ford and Diane Towler, world champion ice-dancers (M.B.E.). Others to receive

honours included the sculptor Elisabeth Frink (C.B.E.); Judy Cassab, Australian artist (O.B.E.); the comedian Arthur Askey (O.B.E.); Mrs. Pauline Crabbe, Britain's only coloured woman magistrate (O.B.E.); Eric Robinson, BBC conductor of musical programmes (O.B.E.); Rev. E. C. Varah, organiser of the "Samaritans" (O.B.E.); the organist Ralph Downs (C.B.E.); Carleton Hobbs, actor (O.B.E.); and Angus Macpherson, aged 92, for services to bagpiping (M.B.E.). Among the 19 Australian knights were David Brand, Premier of Western Australia; the artist Russell Drysdale; R. M. Ansett, head of Ansett airlines and transport group; and John David Bates, chairman of the Australian Tourist Commission.

A special honours list marked the Investiture of the Prince of Wales in July. It included the creation of five knights, one Dame, and 23 other honours to people directly concerned with the Investiture, or who had given special services to Wales. Among those receiving knighthoods were Rev. Albert Evans-Jones, recorder of the Gorsedd of Bards and president of the National Eisteddfod Court, for services to Welsh literature; the

singer Geraint Evans; David Joseph Davies, chairman of the Wales Tourist Board; and Robert Charles Evans, Principal of the University College of Wales, Bangor. Lady Olwen Elizabeth Carey Evans, of Criccieth, was created a D.B.E. The Earl of Snowdon, Constable of Caernarvon Castle, was made a Knight Grand Cross of the Royal Victorian Order, an honour in the personal gift of the Queen.

On July 9, the Queen made Sir Humphrey Gibbs, former Governor of Rhodesia, Knight Grand Cross of the Royal Victorian Order for his outstanding loyalty, and a month later created Lady Gibbs a Dame Commander of the Order of the British Empire. Earlier in the year Lord Reith, first director-general of the BBC, and Sir Charles Maclean, Chief Scout since 1959, were made Knights of the Order of the Thistle, the Scottish order of chivalry.

The Order of Merit was brought up to its full complement of 24 members with the appointment on July 14 of Professor Sir Geoffrey Taylor, mathematician and atomic scientist; Lord Penney, former chairman of the Atomic Energy Authority;

Home-built miniature hovercraft lined up for an amateur race at Goodwood in September 1969.

Latest in Hovercraft

Above: left, a 48-ton 70-knot British hovercraft, suitable for civilian or military use, which started Royal Navy trials in November 1969; *right,* the "Naviplane N300 Croisette," a new French hovercraft carrying 90 passengers at 56 m.p.h., which went into service between Nice and Cannes in June 1969. *Right:* the new 165-ton Hoverlloyd cross-Channel hovercraft which started a Ramsgate–Calais service in April 1969. In spite of the growing use of hovercraft the world over, the British hovercraft industry met severe financial difficulties during the year.

Dame Veronica Wedgwood, historian and writer; and Malcolm MacDonald, retiring special government representative in Africa.

On Oct. 24 it was announced that Anthony Grey, the British journalist released by the Chinese after having been under house arrest for 26 months in Peking, had been awarded the O.B.E.

House of Commons. The U.K. Ministry of Public Building and Works published on Jan. 20, 1969, plans for a six-storey extension to the House of Commons. The scheme provides for a bigger building than that envisaged by Sir Leslie Martin's plan in 1965, which involved the use of land at the corner of Bridge Street and the Victoria Embankment. The new plan extends the building from the Thames to Whitehall, and involves the demolition of Norman Shaw's Scotland Yard building. The extension, which will contain up to 350,000 sq. ft. of rooms, will be connected to the existing House of Commons by a tunnel under Bridge Street. New government offices are also envisaged in the plan, which includes Sir Leslie Martin's suggestion of a tunnel to be built under the Thames from Lambeth Bridge to Charing Cross Underground station, in order to reduce the flow of traffic through Parliament Square. It will be at least eight years before the new building, estimated to cost £5 million, is completed. The design will probably be the subject of a competition open to all British Commonwealth architects, and, after allowing two years for approval of the design, the building will take a further five or six years. See also pp. 368, 369.

Housing. The Minister of Housing and Local Government announced on Jan. 22, 1969, that the number of new homes built in Great Britain in 1968 was 413,700, the highest figure ever achieved. Local authority houses were fewer— 191,722 compared with 203,918 in 1967—but privately built homes increased to 221,993 from 200,438 in 1967. The fall in the number of local authority houses was largely due to a reduction in government grants which was part of the July 1967 economy measures. This reduction still applied during 1969.

Housing tables published on Feb. 26 by the U.K. Registrar-General showed that at the time of the sample census taken in 1966 more than 2,250,000 homes in England and Wales had no fixed bath (14 per cent of the 15,400,000 households). In Wales alone the figure was 20 per cent. The tables also showed that 1,925,940 (12·5 per cent) had no hot water supply; 274,260 (1·8 per cent) had no lavatory; and 2,464,690 (16·1 per cent) only an outside lavatory. 7,200,000 householders owned their own homes, and 3,900,000 rented them from local authorities or new town corporations. Only 442,000 homes were shared by more than one household; but more than 180,000 (1·2 per cent of all dwellings) were overcrowded. Over-

Hydrofoil. The all-aluminium *Plain View*, a U.S. Navy vessel and the world's largest hydrofoil, is 220 ft. long, displaces 300 tons, and can exceed 40 knots.

crowding was highest among unskilled workers' families, where 3·1 per cent of households had more than 1½ people per room, which is the level beyond which overcrowding officially occurs. The lowest density of occupation was among self-employed professional workers, with a density of 0·45 people per room, compared with 0·66 for skilled manual workers, and 0·67 for members of the Armed Forces.

Humber, River. Approval for Britain's longest suspension bridge, which will span the Humber between Hull and Grimsby, was given by the government at the end of April. The bridge, to cost £20 million, will have a central span of 4,500 ft., compared with the 3,300-ft. Forth bridge and the 3,200-ft. Severn bridge, and will be in service by 1976. After the necessary preparatory work, construction will start in 1972.

The Queen Elizabeth dock, a 28-acre extension to the King George V dock, which cost £6,750,000, was opened at Hull by the Queen on August 4, 1969.

Hunt Report (Industrial Areas). The U.K. Minister for Economic Affairs announced on April 24, 1969, that the Yorkshire coalfield; Erewash Valley, Derbyshire; parts of Humberside; some districts of N.E. Lancashire; a large part of S.E. Wales; Leith; and Plymouth were to benefit from a £20 million aid scheme. This statement followed the publication by a nine-man committee, headed by Sir John Hunt, of a report on the problems of "grey" industrial areas affected by government aid to neighbouring development zones. One of the major recommendations of the 27 made in the report was that a national attack on derelict land should be made, involving the formation of a reclamation agency with the National Coal Board's open-cast executive as its nucleus, and aimed at reclaiming 67,000 acres by 1984. The committee estimated the cost at £7 million a year, compared with the present £1 million spent on land reclamation. To help to raise this sum it suggested that the Government should provide £5 million a year by extending its 85 per cent

capital grant payments, so far restricted to development areas. The committee's recommendations for de-scheduling Merseyside as a development area, and easing some building restrictions outside such areas, were rejected by the Government, as were proposals that the whole of Yorkshire, Humberside, and the North West should qualify for a new 25 per cent building grant and increased training assistance.

Hunt Report (Royal Ulster Constabulary). Following the troubles in Northern Ireland during the summer of 1969 a three-man committee, under the chairmanship of Lord Hunt (of Everest fame), was set up to examine the role of the Royal Ulster Constabulary and the Ulster Special Constabulary (the "B" Specials), and to make recommendations for the efficient enforcement of law and order. Their report, published on Oct. 10, 1969, made 48 separate recommendations. Chief of them were the replacement of the controversial 8,000-strong all-Protestant "B" Specials force by two bodies, one to be a locally recruited part-time force of 4,000 men under the control of G.O.C. Northern Ireland, and the other a regular reserve to assist the police in times of emergency. The Royal Ulster Constabulary, the report said, should be relieved of all duties of a military nature, the carrying of firearms being phased out, but the strength of the force should be increased. Roman Catholics should be encouraged to join the force, the uniform of which should be changed from green to blue. A police authority should be set up, the membership of which should reflect the proportions of different groups in the community. The recommendations were accepted by the N. Ireland Government.

Hydrofoil. The world's largest hydrofoil, *Plain View*, built by the Lockheed Shipbuilding and Construction Co., Seattle, U.S.A., started her U.S. Navy test programme in the spring of 1969. *Plain View*, which has an all-aluminium hull, is 220 ft. long, displaces 300 tons, and has two gas-turbine engines which give a speed of over 40 knots.

ij

Ifni, Africa. Under a Spanish–Moroccan treaty signed on Jan. 4, 1969, Spain agreed to return to Morocco her colony of Ifni in N.W. Africa. This small port, on the Atlantic coast and bounded by the Asaka River, is 580 sq. miles in area, and has a population of 50,000, mainly nomads. Ifni was ceded to Spain by Morocco in 1860, but the occupation was nominal until April 6, 1934, when the Spanish flag was hoisted for the first time.

Income and Expenditure. The U.K. Department of Employment and Productivity published in October 1969 a family expenditure survey report for 1968. It stated that the average total income of the 7,184 families surveyed was £29 19s 7d a week in 1968, a 5·2 per cent increase on the 1967 figure of £28 5s. The husband contributed £22 1s 5d of the total, the wife £3 7s 2d, and other members £4 11s. The report also revealed that about 11 per cent of households in the survey had incomes of less than £10 per week. The average cost of housekeeping went up by £1 6s 7d a week in 1968 to £24 18s 7d. The largest weekly expenditure was on food, which took £6 11s 9d, including eating out in restaurants; this was 4s 4d a week more than in 1967. Rent and housing costs increased by 9s 4d to £3 3s 2d a week; and the amount spent on vehicles, including running costs, spares, and accessories, plus train and other fares, increased by 8s to £3 5s 5d. Clothing bills increased by 4s to £2 4s 2d; fuel, light, and power by 1s 9d to £1 11s; alcoholic drinks by 10d to £1 0s 6d; cigarettes, tobacco, and cigars by 7d to £1 5s 9d. Services, including entertainment, telephone charges, gifts, and legal fees, however, cost £2 5s a week, which was 1s 3d less than in 1967; and the amount spent on gambling also fell to about 1s 10d a week, compared with just over 3s in 1967.

Each £1 spent in 1968 was accounted for as follows (with a comparison of the same figures in 1958):

	1968 s. d.	1958 s. d.
Food (household expenditure)	4 2	5 3
Alcoholic drink	1 3	1 2
Tobacco	1 2	1 4
Housing, fuel and light	3 5	2 10
Clothing and footwear	1 8	1 11
Purchase and running costs of cars and motorcycles	1 9	1 0
Household durable goods	11	1 0
Other goods	1 10	1 11
Travel	8	8
Entertainment and other services	3 2	2 11

The Central Statistical Office stated in September 1969 that the gross national product in the U.K. in 1968 was over £36,500 million (about £660 per head of the population). Total personal income was £36,000 million (an increase of $7\frac{1}{2}$ per cent over the 1967 total), and total personal expenditure was £27,000 million. In 1967 family incomes (husband and wife) of over £2,000 a year *before tax* numbered 1,750,000; those between £1,000 and £2,000 numbered 9,500,000; those between £500 and £1,000 numbered over 9 million; those less than £500 numbered 7,250,000. Incomes of more than £2,000 a year *after tax* numbered 1 million, and those over £5,000 *after tax* numbered fewer than 65,000.

A survey of spending by girls between the ages of 10 and 19, produced for the International Publishing Corporation's young magazine group, was published in September 1969. It showed that of the £595 million in their pockets each year, they spent more than one-third (£228 million) on clothes and shoes: £150 million went towards skirts and dresses (9 per cent of their net income), stockings, tights, and socks ($8\frac{1}{2}$ per cent), and shoes (8 per cent). In pocket money and net earnings the average teenager has a weekly income of £3 2s; three out of five boys and girls receive £1 a week or less, but the average for the 15-year-olds and over is about £6 6s a week.

A Common Market Commission report published in September 1969 showed that the average Italian family spends 47 per cent of its income on food, drink, and tobacco, compared with 39 per cent in Great Britain, and 37 per cent in France.

Information given in the August 1969 issue of *Industry Week*, a journal supported by the Confederation of British Industry, showed that the varying salaries received by heads of companies with average annual sales from £436,666 to £20,800,000, in seven major countries were: in Switzerland £14,987; in France £14,308; in Germany, Holland, Italy, and Belgium, over £12,500; and in Britain, £11,187.

Australia. The average annual income in Australia in 1968 varied between $A1,342 and $A1,628 according to State. The Commonwealth Statistician reported in March 1969 that the average in Victoria was $A1,628, in New South Wales and the Capital Territory $A1,589, in Western Australia $A1,450, in Queensland $A1,381, in Tasmania $A1,351, and in South Australia $A1,342. In Western Australia the percentage increase over the previous year was 6·2; this leap, due to the boom in minerals, was over twice the national average increase of 2·7 per cent. In other States the percentage increase was: Queensland 3·6; Victoria 2·9; Tasmania 2·7; New South Wales and A.C.T. 2; and South Australia 0·4.

New Zealand. Figures given in April 1969 by the N.Z. statistics department showed that doctors were the highest-income group in the country. In 1967–68 medical practitioners, including surgeons, specialists, and physicians, had an average income of $NZ8,550, compared with $8,480 in 1966–67. After doctors the wealthiest were lawyers, with an average of $7,800 compared with $7,700 in 1966–67; dentists with $7,500, compared with $7,440; and public accountants with $6,500, compared with $6,420. Lower in the list of the self-employed were those engaged in road freight transport with an average of $3,300, compared with $3,380 in the previous year; dairy farmers showed the same figures. Then followed sheep farmers with $3,200 ($3,450) and building construction workers $3,000 ($3,200). The list of salary- and wage-earners was headed by company directors and managers with an average of $5,160 ($4,970). Then followed professional and technical workers, $2,420 ($2,190); craftsmen, production process workers, and labourers, $2,140 ($2,090); and clerical workers, $1,850 ($1,800). The number of people with incomes of $10,000 and more fell from 6,480 in 1966–67 to 5,980 in 1967–68. More people (a total of 224,810 in 1967–68) were in the $2,000–$2,399 income group than in any other.

Independent, The. This is the name of Western Australia's new Sunday newspaper, which went on sale in Perth on April 27, 1969. The first completely new newspaper to be printed in Western Australia for 70 years, it will later become a daily paper, probably early in 1970.

Indian Princes. The decision of the Congress Party, taken in 1967, to abolish the privy purses and other privileges of former princes of India who merged their states into the Union of India on its formation or since, had still not been made operative in mid-1969. Negotiations between the Government and the Concord of Princes broke down in May over the princes' proposal that the grants should be gradually reduced rather than suddenly stopped. The Congress Party was split on the issue when the Communist opposition tabled a resolution in Parliament that the grants should be immediately abolished. About 500 princes are involved, receiving between them £2 million tax-free per year. Their grants vary between £200,000 a year and £15 a year; a hundred of them receive over £10,000 a year each.

Industrial Bravery Award. This U.K. award, the only one of its kind made specifically for bravery at work, is sponsored by a manufacturer of protective footwear; on March 11, 1969, ten industrial workers went to the House of Commons to have their names placed on the "Plus 50" Roll of Industrial Heroism, and to receive inscribed silver salvers to mark the occasion. The awards went to: Alan Mitchell, a 45-year-old central

Industrial Bravery Award. The first ten winners of the "Plus 50" industrial heroism awards are named in left to right order in the accompanying text.

Iron Ore. On June 26, 1969, the Governor-General, Sir Paul Hasluck, opened the largest iron-ore development project in Australia—the vast mineral deposits in the Mt. Newman complex in Western Australia. During the ceremony Sir Paul unveiled an inscribed cairn on Mt. Whaleback, the prime ore body of the complex, and then touched off an explosion to produce the three millionth ton of ore since full-scale mining began here in March 1969. The complex includes the open-cut mine and plant, a railway, the nearby town of Newman, and large-scale ore-handling and shipping facilities at Port Hedland.

An iron-ore find with a market potential of at least 3 million tons was reported in April in the Hampshire area of Tasmania, 16 miles from Burnie. A spokesman for Tasmanian Exploration Syndicate said it is high-grade ore, and that there is a possibility of finding a further 2-million-ton deposit.

The largest mineral contract ever signed was announced on April 20, 1969, when Western Australia's Minister of Industrial Development gave news of an agreement to supply to Japan £58 million worth of iron ore from the Robe River area in the north-west of W. Australia. The quantities named in the agreement are 87 million tons of pellets over 21 years, and 37 million tons of sinter over 15 years. Deliveries will begin in late 1971 or early 1972 from Cape Lambert, where a vast pelletising plant will be built.

heating fitter from Redditch, Warwickshire, who rescued a man from a fire following a gas explosion; Peter Kemp, a 40-year-old lorry driver from Kilburn, Derbyshire, who, on seeing a driverless lorry on the M1, leapt from his own vehicle on to it, and brought it under control; Mansell Gardiner, aged 45, a fireman from York, who by uncoupling a blazing oil tanker from a goods train averted a major disaster; Charles Davies, aged 31, and Albert Burrow, aged 54, from Tiverton, Devon, who rescued and attempted to revive a man from an ammonia-fume-filled building; and shipyard workers William Pattison, aged 46, from South Shields, and James Thompson, aged 44, Gordon Cliff, aged 37, and Leslie Perera, aged 40, all from Sunderland, who went without breathing apparatus into a ship's hold filled with lethal paint fumes, in an attempt to rescue a trapped man. The only woman recipient, Betty Slatcher, aged 53, an ambulance driver who is only 5 ft. tall, was given her award for forcing an entry into a burning house that she was passing while driving her ambulance, and carrying three children to safety, undoubtedly saving their lives.

Innisfail, Queensland. The Australian government's tropical research laboratories here came into the news in 1969 when a British M.P., a member of the Commons select committee on science and technology, stated that tests in the field of chemical and biological warfare were being carried on there. The Australian Minister of Supply denied the allegations and invited the M.P., Tam Dalyell, Labour member for West Lothian, to visit the establishment at Innisfail. When he did so in May, he withdrew his remarks and admitted that the tropical research unit "does not have and never has had the capability for carrying out experiments of a significant nature in chemical and biological weapon testing." The research unit at Innisfail is jointly supported by the governments of Australia, Canada, the U.S.A., and the U.K.

Insulin. Dr. Dorothy Hodgkin, British scientist and winner of the 1964 Nobel prize for chemistry, announced on Aug. 13, 1969, that work at research laboratories at Oxford University had led to the discovery of the crystalline structure of insulin. She and her colleagues found that the atoms in an insulin molecule could be accurately located by the introduction of "foreign" atoms, which cause distortion of the normal pattern visible by X-rays. The discovery should make possible the synthesisation of insulin, instead of the present expensive production from natural elements.

Invergordon, Ross and Cromarty, Scotland. On Aug. 1, 1969, work began on the site of a £60 million refinery and petro-chemical complex here, which is expected to go into production by mid-1972, employing 400 people. The plant is designed to produce per year 2 million tons of naphtha, 500,000 tons of fuel oil, 500,000 tons of aromatics and derivatives, 400,000 tons of olefins, and 1 million tons of tail gases, which will be used to generate 250 megawatts of power in the plant. The total annual output will be worth an estimated £40 million, more than half of which will be for export.

Jade. It was reported on Nov. 18, 1969, that the world record price of £27,000 for a piece of jade had been paid for a carving of a recumbent jade horse. It is of the Ming dynasty, probably dating from about 1520, and was exhibited at Spink's, London, during September.

Jaundice. The isolation of a virus that causes infectious jaundice (infective hepatitis) was announced by a team of doctors at the London School of Hygiene and Tropical Medicine on Dec. 3, 1969. The discovery should enable research scientists to produce a vaccine to combat or prevent the disease. The

Iron Ore. Explosion touched off by Sir Paul Hasluck, Australia's governor-general, to produce the three millionth ton of ore from Mount Newman, W. Australia.

Jewels. The highest price ever paid for a single jewel was given in October 1969 for this flawless 69·42-carat diamond 1½ inches long and 1 inch wide.

virus was found in the blood of patients being treated for serum hepatitis (caused by the use of infected hypodermic needles by drug addicts) and for epidemic hepatitis (a more common but less dangerous form of jaundice). The leader of the team, Dr. A. Zuckerman, said that the virus is unique, as far as he knew, in being able to co-exist in the bloodstream with its antibody.

Jewels. At an auction held in Geneva on May 1, 1969, a 32·07-carat emerald-cut diamond ring mounted as a single stone, given to the late Nina Dyer by Prince Sadruddin Khan, fetched £111,947. This was believed to be the highest price ever fetched at auction by a single jewel. But it was far exceeded on Oct. 23 when another diamond ring fetched £437,000 at an auction at the Parke-Bernet galleries in New York. Bought by Cartier's, the Fifth Avenue jewellers, and resold to Richard Burton the following day for an undisclosed sum, the diamond in the latter ring is a 69·42-carat, pear-shaped, almost colourless, and flawless stone 1½ inches long, 1 inch wide, and about three-quarters of an inch thick.

Jockey Club. At their respective meetings on Dec. 2 and Dec. 9, 1968, the U.K. Jockey Club and National Hunt Committee passed regulations agreeing to amalgamate, and approved the constitution of the combined new body, to be called the Jockey Club. The body came into being on Dec. 12, 1968, and took over the functions and powers of the old Jockey Club and National Hunt Committee on Jan. 1, 1969. Rules based on the two existing codes of racing came into effect on that date, as did certain new rules dealing, among other things, with club and company ownership of horses. The founding of the new body was intended to continue the improvement in the administration of racing which began with the establishment of the Turf Board in 1965. It is beneficial to the racing industry that a single governing body can speak on behalf of all forms of racing in negotiations with the Government and other bodies.

Journalism Awards. The annual Hannen Swaffer awards to British journalists for the year 1968 were announced in March 1969. The recipients were:

Journalist of the year—Victor Zorza (*Guardian*)
Young journalist of the year—Kevin Rafferty (*Sun*)
International reporter—Walter Partington (*Daily Express*)
News reporter — Harold Jackson (*Guardian*)
Descriptive writer — Angus McGill (*Evening Standard*)
Sports writer—Chris Brasher (*Observer*)
Critic—Peter Black (*Daily Mail*)
Women's page—Marjorie Proops (*Daily Mirror*)
Provincial journalist — Len Doherty (*Sheffield Star*)
Campaigning journalist — Peter Harland (*Bradford Telegraph and Argus*) and Michael Leapman (*Sun*)
Special award — Henry Longhurst (*Sunday Times*) for his golf reporting.
The judges unanimously agreed in commending the *Sun* for the number and variety of campaigns undertaken in the public interest.

Justice. A shortage of judges and court staff threatens the administration of justice in many countries, according to a report by the World's Association of Judges meeting in Bangkok in September. A tenfold increase in the past 10 years in the number of cases coming to the courts was reported, and governments were criticised for failing to increase the number of judges in line with the increase in world population. Whereas West Germany has one judge for every 4,000 of its population, France one for every 12,500, and the Scandinavian countries one for every 25,000, England has only one for every 100,000.

Kejimkujik, Canada. This is the name of Canada's 19th and newest national park, situated in south central Nova Scotia. Officially opened in September 1969, the 145-square-mile park includes a large camping area, a supervised swimming beach, boating facilities, a canteen, three picnic areas, and three nature trails. In some parts, it is completely wild, and travelling is by canoe or on foot. The whole area is threaded by numerous rivers, and contains some 35 shallow lakes. With the exception of fish, all wild life, including the white-tailed deer, beaver, muskrat, and squirrel, is protected. About 100 species of birds, including the blue and grey jay, robin, junco, warbler, and gull, are known to nest in the park.

Kennedy Memorials. The house at Brookline, Mass., where President John F. Kennedy was born in 1917 was on May 29, 1969, made a national historic site, when his mother, Mrs. Joseph P. Kennedy, ceremonially handed over the deeds to a representative of the Federal government.

Keraudren, Cape, Western Australia. The Federal government of Australia announced on Feb. 6, 1969, that two committees were to be set up to study the feasibility of a plan to build a port with nuclear explosives at Cape Keraudren, and said that U.S. assistance would be sought. To provide a deep-water harbour for ships to carry iron ore, deposits of which are found some 30 miles from Cape Keraudren at Mount Goldsworthy and Nimingarra, it would have been necessary to blast out a crater about 6,000 ft. long and 200–300 ft. high at the sides. If the plan had been carried out, this tiny isthmus jutting into the Indian Ocean would have been the site of the world's first harbour to be excavated by nuclear blasting. But on March 29 the proposal was abandoned, the Australian and U.S. Atomic Energy Commissions having decided that there was insufficient basis for proceeding with the feasibility study. The mining company concerned had meantime revalued the economics of developing the iron-ore deposits and concluded that, for the time being, the creation of the harbour was not justified.

Kennedy Memorials. The President's mother handing over the deeds of his birthplace in Brookline Mass., which was declared a national historic site.

Kwinana, Western Australia. It was stated in February 1969 that Alcoa of Australia Ltd. intends to expand its alumina refinery here to an annual capacity of 1,040,000 metric tons. This will be the fourth expansion since the plant began production in 1963, and will make the refinery five times the size of its original installation. Construction plans were announced in May, when it was said that the cost would be $A50 million.

Kyoto, Japan. A 10-storey, windowless, ferro-concrete building, claimed to be the world's first "apartment house tomb," was completed in Kyoto at the beginning of 1969. It was built to house the remains of 14,313 people, each in an apartment resembling a Buddhist household shrine, and was erected because of the shortage of burial places and the overcrowding of existing cemeteries in the city. Costing nearly £3 million, it took almost two years to build. The building is equipped with lifts, and there are three classes of apartments, ranging from the de luxe, costing about £1,160, to the economy class, costing about £350. When the door of an apartment containing ashes is opened the miniature shrine is automatically illuminated, and when an electric heater is switched on aromatic smoke is produced.

Kyoto, Japan. Windowless 10-storey communal tomb, in which each of 14,313 deceased Japanese has an apartment—de luxe, standard, or economy class. Lighting and the burning of incense are provided at the touch of a switch.

Lasers. Details of one of the latest warfare training techniques to be developed by British scientists were given at the beginning of October 1969. Instead of using blank shells, which cost up to £75 each, a laser beam is now used to scan and fire at an "enemy" tank. The laser projector is strapped to a gun barrel; the opponent tank is equipped with a receiver which emits a smoke charge when hit by the laser beam. Called "Sionfire," the laser method has been produced by the Solartron company of Farnborough, Hants.

Lauder, Sir Harry. A commemorative plaque to this famous Scottish entertainer (1870–1950) was unveiled at Longley Road, Tooting, Wandsworth, London, on July 8, 1969, on a house where Lauder lived from 1903 to 1911. During the ceremony dignitaries joined in choruses of Sir Harry's songs, and, as the plaque was unveiled, "Highland Laddie" was played on bagpipes.

Leasehold Reform. Following some manifestly unjust test cases in which an absurdly high price was fixed by the U.K. Lands Tribunal for the purchase by leaseholders of the freehold of the land on which their houses stood, an amendment to the 1969 Housing Act was introduced in May to restore the intention of the Leasehold Reform Act of 1967. In test cases a leaseholder seeking to buy his freehold had been treated as a bidder for the land in the open market, although in the vast majority of cases he was the only interested party. The amendment abolished this anomaly.

Legal Representation. New rules for the training of barristers in the U.K. were published by the Senate of the four Inns of Court on March 31, 1969. The major changes, which come into force in 1970, require for the first time that intending legal practitioners shall undergo compulsory education in practical disciplines. The first part of the training will be the traditional education in the principles of law, taken at either a university or a professional school, and the second, compulsory only for those intending to practise in the U.K., will be a new form of training for practice, run wholly by the profession. Because the nature of the examination will make it difficult to pass without this practical training it is expected that the number of part-time students qualifying while in full-time employment may be reduced. Whereas students are now accepted with two grade E "A levels" the new rules demand grade C passes. The requirement that a bar student "keep term" by dining for two years before qualification is to be altered so that the dining requirement can be fulfilled during the training year, so making it possible for a university law student to delay his decision on which branch of the profession to join until he completes his studies. The number of teaching staff is to be increased, and fees will rise by 40 per cent.

From Oct. 1, 1969, any solicitor in effective practice for three years and with sound experience of advocacy and court procedure can transfer to the Bar without any obstacle or delay other than six months' pupillage (the unpaid period spent as assistant to an experienced barrister). Previously it was necessary for any solicitor with less than five years' experience, regardless of his knowledge of advocacy, to take all the Bar examinations, go through one year of pupillage, and keep dining terms at one of the Inns of Court for two years.

During this "dining" period he was barred from earning his living as either a solicitor or barrister. Solicitors with less than three years' practice or with little experience of advocacy and court procedure are still required to take examinations in procedure and evidence, and may be required to do one year's pupillage and to attend practical courses.

Leisure. A U.K. government social survey report, *Planning for Leisure*, published on Sept. 30, 1969, stated that watching television ranks as the foremost leisure occupation of both men and women in Britain. National population samples, samples from London, and samples from the new towns were surveyed in 1965 and 1966. In the national and new towns samples the second most popular pastime for men was usually gardening, with some form of physical recreation third, while women use their leisure time to pursue crafts and hobbies, chiefly knitting. But television occupies about 25 per cent of leisure time, and no other single activity occupies as much as 10 per cent. In the central London sample, gardening, knitting, and physical recreation were much less popular, and television less important; young single people spend most of their leisure in physical recreation, and young men do not spend more time watching television than in sport until they became fathers.

Le Tremblay, France. Work on a project designed to provide a vast park for leisure, physical recreation, and sports continued on the site of the former race-track here, 6 miles east of Paris, during 1969. The site had already been levelled by bulldozers in the last four months of 1968. The first of its kind in France, the park is planned for people of all ages, and will provide facilities for all types of sport. It will include a huge central clubhouse, with a hall, rest room, discotheque, television rooms, film club, bar, a restaurant to seat 600 people, and a kindergarten with a paddling pool. The architect, Alain Bourbonnais, has planned the park so that the edges are raised round a central plain. This central area will be used for free recreation and leisure pursuits, and the outer circle for sports facilities. In bad weather, shelter will be provided by covered galleries encircling the various sports centres and halls. It is hoped that the athletics ground and three football pitches will be completed by 1970; the tennis courts, riding centre, and archery section by 1971; and the swimming pools, covered skating rink, and central clubhouse by 1973. It is expected that the park, which covers an area of just under 200 acres, will have as many as 20,000 visitors each day during holiday periods. The total cost of the project has been estimated at about £7 million.

Leukemia. A new drug, code-named ICRF 159, during preliminary trials produced notable improvements in the health of some leukemia patients in 1969. In March the *British Medical Journal* published an account of trials carried out by five doctors and research workers from the Imperial Cancer Research Fund and the Westminster and Lewisham Hospital, London. ICRF 159 was given to nine patients, aged two to 75, who had passed beyond conventional treatment and were in the last stages of the disease. The drug had some effect on the blood cells of all but one, although five of these eight subsequently died. One boy, aged 11, given ICRF 159 in November 1968 recovered sufficiently to return to school; another, aged 2, dying when admitted to hospital, was discharged, alive and well, after 4 weeks.

Researchers at Glasgow University announced in November that they had for certain identified a virus that causes leukemia, and had discovered that it can live in the cells of cats, dogs, pigs, and human beings. They isolated the virus of feline leukemia; when injected into dogs, pigs, and human beings it lived. Nevertheless they emphasised that there is no evidence that human beings can contract the disease from their pet animals.

Level Crossings. Following the recommendations of a public inquiry into the disaster at Hixon, Staffs, on Jan. 6, 1968, when an express train crashed into a 150-ton transporter on a level crossing, and 11 were killed and 40 injured, the U.K. Ministry of Transport announced in September 1969 a new design of warning sign to be erected at all the 207 automatic half-barrier crossings in the country. The ordinary level-crossing symbol of a gate will appear above verbal instructions to stop when the lights are showing, and to drivers of large (over 55 ft. long or 9 ft. 6 in. wide or 32 tons total weight) or slow (5 m.p.h. or less) vehicles to telephone to obtain permission to cross. Light signals will be altered to show a steady amber before the flashing red. The barrier operation will be altered by British Rail so that when a second train is due within 52 seconds' travelling time

Lifeboat. Experimental glass-fibre-reinforced plastic lifeboat, 41 ft. long, being put through her paces by the R.N.L.I.

after a preceding train the barriers will remain down and the red lights will continue to flash. Failure by drivers to obey the signals and instructions will be a "totting-up" offence.

Lifeboats. The annual report of the Royal National Lifeboat Institution, given at the annual meeting in London on March 25, 1969, showed that a record number of calls were answered in 1968, and 1,003 lives saved. For the first time, inshore rescue boats, mostly inflatable craft with outboard motors operated by a two-man crew, and fast rescue boats, were launched more frequently than the conventional lifeboats—1,178 times compared with 1,116—and saved 506 lives compared with 497. The report also stated that over 90,000 lives had been saved since the founding of the Institution in 1824.

It was at the 1969 meeting that Coxswain Daniel Kirkpatrick of Longhope was to have received a second bar to his silver medal for gallantry in the rescue of 15 men from the 352-ton trawler *Ross Puma*, in a blizzard off Hoy in April 1968. But Coxswain Kirkpatrick was tragically drowned with the rest of the Longhope lifeboat crew on March 17, after the lifeboat turned over in high seas when on the way to aid a Liberian cargo vessel. He would have been the only man to receive the Institution's silver medal three times. The five other crew members who were accorded the Institution's thanks for their part in the *Ross Puma* rescue also were drowned, and included Daniel Kirkpatrick, son of the coxswain.

A new experimental R.N.L.I. lifeboat underwent trials in January 1969. The 41-ft.-long boat, which has a glass-fibre-reinforced plastic hull, has an operative duration of 26 hours at a cruising speed of 17 knots. After evaluation at selected lifeboat stations in Britain, it may prove to be a forerunner of faster lifeboats at lower construction costs than the conventional type.

Details of a ship's lifeboat that can be catapulted automatically into the sea from the hull of a sinking ship were

given in January 1969. Compressed air blows a flanged plate off the side of the vessel, and the self-inflating rubber dinghy, contained in a glass-fibre capsule, shoots out. Another inflatable lifeboat was under production by Firestone Fabrics company in Magnolia, Arkansas, U.S.A., in 1969. Designed to hold 15 people, it can be folded into a 2 ft. by 4 ft. package. In emergency it is inflated with two bottles of compressed carbon dioxide.

Lighthouse. An unmanned offshore lighthouse at Frederick Reef on the Queensland coast 450 miles from Brisbane, has been constructed entirely of nickel stainless steel, which stands up well to corrosive attack and requires little maintenance. The 100-ft. structure supports a small rotating beacon, clearly visible in daylight and a good radar target. The self-supporting stainless steel column has a diameter of 9 ft. 6 in. at the base and 3 ft. 4 in. at the top, and is constructed of eight cylindrical sections weighing a total of 25 tons. The foundations comprise six steel piles, driven down into the firm coral base.

Lighthouse. "Lanby" (Large Automatic Navigational Buoy), designed to replace lightships, carries a light with a 16-mile range and a fog signal audible at a distance of 3 miles.

Literary Awards. Prizes to authors awarded in 1969 included the U.K. Arts Council prizes of £1,000 each for the best volume of English translation in prose shared between Christine Brook-Rose and William Weaver, for the best volume of English translation in poetry to Michael Hamburger for *Poems and Fragments* by Holdarlin, for the best book for young children shared between Kevin Crossley-Holland, author, and Margaret Gorden, illustrator, for *The Green Children*, and for the best book for older children to Leon Garfield for *Smith*; the Royal Society of Literature awards, under the W. H. Heinemann bequest, to Gordon S. Haight for *George Eliot*, to V. S. Pritchett for *A Cab at the Door*, and to Jasmine Rose Innes for *Writing in the Dust*; the 1968 Winifred Holtby memorial prize, awarded annually for the best regional novel of the year by an author under 37, to Catherine Cookson for *The Round Tower*; the James Tait Black memorial prize for the best novel of 1968 to Maggie Ross for *The Gastropod*, and for the best typographical work of 1968 to Gordon S. Haight for *George Eliot*; the Somerset Maugham award to Angela Carter for her novel *Several Perceptions*; the annual *Guardian* award of 100 guineas for the best work of children's fiction in 1968 to Joan Aiken for *The Whispering Mountain*; the 1968 Duff Cooper memorial prize to Roy Fuller for *New Poems*; the Eleanor Farjeon award for 1968, presented by the Children's Book Circle, to Mrs. Anne Wood, founder of the Books for Children groups and founder and editor of the magazine *Books for Your Children*; the John Llewelyn Rhys memorial prize to Melvyn Bragg for his novel *Without a City Wall*; the annual Scott-Moncrieff Prize of £400 for the best translation into English of a French 20th-century work to Terence Kilmartin for his translation of *Antimémoires* by André Malraux, and *Pitié pour les Femmes* by Henry de Montherlant (a special award of £50 was also made to Anthony Rudolf for his translation of the selected poems of Yves Bonnefoy); the Académie Française Grand Prix to Pierre Moustier for *The Partition*; the £1,000 Macmillan-Panther prize for first crime novel (which also wins $2,000 from a U.S. publisher) to Peter Lovesey for *Wobble to Death* (to be published in March 1970); the *Guardian* annual fiction prize for "work of originality and promise" to Maurice Leitch for *Poor Lazarus*; the Prix Femina to Jorge Semprun for his novel *Le Deuxième Mort de Ramon Mercador*; the Medicis prize to Hélène Cixons for her novel *Dedans*; the first award of the annual £50 Mary Elgin prize instituted by her husband and Hodder and Stoughton in her memory, to Helena Osborne for *The Arcadian Affair*; the Prix Goncourt to Félicien Marceau (pen name of Louis Carette) of Belgium, for his novel *Creezy*; the Spanish Planeta prize, worth nearly £7,000, to Ramon J.

Sender for his novel *En la Vida de Ignacio Morel*; the city of Paris Grand Prix to Jean Rousselot for his collected poems; the first annual trophies by the English Centre of International PEN to John Fowles for *The French Lieutenant's Woman* (fiction), S. Runciman for *The Great Church in Captivity* (non-fiction), and Mary Theresa Reynolds for *Myself, My Sepulchre* (fiction, under-25); the W. H. Smith £1,000 prize to Robert Gittings for his biography *John Keats*; the Queen's Gold Medal for poetry to Stevie Smith; the 1969 Grand Prix National des Lettres to Jules Roy, for his literary work as a whole.

Australia. The Rothman prize went to Professor Manning Clark for the second volume of *A History of Australia*; the Weickhardt award to Thomas Keneally for *Three Cheers for the Paraclete*; the Sidney Myer charity trust awards for poetry to Bruce Dawe for *An Eye for a Tooth* and to David Campbell for *Selected Poems 1942–68*; a new award sponsored by the Victoria Chamber of Automotive Industries, for an Australian pictorial and documentary work to Peter O'Shaughnessy, for *The Restless Years*, a chronicle of Australia in the making.

U.S.A. The 1969 National Book Awards for arts and letters went to Norman Mailer for *Armies of the Night*; for fiction to Jerzy Kosinski for *Steps*; for poetry to John Berryman for *His Toys, His Dream, His Rest*; for history and biography to Winthrop D. Jordan for *White over Black*; for the sciences to Robert J. Lifton for *Death in Life*; for children's literature to Meindert deJong for *Journey from Peppermint Street*; for translation to William Weaver for his translation of Italo Calvino's *Cosmicomics*.

Liverpool. Plans for the construction of an artificial island, 3,800 ft. long, in Liverpool Bay 11 miles from the mainland, off Rhos Point, near Rhyl, Flintshire, N. Wales, were announced by the Mersey Docks and Harbour Board, on May 15, 1969. It will be a terminal for the giant oil tankers, up to 750,000 tons, which are in prospect and which could not enter the port of Liverpool. Storage tanks capable of holding $1\frac{1}{4}$ million tons of oil will be part of the structure, which will be linked to the mainland by underwater pipelines. The island will allow a turn-round time of 24 hours for the largest tankers, and will increase the port of Liverpool's handling of oil from the present 14 million tons to about 80 million tons a year.

Contracts for the completion of the £3$\frac{1}{2}$ million development of Liverpool dock's terminal were reported to have been placed in July 1969. The new development, which will cater for bulk-grain-carrying ships of up to 75,000 tons dead-weight, will have a discharging capacity of 2,500 tons an hour, and ultimate silo storage accommodation for 200,000 tons. The berth will be 850 ft.

long and 48 ft. deep, and there will also be an inlet dock for barges and vessels of up to 10,000 tons alongside the main jetty. The terminal will be capable of dealing with grain distribution by road, rail, and water.

Lloyd's London. From Jan. 1 1970, women are admitted as members of Lloyd's, the world's greatest insurance organisation, for the first time in its long history. A vote by a 16-man committee made this decision, which was announced in February 1969. Candidates must be of British nationality by birth or naturalisation, and permanently resident in Britain. They must also be able to prove that they have assets of £750,000, and are able to pay a deposit of £15,000. Women are not allowed to take an active part in underwriting, but can underwrite through an agent, but they are able to join the full range of syndicates and are also able to lunch in that hitherto entirely male preserve, the Captain's Room.

Local Government, Royal Commission on. This body, set up in 1966, under the chairmanship of Lord Redcliffe-Maud (then Sir John Maud), published its report, popularly called the Maud Report, on June 11, 1969. It found that the large number of local government areas and the multiplicity of local authorities in England (the Commission was not asked for its views on Wales or Scotland) militate against efficiency, and recommended a complete reconstruction of local government. All existing councils (county, county borough, borough, urban district, and rural district) would be abolished, and England, excluding Greater London, would be divided into 61 new local government areas, grouped into eight provinces. Three of the 61 areas would be new metropolitan areas resembling Greater London: (a) Merseyside; (b) "Selnec" (S.E. Lancs, N., E., and Central Cheshire, N.W. Derbyshire, and a part of the W. Riding of Yorks), more or less identified with the Manchester area; and (c) West Midlands, approximately the Birmingham area. These three, like Greater London, would include a number of metropolitan district authorities. The other 58 areas would be governed by "unitary authorities," each covering both urban and rural areas.

The eight provinces would be: 1. North East (Northumberland and Durham); 2. Yorkshire; 3. North West (Cumberland, Westmorland, and Lancs); 4. West Midlands (Staffs, Worcs, Warwicks, Shropshire, and Herefordshire); 5. East Midlands (Derbyshire, Notts, Leics, and Rutland); 6. South West (Cornwall, Devon, Somerset, Glos, Wilts, and Dorset); 7. East Anglia (Cambridgeshire, Hunts, Norfolk, Suffolk, and N.E. Essex); 8. South East (Oxfordshire, Northants, Beds, Bucks, Herts, Berks, Essex, Surrey, Kent, Hants, Sussex, and Isle of Wight). Each would

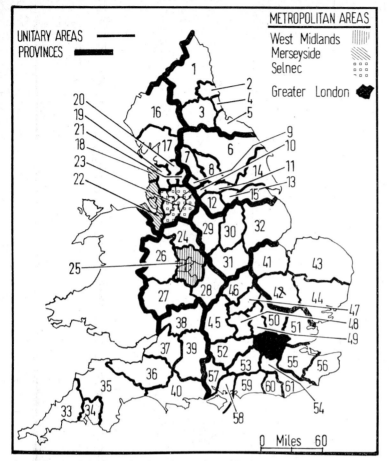

Local Government. Map showing the division of England into 8 provinces and 61 unitary areas, plus Greater London, as proposed in the Maud report.

arrangements, and finance, the number of Scottish local authorities would be cut from 430 (4 cities, 33 county councils, 21 large burghs, 176 small burghs, and 196 district councils) to 44. The seven recommended regional authorities are: Highlands and Islands, North-east, West, Central, East, South-west, and South-east. These authorities would be responsible for the main local government functions, including major planning, transport, water, refuse disposal, tourism, social services, and protective services. The district authorities' responsibilities would include local planning, building control, housing improvement, parks, museums, art galleries and libraries, refuse collection, and administration of justice.

Loch Ness Monster. A fortnight's full-scale scientific investigation of Loch Ness to attempt to decide once for all on the existence or otherwise of the monster began on Sept. 15, 1969. Sponsored by the Loch Ness Phenomena Investigations Bureau Ltd., Independent Television News, and the *Daily Mail,* it involved the use of bait, underwater noise-making machines, anti-submarine sonar "curtains," underwater television cameras, a tank-gun night sight capable of "seeing" a mile in darkness, a one-man submarine from Atlanta, Georgia, and several divers. No sign of the monster was detected.

The oceanics department of Vickers of Barrow stated on Aug. 19, 1969, that their 16-ton submarine *Pisces,* by descending to a depth of 820 ft. in Loch Ness, had established that the Loch is at least 70 ft. deeper than is indicated on Admiralty charts. It was also reported that a chasm about 320 ft. deep had been discovered 500 ft. down.

Lomonosov Gold Medals. The winners of the 1969 Lomonosov gold medals, awarded annually to one Soviet and one foreign scientist, were announced at the beginning of January. The bio-chemist Vladimir Engelhardt, who is head of the Institute of Molecular Biology in Moscow and whose particular sphere is the biosynthesis of protein and its relation to heredity and the structure of nucleic acids, received one medal. The other went to Istvan Rusznyak, of Hungary, a scientist of international fame and president of the Ukrainian Academy of Sciences, whose special field is metabolism.

London. On March 20, 1969, the Greater London Council published its long-term development plan for inner and outer London. Based on an estimate that the population will fall by 1981 from the present 7,900,000 to 7,300,000, the plan covers every aspect of living in London in the future and touches upon development in almost every one of the 32 metropolitan boroughs, to whom carrying out the details of the plan will be entrusted. On transport the plan reaffirms the necessity for three ringways—

have a provincial council, elected by the unitary and metropolitan authorities within its borders, with 20–25 per cent of co-opted members, which would draw up the broad strategic plans for the province; in effect the provincial councils would replace the present regional economic planning councils.

The "unitary authorities," forming the executives to carry out the plans of the provincial councils, would be responsible for all services (education, housing, employment, transport, health, personal and social services). The minimum population for a unitary authority area would be about 250,000, and the maximum size of its council 75 members. Within each unitary authority area elected local councils, replacing existing borough, urban district, rural district, and parish councils, would have the duty to represent local opinion and the right to be consulted on local affairs, and would have the power and money to add to local amenities such as parks, greens, swimming pools, community centres, museums, theatres, and concert halls, and perhaps to provide some main services such as housing, roads, and conservation. Altogether 1,310 councils

would be replaced by 81 main authorities, and in the three new metropolitan areas 159 would be replaced by 23.

The report, in three volumes, contained 405,000 words and many maps. Three members of the Commission expressed reservations on some points, and one totally disagreed with the others; his minority report, occupying one whole volume, preferred the setting up of 37 "city regions." On the day of publication the Government accepted the Commission's main recommendations in principle. If adopted the proposals may be realised by 1975.

Scotland. On June 9, 1966, a 9-member commission was set up under the chairmanship of Lord Wheatley, Senator of the College of Justice in Scotland and M.P. for East Edinburgh, to "consider the structure of local government in Scotland . . . and to make recommendations for authorities and boundaries . . ." In its report, published in September 1969, the commission recommended a two-tier system of local government, consisting of seven regional authorities and 37 district authorities. In their plan for a complete reform of boundaries, functions, electoral

R1 in the centre, R2 about 7 miles out, and R3 about 12 miles out—and makes proposals for more controlled car-parking; a redesigned bus service, with rail-bus-car interchange points in the suburbs; a new underground railway (the Fleet Line); a new railway terminus near Blackfriars, to replace Holborn Viaduct and the present Blackfriars; the rebuilding of Victoria and London Bridge stations and redevelopment of King's Cross and St. Pancras; and better interchange facilities between the main rail termini, possibly by running British Rail trains over London Transport tracks.

The plan expects that by 1981 9 per cent of London's present housing (216,000 dwellings) will be obsolete, and by 1991 a further 14 per cent (347,000 dwellings). Schemes and places for rebuilding are included in the plan, which particularly emphasises the need to preserve the Green Belt and other open spaces, and to increase neighbourhood parks until there is a park of at least 50 acres within three quarters of a mile of every home and one of 150 acres within 2 miles. The character of Central London as the cultural and artistic centre, and of the City as the financial centre, is to be preserved, but institutions such as the University of London are to be encouraged to move units to sites outside London where possible. Pentonville and Holloway prisons and Spitalfields and the Borough Market are to be removed. To decentralise London's attractions six major "strategic centres" for shopping and cultural activities are proposed: these are at Croydon, Ealing, Ilford, Kingston, Lewisham, and Wood Green, each serving a population of about 750,000. A new type of centre for people who use their cars for shopping is proposed for Brent Cross, Hendon. The plan names 56 "future action areas" due for comprehensive development, and 28 where change and improvement are desirable. A large number of "amenity areas" of metropolitan importance, to which special consideration must be paid in redeveloping their surroundings, are named; they range from Westminster Abbey to Hampton Court, from St. Paul's to Harrow School, from the Tower of London to Hadley Common, and include almost every historic building, traditional landmark, and beauty spot in the Greater London area. The G.L.C. promises to make grants to Thames-side councils for riverside improvements. A Thames barrage, and redevelopment of the St. Katharine, London, East India, and, partly, Surrey Commercial docks are mentioned; new power stations at Barking and Croydon are proposed.

The plan was put forward as a "flexible policy framework," which can be adjusted in detail by individual boroughs' plans and perhaps altered on a large scale by the Government's plans for the S.E. England region as a whole.

City. The planned reconstruction of the west wing of Guildhall precinct

London (City). A modern extension to Guildhall, seen from Basinghall Street. It was opened in May 1969.

was announced in August 1969. A seven-storey administrative block containing conference and committee rooms, dining-rooms, bedroom accommodation, and robing rooms for aldermen and members of the City Corporation are all included in a £3 million scheme. There will also be a two-storey underground car park. The west crypt of Guildhall itself also is to be restored. A £2,835,000 scheme to widen King William Street by 1972 in order to cope with the extra traffic that will by that time be using the new London Bridge was proposed to the City's Court of Common Council in October 1969. The scheme involves the initial creation of a five-lane highway, which would be widened later to six lanes in the 1975–80 road programme.

Doors of English oak were hung at the new Warwick Lane entrance to the east wing extension of the Central Criminal Court, Old Bailey, on March 10. The doors, 20 ft. high and each 10 ft. wide, were made from timber from a selected oak in the grounds of Lord Walpole's estate near Norwich, Norfolk. The tree was felled in 1958 and matured before being sawn into planks in 1966, and kiln-dried.

Riverside. On July 8 the City of London Corporation announced proposals for a £9 million redevelopment plan on the north bank of the Thames between Blackfriars Bridge and Southwark Bridge. The main proposals affect the area from Blackfriars to Trig Lane, south of Queen Victoria Street, with a further section at Queenhithe. Nine acres on the riverside will be cleared of old warehouses. A major new 75-ft.-wide road with service roads, part of a southern route to the Tower of London, will take up 2½ acres; over 1,000 ft. of the new highway and part of a loop overpass will provide space for new buildings. These will include a new City of London School replacing the

premises in John Carpenter Street; the school, accommodating 750 boys, will include a great hall, a small hall, a library, two gymnasia, a chapel, and a swimming pool. To the west of the school will be a £2 million telecommunications centre, and the plans provide the Post Office with an additional building within 100 yards of the existing Faraday Building in Queen Victoria Street, and connected to it by a tunnel. The Mermaid Theatre will be retained, but provisions made for its possible enlargement and the complete redevelopment of its surroundings. Proposals are made for the retention of some historic buildings in the area, including St. Benet's Church and the Vintners' Hall. The vista from the south transept of St. Paul's Cathedral is to be extended to the river, where a landing jetty for visitors is proposed. A riverside skyline 15 to 20 ft. lower than that of existing buildings on the north bank is proposed, with new buildings not higher than four or five storeys. As Faraday House obscures the view of St. Paul's from across the river, it is proposed that three storeys, or about 40 ft., should be removed. If the scheme is approved the roads should be completed by 1972, and the whole scheme by 1977.

Planning application for a £10 million redevelopment scheme occupying about four acres of a five-acre site immediately to the west of Blackfriars Bridge on the south bank of the Thames was considered at a public inquiry on July 9, 1969. The plans provide for a hotel of 750 bedrooms in two blocks, each about ten storeys high and facing the river. The remaining river frontage would contain two blocks of flats, each about seven storeys high, and a section of riverside walk to replace the wharves and warehouses. In addition to the 200 flats there would be a restaurant, shops, and other accommodation. The whole

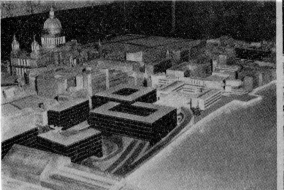

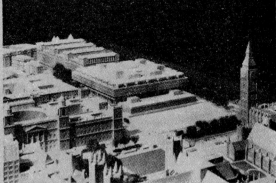

MODELS OF THE

Above. Left: £9 million development plan for the north bank of the Thames between Blackfriars and Southwark Bridges between St. Paul's and the river. *Right:* Whitehall plan, showing new Government office building (*centre*) and, between it and Big Ben, the site of a new Parliamentary building in Bridge Street. *Centre:* layout of the proposed scheme for the 25-acre St. Katharine Dock downstream of the Tower of London and Tower Bridge.

LONDON-TO-BE

Below. Left: the proposed yachting marina that is to be the heart of Thamesmead —the Woolwich-Erith housing estate that will ultimately house 60,000 people. Photos of the tower blocks and linear housing featured in the scheme are to be found in page 155. *Right:* this hotel at Gloucester Road station near the West London Air Terminal, if approved, will have over 2,000 bedrooms, a roof-level night-club, and sports facilities in the basement.

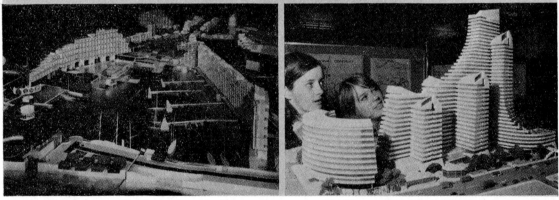

project is designed to provide views of the Thames and to allow the maximum amount of light. A 20-storey tower block of offices over 200 ft. high and containing 350,000 sq. ft. of floor space, is proposed for the centre of the site, with parking space for more than 500 cars beneath it.

St. Katharine Dock was sold on Jan. 21 to the Greater London Council by the Port of London for £1½ million. The dock, which covers an area of 25 acres, is to be developed to include private houses, a hostel, schools, a park for coaches, a commercial exhibition centre, a hotel, a sports centre, an entertainment complex, a yachting marina, and at least 300 council homes. The marina is to be large enough to accommodate 360 boats, including sea-going craft.

After improvements costing £1 million the old Blackwall tunnel was reopened on April 4, carrying north-bound traffic from Greenwich to Poplar. New lighting, ventilation, and an electronic traffic control system were installed, and the previous tight corners eased.

It was announced in October 1969 that a £1 million pumping station was being installed at Chancellor's Road, Hammersmith, as part of a £2½ million flood relief scheme for west London. The station's automatic pumps, 50 ft. underground, will be capable of raising 1,500 tons of water a minute, passing it through two outfalls into the Thames below Hammersmith bridge. As the station will drain water through new sewers stretching for two miles in two directions, and help to dispose of surplus

water from as far away as Wormwood Scrubs and Ladbroke Grove, thousands of people living in west London will be relieved of the threat of floods when it comes into operation in February 1970.

East End. A report published on June 9, 1969, by the Psychiatric Rehabilitation Association, showed that the East End of London has a rate of mental illness far above the national average. A comparison of the discharge rates for patients from psychiatric hospitals in Tower Hamlets and Hackney on the one hand and Greenwich and Bexley on the other showed an overall difference of 52 per cent between the two east and the two south London boroughs. The number of schizophrenics in the East End is 50 per cent above the national average of 7·4 per 10,000 population. In Stepney the number of schizophrenics is $2\frac{1}{2}$ times the national average; cases of depressive illnesses are 90 per cent above the national rate; and cases of alcohol and drug addiction 153 per cent higher.

Westminster. Plans for re-building the western side of Parliament Square were announced by the Minister of Public Building and Works on Nov. 18, 1969. The area involved stretches from Broad Sanctuary on the south to Great George Street on the north, but the old Middlesex Guildhall is left untouched. The Ministry, which is co-operating with the Institution of Civil Engineers in the plan, is to contribute a government conference centre. The proposals for a huge new Parliamentary building, in Bridge Street, put forward in April 1968, took concrete form in December 1969 when a model was put on display to M.P.s in the House of Commons. A second project was included in the exhibition. This would involve taking north-south traffic out of Parliament Square by building a by-pass in the form of a £16 million riverside road tunnel nearly a mile long. It would run from Hungerford Bridge to Lambeth Bridge, and would create 10 acres of new riverside land, which would be landscaped. A public riverside walk would be made in front of the terrace of the Palace of Westminster.

West End. It was announced on April 2, 1969, that the Mall would be permanently closed to traffic and given over entirely to pedestrians on Sundays. Band concerts were also to be held there at weekends. Details of a £4 million scheme for offices and flats on a site facing the Mall were announced on April 18. It is part of a tentative plan which could embrace the whole area between The Mall, Cockspur Street, Spring Gardens, and Carlton House Terrace. The buildings, which will occupy a largely derelict area at the rear of Carlton House Terrace, will consist of three linked blocks. Two of them, with about 145,000 sq. ft. of net usable space, will be occupied by the British Council, and the third will contain 17 two-storey maisonettes and an underground car park on four levels to accommodate 340 cars. This residential block will face Waterloo Gardens.

Between 30 and 40 shops described as of "the highest elegance" are being built in Brompton Road, Knightsbridge, at an estimated cost of £500,000. Built in three storeys, and taking the form of a vertical arcade, the shops, including a restaurant and bar, beauty salons, sauna baths, travel agents, ticket bureaux, car hire firms, and bookstalls, are to be known as Escalade.

North. Sir Frederick Gibberd was the winner in October 1969 of the £3,000 prize for the design of a £750,000 mosque to be built at the north-west corner of Regent's Park for London's Moslem community. There were 52 entries in the competition, 41 of them from abroad. Sir Frederick's design includes a main congregation hall for 1,000 people, with a similar sized lower hall in the basement; a dome about 75 ft. high above the main hall; and a 150-ft.-high minaret rising from a pool in the forecourt. The main walls of the building will be of precast concrete units faced in white Portland stone; the dome will be covered with gold anodised aluminium, and the pinnacle of the minaret faced in dove-grey mosaic.

A four-part plan for a £10 million cultural and shopping centre, to be known as the Swiss Cottage Centre, and to be situated on an 8-acre site bounded by Eton Avenue, College Crescent, Winchester Road, and extending towards Finchley Road, was announced on Sept. 30, 1969. The first £2 million part includes a bank, a hotel, the Central School of Speech and Drama, and part of a new hostel development. The second part, costing £4$\frac{1}{2}$ million, will include underground car parks for 750 cars, service areas, some council offices, part of the hostel, a theatre, cinemas, a college of music, a multi-purpose hall, a boiler plant, and a bridge over Finchley Road. The £1 million third part includes an arts centre, a sports centre, and the rest of the boiler unit, while the fourth part, as yet uncosted, will be the second stage of the Central School of Speech and Drama. The centre has been designed by the architects Sir Basil Spence, Bonnington, and Collins, and will complement the library and swimming pool opened in 1964.

A plan to develop the canal which travels for 50 miles through 11 London boroughs for leisure purposes was revealed on Oct. 14 by the London Canals Consultative Committee, set up in 1966 by the Greater London Council. The committee included in its suggestions the creation of parkland at Tower Hamlets; a garden round Islington tunnel; rowing and fishing clubs for children at Hackney; the extension of the St. Pancras yacht basin; and canalside walkways elsewhere.

South. The Greater London Council announced on May 9 its plan for the reconstruction of the famous Lambeth Walk. To start in April 1970 and to cost £6 million, the scheme includes a pedestrian precinct to contain the street market and shops, with a first-floor walkway giving access to flats on either side, and two pedestrian bridges across the precinct. Rebuilding will be in three phases, the first, due for completion in 1971, providing 17 shops with dwellings, a public house, a dental centre, and an old people's clubroom.

Planning permission has been given for a £4 million development scheme for Kennington Oval, which will provide Surrey County Cricket Club with new buildings and security of tenure. At no cost to itself the Club will have terrace seating, some covered, for 22,000, with about 4,000 seats for members. There will also be 500 flats of one and two-bedroom types, eight shops, a supermarket, a restaurant and bar for spectators, pavilion and club restaurant, and offices for the Professional Golfers' Association and Surrey Supporters' Association. The landlords, the Duchy of Cornwall, will receive a more appropriate income from the Oval's 10-acre site, and the Surrey C.C.C. will have a lease for between 30 and 40 years from the Duchy.

A revised plan for the development of Brixton town centre was submitted to the Lambeth council by the development committee on July 9, 1969. Proposals made in 1967, which provided for the redevelopment of the whole 84 acres over a period of 20 years, at a cost of £70 million, were withdrawn because of restrictions on public spending. The new plan is still designed to ease traffic congestion, and replace obsolete buildings and layout with an efficient town centre, but will affect only 61 acres in the first 17 years, and cost an estimated £47 million. The modified road plan does not involve the creation of new roads, but will be based on existing road systems requiring only improvements.

Transport. The Greater London Council chief transportation officer said on May 9, 1969, that the average speed of traffic in central London had increased by almost 3 m.p.h. in the ten years 1958–68, in spite of a 22 per cent increase in the amount of traffic. Average speed in 1958 was 8.3 m.p.h., and in 1968 was 11.1 m.p.h.

Publication of the London Transport Board's 1968 accounts in April 1969 showed a decreasing number of passenger-journeys by bus, coach, and Underground. Bus and coach journeys fell by 33 million to 1,946 million, and Underground journeys by 6 million to 655 million despite the opening of the Victoria Line. The 1968 loss amounted to £10 million, about £1 million less than in 1967. Under the Transport (London) Bill the Greater London Council was empowered to take over London Transport, but the Council stated it would do so only if and when London Transport was in a position to show profit of £2 million a year. Estimates having indicated that this happy situation was in prospect, the G.L.C. took over London Transport and a new London Transport Executive was set up on Jan. 1, 1970.

The third stage of the Underground's Victoria line, between Warren Street and Victoria, was opened by the Queen in March, when through journeys between Walthamstow Central and Victoria became possible.

The chairman of the Greater London Council's planning and transportation committee gave on March 13 detailed plans for the $2\frac{3}{4}$ miles of the controversial West Cross Route running south to north across West London from the Thames at Chelsea. The new road continues the route at present under construction from Western Avenue to

Holland Park Avenue, and will mean the displacement of 800 families. In an attempt to help people whose homes will be blighted by noise and visual intrusion, the Council has studied sites on the proposed route that could be landscaped and planted with trees, and have special "noise-shields" erected along the motorway. This could add £2·2 million to the £36·5 million cost of the new road. The route of the new road is planned to run over or alongside railways, in order to disturb as few people as possible, and will take much heavy traffic off residential and shopping streets in West London such as Earls Court Road, Warwick Road, and Holland Road.

On July 17 the Council announced details of the proposed South London Ringway 2 motorway, including the 11-mile section between Norbury and Falconwood, a semi-circular route linking the new Thames crossings at Thamesmead and in the Barnes area with the North Circular Road to create a highway completely circling inner London. The 11-mile eight-lane stretch of road, narrowing to six lanes in some sections, will cost nearly £158 million, and will, as it cuts through densely populated suburbs, destroy 2,189 homes and several golf courses. The chairman of the Council's planning and transportation committee said that full market value and the cost of legal, removal, and similar charges would be paid to those whose homes would disappear, and it was hoped to obtain government permission to pay compensation to those people on the fringes of the new route who would suffer.

Air Pollution. The report of the Greater London Council's scientific adviser for 1967, published in February 1969, said that London air is becoming noticeably cleaner; analysis of air checks taken at seven points in inner London has shown that pollution by smoke and sulphur dioxide continues to diminish. Conditions leading to "London smog" have not occurred since December 1962. Buildings and monuments, including St. Paul's Cathedral, which have been cleaned during the past few years should keep their improved appearance for a considerable time. The report also said that fall-out from the fifth Chinese nuclear test (in 1966) was easily detected two weeks later from dust samples in London; the sixth test (in 1967) did not produce early contamination; but the seventh test (later in 1967) produced measurable amounts. The amount of radioactivity was too small, however, to have any appreciable health significance.

London Airport (Heathrow). The new No. 1 passenger terminal, costing £9 million, was opened by the Queen on April 17, 1969. It is used for all domestic and European flights by B.E.A., British Air Services (Cambrian and B.K.S.), Autair, and Aer Lingus, and it is expected

that over 7½ million passengers will pass through it in its first year. The old Europa building, used by European airlines, has been renamed Terminal No. 2. Long-distance flight departures will take place from No. 3 terminal, and a new terminal for long-distance flight arrivals will be built alongside.

The builders of the new No. 1 terminal building were Tersons, and the architects Frederick Gibberd and Partners. The building is a long narrow rectangle surrounded by a continuous gallery and divided horizontally into two levels—one for arrivals and one for departures—with a multi-storey car park alongside. The long frontage provides 600 ft. of kerb space for setting down passengers arriving by car; those arriving by airport bus are set down inside the building. Passengers' baggage was to be moved entirely by automated and partly computer-controlled conveyor belts from the check-in points to tractor-drawn trolleys on the airside of the terminal, at the rate of 2,400 pieces per hour and a speed of 180 ft. per minute. This mechanism, however, developed fatal flaws that produced chaos in baggage handling during the holiday months.

Air France's new cargo terminal was officially opened in July 1969, after a two-month run-in period for staff and equipment. The building is divided into an automated warehouse area, a mezzanine area for storage of loaded pallets, and two floors of offices. Five hydraulic lifts, three with weighbridges, are used to lift the loaded pallets to the storage area, and also descend below ground level to facilitate pallet stacking. When the pallets reach the mezzanine floor they are transferred to a mechanical transporter running the length of the floor. In planning the terminal, which cost about £1 million, Air France designed the working system to take account of

future more advanced developments including computer systems.

Other major building projects taking place during 1969 at Heathrow included a new cargo terminal and tunnel, costing £25 million; a new "jumbo jet" terminal costing £10 million, and "jumbo jet" hangar for B.O.A.C., costing £4 million; and the extension by June 1970 of the No. 1 runway from 9,300 ft. to 12,800 ft., costing £2,100,000.

The number of passengers passing through Heathrow during 1969 was expected to be 15,380,000, and it was estimated that there would be 248,900 aircraft movements; forecasts for future years were given as 19,880,000 passengers and 289,500 aircraft movements in 1971, and 24,290,000 passengers and 313,400 movements in 1973. The new cargo terminal, covering 155 acres, is expected to handle 500,000 tons of cargo in 1970 and 1 million tons by 1975. Heathrow will be the third largest port in Great Britain, after the seaports of London and Liverpool.

Under the 1968 Finance Act simplification of customs clearance was introduced at Heathrow early in 1969. Passengers having "nothing to declare" go straight to the "green" channel and out of the airport, but may be stopped by customs officers for a "spot check" on their luggage. Those with dutiable goods go to the "red" channel to declare their imports.

Lowther Park, Westmorland. A wild-life reserve, created by Lord Lonsdale in conjunction with Associated Pleasure Parks, was opened to the public on May 20, 1969. In the park, which covers 130 acres and cost £25,000, can be seen four species of deer, Australian red-necked wallabies, llamas, Highland cattle, Ankoli cows from Africa, and flamingoes, geese, cranes, and swans.

London Airport (Heathrow). Interior of the new No. 1 passenger terminal opened in April 1969, the exterior of which is illustrated in page 158. The new terminal is used for domestic and European flights by British airlines.

Lundy. This island in the Bristol Channel, 11 miles off the North Devon coast, was put up for sale on March 25, 1969. Its last owner, Albion Harman, died in 1968, and his two sisters, who shared the ownership, authorised its sale because its upkeep was too costly for them. It was announced on May 22 that a British businessman, Jack Hayward, living in the Bahamas, had given £150,000 to enable the National Trust to buy and preserve the island. The Landmark Trust, founded in 1964, agreed to take a long, full repairing lease on Lundy, and when this expires will make an endowment to ensure that the island does not involve the National Trust in further financial responsibilities. An appeal for £75,000 to restore buildings on the island and make it self-supporting was launched on the same day as Mr. Hayward's gift was announced.

Luton, Beds. An independent report on Luton airport, commissioned by the Luton corporation, was presented on July 23, 1969. It recommended an £18 million expansion to make the airport into a major international air terminal capable of handling 15 million passengers by 1990. It proposed that a new north-south runway, 11,500 ft. long, should be built to international standards, which with a passenger terminal would entail the acquisition of nearly 2 square miles of farm land. If either Wing or Nuthampstead were to be chosen as London's third airport, Luton would be unable to continue as an air transport airport because of congestion of air space, but if Foulness were chosen it could continue to serve in a complementary role to the other London airports.

Madrid, Spain. It was announced in September 1969 that a 33-storey building, to be known as Valencia Towers, is to be built in the centre of Madrid, at the junction of three main streets. The building, designed by Javier Carvajal, architect of the prize-winning Spanish pavilion at the New York World's Fair, will have five storeys below ground, and parking space for 450 cars. An overhead cable railway which came into operation in Madrid in September had by mid-November carried 250,000 passengers, the average daily number being 3,200.

Man. Olduvai Gorge, Tanzania, the hunting ground of Dr. Louis Leakey, who has found there fossil fragments of man-like creatures from about 2 million years ago, appeared in 1969 to have a rival in the Omo Valley, of similar geological structure, which runs north into Ethiopia from the edge of Lake Randolph, Kenya. French, Kenyan, U.S., and U.K. parties

Madrid. The Casa de Campo cable railway came into operation in September 1969. It provides a fine view over the city.

visited it in 1967–68. Preliminary reports on the U.S. expedition were made in 1969, when Prof. Clark Howell of the University of Chicago claimed the discovery of pre-human fossil fragments from 3 to 4 million years old. The fossils indicate the simultaneous existence of two types of Australopithecus, the oldest known ape-man. Discoveries at Olduvai and Omo seem to confirm that Africa was indeed the cradle of human evolution.

Manoel Island, Malta. An £8 million project for the development of this island, off Valletta, as a yachting marina, put before the Malta government by a British consortium of bankers and surveyors, was approved in January 1969. The development will give permanent employment to 300 people in the first year, rising to more than 1,400 in the fourth year. When it is finished, the marina will be able to accommodate up to 1,800 yachts, averaging 40 ft. long.

Mass Radiography. Under advice from the U.K. Department of Health to hospital boards mobile chest X-ray units are to be phased out because, although several million people a year use them, the Department feels that the number does not justify the £1 million annual cost. When this was announced at the beginning of December 1969 it was stated that anyone wanting a chest X-ray will have to ask his doctor to refer him to a hospital. The mobile units, which were set up for diagnosis of tuberculosis, discovered 2,847 cases out of 3 million people in 1967, compared with 8,720 out of a similar number in 1954. Recently the majority of people requesting an X-ray have been most concerned over lung cancer, and in 1967 the units found 724 cases of malignant cancer.

Melbourne, Victoria, Australia. Excavation work on the second stage of Melbourne's international class underground theatre centre started in the spring of 1969. It will include a 2,500-seat concert hall, a theatre with a 200 ft. stage and seating for 1,700, a 750-seat playhouse, a lecture and experimental theatre with audience capacity adjustable between 300 and 1,000, a museum for the performing arts, and possibly a rehearsal and broadcasting studio for the Australian Broadcasting Commission and its Orchestras. A 430-ft. spire will contain a restaurant, cafeteria, meeting rooms, and offices. The site, an ancient course of the Yarra river, is a hole 90-ft. deep and $2\frac{1}{2}$ acres in extent. The mud that is scooped out will be replaced round the theatre complex, providing noise insulation and acting as a barrier against temperature changes. The whole complex of theatres and halls, seating in all nearly 6,000 people, will complete a $A38 million project to house all the visual and performing arts under one roof. The first major stage, completed in 1968, comprises an art museum including 6 miles of exhibition and storage galleries, a courtyard theatre, a multi-purpose "great hall," and another large hall for travelling exhibitions. The architect, Sir Roy Grounds, has said that the completed centre will give Australia at least the equivalent of New York's Lincoln Centre or London's South Bank.

The Victoria government in March 1969 agreed in principle to a scheme for the reconstruction of the Flinders Street station and the complete redevelopment of the station area. A spokesman for the company managing the project said that it involved building over Melbourne's central railway yards for four city blocks. Two decks would be built over the railway lines. The lower one would be used as a

Melbourne. The 372-ft. A.M.P. tower, at present the tallest building in Victoria, was completed in 1969.

pedestrian concourse and a parking area; shops also would be built on this level, together with taxi and bus terminals. The second deck would be a base for the construction of high-rise commercial buildings and community facilities. The scheme would cost about $A100 million. Another plan—to build a 17-storey city block in Flinders Street, to incorporate 170 flat units, was announced in May; the building will cost $A2½ million.

The tallest building in the State of Victoria, and the tallest steel-frame building in Australia, will be the 503-ft. 41-storey headquarters of the Broken Hill Proprietary Co. Ltd., in Melbourne, to be erected on the site of the historic Menzies Hotel, at the corner of Bourke and William Streets. It will also be the first Australian office building to be run on the total energy system, using natural gas for all services, including the generation of electricity. The cost of construction, which began in December 1969, will be $A16 million. The method of construction is borrowed from aircraft techniques: a stressed-skin over light, stiffened frames, all loads being carried by the outer steel skin and the central services core. Only 20 lb. of steel are to be used per sq. ft. of floor area. The building's weight will be contained by the façade, which is strengthened by three braces (inverted Vs running over two floors at the base, half-way up, and at the top) distributing the load evenly to the four principal steel columns in each 126-ft. face. Apart from the central core, there will be no interior columns. Interaction between the façade and the core will be carried by lightweight concrete floors with steel decking acting as membranes. The façade will be reinforced by a $\frac{3}{8}$-in.-thick carbon steel welded skin, designed to absorb high building wind loadings.

Australia's longest and widest road bridge is being built at Spotswood, one of the western suburbs of Melbourne. It will be 3 miles long and more than 120 ft. wide, and will rise 176 ft. above the Yarra at the bridge's highest point. It will be completed in 1971 at an estimated cost of $A42 million. The West Gate Bridge, as it has been named, will be three times the length of the Sydney Harbour Bridge.

Melbourne's new $A12 million overseas container terminal was officially opened on March 7, 1969. Facilities at the new dock allow for the unloading of 25,000 tons of cargo and reloading of 25,000 outward tons within less than 48 hours.

Mergers and Take-overs. The City of London's panel on take-overs, and the code of conduct laid down by them, were given new force on May 1, 1969, when the panel acquired a strengthened executive and the rules were revised. The new chairman of the panel is Lord Shawcross, and its first director-general is Ian Fraser. Changes in the rules, mostly minor, are intended to offer more com-

plete protection to shareholders and to diminish the effects of rumours of take-over bids. An offer must be declared unconditional within 60 days, or withdrawn. In the case of a partial bid, the offeror may not deal in the offeree's shares during the offer period. A declaration of intention to make a bid must be carried out, and, once made, a bid cannot be withdrawn without the panel's consent unless there is a rival bid. The panel has no powers to punish offenders against its code, but it reports them to the Board of Trade, the Stock Exchange, and the Issuing Houses Association, who can suspend or expel them. The panel can also ask the Stock Exchange to suspend dealings in a company's shares during a bid whenever it considers it necessary. In June unit trusts, investment trusts, and issuing houses were brought under the same code of conduct.

Two of the largest mergers proposed in 1969 did not take place. That between Unilever and Allied Breweries was called off after a delay of four months in obtaining official permission had so affected share prices that the proposed terms would have been too costly. A £45 million bid by the Rank Organisation for the De La Rue Company was forbidden by the Monopolies Commission on the grounds of "public interest"; later it was disclosed that key executives and directors of De La Rue had threatened to resign if the merger took place, and this the Commission interpreted as "a real and serious risk of damage to the efficiency of De La Rue's business . . . and overseas trading connections." This was the first merger or take-over to be forbidden on those grounds.

Mersey Tunnel. The U.K. Minister of Transport said in July 1969 that the new Liverpool—Wallasey road tunnel, due for completion in 1971, is to be duplicated

Metric System. One of the first British ships to show draught readings on bow and stern in both metric and linear measure sailed in the summer of 1969.

by a parallel tunnel costing an additional £8 million; both tunnels, adjacent to each other, will carry two lanes of traffic. Linking the centre of Liverpool with the new £15 million Mid-Wirral Motorway (M53), they will, it is hoped, relieve traffic congestion on both sides of the Mersey. See also p. 70.

Methodist Church. The introduction of the symbolic gesture of a handclasp, equivalent to the kiss of peace in Roman Catholic and Orthodox worship, into the Holy Communion service of the Methodist Church was announced in February 1969. It will be used experimentally for three years. The handclasp has been in use in the Communion Service of South India since 1947, and at ecumenical assemblies when the liturgy of the Church of South India has been celebrated.

The first Australian woman to become a Methodist minister was ordained in Perth, Western Australia, on Oct. 17, 1969. She was Miss Margaret Sanders, aged 27, who, after education at Perth Modern College, the Western Australian University, and the Melbourne College of Divinity, holds four degrees.

Metric System. From March 3, 1969, chemists in the U.K. gave patients who had been prescribed liquid medicine a standard 5-millilitre plastic spoon with which to measure the dose. More than 3 million such spoons had been distributed to Britain's 13,500 retail pharmacies. Medicine bottles also became metric, with six sizes ranging from 50 to 500 ml.

It was publicly stated at the annual meeting of the British Association's education section that from the beginning of 1970 the teaching emphasis in all primary schools would be on metric units first, and only secondarily on the essential imperial units. The deputy director-general of the British Standards Institution, who made this statement, also said that by 1974 most of the building industry would have gone metric, and that a complete reappraisal of products and designs would have taken place.

Mexico City. The first underground railway in Mexico City was opened in June 1969, when the first 7½-mile section came into operation; it had taken only 2 years to build. The full network of three lines, totalling 26 miles, will be completed by the end of 1970. The trains closely resemble the Paris Metro and Montreal underground trains and were supplied by the same company, R.A.T.P. Running on rubber tyres, they comprise six carriages each.

Miami, Florida, U.S.A. A new marina here, which includes a glass-enclosed restaurant and walkway, was completed in October 1969. The old fishing harbour was demolished to make way for the marina, known as Miamarina, which is also the official home of the Miami charter fishing fleet. An artificial island port, called Dodge Island, was also created off Miami, with which it is linked by a causeway. It will eventually have five berths, of which two had been completed by August, and its steel and concrete buildings are of extremely advanced architectural style.

Midsummer Prize. Elisabeth Lutyens, founder of the English school of atonal composers, became the second winner of this annual City of London prize, and received a cheque for £1,500 at the midsummer banquet for the arts at Mansion House on June 24, 1969. The prize, instituted in 1968 by the then Lord Mayor, Sir Gilbert Inglefield, is given to "an artist, writer, musician, man of letters or science, who has made a major contribution to the British cultural heritage, but has received inadequate financial recompense for his work."

Milan, Italy. The second underground railway line, called the Green Line, or No. 2 Line, in Milan was completed by the summer of 1969 and came into operation in October. Linking the No. 1 line with the central railway station, it runs between Cascina Gobba and Caiazzo Square, a journey taking 15 minutes.

A library of 18,000 volumes opened at the railway terminal here during 1969. The only one of its kind in Europe, by September it had about 300 members, mostly railway employees. No fee is charged for use of the reading room, which was used by between 30 and 40 people a day, but a small fee is charged for borrowing books.

Milford Haven, Pembrokeshire. Details of a £12 million port development scheme were given by the general manager of the Milford Haven Conservancy Board on Jan. 14, 1969. A major part of the development is a £5 million blasting and dredging operation to chisel out the corners of the main navigational channel, making it possible for 250,000-ton super-tankers to sail safely to the four oil jetties whatever the state of the tide. The three international oil companies with installations on the Haven—B.P., Esso, and Texaco—will strengthen and extend their ocean jetties, and build storage tanks capable of holding the enormous cargoes of crude oil anticipated. The scheme, the biggest and most costly ever undertaken in Great Britain, will make Milford Haven the country's leading refining centre, and by the end of 1970 it will probably be the second biggest oil port in western Europe.

Milton Keynes, Bucks. The interim planning report for the proposed new city of Milton Keynes in north Buckinghamshire—first outlined in the publication *South-East Study* in 1963—was published on Feb. 4, 1969. By the end of the century, the £600 million new city is expected to have a population of just over 250,000, its framework taking in the

"Miss International 1969." The winner of this world-wide beauty contest, held in Tokyo in September, was a British girl, Valerie Susan Holmes (*centre*). The five girls seen here are (*left to right*) Jeannette Biffiger (Switzerland), 4th; Satu Ostring (Finland), 2nd; Susan Holmes; Maria Lacaya (Nicaragua), 3rd; and Usanee Phenphimol (Thailand), 5th.

"Miss Universe." The 1969 winner of this beauty contest at Miami Beach, Florida, in July, was "Miss Philippines" (Gloria Diaz) (*centre*). The five girls in this photograph are (*left to right*) "Miss Australia" (Joanne Barrett), 3rd; "Miss Finland" (Harriet Eriksson), 2nd; Gloria Diaz; "Miss Israel" (Chava Levy), 4th; and "Miss Japan" (Kikuyo Chauka), 5th.

"Miss World." The winner of the 1969 "Miss World" beauty competition, held at the Royal Albert Hall, London, on November 27, was "Miss Austria" (Eva Rueber-Staier) (*centre*). The five girls shown here are "Miss Guyana" (Pamela Lord), 4th; "Miss U.S.A." (Gail Renshaw), 2nd; Eve Rueber-Staier; "Miss Germany" (Christa Margraf), 3rd; and "Miss Venezuela" (Marcia Rita Piazza), 5th.

towns of Stony Stratford, Wolverton, and Bletchley, as well as 30 existing villages and about 22,000 acres of farmland. In broad terms the city roads will be based on a grid system one kilometre square, and the squares will contain homes and factories, no home being more than 10 or 15 minutes from work. Each of the residential areas will have a population of about 5,000, and planning is intended to allow easy interconnection with adjoining neighbourhoods. A highly developed public transport system is planned. A resident will dial his destination from his nearest bus stop; a central computer will pick on the nearest bus to him and radio instructions for it to go to the bus stop. Another feature of the transport system is a service of electric battery-powered cars, carrying two people, and running along a magnetic track built into the road. The passengers will dial their destination and a computer will despatch the car by the shortest route. A tentative start on the preliminary stages of the new city is to be made in 1970.

"**Mimic.**" This is the shortened name of the Multiple Image Maker and Identification Compositor, developed in the U.S.A. to produce from witnesses' descriptions an image of a wanted person. Details of the system were given in February 1969 when it was announced that police in Great Britain were testing it. The equipment, resembling a small television set, is electrically operated to feed six rolls of 35 mm. film simultaneously through a back projector on to a screen. Each film carries a particular feature—nose, eyes, etc.—and accessories, including spectacles and moustaches and beards, all of which are drawn by artists. The films are run through at a speed selected by the operator, and automatically superimposed until the likeness required is seen on the screen. Unlike the line drawing of the "Identikit" system, "Mimic" shows facial contours as well as outlines, and more than 100,000 facial combinations can be produced. Each feature is coded for international communication by computer. Attached to the equipment is a Polaroid camera, which takes an "instant" photograph of the finished picture.

Mohole. The Soviet project to drill five immensely deep boreholes in different areas of the U.S.S.R. was reported in February 1969 to be well under way. The final drilling stage of the boreholes in Azerbaijan and the Caspian is to start in 1972 and the rest in 1973. It is estimated that each will take 5–6 years to drill to the required depth of 15–18 km. For the first stage of the drilling—down to about 8 km.—drill pipes of 9-in. diameter are used instead of the usual $6\frac{5}{8}$-in. or $5\frac{3}{4}$-in.; and for the second stage, when the boreholes are drilled down to 15 or 18 km. new techniques and equipment will have to be adopted. First-stage drilling

was reported to have been carried out in the Kola Peninsula in the north, and in the Caspian depression; in the latter the Aral Sea well had reached a depth of some 7 km., at which depth geologists obtained samples of sedimentary rocks possibly indicating large oil and gas reserves. As the chief purpose of the project is to obtain a better idea of the composition of the upper mantle and lower layers of the Earth's crust the five areas have been chosen for their differing geological structures.

Montreal, Canada. The Canadian Minister of Transport announced in March that the new international airport for Montreal is to be built near the town of St. Jerome, about 26 miles N. of Montreal and 17 miles from the existing airport at Dorval, which is on the western outskirts of the city. Fog and rain are said to be less frequent in St. Jerome than elsewhere in the Montreal region.

Morecambe Bay, Lancs. An interim report by a study group at the Department of Economic Affairs on the proposal to build a barrage across Morecambe Bay was published on May 12, 1969. The report pointed out the advantages that would accrue from the 11-mile-long barrage, with a road on it: transport, industrial development, and holiday facilities would all benefit. The road would save £18 million a year in transport costs and would particularly benefit the isolated Barrow-in-Furness area. The idea of a tidal power station had been abandoned, but the barrage would create a fresh-water reservoir of 41 sq. miles, holding 30,000 million gallons, round which could be built facilities for water sport, hotels, restaurants, caravan sites, golf courses, and swimming baths. The effects on fishing are less easy to assess: commercial fishing would probably suffer, salmon and trout fishing would be much reduced, and the shrimping industry might be wiped out. "Polders" of reclaimed land would not be useful for agriculture, the report stated, but could be put to other uses. A tidal model of the Bay and barrage, built at the Hydraulics Research Station, Wallingford, Berks, is being used to discover the effects of the barrage on silting along the near-by coast, including the ports of Heysham and Fleetwood. The study group's final conclusions will not be drawn until 1971–72.

Moscow. Europe's highest tower, officially named "Seventh Heaven," was opened to the public in Moscow in February 1969. Designed by Nikolai Nikitin, the tower is 1,600 ft. high, compared with the Eiffel Tower's 1,056 ft., and the 620-ft. G.P.O. tower in London. It rests on 10 clawlike pinions which are embedded to a depth of 16 ft. in the ground, has a revolving restaurant at the top, and will eventually broadcast six television channels and six short-wave radio transmissions.

Motor-cycles. Figures issued in May 1969 showed that the number of motor-cycles registered in Australia increased by 32·2 per cent over the previous year's figure, to a total of 22,887. Most of the machines were Japanese, the top-selling makes being Honda (10,434), Yamaha (3,164), and Suzuki (2,174). Even this high figure did not show the true number of motor-cycles in the country, since the considerable numbers of machines sold to sheep and cattle stations do not have to be registered. The low cost of running a motor-cycle was given as the major reason for its increasing popularity.

Motoring Offences. A U.K. Home Office report on offences relating to motor vehicles in England and Wales during 1968 was published on July 29, 1969. The total number of offences dealt with by prosecution was 1,472,879, a decrease of 1 per cent on the 1967 figure. Convictions for drink-and-driving offences rose from 9,460 in 1967 to 20,399 in 1968; 16,411 of these cases were brought under the breath-test section of the Road Safety Act, 1968, in its first full year of operation. The total number of convictions in the magistrates' courts was 1,381,159, a decrease of 1·6 per cent on the 1967 figure; fines were imposed in 95 per cent, compared with 96·1 per cent in 1967. Prison sentences imposed in magistrates' courts numbered 2,652, a decrease of 43·8 per cent on the 1967 figure, and those imposed in higher courts numbered 1,189, the same number as in 1967. There were about 10,000 more convictions for speeding in 1968 than in 1967, and the average fine for this offence rose from £6 13s in 1967 to £6 18s 3d in 1968. During 1968 there were 104,642 disqualifications, an increase of 2,889 on 1967; this figure includes 20,675 disqualified under the "totting-up" provision, an increase of 312.

Museums. Work on a "museum for posterity" was started at the beginning of 1969 at the Permafrost Institute in Igarka, in the Taimyr national district, U.S.S.R. The museum is 24 ft. below ground, where there is a constant temperature of – 2 to – 5 degrees C. Among items placed in the "museum" are: examples of northern fauna and flora; files of *Pravda* and other national newspapers for the years of the Second World War, hermetically sealed and marked "to be opened on May 9, 2045"; and details of current research on permafrost, including specifications for pipelines and buildings.

A ceremony marking the completion of a new National Museum of Modern Arts was held on June 12 in Kitanomaru Park near the Imperial Palace in Tokyo, Japan. The 4-storey museum has floor space of about 131,585 sq. ft.; it will show modern Japanese paintings, sculpture, and handicrafts.

Lord Montagu of Beaulieu announced on May 20, 1969, a plan to transform his collection of motor-cars into a national motor museum where the latest British cars would be exhibited as well as veteran and vintage models. The new museum, which would cost £750,000 to build, would be on a fresh site in the park at Beaulieu. Lord Montagu said he would create a charitable trust to run the museum and seek support from industry, particularly from the motor industry. He would make his own collection of cars and books, valued at about £400,000, exclusively available to the trust, and needed £500,000 from industry.

n

National Health Service. Statistics published by the U.K. Department of Health and Social Security on Oct. 13, 1969, showed that the number of Commonwealth and foreign doctors serving in Britain's hospitals increased from 11,735 in 1949 to 21,232 in 1968. In the training grades the proportion increased from 40 per cent in 1964 to 48 per cent in 1968; in the senior house officer grade from 55 per cent to 66 per cent; and in the registrar grade from 45 per cent to 54 per cent. The 1949 total of 137,636 hospital nursing staff increased to 255,641 in 1968. Despite a 5 per cent decrease in the number of hospitals and a 4 per cent decrease in the number of beds between 1959 and 1968, the number of in-patients rose by 29 per cent to over 5 million, and the number of new out-patients by 23 per cent to over 15 million, in the same period. The cost of the national health and welfare services rose from £718 million in 1958–59 to £1,490 million in 1967–68. The number of prescriptions rose from 202,011,000 in 1949 (when they cost £30,331,000) to 271,206,000 in 1967 (when they cost £146,201,000).

National Monuments. The U.K. Ministry of Public Building and Works announced on May 2, 1969, that during 1968 the record number of 10,809,100 people visited national monuments and places of historic interest in the care of the state. For the first time gross receipts exceeded £1 million, the admission fees totalling £722,959, and sales £306,981. The Tower of London again had over two million visitors, of whom 1,184,900 saw the crown jewels, an increase of nearly 340,000 over 1967; 1968 was the first year in which the jewel house had had more than one million visitors. Stonehenge, with 483,000 visitors, also had its busiest year. Fountains Abbey, with 155,600 visitors, was again the most visited place in the North, and Edinburgh Castle, with 483,400 visitors to the historic apartments, was the most frequented place outside Greater London. Kenilworth Castle's 111,700 visitors was another record number.

National Theatre. After 60 or more years, the British National Theatre building was at last begun when Jennie Lee, Minister for the Arts, and Desmond Plummer, G.L.C. leader, shovelled concrete into the foundations on Nov. 3, 1969.

National Theatre. At long last in October 1969 work at the Prince's Meadow site on the south bank of the Thames adjoining Waterloo Bridge, London, was begun on excavation and substructure for the British National Theatre. Completion of the building is due in 1973, the cost being £7,600,000. The Government and Greater London Council will contribute £3,750,000 each, while the Shakespeare Memorial Trust will provide £100,000. Thus 61 years after the project was first proposed the nebulous National Theatre appeared to be taking shape. In the 1908 proposals the theatre was intended to be built by 1916, but the First World War intervened; a second proposal, to build on a site in South Kensington facing the Victoria and Albert Museum, which was actually purchased and a foundation stone laid there in 1936, was foiled by the Second World War; a third attempt to make the dream a reality resulted in the leasing of a South Bank site between Hungerford and Waterloo Bridges in 1946, an Act of Parliament was passed in 1949, and the then Queen Elizabeth (now the Queen Mother) laid another foundation stone in July 1951. But that site, too, was later abandoned, and the foundation stone moved to the Prince's Meadow site.

National Trust. A report on the National Trust, made by an independent committee set up in August 1967 under the chairmanship of Sir Henry Benson, was published on Jan. 17, 1969. Among its major recommendations were the extension of public access to historic buildings; the phasing out of the Enterprise Neptune campaign and its replacement with a £5 million property

improvement appeal, since an estimated £4,750,000 is needed for work on the Trust's properties; and a drive for more members, to increase the present number to 500,000 within the next 15 years. The report recommended changes in the method of election of members to the council, in the arrangements for annual meetings, in the classes of membership, and in the rights of Trust members.

In its annual report for 1968–69, published in September 1969, the Trust said that it was able for the first time to give information about where its 171,076 members live. The largest number, about 25,000, live in London, while the county with the highest number is Surrey, with about 17,300 members, followed by Sussex with 9,600, and Kent with 8,800. The number of members expressed as a proportion of the population, however, shows that Surrey leads by 1·8 per cent, followed by Dorset with 1 per cent, Westmorland with 0·9 per cent, and Sussex with 0·8 per cent. At the other end of the scale are Carmarthenshire with 0·03 per cent; co. Durham with 0·04 per cent; Glamorganshire and Monmouthshire with 0·07 per cent; and Derbyshire and Huntingdonshire with 0·08 per cent. There are 2,200 Trust members living outside the U.K., and of these about half live in the U.S.A.

In 1969, 2,660,667 members of the public visited the Trust's properties that make an admission charge; and the income was £330,000 (£30,000 more than in 1968). These properties also received 195,404 visits from Trust members, an increase of 7,500 over the 1968 figure.

A decision important for the future of the Trust was made by the Minister of Housing and Local Government in March 1969 when he refused to confirm a compulsory purchase order for Rainbow Wood Farm, made by the Bath city council, and also refused planning permission to use the land as playing fields. The compulsory purchase of Rainbow Wood, which is the property of the National Trust, was the subject of a public enquiry in November 1968; Bath council wished to use it as playing fields to replace others which had been given to the University of Bath. The director-general of the Trust saw the Minister's decision as a recognition of "the Trust's right to hold land in perpetuity" and as a sign that "it is not open to every public authority lightly to propose the seizure of National Trust land as an easy way out of their difficulties."

Natural Gas. A 12-year contract for Europe's first total energy scheme using natural gas was signed on July 9, 1969, by the East Midlands Gas Board and John Player and Son, the tobacco company. A £6 million cigarette factory is to be built on a 45-acre site at Lenton, Nottingham, and the gas will be used to drive turbine alternator sets which will provide power, lighting, process steam, and full air conditioning for the factory.

Natural Gas. The 24-in. pipeline carrying North Sea gas across the country to South Wales crossed the Severn at Chaceley, near Tewkesbury, Glos., in July.

The contract contains a guarantee that the maximum period without gas in any year will not exceed a total of 30 days, the annual gas load being about 10 million therms.

The biggest British contract for the supply of natural gas was signed on Aug. 18, 1969, by the Gas Council and Imperial Chemical Industries. I.C.I. will pay about £250 million over a 15-year period for about 1,000 million therms a year, at a price ranging from 4d a therm upwards according to the use to which the gas is put and on the location of the plant to which it is supplied. (Domestic users pay an average of 1s 10d a therm.)

On Sept. 24, 1969, the Shell group announced that it will sell to Japan liquefied gas valued at £650 million over a 20-year period, starting in 1972–73. Shell will supply more than 500 million cubic ft. of gas a day from its offshore fields in Brunei; the gas will be transported 2,500 miles to Japan in six specially designed 460,000-barrel capacity tankers. Rival bids for the contract were put in by British Petroleum, a Soviet state organisation, and two U.S. companies. Brunei gas, being sulphur-free, is particularly valuable to Japan in her effort to combat air pollution.

Storage. It was announced on March 31 that the plan to establish Britain's first underground reservoir for natural gas at Sarsden, Oxfordshire, had been temporarily abandoned. Test bore-holes drilled during 1968 showed that the porous rock strata lacked the required storage capacity. The alternative site is at Lockton, near Scarborough, Yorks.

Developments: Inland. The Gas Council announced on April 17 that it was applying for planning permission to develop the two biggest inland wells in Great Britain (at Lockton, N. Yorks), which have estimated reserves of 250,000 million cubic ft. and are capable of producing 100 million cubic ft. per day (one twelfth of the gas requirement of the whole country). Home Oil of Canada is the Council's partner at Lockton. An 18-inch underground pipeline will conduct the gas 10 miles to a £3 million processing plant at Pickering, which is outside the N. Yorks Moors National Park. If permission is given, the Pickering plant will come into operation at the end of 1970.

North Sea. Also on April 17 the Ministry of Power published a White Paper on North Sea gas. This showed that potential supplies there could produce 3,500 million cubic ft. per day (half a million cubic ft per day more than previous estimates). It is expected that later discoveries will increase potential production to 4,000 million cubic ft. per day by 1975. For example, the Hewett field, 20 miles off the Norfolk coast, was stated in April to be capable of producing 2,000 million cubic ft. of natural gas a day, which is more than three times the figure stipulated in the Gas Council contract.

The Gas Council announced on Nov. 28, 1969, that it had signed 25-year contracts worth £36 million with the Mobil and Arpet oil groups for supplies of natural gas from the Leman field. The price ranges agreed in the contracts average almost 2·87d. a therm, varying according to the amount taken from 2·87d. to 2·83d. a therm until 1983, and subsequently from 2·87d. to 2·75d. a therm. Natural gas above the contract quantity is to be charged at 2·025d. throughout.

The Amoco-Gas Council group started to bring natural gas ashore from the North Sea Leman Bank field on April 18. Initial deliveries were 50 million cubic ft. per day, but reached 160 million cubic ft. per day in May, and were expected to rise rapidly to 350 million cubic ft. a day. The gas was pumped ashore through a 38-mile 30-in. pipeline to the terminal at Bacton, Norfolk. Shell-Esso's production well in the Leman Bank field, however, suffered a four-month shut-down, from the beginning of February to June, due to leakage.

In December 1969 the Gas Council announced plans to build a third major terminal north of Mablethorpe, Lincs, to handle supplies of natural gas from the North Sea. The proposed terminal, which will have an ultimate processing capacity of about 3,000 million cubic ft. of gas a day, will at first take deliveries of gas from the Conoco-National Coal Board partnership's new Viking field. The initial cost of the project will be about £5 million, but the final cost might reach £10 million if and when the ultimate capacity is used.

New discoveries in the North Sea continued during 1969. The National Coal Board and the American-owned Continental Oil group announced on March 14 a strike about 65 miles off Great Yarmouth, and about 6½ miles N.W. of a 49-million-cubic-ft. well announced in December 1968. The new strike's test yield of 55 million cubic ft. a day is larger than that of either of the group's two previous wells. A month later Shell-Esso announced a new find about 60 miles from the Norfolk coast. This was the 200th North Sea find of natural gas since exploration first started in 1964. The Hamilton Group announced on July 23 a possibly significant discovery about 90 miles E. of Flamborough Head, at the comparatively shallow depth of 5,500 ft. Another shallow-depth find was revealed on September 23 when Total Oil Marine U.K., a subsidiary of a French oil group, announced a strike 10 miles from Scarborough. Later in the same month the new field called Viking, worked by a partnership of Continental Oil and the National Coal Board, was confirmed as the third largest in the North Sea, after Leman Bank and Indefatigable. (Viking adjoins Indefatigable.) The development well indicated a potential supply of over 53 million cubic ft. per day.

On September 23, the Ministry of Power invited bids for concessions in a further 140 "blocks" (14,000 sq. miles) of the North Sea and Irish Sea. In the former the area is in the north near the Norwegian zone; in the latter, only companies forming partnerships with the Gas Council or National Coal Board will be granted concessions. The total area of the continental shelf open to exploration was thus extended to 124,000 sq. miles. It was officially stated on Nov. 10, 1969, that the latest estimate of recoverable gas in the U.K. continental shelf is 27 trillion cubic ft.

After at least £25 million had been spent on drilling operations for oil and natural gas in the Dutch sector of the North Sea, results, it was said in November, had proved disappointing. Oilmen in The Hague, however, pointed out that drilling plans had been hampered by the unsettled zones dispute involving Denmark, Holland, and West Germany.

Australia. Brisbane became the first Australian city to be supplied with natural gas on March 17, 1969, when the premier of Queensland ceremonially opened a valve in the 300-mile pipeline from the Roma field. The pipeline, started in April 1968, was completed in January 1969 at a cost of $A11 million;

when the field is in full operation in the early 1970s it will deliver 50 million cubic ft. of gas per day to Brisbane. The conversion of 80,000 appliances in homes and factories is expected to take a year. The chief user of natural gas is the Australian Pacific nitrogenous fertiliser plant on Gibson Island at the mouth of the Brisbane river, which consumes some 13 million cubic ft. per day.

The 108-mile pipeline from Bass Strait to Melbourne came into use in 1969, and big reductions in gas fuel costs in Victoria were announced on February 25. The reductions, which will take place in stages as appliances operated by 420,000 customers are converted to natural gas at the rate of 6,000 a week, range from 54 per cent for a major company using 360,000 therms a year to 10 per cent for small households with only a gas cooker using 120 therms.

The discovery of a possible new natural gas field in the Roma district of Queensland was announced in May. The first on the western side of the Grafton Range, the field is 12 miles N.E. of Roma. Gas was struck at a depth of more than 3,500 ft.; the flow rate was estimated at 4½ million cubic ft. a day.

In November 1969 West Australian Petroleum announced another big flow of natural gas from its Dongara field, 200 miles north of Perth. Gas flows from the Dongara No. 15 well were reported to be at a daily rate of 10 million cubic ft. through a half-inch surface choke, equal to the best obtained in the area.

Nature Reserves. The British Nature Conservancy announced on June 3, 1969, that the estuary of the Dovey, in Cardiganshire and Merionethshire, comprising 3,525 acres of unspoilt foreshore and salt marsh, had been leased from the Crown Estate Commissioners, and declared a new National Nature Reserve.

The estuary is notable for its exceptional bird life. During the winter months it holds up to 3,000 ducks, mostly mallard, wigeon, and teal, with some golden-eye; small numbers of white-fronted geese roost between October and April; and several species of waders, including dunlin, redshank, sanderling, and curlew, frequent the estuary especially while on passage. With the help of local residents, wildfowlers, and naturalists who are represented on a management advisory panel, the Conservancy has established a wildfowl refuge in the eastern part of the reserve. Outside this refuge wildfowling will continue under permit in agreed shooting zones.

The Nature Conservancy also announced an extension to the 57 acres of woodland in the Coed Camlyn reserve on the southern slopes of the Vale of Ffestiniog, Merionethshire, bringing the total area up to 157 acres. Coed Camlyn which consists mainly of sessile oak with some birch, and an abundant ground cover of bilberry, is one of the best examples of deciduous woodland in North Wales. An extension of 16 acres has been added to the 52 acres of Coed Y Rhygen reserve, also in Merionethshire, which is noted for its abundant mosses growing on boulders and tree-trunks under conditions of very high rainfall and humidity.

On Dec. 2, 1969, the Nature Conservancy announced a new nature reserve at Cors Erddreiniog, Anglesey, a 78-acre valley area 4 miles north of Llangefni. The reserve contains one of Britain's few "living" fens, where peat continues to be laid down. The fen contains several rare plants, and has developed from a lake which existed after the last Ice Age about 10,000 years ago. On the same day the Conservancy also announced that the Oxwich nature reserve, Glamorgan, is to be extended by 22 acres.

Nickel. Site of the lease held by Poseidon N.L. at Windarra, Western Australia, where a nickel find sent up its shares from a few shillings to over £100 each.

Nazareth. A French archaeological team uncovered the skeleton of a child, aged 10–13, near Nazareth in August 1969. The child is thought to have been ceremoniously buried 50,000 years ago, which would make this the oldest human grave ever found. In the grave, by the side of the child, were the skull and antlers of a horned animal covered with stones, apparently sacrificed at the time of the burial to accompany the child into the next world.

"New Scientist" Award. The winner of the 1969 £1,000 award by the *New Scientist* weekly magazine was announced on May 29, 1969. It went to Dr. Brian Josephson, who is assistant director of research in the department of physics at Cambridge University, and a research fellow of Trinity College, Cambridge, for his fundamental work in the theory of electrons in superconducting metals.

Niagara Falls. During the summer of 1969 the northern (U.S.) branch of the Niagara river, between Niagara Falls city and Goat Island, was temporarily dammed in order to dry up the river and shut down the American Fall. Hundreds of tons of rock eroded from the brink of the Fall had accumulated at the base, and the damming of the river was carried out to allow geologists to examine the rock in order to devise ways of cleaning the base and thus preserving the full beauty of the Fall. This was the first time that Niagara had ceased to flow. The Falls were "dry" from June 12 to Nov. 25, when the dam was breached and the water flowed again.

Nickel. The most astonishing development in mining in 1969 was the immense growth in price of the shares of Poseidon NL, a small Adelaide

Niagara Falls. In 1969 the American Fall ceased to flow for the first time, when a dam was erected so that the debris at the Fall's base could be examined.

Nobel Prize-Winners 1969

Above: Prize-winners in Stockholm at the presentation of their awards by King Gustav of Sweden. They are (*left to right*) Prof. Murray Gell-Mann, U.S.A. (Physics); Prof. Derek Barton, U.K., and Prof. Odd Hassel, Norway (Chemistry); Profs. Max Delbruck, Alfred Hershey, and Salvador Luria, all U.S.A. (Medicine). *Left:* Samuel Beckett (Literature). *Right:* Prof. Ragnar Frisch (Norway) and Prof. Jan Tinbergen (Netherlands), who shared the Bank of Sweden's Economics prize instituted in memory of Alfred Nobel and awarded for the first time in 1969.

company formed in 1953 to prospect for tungsten in the Northern Territory of Australia, which announced in October the discovery of nickel ore at Windarra, 140 miles N. of Kalgoorlie, Western Australia. The company's shares, which then stood at 8s. reached the fantastic price of £106 each during December. Test drilling of an outcrop of rock 1,000 ft. by 650 ft. showed a concentration of nickel in the ore of 3·56 per cent between 145 and 185 ft. beneath the surface. Windarra became a "gold rush" spot immediately, and shares in companies owning leases on adjacent areas shared in the rise. But Poseidon's discovery was only one of several valuable finds of nickel in Western Australia during the year: in March two finds near Higginsville, 416 miles E. of Perth, were announced, one of an estimated value of £12 million at Widgemooltha, and the other valued at £35 million at Redross; in July, Great Boulder and North Kalgurli reported a discovery of nickel at Scotia, N. of Kalgoorlie, and in October the same partnership reported having found an estimated £25½ million worth at Carr Boyd Rocks, 30 miles N.E. of Kalgoorlie. These discoveries were given greater value by a world shortage of nickel caused by a strike in the Canadian mines of International Nickel that began on July 10 and lasted until Nov. 14.

Nobel Prizes. The 1969 Nobel Prizes, worth about £30,000 each, were awarded as follows:

Peace. The International Labour Organisation (I.L.O.), in recognition of its work during its 50 years of existence.

Literature. Samuel Beckett, Irish-born playwright, whose best-known play is *Waiting for Godot.*

Medicine. Shared by three American scientists for their contribution in the field of molecular genetics involving virus structures and bacteria infection: Dr. Max Delbruck, professor of biology at California Institute of Technology, Pasadena; Dr. Salvador E. Luria, professor of microbiology at Massachusetts Institute of Technology, Cambridge; and Dr. Alfred D. Hershey, director of the Genetics Research Unit at Carnegie Institution of Washington, Long Island, New York.

Chemistry. Shared between Prof. Derek Barton, Imperial College of Science and Technology, London, and Prof. Odd Hassel, Oslo University, for their work in developing and applying the concept of conformation.

Physics. Prof. Murray Gell-Mann, Californian Institute of Technology, Pasadena, for his work on classifying subatomic particles and their relationships.

The Nobel Memorial Prize in Economic Sciences, announced by the Bank of Sweden in 1968, and awarded for the first time in 1969, was shared by Prof. Ragnar Frisch of Norway and Prof. Jan Tinbergen of the Netherlands.

Norfolk Broads. A report compiled by a consortium of local authorities and other interested bodies on a new plan for the Norfolk Broads, expected to cost £4,413,500, was published on Oct. 1, 1969. The report envisages new waterways and moorings, country parks and a network of footpaths. It stated that by the turn of the century it expects over 20,000 craft to be in use on the Broads, including 8,000 hired craft. At present there are about 6,500 craft in use during the holiday season, of which a third are hired.

Norwich, Norfolk. The city's planning officer reported in August 1969 that the experimental closing of London Street, one of the two main central shopping streets, to all but pedestrian traffic since July 1967 had been an unqualified success. The survey had shown that it was not necessary to provide alternative traffic routes; that shoppers strongly favoured traffic-free shopping; motorists supported the project; and shopkeepers had benefited from increased trade and better working conditions. There are plans to extend the idea to other shopping streets in the central area.

Nuclear Power. "Dragon," the experimental high-temperature reactor at Winfrith Heath, Dorset, a British conception supported by most of the countries of Western Europe, had by 1969 become a practical commercial proposition after 10 years' work. Much smaller than other reactors, it is also much cheaper. A 1,260-megawatt Dragon-type power station would cost only two-thirds of the money required for an advanced gas-cooled reactor, and would even be £10 per kilowatt cheaper to build than the latest type of coal-fired power station. Moreover, nuclear fuel costs only about one-third of the price of coal.

The higher operating temperature of "Dragon" is made possible by enclosing the fuel in ceramic particles instead of metal cases, and by using helium instead of carbon dioxide as a coolant. The helium could drive gas-turbines directly or could boil water for steam to drive conventional steam turbines.

Australia. It was announced in October 1969 that Australia's first nuclear power station will be built at

Jervis Bay, N.S.W. World tenders for the station of 500 megawatts will be invited in 1970, and it will be completed in 1976. The station will be built and owned by the Federal Government and operated by the N.S.W. Electricity Commission; power produced will be fed directly into the N.S.W. grid. The plant will use Australian fuel, mainly uranium.

Nursing. Britain's first university degree in nursing is to be created by Manchester University. The degree course will combine practical training with 84 weeks of academic studies and 24 weeks' vacation, the same as the four-year diploma course, which was started in 1959. It is anticipated that the degree will be a basis for post-graduate and research studies, and will also widen the opportunities for those wishing to make nursing a career.

Nuthampstead, Herts. The Roskill Commission gave on April 1 site information details of Nuthampstead, one of the four sites short listed for London's third airport. The total land required for the airport would be at least 7,500 acres; about 1,000 people are currently living in this area. A two-runway airport would have an "intrusive" noise level affecting 18,500 people; if there were four runways the same noise

level would affect 51,000 people. "Intrusive to annoying" levels would affect 3,000 people if there were two runways, and 10,000 if four, while "annoying" levels would affect 4,500 people. At full capacity of two runways 45,000 people would be employed at the airport by the mid-1980s, and 65,000 by the mid-1990s. If two runways were used to full capacity it is thought that 45 million people would use the airport each year; the number would increase to over 100 million if four runways were used. In order to cope with this traffic new high standard dual-carriageway links to the M1 for London traffic, and to the A1 for Midlands and Northern traffic, and rail facilities to a London terminal would be required.

During the public inquiry in June it was stated that an airport at Nuthampstead could have a disastrous effect on Cambridge University's radio-astronomy complex at Land's Bridge in south Cambridgeshire, where £2½ million radiotelescopes had been erected because it was an area free from electrical disturbance. The interference caused by an airport would be fatal to the world lead Britain had established in radio-astronomy. Four important scientific laboratories in north Hertfordshire also would be affected by aircraft noise and vibration.

Obesity. A report, "Obesity and Disease," published by the Office of Health Economics on April 1, 1969, said that one Briton in five is clinically too fat, and that any person carrying 10 lb. of excess fat has less chance of living a long healthy life than one smoking 25 cigarettes a day. It estimated that 2,300,000 prescriptions for slimming preparations were written by doctors during 1967, and that about 100 million tablets or capsules were prescribed, at a cost estimated to be about £3 million a year. In 1965 the market value of slimming foods was about £20 million, and it increases at the rate of 15 per cent a year. The report said that half those starting a slimming course fail to complete it. Overeating is often caused by loneliness, unhappiness, grief, depression, anxiety, tension, frustration, and boredom; in a study of 500 patients it was found that 370 ate more when they were nervous or worried and 95 ate more when idle or bored.

Oceanology. The recent emergence of this word (meaning "study of the oceans") to extend or replace the older term *oceanography* (meaning "descrip-

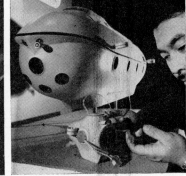

Oceanology

The new science of oceanology was engaging the attention of governments all over the world throughout the 1960s, and many new underwater vehicles were designed and built and much subterranean exploration undertaken. The first international conference and exhibition on the subject was held in England in February 1969, when 200 companies from 11 countries showed their oceanological wares.
Above left, the United Kingdom Minister of Technology, who opened the exhibition, examining the model of a British underwater vehicle, "Bacchus," made by the British Aircraft Corporation; *right,* model of a deep submersible work vessel, with a projecting pincer arm, and separable work pods which can operate independently—a U.S. exhibit at the show. *Left,* Russian survey ship, equipped for underwater prospecting for minerals, which attended the exhibition.

Oil. At this B.P. drilling site on Alaska's North Slope where vast deposits were found in 1968–69, temperatures are often 50 or 60 degrees below zero Centigrade. *Right:* Sikorsky "Skycrane" helicopters bring in all the material and equipment.

tion of the oceans") indicates the shift of emphasis that has taken place in sea-studies. Whereas earlier their most important aspect was the mapping and charting of currents, depths, reefs, and other hazards, modern interest is concentrated upon the sea as a source of scientific knowledge and of raw materials.

In 1968 Pres. Johnson of the U.S.A suggested that the 1970s should be declared an International Decade of Ocean Exploration. The first step towards this was taken in Great Britain in February 1969 when the first inter-national exhibition and conference devoted exclusively to the subject were held over five days at the Hotel Metro-pole, Brighton, Sussex, and in the near-by harbours at Newhaven and Shoreham. The exhibition "Oceanology Inter-national 69," opened on February 17 by the U.K. Minister of Technology, included exhibits by 200 companies from 11 countries, and at the conference over a hundred papers were delivered by experts from all over the world. Most of these were scientific, but others covered the political and legal aspects of oceanology, involving the ownership of the sea bed and continental shelf, territorial waters, fishing limits, and similar matters.

Oceanology International 69 was sponsored by the British Industrial Society for Underwater Technology, but this is only one of the many British bodies concerned with the subject. Others are the National Institute of Oceanography, the National Environment Research Council, the Ministry of Technology, the Ministry of Agriculture, Fisheries, and Food, the Royal Navy, and a dozen other departments and ministries. The establishment of an interdepartmental Advisory Committee on Marine Tech-nology to co-ordinate their activities was announced in Parliament on Feb. 5, 1969, and the Committee published its first report on Dec. 8. British annual expenditure on exploitation of the sea totals about £12 million, compared with £100 million by the U.S.S.R. and £300 million by the U.S.A.

What is thought to be the oldest surviving patch of oceanic floor in the world was discovered by the U.S. research vessel *Glomar Challenger* in an area to the east of the Marianas, half-way between New Guinea and Japan. It consisted of thick layers of sediment deposited over at least the last 140 million years, according to a report published in August 1969.

Oil. Unquestionably the most important development in 1969 was the news that came from the Northern Slope of Alaska. Following Atlantic Richfield-Humble's announcement in July 1968 of a rich strike at Prudhoe Bay, British Petroleum, which then owned a lease of 96,000 acres adjacent, stated on March 13, 1969, that it had struck oil in "encourag-ing" quantities in porous sandstone at 8,000 ft. down. Rumours that this was an exceptionally large strike were con-firmed on Sept. 28 when B.P. stated that the deposit had been independently assessed at 4,800 million recoverable barrels, worth £2,000 million. When in full production the wells will produce 600,000 barrels (worth £250,000) a day. These figures made B.P.'s field at Prudhoe Bay about the same size as the East Texas field, which is the largest in the U.S.A. and one of the ten largest in the world.

To help to market this immense find, B.P. in March purchased for $400 million two refineries and 10,000 filling stations from the Atlantic Richfield and Sinclair companies, and in June an-nounced that its U.S. interests would be merged with Standard Oil of Ohio (Sohio), whose marketing expertise would match the vast quantity of Alaskan oil that B.P. would have to dispose of. Later the question of the legality of the B.P.-Sohio merger was raised in the American courts, but the merger was allowed on certain conditions.

In September the greatest auction of oil leases ever held took place at

Oil. At the biggest bonanza in modern oil history, the auction of leases of 450,000 acres in Alaska brought in bids of over 900 million U.S. dollars.

Anchorage, when the State of Alaska offered 10-year leases of 179 tracts (450,000 acres) of possibly oil-rich land. B.P. in conjunction with the U.S. Gulf Oil company bid more than £38 million for the first six lots offered (the Colville River delta, 100 miles N.W. of Prudhoe Bay). All the major oil companies took part in the two-day sale, which realised the huge sum of £375 million; the average price was £830 per acre for leases of land which, in 1965, fetched as little as £5 10s. per acre. The highest price paid in the auction—and the highest ever paid for oil land in the U.S.A.—was £30 million for a single tract, representing a price of £11,5C0 per acre, given by the Amerada-Hess-Getty consortium; this tract is directly adjacent to the Prudhoe Bay fields belonging to B.P. and Atlantic Richfield. The problem of transporting oil from this remote area led during the year to the making of the North West passage by the tanker *Manhattan* in September (see p. 61) and the planning of an 800-mile pipeline to the south coast of Alaska (see under Pipelines).

Russian oil production looked less hopeful in 1969. Both Baku on the Caspian Sea and Bashkiria, the "second Baku," on the middle Volga began to slow down, and the vast resources discovered in Western Siberia, centred on the town of Tyumen, proved difficult to exploit. Permafrost goes down almost 2,000 ft. in this area, creating delays in production. Accordingly the U.S.S.R. had to reduce exports of oil, and to seek new supplies from Iraq, Persia, and Libya.

Europe. The vice-president of the U.S. International Drilling Company (Contracts) announced on June 20 that high-grade oil had been discovered in the North Sea on the border of the British and Norwegian drilling areas, while gas drilling operations were being carried out. Gulf Oil in partnership with the U.K. National Coal Board started drilling in the Irish Sea, in the summer of 1969, the first "wild-cat" well ever put down there. The Gulf–NCB's production licence covers 1,222 sq. kilometres (about 472 sq. miles) in five blocks off the Lancashire coast N.W. of Liverpool. The first test was made off Formby, where British Petroleum discovered Great Britain's first small oilfield in 1939. The Irish Sea exploration area covers 15,000 miles of the continental shelf between Great Britain and Northern Ireland, as well as a large part of the U.K. shelf farther south. The boundary with the Irish Republic has yet to be decided. Most of the oil companies taking part in the North Sea operations have exploration (but not production) licences for the Irish Sea, and geologists are optimistic about the chance of finding hydrocarbons there.

Australia. There was a considerable increase in oil production in Australia in the financial year 1968–69 when total production of crude oil amounted to

14 million barrels, compared with 12 million barrels in 1967–68. Of the 1968–69 total nearly 12 million barrels were produced at Barrow Island, Western Australia, and the remaining 2 million in Queensland. In 1968 Australian refineries produced 151 million barrels of marketable petroleum products, 9·8 per cent more than 1967. Consumption during 1968 was almost 150 million barrels, 10 per cent higher than in 1967; consumption of motor spirit was 56 million barrels, 6 per cent more.

Australia's biggest oilfield, in Bass Strait, went into production on Oct. 8, 1969. Developed by Esso Standard Oil, Australia, Pty. Ltd., and the Broken Hill Proprietary Co., the field is estimated to contain more than 1,500 million barrels of recoverable oil, which may be added to as exploration continues. Oil is being sent by pipeline to refineries near Melbourne. The Esso-BHP partnership had reported in April that indications of oil had been found in yet another location in Bass Strait, off the coast of Victoria, at 7,000–9,000 ft. This discovery was in Mackerel No. 1 well to the south of the proved Halibut field, and about 50 miles from the Gippsland shore.

A map issued in March by the Department of National Development showed that nearly 1,700,000 sq. miles of the country are at present under title for petroleum exploration and development. Western Australia has the largest area, with 549,854 sq. miles; Queensland is next, with 327,714 sq. miles; then come South Australia, with 323,844 sq. miles, and the Northern territory with 156,318 sq. miles.

New Zealand. A big oil strike off the west coast of North Island was reported on March 20 by the Shell-British Petroleum-Todd Oil Services, Ltd. The well, Maui-One, was 33 miles offshore, at a depth of 360 ft. of water. In addition to the oil it has produced natural gas and condensate.

Storage. At Le Dauphin, near Manosque in the department of Basses Alpes, France, a novel scheme for the storage of crude oil was put into operation in 1969. Large seams of salt in the rock were dissolved and washed out with water, and the cavities filled with oil. As much as 5 million cubic metres (6,540,000 cubic yd.) of storage space was created in this way. A large reservoir to receive the salt water was excavated near by. A huge underwater storage tank for oil from the offshore Fateh field in the Persian Gulf is described and illustrated on p. 72.

Pollution. Active steps were taken in 1969 by the governments of many nations to combat the growing pollution of the sea by oil spilled and discharged by tankers and other ships. In Bonn, West Germany, on June 9, seven North Sea countries signed an agreement committing themselves to warning one another as soon as there are signs of pollution. They are

also obliged to exchange information on methods of fighting such danger, and to provide mutual aid. Signatories to the agreement were Belgium, Denmark, France, Great Britain, Norway, Sweden, and West Germany. The agreement came into force on Aug. 9.

At a plenary session in October of the Intergovernmental Maritime Consultative Organisation (IMCO), an organ of the United Nations, representatives of 34 nations approved the addition of new and more stringent regulations to the convention on pollution signed in 1954 and amended in 1962. That convention forbade the discharge of oil within 50 miles of land and placed a total ban on the discharging of oil by ships of more than 20,000 tons built after 1967. The new regulations prohibit ships from discharging tank washings of more than 100 parts of oil in 1 million parts of water in any sea area, and limits the discharge of tanker residues within 50 miles of land to one fifteen-thousandth of cargo capacity.

On Nov. 28 two more conventions were adopted, which allow countries to intervene when their shores are threatened by oil pollution, and place strict liability for damage on ship-owners. One convention sets liability at £56 per gross registered ton of the ship, to a limit of £5,800,000, and lays equal responsibility on all ships involved in the discharging of oil. This convention will come into force 90 days after ratification by 15 countries. The other convention allows coastal countries to take preventive measures when oil threatens their interests, including fishing, marine and wildlife, and tourist attractions. This convention requires eight signatures, including five from countries with oil tankers totalling more than a million gross tons.

It was announced in the U.K. House of Commons on June 16 that in future the government would arrange and pay for the clearance of oil slicks *at sea* where it is obvious that the coast is threatened. But local authorities would continue to be responsible, with the assistance of a government grant, for dealing with oil pollution on their beaches or up to about a mile offshore.

Ombudsman. The second annual report, covering 1968, of Sir Edmund Compton, U.K. Ombudsman, was published on Feb. 20, 1969. He stated that he had not come across any decision which indicated bias or perversity on the part of the person taking it. Of the 1,340 cases received from M.Ps (which included some carried over from 1967) he rejected 54 per cent as being outside his jurisdiction. He completed investigations in 374 cases, in 38 of which he found that there had been elements of maladministration. The Inland Revenue accounted for 13 cases; the Department of Health and Social Security for seven; the Home Office for four; the Foreign and Commonwealth Office, and the Ministry of Housing and Local Government each accounted for three; and the Ministry of Transport for two; and there was one each against other government departments and authorities. Among matters investigated in 1969 was maladministration in the Inland Revenue department. In a report published on Sept. 17, 1969, Sir Edmund stated that he found 30 cases of maladministration in 79 complaints. The chief subjects of complaint were the sudden unexpected demand for payment of arrears to tax for earlier years, and undue delay in the repayment of tax overpaid.

It was announced at Stormont on March 4, 1969, that the ombudsman for Northern Ireland, creation of which office was promised in November 1968, will be the British ombudsman, Sir Edmund Compton, who will combine the duties of both offices. In May it was stated that his field of inquiry in Northern Ireland will be extended to include citizens' grievances against public bodies and authorities outside central government—although these are excluded from his terms of reference in the rest of the U.K.

Onions. A team of four doctors at Newcastle University's department of medicine announced in February 1969 that they had discovered that onions have a medical property which improves the blood's capacity to dissolve internal blood clots. Work is continuing in an attempt to isolate the chemical responsible for this anti-coagulant effect, since it could prove valuable in fighting coronary and cerebral thrombosis.

Opals. During 1969, after a German digger had discovered one of the best finds of opals in Lightning Ridge, Australia, the town was inundated with prospectors, the population increasing from 50 to 1,500, a third of the arrivals professional miners, and the rest part-timers. Claims were staked, and 434 holes sunk straight down, ranging in depth from 10 ft. to 90 ft. Men, women, and children were all reported to have joined in the opal rush, many of them finding stones worth thousands of dollars. On Dec. 2, a world record price of $A168,000 was paid in Adelaide to four miners who had found a 220-oz. crystal opal in Andamooka in November. The opal, split into two portions of 162 oz. and 58 oz., is the largest ever found in Australia, the previous largest being the 143-oz. "Olympic Australia" found near Coober Pedy in August 1956.

Open University. An announcement on Jan. 27, 1969, that the U.K. Government had accepted the plans for a radio and TV university (formerly called the University of the Air) was followed by rapid developments. Having been granted its royal charter, the Open University became an autonomous institution from June 1. The vice-chancellor, Dr. Walter Perry, said on June 3 that the university had recruited 40 academic staff from

1,100 applicants, and that the same number would be recruited at the beginning of 1970. Overheads for a full year of operation were estimated at £3·5 million, including the cost of BBC programmes, but the cost for each student should be below the cost in the established universities. Staff and students would be eligible for election to the two executive bodies, council and senate, he said, and membership would reflect its regional organisation. The university's permanent home will be in the new city of Milton Keynes, Bucks.

On July 22 Dr. Walter Perry stated that students would be selected according to national need, social justice, degree of motivation to complete a course, and their ability to benefit from a course. Some form of selection was inescapable since research indicated that there might be over 100,000 applicants in the first year. Students for commencement in 1971 will be registered in January–July 1970. A student will require six course credits to get an ordinary degree, and eight for an honours degree. The formal presentation of the royal charter to Sir Peter Venables, chairman of the university council, and the installation of Lord Crowther (formerly Geoffrey Crowther, editor of *The Economist*) as first chancellor, took place at the Royal Society on July 23.

Further information was given by Dr. Perry on Nov. 29, when he said that the minimum outlay for an ordinary degree of Bachelor of Arts will be £140 if it is sat after three years, or £180 if taken with honours after four years. There will be an initial registration fee of £10, and a single foundation course, including summer school accommodation and board, will cost £40. If two courses are taken at the same time the charge will be £50. After the foundation level the courses cost £20 each. No more than two courses can be taken in a year, and it is expected that most students will take four or five years to qualify. Students, who must be able to devote at least 10 hours a week to each of the courses they are studying, will receive study material at regular intervals, as well as assignments which must be completed to schedule. Television programmes will appear on BBC 2, and the radio section will be on the v.h.f. waveband on Radio 3 and 4, all timed for early evening, and for Saturday and Sunday mornings. During their first year of study students will also be expected to attend a summer school lasting up to a fortnight.

Three major adult education courses, to start in January 1970, to prepare students for commencement were announced by the BBC on September 19. Each comprising a series of radio or TV programmes supplemented by a text-book, they will deal with mathematics, literature, and sociology. The foundation courses of the university, in mathematics, science, the humanities, and "understanding society," will begin in January 1971.

Ord, River, Western Australia. A second flood-prevention and irrigation dam is to be constructed across the Ord River, in remote N.W. Western Australia, 1,700 miles from Perth and about 200 miles S.W. of Darwin. The project will include a large rockfill dam, a separate spillway, and diversion tunnels. Its objective is to prevent severe seasonal flooding of the river and to impound water for irrigation of 152,000 acres of land now subject to severe drought. The dam will be 250 ft. high and 1,100 ft. wide at its crest. Construction will involve placement of 2,400,000 cubic yards of rockfill. A separate spillway 7,000 ft. long and 90 ft. deep will be excavated through a granite saddle on one bank of the river; this will require the removal of 650,000 yards of material. Two $14\frac{1}{2}$-ft. diameter tunnels, each 800 ft. long, will be dug. The contractors, Dravo Proprietary Ltd. of Perth, have planned construction to permit flooding at the dam site during the spring of 1970 and to resume work immediately thereafter. The project, which will take three years to complete, is being financed by the Western Australian Government with assistance from the Federal Government. It is expected to make the raising of cotton feasible on land which is at present subject to alternate periods of severe drought and heavy monsoon floods. The latter can total more than a million cubic ft. of water per second.

Ordnance Survey. A new headquarters at Southampton for this official U.K. map-making department was opened by the Queen on May 1, 1969. The Survey began during the 1745 rebellion led by Bonnie Prince Charlie when the English army under the Duke of Cumberland required reliable maps of Scotland if the rebels were to be rounded up after Culloden. An engineer named William Roy was given the task, which was never finished; 20 years later he suggested a national survey, and this was undertaken by his successors, the first map being published in 1801. The Survey remained a section of the Board of Ordnance (artillery) until after the Second World War, when its military connection was partially severed, and it became a wholly civilian establishment in 1968 under the Ministry of Housing and Local Government. Originally housed in the Tower of London, it was moved in the mid-19th century to a converted military asylum in Southampton; after the bombing in 1940 it inhabited temporary buildings in Southampton and Chessington; in 1962 approval was given for its new permanent home, on which work started in 1965.

The new buildings house about 1,500 draughtsmen and 400 printers. The basic series of maps which they produce range from a scale of 50 inches to the mile to that of 16 miles to the inch. They are: (a) the 1/1,250 series for urban areas, a scale large enough to show the width of streets and even pavements, and the 1/2,500

Ordnance Survey. The new headquarters of the official U.K. map-making body were opened by the Queen in May. 1,500 draughtsmen and 400 printers work here.

series for cultivated rural areas, showing single fields ; (b) the 6 in. (1/10,560) and 1/25,000 series, which are derived from the larger maps by photography ; and (c) the 1 in., $\frac{1}{4}$ in., 1/625,000, and 1/1,000,000 series of specially drawn small-scale maps. A large range of specialised maps, e.g. tourist maps, archaeological maps, is also produced. Frequent revisions are made ; altogether, on average 40 new or revised map sheets are published every working day.

Organists, College of. Australia established her own College of Organists with centres in all States in March 1969. Prof. George Loughlin, dean of the faculty of music at the University of Melbourne, is its president. The College aims to improve the standard in organ building and church music generally, and awards diplomas and fellowships. Membership is open to all organists and choirmasters, and all those interested in organ-playing and church music. The first examination for associateship of the College was held in July.

"Origin." This is the name of the Australian aborigines' first regular newspaper, a fortnightly tabloid which began publication in the first week of August 1969. It is published in Adelaide by Mrs. Margaret Kappe, a journalist interested in aboriginal welfare.

Osaka, Japan. The international airport at Osaka, the location of Expo 70, is being expanded. Eight foreign airlines at present serve it, and the number of air travellers it handles is four million a year, including domestic flights. As at least fifteen foreign carriers have asked to operate special flights into Osaka for the 1970 Exposition, the authorities have drawn up a plan to enable the airport to handle 10 million passengers a year. A new runway was opened during 1969, and a new terminal building, costing about £9$\frac{1}{2}$ million, opened in February. This eight-storey central block houses a hotel, customs office, restaurants, shops, and administration offices, and will be used by nine foreign airlines, including B.O.A.C. A new road connects the

airport with the Expo 70 site, only five minutes' drive away.

Oxford. The Oxford city council approved on March 31, 1969, the construction of a £31 million relief road across Eastwyke Farm, south of the line of the Christ Church Meadow road. This final decision came four years after a 60 to 1 vote by the Council for a road across Christ Church Meadow, which was subsequently rejected by the Ministry of Housing and Local Government.

Oxford, University of. The committee set up in 1967 to study the university's relations with its junior members, under the chairmanship of Prof. H. L. A. Hart, published its findings (the "Hart report") on May 15, 1969. It recommended reform of the disciplinary system and also student representation on academic decision-making bodies. The disciplinary rules, it said, should be made and annually revised by a rules committee of six senior and six junior members, and junior members should be on standing joint committees on the syllabus, library facilities, teaching arrangements, and examinations. On academic matters, however, teachers should have final authority. The powers of the proctors should be curtailed and "secret trials" by them of erring students should be abolished, to be replaced by a disciplinary court for serious charges.

For students intending to read science the admission requirement of two foreign languages was reduced to one in February 1969. Insistence on two languages was believed to have contributed to the decline in applications from science students. Cambridge University had made the same move in 1967.

A new degree course in human sciences, intended to cover both the biological and social aspects of man, was approved by Oxford University congregation on Nov. 18, 1969. Its syllabus will include genetics, ethology (the science of character formation), psychology, geography, sociology, and anthropology.

pq

Paddle-steamer. The last commercial paddle-steamer on the south coast of England, the British Rail Isle of Wight ferry, the *Ryde*, made her farewell cruise from and to Portsmouth on Sunday, Sept. 7, 1969. She had been on the Solent ferry service for 32 years.

Papua—New Guinea. The results of the 1966 census, published in February 1969, gave the total population of Papua-New Guinea as 2,184,986, including 34,669 non-indigenous persons. 51 per cent are under 21 years of age. Of the indigenous population 572,215 are "subsistence workers," *i.e.* live on the produce of their own agricultural labour and have no cash income ; 442,109 hunters, farmers, or fishers have some cash income ; and 233,642 are employed persons earning money. The largest town, the capital, Port Moresby, has a total population of 41,848 ; Lae has 16,546, and Rabaul 10,561. Roman Catholics comprise 31 per cent of those professing a religion, and Lutherans 27·6 per cent ; 7 per cent have no particular religious belief. Educational standards are low among the indigenous population, of whom only 14,500 have received any secondary education.

Industry. A gigantic deposit of 500 million tons of high-grade copper ore has been discovered on Bougainville Island. Production by open-cast mining will begin in 1972. A preliminary agreement to supply 950,000 tons of copper to Japan over 15 years was signed in February 1969 ; the value of this quantity is $A1,000 million at ruling copper prices. Over 1,500 men will be employed in the mine.

Archaeology. Exploration and excavation undertaken since 1960 in the Western Highlands of New Guinea show continuous human existence there for at least 11,000 years. Stone axes used by hunters were chiefly made by flaking, but some show evidence of sharpening by grinding ; dated at 9000 B.C., they are among the oldest ground axes found anywhere. Agricultural tools of wood and stone, radiocarbon-dated at 350 B.C., closely resemble those in use until recent years in the area, where the Stone Age persisted until after the Second World War.

Paris. In March 1969 most of the famous old Paris food market, Les Halles, was removed to the suburb of Rungis, where it occupies a 500-acre plot 6 miles from the centre of the city. The flower, fruit, vegetable, and sea-food wholesalers all moved, leaving behind only the wholesale meat traders, who will move to new quarters at La Villette in 1970. The new £40 million market at Rungis, which is capable of handling 1$\frac{1}{2}$ million tons of food per year and will be expanded to

New Developments in Paris

Most of the sections of the Paris central markets moved in March 1969 from the famous old Les Halles in the centre of the city to the suburb of Rungis, six miles out; *left*, scene during the first night of the operation of the new vegetable market. New railway developments also marked the year.

Below: left, the new Gare Montparnasse, where the platforms are surrounded by huge new blocks of offices; *right*, Place de la Nation station on the new east-west express Metro, the first section of which, from Boissy-St.-Léger to La Nation, was opened in December.

Bottom: the new airport, Paris Nord, at Roissy-en-France was taking shape during the year. *Left*, building the supports that will carry Runway 1 over the A1 motorway. *Right*. model of the first passenger terminal, with car parks in the upper storeys.

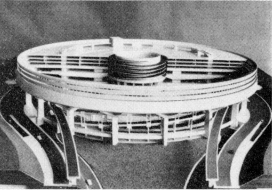

handle 2 million tons, has the latest equipment, including a container-handling facility at the rail spur specially built to serve the market, and a computerised telex-linked indicator board showing arrival quantities and prevailing prices, not only at Rungis but at other markets in France and in the Common Market. The new market is financed half by the Government and half by bank loans. According to a decision of the Paris city council on July 11 a complete underground city, including business, sport, and cultural centres, will be constructed under Les Halles.

At Parly II, a modern suburb near Versailles, the largest regional commercial centre in Europe was opened in 1969. The huge building, with a floor area of nearly 14 acres, contains four department stores and a hundred shops, two cinemas, restaurants, and branch offices of banks and insurance companies. The car park covers over 17 acres. This is the first of 14 such centres planned for the greater Paris area.

The new Gare Montparnasse, the biggest post-war railway project in France, was officially opened in March 1969. Passengers arriving and departing by car are carried to and from the sub-basement car park and taxi-stand by escalators; a "travelator" links the adjacent Metro station. The large concourse and platforms of the new station are two floors above the street level. The Montparnasse station handles about 7,000 arriving and 7,000 departing passengers each day in winter; in summer the number rises to 100,000, since the station is the terminus of lines running to holiday resorts on the Channel and Bay of Biscay.

The first stage of a new "metro express" suburban railway that will cross Paris from west to east was opened in December. The complete line will run from Saint Germain-en-Laye in the west to Boissy-St.-Léger in the east; the section opened joins Paris (La Nation station) to Boissy-St-Léger. Speeds of up to 65 m.p.h. are attainable on the new line.

The foundations of a new airport, to be called Paris Nord, at Roissy-en-France, about 12 miles from the city by the A1 motorway, were laid in 1969 and completion of the first stage is expected in 1972. This will include a $2\frac{1}{2}$-mile-long runway, a freight terminal, maintenance hangars, and a passenger building capable of handling 6 million passengers a year. The whole airport, with an area of over 7,400 acres, is expected to be finished by 1985, when it will have five terminal buildings capable of coping with a total of 30–35 million passengers and over 2 million tons of freight a year. A central building will house offices, restaurants, cinema, hotel, and exhibition halls. The permanent staff will number more than 50,000.

The new terminals will be "drive-in" buildings with car parking in the upper storeys. Having dealt with the formalities of baggage, passport, etc., without leaving his car, a passenger will park it "upstairs" and take one of the 15 lifts down to the departure level, where automatic transport will carry him to the appropriate telescopic covered corridor leading to his aircraft. The airport will have four east–west runways, the longest being nearly 3 miles, and one north-south runway for light aircraft. Runway 1 will be carried on a bridge over the A1 motorway; three other bridges will also cross the same road. As Roissy comes into operation, the Le Bourget airport will become a vertical take-off and landing airport.

Passports. New regulations to impose stricter control over passports were announced by the Canadian Secretary of State for External Affairs in January 1969. The principal change requires passport applicants to produce documentary evidence of their claim to Canadian citizenship: birth certificates or Canadian citizenship certificates are acceptable for those born in Canada, or proof of Canadian registration for those born abroad. Because of the increase in the number of passports lost or stolen each year and the consequent security hazard, the renewal of passports was abolished. They are now limited to a single five-year term, after which new ones must be obtained. The fee for a standard Canadian passport was increased from $5 to $10, and a businessman's passport now costs $12.

Pearls. A pear-shaped, 203·84-gram pearl said to be La Peregrina, the controversial "Wandering Pearl" worn by Mary Tudor, was sold at a New York auction on Jan. 23, 1969, for £15,400; the anonymous purchaser was later revealed to be Richard Burton. Found in the 16th century, the pearl was given to Philip II of Spain who, in turn, presented it to Mary I of England. On her death it was returned to Spain and remained with the Spanish crown jewels until Joseph Bonaparte abdicated in 1813. Controversy about La Peregrina arose when the Duke of Alba, chamberlain to ex-Queen Victoria Eugénie, claimed that the true pearl was locked away in a safe-deposit box; but the auctioneers said they were convinced of the authenticity of the pearl sold in January.

Pelican Crossings. A new type of push-button pedestrian-controlled crossing, called Pelican (PEdestrian LIght CONtrolled), came into operation in London on July 14, 1969, when the Minister of Transport switched on the first one outside the Royal Albert Hall. Others will be placed in London, Reading, Bristol, and Lincoln. The Pelican is intended to replace the complicated and unpopular X-way crossings, which will be phased out over the next two years; instead of the white "X" signal the Pelican crossing will show a green signal to drivers until a pedestrian presses a button to start the signal sequence. Under the Pelican system a driver sees lights resembling conventional traffic lights—green, amber, and red—but in addition a flashing amber light which means that he must give way to pedestrians, and may proceed only if the crossing is clear. To the pedestrian a red figure of a man indicates that he may not cross; after pressing the button he must wait for the "green man" signal which means that he may cross with care, having priority. When the lights are about to change the green man flashes and the pedestrian should not start to cross. The pushbutton control box is painted yellow and carries an explanatory notice of the pedestrian-operated signals.

Pennies. At a sale of English coins at Glendening's, the London auctioneers, in March 1969 a George V 1933 penny was sold for £2,600. The penny, which officially does not exist, was described as "extremely fine, toned and exceedingly, rare." Officially, only six 1933 pennies were produced; three were laid under foundation stones, one is in the British Museum, and two are in the Royal Mint's own collection.

Pensions. The U.K. government published its new earnings-related pensions scheme as a White Paper on Jan. 28, 1969. The scheme, described as the most fundamental change in social security since the present scheme began over 20 years ago, is due to operate from April 1972. It will require increases in national insurance contributions of up to 19s 2d a week for all but the lowest paid, and women for the first time will pay at the same rates as men. Employees will pay $6\frac{3}{4}$ per cent of their earnings as contributions up to a ceiling salary of £33 a week, while employers will pay $6\frac{3}{4}$ per cent of their total pay-roll with no earnings ceiling. All contributions will be collected through P.A.Y.E., so abolishing the insurance stamp card. To offset rising prices there will be a two-yearly review of pensions and contributions. The scheme fully matures in 1992, and those who reach retirement before that date will receive only a proportionate increase in their pensions. There will be partnership with existing private pension schemes, and those people who change their employment will be entitled by law to preserve their pension rights. Widows will receive all their husbands' earnings-related benefits for life, and provision is made for the first time for widows who are under 50 when their husbands die.

A White Paper published on Nov. 5, 1969, set out terms for partial contracting out of the new scheme. Terms were given for the 12 million members of private occupational pension schemes, including the 5,300,000 already contracted out of the present State scheme. The White Paper proposed that these people should not pay the full State contributions (but 1·3 per cent less) so that they will receive a lower pension from State (1 per cent less for men, and 0·55 per cent less for women), with the private schemes making up the amount to at least the total State pension received by those contracted in. Although the higher contributions would be compulsory from the start of the scheme, the full benefits would only be enjoyed after contributions had been made for 20 years; then a man earning $1\frac{1}{2}$ times the national average wage would receive a pension amounting to 60 per cent of the national average wage plus 25 per cent of the difference between that and $1\frac{1}{2}$ times the national average wage.

Increased allowances for some of Britain's 520,000 war pensioners and widows came into operation in November 1969. An unemployable disabled pensioner who is under 65 with a dependent wife now receives at least £21 10s compared with the previous £19 10s 6d. The basic rate, with no additional benefits, for a private soldier on a 100 per cent disability pension rose by 16s to £8 8s a week; the less severely disabled received proportionate increases. A war widow's basic pension increased from £5 17s to £6 10s, and a widow with two children on maximum allowances now receives another £1 5s, making her pension £14 14s a week. In a full year the increased pensions will cost £11 million.

Perranporth, Cornwall. A 14th-century open-air theatre at Piran Round near here was brought into use for only the second time in several centuries in the summer of 1969. *The Cornish Cycle*, a cycle of three religious plays written in 1350, was performed for the first time for three centuries. The theatre consists of a raised circular bank capable of seating 1,500 people round a deep ditch that surrounds a circular stage of about 2,000 sq. ft. Restoration of the site cost £1,500.

Perth, Western Australia. It was reported in June 1969 that Perth, capital of Western Australia, will spend $A23 million on a cultural centre to be built north of the central railway station and to incorporate a museum, a new State library building, a new art gallery, and a new building for the Education Department. The first stage, costing $A1,600,000, will be the museum.

Pesticides. DDT and the other chlorinated hydrocarbons, aldrin and lindane, were banned in Denmark from Nov. 1, 1969, on the grounds that they are dangerous to animal and plant life and, in the long term, to human health. The ban applies to the manufacture and sale of the products, whether they are intended for industrial, home, or agricultural use. Sweden introduced a similar ban in March 1968.

On Dec. 17, 1969, the U.K. Advisory Committee on Pesticides and Toxic Chemicals published their report on the chemicals aldrin, camphechlor, chlordane, DDT, dieldrin, endosulfan, endrin, TDE, and heptachlor. Although the committee found that the use of these pesticides did not constitute the serious health hazard many people had feared, it recommended the withdrawal of some uses of aldrin, dieldrin, and DDT on farm crops when an alternative becomes available, and urged that DDT should cease to be used in paints, lacquers, oil-based sprays, and in dry cleaning. It also included in its recommendations the banning of dieldrin and DDT for mothproofing and insect control in the home. This report led the Minister of Agriculture to announce on the same day that DDT as an ingredient in fly sprays, used in the home and garden, was to be phased out in 1970, and that other uses of DDT and pesticides in the organo-chlorine group, including aldrin and dieldrin, would be subject to further restrictions. On Dec. 18 the West German government also banned the use of DDT and other organo-chlorine pesticides.

Peter, St. A commission appointed by the Pope stated in November 1969 that one of the Roman Catholic Church's most revered relics in St. Peter's Basilica —St. Peter's throne—could not in fact have been used by St. Peter. It found that the throne dated from the Emperor Charles the Bald, in A.D. 875, and only came to be known as St. Peter's throne through an accident of historical usage. After suspicions of the wooden throne's authenticity were raised in 1968, it was submitted to carbon-14 and other radiological tests which revealed its true date.

Pipelines. It was estimated in 1969 that the total world mileage of pipelines is over 1 million miles, 70 per cent of which carries natural gas, 20 per cent crude oil, and 10 per cent refined petroleum products. In 1968 new pipelines laid totalled 27,000 miles, of which 17,000 miles were laid in North America. The new American pipes included 1,000 miles in the offshore area of Louisiana; a 1,000-mile 36-inch line for natural gas from western to eastern Canada via the U.S.A.; and a doubling of the capacity of the 2,000-mile line carrying crude oil

Pipelines. Laying the Israeli oil pipeline from Eilat to Ashkelon, which bypasses the blocked Suez Canal. The 42 in. pipe will carry 25 million tons a year.

from Edmonton to Chicago and Ontario. Other pipes completed in 1968 were the 1,060-mile 8-inch oil products line from Dar-es-Salaam, Tanzania, to Ndola, Zambia, the longest pipe in Africa; the 280-mile 40-inch transalpine line carrying crude oil from Trieste to Ingolstadt, southern Germany; and a total of 2,000 miles of line, of which half is 48-inch, in Russia.

In 1969 a 280-mile 10-inch natural gas line, the first major trunkline in Australia, was laid between Roma and Brisbane, and in the U.K. a 245-mile pipe between Merseyside and the Thames estuary came into operation in March. In this last, oil and oil products—petrol, paraffin, diesel oil, aviation spirit, and gas oil—are pumped 24 hours a day in batches of 700,000 gallons minimum at a speed of 8 m.p.h. Products of the four major companies using the line (Shell-Mex and B.P., Texaco-Regent, Mobil, and Petrofina) are separated in the pipe by big inflatable rubber balls; control of the valves is managed by a computer at Kingsbury, near Tamworth, Staffs. This pipeline, which took three years to build, cost £16 million.

Projects due for completion soon include an 800-mile 48-inch pipe to carry crude oil from the new wells on the North Slope of Alaska to Valdez on the Gulf of Alaska in the south (to be completed in 1972); a 700-mile 40–42-inch pipe to carry associated natural gas from the oilfields of southern Iran over 9,000-ft. mountains to the Russian border (due to come on stream in 1970); a 400-mile 34-inch crude oil line in Algeria from desert wells to the Mediterranean; a 200-mile network to carry oil and gas ashore from wells discovered in Bass Strait, Australia; and a 2,500-mile natural gas network in Great Britain, to be laid at the rate of 450 miles a year.

Plans for a cross-U.S.A. pipe were announced by the three major oil

companies drilling for oil on the Alaska North Slope—B.P., Atlantic-Richfield, and Humble—in July 1969. It would run from the Pacific coast of the state of Washington by way of Chicago to the east coast—a distance of about 2,600 miles—and would cost over $1,000 million.

The average diameter of pipes increases every year. The norm of 30 inches of a few years ago is now 42 inches, and one short line of 52-inch diameter has been laid under the sea off Kuwait to supply the gigantic 300,000-ton tankers that ply from the Persian Gulf to Bantry Bay.

Planetarium. The planetarium at Armagh, Northern Ireland, which was opened on May 1, 1968, and in that year won the British Travel Association's "Come to Britain" award, received in 1969 the Ulster Award presented annually by the New Ireland Society and the Northern Ireland Tourist Board for "an outstanding educational, cultural, and tourist asset to the country." By the beginning of March 1969 more than 35,000 people had visited the planetarium. Plans have been made to extend the museum section with a permanent display of ancient astronomical instruments.

Police. The Sussex constabulary experimented during 1969 with a mobile facsimile system which is being developed by Muirhead Ltd., Beckenham, Kent. With the equipment, which uses existing radio wavelengths, photographs, Identikit pictures, lists of missing cars, and sketches of road blocks or buildings under observation, transmitted from the operations room at county headquarters, Lewes, to mobiles over a wide area are reproduced by a machine in each car. The equipment is automatically switched on by headquarters, and can transmit at any time, to an unmanned car or to a single manned car on the move. It cannot be intercepted by criminals monitoring police speech channels.

Ponies. The U.K. House of Commons gave on May 9, 1969, an unopposed third reading to the Ponies Bill, under which ponies can be exported only for breeding, riding, or exhibition. The purpose of this private member's bill was to prevent the export of ponies to the Continent for slaughter, by placing on them a high minimum price which would make slaughter uneconomic. The price was fixed at £100 for horses and £70 for ponies, but the latter figure was amended to £40 for Shetland ponies under 10½ hands. The defined height of other ponies is 14½ hands. It was stated in the debate that by 1970 the National Coal Board will be disposing of 2,000 pit ponies displaced by machines, and these will be covered by the Bill.

Population. Statements at a Budapest conference of the International Planned Parenthood Federation in September

1969 included these striking observations: at the present rate of world population growth there will be more people alive in 1980 than have died since the beginning of history; and if the rate of population growth is to be kept within reasonable limits families must be restricted to an average of 2·2 children. Other population forecasts made during the year included the official statement that the population of Great Britain is expected to increase by 13 million to reach 68,190,000 in the year 2000. The under-20s will form one-third of the total, compared with 30·9 per cent in 1969; the over-65s will form 11·9 per cent, compared with 12·5 per cent in 1969. In the over-50s age group women will outnumber men, but among the under-50s there will be 1 million more men than women; in the marriageable age group of 15–34 there will be 400,000 more men than women. By the year 2000 New Zealand's population will be 4,750,000, assuming a yearly 5,000 net inward migration, according to projections made by the Department of Statistics in March 1969. The report said that New Zealand will have a population of more than 3,000,000 by 1975, and predicted a steady increase in the annual growth rate, reaching a peak in the period 1980–85, declining in the following decade, and rising again in the period 1995–2000. The population of India, which was over 520 million in 1969, will reach 723 million by 1981; in the light of this forecast it was unfortunate that the Indian Government's programme of contraception and sterilisation received a setback in 1969, when the number of people taking advantage of it fell by about 30 per cent.

England and Wales. Figures published by the U.K. Registrar-General in January 1970 showed that the population of England and Wales was 48,826,800 in June 1969, an increase of 234,000 over June 1968. This figure compares with an average annual increase of only 170,000 between mid-1951 and mid-1956, and of 358,000 between mid-1961 and mid-1966. The latter period included the "boom" year for net immigration (the year ending on June 30, 1962), when 207,000 were added to the population by this means alone. The number of people living in Greater London on June 30, 1969, was estimated at 7,703,000, and the number living in the outer London area at 5,253,000.

Australia. The total population at the end of 1968 was estimated at 12,174,000 an increase of about 244,000 since the end of 1967. These figures were issued in Canberra in March 1969 by the Bureau of Census and Statistics. New South Wales, with 4,430,000, had the biggest State population at the end of 1968, and Victoria was the second most populated State with 3,357,000.

New Zealand. The Government Statistician announced in September 1969 that the total population at June 30, 1969, was 2,776,737. In the past three years the gains in total population from all sources were: 1966–67—49,454 (1·9 per cent increase); 1967–68—25,195 (0·9 per cent increase); 1968–69—25,898 (0·9 per cent increase). At June 30, 1969, there were, for the first time since 1945, approximately 2,000 more females than males in the total population; this is explained by the greater emigration of males. But in the Maori population alone there were almost 3,000 more males than females.

Norway. According to figures given by the Norwegian Central Bureau of Statistics in January 1969 the population of the country increased by some 33,000 during 1968 to approximately 3,835,000. A quarter of the population are under 15 years of age, and a quarter over 53 years.

U.S.A. The Census Bureau reported on Sept. 3, 1969, that the population on July 1, 1969, was 201,921,000, an increase of more than 2 million since July 1968, and an increase of 22 million since the 1960 census. The population of California (19,994,000) exceeded that of New York State (18,321,000) for the first time. After those two the states with the greatest population were Pennsylvania (11,803,000); Texas (11,187,000); and Illinois (11,047,000).

Port Adelaide, South Australia. In June 1969 the South Australian Government signed a $A100 million agreement for a housing development project at Port Adelaide. One of the biggest civil engineering projects ever undertaken in South Australia, it will be a joint venture of the State Government and private investors. On a 1,600-acre site, now swampy wasteland and sandhills owned by the State government, will be constructed more than 4,000 houses, a 40-acre regional shopping centre, and two schools; after the dredging of a lake about 3 miles long and covering 200 acres, a 2,000-metre championship rowing course, a small boat basin, and extensive foreshore recreational areas will be created. A light industrial area also will be provided. The development is to follow the course of an old river bed which will be dredged of 6 million cubic yd. of soil to fill about 1,000 acres of nearby land.

Portglenone, co. Antrim, N. Ireland. In the spring of 1969 the Northern Ireland Ministry of Agriculture opened a forest at Portglenone on the banks of the river Bann as a recreational area. Comprising about 100 acres, it includes a nature reserve managed by the Ministry and the Royal Society for the Protection of Birds, and a landing stage which gives access to the forest from the river.

Port Moresby, Papua. On Aug. 10, 1969, the new St. Mary's War Memorial Roman Catholic Cathedral was blessed and opened. The cathedral, which uses native art and artifacts in its design, can seat up to 600 people in the pews, which are arranged in the form of a fan, so that no one in the congregation is more than 50 ft. from the altar.

Postmen. A new all-grey uniform for postmen in the U.K. was introduced in Scotland, Northern Ireland, and the North of England in the spring of 1969. Made of worsted and Terylene it is single-breasted and no longer has the traditional red piping, the last link with the first scarlet uniform of 1793. By the autumn of 1970 every postman will have been issued with the new uniform.

Potash. Construction work was formally inaugurated at Great Britain's first potash mine at Boulby near Staithes, North Yorkshire, on April 16, 1969. The mine, known as Cleveland Potash, is a joint venture by I.C.I. and a mining company, Charter Consolidated. Twin 18-ft.-diameter shafts are being sunk to a depth of 4,000 ft., where the potash

Police. Radio transmitting system for sending photos of wanted persons and similar information in facsimile from headquarters to mobile patrols.

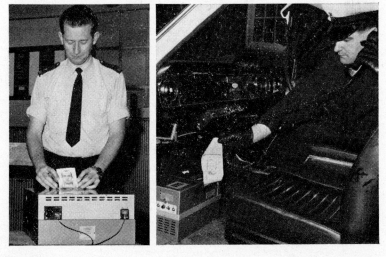

seams are; the shafts have to pass through hundreds of feet of water-bearing sandstone, but new techniques ensure that the mine is kept absolutely dry. A saving of £14 million a year in potash imports will be possible when the mine comes into production at the end of 1973.

Potholing. On Aug. 10, 1969, Anna Taparkova, aged 23, of Bulgaria claimed a world record for the deepest cave descent by a woman when she reached a depth of 3,681 ft. in the Gouffre Berger Cave, near Grenoble, France. The previous record was held by Jacqueline Bocquet, of Grenoble, with a depth of 3,123 ft. The French speleologists Jacques Chabert (28) and Philippe Englender (30) figured again in 1969 in the "cavern-squatting" records. On January 15 they were brought to the surface from a cave 260 ft. below the surface near Grasse, in the South of France, where they had spent five months. Again in March, with Gerard Cappa, they endured a 6-day period of complete isolation in simulation of an orbital flight, and observations of their sleeping and working periods were made.

Prisons. On Oct. 8, 1969, the U.K. Home Secretary opened Great Britain's first experimental industrial prison, Coldingley, near Bisley, Surrey. In the £1,600,000 prison, inmates working a 40-hour, five-day week are trained to trade union standards in laundry work, the manufacture of steel shelving, and making road signs. The prisoners can earn up to 33s per week, paid in cash, which can be spent at the canteen.

The parole system introduced in Great Britain in 1968 was admitted in 1969 to be somewhat less than successful. Figures given in April showed that of 10,484 prisoners considered for parole up to the end of March 1969, 8,922 were

Potholing. Three French "speleonauts" emerging from a 6-day underground "simulated orbital flight." They are (*left to right*) Gerard Cappa, Jacques Chabert, and Philippe Englender; the latter two had earlier spent 5 months 260 ft. down.

refused. Of the 1,562 prisoners granted parole, 41 were recalled, just over half of them because they committed further offences. Nearly 900 who qualified to be considered for parole refused to allow their cases to be examined.

Pulitzer Prizes. The 1969 Pulitzer prize for drama went to Howard Sackler for his play *The Great White Hope*, based on the life of Jack Johnson, the Negro heavyweight boxing champion. The prize for fiction was won by N. Scott Momaday, for *House made of Dawn*. General non-fiction prizes went to René Jules Dubos for *So Human an Animal*, and to Norman Mailer for *The Armies of the Night*. The prize for poetry was awarded to George Oppen for his volume of verse *Of Being Numerous*. The biography prize went to B. L. Reid for *The Man from New York: John Quinn and his Friends*, and the history prize to Leonard W. Levy for *The Origins of the Fifth Amendment*. Prof. Karel Husa, Czechoslovak-born director of the Cornell Symphony, won the music award. The *Los Angeles Times* won two prizes in journalism, one for meritorious public service for a series of articles exposing irregularities within Los Angeles city government commissions, and the other to William Tuohy for his international reporting as a war correspondent in Vietnam, first of all for *Newsweek* and then for the paper. The prize for national reporting went to Robert Cahn of the *Christian Science Monitor*, for a series on national parks. John Fetterman, of the *Louisville Times and Courier-Journal*, took the award for general local reporting; John Fischetti, of the *Chicago Daily News*, the cartoon award; Edward T. Adams, of Associated Press, the spot news photography award; and Moneta Sleet, jr., of *Ebony* magazine, the award for feature photography.

Pyrosomas. Rare denizens of the ocean were seen by big-game fishermen about 5 miles off-shore from the Sydney suburb of Malabar in July 1969. These were giant pyrosomas, members of a genus of free swimming, brilliantly phosphorescent, pelagic, compound ascidians, the colonies of which form a hollow cylinder closed at one end. The fishermen estimated one of the pyrosomas to be 45 ft. long, making it the largest ever discovered. Little is known about these creatures. They are made of millions of individual living organisms which take water in through their mouths to obtain food. The first sighting of this species of giant pyrosoma was made by the *Challenger* Expedition of 1873–76. Until 1967, when three specimens were seen near Sydney, it had been known only from the North and South Atlantic, the Indian Ocean and the north-west Pacific Ocean. The 1969 sightings are only the second from the South Pacific.

Quebec, Canada. The upper house of the Quebec legislature was abolished at the

end of 1968. The intention of introducing this reform had been announced in February 1968; the lower house (the Legislative Assembly) passed the bill on November 28, and the upper house (the Legislative Council) on December 13. At the same time the lower (and now only) house was renamed the National Assembly of Quebec.

"Queen Elizabeth." The 28-year-old 83,000-ton former transatlantic liner was finally sold in July 1969 to an American company, the Queen Ltd., for £3½ million. The company plans to transform the liner, which will remain at Fort Lauderdale, Florida, into a complex of shops, theatres, and restaurants, with an hotel and convention facilities. In addition, 209 acres of adjoining land in the Fort Lauderdale–Hollywood area will be developed for use as an entertainment area.

Queen's Awards to Industry. The fourth annual list of companies that have won these awards for achievement in the export field, or for technological innovation, or for both, was published on April 21, 1969. From about 1,000 applications, 99 were selected for awards, 69 being for export achievement, 24 for technological innovation, and 6 for both. Four companies maintained their record of receiving an award each year since the inception of the scheme: they were I.C.I., Marconi, Rolls-Royce, and Martin-Baker Aircraft Co. Award-winners included small as well as large companies: 30 per cent of the awards went to companies employing fewer than 250 people. Even smaller successful companies, employing fewer than 50 people, included a slate quarry at Coniston and a firm that makes about a third of the world's production of eutectic ferro-titanium (used in stainless steel manufacture). Other award-winners ranged from ATV (for export of films) and BBC (for technological innovation) to M.Y. Dart Co. of Barnet who make and sell dartboards and darts, 80 per cent of which are exported; from Glaxo (pharmaceuticals) and Gillette (razor blades) to Holland and Holland (sporting rifles); from Short Bros. and Harland (anti-aircraft weapons) to J. C. Wells (bespoke tailoring).

Queen's University, Belfast. This university purchased the library of Thomas Percy, the eminent 18th-century literary scholar, for £90,000, at an auction at Sotheby's in London on June 23. The library, which was the only collection of its kind left in private hands, contains over 1,800 titles bound in about 880 volumes. Thomas Percy, who lived from 1729 to 1811, was Bishop of Dromore, co. Tyrone, and after his death the library was bought by the Earl of Caledon, in whose family it remained. The university raised the money for the purchase from private donors, banks, grants, and its own funds.

Rabies. On Oct. 15, 1969, at Camberley, Surrey, a mongrel dog, released from quarantine kennels in Kent after the 6-month period required after being brought to the U.K. from Germany, died of rabies, the first case in Britain for 47 years. Before dying the dog ran amok for about half-an-hour, during which it killed a cat and bit two people. Because of the possibility that it had also bitten other animals the Ministry of Agriculture mounted a campaign to rid 2,000 acres of common land in the area of wild life, using a type of cyanide gas, and employing beaters to drive the animals into the open where they were shot. Six months' quarantine was also imposed on all dogs in the district, during which time they were all ordered to be muzzled. None of the 130 animals and birds killed in the shoot showed any sign of the disease. Two other cases of rabies at the same kennels occurred later, and all dogs released from the kennels during the past four months had to be muzzled and leashed. Finally on Dec. 4 the Minister of Agriculture announced that the quarantine period was to be extended from 6 to 8 months, and the 33 dogs which had been released from the kennels, or which might have been in contact with the Camberley dog, were recalled for the full 8 months. From Dec. 15, the importation into the U.K. of a wide range of exotic animals susceptible to rabies, including bush babies, marmosets, gorillas, genets, and chipmunks, was forbidden unless they were consigned to approved zoos or research establishments.

Race Relations. An 838-page report, "Colour and Citizenship," published by the U.K. Institute of Race Relations on July 10, 1969, stated that by 1986 the coloured population of Great Britain will have increased to over 2 million, representing between 4 and $4\frac{1}{2}$ per cent of the population. The report recommended that aliens and Commonwealth citizens should be put on an equal footing, and that responsibility for integration policy should be transferred from the Home Office to the Department of Health and Social Security. Other proposals included the setting up of a department of education to cover the teaching of immigrant children, with large education authorities possibly employing a special adviser or classroom policy for these children; that town halls should consider rehousing on the basis of need, not length of residence; that in the field of employment both unions and management should ensure equal opportunity, and records distinguishing employees by their ethnic origin should be kept at all levels of employment; that the training of the police should give more emphasis to social studies, and that there should be special recruiting programmes to encourage immigrant and coloured recruits into the police force. The report recorded that the number of people who were tolerantly inclined towards immigrants had risen from 50 per cent in 1958 to 73 per cent in 1968, while those inclined to prejudice had fallen from 49 per cent to 27 per cent.

Figures published by the U.K. Race Relations Board on Nov. 25, 1969, showed that during its first year of work 1,562 complaints of racial discrimination had been received. Of these, 334 complaints fell outside the scope of the Act or were withdrawn, and 531 were still being considered. Of the remaining 697 cases the Board found that discrimination had occurred in 152, but not in 545 others. Of the 152 cases of proved discrimination, 31 of them were employment complaints. The Board also stated that victims of racial discrimination had been given cash payments of up to £100 as compensation from those responsible, mostly in instances where the discrimination was considered to have involved loss of earnings or job opportunities.

Radar. It was announced in February 1969 that scientists at Loughborough University, working on an early warning system that would enable aircraft pilots to change course to avoid flocks of birds, had discovered that birds, bats, and insects all produce different and identifiable radar echoes. High-speed photographs of the wing-beat patterns of different species of birds and insects were compared with the echoes produced on the radar screen, and it was found that the reflected radar beam fluctuates according to the pattern of the wing beat. Comparatively simple equipment is sensitive enough even to identify, for example, a male from a female locust in flight.

Radio Awards. The Writers Guild of Great Britain radio awards for 1968 were presented on March 5, 1969. They were as follows:

Features script—David Franklin, for *Cambridge Revisited.* Comedy or drama series or serial script—Stewart Farrar, for *Watch the Wall, my Darling.* Drama script—John Boland for *Uncle Guy.*

Radio Telescope. The world's largest radio telescope of its kind is to be sited on the former Bedford to Cambridge branch railway line which directly adjoins the Mullard Radio Astronomy Observatory, the director of which, Sir Martin Ryle, F.R.S., will control the new project. The Science Research Council is to pay for the telescope which will cost about £2,100,000. These decisions were announced on February 6, when it was said that the telescope should be completed by 1971. It will consist of four movable and four fixed reflectors, each 42 ft. in diameter, strung out in a line over 3 miles; a computer will keep them in step with the Earth's rotation. New rails are to be laid on the old track, and it is on these that the movable reflectors will run. The chief purpose of the radio telescope will be to examine the structure of quasars. The control room is to be on the site of the former Lord's Bridge station, disused since the closure of the Cambridge to Bedford line.

"Rangatira." This is the name of a new inter-island ferry to be built by the Newcastle-upon-Tyne firm of Swan Hunter to replace the *Wahine*, which sank in Wellington Harbour, New Zealand, on April 10, 1968, with the loss of 51 lives. The *Rangatira* will have cabin accommodation for 844 passengers and will carry over 200 cars, or equivalent number of sea-freighter units and motor vehicles. It will have a maximum speed of 22 knots. Delivery will be in November or December 1971.

Registration, Certificates of. On April 1, 1969, changes in the registration of births, still-births, and deaths were introduced in England and Wales. The chief change is that the entry in the register must now include the birthplaces of the parents of a baby, and that of the deceased in a death. The shape of birth and death certificates, which for more than 130 years have shown particulars in a horizontal row of headed columns, has been replaced by an almost square form, with spaces for particulars running vertically.

Representation of the People Act. The main provision of this Act of the U.K. Parliament, published as a Bill on Nov. 7, 1968, and enacted on April 17, 1969, was that the minimum age of voting was reduced from 21 years to 18 years at both parliamentary and local government elections. The Act included the raising of the limit on candidates' expenses at parliamentary elections from £450 to £750, and at local government elections from £25 to £30, broadcasting being exempted from the calculation of such expenses. It also extended the polling hours at parliamentary elections from 9 p.m. to 10 p.m.

Reservoirs. Work on the largest artificial lake in France, the Marne reservoir, began near Saint-Dizier, about 120 miles east of Paris, during 1969. The reservoir, which will cover 25 sq. miles, coupled with the Seine reservoir that went into service in 1966, should not only reduce the crest of the Seine at Paris by $3\frac{1}{2}$ ft., so ridding the city of flood dangers, but also ensure water supplies for the 10 million inhabitants of the Paris region during droughts. During the construction of the reservoir three small villages south of Saint-Dizier will be flooded, displacing about 300 people; 12 miles of dikes will be constructed and several roads and bridges relocated. Water from the Marne will be delivered to the reservoir by a canal. The whole

Roads. Typical of the complex multi-level road junctions of today is the Bagnolet interchange in France (*left*), part of the first section of the Paris–Strasbourg motorway. New methods of road construction in the U.S.A. include reinforced concrete (*right*), the steel rod network being laid first and the concrete then poured over it by a road-wide spreader which is constantly fed with fresh concrete from a mobile mixer alongside.

project, including construction and land purchase, will cost an estimated £20 million. In August 1969 it was reported that a new lake-side village named Sainte-Marie-du-Lac is to be built on the shore of the reservoir.

Work on a reservoir which will have a perimeter of more than 3 miles, and a capacity of 8,300 million gallons, began at Datchet, near Windsor, Berks, in November 1969. It will be the largest reservoir owned by the Metropolitan Water Board.

Rhodes Scholars. For the first time since the Second World War German Rhodes scholars will be going to Oxford University from October 1970. It was announced in March 1969 that the Cecil Rhodes trustees had decided to institute two scholarships a year for men from West Germany.

Rifampicin. This is the name of a new antibiotic drug, a synthetic derivative of rifomycin, which was first discovered in Italy in a fungus inhabiting the pine woods of S. France. It is used in Italy for treating tuberculosis, and may have other valuable uses. In March 1969 Glasgow University scientists and an Israeli group in Jerusalem both found that in animals rifampicin appears to inhibit the growth of certain viruses, viz. those causing vaccinia (related to smallpox), smallpox itself, cowpox, and an adenovirus (one of the causes of the common cold). The antibiotic appears to operate by inhibiting an enzyme present in a virus without damaging the body cell containing the virus.

Road Safety. The annual report by the U.K. licensing authorities, published in July 1969, showed that of all goods vehicles subjected to roadside spot checks by Ministry of Transport examiners between Oct. 1, 1967, and Sept. 30, 1968, 37 per cent were found to be unsafe. Of almost $1\frac{1}{2}$ million goods vehicles licensed during this period, nearly 50,000 (9 per cent) of all vehicles checked were found to be so defective that they were ordered off the road. Prosecutions for goods vehicles offences increased by 32 per cent, to 35,849

successful prosecutions, the most common offences being the failure by drivers to keep proper records of driving hours. Since 1963 the number of drivers of goods vehicles receiving summonses has doubled, and those issued against their employers increased by almost a third.

From Oct. 1, 1969, safety belts were included in the annual motor vehicle tests under the U.K. Ministry of Transport. Vehicles required by law to have such belts are not issued with a test certificate unless the belts are fitted. (Belts must be fitted to the front seats of all cars registered after Jan. 1, 1965, and of light vehicles under 30 cwt. registered after April 1, 1967.)

Under new U.K. Ministry of Transport rules, laid before parliament on Aug. 6, 1969, burst-proof doors and collapsible steering columns will have to be fitted to all new cars registered in the U.K. after July 1972. These regulations follow a 10-year study by the Road Research Laboratory which showed that 50 per cent of all people thrown out of a car in a crash are killed; a third are seriously injured; and all the rest are injured to some extent. But only 27 per cent of passengers who remain in a car after a crash are killed; 36 per cent are seriously injured; 29 per cent are slightly injured; and 8 per cent escaped injury altogether.

New regulations requiring a minimum depth of $\frac{1}{16}$ in. in the tread of motor vehicle tyres came into effect in New Zealand on May 1. These regulations cover all motor vehicles capable of speeds of over 20 m.p.h., and trailers with a gross laden weight of more than 10 cwt., unless they are being towed by vehicles incapable of speeds of more than 20 m.p.h. The $\frac{1}{16}$-inch minimum also applies to motor-cycles, but the tyres of powered cycles are required to have only a clearly visible tread pattern. The minimum tread depth is required over at least three-quarters of the width of the tyre.

Two electrical engineers, G. J. Mollison and his son P. R. Mollison, who live in North Perth, Western Australia, gave details in March 1969 of their invention of a mechanism which, when a car is in a collision, automatically switches off the ignition and applies the brakes. On impact the movement of a

spring-based stationary weight triggers off the mechanism which is wired to the electrical and braking systems, but it is activated only by a sideways or frontal knock so that light bumper clashes, or downward jolts, do not set it off.

A British firm has developed a device to warn drivers when the air pressure in their tyres drops below the required pressure. When this happens a small fitting on the top of the tyre valves springs up and actuates a tiny radio transmitter which switches on a flashing light or buzzer fixed to the dashboard. A device to give warning that a vehicle is reversing was demonstrated in Auckland, New Zealand, in February. The word "Backing" appears in red with a flashing white light beneath it when reverse gear is engaged; a horn also sounds at intervals. The inventor, E. J. Murtagh,

Road-Rail Vehicle. This bus, fitted with both tyred wheels and flanged railway wheels, is for linking Australian rural branch lines. The whole bus is jacked up when the rail wheels are to be brought into use.

said that it had been approved by the New Zealand Carriers' Association and Lorry Drivers' Association.

Roman Catholic Church. According to figures revealed in the September 1969 issue of the international journal *Herder Correspondence* the number of Roman Catholic priests throughout the world who had applied to be released from their vows on grounds of celibacy between 1963 and 1968 was 7,137. In 1968 the rise in applications reached the record number of 1,026 secular priests, of whom 82 per cent were released, and 1,237 priests in religious orders, of whom 71 per cent were released. In January, February, and March 1969 the number of applications from secular priests was 675, and the Turin newspaper *La Stampa* forecast that 3,000 priests would probably leave the Church to get married by the end of the year.

The Vatican announced in February 1969 new rules for entry into religious orders. Heads of religions are authorised to call in "a prudent and qualified psychologist known for his moral principles" to help them decide whether or not a novice monk or nun has an "authentic" religious vocation. Novices may also replace the traditional vows of chastity and obedience by binding promises, until their minds are committed, and they are also allowed to live outside the religious homes so that they may "achieve gradual spiritual and psychological adaptation to the religious life of today's world."

On Aug. 21, 1969, some of the rigid rules governing 15,000 cloistered nuns were relaxed, permitting the superior of a convent to allow nuns to leave the convent on a special occasion or on a regular basis after asking the authorisation of the local bishop. It is no longer regarded as a mortal sin for nuns to go outside their cloistered convents, and the rule under which laymen could be excommunicated for entering cloistered convents was suspended. The Pope, however, rejected any suggestion that enclosure should be ended, or that cloistered nuns should be allowed to turn to social work for the needy.

The U.S. National Conference of Catholic Bishops announced on Jan. 31, 1969, that for the first time in the U.S.A. women were permitted to take an active part in the services of the Church. Following a request by the American bishops the Vatican had agreed that women, particularly those who were members of religious orders, should be allowed to serve as lectors, commentators, and song leaders at Mass where men were not available.

The revised missal (prayer-book) requested by the Second Vatican Council was published on May 2, 1969, and came into use on November 30. It includes the reformed Mass, which allows parish priests some freedom in arranging the service and provides for greater congregation-participation. For example, lay men and women are permitted to read the lessons from the Old and New Testaments, although that drawn from the Gospels is still reserved for priests. Changes in the wording and in the rites of the Eucharist are included in the new missal, which was described as clearer in expression, more realistic, and more authentic in its emphasis on the Bible. The ceremony of the Mass had remained almost unchanged since 1570.

A new marriage rite which came into effect at the beginning of July, allows the couple, instead of saying only "Yes" or "I do," to say : "I take you for my lawful wife, to have and to hold, from this day forward, for better, for worse, for richer, for poorer, in sickness or in health, till death do us part." The Vatican's Congregation of Rites, which approved the new rite on March 19, said that the changes would open the way in Latin countries and other nations for ceremonies similar to those which are traditional for Roman Catholics and Protestants in Britain, U.S.A., and other English-speaking countries. Under new rules published by the Vatican in June babies being baptised will no longer be asked by the priest to renounce Satan, all his works and all his pomp. These ritual questions will now be addressed directly to the parents, who will play a more active part in the ceremony.

The nomination of 33 new cardinals, bringing the total to the record number of 134, was announced on March 28, 1969, and the ceremonies of their induction took place at the end of April. The list included five Italians, five from Latin America, four from N. America, three from France, two from Spain, and one each from China, Korea, the Philippines, Madagascar, the Congolese Republic, and Scotland. The Scottish cardinal, the first since Cardinal David Beaton or Bethune, who was murdered by Protestant reformists in 1546, was Archbishop Gordon Gray of St. Andrews and Edinburgh, who on his appointment in 1951 was one of the world's youngest archbishops and is a leader in the movement towards Christian unity. In addition to the customary pledges of faith and obedience the new Cardinals had for the first time to take a vow of secrecy, promising not to divulge, without the consent of the Holy See, any instructions entrusted to them directly or indirectly.

On April 5 the Pope ordered that the dress of cardinals should be simplified in accordance with "the changing circumstances of the times." The broadbrimmed, flat, red plush hat, the 30-tasselled galero, the most symbolic of all the items of cardinals' dress, was abolished; instead, a cardinal will receive a red biretta from the Pope. The phrase "receiving the red hat" has, for centuries, been synonymous with being elevated to the College of Cardinals, although, in fact, it was never worn by a contemporary cardinal but remained on display in his titular church in Rome, and was hung over his tomb after his death.

In all, 35 modifications in dress, style of address, and coats of arms of cardinals and lesser prelates were listed in a five-page instruction from the Vatican Secretariat, the general trend being a substantial reduction in the use of red and the encouragement of black trimmings and accessories.

At the close of the second international Synod of Bishops in October 1969 the Pope promised that the ordinary synod should meet at least every two years instead of, as hitherto, at the desire of the Pontiff; that the synod secretariat, at present consisting of one bishop and a few secretaries, should become a permanent entity in Rome, and its members augmented to include diocesan bishops from abroad; and that he would give "maximum consideration" to those subjects the bishops wish to be included in the next synod agenda. He had announced on April 28 the setting up of the theological commission which the international synod had called for at their first meeting in October 1967.

Roman Catholics in Great Britain were given in 1969 the right and opportunity to criticise their priests and bishops and to put forward constructive ideas about the government of their Church. Cardinal Heenan, Archbishop of Westminster, in a pastoral letter read on February 16, announced plans to hold elections, and for the laity for the first time in the 1,372 years of the Church's history to be given a voice in the running of the archdiocese of Westminster. After Easter a pastoral council of priests, representatives of religious orders, and laity was set up, and smaller elected councils began to be formed throughout the country.

Australia. Concern over the high rate of defection from the priesthood led the Church to appoint a committee to survey the problem and prepare a programme to combat it. When this decision was announced in November 1969 a spokesman for Sydney Archdiocese said that there was a shortage of priests, as many were leaving the priesthood and relatively few entering it, while the Roman Catholic population was expanding rapidly. While no official figure has been given it is believed that between 180 and 200 priests left the priesthood during 1968 and 1969. Among their number was Dr. John Burnheim, one of the church's leading priests and intellectuals, who abandoned his priesthood after 20 years, and left the Church in November 1969.

More than 80 priests attended a two-day conference at Coogee in October to discuss their vocation from the personal and parish viewpoints, including involvement in secular problems, in-service training, and celibacy. They decided to call a national convention of priests in May 1970 to consider the formation of a National Association of Priests, which, they felt, would give them a greater voice in the decisions made in the Church.

Rome. The new Byzantine-style church attached to the Ukrainian Catholic University in Rome was opened on July 1, 1969, by a Ukrainian archbishop freed from a Russian prison. The cost was found by Ukrainian exiles all over the world.

of 1969. The forest, which is on the slopes of the Mourne Mountains, overlooking the village of Rostrevor, covers an area of more than 4,000 acres. An interesting feature is the Cloghmore Stone, a large granite boulder lying on a bed of slate, which legend says was thrown by the giant Finn McCoul from the far side of Carlingford Lough, but which scientists believe was carried to its present resting-place by the melting ice as it retreated after the Ice Age.

Royal Regiment of Wales. This regiment of the British army was formed in 1969 by the amalgamation of the South Wales Borderers and the Welch Regiment, two regiments with nearly 600 years of service between them. The new regiment's colours were presented by its colonel-in-chief, the Prince of Wales, at a ceremony at Cardiff Castle on June 11. On the new regiment's collar badge the Borderers' circlet of immortelles surrounds the Welch Regiment's dragon.

Rome, Italy. A new Byzantine-style church for Ukrainian exiles was opened here on July 1, 1969. It is joined to the new Ukrainian Catholic University, and both were built mainly with money contributed from Ukrainian exiles in America, Canada, and West Germany. Situated just outside Rome's western city limits, the university and church are the only ones of their kind in Italy.

Roskill Commission. This Commission, set up in May 1968 to examine all suggested sites for a third London airport, published on March 3, 1969, the names of four possible sites for a four-runway airport. They are: Cublington, Bucks, near Leighton Buzzard, and near the electric railway to Birmingham and Lancashire, 12 miles from the M1 and 39 miles from London; Thurleigh, Beds, near the mainline railway from St. Pancras to Leicester, Nottingham, and Yorkshire, 7 miles to the west of the Great North Road, and 51 miles from London; Nuthampstead, north-west of Stansted on the Cambs-Herts border, 39 miles from London; and Foulness, on the Thames estuary off the Essex coast, 42 miles from London. The report said that all these sites were found to offer "advantages in respect of important criteria such as site costs, air traffic control, defence, noise, and surface access (including user and capital costs)." Stansted, Essex, was rejected in favour of Nuthampstead. The Commission then proceeded to investigate the four alternatives, holding hearings at each place to receive evidence from promoters and objectors. See also under Cublington, Foulness, Nuthampstead, Thurleigh.

Rostrevor Forest, co. Down, N. Ireland. The Northern Ireland Ministry of Agriculture opened another forest drive to the public here during the summer

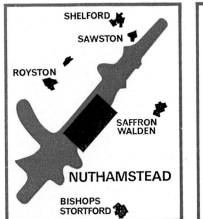

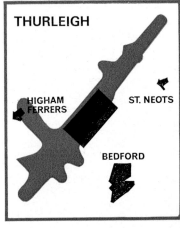

Roskill Commission. Maps based on information given by the Commission inquiring into the siting of the third London Airport. The black oblongs show the positions of the four suggested airports, and the coloured patches the areas that would be affected by aircraft noise.

Courtesy of The Guardian

Sailly-le-Sec, France. In a brief ceremony in Sydney, N.S.W., on June 18, 1969, veterans of the 3rd Division of the A.I.F. repaid a debt of gratitude to a small village in France, incurred during the First World War. A cheque for $A1,000 was handed to the French ambassador to help in the completion of a youth centre at Sailly-le-Sec in Picardy, where members of the Division fought for three months in 1918 and were fed by the villagers. Following a visit to the village by a veteran in 1968, it was decided that former members of the Division—now few in number—should repay the kindness shown to them. The gift of a thousand dollars was raised from their pensions—a graceful tribute after more than half a century.

Saints. In the revision of the Roman Catholic Church's Liturgical Calendar published on May 9, 1969, to come into force on Jan. 1, 1970, the names of over 30 saints were permanently removed on the ground of doubt of their existence. (Over 200 unnamed saints—normally described as "fellow martyrs"—also were removed.) Among the 30 are such popular saints as St. Christopher, patron of travellers; St. Barbara, patron of gunpowder and artillerymen and protector against lightning; St. Catherine of Alexandria, who gave her name to the firework the Catherine wheel; and the lesser known St. Susanna, St. Eusebius, St. Ursula, St. Margaret of Antioch (patron of pregnant women), St. Anastasia, St. Eustace (patron of hunters), St. Martina, St. Venanzio, and St. Domitilla. Masses will not be said on their name days in future; churches bearing their names may continue to do so, but no new church may be dedicated to any of them; and Catholics will be discouraged from giving their names to their children in baptism. For another class of saints the Calendar demoted the feast day from obligatory to optional; included in this is England's and Portugal's patron St. George, the children's, thieves', and pawnbrokers' patron St. Nicholas (Santa Claus), St. Januarius (of liquefaction-of-blood fame), Saint Maria Goretti (a recent creation), St. Louis of France (King Louis IX), and St. Elizabeth of Portugal. The angels Michael, Gabriel, and Raphael will in future all share the same feast day. In general all the accepted saints have their feast days on the day of their death. The Calendar recognised some new saints—St. Sir Thomas More (author of *Utopia* and opponent of Henry VIII), the Martyrs of Uganda, the Martyrs of Nagasaki, the Martyrs of North America, St. Martin Chanel (Oceania), and St. Martin d'Porres (S. America). The effect of the revision is to spread the saints more widely both

geographically and chronologically. In the previous Calendar the majority of saints were early martyrs of the 1st century A.D. in the Mediterranean region; of the 153 saints given obligatory feast days in the new Calendar, 126 are European, 14 Asian, 8 African, 4 North American, and 1 Australian, and the first 10 centuries A.D. now yield 64 saints, and the second 79. The new Calendar results from a 15-year investigation by a 36-member commission under the Sacred Congregation of Rites.

By contrast the Church of England's Liturgical Commission report, published on Jan. 23, proposed 34 new saints for the calendar. Among them were a number of non-Anglicans, including David Livingstone, the missionary-explorer, a Free Churchman; George Fox, the Quaker leader; John and Charles Wesley, the Methodist leaders; and John Bunyan, author of *Pilgrim's Progress.*

On April 10 the Pope authorised changes to the 300-year-old regulations governing sanctification which will shorten by several years the time necessary for a Roman Catholic to achieve sainthood. Under the old laws there were two investigations before beatification (the preliminary to sainthood), one by the bishop of the region in which the candidate was born, and the other by the Sacred Congregation of Rites. The Pope abolished the second trial.

Salvation Army. After a 45-member grand council meeting held at Sunbury-on-Thames, Middlesex, it was announced on July 23 that Commissioner Erik Wickberg, aged 65, had been chosen as the Salvation Army's ninth—and first non-British—general. General Wickberg, who had been chief of staff and second in command for eight years, took up his position in September, when General Frederick Coutts retired at the age of 70. He was born in Sweden.

Saints. Statue of the newly sainted Sir Thomas More, at Chelsea Old Church, London, unveiled in the presence of Cardinal Heenan and the Archbishop of Canterbury.

Samarkand. Building methods used in the latest Moscow skyscrapers are helping to restore the famous Bibi-Khanym Mosque in Samarkand, built in 1404 by order of Tamerlane the Great in memory of his favourite wife. The mosque, which had a cupola weighing 757 tons, has suffered greatly from both earthquakes and subsidence. In the restoration work the cupola was supported on 60 jacks while the structure was reinforced by precast units, steel struts, and cement forced into the old brickwork. Restoration of the facing of the mosque and its frescoes also is being done.

"Saturday Evening Post". This famous U.S. magazine, first published in 1821, a development of the "Pennsylvania Gazette" founded by Benjamin Franklin in 1728, ceased publication with its Feb. 8, 1969, issue. Circulation had fallen by almost 3 million in ten years, and the consequent sharp drop in advertising revenue had brought about a financial loss of more than £2 million in 1968.

S.A.Y.E. The U.K. government introduced its "Save As You Earn" scheme on Oct. 1, 1969. People prepared to enter into a contract to save regularly each month for five years will be entitled, at the end of that period, to a bonus equivalent to one year's savings on which there will be no form of taxation. If the completed savings are left for a further two years the saver will have his tax-free bonus doubled; but if the completed savings are withdrawn between the fifth and seventh year the five-year bonus only will be paid, and savings withdrawn before five years will earn only $2\frac{1}{2}$ per cent compound interest. The minimum amount a person is allowed to save under the scheme is £1 a month, and a maximum £10 a month.

Scarlatti, Alessandro. It was reported in April that a 300-year old manuscript of an oratorio by this Italian composer, who lived from 1659 to 1725, had been discovered in Morristown, New Jersey, U.S.A. The work, entitled *La Giuditta,* and dated March 1693, Naples, Italy, was found in a collection of rare printed materials in the Morristown National Park Library; bound in with it was a three-page handwritten, signed letter by the composer containing performance notes.

Schubert, Franz. The manuscript of a fantasy for piano by Schubert, discovered in the attic of a house in Knittelfeld in southern Austria, in May 1968, was authenticated in early 1969. This major musical discovery, known as the *Grazer Fantasie,* is thought to have been composed by Schubert in about 1817, when he was 20 years old. It was given its first full performance in Graz in the autumn.

Science Fair. Six teams of schoolchildren travelled to London for the final contest of the "Science Fair '69" competition organised by the *Sunday Times* and the BBC. The winners were Golspie High School, Sutherland, Scotland, whose team of two girls and a boy had carried out a long-term project on the trout in Scottish lochs. Their aim was to provide a means of classifying all the lochs in the 2,000 sq. miles of Sutherland, and improve the fishing in them; their work was recognised and supported by the Highlands Development Board. On their return to Golspie the young scientists were given a welcome more usually reserved for victorious football teams. The junior winning team came from J. H. Whitley School, Halifax, whose project was designed to test motorists' vision. The group built their own equipment to test binocular and peripheral vision, their earlier work having suggested a correlation between accidents and poor vision.

Golspie High School, together with H.M.S. Conway School, Anglesey, which came second, won the right to represent Britain in the European Science Fair held in Eindhoven, Holland, in May. On May 24 it was announced that the jury of European professors had been so impressed by the work of both teams that they not only awarded them £1,000 each but also made them special grants for the purchase of materials to continue their work.

Scientology. The U.K. Secretary for the Social Services announced on Jan. 27, 1969, that an inquiry into the "practice and effects" of Scientology was to be held. It would be conducted in private by Sir John Foster, Conservative M.P. No report of his findings had been published by the end of the year. On March 18 a commission of enquiry into Scientology, and its opponents' charges that it had brought undue

Science Fair. The two girls and a boy from Golspie High School, Sutherland, who won the 1969 contest, received a "cup-winners'" welcome on their return home.

pressure to bear on its members and had caused family estrangement, opened in Wellington, New Zealand. The N.Z. ombudsman and a former editor of the *Auckland Star* formed the commission. Nothing was found to support the charges, and the sect was allowed to continue to operate in the country. The originator of the sect, Lafayette Ron Hubbard, and about 200 of his followers, who had been living in two ships moored in Corfu harbour since August 1968, were suddenly expelled as "undesirables" by the Greek government in March 1969.

On November 14, 1969, three High Court judges ruled that the Scientologist's chapel at Saint Hill Manor, East Grinstead, Sussex, was not a place of religious worship, and dismissed an appeal against the Registrar General's refusal to register it as a place of worship under the 1855 Places of Worship Registration Act.

Scouting. The 1969 census figures for the British Scout Association, published in October 1969, showed that membership in the cub scout section had gone up by 2,604; the scout section by 322; venture scouts by 668; adult leaders and administrators by 273; and others by 38. The total number of Scouts in the U.K. was 531,011.

Segrave Trophy. This U.K. award for transport achievement was in 1969 given to Wing Commander Kenneth Wallis, a pioneer of light autogyros and holder of the altitude record for that type of aircraft. The trophy commemorates Sir Henry Segrave (1896–1930), the British holder of speed records in racing cars and motor boats.

Seville, Spain. Work began at the beginning of 1969 on the new canal linking Seville with the sea, approved

by the Cortes in 1965. Expected to cost £20 million, the work will take seven years to complete, will create employment for about 500,000 people, and will open the south-west of Spain for massive farming and industrial development. The canal, which will be 42 miles long, nearly 400 ft. wide, and 32 ft. 6 in. deep, will allow passage for freighters of up to 20,000 tons and of passenger ships of up to 24,000 tons. It will also irrigate some 500,000 acres of land, which will become a major cattle-raising zone. Seville is already Spain's only inland port, but the Guadalquivir river and the Alfonso XIII canal are inadequate to handle all her potential traffic because of the need for constant dredging.

Sewing Machine. The world's smallest sewing machine, the size of a cigarette lighter and weighing only 40 grams ($1\frac{1}{2}$ oz.), is being manufactured in Japan, where it went on sale in 1969. Called the "Finger Stitcher," the machine is operated by pressure from the thumb which, when it depresses a plunger, makes a stitch. A spring returns the plunger for the next stitch.

Sewing Machine. The world's smallest sewing machine, a Japanese device, is operated by pressure from the thumb.

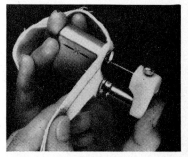

Sheep. It was announced in January 1969 that a group of scientists working for the U.S. Department of Agriculture had developed a chemical, cyclophosphamide, that causes sheep to shed their fleeces spontaneously, or at least by hand-plucking. During the summer of 1968 a series of experiments were carried out at the Animal Husbandry Research Division, Beltsville, Maryland, during which 28 sheep were treated with various doses of the drug, administered both orally and intravenously. It was found that, while strong doses proved to be toxic, weaker ones caused a narrowing of the hair at the point of growth so that the fleece was easily removable by hand a week later. It appears that the drug restricts wool growth for probably less than a day, after which normal growth is resumed.

Australia. Figures released by the Federal Statistician showed that Australian sheep numbers recovered at last in 1969 from the disastrous 1965 drought in the eastern states. Between the annual counts of livestock numbers in 1965 and 1966 the number of sheep and lambs in Australia fell from 170 million to 157 million. It then began a slow recovery, but it did not exceed the 1965 figure until the annual count in March 1969, when there were 176 million, an increase of about 5½ per cent over March 1968. In New South Wales and Queensland, the two states worst hit in the 1965–66 drought, however, the numbers had still not reached the 1965 level: New South Wales with 68 million sheep and lambs, and Queensland with 20 million, were each 4 million below the 1965 figure.

The ban on the export of Merino rams from Australia, introduced in 1929, was lifted by the government in March 1969, at the request of the Australian Wool Industry Conference, supported by the International Wool Secretariat. Prohibition of the export of Merino ewes and of Merino ram semen for artificial insemination is to be maintained, however, and extended to fertilised Merino ova. The maximum number of rams that can be exported in the first 12 months is 300.

A grazier, K. G. Downie, living in Bothwell, Tasmania, has developed a new breed of sheep which experts say is likely to win widespread acceptance. Information about the breed, named Cormo, was given in March when the first Cormos were sold. With the aim of producing a sheep which would combine high body weight and fertility with a heavy, good quality fleece, the Cormo was developed by crossing best quality Corriedale rams with superfine Merino ewes. Mr. Downie built up a flock of 4,600 Cormos, which have a lambing percentage of 130 and an average fleece weight of 11½ lb. A further advantage is that the Cormos' strong, tight fleece will not allow dirt and scrub to penetrate when the sheep have to forage in rough bush country.

Sheep. The Cormo, a new Australian crossbreed, showing the fine dense fleece impenetrable by dirt.

The development by Australian scientists of a vaccine to protect sheep against footrot was announced in November 1969. The new vaccine is the outcome of five years of intensive study by scientists working at the CSIRO's McMaster Laboratory in the animal health division. Tests have shown that the vaccine will also cure a high percentage of established cases of the disease, which has been costing Australia $A16 million a year in treatment and loss of production. It is expected that production of the vaccine will begin during 1970, and scientists are seeking the most effective method of vaccination.

India. The Australian Minister for External Affairs announced in May 1969 that a sheep-breeding centre would be established at Hissar, India, as a joint venture by India and Australia. The development of the centre over a period of eight years would cost an estimated $A2,200,000 to which Australia would contribute $960,000 under the Colombo Plan. Australia will supply 5,000 Corriedale ewes and 110 rams, as well as equipment for shearing, disease control, fodder conservation, and irrigation, and the machinery essential for clearing and levelling the 7,000-acre site. Three Australian advisers will be appointed to the centre and a technical advisory committee from the New South Wales Department of Agriculture will be set up to assist in the organisation.

Sheffield, Yorks. Work on a theatre at Arundel Gate, Sheffield, to replace the Sheffield Playhouse started during 1969. The £910,000 project includes two auditoriums, one to seat 1,000 people, and a studio theatre to seat 250 people. Together the auditoriums will form an octagon with the seating round three sides of a promontory stage. Sheffield corporation and the Arts Council are jointly contributing £650,000 towards the cost.

Silk Road. The famed romantic "golden road to Samarkand" along which for centuries caravans from China carried silk and spices to the capital of Tamerlane the Great was partially re-opened as a trade route between China and Pakistan in August 1969. It had been closed since the establishment of Communist rule in China in 1949. In 1963 China and Pakistan agreed to reconstruct the mountainous 200-mile-long stretch over the Karakoram range between Lup Zag in Sinkiang and Gilgit in Kashmir, and this was re-opened in 1969. The first caravan from China—of 16 merchants and 50 camels—arrived at Gilgit on Aug. 24. One caravan from each country travels the road each month, carrying textiles, leather goods, herbs, and metal goods from Pakistan to China, and hides, tools, silk, and electrical and household goods from China to Pakistan.

Smoking. Figures given by the U.K. Tobacco Advisory Committee on Feb. 11, 1969, showed there was a decline in the consumption of tobacco in Great Britain during 1968 when 253·4 million lb. were consumed, compared with 255·4 million lb. in 1967. More people smoked smaller cigarettes for, although 121,800 million cigarettes were smoked, they contained only 220·2 million lb., compared with 221·3 million lb. in 1967. The trend towards filter-tipped varieties continued, for 86,100 million were smoked in 1968, compared with 78,500 million in the previous year. Consumption of pipe tobacco fell by 700,000 lb. to 13·2 million lb., and a total of 1,180 million cigars were smoked during the year. A decline in cigarette smoking was also reported on Jan. 5, 1969, by the U.S. Department of Agriculture, which stated that over a thousand million fewer cigarettes were smoked in the U.S.A. than in 1967.

The British Safety Council published on Oct. 20, 1969, a booklet, "Smoking and Lung Cancer," which stated that 70,000 people die in Great Britain each year from diseases directly attributable to smoking. Further, out of a total of 255 million man-days lost to British industry in 1968, 32 million were lost through respiratory diseases, three quarters of which can be attributed to cigarette smoking. Eight times as many people are killed by lung cancer as by road accidents. But in 1968 the average consumption of cigarettes by adults was 2,830 in the U.K., compared with 3,450 in Canada, and 3,680 in the U.S.A. The Safety Council recommended that smoking advertisements should be banned from cinemas, that producers should prohibit smoking in television plays and discussions, and that manufacturers should be compelled by law to print a warning about health hazards on cigarette packets.

Young Smokers. Two California, U.S.A., smoking research teams reported at the beginning of February 1969 that smoking causes measurable changes in the heart and lungs of young and healthy people, and that cigarette-smoking even in moderation for a comparatively short period can produce potentially harmful effects. One study, among 800 students at San Fernando Valley State College, showed that smokers have a significantly higher heart rate and blood pressure during exercise than non-smokers, and that their blood clots faster and contains a higher level of fatty acids than that of non-smokers. A second study, of the sputum of students at the University of California, Santa Barbara, showed that abnormal lung cells suspected of being in a pre-cancerous stage occurred in 14·3 per cent of the students who smoked and in only 4 per cent of the non-smokers.

A U.K. government social survey report, "The Young Smoker," compiled from questionnaires completed anonymously by 5,601 boys between the ages of 11 and 15 from 60 schools in 1966, was published on Oct. 2, 1969. It showed that 45 per cent had smoked by the age of 11, and over 80 per cent by the age of 15. Filter-tipped cigarettes were preferred by 87 per cent of the boys, whereas in a survey of adult men only 31 per cent admitted choosing this type of cigarette. The report said that there are two main reasons why boys start smoking: to appear "manly," and to attract girls. The heaviest smokers (20 cigarettes or more a day) said they enjoy it too much to give it up, but nearly 50 per cent said they want to stop, either because of their parents' disapproval or because of the risk to their health. The survey recommended that health education should concentrate on trying to increase disapproval of smoking by emphasising not only the risks of lung cancer but also minor health hazards, by persuading boys that smoking is not a sign of manliness and maturity, and by asking parents to dissuade their children from smoking.

In Australia, a survey, made between October 1967 and February 1968 and based on information given by nearly 26,000 children between 9 and 16 years old at 33 primary and secondary schools, showed that, at the age of 15 years, 37·4 per cent of schoolboys and 14·7 per cent of schoolgirls were regular smokers. Those who smoke do so for a variety of reasons—34 per cent of boys and 23 per cent of girls because they are bored or lonely, and 34 per cent of boys and 42 per cent of girls because their friends smoke. Among the regular smokers more than a third said that they were aware of a possible risk to health.

Australia. The managing directors in Australia of W.D. and H.O. Wills, Rothman's, Philip Morris, and Godfrey Phillips announced in June 1969 that a research foundation is to be set up to investigate the relationship between smoking and health. The project, which will take five years, is expected to receive about \$A1 million for research. On the scientific advisory committee of eight members, four will represent the tobacco

and cigarette manufacturers, and four will be scientists. Meeting in Adelaide in the same month Federal and State ministers agreed to recommend to their governments that cigarettes should be labelled with a warning of the dangers of smoking, and that packets should be labelled to notify the nicotine content. In addition, the ministers decided to recommend restrictions on the advertising of cigarettes in the press, on radio, and on television, the precise nature of the restrictions to be decided by each government.

Social Responsibility in Science, British Society for. This is the name of an organisation formed by a group of more than 100 leading scientists to examine the moral and social aspects of both research and science education in Britain. The foundation of the society was announced in February 1969, and its inaugural meeting was held at the Royal Society on April 19. Its objects are to stimulate an awareness among scientists of the social consequences and responsibilities of their work; to draw attention to the political, economic, and social pressures confronting research workers; and to identify those areas of research that are likely to have a major effect on human life and its environment. Members share with the general public a feeling of uneasiness at the general lack of control of technological "advances" and the apparent irresponsibility of many scientists who allow their discoveries to be exploited for purposes harmful to society as a whole. Examples include nuclear, biological, and chemical weapons, of course, but also methods of changing individual personality by chemical or electrical means, and the effects on society of genetic control, the creation of "test-tube babies," and the manipulation of heredity principles to produce human "types" to order. The Society intends to detect such scientific developments at the early stages, and draw to them the attention of the public and the government; to lead opposition to scientific or technological policies that may produce undesirable effects on society; and to demand reform of the education of scientists to make them more aware of their responsibility to society. A similar society already exists in the U.S.A.

Speed Limits. When the metric system is officially introduced into the U.K. in 1975, the speed limit on motorways may be 120 kilometres an hour— 75 m.p.h.—if driving behaviour improves. The Minister of Transport, announcing this on March 5, 1969, said that there would be more 40 m.p.h. limits on main urban traffic routes, some experimental 60 m.p.h. restrictions on those stretches of roads with bad accident records, and more 50 m.p.h. limits. The scale of speed limits under the metric system will be: 50 km.p.h. (31·1 m.p.h.); 65 km.p.h. (40·4 m.p.h.); 80 km.p.h.

(49·7 m.p.h.); and 100 km.p.h. (62·1 m.p.h.). The cost of converting road signs, which should be complete by 1975, will be £1½ million and £2 million.

In May the Minister said that the motorway and non-motorway speed limit for towed caravans would be raised from 40 m.p.h. to 50 m.p.h., and the motorway limit for heavy lorries reduced from 70 m.p.h. to 60 m.p.h. The non-motorway speed limit on light goods vehicles of up to 30 cwt. was raised from 40 m.p.h. to 50 m.p.h. on March 5.

On March 22 a maximum speed limit of 100 km.p.h. (62·1 m.p.h.) came into force on 1,000 miles of main roads in France for a trial period. If the accident rate falls on these roads the limit may be made permanent. No restrictions were placed on motorway speeds.

Stamps and Stamp-Collecting. On Oct. 1, 1969, after more than 300 years as a department of state, the British General Post Office became a public corporation headed by a board and a chairman, Viscount Hall. The change had its most immediate effect in the Channel Islands, for on the same day Guernsey and Jersey assumed control of their own postal services. United Kingdom stamps, including the regional stamps first issued in 1958, ceased to be valid for postage from and within the Channel Islands; instead, both islands issued complete new series of stamps ranging from ½d. to £1. Those for Guernsey showed views of the island and the coats-of-arms of Alderney and Sark, whose post offices were placed under the control of the States of Guernsey Post Office Board. The Jersey stamps were also pictorial. Both series included portraits of the Queen.

In Britain the year saw the completion of the long series of definitive stamps with the portrait of the Queen by Arnold

---

British and Commonwealth Stamps issued in 1969

1st row. (*Above*) Jersey, 6d, Jersey cow; (*below*) New Zealand, 2½ cents plus 1 cent, Health, cricket; Samoa, 7 sene, 7th anniversary of independence, hibiscus blossom; British Solomon Islands, 8 cents, 3rd South Pacific Games, football; (*above*) Canada, 6 cents, curling; (*below*) Australia, 5 cents, 50th anniversary of ILO.

2nd row. Great Britain, 1s, *S.S. Great Britain;* 1s, Investiture of the Prince of Wales; 5d; 50th anniversary of the first non-stop Transatlantic flight.

3rd row. Cayman Islands, 4 cents, royal poinciana; Great Britain, 9d, first flight of the Concorde; Seychelles, 20 cents, Apollo 11 Moon-landing.

4th row. Virgin Islands, 4 cents, 75th anniversary of the death of R. L. Stevenson, *Treasure Island;* Trinidad and Tobago, 15 cents, coat-of-arms; Great Britain, 2s 6d; Grenada, 10 cents, cricket.

5th row. Guernsey, 6d, King Charles II and Alderney coat-of-arms; New Hebrides Condominium, 25 cents, 3rd South Pacific Games, relay race; Cook Islands, 30 cents, Scout Jamboree at Christchurch, New Zealand, Lord Baden Powell.

398

Machin, R.A., when the high values—2s 6d, 5s, 10s and £1—were placed on sale. In the same design as the lower values but in a larger format, these stamps continued a long tradition by being recess-engraved instead of being printed by photogravure, the process used for low value definitives and for almost all commemoratives. The British scene was reflected in a series of six stamps showing historic ships including *Queen Elizabeth 2* and *Mauretania*, and in another series of six with views of cathedrals. The investiture of the Prince of Wales was commemorated by five large stamps, three of which had stylised views of Caernarvon Castle. There were complaints that the design of the 9d stamp, which is used mainly on letters sent abroad, would be incomprehensible to foreigners, for its picture of a Celtic cross at Margam Abbey, Glamorgan, was innocent of any explanatory inscription.

Among the anniversaries celebrated by special British stamps were the 20th of NATO (founded in 1949), the 50th of the first non-stop Transatlantic flight by John Alcock and Arthur Whitten Brown, and the 50th of the first England-to-Australia flight by the brothers Ross and Keith Smith with their mechanics W. H. Shiers and J. M. Bennett. This last anniversary was also celebrated in Australia with three stamps, all 5-cent values printed in the same sheet in the arrangement known to philatelists as *se tenant*. One showed the Vickers Vimy aeroplane in which the flight was made, and the others paid tribute to the work of H. N. Wrigley, A. W. Murphy, P. McGuinness, and Hudson Fysh in surveying a trans-Australia route in preparation for the Smith brothers' flight.

In common with Britain and many other countries both Australia and New

---

Foreign Stamps issued in 1969

1st row. German Democratic Republic, 50 pfennigs, 50th anniversary of the League of Red Cross Societies; Rumania, 40 bani, yellow tiger-moth; Norway, 50 öre, centenary of the Norwegian transport system; Rwanda Republic, 20 centimes, Touareg head-dresses.

2nd row. Ireland, 4 pence, Celtic brooch; Portugal, 3½ escudos, "Europa"; South Africa, 2½ cents, Dr. Christian Barnard and Groote Schuur Hospital; Switzerland, 10 centimes, 50th anniversary of Swiss Girl Guides.

3rd row. Afghanistan, 1 afghani plus 1 afghani, Mothers' Day; Austria, 2 schillings, Armed Forces; Turkey, 50 kurus, Kemal Ataturk; United Nations, 15 cents, Santiago, Chile, headquarters.

4th row. Paraguay, 20 centimos, Olympic Games champions, David Hemery (Great Britain); Mongolia, 15 mongo, peasant costume, Sakhchin woman; France, 1 franc, bas-relief, Amiens Cathedral.

5th row. Poland, 40 groszy, fox-terrier; Belgium, 3 francs, Day of the Stamp, mail-train; Hungary, 5 forint, centenary of the birth of Mahatma Gandhi; Argentina, 20 pesos plus 10 pesos, child welfare, suiriri duck.

Zealand issued stamps to commemorate the 50th anniversary of the International Labour Organisation. The New Zealand stamp featured the ILO emblem, two hands holding spanners, but the Australian was a symbolic design of concentric circles. Particularly colourful were the New Zealand series which marked the centenaries of Otago University and of the New Zealand Law Society, while the annual Health stamps showed boys and girls playing cricket and a portrait of Dr. Elizabeth Gunn, organiser of the first children's health camp in 1919. Canada's most attractive series depicted wild birds in their natural colours, and there were interesting new pictorial definitive series from the Cayman Islands, Trinidad and Tobago, the Pitcairn Islands, and Swaziland. Sierra Leone again showed its penchant for unusual designs by issuing stamps in the shape of a tiny anvil to publicise its exports of iron ore, and Gibraltar marked its new constitution by four stamps perforated in the shape of the Rock.

The most outstanding event of the year, the first landing of the American astronauts on the Moon, was celebrated by special issues in many countries, including some of the Communist-ruled states which normally confine their philatelic tributes to the achievements of Russian cosmonauts. Hungary issued miniature sheets containing one large stamp showing Neil Armstrong and Edwin Aldrin on the Moon, and similar stamps, also in miniature sheet form, came from Belgium, Grenada, and the Rwanda Republic. Among all the elaborate designs that of the Mexican commemorative was strikingly different: it showed simply a single footprint on the Moon's surface.

France and countries of the French Community celebrated the bicentenary of the birth of Napoleon I with special stamps and postmarks. The French 70-centimes stamp was a conventional pictorial with a portrait of Napoleon as a young officer and a view of the house in Ajaccio where he was born, but many of the Community issues reproduced in full colour some of the splendid portraits and battle scenes by imperial painters such as David and Gros. A remarkable stamp from the Federal Republic of the Cameroons, showing David's "Napoleon crossing the Alps," was embossed on gold foil and had a face value of 1,000 francs, about 33s sterling. The centenary of the birth of Mahatma Gandhi was also marked by issues from many countries, Britain's 1s 6d stamp being the first to honour anyone not of British birth and the first to be designed by an overseas artist, Biman Mullick, of India.

The world's oldest society for stamp collectors, the Royal Philatelic Society, celebrated its centenary by staging an exhibition at its London headquarters, to which the Queen paid a visit. The Queen herself owns one of the most valuable stamp collections ever formed. It was begun by her grandfather, King

George V, while he was a young naval officer and was continued by her father, King George VI, who was an enthusiastic and knowledgeable philatelist. The keeper of the royal philatelic collection, Sir John Wilson, retired in July after more than 30 years' service and was succeeded by Mr. J. B. Marriott, housemaster of Girdlestoneites at Charterhouse. Other notable exhibitions during 1969 were held in Sofia to mark the 90th anniversary of the first Bulgarian stamps, and in Johannesburg to mark the centenary of the first stamps of the Zuid Afrikaanse Republiek.   **C. W. Hill**

Stanhope Gold Medal. This award is given annually for the bravest deed in the U.K. and Commonwealth which is not already recognised by a Sovereign's gallantry award. It was announced in April 1969 that the medal for 1968 had been awarded to Robert Ryan, aged 24, who saved one man's life and attempted to save another from a deep crevasse of melting snow and ice on a glacier in New Zealand. Ryan, who is an Australian, works as a ranger for the Mount Cook National Park Board.

Stansted, Essex. Once the officially designated site for London's third airport, Stansted was omitted from the list of four sites submitted by the Roskill Commission report published on March 3, 1969, Nuthampsted, 8 miles to the north west, being selected in its place. The inhabitants of Stansted, who had mounted a long and active publicity campaign against its selection, were rightly elated by this decision. See Roskill Commission.

Steel. Details of the development of the strongest steel ever made, announced at a December 1968 meeting of the Japan Metallurgical Society, were published in January 1969. Called "IN-U Steel," it is a composite ultra-high-tension steel developed by the director of technical research at the Ishikawajima-Harima Heavy Industries Co. The steel has enough tensile strength to resist up to 250 kilograms of pressure per sq. millimetre (about 400,000 lb. per sq. in.). Its inventor got his idea from the method of making Japanese swords, in which many sheets of metal, each with different ingredients, are placed one upon another and tempered. A sword made in this way, although strong enough to cut through a steel helmet, is apt to be brittle and liable to snap. The scientist hit upon the idea of sandwiching thin sheets of copper, nickel, and other metals, only 10 microns thick, between sheets of strong steel, and in this way finally developed "IN-U Steel." He claims that the new steel is characterised by low cost, great strength, and light weight, and that it will not only be used for a wide range of products, such as super-high-speed engines and gas turbines, but will also meet the needs of space science.   Ishikawajima-Harima

Heavy Industries said it had applied for patent rights, notably in Great Britain, the U.S.A., and West Germany.

Steel Industry. The U.K. Steel industry was nationalised in July 1967, when the 14 largest steel companies and their 200 subsidiaries were placed under the sole ownership of the British Steel Corporation. The B.S.C., which in volume of sales is the third largest steel producer in the Western world, after the American U.S. Steel and Bethlehem Steel companies, employs 250,000 workers, and its sales are worth £1,000 million a year; in 1968 its output was 22,900,000 ingot tons out of the British total of 25,100,000 ingot tons. (The remaining 2,200,000 ingot tons were produced by the 200 independent steel companies which were not included in the nationalisation scheme.) Three major developments were announced by the B.S.C. in the first quarter of 1969. First, it decided to re-equip the industry at a cost of £1,000 million over the next six years, to increase output to between 30 million and 34 million tons a year by 1975. Secondly, it planned to increase its prices by 7·3 per cent (the Prices and Incomes Board subsequently reduced this to 5 per cent). Thirdly, it decided in March to reorganise the structure of the industry as from October. Hitherto the companies owned by the B.S.C. had retained their names, and had been administered on the basis of four geographical regions. Under the new scheme organisation is according to product and not location, and all the companies' assets and undertakings are transferred to the B.S.C., so that the companies' names will eventually disappear.

The 200 independent companies, employing over 95,000, are engaged chiefly in the processing of crude steel which they buy from the B.S.C. and make into bars, sheets, and forgings; they also produce much of the alloyed and stainless steels and most of the steel used in making tools. Their refined products earn more than crude steel, and account for over a third of the turnover of the entire industry. Most of these companies belong to the British Independent Steel Producers' Association (B.I.S.P.A.).

Raw Materials. The chief raw material used in the British steel industry is iron and steel scrap, of which 14 million tons were used in 1968 in making about 25 million tons of crude steel. The other raw material is pig iron made from iron ore which was formerly mostly home produced but is now chiefly imported. U.K. iron ore contains a low percentage of iron (25 to 30) compared with the 64 per cent of the newly discovered Australian deposits. In 1968 imported ore, at 16,800,000 tons, was 40 per cent more than local ore; the chief supplier was Sweden (4,700,000 tons), and second was Canada (3,200,000 tons). Between 1½ million and 2

million tons each came from Mauretania, Liberia, Venezuela, and Russia. A great increase is expected in imports from Australia. Whereas ore-carrying ships of 20,000 or 30,000 tons or less are economic for the short runs from European suppliers, large distances require 100,000-ton, 150,000-ton, or even 250,000-ton carriers. At present big carriers cannot be accommodated at British ports; they have to unload at Rotterdam, where the ore is reloaded into smaller ships; in 1968, 500,000 tons of ore had to be transhipped in this way. Enlargement and deepening of British ports adjacent to steel-producing areas are therefore being planned or are under way; at Port Talbot, South Wales, a harbour capable of berthing 100,000-ton or 150,000-ton ships is nearing completion, and deep-water terminals are planned for the Clyde and the Tees, and possibly the Humber.

Stirling, University of. At the beginning of 1969 work began on the first contract, for three buildings worth £680,000, for student accommodation at this university. The buildings, which will provide places for 638 students, are expected to be completed by September 1970, when the university will have 1,100 students. In order to achieve the authorities' long-term plans for two-thirds of the students to be in residence on the site, 2,000 study-bedrooms with ancillary accommodation will have to be built by 1973. See also pp. 156, 158.

Stone Age. It was reported on Dec. 9, 1969, that during excavations at Beachport, 250 miles S.W. of Adelaide, South Australia, a haul of Stone Age tools, highly polished bone points, and the remains of fish, shell-food, animals, and birds had been discovered. Describing it as one of the richest discoveries of prehistoric material to be found in southern Australia, the curator of Anthropology at the South Australia Museum, Robert Edwards, said that it gave firm evidence that Beachport was once a manufacturing site for Stone Age technology, and was a further indication of the spread of early man through Australia.

Storms. The annual report of the U.K. Meteorological Office covering 1968 and published in September 1969 referred to several records set up during the gales and floods of January, July, and September 1968. In January the highest confirmed wind speed in England and Wales of 134 m.p.h. (116 knots) was recorded at Great Dun Fell, Westmorland; in July hailstones as big as tomatoes fell at Cardiff; and in September 2·2 in. of rain fell in 42 minutes at Purleigh, Essex.

The Meteorological Office report added that gales and floods of the severity experienced in 1968 cannot be expected more frequently than once in a century.

Stratfield Saye, Berks. Plans for creating a recreational centre at the Duke of Wellington's estate, Stratfield Saye, near Reading, Berks, were announced in August 1969. About 750 unproductive acres of the 10,000-acre estate are being set aside for the centre, which will include a championship golf course, a heated swimming pool, 40 acres of gravel pits for sailing and fishing, a riding school, picnic places, restaurants, and car parks. It is believed that such a centre would attract 100,000 visitors yearly.

Strontium-90. The amount of radioactive strontium-90 present in the bones of human beings continued to decline in 1967, according to a Medical Research Council report published on April 11, 1969. This isotope, which is created by atmospheric nuclear tests, is dangerous to man because when it is present in food and drinking water the body is unable to distinguish it from calcium and erroneously uses it to make bone. Levels of strontium-90 in human bones rose until 1964 as a direct result of nuclear tests carried out in the atmosphere before the partial test ban treaty was concluded.

Students. The University Grants Committee reported on Feb. 25, 1969, that the number of full-time students at British universities in 1967–68 was 200,121, of whom 17½ per cent were postgraduate students. The Committee stated that the government had undertaken to provide resources for a total university population in 1971–72 of between 220,000 and 225,000 full-time students; this implies a rate of growth in the universities of only about 3 per cent a year, compared with the average annual growth rate during the emergency expansion period (1962–63 to 1967–68) of about 13 per cent.

The Association of Commonwealth Universities on April 2 stated that more than 16,000 overseas students were enrolled at British universities in 1968. Just over half were from Commonwealth countries. The largest groups, 2,018, came from America; India sent 1,429, the second largest; Pakistan sent 899, Canada 784, and Norway 678. The most popular subject for study was engineering and technology, for which 4,371 students enrolled, followed by social, administrative and business studies with 3,048, and biological and physical sciences with 2,717.

Japan. According to the Education Ministry, student enrolment at four-year universities totalled 1,270,000 (1,040,000 men, and 230,000 women) on May 1, 1968, while on the same date 255,000 students were attending junior colleges (45,000 men and 210,000 women). The total enrolment of 1,525,000 was more than twice the 1958 figure. One out of every five people of university age now attends a school of higher education, and it is estimated that in or about 1975 this figure will have risen to one out of every three. There are 377 four-year universities and 468 two-year colleges in Japan, 669 of the total number being under private management. The teaching staff of the four-year universities numbered 71,786 in 1968, compared with 66,738 in 1967, but the number of students per teacher increased by 0·3 to 17·7. At junior colleges the teaching staff totalled 14,829 in 1968, an increase of 1,380 over 1967, and the number of students per teacher stood at 17·2, a reduction of 0·3.

Submarines. The fourth British Polaris-carrying submarine, H.M.S. *Revenge*, was commissioned at Birkenhead on Dec. 5, 1969. On Dec. 12 the second French nuclear-powered submarine, *Le Terrible*, was launched at Cherbourg; it is expected to become operational by the end of 1972. The first French submarine of this type, *Le Redoutable*, launched in 1967, will be operational in 1971; the third, *Le Foudroyant*, is due to be laid down at the beginning of 1970.

Escape and Rescue. A new British escape suit for submariners was demonstrated in Loch Shira off Loch Fyne, Argyllshire, in April 1969. It consists of an orange-coloured "overall" suit with hood, which completely encloses the user and which is inflated through a tube in the sleeve just before the wearer leaves the submarine. In the demonstration, escapers shot to the surface from a submarine submerged 150 ft. below. The suit was developed by the Submarine Command Escape Unit, Gosport, Hants.

A "deep submergence rescue vessel" capable of submerging to a depth of 3,500 ft. and rescuing up to 24 men at a time from a sunken submarine was constructed for the U.S. Navy by the American Lockheed company during 1969. Resembling a small submarine, it locks on to the sunken vessel's escape hatch, through which escapers climb into it. A feature of Lockheed's escape vessels is a circular "air bar," from which rescued sailors suffering from oxygen-lack can inhale pure air through face masks, as soon as they have been taken aboard. The air-filtering system was developed from those used in astronauts' capsules.

Sussex, University of. A new £1¼ million biology, biochemistry, and experimental psychology building was opened here by Sir Peter Medawar, director of the National Institute for Medical Research, on June 20, 1969. The building, which cost more than £750,000, was built in two stages over a four-year period, the second stage being completed in May 1969.

The Gardner Centre for the Arts, named after Dr. Lyddon Gardner, former chairman of the university's building committee, who died early in 1969, came into use for drama and music in November 1969. Built around a drum-shaped

Submarines. *Left:* the new British all-enveloping escape suit, which is inflated through a tube in the sleeve. *Right:* circular "air-bar" in a U.S. underwater vessel for resuscitating oxygen-starved rescued submariners who sit in a ring round it and inhale pure air through face masks.

theatre seating 486 people, the Centre cost £321,000. Dr. Gardner bequeathed £176,000 of this amount, and the rest was made up of £60,000 from the University Appeal Fund; £58,000 from the University Grants Commission; £20,000 from the Gulbenkian Foundation; and £7,000 from the Arts Council.

Swansea, Glam. On July 3, 1969, the Prince of Wales, during the four-day tour which followed his Investiture, announced to a crowd gathered outside Swansea Guildhall that the Queen had decided to confer city status on Swansea. The city, which grew up round a castle, had been a borough since the 12th century.

Swearing. Eavesdropping by 150 American student researchers who listened to the conversations of more than 3,000 people was the basis of a report of profanity made by an American psychologist to the Midwestern Psychological Association meeting at Detroit in May 1969. They found that U.S. factory and construction workers use one swear word in every four that they speak, college students one in every 14, and secretaries only one in every 200. Most swear words consist, they discovered, of four letters, the commonest in use being "damn." In American co-educational establishments, it was found, girls swear and tell "smutty" stories as much as boys.

Swindon, Wilts. The Swindon borough council, Wiltshire county council, and Greater London council published on Jan. 31, 1969, a study for the possible future expansion of Swindon. The figure of 75,000 additional immigrants from London has been set by the Minister of Housing and Local Government, and by 1986 the population in

the new city area will be 241,000, compared with 121,000 in 1966. To house this population some 37,000 new dwellings will be needed. The study proposed the development of about 13,000 acres of land, which, including the existing town, would give a total of 21,000 acres. Each main residential commuter area would have a population of between 5,000 and 8,000; to reduce traffic problems industrial estates would be distributed in units of 100 to 150 acres through the urban area. The centre of the town would be retained and developed as a regional centre. The total capital investment required was estimated at £315 million.

Sydney, N.S.W. Plans by the New South Wales government to spend $A75 million on developing Botany Bay as a second major port for Sydney were announced in March. The development, which will be in four stages spread over 15–20 years, will create a deep-sea port capable of handling vessels of up to 100,000 tons, and a large industrial and transport complex on the foreshore. A channel 70 ft. deep will be dredged at the entrance to the Bay, island break-waters constructed, and a large area reclaimed, using the sand dredged from the Bay. Part of the reclaimed area, when developed for port purposes, will provide about 11,000 ft. of longshore wharfage compared with the 42,000 ft. now available in the whole of Sydney Harbour. It was at Botany Bay that Captain James Cook made his first landing on Australian soil in 1770.

The cargo container terminal at Balmain, Sydney, came into use on March 18, 1969, three days ahead of its scheduled official opening, when the Australian-built container vessel *Kanimbla* berthed there on its maiden voyage, carrying a cargo of pig iron from New-

Sydney, N.S.W. Model of what will be Sydney's tallest building, the 51-storey 612-ft.-high A.M.P. office block, which will stand behind A.M.P.'s block on Sydney Cove.

cost $A20 million on the site of an old dance hall, the Trocadero, and some other buildings. It will consist of a 42-storey tower rising to 475 ft. above George Street. The cinema centre will have five theatres, and there will also be a restaurant, swimming pool, and plaza. A development site of 25,600 sq. ft. in the centre of the city, including the historic Theatre Royal, was sold at auction for $A7,250,000 on Sept. 25. This price, equal to $A283 a sq. ft., is believed to be a record for an auction in Australia. The property has frontages on King and Castlereagh Streets. The present Theatre Royal building was opened in 1872 after two theatres on the same site had been destroyed by fire.

In a debate in the N.S.W. parliament in March it was stated that the Sydney Opera House will be completed by 1972, at a final estimated cost of $A85 million.

Tankers. The largest ship ever built in Great Britain, the *Esso Northumbria*, an oil tanker of 253,000 deadweight tons, was launched by Princess Anne on May 2, 1969, at the Swan Hunter group's yard at Wallsend-on-Tyne. She is the first of four such vessels ordered by Esso from Swan Hunter and from Harland and Wolff, Belfast.

Tate Gallery, London. The £2 million plan for extending the gallery was shown for the first time at the Tate on Jan. 23, 1969. The proposals involved the construction of a new front along the whole width of the site, overlooking the Thames. The exhibition space would have been nearly doubled, with all the permanent collection on one floor; and space would have been available for the Henry Moore gift of 24 of his major works. The plans included a lecture theatre with 240 seats, and a 200-seat restaurant overlooking the river. The exhibition was open to the public, who were invited to give their opinion of the plan on printed slips.

The scheme at once aroused bitter criticism from those who objected to the destruction of the old façade, portico and steps, and on Feb. 1 the Historic Buildings Council, advisers to the Minister of Housing and Local Government, announced its own opposition. The general public showed the same opposition in their answers on the slips given out at the exhibition and in a random sample poll taken on Feb. 6. Affection for the existing portico and steps was strong. Finally the plan was abandoned, and on July 8 the Prime Minister told the House of Commons that the Government had decided to make available to the gallery trustees the adjacent Millbank site at present occupied by Queen Alexandra's Military Hospital. A decision to build a new

"Teklan". Although warm, soft, and light, this new Courtauld's man-fibre clothing material is entirely and permanently flame-resistant. It is especially suitable for children's nightdresses.

500-bed hospital on army land at Woolwich had made the site available. He also announced that the Calouste Gulbenkian Foundation had made a £250,000 gift to the Tate for the construction of a gallery to house temporary exhibitions. This was the largest single gift ever made by the foundation in the United Kingdom, and was given to mark the centenary of the birth of its founder.

Tea and Coffee. Figures released by the Australian Bureau of Census and Statistics in October 1969 showed that since 1964 tea consumption in Australia had fallen while the consumption of coffee had risen. In the financial year 1968–69, 63 million lb. of tea were consumed, a fall of nearly 3 million lb. from the 1964 total, while coffee consumption rose from 27 million lb. in 1964 to 33 million lb. in 1968–69.

"Teklan." This is the name of a new modacrylic fibre produced by Courtaulds, claimed to be the first British-produced clothing fibre that is "totally, inherently, and permanently flame resistant." It was exhibited at a London trade exhibition in March 1969, when it was described as hard-wearing, soft, warm, and light, and specially suitable for nightdresses, children's wear, toys, furnishings, and industrial clothing.

Tektite I. This is the name of an underwater laboratory in which four U.S. scientists spent a record 60 days (Feb. 17–April 16, 1969) on the sea bed 50 ft. down off St. John, in the Virgin Islands. The experiment was sponsored by NASA, the U.S. Navy Department, and the U.S. Department of the Interior. The biological research programme carried out in the laboratory included studies of

castle. Balmain was thus the first of Australia's three container ports to become operational: the others are at Melbourne and Fremantle.

Plans for what will be Sydney's tallest office block (by 12 ft.) were submitted to the city commissioners on March 27, 1969. Designed for the A.M.P. Society, the building, of 51 storeys, 612 ft. high but only 90 ft. deep, will be erected on the 1½ acres bounded by Bridge Street, Philip Street, and Young Street, and will be surrounded by open space of 1·2 acres. The floor space of 550,000 sq. ft. will accommodate up to 5,000 people. Together with the Society's 383-ft.-high building at Sydney Cove, it will be called the A.M.P. Centre. A two-level plaza—the upper landscaped with trees and seats, the lower a shopping area—is included in the plan, as is parking for 275 cars on two basement levels. Completion, at a cost of $A21 million, could be in 1974. The architect is Graham Thorp. The planned erection of what will be Sydney's third highest building, 437 ft. high, with 34 storeys, had been announced in February. This is to be erected in York Street. The tallest building in Sydney at present is the cylindrical tower block in Australia Square, which has 50 storeys and is 600 ft. high.

Other building applications made to the city commissioners by the end of March included: in George and Pitt Streets blocks of 42, 39, 30, and 20 storeys; in Clarence and Kent Streets blocks of 45, 34, and 26 storeys; in Macquarie Street a 21-storey block; and new offices and shops in King, Hunter, and George Streets, Martin Place, and Circular Quay. On June 2, the city commissioners approved the building of a combined hotel and cinema block, to

phytoplankton and zooplankton, especially in relation to measuring the productivity of marine life; the identification and mapping of sediments in the bay where it was anchored; and the study of the formation of deposits from marine animals. The four scientists lived and worked in two interconnected cylinders, each 18·1 ft. high and 12·5 ft. in diameter; at a pressure of 36·9 lb. per sq. in. it was possible for them to breathe a nitrogen-oxygen mixture. On returning to the surface they had to spend 20 hours in a decompression chamber.

Tektites. These are small glassy objects found on the surface of the earth in particular places, one group in Australia, another in Czechoslovakia, and perhaps the largest in the Philippines. Many have shapes which indicate that aerodynamic forces acted on them when they were molten or partially molten, and it is generally believed that this happened as they entered the earth's atmosphere from outside. Some astronomers have argued that they originally came from the moon, the result of material being "splashed" off by meteorite collision. During 1969 Dr. Dean R. Chapman, of NASA's Ames Research Centre, announced that after ten years' work he had identified the source of the tektites in Australia as the Tycho crater on the moon, believed to have been scooped out by a meteorite relatively recently—70 million years ago. Computed trajectories, he claimed, had shown that only a shower of objects originating at Tycho and travelling in the same direction as the Rosse ray, which projects for over 600 miles from the crater, could have produced the landing pattern shown on earth.

Objections to the theory of a lunar origin for tektites include the questions why they should land on the earth which is a very small target when seen from the moon, what was the focusing procedure that kept them on so well defined a course, and why there are no tektites at all over such a large area as the Soviet Union. A mathematical examination by Dr. R. A. Lyttelton, the Cambridge astronomer, has shown that the impact of a Tycho-sized meteorite on the earth would result in vaporised materials being thrown out through the atmosphere. The solid objects formed from this by condensation would, in many cases, be returned to the earth, by a focusing effect of the earth's gravitational field, to a point diametrically opposite the impact. Varying times of flight, caused by different trajectories taken by the objects, would result in a spread of them as the Earth rotated.

Telescopes. The Anglo-Australian 150-inch Southern Hemisphere telescope at Siding Spring Mountain, near Coonabarabran, New South Wales, was under construction in May 1969. The cost of $A11 million is being shared by Australia and Great Britain. The director of Mt. Stromlo and Siding Spring Observatory, Prof. Olin Eggen, said that when the telescope is completed it will be as sophisticated as any ever constructed. The contract for casting the primary mirror blank was given in 1967

to a U.S. company at Toledo, Ohio; the grinding and polishing of the mirror and other optical components, and the construction of the tube, are the task of a Newcastle upon Tyne company, Grubb Parsons and Co. Ltd., who were given the contract for this work in March 1969. It is hoped that the telescope will become operational in 1974.

A new 107-inch telescope, built at the Westinghouse Sunnyvale division in California, was used at the University of Texas McDonald Observatory on Mount Locke during 1969 to study the planet Mars. Studies of the pressure, temperature, and composition of Mars will assist in the planned landings of space vehicles on the planet.

Work on a unique new telescope in a 136-ft.-tall observatory situated on a 9,000-ft.-high ridge in the Sacramento Mountains of New Mexico was completed in 1969. Made of fused silica, the 64-inch-diameter mirror is said to be the purest ever made. The telescope, which cost $3·3 million, is to be used to study solar flares and sun spots, to assist in the production of accurate forecasts of radiation caused by sun eruptions. Such radiation could be harmful to astronauts in spacecraft travelling outside the earth's protective atmosphere.

Television and Radio Festivals. At the Monte Carlo festival on Feb. 14, 1969, Freddie Jones received the Golden Nymph award when he was named actor of 1968 for his performance in the final episode of *The Caesars,* a Granada production. This was the only British entry to receive an award at the festival. The two chief awards went to an Italian production, *The World of Pirandello,* and a Czechoslovakian programme, *The Ballad of the Seven Hanged Men*, which also won the press jury's award.

At the 1969 Montreux festival of light entertainment TV on May 2, the Golden Rose went to a Swiss musical, *Holiday in Switzerland.* Britain's Marty Feldman gained the Silver Rose, for *Marty;*

Telescopes. *Top:* 107-inch telescope at the University of Texas McDonald Observatory on Mount Locke, for studying Mars. *Left:* 64-inch fused silica mirror telescope in the Sacramento Mountains, New Mexico. *Right:* the mirror for the 150-inch Southern Hemisphere telescope at Siding Spring Mountain, N.S.W., at the Newcastle, U.K., works where it is being ground and polished.

and the Bronze Rose went to Spain for *La Ultima Moda* (The Latest Fashion).

In the annual competition for the Italia Prizes, held in Mantua in September 1969, the 10,000 Swiss francs (£960) prize for the best television documentary went to the BBC's *Signals for Survival*, a programme on seagulls. O.R.T.F. (France) won the 15,000 Swiss francs (£1,400) prize for an original television dramatic production, *The Separation*; the 15,000 Swiss francs prize for a radio musical composition, *Cries*; and a second prize of 7,500 Swiss francs (£700) for a radio literary or dramatic work, with *Eyewitness on the Spot*. Czechoslovakia won the 10,000 Swiss francs award for an original musical production with *The Labyrinth of Power*, and the 15,000 francs radio drama prize for *The Inevitable End of the Marathon Runner*. Some 120 television and radio programmes from 31 countries were entered in the competition.

Television Awards. The 1968 awards of the British Guild of TV Producers and Directors were presented on Feb. 14, 1969. The BBC gained 13 of the 18 awards, ITV won four, and one—the foreign television programme award—went to the producers, directors, cameramen, reporters, and technicians of the Czechoslovakian TV service for "their integrity and courage during the past year." The guild's highest honour, the Desmond Davis award, went to Ken Russell, BBC director, whose work included imaginative documentaries on Elgar and Isadora Duncan. Marty Feldman was named as television personality of 1968, and his series *Marty* won the best light entertainment award for its producer, Denis Main Wilson, and the script award for Feldman and his co-writer Barry Took. Other awards were:

Actress of the Year—Wendy Craig, for her part in *Not in Front of the Children* (BBC)

Actor of the Year—Roy Dotrice, for *Brief Lives* (BBC)

Richard Dimbleby award—Julian Pettifer, for reports from Vietnam and the U.S.A. (BBC)

Best drama production—*Parachute*, produced by Anthony Page (BBC)

Specialised programmes—*The World of Coppard*, produced by Jack Gold (BBC)

Design—Roy Oxley, for *Portrait of a Lady* (BBC)

Lighting—Tom Moncrieff, for *The Black and White Minstrel Show* (BBC)

Special awards—News at Ten (ITN); Brian Cowgill, David Coleman, and the BBC Olympic Games production team

Mullard award (for significant contribution to science understanding)—Dr. Robert Reid and Peter Goodchild, for *Doctors' Dilemma* (BBC)

Shell international award (for contribution to understanding of trade and industry)—Anthony Firth for *Big Fish, Little Fish* (Independent).

The Writers' Guild of Great Britain awards for 1968 were presented on March 5, 1969. All but one were given for BBC programmes. They were:

Best comedy writer—Johnny Speight, for *Till Death Us Do Part* (for the second year running)

Best original tele-play—David Mercer, for *Let's Murder Vivaldi.*

Documentary script—Robert Erskine, for *The Glory that Remains of Persia and India.*

Light entertainment script—Team of writers for *Marty*, including Barry Took.

Dramatisation—Jack Pulman, for *Portrait of a Lady*

Writer of British series—Julian Bond, for *A Man of our Times* (ITV)

The 1968 awards of the Royal Television Society were presented on May 9, 1969. The silver medal for "outstanding artistic merit in front of the camera" went to Derek Nimmo (BBC, *All Gas and Gaiters* and *Oh, Brother!*), and that for merit "behind the camera" to Peter Morley, director and producer of *The Life and Times of Lord Mountbatten* (ITV). The television manufacturing company Pye gave special awards for colour TV: that for the "most memorable moment" was awarded to Col. Frank Borman and the crew of the Apollo 8 spacecraft; the chief technical prize went to a BBC research engineer, Robin Davies, for his solution to the problem of converting U.S.-standard pictures to European standards; and awards for the "outstanding personality in the medium of colour" were given to Marty Feldman for his BBC-2 comedy show *Marty*, and to Suzanne Neve (Holly in *The Forsyte Saga*) who starred in the BBC-2 serial *Portrait of a Lady.*

The 1969 Asian Broadcasting Union prize, given annually for the best television documentary, went to the Australian Broadcasting Commission film *The Cry of Nukumanu*, which defeated entries from Great Britain, Germany, India, Japan, New Zealand, Singapore, South Korea, and the U.S.A. The programme looked at life on a remote atoll in the Solomon Islands, where a tiny community faces the break-up of its traditional way of life.

Telford, Shropshire. The final draft of the plans for the new city of Telford was handed to the development corporation on July 16, 1969. The city will include the present towns of Wellington, Oakengates, and Dawley, and will have a completely new centre just south of the A5 at Malins Lee, which, it is hoped, will be established by 1976. Over the next 25 years homes and jobs will be provided for 225,000 Midlanders. Groups of 200 to 400 homes will be built to form local communities of about 8,000 people, based on primary schools; these communities will be grouped in threes, forming districts, each with local shopping, library, and recreation facilities. An urban motorway will ring the

city, which will be built on a grid system to allow for growth, and primary and secondary roads will link the separate districts. At the centre of the city there will be a 600-acre park. Of the 48,000 new homes, 23,500 will be privately owned and the remainder rented. By 1991, 99,000 new jobs in the city will be needed, of which 28,000 could be provided by the expansion of existing industries, and 23,000 by new industry.

Telford Gold Medal. It was announced in August 1969 that this medal, the highest award given by the U.K. Institute of Civil Engineers, had been awarded to Letitia Chitty, aged 72, an authority of stress in structures. She was given the medal for her "outstanding series of papers ... culminating in her review of the work of the Arch Dams Committee ..." Another gold medal winner, also announced on the same day, was Professor P. W. Rowe of Manchester University, who received it for his contributions to soil mechanics.

Territorial Army. The decision to abolish the T.A., announced in November 1968, was carried out in 1969. Members were encouraged to join the army reserve, now called the "Volunteers," which became the sole reserve force with an establishment of 54,000. The "Ever-Readies" (Category One reservists) were also abolished as a separate body, and absorbed into the Volunteers. To preserve the titles of most Territorial Army regiments, about 100 cadres of eight officers and N.C.O.s were formed and attached to the Volunteers and based on the local drill halls. They maintain the regimental tradition by, for instance, preserving the regimental silver. The abolition of the T.A., numbering about 10,000 men, will save about £3 million a year, but leaves the U.K. without any home defence force, since the Volunteers are solely a reserve for the Rhine army.

Thalidomide. The trial of seven executives of the West German company that manufactured this drug, on charges of causing bodily harm with intent and through negligence, negligent killing, and the violation of drug laws, continued during 1969 at Alsdorf, where it had started on May 27, 1968. In April talks on the possibility of an out-of-court settlement with parents of children allegedly born deformed because of their mothers' use of the drug were held, but they proved abortive and the trial continued.

In Great Britain it was announced on Feb. 11 that another 150 parents of "thalidomide babies" were to start actions for damages against Distillers Company (Biochemicals) Ltd., the British licensees of the German manufacturers, bringing the total number of lawsuits pending against the company to 250. As these new applications to start actions were outside the legal time limit, special leave from the High Court had to be obtained. On Feb. 19, 1968, a basis for settlement had been announced for actions on behalf of 62 children; in these cases negligence allegations against the company were withdrawn, and it was stated that each child would receive 40 per cent of the damages payable if the actions had been successful. The same principle was applied in the first of the new actions in July, when two boys, one armless and one virtually limbless, were awarded £12,850 and £20,800 respectively, and the mother of one received £2,900 for shock, this sum also being 40 per cent of the full award of £7,250. Another thalidomide victim, a girl now 8 years old, born without arms and legs, was awarded £20,800 agreed damages in the High Court on Dec. 19. Her mother was awarded £2,000 agreed damages, and her father £2,150.

In Sweden, an agreement compensating 100 deformed children was signed on Sept. 26, 1969, between a pharmaceutical company that sold the drug and representatives of the Swedish Society for Thalidomide Victims. The company agreed to make an annual payment of £48,000 a year to be divided between the children as long as they live. The payments were made retroactive from January 1968, and will be linked to the cost-of-living index. This compensation was slightly more than 50 per cent of what the children would have received if full damages had been awarded to them by the courts. In Norway a total sum of about £5,825 per year for life was awarded to 13 disabled children, to be divided according to disability.

Thamesmead, Kent. Building of this new town on marshes at Woolwich—Greenwich continued during 1969. The Minister of Transport stated on March 11 that he favoured a tunnel rather than a bridge across the Thames at Thamesmead, and was prepared to make a 75 per cent grant towards the cost of a suitable scheme. Although a tunnel will be more costly, a bridge would involve the loss of 80 acres of residential land, enough to provide 2,150 homes. Figures given by the G.L.C. showed that a tunnel would cost £20 million, including servicing, and a bridge, on a comparable basis, £12 million for the building and £2 million because of the loss of housing. The cost of creating Thamesmead is estimated to be £211 million, of which the G.L.C. is expected to find £100 million; the Inner London Education Authority more than £14 million; Bexley £5 million; Greenwich £2½ million; the government £9 million; and other developers more than £80 million. The town is designed to house 60,000 people by the 1980s. See also p. 155.

Thermopylae, Greece. A £1 million communications satellite ground station is to be built at this historic pass which the Spartan king Leonidas defended against the Persians in 480 B.C.

Greece will become a member of the International Communications Satellite network when the station comes into operation in 1970. The system will assure reception and transmission of television and allow telephone and telegraph traffic between Greece and other parts of the world through an Intelsat III satellite, in orbit 23,000 miles over the Atlantic at the Equator.

Thurleigh, Beds. An information study on this possible site for London's third airport was published on May 28, 1969. The Royal Aircraft Establishment's airfield, Thurleigh, is ten miles north of Bedford. The 7,500 acres required for a four-runway airport is largely agricultural; about 2,000 people live in the area. It would be necessary for Thurleigh to be linked by a new rail complex to a London terminal, and for new roads to be built to the M1 and the A1. The commission estimated that, when completed, the airport would handle about 100 million passengers a year, and would create 65,000 jobs when running at full capacity. More than 24,000 people would be affected by "intrusive" noise if four runways were used, and 11,200 people if two runways were used. With two runways in operation 4,100 people would find the noise "annoying," and 5,200 "intrusive-annoying"; with four runways in use 6,200 would experience the former level of annoyance and 6,400 the latter. The public inquiry into Thurleigh as the airport site opened at Bedford on Sept. 8.

Tidbinbilla, A.C.T. A new 210-ft.-diameter space communications antenna, costing approximately $A10 million, is to be built at the deep space tracking station here. The new dish, which is modelled on the giant radio telescope at Parkes, N.S.W., will be six times more sensitive than the existing 85-ft. dish at Tidbinbilla; it will be used to send commands to and recover data from planetary missions in the 1970s and 1980s, including orbiting and landing missions on Mars. Fabrication of the antenna began in the U.S.A. in 1969, and work on the 5,000-ton reinforced concrete pedestal on which it will stand was begun on the site. The new station will be operational in 1973.

Tokyo. The population of the Japanese capital increased by almost 154,000 during 1968 to reach an estimated 11,353,724, according to figures published in March 1969.

Tolpuddle, Dorset. One of Great Britain's most famous trees, the sycamore under which six farm labourers, faced with a reduction in their 9s-a-week wages, met in 1834 and formed the first trade union, was reported in May 1969 to be in danger of falling down. The tree, which stands on the village green here, 7 miles from Dorchester, Dorset, is a favourite visiting place for tourists, and a constant reminder of the Tolpuddle

Tolpuddle. The ancient "Tolpuddle Martyrs" tree, under which the trade union movement was born, is in danger of collapse.

Martyrs, who for their crime in forming a trade union were sentenced to transportation to Australia for seven years but, thanks to a national outcry, were given a full pardon after two years. The trunk of the tree has been eaten away by fungus; preservation work by forestry experts employed by the National Trust involved the propping of a 10 ft.-high overweight branch, reinforcing the trunk with steel rods, and treating the fungus with chemicals. If the work proves unsuccessful and the tree has to be felled, a cutting from it will be planted on the village green.

"Tony" Awards. These annual American theatre awards, Broadway's equivalent of Hollywood's Oscar, were presented in New York on April 20, 1969, for theatrical achievement during 1968. British artists won five major awards: Sir Laurence Olivier received a special award honouring Britain's National Theatre and his contribution to it; Rex Harrison an award for his great contribution to the theatre; Angela Lansbury the award for best performance in a musical (*Dear World*); Loudon Sainthill the award for best costume designer in the Broadway version of *Canterbury Tales*; and Peter Dews the award for best director of a dramatic play (*Hadrian VII*). Another British actress, Vanessa Redgrave, shared an award (for her part in *The Great White Hope*) with Dustin Hoffman. James Earl Jones won the best actor award for his part in *The Great White Hope*, and Julie Harris the best actress award for her performance in *Forty Carats*. The best musical of 1968 was *1776*, which also gave Peter Hunt the best director of musicals award. The best actor in a musical was Jerry Orbach, for his role in *Promises, Promises*. Leonard Bernstein won a "Tony" for his contribution as a composer. The Negro Ensemble company, a repertory company founded in 1968, won a special citation.

"Torrey Canyon." Compensation of £3 million for loss and damage caused when the tanker *Torrey Canyon* went aground off the Isles of Scilly in March 1967 was paid by the owners, the U.S.-controlled Barracuda Tanker Corporation, and the charterers, the Union Oil Co. of California, on Nov. 11, 1969, at the Foreign Office in London. The money was shared equally by the British and French governments. Its share of £1,500,000 reimbursed the British Government, who paid out 80 per cent of the cost of losses to local authorities and other public and dock authorities for oil clearance. The owners and charterers also agreed to pay up to £25,000 to individuals and firms in both countries who are able to show losses not covered by insurance or other relief.

Tourism. The U.K. Development of Tourism Act became law on Aug. 25, 1969. The Act contains enabling powers for the registration of hotels and tourist accommodation, provides for grants and loans to hotels, and establishes a new tourist organisation. Four tourist bodies were set up: the British Tourist Authority, and the English Tourist Board, both responsible to the Board of Trade; the Scottish Tourist Board, responsible to the Secretary of State for Scotland; and the Welsh Tourist Board, responsible to the Secretary of State for Wales. The British Tourist Authority, which replaces the British Travel Association, will have a government grant of £3½ million a year for promotional and research activities, and to pay the salaries of its staff of 400.

Figures issued by the U.K. Board of Trade in August 1969 showed that 1968 was the first year in which overseas visitors to Great Britain spent more than British nationals travelling abroad. Visitors spent £282 million (a 20 per cent increase over 1967), while British travellers spent £271 million overseas (a decrease of £3 million on 1967), although the number travelling abroad was 1 per cent more than in 1967. More British people went to Spain, Eire, and the whole of the sterling area, with the exception of Australia and New Zealand; and fewer went to Italy, Switzerland, Austria, and France. Average spending by British travellers fell to £34 6s. per visit, compared with £35 4s. in 1967, and £39 18s. in 1966. Of these British travellers, 68 per cent went abroad on holiday, 14 per cent on business, and the remainder for study. Of the 4,800,000 visitors to Britain (a 13 per cent increase over 1967) 4,300,000 spent an average of £56 a visit.

The annual report of the British Travel Association, published on Oct. 3, 1969, showed that in 1968 for the first time the number of overseas visitors to Britain exceeded 4 million. In addition, there were 783,000 tourist arrivals from the Republic of Ireland. The visitors included 106,000 from Australia and New Zealand; 276,000 from Canada; 507,000 from France (a 12 per cent increase over 1967, and the first time the yearly figure had exceeded half a million); 356,000 from Germany (a 21 per cent increase); 253,000 from Holland (a 20 per cent increase); 167,000 from Belgium and Luxemburg (a 30 per cent increase); and 878,000 from U.S.A. (a 5 per cent increase).

A survey carried out by the British Travel Association and the Greater London Council showed that Nelson's Column is the biggest tourist attraction in London; 93 per cent of overseas visitors and 82 per cent of British tourists make Trafalgar Square a "must" in their sightseeing. The next five most popular attractions are Buckingham Palace, the Houses of Parliament, Hyde Park, Westminster Abbey, and the Tower of London.

Northern Ireland. Figures given by the Northern Ireland Tourist Board in March 1969 showed that the tourist revenue in the year ending September 1968 was £28·4 million, £1·9 million more than in 1967. The total number of visitors, either on business trips or on holiday, was 1,197,000, a 10 per cent increase over 1967. It was estimated that over 740,000 visitors came from Great Britain, and 375,000 from Eire. Overseas visitors increased to 85,000, compared with 80,000 in 1967, about 65 per cent of them coming from the U.S.A.

Australia. Visitors to Australia in 1968 increased by almost 30 per cent to 253,000, much of the increase being accounted for by U.S. troops on recreation leave. In 1967, 7,000 U.S. servicemen visited Australia, and in 1968 the figure rose to 63,000.

New Zealand. During 1968 a total of 221,129 overseas tourists visited New Zealand, an increase of 22,117 over the 1967 figure.

Norway. About 3,760,000 tourists visited Norway during 1968, compared with 2,670,000 in 1967. The number of Scandinavian visitors went up by 2·3 per cent, with 2,780,000 from Sweden, and 270,000 from Denmark. The number of tourists from other countries increased by 3·4 per cent, with 145,000 from West Germany, 140,000 from Finland (12 per cent down), 124,000 from Great Britain (1 per cent down), and 120,000 from the U.S.A. In addition, there were 1·9 million one-day visitors from Sweden and Finland. Only 34,000 French tourists went to Norway in 1968, a 3 per cent decrease on the 1967 figure, but the number of Dutch tourists increased by 20 per cent to 55,000.

Japan. In 1968, 541,716 Japanese went abroad, 27 per cent more than in 1967. Of this total, 198,000 went to the Ryukyus; 83,000 to the U.S.A.; 65,000 to Taiwan; and 47,000 to Hong Kong. During the same year 519,004 foreign tourists visited Japan, 9 per cent more than in 1967; half of the total number were Americans, 9 per cent South Korean, and 6 per cent Chinese from Taiwan.

U.S.A. According to figures given by the International Union of Travel Organisations in October 1969 the number of U.S. tourists visiting Europe in 1968 rose by one per cent over the 1967 figure to 5,857,000. The average expenditure per tourist, however, fell by 2·9 per cent, from $167·60 in 1967 to $162·70 in 1968. The total spent by U.S. tourists in 16 European countries in 1968 was $953 million.

Traffic. Figures given by the British Road Federation in July 1969 showed that traffic congestion is worse in Great Britain than in any other major country. There are 59·2 vehicles for every mile of road in Britain, compared with 48·3 in Germany and 45·1 in Italy, while France and the U.S.A. have less than 26 vehicles to the mile. On trunk and secondary roads in Britain there are only 11½ yards for every vehicle.

Control. A remote-controlled system of signals to drivers using the M4 motorway came into operation on March 21, 1969. The "urban" signals, mounted on overhead gantries about 500 yards apart, show advised maximum speeds and other instructions for each lane of the motorway for about 2 miles from the Chiswick roundabout; "rural" signals then operate to Langley, Bucks, the interchange point with the A4 road.

Transplant Surgery. A committee of eleven, appointed in the U.K. in January 1969 to advise on problems arising from the transplantation of organs, gave its views in a White Paper published in July. Regarding donors of organs, six members of the group were in favour of a "contracting-out" scheme, under which it would be assumed that everyone was a willing donor unless he had objected during his life; and five, including the committee chairman, Sir Hector MacLennan, President of the Royal Society of Medicine, were in favour of a "contracting-in" scheme, under which a potential donor must have positively stated his willingness to become one. They suggested the experimental establishment of a single public central register for recording the names of those consenting (and objecting) to the use of their organs after death. Regarding the determination of the moment of death, they said that before organs are removed death should be certified by two doctors, one of whom should have been registered for at least five years; and the fact should be recorded at the time on record forms provided for the purpose so that each doctor could record his findings independently. In cases where a patient was being kept alive by artificial means the decision to continue or discontinue such support must be made without regard to the possibility of a transplant being made.

Delegates to an international symposium in Madrid in July agreed—but by no means unanimously—on a definition of death which is expected to form the basis for legislation in many countries. Death is defined as the moment when the brain ceases to perform its vital functions and fails to react to medical stimuli, but a final decision on death should be made only on the recommendation of experts after they have conducted internationally approved medical tests, including the electro-encephalograph, over a minimum of 24 hours. The delegates warned that these criteria do not apply unreservedly to children, and are not applicable in cases involving drugs.   Regarding transplants the delegates recommended that the doctor who signed the death certificate should not be involved in a transplant operation, and that the dead or moribund donor should not be capable of breathing without medical devices.

The planning unit of the British Medical Association in a report on "Priorities in Medicine," published on Jan. 10, 1969, said that more basic knowledge was needed before heart and lung transplants could be considered generally acceptable methods of treatment, and pressed for encouragement to be given to other forms of transplant operations, particularly of the kidney. Seven thousand people die from chronic kidney disease in Great Britain every year. It has been estimated that the lives of 2,000 of them could be saved by the use of long-term dialysis ("kidney machine"), but the direct cost of this would be about £30 million a year, plus the services of 10,000 skilled personnel. A kidney transplant, at a cost of £6,000 per patient, is a better investment. About 1,000 of those who die every year from chronic renal failure are aged between 15 and 44 years, and many might be saved by transplants from 600 donors. On the other hand, there are 15,000 deaths from chronic heart disease in Great Britain each year of people between the ages of 20 and 54, and there is no potential supply of donors on such a scale. The real value of the heart transplant operation, the report suggested, would be for children with congenital heart disease, and young adults with rheumatic heart disease. See also Heart Transplants.

Transport Authorities. Following the Transport Act, 1960, which was intended to decentralise to a large extent the administration of transport so that regional and local councils would have more authority over transport in their own areas, regional passenger transport authorities were set up in April, 1961, for Merseyside; South East Lancashire and North-East Cheshire (SELNEC); Tyneside; and the West Midlands. A fifth authority for the Greater London area, came into operation under the Greater London Council on Jan. 1, 1970. See also under London.

Treasure. *Above: left,* bronze cannon, recovered from the wreck of Sir Cloudesley Shovell's flagship *Association* were sold for £3,000 each; *right,* builder's labourers with the hoard of 10,000 13th-century silver pennies they found in Colchester. *Right:* five early Iron Age gold torques earned their finder £45,000.

Treasure. It was announced by the British Museum on Feb. 7, 1969, that Malcolm Tricker, a building worker, who found five Early Iron Age gold torques (collars) near Ipswich, Suffolk, in October 1968, was to be paid £45,000. The torques are described as "unique"; four of them have their ring terminals decorated in the same style as the famous torque found at Snettisham in 1950.

On Feb. 13 two workmen found a hoard of 10,000 13th-century silver pennies on a building site at Colchester, Essex. The coins, which were in a heavy lead casket, were only a few feet from the place where another hoard was found in 1902.

It was reported in June that gold and silver coins, an anchor, and other objects had been recovered from the wreck of a Spanish Armada ship off the North Antrim coast of Northern Ireland, and that many of the discoveries had been undergoing treatment at the conservation department of Queen's University, Belfast. The ship was the *Gerona,* lost in the great storm of 1588 with nearly 1,800 men. The search was carried out by Robert Stenuit, a Belgian writer, and a team of two other Belgians and two Frenchmen, who paid a brief visit to the wreck in 1967, worked there for five months in 1968, and continued their recovery work in 1969. Another Armada galleon, the *Santa Maria de la Rosa,* which sank off Blasket Island, Co. Kerry, was investigated by divers in 1969, and yielded cannon balls, musket parts, and gold medallions; it was supposed to be carrying gold and silver plate, jewellery, and 30,000 ducats.

In 1707 a squadron of five British ships, with their commander Admiral Sir Cloudesley Shovell and 2,000 men, were lost off the Scilly Isles. Divers have been prospecting in the area for several years. Treasure from Shovell's flagship, *Association,* brought up between July 1967 and June 1968, was sold at Sotheby's on July 14, 1969 for a total of £12,354. Two French 17th-century cannon went for £3,000 each; coins fetched over £5,000, a toothpick case £115, and an inkwell £18. In July divers operating on the wreck of the *Romney,* a 50-gun man-of-war of the same squadron, discovered English silver and gold coins, Portuguese gold coins, Spanish pieces of eight, and gold rings.

Trucks. An Australian manufacturer of construction and mining equipment at Rydalmere, N.S.W., completed in 1969 the largest rear dump truck at present in operation anywhere in the world. Information about the truck, the 120A Haulpak, was given in April. It has a capacity of 120 tons; a 1,000 h.p. engine; and tyres over 8 ft. tall and weighing over a ton each. It has an overall length of 35 ft., and is 16 ft. high, and 18 ft. wide. It has no transmission or differential, but instead power from the GM diesel engine is transmitted through a generator directly to self-contained electric motors fitted in the rear wheel hubs. Six of these trucks will be used for hauling iron ore in open-cut mines in Western Australia, and the truck is already in use in the U.S.A. and South Africa.

Tulloch. This horse, a champion of the Australian turf, died near Coonabarabran, N.S.W., on June 29, 1969. With a record of 36 wins, 12 seconds and 4 thirds from 53 starts, Tulloch became the top stakes winner of Australia with $A220,247. His wins included the 1961 Brisbane Cup (2 miles) carrying 9 stone 12 pounds, as well as, at various times, the Queensland Derby, the Victoria Derby, and the A.J.C. Derby. He held the Australian record for $1\frac{1}{2}$ miles with the time of 2 minutes 26.9 seconds. A New Zealand-bred horse, Tulloch was bought in that country as a yearling for $A1,575.

Tunnels. The longest conduit tunnel in Europe was completed in Spain in March 1969 after four years' work. The 9-mile-long tunnel in the province of Salamanca was excavated out of solid rock to bring water from the reservoir of the river Tormes to the Vilarino power station, where the turbines will generate 1,324 million kWh in an average year.

Unidentified Flying Objects. The report of a U.S. Government-appointed committee which investigated the mystery of unidentified flying objects over a period of 18 months was published in January 1969. The investigation was carried out at the request of the U.S. Air Force by a team of scientists from the University of Colorado under the direction of Dr. Edward Condon. The report confirmed the air force's conclusion that there is "no evidence to justify a belief in flying saucers." Excluding hoaxes, nine out of ten flying saucers had proved to have a natural explanation, being either aeroplanes, weather beacons, balloons, space satellites, street lights, or clouds and other natural phenomena. Of 35 photographs of unidentified flying objects, nine were found to be fakes; seven were possible fakes; seven were natural or man-made phenomena; and the re-

maining 12 provided insufficient evidence for any conclusion.

Universities. Figures given by the U.K. Department of Education and Science on October 3, 1969, showed that of 200,121 full-time students at British universities in 1967-68, 145,277 were men and 54,844 women. The proportion of women was 27·4 per cent. The total showed a considerable increase over 1966-67 when there were 184,799 full-time students. The number of part-time students rose from 18,555 in 1966-67 to 19,378 in 1967-68. The number of first degrees obtained in 1966-67 was 36,256, compared with 31,887 in 1965-66; this represented a rise of only 5 per cent in science degrees, compared with increases of 19 per cent in engineering and technology, and 18 per cent in social, administrative, and business studies. See also under Students.

The U.K. Universities Central Council on Admissions reported in April, 1969 that applications for science and technology courses were increasing slowly but that those wishing to read sociology had declined considerably. At the end of January, when about 95 per cent of applications for courses beginning in October, 1969 had been received, there were 10,000 fewer applications for sociology than in 1968. Applications for other social sciences, especially business studies, economics, geography, government and public administration, and law all showed an increase. Universities also reported a significant increase in options for mixed courses in the environmental, physical, and biological sciences groups of studies; there were increases also in applications for courses in mathematics and engineering.

It was announced in March 1969 that up to 40 women undergraduates are to be admitted to a men's college at Cambridge—Churchill College—in the October of either 1972 or 1973. Admission standards will be the same as for men. In May, King's College, Cambridge, founded in 1441, also decided to admit

up to 35 women as undergraduates for the first time in 1972 and 1973. To make room for them the number of male entrants will be reduced from an average of 91 to about 80 each year.

The Easter conference of the National Union of Students voted on April 11, 1969, to rescind the joint statement made in November 1968 by their executive and the Association of Education Committees on management and discipline in art, technical, and education colleges run by local authorities. The conference demanded one third student representation on governing bodies, and negotiations for new disciplinary procedures.

During 1969 four new universities in the Soviet Union were opened, each with six departments of natural sciences and the humanities. They are in Gomel (Byelorussia), Krasnoyarsk (Siberia), Kuibyshev (on the Volga), and Ordjonikidze (Northern Caucasus). All the Soviet republics now have universities.

Uranium. A valuable discovery of uranium was made about 230 miles north of Mount Isa, Queensland, Australia. It was stated on February 11, 1969, that drilling had revealed a minimum grade of 6 lb. of uranium oxide per ton of ore, by far the highest grade of uranium so far found in Australia.

The discovery of a new vein of uranium at Guijo de Avila, near Salamanca, Spain, was announced in October 1969. Initial tests suggested a deposit of substantial quantity.

Variety Club Awards. The 1968 awards to actors and actresses by the Variety Club of Great Britain were presented on March 11, 1969. They were:
Showbusiness personality—Tom Jones
Joint ITV personalities—Ronnie Corbett and Tommy Cooper
Joint BBC TV personalities—Marty Feldman and Rolf Harris
Stage actress—Jill Bennett, for her performance in *Time Present.*
Stage actor—Sir John Gielgud, for his performance in *Forty Years On.*

Victoria Cross. The two Australian soldiers serving in Vietnam who won the V.C. for gallantry in the same action in May 1969: Warrant Officer Rayne Simpson (*left*) of Sydney, and Warrant Officer Keith Payne of Stafford Heights, Queensland.

Film actress—Maggie Smith, for her performance in *Hot Millions*.

Film actor—Ron Moody, his for performance in *Oliver!*

Most promising star—Alan Bennett, for his performance in *Forty Years On*.

Radio personality—Jimmy Young.

Special award—Dame Sybil Thorndike, for her long service to the theatre.

Venice, Italy The president of the city's public works council, stated on Jan. 28, 1969, that by 1990 Venice will have sunk another 10 inches into the deep silt on which it was built almost a thousand years ago. The sea would have risen about 6 inches, a phenomenon observed every 100 years. The steady removal of subterranean water and new canal-digging had weakened the ground below the city.

A £1·3 million project, sponsored by the Italian tourist board, for a congress hall and an artists' colony in the Castello gardens was proposed at the end of January. The congress hall, designed by Louis Kahn, the American architect, would seat 2,500 people when used as a single auditorium, and could be divided by curtains to form a theatre-in-the-round seating 550. This auditorium would be built of concrete and suspended in a curve between columns, allowing people to sit or walk beneath it. One entire side of the hall would consist of a window giving views across the Biennale gardens and the lagoon towards San Giorgio Maggiore. The artists' colony would be in permanent residence in a second building, which is intended to replace the existing Biennale pavilion. Huge sliding doors and roof panels would permit it to be either an enclosed room or an open courtyard. The ground floor would be devoted to workshops, and the first floor to art galleries. The artists would live in flats on the top floor.

Victoria Cross. The Victoria Cross was awarded to two Australian soldiers serving in Vietnam during 1969. Both showed gallantry in action in Kontum province in May. Warrant-Officer Rayne Stewart Simpson, aged 43, of Sydney, N.S.W., while serving with the U.S. "Green Berets," made himself a focal point for enemy fire while leading his men to the assistance of another platoon, carrying a wounded man to safety before crawling to within 10 yards of the enemy to throw grenades into their positions. Five days later, when his U.S. battalion commander was killed he organised two platoons, and in the face of heavy fire moved forward to cover the initial evacuation of casualties. The citation said that "at the risk of almost certain death" he tried to reach the body of his commander, but was stopped by heavy fire. When the position became untenable he fought on alone, preventing the enemy advance until the wounded had been withdrawn. A veteran of the Second World War, the Korean war, and the anti-terrorist campaign in Malaysia,

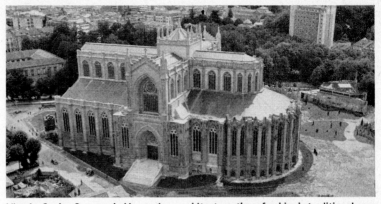

Vitoria, Spain. Surrounded by modern architecture, the refreshingly traditional new cathedral at Vitoria, which was dedicated in 1969.

W.O. Simpson became the first living Australian to receive the V.C. for service in Vietnam.

The second recipient of the V.C. was Warrant-Officer Keith Payne, 36, of Queensland. In the Australian army since 1951, W.O. Payne went to Vietnam in January, after serving in Japan, Korea, and Malaya; he is married with five sons. Although wounded, W.O. Payne exposed himself to enemy fire in encouraging S. Vietnamese troops to hold positions under attack, organised a rearguard action to allow his battalion to withdraw, and later was instrumental in rescuing 40 Allied soldiers left behind.

Victoria Line. The third stage of London's new Underground railway, the Victoria Line, was opened by the Queen on March 7, 1969. Comprising the stretch between Warren Street and Victoria, this stage completed the main Walthamstow-Victoria section, linking the northern termini at King's Cross, St. Pancras, and Euston, with the chief southern terminus, Victoria, via the West End. Construction of the line, which started in September 1956, cost £70 million. A southern extension from Victoria to Brixton, due for completion in the early 1970s, will cost a further £19 million.

Wages. The U.K. Department of Employment and Productivity stated on Jan. 31, 1969 that in the 12 months ending Oct. 31, 1968, the average weekly earnings of over 6 million manual workers in the main manufacturing industries rose to £23 a week, an increase of 7·6 per cent over the previous 12-month period. The average for women industrial workers, £11 6s., showed a 7 per cent rise.

Walking. A new world non-stop walking record of 201 miles 720 yards was set up by Bob Thistle, aged 49, when he completed 47 laps of the perimeter

track at Marham R.A.F. station, Norfolk, in 55 hours 21 minutes on April 6, 1969. He lost a stone in weight during the walk.

Warrenpoint, Northern Ireland. Harbour improvements and extra berthage planned for Warrenpoint were announced in the summer of 1969. Tenders for the improvements, which will cost £1,630,000 are to be invited in June 1970, and the first berthage is expected to be available by October 1971, and two further berths by the middle of 1972. The modernised harbour, which will have improved road access, will be able to handle shipping at present using Newry, where the now obsolete ship canal and dock basin will be closed.

Washington, D.C., U.S.A. After more than ten years of planning, negotiation and controversy, it was agreed by Congress on Sept. 24, 1969, that funds should be made available for the construction of an underground railway. By late 1972 or early in 1973, high-speed electric trains will run on the first 6-mile line, and the full 98-mile network will be completed by 1980.

Waste Paper. According to a statement by the Joint Waste Paper Advisory Council in March 1969, about 6 million tons of waste paper arises annually in Great Britain, of which 90 per cent would be re-usable if it were collected. The re-use of waste paper confers a large saving in the import bill for wood pulp for making new paper. In 1968, 1,800,000 tons of waste paper were re-used—about one third of the paper industry's total requirements of raw material. Since 1967 demand has risen by 200,000 tons a year. The world's largest factory and wharf for the handling of waste paper were opened at Charlton, S.E. London, at the end of February 1969; by 1971 it will be handling 1,000 tons a day, yielding an import saving of about £20 million a year.

Wealth. Figures published by the U.K. Central Statistical Office on Jan. 15,

Windsor. A little chapel created in the wall of St. George's Chapel received in March 1969 the remains of King George VI, who died in 1952.

1969, showed that in 1966 the total gross wealth held by individuals in Great Britain was estimated at £85,114 million. This comprised £22,795 million in landed property owned by 6,501,000 people, and £62,319 million in personal property. Of the latter, more personal wealth was in shares and debentures than in any other investment, viz. £12,236 million, held by 1,967,000 people. Insurance policies valued at £11,400 million were held by 10,642,000 people. National Savings Certificates were held by 6,525,000 people, accounting for £2,299 million; 17,594,000 people had £9,264 million in their bank accounts, including the Post Office and Trustee Savings Banks; and it was estimated that a further £201 million was held in cash in people's homes. 14,000 people had individual fortunes of more than £200,000, and about 30,000 were worth from £100,000 to £200,000. At the other end of the scale, 2,739,000 were worth between £3,000 and £5,000, and there were 6,335,000 owning less than £1,000 each.

Westernport, Victoria, Australia. The announcement that the directors of three major steel firms—Broken Hill Pty., John Lysaght (Aust.) Ltd., and Guest, Keen, Nettlefold—had agreed in principle to the building of a new steelmaking and rolling plant on the shores of Westernpoint Bay, Victoria, Australia, was made simultananeously in both Melbourne and London in May 1969. The mill, which was expected to come into operation in 1972, will supply principally southern Australia with uncoated and coated steel sheet and coil.

West Indies, University of the. Work on the $2,131,000 expansion programme for this university, through the co-operation of the Canadian International Development Agency, started during

1969. The programme—which includes the construction of six university centres in the Windward and Leeward Islands, a student residence in Barbados, and a faculty club in Trinidad— is part of a five-year $5 million plan of Canadian assistance to the University which began in 1966. As well as buildings, the plan provides for scholarships and fellowships and the provision of Canadian lecturers and professors. In 1948 the University of the West Indies had only one centre, at Kingston, Jamaica, with a total enrolment of 33 students; in 1968 it had additional centres in Trinidad and Barbados, with a total enrolment of 3,614 students. The six centres in the programme are on the islands of Dominica, Grenada, Montserrat, St. Kitts, St. Lucia, and St. Vincent.

Windsor. On March 24, 1969, the remains of King George VI were transferred from the crypt of St. George's Chapel, where they had lain since his death in 1952, to their final resting-place in the new George VI Memorial Chapel, which was dedicated on March 31 in the presence of the Queen. The new chapel, created in the wall of St. George's Chapel between the north transept and the choir, contains the black marble vault, a small altar, and on the wall above a relief portrait of the King, sculpted by Sir William Reid Dick. It is enclosed by a wrought-iron gate and lit by stained glass windows designed by John Piper.

Wine. Sales of wine in Australia rose by $13\frac{1}{2}$ per cent to 19,840,000 gallons between June 30, 1967, and June 30, 1968, and in the same period imports increased from 146,995 gallons to 305,404 gallons. One of the reasons for the growing demand is the increase in immigrants from the Continent of Europe.

Woking, Surrey. A large-scale development planned for the central area of Woking will provide 59 shops, 5 stores, 48 flats, 126,000 sq. ft. of office space, a dance hall, a garage, and a multi-storey car park. The shops, approached by pedestrian walks, will be on two levels, with three-storey stepped blocks of flats over them; and the offices will occupy a 15-storey block. The site of the development lies between Commercial Road, Church Path, and Church Street.

Woomera, South Australia. It was announced on April 23, 1969, that a space-communications station for defence purposes will be established jointly by the U.S.A. and Australia at Woomera, the rocket-launching site in South Australia. Its exact purpose was not disclosed, but it is supposed that it will receive from and transmit to U.S. military satellites. To be manned by a joint American-Australian staff of 250-300, it was begun in late 1969 and was expected to take a year to construct. The new station is only the latest of the many U.S. space and communications centres in

Australia. Others include the U.S. Navy very-low-frequency station at North-West Cape, W. Australia; a secret space research station at Pine Gap, near Alice Springs; a space phenomena observation station at Alice Springs; and six NASA satellite-tracking stations (at Tidbinbilla, Orroral Valley, and Honeysuckle Creek, all near Canberra; Island Lagoon, near Woomera; Carnarvon, W. Australia; and Cooby Creek, near Toowoomba, Queensland). A navigation satellite station is also planned for Tasmania.

Wythenshawe, Manchester. The foundation stone of the long-awaited civic centre here was laid on Sept. 26, 1969. To cost £1·3 million, the centre will include a theatre, library, indoor recreational accommodation with a sports hall and public hall, and two swimming pools. There will be a restaurant, bar, and an exhibition area.

X-Rays. An exhibition illustrating the use of X-rays in art detection, organised by the Burlington Magazine, was held in London during March 1969. The exhibition included two of four panels of a 16th-century Spanish altar piece belonging to the Wellcome Institute; use of X-rays at the Courtauld Institute of Art having revealed under the surface eight religious paintings dating from 1300, the later paintings were sacrificed and months of painstaking work with a micro-

X-Rays. Months of work with microscope and scalpel removed 16th-century Spanish Altarpiece paintings to reveal more important 12th-century works underneath, which had been detected by means of X-rays.

York. Four items of ecclesiastical treasure found in a 700-year-old tomb in the Minster—a wooden crozier, a paten, a ring, and a chalice.

scope and scalpel removed them to reveal the more important work beneath. A previously unknown painting by Picasso of a woman beneath the paint surface of his *Girl Holding a Dove* also was shown at the exhibition.

When the painting *The Adoration of Magi*, by the 17th-century Flemish artist Jordaens, was sent by its owners, the Cherbourg Art Gallery, to the Louvre laboratory for restoration, photographs taken under lateral light beams revealed a smaller, second panel within the work. In June 1969 this was identified as a painting of the Holy Family, of higher quality than the *Adoration* that covers it.

X-Ray Stars. A joint discovery by Dr. P. J. Edwards, a senior lecturer in the physics department at the University of Otago, and F. Knox and P. Burtt of the Department of Scientific and Industrial Research in Wellington, New Zealand, has shown that X-ray stars more than 1,000 light-years away affect the earth's atmosphere during the night. By a new technique X-ray stars were monitored from the ground instead of, as was previously the only possible method, from rockets, high altitude balloons, or satellites. The discovery was that an X-ray star "pushes" the ionosphere closer to the earth's surface by about half a mile, this movement being detected by sensitive radio receivers.

York. A £2 million plan to preserve the historic walled city in the centre of York from the encroachment of industry and traffic was published on Feb. 14, 1969. It was the first of four studies commissioned by the Minister of Housing and the councils concerned with the conservation of historic towns and cities. The plan proposed that all through-traffic and 24 acres of industrial development should be removed from the walled city, and the resident population there increased from 3,500 to 6,000, new housing being built. Historic central shopping streets should be paved from wall to wall and closed to all traffic after 10 a.m. Only residents would be allowed

to drive in narrow streets, except on four roads leading to multi-storey car parks, two of which would be built inside the city walls, and two just outside. These car parks would increase the present parking capacity from 190 to 5,000. The report assumes that the Government would make a 50 per cent grant towards the work of conservation, and proposes that the local authority should make a 40 per cent grant for repairs and conversions.

During excavations for the £2 million restoration work on York Minster, the 700-year-old tomb of a former Archbishop of York, Geoffrey de Ludham, Archbishop from 1258 to 1265, was discovered, and it was opened on Feb. 3, 1969. The tomb was found in the south transept of the Minster, near the place where the tomb of another Archbishop, Walter de Grey, was dicovered in January 1968. After vestments, a chalice, paten plate, ring, and crozier were removed from the coffin was resealed. Several of the articles from both tombs will be placed in the museum that is planned for the Minster.

York, University of. A 500-seat concert hall, together with lecture and practice rooms, a library, and an electronic music laboratory, was opened here as part of the music department on March 1, 1969. The fan-shaped hall has walls of bare painted stone and matt wood, and a ribbed roof of aluminium. The hall was paid for by Mr. and Mrs. Jack Lyons and is called the Lyons Concert Hall. The music department at York is one of the largest in Great Britain.

Yorkshire (W. Riding). Plans for a £140 million inter-urban highway scheme to link Leeds, Bradford, Halifax, Huddersfield, Dewsbury, and Wakefield were stated in August 1969 to have been approved in principle by the towns' local authorities. The scheme includes the extension eastward of the M62 from the A1 towards Goole, and the extension of the M1, which runs near Leeds, to join the A1 near Doncaster. It is also planned

to build link roads between the M62 and M1, and a new motorway between Bradford and the M62 via the Aire Valley.

Yosemite National Park, California. Park rangers reported in May 1969 that the Wawona tunnel tree, one of America's oldest tourist attractions, had fallen after an unusually severe winter. Since 1881, when a scar in the trunk of the 234-foot-high tree was enlarged to an opening 8ft. wide and 9ft. high, millions of tourists have driven through it. The tree, a Sequoia redwood, a species native to California, had a circumference of 83 ft., and was estimated to be about 2,000 years old.

Youth Hostels. A new scheme under which youth hostels in England and Wales are to be graded into four categories—simple, standard, superior, and special—with differential charges, was approved by the Youth Hostels Association's National Council at its annual meeting in March 1969. To allow for careful investigation of the facilities provided at the Association's 263 youth hostels, the new scheme, will not come into operation until 1971. It is anticipated that most hostels will fall into the standard category; the "simple" category will probably be found to outnumber the "superior" and "special" classes.

The Y.H.A. reported in October that provisional membership figures for 1969 had reached 221,389, and that 80,000 of this number were over the age of 21. The total represents an increase of 3,547 over the 1968 figure, and a rise of more than 25,000 since 1959.

Zadar, Yugoslavia. A new airport was opened here at the beginning of the summer of 1969. It is the sixth on the Adriatic coast, the others being in Pula, Split, Dubrovnik, Titograd, and Tivat. This development has increased the accessibility of the central coastal area of Yugoslavia to tourists. During 1968, 72,000 landings and take-offs took place on airports in Yugoslavia and the 1969 figure was expected to increase to as many as 83,000.

Zoos. A new 50-acre zoological garden, costing about £2 million, is to be opened in Madrid in the autumn of 1970. It is being laid out in the Casa de Campo. Railings will be eliminated wherever possible, and the animals will be allowed to wander freely in enclosures separated from the public by deep ditches. Visitors will be able to travel round the lions' compound in a monorail train with glass walls, and 6- or 8-seater boats will travel through a canal in a large free-flight aviary, similar to that at London Zoo. Children will have their own special zoo where they can meet some of the smaller animals, see films, and play in an adventure playground. The new zoo in Madrid will also contain restaurants, conference and exhibition halls, and an animals' hospital.

INDEX

This Index comprises references to all the important subjects mentioned or illustrated in pages 5–284 of the Year Book. "Names in the News" and "Fact Digest", which are arranged in alphabetical order, are not indexed here.

Page references to illustrations are in italic type, but where an illustration is in the same page as its related text it is not separately noted. Dates refer to the section "The Year 1969 in Headlines" in pages 6–29. The abbreviation f.p. ("facing page") refers to illustrations in the plate facing the page given. Names beginning with Mc are entered as if spelt Mac, and names beginning with St. are entered as if spelt Saint in full.